THE SEDUCTIVE SAPPHIC EXPLOITS OF

MERCEDES DE ACOSTA

HOLLYWOOD'S GREATEST LOVER

DARWIN PORTER & DANFORTH PRINCE

MERCEDES DE ACOSTA
A WOMAN IN TURMOIL
(1892-1968)

In 1960, eight years before her death, in ill health and desperately in need of money, the self-described "poet and predatory lesbian," Mercedes de Acosta, wrote and published a controversial memoir (*Here Lies the Heart*).

Instantly, it generated screams of outrage from the scores of women she had defined as her lovers during the course of her long, promiscuous, and socially well-connected life. But whereas many of them rejected and condemned her for her candor, she became widely celebrated by thousands of new-found fans, many of them feminists who "adopted' her as a cultural celebrity.

In 1965, three years before her death, she met and befriended Darwin Porter, the intellectually curious senior co-author of this book.

During their subsequent conversations and interviews (many of which transpired at his home in Manhattan and later, within Magnolia House on Staten Island), she expanded and amplified the information which had already appeared within her (by now notorious) book, fleshing out incidents which had been censored by over-zealous editors.

As her conversations with Darwin evolved, Mercedes remained firmly (some said "ferociously") protective of her self-anointed role as a Muse, Encourager, and Enabler of women experimenting with (or deeply entrenched in), episodic instances of same-sex love.

In 2020, bolstered by the conviction that many of Mercedes' intellectual contributions to her era were culturally meaningful and historically important, Blood Moon Productions proudly published this, the third installment of its Magnolia House Series.

We dedicate this book to one of the most fascinating and genuinely well-connected women of her era, Mercedes de Acosta, a woman with a brave heart.

REST IN PEACE MERCEDES
Here Lies the Heart

Magnolia House was familiar to Mercedes de Acosta. It's the Headquarters of Blood Moon Productions. What is Blood Moon Productions?

"Blood Moon, in case you don't know, is a small publishing house on Staten Island that cranks out Hollywood gossip books, about two or three a year, usually of five-, six-, or 700-page length, chocked with stories and pictures about people who used to consume the imaginations of the American public, back when we actually had a public imagination. That is, when people were really interested in each other, rather than in Apple 'devices.' In other words, back when we had vices, not devices."

—The Huffington Post

Biographies that Focus on the Ironies of Fame
www.BloodMoonProductions.com

Award-Winning Entertainment About
How America Interprets Its Celebrities

The Seductive Sapphic Exploits of
MERCEDES DE ACOSTA
Hollywood's Greatest Lover

Volume Three of Blood Moon's "Magnolia House" Series
by Darwin Porter and Danforth Prince

Copyright 2020, Blood Moon Productions, Ltd.
All Rights Reserved
www.BloodMoonProductions.com
Manufactured in the United States of America

ISBN 978-1-936003-75-4

Conception, Covers, & Book Design by Danforth Prince
Distributed worldwide through Ingram's Lightning Source and Internet vendors
which include Amazon.com

OTHER INTRIGUING TITLES FROM BLOOD MOON PRODUCTIONS

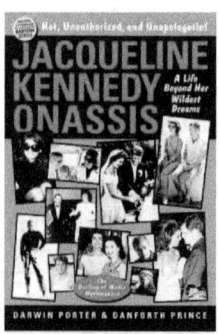

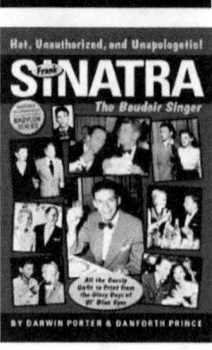

Here's Part of the Coven of Legendary Women Who Were Exposed in the Confessions of Mercedes de Acosta

Silent Screen Vamp **Jean Acker**

Philanthropist and arts patron **Rita Stokes Lydig**

Stage star and the former Toast of London, **Tallulah Bankhead**

Stage diva **Ethel Barrymore**

"The aristocracy of Broadway," **Katharine Cornell**

"The Mother of Modern Dance," **Isadora Duncan**

"The world's most fabulous woman," **Marlene Dietrich**

Italy's most celebrated actress, **Eleanore Duse**

Socialite, trendsetter, and interior decorator, **Elsie de Wolfe (Lady Mendl)**

Torch singer, heiress, and murderess
Libby Holman

Silent screen megastar
Jeanne Eagels

"The Good Witch of the North,"
Billie Burke

Greta "The Divine" **Garbo**

John Barrymore
shown here with his third wife,
Dolores Costello

French cabaret entertainer and model
for Toulouse-Lautrec:
Yvette Guilbert

Russian *prima ballerina*
Tamara Karsavina

Violet Ward "and her lover"
circa 1900 at the Alice Austen
House, as photographed by
Queer Icon & long-time Staten
Island resident **Alice Austen**

Photographer pioneer
Gertrude Kasebier

Broadway Über-Diva
Eva Le Gallienne

Comedienne and Stage Star
Beatrice Lillie

Broadway investor and theatrical agent **Bessie Marbury** (left), with **Elsie de Wolfe**

Philanthropist & Activist
Anne Morgan,
daughter of J.P. Morgan

Suicidal Hollywood star
Ona ("Belle Watling") **Munson**

"Force of Nature" & Silent Screen Diva
Nazimova

Rudolph Valentino's second wife
Natacha Rambova

Art Connoisseur and *Zeitgeist* star
Gertrude Stein

Novelist, philanthropist, and Francophile, **Edith Wharton**

PREVIOUS WORKS BY DARWIN PORTER
PRODUCED IN COLLABORATION WITH BLOOD MOON

BIOGRAPHIES

Judy Garland & Liza Minnelli, Too Many Damn Rainbows

Historic Magnolia House: Celebrity & The Ironies of Fame

Glamour Glitz & Glitter at Historic Magnolia House

Burt Reynolds, Put the Pedal to the Metal

Kirk Douglas, More Is Never Enough

Playboy's Hugh Hefner, Empire of Skin

Carrie Fisher & Debbie Reynolds, Princess Leia & Unsinkable Tammy in Hell

Rock Hudson Erotic Fire

Lana Turner, Hearts & Diamonds Take All

Donald Trump, The Man Who Would Be King

James Dean, Tomorrow Never Comes

Bill and Hillary, So This Is That Thing Called Love

Peter O'Toole, Hellraiser, Sexual Outlaw, Irish Rebel

Love Triangle, Ronald Reagan, Jane Wyman, & Nancy Davis

Jacqueline Kennedy Onassis, A Life Beyond Her Wildest Dreams

Pink Triangle, The Feuds and Private Lives of Tennessee Williams, Gore Vidal, Truman Capote, and Famous Members of their Entourages.

Those Glamorous Gabors, Bombshells from Budapest

Inside Linda Lovelace's Deep Throat,
Degradation, Porno Chic, and the Rise of Feminism

Elizabeth Taylor, There is Nothing Like a Dame

Marilyn at Rainbow's End, Sex, Lies, Murder, and the Great Cover-up

J. Edgar Hoover and Clyde Tolson
Investigating the Sexual Secrets of America's Most Famous Men and Women

Frank Sinatra, *The Boudoir Singer. All the Gossip Unfit to Print*

The Kennedys, *All the Gossip Unfit to Print*

The Secret Life of Humphrey Bogart *(2003), and*
Humphrey Bogart, The Making of a Legend *(2010)*

Howard Hughes, *Hell's Angel*

Steve McQueen, *King of Cool, Tales of a Lurid Life*

Paul Newman, *The Man Behind the Baby Blues*

Merv Griffin, *A Life in the Closet*

Brando Unzipped

Katharine the Great, Hepburn, *Secrets of a Lifetime Revealed*

Jacko, His Rise and Fall, *The Social and Sexual History of Michael Jackson*

Damn You, Scarlett O'Hara,
The Private Lives of Vivien Leigh and Laurence Olivier

FILM CRITICISM
Blood Moon's 2005 Guide to the Glitter Awards
Blood Moon's 2006 Guide to Film
Blood Moon's 2007 Guide to Film, and
50 Years of Queer Cinema, 500 of the Best GLBTQ Films Ever Made

NON-FICTION
Hollywood Babylon, It's Back! and *Hollywood Babylon Strikes Again!*

NOVELS
Blood Moon,
Hollywood's Silent Closet,
Rhinestone Country,
Razzle Dazzle
Midnight in Savannah

OTHER PUBLICATIONS BY DARWIN PORTER
NOT DIRECTLY ASSOCIATED WITH BLOOD MOON

NOVELS

The Delinquent Heart
The Taste of Steak Tartare
Butterflies in Heat
Marika (a roman à clef based on the life of Marlene Dietrich)
Venus (a roman à clef based on the life of Anaïs Nin)
Bitter Orange (a roman à clef based on the life of Anita Bryant)
Sister Rose

TRAVEL GUIDES

Many Editions and Many Variations of The Frommer Guides, The American Express Guides, and/or TWA Guides, et alia to:

Andalusia, Andorra, Anguilla, Aruba, Atlanta, Austria, the Azores, The Bahamas, Barbados, the Bavarian Alps, Berlin, Bermuda, Bonaire and Curaçao, Boston, the British Virgin Islands, Budapest, Bulgaria, California, the Canary Islands, the Caribbean and its "Ports of Call," the Cayman Islands, Ceuta, the Channel Islands (UK), Charleston (SC), Corsica, Costa del Sol (Spain), Denmark, Dominica, the Dominican Republic, Edinburgh, England, Estonia, Europe, "Europe by Rail," the Faroe Islands, Finland, Florence, France, Frankfurt, the French Riviera, Geneva, Georgia (USA), Germany, Gibraltar, Glasgow, Granada (Spain), Great Britain, Greenland, Grenada (West Indies), Haiti, Hungary, Iceland, Ireland, Isle of Man, Italy, Jamaica, Key West & the Florida Keys, Las Vegas, Liechtenstein, Lisbon, London, Los Angeles, Madrid, Maine, Malta, Martinique & Guadeloupe, Massachusetts, Melilla, Morocco, Munich, New England, New Orleans, North Carolina, Norway, Paris, Poland, Portugal, Provence, Puerto Rico, Romania, Rome, Salzburg, San Diego, San Francisco, San Marino, Sardinia, Savannah, Scandinavia, Scotland, Seville, the Shetland Islands, Sicily, St. Martin & Sint Maarten, St. Vincent & the Grenadines, South Carolina, Spain, St. Kitts & Nevis, Sweden, Switzerland, the Turks & Caicos, the U.S.A., the U.S. Virgin Islands, Venice, Vienna and the Danube, Wales, and Zurich.

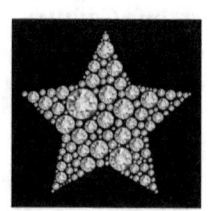

BIOGRAPHIES

From Diaghilev to Balanchine, The Saga of Ballerina Tamara Geva

Greta Keller, Germany's Other Lili Marlene

Sophie Tucker, The Last of the Red Hot Mamas

Anne Bancroft, Where Have You Gone, Mrs. Robinson?
(co-authored with Stanley Mills Haggart)

Veronica Lake, The Peek-a-Boo Girl

Running Wild in Babylon, Confessions of a Hollywood Press Agent

HISTORIES

Thurlow Weed, Whig Kingpin

Chester A. Arthur, Gilded Age Coxcomb in the White House

Discover Old America, What's Left of It

CUISINE

Food For Love, Hussar Recipes from the Austro-Hungarian Empire, with collaboration from the cabaret chanteuse, Greta Keller

AND COMING SOON FROM BLOOD MOON
Jane & Henry Fonda
To Each His (or Her) Own

CONTENTS

CHAPTER ONE   **PAGE 1**
    HERE LIES THE HEART
    MERCEDES DE ACOSTA— MUSE, MENTOR, ENABLER, & SEDUCTRESS OF THE WORLD'S MOST FAMOUS WOMEN

CHAPTER TWO   **PAGE 9**
    THE LOST GENERATION
    A TALE OF TWO SISTERS— HOW MERCEDES DE ACOSTA AND HER RICHER, MORE BEAUTIFUL SISTER, **RITA HERNÁNDEZ DE ALBA DE ACOSTA STOKES LYDIG**, MOVED WITHIN THE UPPER ECHELONS OF GILDED-AGE SOCIETY EXPLORING THE PRETENSIONS, PRIVACIES, & PECCADILLOS OF THE "FIN DE SIÈCLE"

CHAPTER THREE   **PAGE 67**
    "LA DUSE"
    ELEANORA DUSE— ITALY'S BELLE-ÉPOQUE ANSWER TO SARAH BERNHARDT

CHAPTER FOUR   **PAGE 73**
    THE GODDESS OF MODERN DANCE
    ISADORA DUNCAN— DANCE AS A REVOLUTIONARY CELEBRATION OF LIFE

CHAPTER FIVE   **PAGE 79**
    LONELY ARE THE BRAVE
    EVA LE GALLIENNE— ONE OF BROADWAY'S MOST ADMIRED *GRANDE DAMES*, AMERICA'S ANSWER TO SARAH BERNHARDT

CHAPTER SIX   PAGE 107
   SELF-ENCHANTED, IMPERIAL, UNFORGETTABLE
   NAZIMOVA— EMPRESS OF SILENT FILMS, QUEEN OF METRO

CHAPTER SEVEN   PAGE 145
   MERCEDES' SEDUCTIONS OF VALENTINO'S WIVES
   JEAN ACKER & NATACHA RAMBOVA— HOW "THE SHEIK OF ARABY" GOT CUCKOLDED, BY A WOMAN, TWICE.

CHAPTER EIGHT   PAGE 161

   MERCEDES' AFFAIR WITH *LES DEMOISELLES DE LA RUE DE FLEURUS*
   GERTRUDE STEIN & ALICE B. TOKLAS— THE WORLD'S MOST CELEBRATED LESBIAN COUPLE

CHAPTER NINE   PAGE 177

   THE VENUS'S FLYTRAP FROM ALABAMA & "THE DARLING SHE-DEVIL"
   TALLULAH BANKHEAD AND HOPE WILLIAMS:

CHAPTER TEN   PAGE 225
   EAGLES FLY HIGH
   JEANNE EAGELS— BEAUTIFUL, DOOMED, AND UNINHIBITED, AN ACTRESS OF MYTH AND LEGEND.

CHAPTER ELEVEN   PAGE 271
   AMERICA'S OBSESSION WITH GIRLS YOU'D NEVER BRING HOME TO MOTHER.
   RAIN
   IT'S A HIT! STAGE AND FILM PORTRAYALS OF AMERICA'S MOST NOTORIOUS PROSTITUTE, SADIE THOMPSON BY JEANNE EAGELS, GLORIA SWANSON, JOAN CRAWFORD, TALLULAH BANKHEAD, & RITA HAYWORTH. WHICH OF THEM PORTRAYED THE MOST CONVINCING SLUT?

CHAPTER TWELVE   PAGE 297
   "THE HAPPIEST MARRIED HOMOSEXUAL COUPLE OF THE THEATER WORLD"
   KATHARINE CORNELL & GUTHRIE McCLINTIC
   MERCEDES & TALLULAH SEDUCE THEIR BELOVED "KIT" AS McCLINTIC FALLS FOR A YOUNG ACTOR NAMED KIRK DOUGLAS

CHAPTER THIRTEEN — PAGE 313
"STAR CRAZED" BEFORE ANYONE CALLED IT BY THAT NAME
MERCEDES' MANIA FOR CELEBRITY CHASING
DIAGHILEV, NIJINSKI, & STRAVINSKY; JEAN COCTEAU (FRANCE'S ENFANT TERRIBLE); ETHEL (HIGH PRIESTESS OF THE AMERICAN THEATER) BARRYMORE; JOHN BARRYMORE & HIS WIFE, MICHAEL STRANGE; ALDOUS ("BRAVE NEW WORLD") HUXLEY; CULT SINGER YVONNE GEORGE & SOCIALIST ROBERT DESNOS; THE GREAT RUSSIAN BALLERINA, TAMARA KARASAVINA; PLUS THE HINDU MYSTICS, MEHER BABA & JIDDU KRISHNAMURTI.

CHAPTER FOURTEEN — PAGE 339
"THE FACE OF THE 20TH CENTURY,"
GARBO THE DIVINE
SHROUDED IN MYSTERY, SHE REIGNED AS A GODDESS OF THE MOVIEGOING PUBLIC. HER LEGEND NEVER DIES

CHAPTER FIFTEEN— — PAGE 427
"THE KRAUT"
MARLENE DIETRICH
— COSMOPOLITAN & OMNISEXUAL, SHE WAS THE 20TH CENTURY'S *FEMME FATALE*

CHAPTER SIXTEEN — PAGE 441
THE CONFEDERACY'S MOST FAMOUS WHOREHOUSE MADAM
ONA MUNSON
— MERCEDES' TORRID AFFAIR WITH BELLE WATLING, *GONE WITH THE WIND*'S KIND-HEARTED HOOKER

CHAPTER SEVENTEEN — PAGE 451
MEDIA BUZZ & ZOOMER TIMES
BETTER ACCESS TO A FAMILIAR FRIEND
— MAGNOLIA HOUSE'S ZOOMED-IN VIEW OF MEDIA GURU & GRANDE DAME **ANITA FINLEY**, GUIDING LIGHT BEHIND ONE OF FLORIDA'S MOST-WATCHED WELLNESS & LIFESTYLE PROGRAMS

AUTHORS & SCRIBES — PAGE 467
DARWIN PORTER, DANFORTH PRINCE, & THE RESIDENT GHOSTS AT MAGNOLIA HOUSE

Stained glass at **Magnolia House**, the kind Mercedes de Acosta described as "inspirational" during some of her conversations with Darwin.

After this window (right photo) was commissioned by Darwin and installed at Magnolia House, he dedicated it to the memory of his friend **Mercedes de Acosta,** mentor, guide, and lover to some of the most famous and celebrated women of the 20th Century.

DID YOU KNOW? That Mercedes de Acosta's belief in the healing and restorative power of light filtered through stained glass has been pumped and amplified by new generations of *avant-garde* filmmakers?

In September of 2019, **Blood Moon Productions rented Magnolia House** to an Anglo-French film crew for the crafting of their horror romance, **The Dream Eater.**

Their selection of Magnolia House was partly based on their belief that the stained glass dedicated to Mercedes de Acosta would be a suitable background for the encounter *(depicted above)* of its intuitive teen-aged protagonist with the other-worldly intelligence identified as "An Eater of Dreams."

Mercedes would have understood the ironies.

[Photos courtesy of the film's British producer, **Ciaran Harland** *and its French director,* **Simon Doutreleau.**]

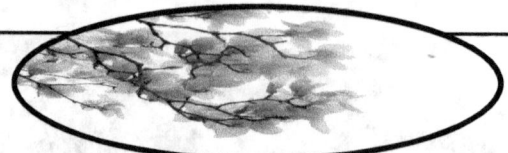

Magnolia House is a historic landmark on Staten Island, the least-visited Outer Borough of New York City. Built in stages between 1830 and 1870, it was designed by one of NYC's then most-fashionable architects, Edward A Sargent.

Set within a 12-minute walk from the (free) Staten Island ferry that accesses Manhattan at intervals of every thirty minutes or less, it's the headquarters of the widely distributed independent press, BLOOD MOON PRODUCTIONS, a feisty wordsmith noted for celebrity biographies that have been reviewed in *THE DAILY MAIL*, the New York *DAILY NEWS*, The New York *POST*, show-biz news reports, and literary journals across the country.

Some visitors liken Magnolia House to a *grande dame* with a centuries-old knack for nourishing high-functioning eccentrics. Many of them, including the infamous **MERCEDES DE ACOSTA**, the focal point of this book, have lived or been entertained here since New York's State Senator Howard Bayne, a transplanted Southerner, moved in with his wife, the daughter of the Surgeon General of the Confederate States of America, in the aftermath of that bloodiest of wars on North American soil, the War Between the American States.

In addition to Mercedes, dozens of celebrities have whispered their secrets and rehearsed their ambitions within its walls. They've included movie vamps from the silent screen, MIDNIGHT COWBOYS, dancers from the dance, BUTTERFLIES IN HEAT, a heavyweight boxing champ, writers from every hue, faded film goddesses, playwrights who crafted blockbusters for both Marilyn (Monroe) and Elizabeth (Taylor), *ultra-avant-garde* diarists, every known variety of *prima donna* and *diva*, including some from the world of opera, and a world-class Olympic athlete.

They've also included Darwin Porter and Danforth Prince, who spent decades here renovating it and within its walls, producing a stream of FROMMER TRAVEL GUIDES and award-winning celebrity biographies.

This book illuminates Mercedes de Acosta and her contribution to the American Century, when dozens of individual movers and shakers—some of them sane and emotionally stable, others not—relayed their stories within Magnolia House.

Mercedes was one of them. **This book reveals some of her secrets.**

For information about reasonably priced "celebrity centric" overnight stays at a *"grande dame"* historic inn with astonishing cultural antecedents, click on:

AIRBNB.COM/H/MAGNOLIA-HOUSE
AND/OR
WWW.MAGNOLIAHOUSESAINTGEORGE.COM

DAISY CHAIN
A Witty, Sometime Cruel, Late-Night Parlor Game Invented by Truman Capote

Whenever he was feeling provocative and bitchy (which was most of the time), a puckish **Truman Capote** would, if the company were amenable, play one of his favorite parlor games. He called it "Daisy Chain."

If the players had a large enough inventory of salacious gossip, and no compunction about revealing other people's indiscretions, "Daisy Chain' could link ANYONE to almost ANYONE ELSE through their previous sexual or romantic indiscretions.

According to Capote, **Mercedes de Acosta**—a socially well-connected eccentric whose lesbian adventures usually defied conventional social circuits—provided some of the most consistently reliable links in his parlor game.

Capote paid a price for his wit: Tennessee Williams described him as "a sodomite's delight, a monster unleashed from virginal portals," and when he got too caustically witty, in print, most of his friends and parlor game playmates brusquely abandoned him forever.

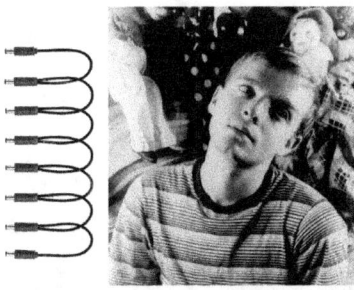

Wallis Warfield Simpson
(aka The Duchess of Windsor)

King Edward VIII abandoned the British throne to marry her. After that, she was both reviled and sought-after as a source of delicious gossip.

Francis Spellman was a predatory homosexual and the Cardinal Archbishop of New York.

At the Vatican, it was no secret that he had "this thing" for acolytes and choir boys.

Here Lies the Heart

CHAPTER ONE
Here Lies the Heart

MERCEDES DE ACOSTA

Inspiration, Enabler, Muse, Mentor, &

SEDUCTRESS

OF THE WORLD'S GREATEST ACTRESSES

Until she was seven years old, the legendary Spanish beauty, **Mercedes de Acosta**, was convinced she was a boy. She tried to convince others of that, too. However, her world came tumbling down on her when a ten-year-old boy challenged her to show him her penis. He took her behind a bathhouse, unbuttoned his pants, and pulled out his penis, playing with himself until it was erect.

At this point, he was joined by five other boys, all of whom produced erections for her. When challenged to show her own privates, she ran screaming back to her bedroom, where she cried for two days and nights.

She later wrote, "On this hot afternoon, everything in my young soul turned monstrous and terrible and dark."

The photo on the right shows Mercedes after she'd lost an eye after surgery for removal of a tumor. Stylish to the last, she wore that patch with a sort of panache.

In her final years, desperately in need of money, she had to sell her jewelry and private papers, including letters from Greta Garbo and Marlene Dietrich, to pay medical bills.

She spent the end of her life, as she told Darwin Porter, "learning just simply and quietly to be."

She was seventy years old in 1966, when she died, the long-time survivor of one of the 20th Century's most fascinating lives.

Darwin Porter cited the legendary Mercedes de Acosta as one of the most fascinating characters of the 20th Century. A poet, novelist, and playwright, he entertained her frequently at Magnolia House and was dazzled by her fabled life, contacts, and personality.

Born in 1893 in New York, and, during her youth, independently wealthy, she was descended from Spain's Dukes of Alba. In time, she grew into one of the most celebrated beauties of her day. Although married to the painter Abram Poole from 1920 to 1935, she was rarely home, busily seducing such towering figures on the screen as Marlene Dietrich and Greta Garbo, as well as the fabulous dancer, Isadora Duncan, and Italy's most acclaimed actress, Eleonora Duse.

"Oh, did I leave out Katharine Cornell, the First Lady of the American Theater, and Alice B. Toklas, the lover of the formidable Gertrude Stein in Paris?" Darwin asked. "By the time I met Mercedes, she already had a reputation as a 'lady killer.'"

"She was a self-admitted celebrity stalker, tracking down everyone from John Barrymore to Igor Stravinsky, from Erich Maria Remarque to Cole Porter, from Jeanne Eagels to Tallulah Bankhead and Douglas Fairbanks, Jr. Many women, some of them major-league cultural icons of the 20th Century, found her irresistible. So did I. As a very young man, I fell under her spell and was always happy to give her money and bring her presents."

Biographer Gavin Lambert described a young Mercedes in her heyday as "dark-eyed, romantically pale, black hair slicked down with brilliantine, with the air of a toreador, especially when wrapped in a black cape and wearing buckled shoes. As a woman chaser, she could be persistent to the point of absurdity."

"Among her male friends were Stravinsky,

When this picture was snapped, **Mercedes** had attended her first bullfight in Madrid. When she told her friends that she'd been horrified by it, they called her "not a true Spaniard."

"If killing pathetic horses and bulls is being a Spaniard," she said, "then I forever renounce being one."

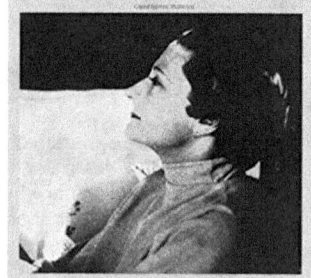

HERE LIES THE HEART
A Tale of my Life
MERCEDES DE ACOSTA

Darwin still retains (and treasures) his autographed first edition of **Mercedes' memoirs**, the one she gave him shortly after its publication in 1960.

At the time, she was seriously ill with a brain tumor, half blind, and walked with a prosthetic leg—a disfigured relic of her former beauty.

Aldous Huxley, and Krishnamurti, none of whom had any patience with fools or friends."

She would meet a woman, such as the celebrated Russian ballerina, Tamara Platonovna Karsavina, who would immediately be enticed into becoming her lover.

Robert A. Schanke, Mercedes' biographer, claimed, "She was flawed and imperfect, a complex woman who impaired several of her relationships and failed to achieve her professional and romantic aspirations. But she was exceptionally lively, intelligent and dynamic, and she had many devoted friends. She was a brave lesbian of her time, and a person who remained kind and loyal to most everyone with whom she crossed paths. The many denigrating portrayals of her may derive from the deep homophobia of her generation."

Her memoir, Here Lies the Heart, was widely attacked in its day, and she was accused of fabricating incidents and "lacing it with half-truths and fantasies." Upon its release in 1960, the book did not sell well, but it was reissued in 2016, and is now considered a major contribution to gay and lesbian history.

In 1955, John Bainbridge, the biographer of Greta Garbo, called Mercedes "a woman of courtly manners, impeccable decorative taste, and great personal elegance, a woman with a passionate and intense devotion to the art of living. She was endowed with a high spirit, energy, electric curiosity, and a varied interest in the arts."

Soon after its debut, her "lavender marriage of convenience" (to the painter Abram Poole, as mentioned) became less and less convenient for him and everyone concerned.

Shortly after marrying him, Mercedes launched a five-year affair with Eva Le Gallienne, one of the most talented and famous of American stage actresses. [For more on

When **Mercedes** was a young woman, the Spanish painter, Ignacio Zuloga, said to her, "All great people function with their heart."

He placed his hand over her physical heart and continued: "Here lies the heart. Always remember to think with it, to feel with it, and, above all, to judge with it."

Photo shows **Mercedes** (looking macho and avant-garde) in the 1930s with an Indian-born mystic.

He was Bhagavan Sri Ramana Maharsi (1879-1950) an "in the news" guru whose lifestyle teachings took café society by storm.

this, refer to Chapter Five of this book. Mercedes wrote two plays for her, including Jehanne de Arc.]

Many of her affairs were with women known in her day but largely forgotten today, including the New York actress Ona Munson, who played the whorehouse madame, Belle Watling, in Gone With the Wind (1939). Munson became critically acclaimed for the way she interpreted the role, although Mercedes later said, "Ona had about as much in common with a Georgia madam as Hitler did with Santa Claus." Ona attended Gone With the Wind's Los Angeles premiere with Mercedes.

***

Mercedes also managed to seduce Alla Nazimova, born in 1879, in Yalta, Russia. In the 1920s and during the Silent era, she became the Queen of MGM. She studied with Stanislavsky and knew Chekhov. In silent films, she earned $13,000 a week, a fabulous fortune in 1915. She welcomed the elite of Hollywood to her legendary hotel, the Garden of Allah.

One of her most celebrated films was Camille (1921), where she played opposite Valentino as Armand. She is still seen on TCM's screenings of Blood and Sand (1941) as Tyrone Power's mother.

Today, Nazimova is mostly remembered as Nancy Reagan's godmother.

***

Mercedes even seduced Pola Negri, the rival silent screen vamp of Gloria Swanson.

"I can take any woman from any man," Mercedes boasted. Garbo, however, remained her closest relationship, except when they were feuding. Their affair began in 1931, when Garbo was beginning to talk on the screen for the first time.

During these 30 years, Garbo wrote Mercedes 181 letters. In 1959, Mercedes, nearly bankrupt, sold her papers, including the Garbo letters.

One night in front of a fireplace at Magnolia House, she told Darwin, "I could not bear burning Garbo's letters to me. I only hope they are not seen by the eyes of vulgar people."

***

How did Darwin meet such an exotic, rarefied creature? It was arranged, at his request, through a mutual friend, Maria Voigt, a leading jewelry designer for Tiffany's.

As Humphrey Bogart told Claude Rains in the closing reel of Casablanca, "It was the beginning of a beautiful friendship."

It was 1960, and Mercedes had just published her controversial, even notorious, autobiography, Here Lies the Heart.

After reading the book, Garbo—in outrage—ended her long friendship with Mercedes. In contrast, Marlene Dietrich wrote, "I loved the book, darling."

In Paris, Alice B. Toklas said, "Say what you will about Mercedes, she had the most important women of the 20th Century."

After she'd spent the money from her book, Mercedes was broke again. She turned to Darwin, asking him if he'd co-author a book with her on Garbo.

That did not come to be, although he spent a lot of time with her, making copious notes. But at the age of 75, in May of 1968, a few months after a final visit to Magnolia House, Mercedes died.

Darwin, however, incorporated the material she gave him into one of his most successful novels, Marika. Although its namesake was obviously based on Marlene, one of its other main characters was a thinly disguised portrait of Mercedes. In the words of most critics, Marika (aka Marlene) remained Mercedes' dear friend until the end.

Shortly after her death, Darwin told the Hollywood Reporter "Of all the fabulous women who have crossed my path in life, none was like Mercedes de Acosta. Until her last hours, she was passionately devoted to the art of living…and to seduction. She told me that after all the failures, disappointments, and betrayal one goes through in life, you learn at some point to sit in a room watching the sun pour through stained glass."

"In all likelihood, there will never be another woman like Mercedes. For one thing, God no longer makes legendary women like those she seduced."

Other sexual romances inaugurated by Mercedes de Acosta, as relayed by contemporary witnesses and laid out in her memoirs, were with stage star **Eva Le Gallienne** (upper photo), silent film star **Alla Nazimova** (middle photo) and Hollywood's "ultimate vamp," **Pola Negri** (lower photo).

They're more fully described in later chapters.

***

Long after Darwin's friendship with Mercedes ended with her death, latter-day appraisals of her have often been harsh.

Tallulah Bankhead claimed, "Mercedes looks like a mouse in a top-coat."

Maria Riva, the daughter of Marlene Dietrich, dubbed Mercedes as "Dracula."

The famed photographer, Cecil Beaton, found her "charming, kind, clever, and interesting, birdlike and vividly quick. She has glorious enthu-siasms, glorious friendships—and I like her very much."

Mysteries, however, surround many of her other cosmopolitan and in-ternational seductions.

In her book, *The Girls*, and in reference to Mercedes, Diana McLellan, whose column, "The Ear," ran for ten years in the Washington Post, Washington Star, and Washington Times, wrote:

"Cognoscenti marveled at Mercedes' conquests. The writer, Hugo Vickers, cites the late Truman Capote's game of international 'Daisy Chain,' whose object is to link people sexually, using as few beds as possi-ble. In Capote's view, Mercedes was the best card in the world to hold. You could get, he said, to anyone from the Duchess of Windsor to Cardinal Spellman."

More than any other portrait of **Mercedes De Acosta**, this one hints at her wildly romantic "love with abandon and damn the consequences" motif that made her wildly appealing to the (repressed and sexually frustrated) bisexual entertainers of her era's stage and screen.

La Belle Époque, usually defined as the years between 1880 and the outbreak of World War I, was defined as a "Golden Age," but only in contrast to the horrors of "The Great War" that brought it to an end.

Modern viewers interpret these "ultra-feminine," expensively attired duets of highly demonstrative friends—snapped around 1910 during Mercedes' late teenaged years—as attention-grabbing, *avant-garde*, and "screaming" with lesbian implications.

So did Mercedes de Acosta.

CHAPTER TWO
A Tale of Two Sisters

THE LOST GENERATION

How Mercedes De Acosta and her Richer, More Beautiful Sister,

Rita (Hernández de Alba de Acosta Stokes Lydig) Moved Within the Upper Echelons of Gilded-Age Society

Exploring the Pretensions, Privacies, & Peccadillos of the *"Fin de Siècle"*

Art critics interpret Giovanni Boldini's depictions of **Rita de Acosta** as one of the most revelatory portraits of the Gilded Age. The collage assembled above includes details of her shoes—she was said, thanks to the hundreds of very upscale shoes she collected, to have had something of a fetish.

Hailed as one of the most glamourous women in the world, Rita surrounded herself with the *glitterati* of her age. Her salon was a mecca for the world's greatest artistic legends—painters, opera stars, actresses, writers, composers, musicians, and philosophers.

It is not unheard of for two sisters to each become internationally famous. Such was the case with the movie star siblings Olivia de Havilland and Joan Fontaine, and with Constance and Joan Bennett.

Separately and individually, both Mercedes de Acosta and her older sister, Rita Hernández de Alba de Acosta Stokes Lydig (1875-1929), became towering social figures, each interacting at frequent intervals with some of the great cultural figures of the early 20th Century.

But whereas Rita was heterosexual and *fêted* by hostesses across the Eastern Seaboard, the more avant-garde Mercedes—as an outspoken lesbian—was received with a bit more caution. Nonetheless, for decades, their respective social lives orbited each other in all kinds of combinations, most of them loving and mutually supportive.

Mercedes—the "glue" that binds together the various components of this book— was the final child of a family of three boys and five girls. The other siblings included Rita (born October 1, 1875), Joaquín, Enrique, Ricardo, Aida, Maria, and Angela.

Their father was Ricardo de Acosta (1837-1907), a Cuban steamship line executive and sugar refiner. His parents were from Spain, and as a youth he traveled back and forth between Havana and Madrid.

During the Cuban insurrection against Spain, known as the Ten Years' War (1868-1878), Ricardo sided with Cuban patriots. Spanish soldiers arrested him and, along with two dozen other revolutionaries, he was lined up to face a firing squad. He escaped by jumping off a cliff into the sea, where he was later picked up by an American vessel sailing for Boston.

Adaptable and savvy, he became a Spanish instructor at Harvard University and assimilated well into the booming economy that flourished in the Northern States after the U.S.'s Civil War. After several years, he returned to Havana where he grew rich in the shipping and sugar industries.

In 1871, he married Micaela Hernández de Alba y de Alba (1853-1921), whose

Ricardo de Acosta (1837-1907), father of Mercedes and Rita. Even before she learned to read, Mercedes' father read to her nightly from the works of Shakespeare, Cervantes, and Goethe

Micaela Hernández de Alba y de Alba (1853-1921), mother of Mercedes and Rita. As a young girl, this Spanish aristocrat inherited four million dollars, a vast fortune in her day.

It is not unheard of for two sisters to each become internationally famous. Such was the case with the movie star siblings Olivia de Havilland and Joan Fontaine, and with Constance and Joan Bennett.

Separately and individually, both Mercedes de Acosta and her older sister, Rita Hernández de Alba de Acosta Stokes Lydig (1875-1929), became towering social figures, each interacting at frequent intervals with some of the great cultural figures of the early 20th Century.

But whereas Rita was heterosexual and *fêted* by hostesses across the Eastern Seaboard, the more avant-garde Mercedes—as an outspoken lesbian—was received with a bit more caution. Nonetheless, for decades, their respective social lives orbited each other in all kinds of combinations, most of them loving and mutually supportive.

Mercedes—the "glue" that binds together the various components of this book— was the final child of a family of three boys and five girls. The other siblings included Rita (born October 1, 1875), Joaquín, Enrique, Ricardo, Aida, Maria, and Angela.

Their father was Ricardo de Acosta (1837-1907), a Cuban steamship line executive and sugar refiner. His parents were from Spain, and as a youth he traveled back and forth between Havana and Madrid.

During the Cuban insurrection against Spain, known as the Ten Years' War (1868-1878), Ricardo sided with Cuban patriots. Spanish soldiers arrested him and, along with two dozen other revolutionaries, he was lined up to face a firing squad. He escaped by jumping off a cliff into the sea, where he was later picked up by an American vessel sailing for Boston.

Adaptable and savvy, he became a Spanish instructor at Harvard University and assimilated well into the booming economy that flourished in the Northern States after the U.S.'s Civil War. After several years, he returned to Havana where he grew rich in the shipping and sugar industries.

In 1871, he married Micaela Hernández de Alba y de Alba (1853-1921), whose

Ricardo de Acosta (1837-1907), father of Mercedes and Rita. Even before she learned to read, Mercedes' father read to her nightly from the works of Shakespeare, Cervantes, and Goethe

Micaela Hernández de Alba y de Alba (1853-1921), mother of Mercedes and Rita. As a young girl, this Spanish aristocrat inherited four million dollars, a vast fortune in her day.

lineage descended from the Dukes of Alba, one of the most prominent and prestigious pedigrees in Spain.

Rita grew into a celebrated beauty and socialite, one of "the most picturesque women of the Gilded Age."

The portrait painter, John Singer Sargent, was once asked why Rita, who was considered clever and creative, never found (or developed) an artistic expression of her own.

"Why should she?" Sargent responded loyally and instantly. "She herself is a work of art."

Rita de Acosta Lydig, then one of the richest and most socially sought-after patronesses of the arts in NYC, photographed in 1913 by Baron Adolf de Meyer. Here, the photographer captures her sense of self-entitled *hauteur*.

She always had a fetish, it was said, for shoes.

***

As Rita came of age, she became famous for an extravagant lifestyle that was acted out with flair and high drama in Manhattan, London, and Paris. She was forever surrounded by her hairdresser, masseuse, chauffeur, secretary, two maids, and a valet. In her literary and artistic salon, she frequently entertained painters, musicians, actors, philosophers, and intellectuals.

She also married twice, in both cases to men who were wealthy and twenty years older than herself.

Her first husband was William Earl Dodge Stokes (1852-1926). She was only nineteen when, on January 13, 1895, she became his wife, a role she came to despise.

Although she was only three years old at the time, Mercedes always claimed that she remembered the wedding of her oldest sister, an event covered by *The New York Times*. That newspaper hailed her as "the most beautiful woman in New

Portrait by unidentified artist of **Rita de Acosta Lydig** in then the height of Gilded Age fashion, accessorized with her trademark antique lace. The statuette of the *Virgen de Guadelupe* in the upper right betrays her conservative Hispano-Catholic upbringing.

York." She was known for her porcelain skin, her raven black hair worn in a pompadour, her ruby red lips, and—one of her best features—her dark, flashing eyes.

Rita's mother, a devout Catholic, was disappointed that her oldest daughter's new husband was a Protestant. A truckload of flowers, including orange blossoms imported at huge expense from Florida, decorated the house on the day of her wedding, when it was packed with at least a thousand guests, many of them noted personalities from the Gilded Age. The prestige quotient was "off the charts," and included a scattering of Vanderbilts, Astors, Rockefellers, and Morgans.

Two views of Rita's first husband, the adultery-soaked mega-millionaire who developed the Ansonia Hotel and the Upper West Side of Manhattan, **W.E.D ("Weddie") Stokes** (born 1852, died 1926)

As she grew up, Mercedes learned from Rita that she had not married for love, but for financial security. W.E.D. Stokes became known in Manhattan as the developer of most of the Upper West Side of Manhattan. The most visible and valuable gem in his crown was the Ansonia Hotel at 2109 Broadway at West 73rd Street. Attracting such guests as baseball great Babe Ruth, novelist Theodore Dreiser, the great opera singer, Enrico Caruso, and the composer Igor Stravinski, it became the grandest hotel in New York.

An architect's rendering of the **Ansonia Hotel**, the "*ne plus ultra*" of NYC residences, as developed and promoted by Rita de Acosta's first husband.

On the roof of his hotel, as a means of supplying fresh ingredients for the kitchens downstairs, Stokes established a small farm with cows, 500 chickens, a scattering of ducks, six goats, and even a small bear in a cage. Eventually, New York's Department of Health shut down the rooftop farm.

Stokes (known in the press and to his friends as "W.E.D.," eventually became the president of the Chesapeake Western Railroad. Both he and his wife were devotees of horse racing and both of them traveled frequently to the Kentucky Blue Grass Country, where they bred and raised racers and stud horses.

York." She was known for her porcelain skin, her raven black hair worn in a pompadour, her ruby red lips, and—one of her best features—her dark, flashing eyes.

Rita's mother, a devout Catholic, was disappointed that her oldest daughter's new husband was a Protestant. A truckload of flowers, including orange blossoms imported at huge expense from Florida, decorated the house on the day of her wedding, when it was packed with at least a thousand guests, many of them noted personalities from the Gilded Age. The prestige quotient was "off the charts," and included a scattering of Vanderbilts, Astors, Rockefellers, and Morgans.

Two views of Rita's first husband, the adultery-soaked mega-millionaire who developed the Ansonia Hotel and the Upper West Side of Manhattan, **W.E.D ("Weddie") Stokes** (born 1852, died 1926)

As she grew up, Mercedes learned from Rita that she had not married for love, but for financial security. W.E.D. Stokes became known in Manhattan as the developer of most of the Upper West Side of Manhattan. The most visible and valuable gem in his crown was the Ansonia Hotel at 2109 Broadway at West 73rd Street. Attracting such guests as baseball great Babe Ruth, novelist Theodore Dreiser, the great opera singer, Enrico Caruso, and the composer Igor Stravinski, it became the grandest hotel in New York.

An architect's rendering of the **Ansonia Hotel**, the "*ne plus ultra*" of NYC residences, as developed and promoted by Rita de Acosta's first husband.

On the roof of his hotel, as a means of supplying fresh ingredients for the kitchens downstairs, Stokes established a small farm with cows, 500 chickens, a scattering of ducks, six goats, and even a small bear in a cage. Eventually, New York's Department of Health shut down the rooftop farm.

Stokes (known in the press and to his friends as "W.E.D.," eventually became the president of the Chesapeake Western Railroad. Both he and his wife were devotees of horse racing and both of them traveled frequently to the Kentucky Blue Grass Country, where they bred and raised racers and stud horses.

In a loveless marriage, Stokes soon drifted into countless affairs, usually with teenage servant girls or the daughters of local farmers in Kentucky. As Mercedes later claimed, "Bill liked them young, and I mean barely out of the cradle."

Stokes and Rita produced a son, William Earl Dodge Stokes, Jr., born in 1896. But Rita confessed to Mercedes, "I detest having a child. I can't tolerate even holding the boy. I won't win any Mother of the Year awards. If I get pregnant again, I'll have a doctor terminate it."

Inevitably, in 1900, Rita's marriage came to an unhappy end, when she divorced Stokes and received a widely publicized two-million dollar settlement. At the time, it was a record amount for a divorce settlement in the United States.

Although Rita didn't want (or even like) her child, she was granted custody of her son. In hopes that he would in time inherit Stokes' remaining fortune, she sent him back to his father.

As Mercedes grew older, her mother perceived that she was much too obviously jealous of her oldest child's (Rita's) beauty, social grace, and charm. And although Mercedes seemed to worship Rita, perhaps that was to some extent true.

"Rita could have had any man she wanted," Mercedes said. "She received proposals from royalty in England, from noblemen in France, and from counts in Italy, plus certain titans of industry in America. Once, she took me to Oyster Bay in Long Island to meet the man she called "my dear friend, Teddy."

According to Mercedes, "Rita and Teddy left me in the library to look at some books while they disappeared for a few hours."

Mercedes, of course, was referring to Theodore Roosevelt.

***

In 1902, Rita married once again, this time to Philip Mesier Lydig, a rich and socially prominent officer in the U.S. Army. Once again, and again much to her Catholic mother's regret, Rita's second husband was also a Protestant. At her wedding, she was given away by her brother, Ricardo. Rita's sister, Aida, was Maid of Honor.

Aida would never achieve the fame of Mercedes and Rita, but she did have a distinction. In 1903, when she was nineteen, she became the first woman to fly an aircraft (in this case, a dirigible), solo, over the rooftops of Paris.

[How did it happen? One of the era's most colorful rogues, the Brazilian aviator Alberto Santos-Dumont, was known for flying his miniature dirigibles in and out of central Paris. He had, on several well-publicized occasions, navigated his way from a Parisian suburb to an inner-city restaurant, and

Airborne bravado in the early "lighter-than-air' days of modern aviation:

Alberto Santos-Dumont appears in this photo in his dirigible, barely missing collisions into the rooftops of Paris.

parked his dirigible on the street during dinner.

On the afternoon of June 27, 1903, after a few hours of training and in a moment of humor, whimsy, and charm, Santos-Dumont perched Aida in the pilot's seat, surrendered control of the dirigible to her, and instructed her to take a "test drive." As she flew alone above the rooftops of Paris, Santos-Dumont rode his bicycle along below, flailing his arms in a series of pre-defined signals and shouting directions. Her flight ended at the northern end of Paris' **Bois de Boulogne** during a polo match between the American and British teams. After securing her dirigible and" anchoring it" with ropes, spectators good-naturedly helped the beautiful American teenager climb out of the basket and congratulated her on her achievement. After watching some polo with Santos-Dumont, Acosta climbed back into the dirigible's "passenger basket" and flew the machine back to the Parisian suburb of Neuilly St. James.

As such, Aida became the first woman to pilot any kind of motorized aircraft, a few months before the Wright Brothers flew their aircraft above the sands of Kitty Hawk, North Carolina.

Later in Aida's life, she developed glaucoma in one eye, which led to her becoming a staunch advocate for ocular health. In that capacity, she was named the executive director of the first eye bank in the United States.

Aida's second husband was Henry Skillman Breckinridge (1886-1960), the Assistant Secretary of War from 1913 to 1916. He was also an attorney, representing aviator Charles Lindbergh in the most famous kidnapping case in U.S. history.

***

Two views of Mercedes' and Rita's sister, **Aida de Acosta**, lower photo, flying to a polo match in 1903 during her infamous afternoon above the landmarks of Paris.

Her actions were considered so shocking, so "against the norm" of what a well-bred young woman should do, that her parents did everything they could to erase the incident from speculation.

News of Aida's role as the first "*aero-chauffeuse*" in human history only emerged, accidentally and whimsically, in the 1930s, decades after it happened, during a casual dinner conversation with her then-husband and a family friend.

Although Rita was not in love with her second husband, either, she found it was to her advantage to be married to him. One of the most memorable events of her marriage was when they traveled together to St. Petersburg in Russia. They were guests of Czar Nicholas and his Czarina, Alexandra, at a lavish banquet at the royal palace.

When Russian revolutionaries, on July 17, 1918, massacred every member of the Czar and Czarina's family, including their children, Rita was both enraged and horrified.

***

In 1907, the Acosta family was horrified with news that their patriarch, Ricardo, had committed suicide at a vacation resort in the Adirondack Mountains of New York State.

Depressed over his declining fortunes, Ricardo had traveled alone to the Camp Uncas, an artfully rustic but ultra-deluxe retreat acquired by J. Pierpont Morgan in 1896. Operated as a resort, it was billed as a rustic utopia where the rich and famous could retreat, perhaps with a favorite mistress, for boating, fishing, relaxation, hunting, fine dining, and hill climbing.

On August 24, Ricardo had told the resort's staff that he was headed off for a solo hike. He never came back. His body was later recovered at the bottom of a cliff. Apparently, he had jumped off the cliff to his death.

"My heart was broken," Mercedes said. "This was my first experience with suicide. Throughout my life, I would live through the suicides of many of my closest friends."

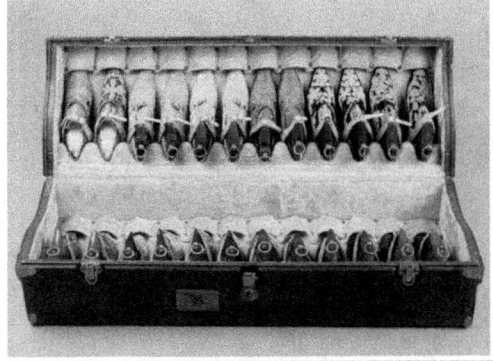

***

"In time, I would make love to some of the world's most beautiful women, notably Greta Garbo and Marlene Dietrich," Mercedes said. "But when I was a girl, my sister Rita symbolized beauty to me. She was one stunning creature."

"Her beauty did not go unnoticed. Many of the great painters and some of the most noted photographers wanted to paint her or to have her pose for photographs. There is little

Everything about Rita de Acosta's persona was the immaculately "*soigné*" after-effect of an armada of coiffeurs, masseuses, makeup artists, couturiers, and shoemakers—in this case, **Pierre Yantory**, whose custom-made shoes are today treasured mementos in the collections of many major-league museums.

Displayed above are shoes crafted by Yantory and later donated to the Costume Institute, a subdivision of New York's Metropolitan Museum. Each was the avant-garde, probably custom-made property of Mercedes' rich, socially prominent sister, Rita.

doubt that my sister, Rita, had an enormous impact on the art and fashion of her heyday," Mercedes claimed.

[Rita's sense of style and fashion, coupled with donations of many seminal articles from her personal collection, led to the launch of the Costume Institute at the Metropolitan Museum of Art in Manhattan.]

"Among other passions, she was a devotee of antique lace," Mercedes recalled. "She designed her own clothes, and her outfits were copied by fashion houses in both New York and Paris."

In Paris, she had her gowns and dresses designed and crafted by Callot Soeurs, one of Europe's leading *couturiers* during the 1910s and '20s. It was operated by the four Callot sisters, who specialized in the antique lace so beloved by Rita. *Vogue* magazine defined the sisters as "foremost among the powers that rule the destinies of a woman's life."

Ladies Home Journal recognized the sisters for having the richest clients of any of the fashion houses. Rita wore a silver Callot Soeurs dress when she posed for Giovanni Boldini in 1911.

At times, Rita would order two dozen outfits from the sisters. When she learned that her husband was being entertained by a mistress with poor taste in clothing, she ordered the sisters to create a stylish wardrobe for her.

Some of Rita's designs were interpreted as scandalous. Men raved about the beauty of her back, so she decided to show off this physical asset by designing a backless gown, a *décolleté* evening gown cut on its backside down to her waistline and (obviously) worn without a *brassière*.

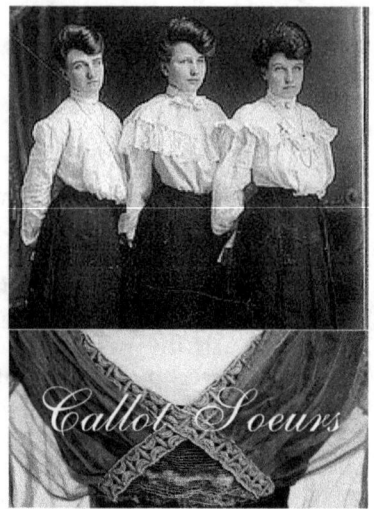

By modern dressmaking standards, **the Callot Sisters**, three of whom appear in the upper photo, were astonishing.

The lower photo is of an "art nouveau on the cusp of art deco" evening dress they designed and crafted, and probably showed as the best of their collections that year, with pride, to Rita de Acosta. It's now a treasured exhibit in the Costume Institute of New York's Metropolitan Museum.

It was the Callot Soeurs who designed and crafted the dress that Rita made famous in the portrait by Boldini, displayed on the first page of this chapter

To introduce this daring new concept in alluring women's fashion, she appeared at the Diamond Horseshoe Box of the Metropolitan Opera House in Manhattan. Lorgnettes and binoculars were lifted from all sides of the audience to gaze upon her, although some newspapers the following morning denounced her backless gown as "indecent."

***

In the early stages of her marriage, Rita commissioned Stanford White to design a stunningly beautiful three-story townhouse at 38 East 52nd Street in Manhattan. Built in the Italian Renaissance style, it was filled with Rita's rare paintings and *objets d'art* she'd collected mostly in Paris and London.

White (1852-1906) designed many homes for the wealthy of his era, as well as numerous public buildings. At the age of fifty-two, he was fatally shot by the mentally unstable millionaire, Harry Kendall Thaw, who was jealous of White's affair with his wife, the actress Evelyn Nesbit. The shooting led to a court case dubbed "The Trial of the Century."

***

Like her first marriage, Rita's relationship with Philip Lydig was also doomed for failure. She first filed for divorce in 1914, but the case was delayed until after World War I. The final divorce decree was granted on July 24, 1919, eight months before Mercedes' own announcement of her loveless engagement to artist Abram Poole.

Actually, Rita did fall in love at least once. The object of her affection was Percy Stickney Grant (1960-1927), the Rector of the (Episcopal) Church of the Ascension at Fifth Avenue and West 10th Street in Manhattan. Regrettably, the pastor's bishop would not grant him permission to marry Rita because she was twice divorced and

Rita de Acosta in a backless, then-scandalous, evening sheath, as photographed by **Baron Adolphe de Meyer,** a fashion photographer at the time for the then-new American edition of *Vogue.*

Rita de Acosta Stokes Lydig was not the first (or last) marital scandal to rock the Episcopal Church, but at the time she fell in love with **Percy Stickney Grant** *(profile portrait, above)* they were each so controversial that the Episcopal Bishop of New York banned their nuptials.

Defying each of their deeply ingrained religious principles, they moved in with one another anyway. rocking and rolling NYC's *haute bourgeousie.*

"a woman of dubious reputation." She was also known to hang out in lesbian circles with her notorious younger sister, Mercedes.

Grant moved in with Rita anyway, without benefit of marriage. He would die at the age of sixty-six in 1927, two years before Rita's own death.

***

Rita became a charter member of the Colony Club, the first women-only private social club in Manhattan. It was founded in 1903 by Florence Jaffray Harriman, wife of J. Borden Harriman.

Stanford White designed the clubhouse at 120 Madison Avenue. It was constructed between 1904 and 1908 and was modeled after an 18th Century building in Annapolis, Maryland.

In her novel, *Tragic Mansions*, Rita described "the tragic futility of fashionable life," and said: "'The display and luxury, the appearance of success and the envy of the world, had blinded me to the real miseries of our existences."

Elsie de Wolfe designed the interior, and her longtime companion, Elisabeth Marbury was one of its founders. Anne Morgan, the daughter of J. Pierpont Morgan, was also one of the founders.

Other members included Madeleine Talmadge Force Astor, wife of John Jacob Astor; Emily K. Rafferty, president of the Metropolitan Museum of Art; and Abby Aldrich Rockefeller.

Like its other members, Rita became a suffragette, campaigning for the rights of women. Rita joined in marches along Fifth Avenue, demanding the right to vote.

After many a march, and many a battle, on August 18, 1920, women won the right to vote with passage of the 19th Amendment to the U.S. Constitution.

***

The Acosta siblings lost their mother on December 5, 1921. She died while visiting Rita at her lavish country home in Bedford Hills, New York. During the final years of her life, she refused to utter one word of English, demanding to be addressed only in Spanish.

In her final days, she told Mercedes that she loved Rita, but that "she stabbed my heart by marrying two Protestants and by living in sin with a minister," a reference to Dr. Grant, the Episcopal priest.

Señora De Acosta had been made aware (by somebody) of Mercedes' own lesbian liaisons, but she dismissed such speculation, claiming, "It is impossible for two women to make love to each other." *[Incidentally, Queen Victoria maintained almost exactly the same point of view.]*

***

Rita published her only novel, *Tragic Mansions*, in 1927 under the name of Mrs. Philip Lydig. It was an overview of life, love, and tangled relationships among the mega-rich of the Gilded Age.

It came out when she was in heavy debt and in ill health.

Some critics interpreted it as part memoir, part scathing social critique. It described "the tragic futility of a fashionable life," suggesting that "marriage without love is a suicide pact."

In the novel's depiction of the ostentation of the Gilded Age families of Newport, Rhode Island, *Tragic Mansions* moves into the same territory that F. Scott Fitzgerald explored in his classic, *The Great Gatsby*, except the he did it so much better.

Tragic Mansions also evoked the novels of Edith Wharton. When Rita and Wharton were younger, each of them fell in love with the same beau.

One New York critic wrote: "The entire book by Mrs. Lydig is tedious and dull, unlike the novels of Mrs. Wharton. She cuts into the underbelly of Manhattan's aristocratic class, exploding their hypocrisy. Lydig makes a feeble attempt at similar introspection by sharing stories using pseudonyms and altered situations. But they fall flat. Her novel is virtually unreadable."

After reading that, Rita cried on and off for the next two days.

Haute, Gilded-Age glamour is evoked here: Above is **Giovanni Boldini's** rendering, symbolically, at least, in the Bois de Boulogne, of **Rita de Acosta** with her megawealthy husband #2, **Philip Lydig.**

***

Rita's extravagant lifestyle finally caught up with her, and on April 7, 1927, she filed for bankruptcy. The news made the frontpage of *The New York Times*, as more than three dozen creditors were demanding immediate payment, which she could not meet.

At the time, she was suffering from a prolonged illness and had undergone several costly surgical operations in the aftermath of an accident she'd suffered.

Months before, Rita and her sister Aida had been driving a horse-drawn cart in Westbury, Long Island. Something seemed to frighten the animal, and it went wild, ramming the cart it was hauling into an embankment. Rita fell out of the cart and was trampled by the horse, which damaged her internal organs. In the agonizing aftermath of the same accident, Aida lost her sight in one eye.

In court, Rita pleaded her own case before the judge. She claimed, "I have no income. I have been too ill to handle my affairs. In fact, I fear that

I am dying."

A former butler testified that Rita spent at least $3,000 a week on morphine, which she was ingesting as a means of relieving the pain of that accident with the horse.

The judge was unsympathetic to her case and ordered that she hold a public auction to meet the demands of her creditors.

At the auction, since Rita was confined to her hospital bed, Mercedes was designated as her sister's representative. But at the last minute, defying her doctors' orders, Rita appeared in an attempt to direct—or at least influence—the proceedings.

In her weakened condition, she watched her treasures go on the auction block. Representatives from the American Art Institute called it "the most important public sale of Gothic and 16th-Century art to take place in the United States."

One by one, items she'd had in her possession for years went for what she thought were shockingly low bids. Treasures included six George III candlesticks, a 16th Century bronze statue, a set of 18th Century Chippendale dining chairs, a Queen Anne coffeepot.

"On and on it went," Mercedes said. "Each sale was a humiliation for her."

Most painful of all were the sale of her masterpieces, including *Portrait of a Philosopher* by Ignacio Zuloaga; and one of several representations of *Venus* painted by Botticelli, art that evoked his even more famous painting with the same name that hangs in the Uffizi Gallery in Florence.

[*Rita's painting by Botticelli had inspired Mercedes in the composition of her play,* Sandro Botticelli, *which a few years earlier had starred her then-lover, Eva Le Gallienne.*]

The entire auction brought in only $400,000. Rita had hoped for at least one and a half million dollars.

***

Mercedes was at the bedside of Rita on the morning she died at the age of fifty-four in Manhattan's Gotham Hotel. She was recovering from her latest operation and had recently been released from the hospital.

"We were sisters, but we were more than that," Mercedes said. "We were friends forming some alliance against the world and our many critics. She never condemned my role as a lesbian, and I never attacked her extravagances. In a lifetime of meeting famous and charismatic women, I never was introduced to one that had the charm and charisma of Rita de Acosta. She was one of a kind."

"The death of my beloved Rita was one of the more severe blows to my already battered heart," Mercedes said. "At times, I envied her and may even have been jealous of her. I saw her suffer through two failed marriages with men she did not love, and I knew that she never found the fulfillment in life she desperately sought. She failed to find happiness...and so did I."

"I cried and cried after Rita's death. Then I woke up one morning and decided I must carry on with my life, forever searching for the contentment

I so desired."

In the wake of Rita's death, Mercedes assembled some special guests for a memorial to share in her grief. The list included Jeanne Eagels, Katharine Cornell, Noël Coward, Constance Collier, Laurette Taylor, Alfred Lunt, Lynn Fontanne, and Clifton Webb and his mother.

"My theater friends stood by me, and I developed a series of kitchen-supper nights where we would gather, many after their performances on Broadway. Sometimes we stayed up until dawn before hustling off to our beds for some much-needed sleep. My kitchen was almost like a late-night club that went on until dawn. These suppers were a great solace to me."

SPECIAL FEATURE

THE DE ACOSTA SISTERS CONFRONT BELLE EPOQUE SOCIETY

"Whatever do you do when every one of your friends is a living legend?"
— Mercedes de Acosta

Beginning when Mercedes was ten, her older sister, Rita, either invited her or accompanied her to gala parties and literary salons in New York and Paris. There, she mingled and conversed with some of the most celebrated figures of her era. Some had shot to fame during the *Belle Époque.* Others were embittered luminaries from what Gertrude Stein had defined as "The Lost Generation."

A parade of figures came and went from their lives: Rodin, Anatole France, D'Annunzio, Edith Wharton, Sarah Bernhardt. They also met lesser-known celebrities whose fame didn't survive their generation: Bourdelle, Henry Bergson, Brieux, Yvette Guilbert, and Jacques Copeau.

According to Mercedes, "Because of Rita and other factors, I was growing up fast with hopes of becoming a woman known on two continents as a writer. From an early age, I found myself chatting with such intellectuals as Unamuno, Ortega y Gasset, or Benevente."

"My contacts weren't confined to actors, directors, writers, and painters. On occasion, I met royalty—King Alfonso XIII of Spain, Queen Maria of Romania, Count Boni de Castellane, Princess Hohenlohe."

"I also became friends with Pierre Yantorny (1874-1936), the most famous and remarkable shoemaker who ever lived. He flattered me, telling me that I had the most beautiful feet he'd ever seen, and he'd seen the feet up close of some of the most famous ladies of his generation." *[Years after her death, Rita's wardrobe—including dozens of spectacularly upscale shoes crafted by Yantory—ended up as part of the Costume Institute of New York's Metropolitan Museum of Art.]*

Although a heterosexual, Rita moved through lesbian salons in Paris or New York with the same ease as she greeted her straight friends. She was equally at ease talking to Gertrude Stein and Alice B. Toklas as she was with Ernest Hemingway or F. Scott Fitzgerald.

"Rita and I entertained homosexual writers like André Gide, Jean Cocteau, or Marcel Proust, but also stood our ground with Ezra Pound, Max Jacob, or Sherwood Anderson, to name a few. These men came and went from our lives. I found it hard keeping up with all their published works."

What follows are thumbnail sketches of some of the celebrities Rita and Mercedes met and entertained over the years. In the early part of the 20th Century, their names were widely known by thousands of people. Today, except for the more widely publicized few, they are largely forgotten and virtually unknown to millennials or members of Generation Z.

"In a different age, certainly, a more gracious time, these figures dazzled the world with their charm and talent," Mercedes said. "They were also flawed. Have you ever met anyone who is not flawed?"

ETHEL BARRYMORE
(1879-1959)

The sister of the equally famous John and Lionel Barrymore, Ethel Barrymore, an actress from Philadelphia, competed with two or three other women for the title of "First Lady of the American Theatre," a title she surely deserved.

Much of her early life was spent in London, where she was shy, recalling "the terror" she felt when she first met Oscar Wilde. By the 1890s, she had decided that her life would be spent upon "the wicked stage," as it was called in those days.

In time, Rita de Acosta befriended Ethel, and a young Mercedes always made it a point to be present whenever Ethel visited. "I had my first big schoolgirl crush on this *grande dame*," Mercedes said. "I prayed I wouldn't turn pea-

Ethel Barrymore, left, as an ingenue, and right, as the gullible and politically imcompetent Czarina Alexandra in MGM's blockbuster *Rasputin and the Empress (1932)*.

green with fright. She inquired about my future, and I could come up with no ambition, no goal. I was tongue-tied. But my infatuation with Miss Barrymore continued, and I would always skip school to attend one of her *matinées*. I remember seeing her in such dramas as *Captain Jinks* and *Alice Sit by the Fire."*

In 1895, Ethel appeared on Broadway in *The Imprudent Young Couple,* co-starring Maude Adams and John Drew, Jr. The following years she also co-starred with them in *Rosemary.*

In 1897, she was in London where she was offered the role of Annette in *The Belief,* co-starring with Henry Henry Irving and Ellen Terry.

During this period, many suitors were attracted to her considerable charms, most notably Sir Winston Churchill, who fell in love with her, began a secret affair with her, and asked her to marry him. She turned him down. Details of their brief affair weren't revealed to the public until sixty-three years after it ended.

Other suitors included the Duke of Manchester, actor Gerald Du Maurier, and writer Richard Harding Davis. In 1909, Ethel married Russell Griswold Colt, who was younger than she was. Together, they produced three children, including future actress Ethel Barrymore Colt, born in 1912.

Mercedes Becomes Embroiled in the Lives of
RASPUTIN & THE RUSSIAN PRINCE WHO MURDERED HIM

As unlikely as it seemed in 1932, Mercedes became involved indirectly in the first motion picture in which Ethel co-starred with her brothers, John and Lionel. She was cast as Czarina Alexandra; Lionel as Grigori Rasputin; and John as Prince Chegodieff.

At that time, Mercedes was employed temporarily as a scenario writer for MGM, working directly with Irving Thalberg, "The Boy Wonder at MGM" He had hired her mainly because of her strong emotional links to Greta Garbo.

One morning, Thalberg summoned Mercedes to his *moderne* office on the second floor of MGM's executive building. Because he liked to clearly establish his power over his "supplicants," his massive desk was set on a platform so that visitors were forced to look up at him as they made their respective arguments, sales pitches, and pleas.

Rasputin "the Mad."

After his murder, his fabled fourteen-inch penis was cut off and preserved in alcohol.

That morning he told her, "I'm considering making a movie about Rasputin and the Russian Czarina." Mercedes may have been the target of this conversation because Thalberg had recently learned that she maintained friendly dialogues with Prince Feliz Felizovich Yusupov (1887-1967), a Russian aristocrat who had married the niece (Princess Irina Alexandrovna) of Czar Nicholas II. Before the Revolution, he'd been one of the richest men in Imperial Russia and had participated in the murder of the notorious Rasputin.

Mercedes and the prince had become friends in Paris. From time to time, she had accompanied him to drag balls and other events where he had dressed as a woman. He was fond of cross-dressing and seducing "studly men," including a string of conquests recruited from the Russian Army. Even after his marriage, Yusupov continued his affairs with men. In Russian during World War I, he had converted a wing of his Moika Palace into a hospital for wounded soldiers. As he nursed some of the better-looking ones back to health, he had insisted on giving them their baths.

Originally, Yusupov had been a "client" of Rasputin, hoping that "the healer," as he was known, might cure him of his homosexual impulses as a means of cultivating a more satisfactory marriage to the beautiful and well-connected Princess Irina. On the night of December 17, 1916, that motive became a ruse to lure Rasputin to Yusupov's residence at Moika Palace.

Details of the murder of Rasputin that mysterious night vary greatly. Mercedes always claimed that Prince Yusupov in Paris had relayed to her many accurate insights into the actual murder.

Apparently, the prince had given Rasputin tea and cakes which were laced with cyanide. The burly Russian peasant mystic and self-proclaimed "Holy Man" survived them, even after swallowing its "chaser," a cyanide-laced glass of Madeira.

When it became obvious that the cyanide wasn't going to kill him, it took a loaded re-

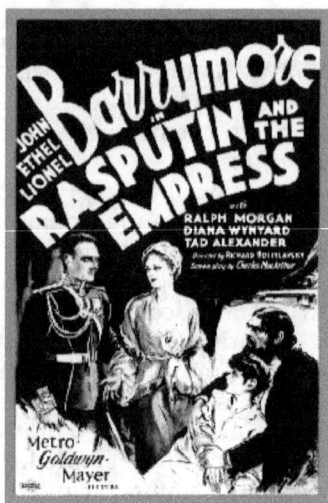

Rasputin and the Empress brought together the three fabulous Barrymores in one movie—John, Ethel, and Lionel. But the film led to outrage, lawsuits, libel judgments against MGM, and the banning of the movie in Britain.

The notion that **Rasputin and Alexandra** had shared indiscretions wasn't as far-fetched as Yusupov's lawyers implied in their suit against MGM

Depicted above is a crude political cartoon that was widely distributed (and widely believed) throughout Russia in the months before the Revolution of 1917, perhaps part of a campaign to discredit the imperious but gullible matriarch of the detested autocrats, the Romanovs.

volver (i.e., a bullet shot directly into his brain) to end Rasputin's life.

"This tale was like fodder for me when I began replicating Rasputin's murder for MGM's movie," Mercedes said.

Rasputin had spent a lot of time with Czar Nicholas II because his oldest son and heir, Alexei, suffered hemophilia. During his tenure at the Romanov court, Rasputin developed many enemies, some of whom considered him a destructive but charismatic charlatan and resented his influence over the Czar. Soliciting the help of Prince Yusupov, they began plotting his assassination.

A problem arose at MGM when Thalberg demanded that Mercedes insert a fictional subplot into her script that suggested that Rasputin had once raped the Princess Irina. Emphatically denying it, Yusupov told Mercedes that his wife had never met Rasputin.

Once again, Mercedes contacted Yusupov in Paris, warning him of what Thalberg wanted inserted into the scenario. That resulted in letters to MGM from Yusopov's attorneys threatening to sue MGM if such an insinuation made its way into the filmscript.

Consequently, Mercedes faced a dilemma: "I knew that if I didn't write that sensational, vulgar, and untrue sequence, Thalberg would fire me. Even after I warned Thalberg that Yusupov might sue, he insisted that the scene be included anyway."

Once again, Mercedes met with Thalberg, revealing that she'd discussed the scene that he wanted directly with Yusopov. When "The Boy Wonder" heard that she'd broken the news to him, he exploded in fury, summoning his secretary to demand that she bring him Mercedes' contract at once. Right in front of her, he tore it into pieces and threw them into his wastepaper basket. She was out of a job.

As Mercedes had warned, when *Rasputin and the Empress* was released, Yusupov, then a British subject, filed suit in London against MGM, charging libel and invasion of privacy. His attorneys notified Mer-

Two views of Mercedes' friend, **Yusupov**, lower photo, with **Princess Irina**, niece of the Czar.

Mercedes alerted the Russian prince that MGM was planning a "libelous" allegation involving his wife and a the possibility that she had been raped by Rasputin.

cedes that she would be summoned to London to testify.

When Thalberg heard that, he ordered that MGM rehire Mercedes. When he met with her, he made no mention of his having fired her.

She later wrote that Yusupov won his libel judgment and was granted damages of a million dollars, although she vastly overstated the amount. MGM was forbidden to show *Rasputin and the Empress* in Britain.

[Actually, the film's working script contained very little material that had been written by Mercedes: What became the final version had been crafted by Charles McArthur, the husband of Helen Hayes.]

[In the aftermath of Yusupov's lawsuit against MGM, all studios made it a point to insert disclaimers into every film's credits. The disclaimers stated that the story line was not based on any actual person or event.]

Mercedes held onto her job at MGM until Thalberg died in 1936. The day after his death was announced, she was fired once again, this time definitively.

JUAN BELMONTE
(1892-1962)

Emerging from Seville in Spain's sun-blasted but historically fecund province of Andalusia, Juan Belmonte became one of his country's greatest and most daring matadors.

He killed his first bull in the ring when he was eighteen. From the beginning, he developed a death-defying technique of standing just inches away from the raging bull. Of course, that meant that he was frequently gored, and he sustained serious wounds. Some of his mistresses said that he liked to show off his many scars from his record-breaking 109 *corridas*.

He became so famous that in January of 1925, Belmonte's image was affixed to the cover of *Time* magazine.

He became a stalwart friend of Ernest Hemingway, the world's famous bullfight *aficionado*. Belmonte appears in two of the

During the Golden Age of bullfighting in Spain, **Juan Belmonte** was hailed as the country's greated matador.

Belmonte's bullfighting technique was unique in the inbred world of matadors. Partly because his legs were bowed and he had difficulty running, he stood erect and nearly motionless within a few inches from whatever bull he confronted. As a result, he was frequently gored, sustaining, it's estimated, 25 serious wounds and dozens of less serious ones.

One such incident occurred in 1927 bullfight in Barcelona, when he was impaled by a bull's horn through his chest and pinned against a wall. Other toreros rescued him. Among the spectators that day were King Alfonso XIII, the Queen of Spain and the Infanta Beatriz.

After lifelong injuries and trauma, when his doctor told him he could no longer smoke cigars, ride his horse, drink wine, or have sex with women, Belmone decided it was time to die. He took a pistol from his drawer and shot himself.

novelist's books, *Death in the Afternoon* and *The Sun Also Rises*.

Rita's de Acosta sometimes shocked her more snobbish guests by including the rough-edged Belmonte in some of her gatherings. One socialite warned Rita, "A bullfighter, my dear, is lower than a prizefighter."

On April 8, 1962, within a week of his 70th birthday, Belmonte shot himself in the head. It was defined as a "copycat suicide," inspired by the suicide of Ernest Hemingway, who had killed himself the same way almost nine months earlier.

JACINTO BENAVENTE
(1866-1954)

In the studio of her friend, Ignacio Zuloaga, the Spanish painter, Mercedes was first introduced to Jacinto Benavente, one of the foremost Spanish dramatists of the 20th Century. His plays included such dramas as *La noche del sábado* (1903) and *Señora Ama* (1908). Each of them relied on dialogue instead of action to convey the author's points and values.

In 1922, Benavente won the Nobel Prize "for the happy manner in which he continues the illustrious traditions of Spanish drama," as reflected in 172 of his works, an amazing output.

Jacinto Benevente in 1920, in San Sebastian with an admirer. He was immune to the charms of women, gravitating instead to the charms of studly matadors.

Mercedes soon learned that he was a homosexual, with a fondness for both aspirant actors and young matadors. Bullfighters were a favorite subject for Zuloago, and Benavento was often present during their posing sessions.

Mercedes was never certain of Benavente's politics. He was defined "as a liberal monarchist and critic of socialism." Later, he became a somewhat reluctant supporter of the dictator Franco, backing him only because he was against the Spanish government's "Republican Experiment" (1931-1936).

Mercedes turned against Benavente when his name was linked to the assassination of Federico Garcia Lorca, the great (and devoutly homosexual) Andalusian poet and dramatist.

In 1936, Spanish Republicans incorrectly claimed, for political reasons, that Benavente had been murdered. Actually, he lived until 1954, dying in Madrid at the age of eighty-seven.

GIOVANNI BOLDINI
(1842-1931)

The moment Rita de Acosta met Giovanni Boldini, the Italian painter was awed by her physical beauty. "My dear, you must come by my studio tomorrow so that I can capture your beauty on canvas. When God created you, he must have had Venus on one side, Helen of Troy on the other. Had you been a handmaiden in the court of Cleopatra, she'd have had you beheaded because she could not stand the competition."

Boldini eventually portrayed Rita in fourteen separate portraits. Mercedes often accompanied her during her visits to his studio. One of his portraits depicted Rita with her second husband, Philip Lydig, walking in Paris' Bois de Boulogne. The portrait now hangs in the Louvre.

Mercedes noted with amusement that Boldini never worked without wearing his bowler hat, regarding it as a good luck charm.

Born in Ferrara, Italy, he later studied in Florence, launching himself as a portrait painter. As his talent became more widespread, he moved to Paris, where he was labeled "the Master of Swish." *[At the time, Swish" was not a politically incorrect gay reference, but a designation of his "flowing" style of portraiture.]*

Sometimes, when Mercedes and Rita visited his studio, they talked to his best friend, Edgar Degas. Many famous people of his day, including the Duchess of Westminster, came and went from his studio.

A self-portrait from 1865 of **Giovanni Boldini**. Mercedes said, "He was highly nervous, energetic, and astute, a little man with a flair for style and chic that no other portrait painter in this century could ever surpass."

ENRICO CARUSO
(1873-1921)

The greatest operatic tenor emerged from the City of Naples to enchant music lovers worldwide. One of the first major singers to be recorded, his voice was captured on records from 1902 to 1920.

Mercedes' early memories of him was his "being gay, sometimes comic, always reacting with his heart to people and events."

Caruso's career spanned a quarter of a cen-

Enrico Caruso and his wife, the American-born socialite **Dorothy Benjamin**. (1893-1955). Their marriage lasted only three years—until his death in 1921.

She later wrote two biographies of her late husband, one of which was adapted into a movie, *The Great Caruso* (1951) where she was portrayed by Ann Blyth and her husband was cast with Mario Lanza

tury and included an astonishing 863 appearances at Manhattan's Metropolitan Opera House. In 1910, he performed as part of the first radio program ever transmitted in America.

Caruso made two films, the first a silent movie, *My Cousin*, released by Paramount in 1918. The following year, he starred in another movie, *The Splendid Romance*. Producer Jesse Lasky paid Caruso the then-astonishing fee of $100,000 for his two appearances. *My Cousin* bombed at the box office, and *The Splendid Romance* was never released.

Mercedes remembered attending one of Caruso's performances, in 1920, at The Met. He also starred at La Scala in Milan; at the Royal Opera House in London; and at the Marinsky Theatre in St. Petersburg.

During his time in New York, Rita often entertained him at her salon, where—much to the awe of Mercedes—he sometimes sang for her guests.

New and younger generations were introduced to Caruso through Mario Lanza, who starred in the film *The Great Caruso* (1951), thrilling movie audiences with his soaring tenor voice.

LINA CAVALIERI
(1874-1944)

Judge for yourself—Was **Lina Cavalieri** the world's most beautiful woman? After a bomb from Allied forces hit her villa in Florence, a priest discovered her body in the ruins, and proclaimed it as "the most beautiful corpse he had ever known."

Lina Cavaliera, an Italian operatic soprano, actress, and monologist [*i.e., a performer who recites dramatic readings*] was born on Christmas Day in a small town fifty miles north of Rome. She lost both parents and became a ward of the state at the age of fifteen. Although she was sent to a Catholic orphanage, as it turned out, she was too vivacious to submit to the strict discipline of the nuns.

As a teenager, she escaped and fled to Paris, where she found work singing in music halls. In time, she became a noted opera singer, appearing at The Met in Manhattan with Enrico Caruso.

During that time, Rita de Acosta entertained her at her gatherings of the artistic elite.

The Russian prince, Alexander Bariatinsky, fell madly in love with Lina, and they sustained a widely publicized affair. Although he wanted to marry her, their wedding was opposed by Czar Nicholas II.

Boldini, who had painted Rita, also arranged for Cavalieri to pose for him. In the press, she was defined as "the world's most beautiful woman," using corsetry to augment her alluring hour-glass figure.

One of her marriages was to Robert

Winthrop Chanler (1872-1930), a painter and a member of the Astor family, but the union did not survive the honeymoon.

Mercedes was a friend of Chanler, describing him as "gargantuan... everything about him—hands, feet, shoulders, head—all were enormous. His voice bellowed like the roaring of the bulls."

As a portraitist, Chanler crafted several portraits of Mercedes. She warned him not to marry Cavalieri, advising him that "the diva is a schemer."

Mercedes was right: Shortly after marrying him, Cavalieri persuaded him to sign a document that turned over all his assets to her. Immediately after he signed it, she left him and went through the courts in a successful bid to commandeer his bank accounts, real estate, possessions.

Cavalieri starred at all the great opera houses alongside the major singers of her day, including Mary Garden (see below) and the French tenor, Lucien Muratore, whom she married in 1913.

After she retired from the stage, she ran a cosmetics salon in Paris, where she launched her own perfume, a scent she marketed as the "Mona Lina."

When Italy entered World War I, she migrated to Hollywood, where she starred in silent pictures. Her best-known film was *A Woman of Impulse* (1918), with Robert Cain and Raymond Bloomer.

After marrying once again, this time to Paolo D'Arvanni, she moved to Florence. Hearing an Allied bomber in 1944, she panicked and fled with her family to a bomb shelter. However, at the last minute, she returned to retrieve her valuable jewelry collection. As she was rushing to rescue it, a bomb destroyed her home, killing her.

The Italian bombshell, Gina Lollobrigida, portrayed Cavalieri in the 1955 film, *Beautiful But Dangerous* (aka *The World's Most Beautiful Woman.*)

CLAUDE DEBUSSY
(1862-1918)

Rita de Acosta's circle of friends reached out to embrace Claude Debussy, who became one of the most influential composers of the late 19th and early 20th Centuries.

Debussy was a boy prodigy, showing such talent that at the tender age of ten, he was admitted to the Conservatoire de Paris, the leading music college in France. Even so, it took many years before he developed a reputation of international renown. He was already forty years old when he shot to fame in 1902 with the only opera he ever completed, *Pelléas et Mélisande.*

Critics claimed that Debussy's music was a reaction against Wagner and the German musical tradition, and showed an early influence from Russia and the Far East. He developed his own style of harmony and orchestral coloring, as reflected in such orchestral works as *Nocturnes* (1897), which became a favorite of Mercedes.

He is often defined as the first Impressionist composer, although he detested the term. "Anyone using that term about my music is an imbecile," he said. Nonetheless, Debussy scholars continue to use it, one of them labeling his work as "the greatest example of an orchestral Impressionist work." Nigel Simeone wrote, "It does not seem unduly far-fetched to see a parallel in Monet's seascapes."

Mercedes knew nothing of Debussy's past, and when she and Rita talked to him, he avoided anything personal. He defined the introspection of one's past as "a vulgar pursuit." That caused both sisters to wonder what he was hiding.

"We must agree that the beauty of a work of art will always remain a mystery," he told the sisters. "We can never be absolutely sure how a work is made. Even I don't know how I created *Prélude à l'après-midi d'un faune* in 1894. We must at all cost preserve this magic, which is peculiar to music and to which music, by its very nature, is of all the arts the most receptive."

One night, he stood on Rita's terrace as she and Mercedes joined him to watch the sun set. "When I gaze at the fading day, with sunset in colors of orange, pink, and yellow, I contemplate the ever-changing beauty of nature. An extraordinary emotion overwhelms me. We do not know if we will live through the day to see another sunset. Life is a gamble. Our lives can be snuffed out in a moment. That is why we must view each dawn as a promise, each sunset as an extraordinary hope that we will live to see another one."

The poet in Mercedes came out when speaking of Debussy. "To listen to his music is to understand him. It's like listening to the rustling of dying leaves as the autumnal winds blow down on us from the north. It also evokes the sounds and secrets of the evening air at twilight time."

A *fin-de-siècle* photo of **Claude Debussy** performing at an intimate gathering, all very "*beau-monde*," avant-garde, and socially correct.

He consistently refused to play the music of *le vieux sourd* (the old deaf man), a reference to Beethoven. "His music is like somebody dancing on my grave."

Claude Debussy with **Emma Bardac**. who became his second wife in 1908. "To a composer, a woman is only a secondary fixture in a man's life, if that. Music is my only mistress."

EMMA EAMES
(1865-1952)

When Mercedes visited Rita's Manhattan home on 52nd Street, she never knew what celebrated figures—painters, writers, singers, photographers—she would meet.

Late one Saturday afternoon, she found herself seated with Emma Eames, the great American soprano renowned for the beauty of her voice. "She was well-bred and reserved, but with a quiet charm," Mercedes recalled.

The daughter of an international lawyer, Eames was born in Shanghai in the year that the Civil War came to an end in America. Her parents soon moved to Maine, where Eames' mother recognized her singing talent and sent her to school in Boston and Paris.

Cast as Juliette, Eames made her professional operatic debut in Gounod's *Roméo et Juliette* at the Palais Garnier in Paris in 1889. She was immediately labeled "the favorite *cantatrice* of the Opéra." In her future, she would perform that same role many times.

In November of 1891, she made her debut at the Metropolitan Opera in Chicago, starring as Elsa in Wagner's *Lohengrin*. She sang at the Met in New York and at the Royal Opera House in London's Covent Garden. In London, where she challenged the Garden's reigning diva, Nellie Melba, the two singers became bitter enemies.

In the years to come, she toured such capitals as Madrid or such chic enclaves as the Monte Carlo Opera House during the 1890s.

Regrettably, she arrived for a performance in San Francisco in 1906 as an earthquake destroyed the city. She survived. Her career ended with a series of concert tours across America, delivering her final performance in 1916 when the world was at war.

Emma Eames as Queen of the Nile in Giuseppe Verdi's *Aïda*.

One critic wrote: "During her prime, Miss Ames, a proud and handsome diva of a certain girth, is imbued with a beautiful, expertly trained soprano voice. It has increased in size over time, enabling her to tackle such roles as Aïda, Santuzza, Tosca, and Sieglinde. However, there is a certain coldness in her interpretations and an aloof stage manner."

At this point, her voice had begun to deteriorate. In 1929, she published her autobiography, *Some Memories and Reflections*.

She married twice, once to Julian Russell Story, the society painter, and then to Emilio de Gogorza, the celebrated concert baritone. She had no fondness for children. Once, when she became pregnant, she went to an abortion doctor. As she told Mercedes, "I don't feel my body should be turned into a breeding factory like a cow. I was made for better things. Instead of changing dirty diapers—how ghastly—I prefer to devote my life to performing the works of Mozart, Verdi, Wagner, and—dare I leave out—Mascagni."

GERALDINE FARRAR
(1882-1967)

One of the greatest American operatic sopranos of her day, Madame Farrar was also a film actress. She was celebrated for both the timbre of her remarkable voice and also for her beauty. She made a glittering addition to Rita's social gatherings where at any appearance she was the center of attention.

As she left through any stage door, she was surrounded by devoted fans, labeled "Gerry Flappers" by the tabloid press.

Born in Massachusetts, Farrar was the daughter of baseball player Sidney Farrar. At the age of five, she began to study music in Boston, and by the time she was fourteen, she was giving recitals.

She created a sensation at the Berlin Hofoper when she made her debut as Marguerite in Charles Gounod's *Faust* in 1901. Her biggest admirer in Berlin was Crown Prince Wilhelm of Germany, with whom she had an affair in 1903.

She later spent three years with the Monte Carlo Opera where, in private, she became known for seducing famous men.

In 1906, she made her debut at The Met in Manhattan in *Roméo et Juliette* and later starred in the Metropolitan's first production (1907) of Puccini's *Madame Butterfly*.

Geraldine Farrar was a great operatic diva, showcasing her brilliance in title roles that included *Madama Butterfly, Carmen*, and *Tosca*. She was also known for seducing famous men ranging from Toscanini to Caruso.

In all, she would appear 672 times at The Met, singing in 29 roles. The most notable included Umberto Giordan's *Madame Sans-Gêne* in 1915 and as the Goosegirl in Engelbert Humperdinck's *Königskinder* in 1910.

She was one of the first performers to make a nationwide radio broadcast in 1907.

She also appeared in silent films from 1915 to 1920. Cecil B. De Mille cast her in a 1915 adaptation of George Bizet's *Carmen*. San Francisco's *Call & Post* said her performance "is the greatest triumph so far in motion pictures."

Another of her notable screen roles was as Joan of Arc in the 1917 silent film *Joan the Woman*.

Her biographer wrote: "Unlike most of the famous *bel canto* singers of the past, who sacrificed dramatic action to tonal perfection, Miss Farrar was more interested in the emotional than in the purely lyrical aspects of her roles. According to her, until *prime donne* can combine the arts of Sarah Bernhardt and Nellie Melba, dramatic ability is more essential than perfect singing in opera."

Mercedes met Farrar on several occasions, later referring to her as "charming and sensuous, a feline beauty who was almost ethereal."

Farrar was also famous for her love live. She sustained a seven-year affair with the Italian conductor, Arturo Toscanini. She also had a notorious affair with Enrico Caruso.

From 1916 to 1923, she was wed to Dutch-born Lou Tellegen, a stage and film actor.

Early in his career, he had performed in Paris in several roles with Sarah Bernhardt, with whom he had an affair. In 1910, the two of them made their motion picture, *La dame aux camélias*. The world's greatest actress was thirty-seven years Tellegen's senior, and *The New York Times* once announced a story about their impending marriage… which never took place.

Then-newlywed **Geraldine Farrar** in love and at home with **Lou Tellegen** in 1916.

He later stabbed himself in the heart seven times with a pair of sewing scissors in an eventually successful suicide.

Before the end of his life, Tellegen did manage to marry four separate times, once to Farrar (1916-1923). In Hollywood, they made three films together.

The latter years of Tellegen's life were tragic. On Christmas Day, 1929, he fell asleep while smoking, and his face was severely burned, requiring plastic surgery. In 1931, he wrote his tell-all autobiography, *Women Have Been Kind*, which was hardly the case in his love life.

At that time, his matinee idol popularity had waned, and he was deeply in debt, facing bankruptcy. As if that weren't bad enough, his doctor told him he had incurable cancer.

At the home of Edna Cudahy, the widow of the meat-packing heir, Jack Cuhady, Tellegen went into one of her bathrooms. There, after shaving and powdering his face, he stabbed himself in the heart seven times with a pair of sewing scissors.

Reporters were keen to ask Farrar for her reaction to the bizarre suicide of her former husband. She answered with, "Why should that interest me?" before walking off.

Farrar herself survived to the ripe old age of eighty-five, dying in Ridgefield, Connecticut, on March 11, 1967. She didn't get her final wish, which for her to live to see another Spring.

ANATOLE FRANCE
(1844-1924)

In Paris, Rita and Mercedes were often invited to the literary salons where the cultural élite of the early 20th Century met.

One one occasion, the sisters were introduced to Anatole France, that distinguished man of letters, with his "sculpted beard." He was a poet, journalist, and novelist who penned several best sellers. A member of the *Académie française,* he had won the Nobel Prize in literature in 1921, "in recognition of his brilliant literary achievements, characterized as they are by a nobility of style, a profound human sympathy, grace, and a true Gallic temperament." It was widely reported that he was the model for narrator Marcel Proust's literary idol, Bergotte, in his masterpiece, *A la recherche du temps perdu (In Search of Lost Time).*

About as grand and talked-about literary figure as was available in *fin-de-siècle* Paris, and almost unknown among present-day French twenty-somethings: **Anatole France**.

"When Rita and I met Anatole, he was beyond his prime," Mercedes claimed. "But that didn't stop him from flirting with us. Perhaps he was just trying to shock or else he really meant it, but he claimed that going to bed with two sisters was one of the greatest sexual adventures a man could ever have."

In French literary circles, he was known for his many affairs. In 1877, he married Valerie Guérin de Sauville, granddaughter of Jean-Urbain Guérin, a miniaturist who had painted Louis XVI.

Among his many liaisons was an affair with Madame Arman de Caillavet, who conducted a celebrated literary salon of the Third Republic. His affair with her lasted almost until her death in 1910.

In the wake of his divorce in 1893, he was said to have had indulged in many liaisons, often with very young women. One of his mistresses committed suicide when he dumped her. His final marriage occurred in 1920 to Emma Laprévotte, but he had only four years to live.

Politically, he was a socialist and an outspoken supporter of the Russian Revolution of 1917. Three years later, he gave his support to the newly formed Communist Party of France. His political beliefs brought on many critical assaults against him both from the left and right.

Two years before his death, he appeared on the *Prohibited Books Index* of the Catholic Church. When asked about this, he told the press, "I consider it a distinction."

MARY GARDEN
(1874-1967)

This Scottish operatic soprano was hailed in her heyday as "The Sarah Bernhardt of Opera." Having met her in Paris, Mercedes found her "highly intelligent, magnetic, and almost puritanical—entirely the reverse of her reputation as a *femme fatale.*"

Although born in Scotland, her parents and her three sisters grew up in Hartford, Connecticut and in Chicago. Much of her later life was spent in France.

One critic commented on her "beautiful lyric voice with its wide vocal range and flexibility," Fame came to her in Paris in the early years of the 20th Century when she was designated as the leading soprano at the Opéra-Comique. She was outstanding in the operas of Jules Massenet, including *Chérubin* (1905), which he wrote especially for her.

Scottish-born Mary Garden was an exceptional singer and actress, with a beautiful lyric voice, a wide vocal range, and a career that was showcased by the classical music and opera impresarios of New York, Chicago, London, and Paris.

Oscar Hammerstein, in 1907, persuaded her to join The Met in Manhattan, where almost from the beginning, critics raved about her. By 1910, she was about the most famous opera star in America, performing in such key cities as Boston, Chicago, and Philadelphia.

She was also an actress and starred in two silent flickers for producer Samuel Goldwyn.

In Paris, Garden took Mercedes to the studio of Lucien Muratore, who had been married to Lina Cavalieri (see above). Born in Marseilles to Italian parents from Piedmont, he was both an actor and an operatic tenor. He was already intimately associated with some of the operas by Massenet, in which he had starred, including *Bacchus.* Later, he became the principal French tenor at the Boston Opera Company. He'd also been a star with the opera companies in Chicago. With his wife, Cavalieri, he had co-starred in the silent movie, *Manon Lescaut,* in 1914.

Mercedes had presented Garden with a copy of her play, *The Mother of Christ,* and she wanted to have it produced in Paris with Muratore as her co-star in the role of Pontius Pilate, the Roman procurator of Judaea.

Mercedes wondered if two great singers should be cast in a play without music, but both artists seemed willing. Plans moved ahead, but then World War I came and the production was abandoned.

Garden retired from the stage in 1934 when she was no longer pleased by the sound of her voice. She moved to Hollywood and became a talent scout for MGM where she was seen in the company of Norma Shearer,

Clark Gable, Joan Crawford, William Powell, and Jean Harlow, among other stars. She worked with Irving Thalberg more than with Louis B. Mayer.

She delivered lectures and recitals across America, most of them devoted to the life and works of Claude Debussy [see above].

For her declining years, she opted to return to her native Scotland where she penned an autobiography, *Mary Garden's Story*.

Alone with her memories, this former Scottish lass lived in the breezy winds of Inverurie in Scotland, dying at the age of ninety-two in January of 1967. Her fame had largely been forgotten by a new generation of music lovers.

ISABELLA STEWART GRANGER
(1840-1924)

In September of 1916, Rita arranged for an exhibition of the works of Ignacio Zuloaga to tour the United States, with the understanding that it would begin in Boston and spend time at the Duveen Galleries on Manhattan. During his crossing of the Atlantic, Zuloago had been afraid that the Germans might attack his ship, but he eventually arrived safely in New York, where he stayed at Rita's house at #8 Washington Square North.

With Rita, Mercedes journeyed with the artist to Boston for the premiere of the Zuloaga Exhibit. There, they were joined by John Singer Sargent [see below], and a remarkable art collector Mrs. Jack Gardner (aka Isabella Stewart Gardner), hailed locally as "The Queen of Back Bay." A great philanthropist and patron of the arts, she eventually founded the Isabella Stewart Gardner Museum in Boston.

Two views of **Isabella Stewart Gardner**: Left: 1888 portrait by John Singer Sargent, and right, her portrait by Anders Zorn, "In Venice" from 1894

It featured Titian's masterpiece, *The Rape of Europa* (1561) and works by Raphael, Matisse, Velázquez, and Rembrandt.

"I found Mrs. Gardner a really inspirational woman," Mercedes recalled. "She lived life on her own terms and was known for her style and taste. She was always viewed as an eccentric. One never knew what outfit she might appear in."

In 1894, Anders Zorn captured her on canvas in his portrait, *Isabella*

Stewart Gardner In Venice. It hangs today as a centerpiece of her museum in Boston.

In 1860, she'd married the wealthy Jack Gardner, then the most eligible bachelor in Boston. The pair traveled the world buying art in the Middle East, in Central Europe, in Turkey, and in Paris. One of their first acquisitions was *The Concert* by the quintessential "Old Master," the Dutch painter Jan Vermeer (1632-1675).

Their collection grew and grew, branching out to include not just paintings but rare ceramics, tapestries, even the original manuscripts of fabled authors.

"Isabella of Boston," as she was known in the press, befriended many of the great artists of her day, including James Abbott McNeill Whistler (1834-1903). He immortalized himself by painting "Arrangement in Grey and Black: Portrait of the Artist's Mother" in 1872.

YVETTE GUILBERT
(1865-1944)

According to Mercedes, "I must have been only twelve years old when I met Yvette, the French cabaret singer and a leading actress of the *Belle Époque*. I remember a party in New York when Sarah Bernhardt was staying with Rita. I spotted Yvette bowing down before 'The Divine One' to kiss her hand."

Guilbert was born in Paris and, as a child, sang in cabarets. She later worked as a teenaged model for Le Printemps, the French capital's venerated department store. By 1886, she was appearing on stage, and in time, became a headliner at the Moulin Rouge in Montmartre, where she was a favorite of Henri Toulouse-Lautrec.

The English painter, William Rothenstein, described her as "virginal,

Three views of the Parisian cabaret entertainer, **Yvette Guilbert.** Far right, *Yvette Guilbert with Black Gloves,* as interpreted by Henri de Toulouse-Lautrec

slender, pale, without rouge. Her songs weren't virginal, but *risqué.*"

She was also a favorite of Sigmund Freud in Vienna and of George Bernard Shaw, who wanted to seduce her.

Although she received raves in general, she also had her critics, none more venomous than the playwright and songwriter, Maurice Lefèvre, who wrote:

> "Let's enter the Chanson Moderne. There she is! Long leech, sexless! She crawls, creeps with hissings, leaving behind the moiré trail of her drool...On both sides of the boneless body hang, like pitiful wrecks, tentacles in funereal gloves. For she will, indeed, lead the burial of our Latin race. Complete negation of our genius. Poor little Chanson, faithful mirror in which men reflect themselves, are you responsible for their hideousness?"

At a private party on the French Riviera, Guilbert once performed for the Prince of Wales (later King Edward VII), catching his lusty eye.

She was a great success in Manhattan at Carnegie Hall, and even went to Hollywood to appear in some silent films, notably in F.W. Murnau's *Faust.* She also starred in some talkies, making her *adieu* to the screen in 1936 in a film called *Let's Make a Dream.*

Upon hearing of Rita's death in 1929, Guilbert wrote to the *Paris Herald:* "Rita de Acosta Lydig, the magnificent patroness of the arts, should receive the Legion of Honor in recognition of her great service she has rendered to French culture."

KATHERINE CORRI HARRIS
(1890-1927)

As described later in this book, Mercedes became intimately involved with John Barrymore and his mistress (and later, wife) Michael Strange. She also knew Barrymore's first wife, Katherine Harris, the American socialite and renowned golfer. Harris had been born into a life of wealth and privilege, and at sixteen, made her debut into high society.

Harris was the first cousin of Philip Lydig, Rita's second husband. Mercedes found that delightful because in some remote way, it meant that she was related to John and Ethel Barrymore through her brother-in-law.

Mercedes never got to know Harris as well as she did Michael Strange. But the two women frequently encountered each other. Barrymore married her in 1910., the tumultuous marriage lasting for seven years. From the beginning, Mercedes was aware that Barrymore was never faithful to his wife.

Harris had a brief stint as an actress of the silent screen, and he got her cast in two of his movies: *Nearly a King* (1916) and *The Lost Bridegroom* the same year. Both films have been lost to history.

Two years later, Harris had her most memorable role as Lily Bart in *The House of Mirth,* based on Edith Wharton's 1905 novel.

"Katherine was a delicate beauty, and a woman of grace and charm, but she was destined to die young," Mercedes said. "John, as I could have predicted, did not turn out to be a good husband."

Since the age of fourteen, Barrymore had struggled with alcohol abuse. Ironically, he was the most influential and idolized actor of his day, yet his private life made him tabloid fodder, as he drifted in and out of scandal.

"When Katherine was first married to John, he was a great male beauty," Mercedes said, "and so famous that almost everyone on the planet knew him as 'The Great Profile.'"

Mercedes attended every stage show she could, watching him perform in *Richard III* and *Hamlet*, among many others.

"I was greatly saddened when John phoned me on the first of May 1927, to tell me that Katherine had died of pneumonia in New York City. Although they'd divorced, they'd remained friends, and he was at her bedside at the time."

Harris had remarried in 1923 to Alfred D.B. Pratt, a stockbroker, but that union lasted for only a few months. She took a final husband in 1925, Leon Orlowski, an ambassador from Poland. But that marriage, too, lasted for only a few months.

"Katherine told me that the only man she'd ever loved was John," Mercedes said.

His first wife never lived to see Barrymore slip into self-parody as the years went

Two views of **Katherine Corri Harris.** Lower photo: with her then-husband, the never faithful **John Barrymore.**

by. And his heavy drinking increased. His once ascetic face became dissipated. On movie sets, technicians worked to reconstruct his spiritual beauty with lights, filters, and makeup. He'd also put on a lot of weight.

Barrymore died in Los Angeles on May 29, 1942, at the age of sixty. America was going through its most agonizing year of World War II, but the actor hardly seemed aware of that.

John Gielgud, who knew Barrymore well, delivered a bitchy assessment of this once-great talent: "John is like a monstrous old male impersonator jumping through a hoop. He should really have been shot."

In his last visit from Mercedes, he said, "What have I become? A much-married ham. An aging satyr. A has-been alcoholic, But I'll go out of life with aplomb and a sense of humor."

Douglas Fairbanks, Jr. weighed in, too: "John is reputed to have indulged in every known vice from homosexuality to drug abuse. He seduced everyone from Tallulah Bankhead to Carole Lombard to Mary Astor. He told me that he spent a full month in a whorehouse in Calcutta. He also claimed that he lost his virginity to his stepmother, Mamie Floyd, when he was only fifteen."

He also revealed what he really thought of women: "You can't trust them as far as you could throw Fort Knox," Barrymore said. "All of them are twittering vaginas."

MALVINA HOFFMAN
(1885-1960)

One of the leading American sculptors, Malvina Hoffman was a New York native who became famous for her life-sized bronze sculptures of such famous dancers as Anna Pavlova and Vaslav Nijinsky. She also created portrait busts of working-class people she collectively defined as "the common man."

To understand the human body better, she once dissected corpses at the College of Physicians and Surgeons at Columbia University.

In Manhattan, she maintained a salon where the artistic elite of her era gathered. Mercedes always remembered it was at that salon that she was first introduced to the great Pavlova *[see below]*.

During World War II, both Hoffman and Mercedes worked for the Red Cross, tending to wounded and blinded men from the Allied nations. "Sometimes, to raise morale, we held parties," Mercedes said. "There, I met Hope Williams and began our life-long friendship. The party was hosted by Mrs. John Jacob Astor at her elegant Fifth Avenue mansion."

In Paris, where Hoffman had a townhouse, Mercedes was a frequent visitor. They sometimes visited a busy foundry on rue Leplanquais in Malakoff (Hauts-de-Seine), a Paris suburb, where sculptures were cast in bronze." *[From those premises, its Master Foundryman, Eugene Rudier also cast sculptures from models crafted by Henry Moore, Degas, Renoir, Robin, Matisse, and many other great sculptors of that era.]*

Malvina Hoffman was one of the greatest American sculptors, known especially for her life-sized bronzes. She was celebrated for her depictions of dancers, notably of the grand ballerina, Anna Pavlova.

Russian Dancers, sculpture in bronze by Malvina Hoffman

In 1929, Hoffman was commissioned by the Field Museum of Natural History in Chicago to travel around the world to create anthropomorphically accurate sculptures of people of diverse nationalities and races. She visited Africa, India, Bali, and other places, completing sculptures in marble, bronze, and stone.

She explained her technique to the press:

> *"To understand the submerged passion that burns in the human eye, to read the hieroglyphs of suffering etched in the lines of a human face, to watch the gesture of a hand or listen for the false notes and the true in a human voice: these are the mysteries that I found I must delve into and try to unravel when I made a portrait."*

GERTRUDE KÄSEBIER
(1852-1934)

Hailing from Des Moines, Iowa, Gertrude Käsebier became the foremost professional photographer in the United States. In the summer of 1899, she was paid $100 for her photograph entitled "The Manger," which was the most ever paid for a photograph at that time. _

Käsebier emerged from a pioneering background. Her father, John W. Stanton, had been part of the Pike's Peak Gold Rush in 1859. He later became Mayor of Golden, the capital of the Colorado Territory.

Käsebier entered the life of Rita de Acosta after asking her to pose for some photos. (Rita obliged.)

In 1874, on Gertrude's 22nd birthday, she wed 28-year-old Eduard Käsebier, a rich and socially connected businessman in Brooklyn. The union produced three children. However, she told Rita, "I hate my marriage. If I hear my husband is heaven-bound, I'll ship off to the Gates of Hell just to avoid him. Nothing is ever good enough for him, especially me."

In 1898, Käsebier watched Buffalo Bill's Wild West Troupe parade

Gertrude Kasebier in 1908, and (right) one of her subjects, **a Native American Sioux**, circa 1900.

down Manhattan's Fifth Avenue toward their big show at Madison Square Garden. She became fascinated with Native Americans and asked his permission to photograph the members of the Sioux tribe accompanying his act. Her request was granted. In the weeks ahead, she was shooting portraits of Chief Flying Hawk and Chief Iron Tail. Those photographs and others are now preserved at the Smithsonian Institution.

ELISABETH MARBURY
(1836-1933)

Elizabeth Marbury was born and reared in one of the most affluent and cultured homes of 19th Century New York. Eventually, she became a legend in her own time. She was a towering literary and theatrical agent and also a producer and author. She helped shape business methods of the modern commercial theater and represented some of the world's most famous literary figures.

None of her theatrical and literary clients was more famous than Oscar Wilde. When he was sent to Reading Gaol (Prison) for homosexuality, she raised money for him by selling his *Ballad of Reading Gaol* to the Pulitzer Newspapers.

Called "Bessie" by her friends, Marbury weighed more than two-hundred pounds and had trouble walking. Her feet were too small to support such a load, and she had to wear steel braces on her legs and use a pair of canes to get about. Most of the literary and theatrical elite who visited her salon found the imposing figure seated in an armchair.

Grande dame (in every sense of the word) and mentor to Mercedes de Acosta, theatrical agent and woman of influence and means, **Elisabeth Marbury**, in 1905

For years, she was the longtime companion—read that as "lover"—of Elsie de Wolfe *[see below]*, a prominent socialite and the world's most famous interior decorator.

Bessie also had a long-lasting and intimate relationship with Elizabeth Arden (1878-1966), who founded Elizabeth Arden Beauty products. Tallulah Bankhead said, "I'm an Elizabeth Arden Girl. I never go out the door without a tube of Elizabeth Arden lipstick."

Born in New York before the Civil War, Bessie was descended from Calvinist Anne Hutchinson, who co-founded Rhode Island after her banishment from the Massachusetts Bay Colony.

As time went by, both Rita de Acosta and her younger sister Mercedes were frequent visitors to whichever home Bessie occupied at the time. The most famous of these was Irving House, a venerably historic structure at Third Avenue at Irving Place in Manhattan. There, they joined a stream of literary and theatrical figures who came and went from her salon.

"In spite of our age difference, Bessie and I became friends until the end of her life," Mercedes said. "I found her an incredible blend of worldliness and childishness, of shrewdness and Victorian innocence. She had the brain of a man, well-balanced and keen."

"She suggested I call her my grandmother but found her too manly for that. We settled on me calling her 'Granny Pa' instead."

During World War I, Bessie, in spite of her weight, devoted much of her time to relief work, helping to ease the suffering of wounded soldiers. She worked in France, winning decorations from both the French and Belgian governments.

"When I went to visit Granny Pa, I knew I was in the presence of a towering giant who enriched the cultural life of her era. After her death, I went and stood in front of her home, imagining all the great talents in literature and the theater who came and went from that address, their lives enriched by Granny Pa. It is unlikely that the world will see the likes of her ever again."

MARIE, QUEEN OF ROMANIA
(1875-1938)

Marie was the last queen of Romania, a position she acquired through her marriage to King Ferdinand, who was king from 1893 until his death in 1927.

Born into British royalty, she was also known as "Marie of Edinburgh." Her father was Prince Alfred, Duke of Edinburgh. Her mother was Marie Alexandrovna, a Grand Duchess of Russia.

Before agreeing to marry Ferdinand, Marie turned down a proposal of marriage from the man who later became the British king, George V.

When Bucharest was occupied during World War I, Marie and Ferdinand fled to Moldavia, where she was a nurse to the sick, the wounded, and the dying, a gen-

Marie, Queen of Romania, appearing here in the ceremonial robes of Romania's richly mythic past. There was much speculation about the identity of that "unlikely suitor" who secretly stayed in Queen Marie's suite in New York. A hotel clerk claimed that it was the swashbuckling Douglas Fairbanks, Sr., at that time one of the most famous men in the world.

uine act of Royal heroism.

Returning to Bucharest at the end of the war, she became a very popular queen.

She embarked on a good will tour of America, drawing large crowds wherever she went. Upon her return, she found Ferdinand gravely ill, with medical complications that eventually led to his death.

Her eldest son, King Carol, became the monarch in his place. Almost immediately, he exiled her from the political scene. After dropping out of public view she went to live in a villa on the Black Sea.

Rumors circulated (none of which were ever verified) that she had become a drunkard and that she staged frequent orgies with studly Russian soldiers.

Mercedes had attended a party in New York to welcome Marie at the beginning of her good will tour of America. She was said to have been escorted by a man whose face was familiar in every household in the United States.

Near the end of Mercedes's drama-soaked life, Darwin Porter pressed her to identify the "adulterous beau" who accompanied Marie to the party that night, but Mercedes would not cooperate. "Even if I told you, you would not believe who escorted her into Rita's salon."

ANNE MORGAN
(1873-1952)

One of the great American philanthropists, Anne Tracy Morgan was the youngest of the four siblings born to the super rich John Pierpont Morgan and Frances Morgan. She grew into womanhood as one of the most famous and commented-on daughters of the Gilded Age.

But instead of living a life of idle privilege, she devoted much of her time to social causes and became acclaimed for her aid to France in both World Wars. Eventually, she became the first American woman appointed a commander of the French Legion of Honor.

Anne Murray Dike, a noted doctor, joined Anne Tracy Morgan in France and the two women fell in love. From 1917 to 1921, they took residence near some of the bloodiest trench lines of World War I and ran an organization known as the American Friends of France, which

The formidable philanthropist **Anne Morgan**, one of the most famous and distinguished women in America and France. Known for her volunteer work during both World Wars, she was sometimes photographed in mannish-looking clothes with her lover, Dr. Anne Murray Dike.

employed several hundred people, many of them volunteers from abroad. Morgan financed the operation partly from her own funds. Included in their operation was a healthy service facility for orphans and a workshop that provided basic furniture to bombed-out families.

She often championed the case of the down-trodden. In 1910, she became a union activist, supporting female workers in the highly underpaid New York garment industry. Morgan herself marched in picket lines. As a key member in the American Woman's Association, she predicted that a female "with ambition, pluck, and energy would one day move up in industry. It requires only evolution."

Morgan also found time to move into the glittering world of celebrities of her era. In 1916, she was one of the backers of Cole Porter's first Broadway musical, *See America First* produced by Elisabeth Marbury *[see above]*.

Among her friends were such cultural icons as Pearl S. Buck, Salvador Dalí, and Katharine Hepburn. In 1940, Morgan gathered up celebrity recipes and published them in a book, *Spécialités de la Maison,* the proceeds going to charity.

Although not a lesbian herself, Rita de Acosta entertained and involved herself in the lives of a quartet of lesbians that included Morgan, Anne Vanderbilt, Elsie de Wolfe, and Elisabeth Marbury.

Morgan joined Marbury and De Wolfe in 1903 in the restoration of their private home, the Villa Trianon. *[Their home is not to be confused with either the Grand or Petit Trianon within the gardens of the château at Versailles.]* Thanks partly to their lavish attention to 18th Century detail and opulence, members of the French press referred to this small, well-upholstered band as "the Versailles Triumvirate."

ADOLPHE DE MEYER
(1868-1946)

Attracted to her stunning beauty, French photographer Adolphe de Meyer wanted Rita de Acosta to pose for his camera. She agreed, joining a coterie of celebrities who included John Barrymore, Billie Burke, Irene Castle, Lillian Gish, dancer Ruth St. Denis, Luise Casati, and even King George V and Queen Mary. In 1913, De Meyer also became the first official fashion photographer for the American magazine, *Vogue.*

In 1899, he made headlines when he married Donna Olga Caracciolo, an Italian noblewoman thought to be the (illegitimate) daughter of King Edward VII. It was not a marriage based on sexual passion, as he was

Très haute mode: the **Baron Adolphe de Meyer** became the first official fashion photographer for the American magazine, *Vogue,* in 1913.

One of his fashionable portraits of Rita de Acosta in a "backless, then-scandalous evening sheath" appears earlier within this chapter.

a homosexual and she was either bisexual or a lesbian. In an autobiographical novel, De Meyer wrote about "the real meaning of love shorn of any kind of sensuality."

He also wrote that "marriage based on too much love and unrestrained passion has rarely a chance to be lasting, whilst perfect understanding and companionship generally makes the most durable union."

When his wife died in 1931, Baron de Meyer became involved with his chauffeur, a young German, Ernest Frohlich, born in 1914. He later adopted him as his son, and he became Baron Ernest Frohlich de Meyer.

Both Mercedes and Rita sometimes called on the couple when they lived in London. England's best-known photographer, Cecil Beaton, called De Meyer "the Debussy of Photography."

In 1912, De Meyer photographed Nijinsky in Paris. It was rumored that he persuaded the dancer to pose not only in the nude, but with an erection. It is not known if those photographs exist today, perhaps somewhere in a private collection.

One of his more famous photographs, which survived World War II bombings, was a profile of actress Jeanne Eagels snapped in 1921. Seated in a chair reminiscent of ancient Greece, she wore a cape accessorized with an ostrich ruff over a dress fashioned from tulle.

Adolphe de Meyer's 1925 fashion photo of a mousseline dress by Chanel.

JOSE ORTEGA Y GASSET
(1883-1955)

This Spanish philosopher and essayist, born in Madrid, enjoyed a certain fame during the first half of the 20th Century, perhaps as much for his outspoken political

Hispanic, intense, and famous—despite his esoteria—as a philosopher worldwide, **José Ortega y Gasset** was influenced by John Stuart Mill, De Tocqueville, Immanuel Kant, and Nietzsche. As Spain entered the trauma of its Civil War and the post World War II Franco regime, he became especially reknowned for his political commentaries, all of which were passionately discussed by Mercedes and Rita de Acosta and the avant-garde members of their entourage, especially the Spaniards.

lamentations than for his esoteric and hard-to-decipher work as a philosopher.

Educated by Jesuit priests in Málaga, the capital of the Costa del Sol, he went on to attend the private, Jesuit-owned University of Deusto in Bilbao, eventually receiving a doctorate in philosophy.

Back in Madrid, he published his two most notable works, *Invertebrate Spain* and *The Revolt of the Masses,* the latter making him internationally famous.

Ultimately, the politics of Spain as it drifted into a dictatorship spearheaded by Franco disappointed him. He went into exile for many years in Argentina, returning to neutral Portugal in 1942 as World War II raged across the Continent. In 1948, he returned to Madrid where he privately continued to voice his dislike of the Franco regime.

Mercedes and Rita sometimes encountered him at the studio of their mutual friend, Ignacio Zuloaga. "Even the most advanced of his students may not have understood him," Mercedes said.

As one of his biographers expressed it, "His philosophy of life went from pragmatic metaphysics to realist phenomenology to proto-existentialism to realist historicism."

IGNACY JAN PADEREWSKI
(1860-1941)

In her New York salon, Rita de Acosta entertained Paderewski, the great pianist and composer and the leading spokesman for Polish independence.

In 1919, he became Poland's prime minister after a stint as its foreign minister, one of the signatories of the Treaty of Versailles that (disastrously) ended World War I. During the course of that war, he had advanced the cause of Polish independence by—among many other campaigns—touring the United States and meeting with President Woodrow Wilson.

It was in New York City that Mercedes was introduced to him. She recalled this event in her life, finding that "He was idealistic and fragile, with a remarkably handsome head."

It was Paderewski the artist more that the politician that Mercedes remembered. She was at Carnegie Hall in 1922 when he delivered a remarkable piano concert, winning rave reviews. He also filled Madison Square Garden's 20,000 seats during an equivalent concert before, in a private railway car, launching his tour of the U.S.

More of the world got to see him in 1936 when he starred in a romance/drama directed by German-born Lothar Mendes. The movie was released in Britain as *Moonlight Sonata* and retitled *The Charmer* for its 1943 debut in the U.S. *[The plot? When a plane makes an emergency landing, passengers who include a swindler/hustler and a piano-playing celebrity (Paderewski) take refuge within the manor house of a gracious Baroness played by Marie Tempest. Ironically, and to Paderewski's horror, the film in which he starred was re-*

leased simultaneously with the destruction of Warsaw by the Nazis.]

In 1940, the artist was living in war-torn London at the time of the Blitz, with the *Luftwaffe* raining death upon the British capital. By now, he was the Director in Exile of the National Council of Poland.

Impulsively but bravely, during the darkest months of the war in Europe and fearing a U-Boat attack, he decided to attempt the dangerous crossing of the Atlantic. He arrived at the Port of New York, where he launched a tour of Canada and the U.S., delivering speeches calling for the liberation of Poland that were broadcast over at least a hundred different North American radio stations.

During the final months of his life, he was thrilled to witness many glowing tributes to his life as a humanitarian as cities across America celebrated the anniversary of his first U.S. tour. It was packaged as "Paderewski Week." More than 6,000 concerts were organized in his honor.

Regrettably, his 82-year-old mind began to fail him at this point, and he began behaving in ways that his associates, with regret, defined as "deranged." When his schedule called for a return engagement at Madison Square Garden, he refused to go onto the stage, claiming that he had already delivered his performance the previous night. Actually, he was remembering his appearance there in 1921, thinking that it had transpired only the day before.

Polish romantic, musician, and nationalist: **Ignacy Paderewski** in his youthful glory.

Marie Tempest, the most celebrated soprano in Victorian light opera and Edwardian musical comedy, co-starred in a silent movie with him. "I found him a most satisfactory lover except that he made demands for some acts that no self-respecting lady would perform, more suited to a whorehouse than to a lady's boudoir."

At this point of his tour, he became desperately ill with pneumonia. He died in Manhattan at 11PM on June 29, 1941. His last words were a lament that he would never get to see the liberation of his country from the Nazis.

The great Polish patriot lay in repose in the crypt of the USS Maine Mast Memorial in Arlington National Cemetery.

In 1992, after *Glasnost* and the collapse of communism in Poland, his remains were transferred to Warsaw and placed within St. John's Arch-Cathedral.

ANNA PAVLOVA
(1881-1931)

From the Russian City of St. Petersburg emerged Anna Pavlovna Pavlova, the great *prima ballerina* of the late 19th and early 20th Centuries. At an early age, she became the principal dancer of both the Imperial Russian Ballet and also of the *Ballets Russes* of Sergei Diaghilev.

Her greatest and most oft-repeated role onstage was a four-minute long solo, *The Dying Swan*. [*Choreographed by Mikhail Fokine it was set to Camille Saint-Saëns's score for* Le Cygne *from* Le Carnaval des animaux. *During the course of her career, Pavlova was estimated to have performed it onstage 4,000 times.*]

Pavlova became the first ballerina to tour the world, stopping for dance performances in India, Australia, and throughout South America.

From 1921 to 1926, she made almost annual tours of the United States. For many ticket holders, it was their first time at a ballet. She even attracted audiences in St. Louis, which at the time was known as "the worst showbiz town in America."

Mercedes attended performances of Diaghilev's ballets in New York, London, and Paris, where she became enchanted with Pavlova's grace and charm.

It was in New York where she finally had an encounter with the prima ballerina. It was at a party hosted by Malvina Hoffman (see above) at her studio on East 35th Street. At the time, Mercedes worked for a committee called "The Lafayette Fund," which raised money for France during World War I. Every week, the committee sponsored charity supper dances at the Vanderbilt Hotel, where an orchestra played and big-name performers entertained.

Afraid of rejection, Mercedes approached Pavlova and asked if she would be a guest artist for their committee. As it turned out, Pavlova had heard of the Lafayette Fund and agreed to perform that Saturday night.

"It was a memorable evening," Mercedes said. "Even the Imperial Russian Ambassador and his chief staff members showed up to see Pavlova. The ballerina appeared in an elaborate headdress and a Russian costume and danced to a Russian folk song played by the orchestra. The applause that followed was thunderous."

Mercedes retreated to one of the empty boxes overlooking the ballroom. She was seated there for about an hour, looking down on the dancers on the floor, including many young men who would be traveling overseas to battle the Kaiser's army.

Suddenly, someone joined her in the

Anna Pavlova, it seems, really did like swans. It's estimated that during the course of her career, she portrayed one that was dying, onstage, more than 4,000 times.

darkness. She turned to stare into the dimly lit face of Pavlova herself.

"I hope I'm not intruding," the dancer said.

"You are most welcome," Mercedes said. "What a mesmerizing performance. You must be tired of being told that you are the world's greatest ballerina."

"It is always music to my ears to hear it again," Pavlova said. "Do you mind if I ask you what you were thinking sitting here all alone looking down at the dancers in the ballroom?"

"I was thinking of death, wondering how many of the young men going off to war would return alive from battle," Mercedes replied.

"I, too, often think of death," Pavlova said. "It is the Russian in my soul."

"I guess I think about it because it is the Spaniard in my melancholy soul," Mercedes said.

For about twenty minutes, the two women talked about death, immortality, and God.

Suddenly, Pavlova rose to her feet, telling Mercedes, "I must go. People are waiting for me."

Mercedes walked with her to the corridor, where she took Pavlova's hand. "Please don't go into the ballroom. Death himself is making an appearance there to select those young people who will be doomed to be killed in the war. I don't want Death to even get near you."

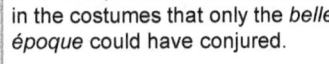

Pavlova, around 1900 and clad in the costumes that only the *belle époque* could have conjured.

"I understand, and I, too, want to avoid Death."

She bent over and her lips lightly touched Mercedes' cheek, and then she was gone, disappearing down the corridor.

"I stood there for a long time," Mercedes said. "At first, I felt that a white moth had touched my cheek—not the lips of a living woman. Then I changed my mind. It was not a moth after all, but a winged white bird, who landed from the air to spend precious moments with me before just flying away."

In 1931, while in transit between Paris and The Hague, Pavlova suddenly became ill. At a hospital, she was told she had pneumonia and needed to undergo an operation. She was also warned that after the operation, she would never be able to dance again. She rejected the doctor's offer of surgery. "If I can't dance, then I'd rather die in this hospital bed."

Death came to her on January 23, 1931, only three weeks short of her 50th birthday.

GIACOMO PUCCINI
(1858-1924)

Giacomo Antonio Domenico Michele Secondo Maria Puccini was hailed as "the greatest composer of Italian opera after Verdi."

His most renowned works were *La Bohème* (1896); *Tosca* (1900); and *Madama Butterfly* (1904). These operas are among the ten most frequently performed operas worldwide. Puccini ranks third behind Verdi and Mozart in operas performed.

A critic wrote, "Puccini's work was rooted in traditional late 19th-Century romantic Italian opera. Later, he successfully developed his work in the realistic *verismo* style, of which he became the leading exponent."

In 1891, Puccini spent much of his time at Torre del Lago, a small community fifteen miles from Lucca opening onto the Ligurian Sea. He told a reporter, "I love hunting. I love cars. I love women, but not necessarily in that order."

He became known both for his music and his numerous affairs, one of which was with Elvira Gemignani, a married woman. He made her pregnant, and she gave him a son, born in 1886. Her husband was a womanizer, and he was eventually shot by the husband of a woman with whom he'd been having an affair at the time. That allowed Elvira and Puccini, in 1904, to get married and "legitimatize" Antonio.

During Puccini's marriage to Elvira, he continued his infidelities, often with singers who performed his works, including Emmy Destinn and Hariclea Darclée, each of whom were well-known and celebrated in their respective heydays.

At a performance of *Madama Butterfly*, Puccini fell in love with Blanke Lendvai, the sister of the Hungarian composer Ervin Lendvai. Their affair lasted until 1911 when Puccini launched an affair with that German aristocrat, Baroness Josephine von Stangel. Their romantic liaison lasted for six years.

Although she never admitted it, Rita de Acosta may have had an affair with the aging Puccini, too. She sat in his box during a performance of

Giacomo Puccini next to the first poster ever crafted for an opera judged by some critics as the best of its genre in human history.

La fanciulla del West (The Girl of the West). She showed up in a backless gown. A woman who also sat in the box with them later reported, "Puccini sat behind Miss De Acosta and never took his eyes off that porcelain back of hers. Finally, at the end of the third act, he rose to take a bow and was then seen leaving the building with De Acosta."

A chain smoker of *Toscano* cigars and cigarettes, Puccini developed throat cancer in 1923. His doctors sent him to Brussels, where he underwent a new and experimental radiation therapy. At the age of sixty-five, he died from complications from the treatment. After surgery, uncontrolled bleeding led to a heart attack.

At the time, the opera house in Rome was presenting *La Bohème*. News reached the conductor, who immediately interrupted the score of that opera and switched to a rendition of Chopin's *Funeral March* as the audience sat in stunned disbelief.

AUGUST RODIN
(1840-1917)

During one of their sojourns in Paris, Rita and Mercedes visited the studio of Auguste Rodin at Meudon (Hauts-de-Seine), on the city's southwestern edge, about 5½ miles from the capital's center. Rodin had already immortalized himself with such sculptures as *The Gates of Hell, The Kiss, The Thinker,* and *The Burghers of Calais.*

In spite of massive criticism, Rodin became the pre-eminent French sculptor of his time, and even today enjoys worldwide acclaim. He rejected traditional sculpture that depicted allegory and mythology, preferring instead to depict the human body with naturalism, celebrating individual character and physicality.

Rodin's growing fame attracted a bevy of notable supporters, including Oscar Wilde and the German poet, Rainer Maria Rilke. At his modest country estate at Meudon, distinguished visitors showed up, including the British king Edward VII.

The modern dancer Isadora Duncan also visited. He immediately wanted her as a model.

The brilliant and eccentric **Auguste Rodin** in a photo from 1891.

In Paris, the Musée Rodin, opened in 1919 at the Hotel Biron, contains more than 6,000 of his sculptures and 7,000 of his drawings. .

Later, Duncan wrote about the experience. "He gazed at me with lowered lids, his eyes blazing, and then, with the same expression that he had before his works, he came toward me. He ran his hands over my neck, breasts, stroked my arms, and ran his hands over my hips, my bare legs and feet. He began to knead my whole body as if it were clay, while from him emanated heat that scorched and melted me."

Mercedes later wrote of her meeting with Rodin. "Awe was my reaction to him, awe for the man for his superhuman work." She was only mildly surprised to see nude models walking about. Once, he suggested to Rita and Mercedes that he might want them to pose nude in a lesbian embrace. "Perhaps he was just joking," Mercedes said. "He never followed through on such a provocative suggestion."

In Britain, Rodin found early acceptance from such notable writers as Robert Browning and Robert Louis Stevenson. In 1914, he donated a large number of his sculptures to Britain.

The female form continued to enchant him, as reflected by the 1899 bronze, *Eva*, set today in the Jardin des Tuileries in Paris.

In 1906, he was enchanted by dancers from the Royal Ballet of Cambodia and produced a series of drawings. He also drew a number of erotic pictures, modeled after nude women in his studio.

Even in his lifetime, Rodin was compared favorably to Michelangelo and was widely recognized. Although his popularity waned after his death, it has come back strong in the modern era.

Rodin enjoyed affairs with many of his models, but his longtime mistress was Rose Beuret, an affair that stretched over fifty-three years. He finally married her in 1917, the year of his death at the age of seventy-seven, only two weeks before he died.

The Age of Bronze by Auguste Rodin.

He was greatly influenced by Michelangelo. "He taught me to model the homan body with naturalism, celebrating individuality and physicality."

JOHN SINGER SARGENT
(1856-1925)

Rita de Acosta formed a close bond with John Singer Sargent, hailed as the greatest portrait painter of his generation.

Born in Florence, part of the Grand Duchy of Tuscany, he evoked Edwardian-era luxury in some 900 oil paintings and more than 2,000 watercolors. He found subjects wherever he traveled, notably to Venice but also to the Tyrol region of northeast Italy and Austria, and to the Middle East. In America, he gravitated to Florida, Maine, and Montana. In Florida, his best-known work, executed in 1917, was a painting entitled *Muddy Alligators*.

During his first trip (1887) to Boston, he painted Isabella Stewart Gardner, that city's most famous art patron *[see above]*.

In 1890, he painted Ellen Terry, the most famous actress in England at the time, as Lady Macbeth. He soon earned a reputation as "the Van Dyck of our times."

Some of his subjects enjoyed world renown. They included Robert Louis Stevenson (whom he painted three times) and two American presidents, Theodore Roosevelt and Woodrow Wilson.

Many of the richest women in the world posed for him, including Alice Vanderbilt Shepard, great-granddaughter of Cornelius Vanderbilt. John D. Rockefeller posed for him in 1917.

John Singer Sargent was a crafter of grandly theatrical portraits of the then-ruling class.

Although widely recognized for his genius as a portraitist, Sargent's contemporaries—many of them modernists—defined him as a talent from another era, way out of touch with current art trends such as Cubism.

A lifetime bachelor, Sargent formed close bonds with his neighbor, Oscar Wilde, and he became a friend of the lesbian author, Violet Paget. He often selected well-built men to pose nude for him, as best evoked by his *Man Standing Hands on Head* displayed at Manhattan's Metropolitan Museum of Art.

Sargent developed a romantic attachment to the handsome and aristocratic artist Albert de Belleroche, which led to a long relationship. They traveled the world together.

One of his clients, Betty Werthheimer, visited Venice with Sargent, later noting, "He was only interested in the Venetian gondoliers." The painter, Jacques-Émile Blanche, who posed for Sargent, said, "He was a notorious figure in Paris, positively scandalous, a frenzied bugger."

Mythological and sumptuous: John Singer Sargent's portrait of **Ellen Terry as Lady Macbeth.**

Although praised and sought out in many quarters, Sargent also had many detractors. Lewis Mumford, five years after his death, wrote: "Sargent remained to the end an illustrator...the most adroit appearance of workmanship, the most dashing eye for effect, cannot conceal the essential emptiness of Sargent's mind, or the contemptuous and cynical superficiality of a certain part of his execution."

Andy Warhol in 1986 said that Sargent "made everybody look glamourous. Taller, thinner. But they all have mood, every one of them a different mood."

In 1980, writing in *Time* magazine, critic Robert Hughes claimed that

Sargent "was the unrivaled recorder of male power and female beauty in a day that like ours, paid excessive court to both."

In 2004, Sargent's *Portrait of Robert Louis Stevenson and His Wife* sold for $8.9 million dollars. That same year, his *Group with Parasols* fetched $23.5 million.

EDWARD STEICHEN
(1879-1973)

Rita de Acosta's beauty also captured the attention of Edward Steichen, a Luxembourg-born artist, who was once the most famous and highest paid photographer on earth.

Rita, with Mercedes, met Steichen in the fashionable salons of Paris. Whereas he was immediately drawn to Rita's allure, he found Mercedes "too mannish."

In 1911, Steichen became the first to publish fashion photographs in the magazine *Art et Décoration*. From 1923 to 1938, he was the photographer for *Condé Nast*, *Vogue*, and *Vanity Fair*. Years later, he directed a war documentary, *The Fighting Lady*, voted Best Documentary of 1945, the year World War II came to an end.

A pioneer in the artistic applications of color photography, Steichen was the first to photographically reproduce the work of many famous artists, notably Picasso, Cézanne, Rodin, and Matisse. Later in his life, as a photographic curator for New York's Museum of Modern Art, he spearheaded the compilation of one of that era's greatest artistic achievements. Seen by at least ten million visitors in seventy countries, it was *The Family of Man*, an "inspirational and healing" exhibition of five-hundred photographs that collectively celebrated the universal aspects of the human experience.

Russia denounced everything about the exhibition as Cold War propaganda.

The work today is on display at Clervaux Castle in northern Luxembourg. Steichen called the photographs gathered together there as "the culmination of my career."

Edward Steichen did more than most men in his field to turn photography into an art form. He became celebrated for his portraits of famous people, notably Greta Garbo, Charlie Chaplin, and (immediately below) Rita de Acosta.

One of the best psycholocal portraits of a brooding and haunted but astonishingly rich and well-connected **Rita de Acosta**, by Edward Steichen.

ARTURO TOSCANINI
(1867-1957)

Toscanini as he appeared in 1908.

His biographer, Harvey Sachs, wrote: "He believed that a performance could not be artistically successful unless unity of intention was first established among the components: Singers, orchestra, chorus, staging, sets, and costumes."

The Italian conductor, Arturo Toscanini, the music director of La Scala in Milan and also of the New York Philharmonic in Manhattan, became one of the most acclaimed musicians of the 20th Century. His late-in-life direction of the NBC Symphony Orchestra (1937-1954) made him a household name throughout the United States.

One critic wrote, "Toscanini was known for orchestral detail and sonority, and his eidetic memory." *[Also known as* **photographic memory***, it's the ability to recall an image from* **memory** *after seeing it only once.]*

Mercedes got to meet Toscanini at one of Rita's galas at her home in Manhattan. She found him "wickedly flirtatious, alive, and keenly aware of the charms of women. At least we had something in common."

He was very blunt with her. "I hear that you are a lesbian. I have always wanted to go to bed with a lesbian to show her what she has been missing."

Mercedes was also introduced to Toscanini's wife, Carla Martini, whom he'd married in 1897 when she was nineteen. She told Mercedes, "No wife in Italy expects her husband to be faithful. We know that when we marry them, we will have to live with their infidelities." Toscanini's many conquests were with famous divas such as Geraldine Farrar *[see above]*. In spite of his other conquests, he stayed married to Carla until her death in 1951. He would live for another six years and would never marry again.

MIGUEL UNAMUNO
(1864-1936)

Mercedes first met Unamuno while visiting the studio of the painter, Ignacio Zuloaga, in Paris.

Born in the Basque region of Spain, Unamuno was a world class essayist, novelist, poet, playwright, and philosopher. According to Mercedes,

"You never knew who would turn up at Zuloaga's studio in Montmartre: Perhaps Benevente (see above), the dramatist, certainly some gypsies and maybe a bullfighter or two."

Mercedes had read Unamuno's most famous novel, *Abel Sánchez: The History of a Passion* (1917), a modern adaptation of the classic Biblical story of Cain and Abel.

Unamuno became a towering figure in the intellectual life of Spain during the years he spent (1900-1924 and 1930-1936) in the scholastic stronghold of Salamanca, where he labored as a professor of Greek and Roman Classics and as one of the university's rectors.

He was removed from his university chair in 1924 by the Dictator, General Miguel Primo de Rivera, despite the protests of other Spanish intellectuals. Unamuno had been a blistering critic of the general and was forced into exile on the Canary Island of Fuerteventura. His house there is now a museum, as is his former home in Salamanca.

Miguel Unamuno was one of a group of Spanish intellectuals and philosophers who influenced thought in his native land. His views—familiar to the Spanish sensibilities of both Mercedes and Rita de Acosta—were always controversial in some quarters.

In spite of Spain's neutrality during World War I, Unamuno was an outspoken champion of the Allies.

Finally, after years of struggle and controversy, Unamuno declared, "I am neither Fascist nor Bolshevik. I am alone! Like Croce in Italy, I am alone."

Mercedes, as a passionate and politicized member of the intellectual avant-garde, befriended Unamuno and visited him at the stylish Basque resort of San Sebastian in the summer of 1930. During her time there, an invitation arrived from King Alfonso XIII. *[Born in 1886, Alfonso XIII was king of Spain from his birth until a decade before his death in 1941. After World War I, Spain threw itself into the corrosive Rif War (1920–1926) in a futile attempt to preserve its colonial grip on northern Morocco. Critics of the monarchy interpreted it as an unforgivable loss of blood and money, and pejoratively nicknamed Alfonso, until the end of his traumatic life,* **el Africano** *("the African") as a political insult.].*

Mercedes' invitation "summoned" her to sit in the Royal box at a bullfight the following day. She did not want to go, but Unamuno persuaded her that it would be awkward for him if she refused a royal invitation.

In her latter-day descriptions of the events of that day, she said she had a foreboding that Alfonso XIII was in his last months as a monarch. "I felt he was very close to losing his throne."

She was right. In 1931, control of the Spanish government returned overwhelmingly to a Republican majority, and Alfonso lost the support of the Army. Although at first he refused to give up his throne, he was eventually forced to and went into exile in 1931, eventually settling in Rome.

ANNE HARRIMAN VANDERBILT
(1861-1940)

Thanks to their many social connections, Rita and Mercedes often moved into the inner circles of such Gilded Age "kingmakers" as the Vanderbilts.

Both sisters became especially friendly with Anne Vanderbilt, who was born in New York as one of eight siblings in the Harriman family. Her first cousin, E.H. Harriman, was the father of New York State's Governor W. Averell Harriman.

Anne could have lived a life of idle privilege, but she devoted much time to philanthropy, helping "those less fortunate than myself." She financed the construction of four large apartment houses on York Avenue in Manhattan, creating homes for tuberculosis patients. In 1916 she hosted a fundraiser for the citizens of Venice who had suffered during World War I.

In Manhattan, she played a key role in the development of Sutton Place, turning what had been a seedy neighborhood into one of the most fashionable places to live in the entire city.

In the restoration of Sutton Place, Anne was joined by Elisabeth Marbury and Anne Morgan. The society pages of *The New York Times* derided the restoration of Sutton Place, referring to it as an "Amazon enclave," a veiled reference to the lesbianism of some of its residents.

Anne's first marriage, in 1884, was to sportsman Samuel Stevens Sands (1856-1889), who was also born into wealth. He died after a fall that occurred during a hunt. The couple had produced two sons.

Her second marriage, on June 16, 1890, was to Lewis Morris Rutherford, Jr. (1834-1901), son of the astronomer, Lewis Morris Rutherford. The newlywed couple produced two daughters.

In 1903, she co-established the Colony

Anne Harriman Vanderbilt was a philanthropist with good values and a knack for marrying spectacularly rich men..

As the second wife of one of the richest of the Vanderbilt heirs, she willingly granted access to her late husband's controversial "urban chateau" (Fifth Ave at 52nd Street in Manhattan, see below) for charity benefits and the war effort.

Club with Anne Morgan and Elisabeth Marbury [See above] the first women's social club in New York. Both Rita and Mercedes became members.

That same year, Anne married her third and richest husband, William Kissam Vanderbilt (1849-1920) in London. That marriage lasted until his death. A philanthropist, horsebreeder, and Vanderbilt heir, he managed his family's railroad investments. His father had been Commodore Cornelius Vanderbilt, who became the richest man in America. Cornelius eventually bequeathed his son the equivalent of about $1.6 billion in today's currency.

In 1879, Anne's husband took over some railroad property at Madison Square Park and developed it into Madison Square Garden. Around the same time, he became one of America's greatest horse breeders, erecting a château in France and establishing a breeding farm near Deauville.

In spite of her three (spectacularly prosperous) marriages, Anne Harriman Vanderbilt was cited as a secret lesbian. According to New York society gossip, she and Rita de Acosta sustained an affair.

EDITH WHARTON
(1862-1937)

A New Yorker, the future novelist was born into a wealthy and socially prominent family who made a fortune in New York City real estate. Her paternal family was named Jones. The expression, "Keeping up with the Joneses," was said to refer to this prosperous, high-reaching family.

Wharton herself, though born during the Civil War, suffered no deprivations. At the end of that war, she joined family members on an extensive six-year tour (1866-1872) of Europe that focused on the cultural highlights of France, England, Germany, and Italy. A mishap occurred when she nearly died from typhoid fever at the age of nine.

As ironic as it seemed, one of America's best-known novelists wasn't allowed to read a novel until she was married. As time went by, her family was scandalized (for them, a writer was akin to being a low-level mistress or a prostitute) when she began to write fiction.

Beginning in 1880, Edith became a socialite in Manhattan, where she keenly observed members of the Gilded Age. She would later dissect them and many of their prevailing dynamics, within her novels.

In 1885, she married Edward Robbins Wharton, a socialite twelve years her senior. He was a sportsman and a gentleman of the upper classes, having emerged from one of the "better" families of Boston. He, too, shared Edith's love of travel. Otherwise, they divided their time between their lavish residence at 884 Park Avenue in Manhattan, and (in summer) their sprawling villa in Newport.

By 1902, their marriage had soured. Edward Wharton suffered from acute depression, often locking himself away for weeks at a time without seeing her. The isolation also made her moody and melancholy, since she knew that divorce was inevitable. They had been long separated when her divorce was granted in 1913.

In the meantime, she launched a torrid affair with Morton Fullerton, a reporter for *The New York Times*.

Long before that, Edith wrote one of her most famous novels, *The House of Mirth* (1905), the first of many chronicles of life in the upper levels of society in Manhattan.

She also built an estate in Lenox, Massachusetts, which was visited by the cream of literary society, including her close friend and fellow novelist, the celebrated Anglo-American, Henry James. He called her estate "a delicate French château mirrored in a Massachusetts pond."

Eventually, she migrated to France, living at 53 rue de Varenne in Paris (7e) in an apartment previously occupied by George Washington Vanderbilt II.

Edith Wharton. Traumatized by her early years as a socialite, and her middle years as an active volunteer near the fighting in Europe of World War I, she spent her latter years writing and working through her often sad memories.

Although most of Paris' American expatriates fled when World War I broke out, Edith remained there as a tireless supporter of the Allied war effort. She helped unemployed women find work and provided housing for Belgium refugees.

In spite of her busy life, she began to write, penning the romantic novel, *Summer*, in 1916, and the war novella *The Marne*, in 1918.

At the end of the war, she settled into an 18th-Century house in Saint-Brice-sous-Forêt, a few miles north of Paris. By 1920, she had finished one of her most enduring works, *The Age of Innocence*. She returned to the United States only once after the war to receive an honorary doctorate from Yale University in 1923.

In 1921, she became the first woman to win the Pulitzer Prize for Literature. She beat out Sinclair Lewis for his satire on American life (*Main Street*). Edith would also be nominated (but not win) the Nobel Prize for Literature in 1927, 1928, and 1930.

Throughout her life, she surrounded herself with famous friends, which is how Mercedes and Rita de Acosta entered the tableau, joining a select group that included Theodore Roosevelt, Sinclair Lewis (he forgave her for taking the Nobel Prize from him), F. Scott Fitzgerald, and the (gay)

French authors Jean Cocteau and André Gide.

Although Mercedes and Rita had entertained Edith on occasion in Paris and also in New York, they never became close friends. Cocteau claimed, "The De Acosta sisters, in my view, were rather jealous of the literary success of Edith, and Rita even wrote a novel to try mining the same territory that Edith did. Most of Mercedes' literary efforts failed as well. The De Acosta sisters, of course, triumphed over Edith in attracting both men and (in Mercedes' case) women into their boudoirs. In romance, they left poor Edith behind in the dust."

In 1934, Edith wrote her autobiography, *A Backward Glance*.

The American National Biography (*a four-volume biographical encyclopedia with more than 17,000 entries and 20 million words*) later claimed, "What is notable about *A Backward Glance* is what it does not tell: her harsh criticism of Lucretia Jones (her mother); her difficulties with Teddy Roosevelt; and her enduring affair with Morton Fullerton." [*Many of these stories came to light when her papers, deposited at Yale, were opened in 1968. In her papers, Wharton described her mother as "indolent, a spendthrift, censorious, disapproving, superficial, icy, dry, and ironic."*]

In later years, many costume dramas with fabulous sets and costumes have been made based on the works of Edith Wharton. One of the earliest was *The Old Maid* (1939), directed by Edmund Goulding, and starring Bette Davis in one of her most memorable roles.

In 1944, *Variety* announced that Joan Crawford would star in *Ethan Frome*, based on the Wharton novel with the same name. However, the project was abandoned but revived in 1960 when it became a CBS-TV production starring Sterling Hayden in the title role.

As late as 1993, director Martin Scorsese made *The Age of Innocence* starring Daniel Day Lewis, Winona Ryder, and Michell Pfeiffer.

ELSIE DE WOLFE
(1859-1950)

This sometimes overwhelmingly stylish New Yorker failed as an actress but became one of the most famous and sought-after interior decorators in the world, replacing the dark and heavy Victorian styles with light, intimate effects and uncluttered room layouts. *The New Yorker* proclaimed, "Interior design as a profession was invented by Elsie de Wolfe."

She made her reputation decorating the homes of Amy Vanderbilt, Anne Morgan, and the Duke and Duchess of Windsor.

She also decorated the home of the coal magnate, Henry Clay Frick, one of the richest men in the United States. In another commission, she brought her style and taste to the interiors of the Colony Club, the first women's social club in America.

Her ideas about decorating first appeared in an influential book, *The House in Good Taste*, published in 1931.

De Wolfe told a magazine reporter, "I opened the doors and windows of America and let in the air and sunshine." She referred to herself as "a rebel in an ugly world."

She set out to be an actress, but her close friends told her she was not very good. One critic, scrambling to come up with something good to say about her onstage performance, said, "She is the leading exponent of the peculiar art of wearing good clothes well."

Much of the literary world, as well as figures from society, flocked to the Washington Irving House (17th Street at Irving Place) in New York City, the residence she shared from 1892-1911 with her rotund lover, Elisabeth Marbury. *[See above.]*

The press often wrote of the De Wolfe/Marbury liaison, referring to "the willowy De Wolfe and the masculine Marbury."

In 1926, De Wolfe upset prevailing opinions about her by marrying Sir Charles Mendl, the British press *attaché* in Paris. The marriage was both platonic and convenient. After the wedding, she made it clear that she preferred to be addressed as "Lady Mendl."

Lord Mendl never had a particularly distinguished career, but he moved up in the world and even had a knighthood bestowed on him. Somehow, he acquired love letters sent by Prince George, the Duke of Kent, to a homosexual gigolo, and the young man was threatening to use them for blackmail. Through his acquisition and "burial" of those letters, Mendl thereby rescued the British Royal Family from a colossal public embarrassment, for which the Duke of Kent remained forever grateful.

In Paris, both Mercedes and Rita were invited into French society's top-notch literary and social circles—especially those run by lesbian hostesses. The most famous of these were hosted by lesbians Natalie Barney and Ro-

Elsie de Wolfe as she elaborately appeared in a 1905 gown. A famous lesbian, she later was voted best-dressed woman in the world. She virtually invented interior decorating.

The parties she hosted at her Sutton Place townhouse in Manhattan were so stylish they helped make lesbian households not only acceptable but chic.

maine Brooks. On Sunday evenings, Rita and Mercedes visited Gertrude Stein and Alice B. Toklas.

Not to be outdone, Marbury and De Wolfe hosted their own "at home" parties at the Villa Trianon in Versailles. *[An opulent private home, it's not to be confused with either the Grand Trianon or the Petit Trianon directly on the grounds of the Palace of Versailles.]*

One party hosted there in June of 1913, attended by both Rita and Mercedes, was so memorable that it was reviewed in the press:

"There were covers set for forty at small tables upon the lawn. Rows of tiny lights marked the flower beds. Garlands of electric bulbs dripped from the trees. Festoons of roses hung from the roof covering the terrace. The fountains played, illuminated by the variety of colored lights...At the foot of the rose garden was the best orchestra to be engaged in Paris. Fortunately, the night was perfect. The stars were shining, the silver moon peeping through the branches, and the air soft and caressing."

De Wolf remained Marbury's lover until the latter's death in 1933. In 1935, Lady Mendl wrote an autobiography, failing to mention her husband.

That same year, experts in Paris hailed Lady Mendl as the best-dressed woman in the world.

She had taffeta pillows embroidered with her motto, "Never complain, never explain." On first seeing the Parthenon in Athens, she had exclaimed, "It's beige—my color!"

Lady Mendl lived until 1950, embracing a vegetarian diet as supervised by nutritionist Gayelord Hauser. Her morning exercises (which included yoga) were widely publicized. At the age of seventy, she could stand on her head, walk on her hands, and turn cartwheels.

She died at Versailles and was cremated, her ashes buried at Père Lachaise Cemetery in Paris.

IGNACIO ZULOAGA
(1870-1945)

Both Rita de Acosta and Mercedes were drawn into the circle of friends and fans who gravitated to the Spanish painter, Ignacio Zuloaga.

Born near the Monastery of Loyola in Spain, Ignacio was the son of a metalworker and damascener. He was also the grandson of the Don Eusebio, the director of the Royal Armoury in Madrid. During his youth, Ignacio worked as a blacksmith and metalworker in the footsteps of his father, but after a short visit to Rome, he was inspired to become a painter. After laboring for years to hone his craft, his first painting was exhibited in Paris in 1890.

He had moved there, at times barely surviving, settling with other artists in Montmartre, but in frequent contact with such towering figures as Toulouse-Lautrec and Gauguin.

Relatively unsuccessful in both Paris and London, he moved back to

Spain, settling is Seville and later in Segovia.

There, he was inspired by the paintings of Murillo and Velázquez. His favorite subjects were flamenco dancers and bullfighters. He also developed a "fetish" for painting dwarves and beggars, preferring muted tones such as grey or maroon.

In May of 1899, he married Valentine Dethomas, having met her through her brother, Maxime, formerly one of his classmates in Paris.

After many failures, he gradually became known as one of Spain's best painters.

Two of his best-known works included *Christ of the Blood* and *A Brotherhood of the Crucified Christ*, on display today at the Museo Reina Sofia in Madrid.

His work was praised by Unamuno *[see above]*, who wrote about Zuloaga's "particularly Spanish Catholic fascination with mutilating penance."

In time, Ignacio entered the orbit of Rita de Acosta, a devoted, free-spending patron of the arts. He later described her beauty and charm, and he almost demanded that she pose for him. There were rumors of an affair. He painted her, trying to capture her ethereal looks on canvas. A few months later, she arranged his first American exposition, in Boston and then in Manhattan.

Rita also purchased his *Portrait of a Philosopher,* which she was later forced to sell at auction as a means of paying her mounting debts.

In 1909, an art critic described the exposition of Zuloaga's works that Rita had helped organize, schedule, and arrange:

> *"It is this racy and picturesque life which Zuloaga seeks above all else to place on record, and it is these popular types unspoiled by ruthless modernism which he pursues into the farthest corners of his native land. In this zealous quest of congenial models, he hesitates at nothing. He will haunt for hours a fiesta on the outskirts of some provincial town, or hasten away to the mountains, passing months at a time with smugglers and muleteers, with the superstitious fanatics of Anso in the extreme north of Aragon, or with the monkish cut-throats of Las Baluecas, a little village on the southern boundary line of Salamanca."*

Zuloaga is depicted in a self-portrait from 1908.

A critic in 1909 reviewed the artist's work, calling it "defiant, almost despotic. It does not strive to enlist sympathy, nor does it fear to be frankly antipathetic. The surfaces are sometimes hard and metallic, reactionary, if you will."

In part because he was already a friend of Rita, Zuloaga also came into the orbit of Mercedes. On a visit to Spain, she was invited to stay at his home in Zumaya, a small fishing village near San Sebastian

One day, he invited her to visit a colony of gypsies, one of his favorite subjects for painting. The gypsies even danced for them to flamenco music. He had made friends with the *gîtanes* (gypsies), and they considered him one of "their own."

"They welcomed me to their camp, even though they were hostile to strangers for the most part," Mercedes said.

He told Mercedes, "I am only happy when I'm with my gypsy friends."

During her stay with him, she made a rare discovery. Displayed in a stone chapel he had built near his villa in Zumaya, he maintained a collection of thirteen El Grecos, including the celebrated *Sacred and Profane Love,* a world-class masterpiece later renamed *The Vision of St. John.*

Now worth millions of dollars, they were later sold to various major-league museums worldwide, with *The Vision of St. John,* noted above, going to the Metropolitan Museum in Manhattan.

During the Spanish Civil War (1936-1939), Zuloaga, unlike Mercedes, took the side of *El Caudillo* (Franco), who eventually evolved into the ruthless dictator of the Spanish state. Zuloaga painted Franco's portrait in 1940.

In a 1939 letter, he wrote, "Thank God and Franco, that at last the war is won and over. We will work with all our strength to rebuild a new Spain—free, great, and unified. That's my dream in art. What a shame that other countries inflicted crime and savage vandalism on my native land."

After Zuloaga's death in 1945, Franco ordered that his image appear on Spain's 500-peseta banknote.

Zuloaga even painted **Rita de Acosta Lydig** (some say unflatteringly) like an imperious and pressed-for-time *grandée* of Old Spain. In it, he emphasized her energy and eccentricity more than her legendary beauty.

Zuloaga's self-portrait from 1942 as it appeared on the 500-peseta banknote commissioned by Generalissimo Francisco Franco, *Caudillo* (dictator) of Spain from 1939-1975.

Many of the artist's early friends, including Mercedes, hated Zuloaga's support for Franco, a repressive, blood-soaked fascist who collaborated with Hitler and the Nazis.

CHAPTER THREE
"La Duse"

ELEANORA DUSE
Italy's *Belle-Époque* Answer to Sarah Bernhardt

LA DUSE!! Her audiences screamed. On the stages of London, Paris, Rome, and New York, her fans threw roses at her as the curtains fell.

She fought some dazzling professional duels with her only stage rival, Sarah Bernhardt. And she fell in love with the dashing Italian politician and poet **Gabrielle D'Annunzio** *[inset photo, top center]* which led to heartbreak and, coincidentally, floods of publicity.

Eleanora Duse (1858-1924) was not only the greatest actress in (recorded) Italian history, but was acclaimed as one of the greatest thespians of all time.

Born in what was the Kingdom of Sardinia, Duse joined a traveling troupe of actors at the tender age of four, when she already showed an amazing talent. "Acting is in my genes," she later said, referring to the professions of both her father and grandfather.

At the age of twenty-one, she fell in love with a journalist, Martino Cafiero. But when she got pregnant, he deserted her. Her infant did not survive childbirth.

From that day forth, she launched numerous love affairs, both gay and straight. When she joined Cesare Rossi's Theatre troupe, she fell for the handsome actor Tebaldo Checchi [the pseudonym of Tebaldo Marchetti], marrying him in 1881. Four years later, the couple had a daughter, Enricheta, but the marriage came to an end when she fell in love with another actor in the troupe, Flavio Ando.

By now, her fame as an actress had spread through Italy, and she was booked for a tour through South America.

When she returned to the shores of Italy, she was so well established that she formed her own production company, functioning as its star, director, and manager. Critics hailed her for her "total absorption in characters she presents on stage."

Eleanora Duse was the first woman to appear on the cover of *Time* magazine, and thirty-four years after her death, she graced a commemorative postage stamp issued in her honor by the Italian nation.

"I am a vagabond, a nomad," she proclaimed.

One of her longest-running affairs was with the Italian poet Arrigo Boito, the librettist for Verdi. The couple were often separated, but their love letters, for the most part, were preserved.

Their affair lasted from 1887 to 1894. The following year, one of the most celebrated of all Italians, Gabrielle D'Annunzio (1863-1938), five years her junior, entered her life.

[General Gabriele D'Annunzio, Prince of Montenevoso, Duke of Gallese, was a journalist, poet, playwright and soldier during World War I, and later, for about a decade, a politician. Sensuous and mystical in his writing, and deeply influenced by the German philosopher Nietzsche, he's sometimes criticized (or condemned) for having influenced the Fascist principles of Benito Mussolini.]

Handsome, dashing, and romantic, D'Annunzio wooed her and she fell under his spell. He wrote four plays for her, for which both of them won wide acclaim. By then, she had become a rival of France's Sarah Bernhardt. [The two grande dames quickly developed a lifelong animosity.]

Bernhardt's allure eventually ended D'Anunzio's affair with Duse. After he awarded the leading role in his latest play, *La Città*, to Bernhardt, an enraged Duse attacked him with claws freshly sharpened. After suffering bloody scratches from her, he fled, ending their highly publicized affair.

Critics were almost evenly divided on the question of which actress was greater: Bernhardt or Duse. During one theatrical season in London, both of them were appearing in different plays in the West End. George Bernard Shaw was one of the many consumers who saw each of their respective performances. He announced to the press that Duse was the greater actress, based on her starring role in *Cosí Sia*.

The leading English actress of her era, Ellen Terry, was more diplomatic, stating, "It is futile to make comparisons between the leading actress of Italy and the leading actress of France. Better far to thank heaven for both of these stars."

In 1896, Duse toured the United States, stopping first to perform in Washington, D.C. President Grover Cleveland and his wife, Frances, attended on opening night. Later, the First Lady held a tea at the White House in honor of Duse, which shocked Washington society. In those days, actresses were regarded as little more than whores.

Duse retired from the stage in 1909 although, near the end of her life, she would make a comeback, embarking on a final tour of the United States.

Around the time of her retirement, she was involved in a lesbian affair with the feminist, Tina Poleti. The couple lived together in a villa in Florence before separating two years later.

In time, she began an affair with the dancer, Isadora Duncan, whom Duse had known for years. Both the dancer and the dramatic actress occupied a villa at the seaside resort of Viareggio.

Duncan had given birth to two children out of wedlock, Deirdre and Patrick, each fathered by Paris Singer, one of the many sons of the sewing machine magnate, Isaac Singer. In 1913, both children had drowned in the care of a nanny when their car went off a bridge and into the Seine in Paris.

While living with Duse, Duncan was seduced on the beach by the sculptor, Roman Romanelli, who agreed to give her another child to replace the ones she'd lost. When Duse heard about this indiscretion, she asked Duncan to leave.

After Duncan's departure, lovers came and went from the Duse household. She became in-

Duse's friend, **Ellen Terry,** was probably the most famous English actress of her era. She appears here as Shakespeare's heroine in *Cymbeline.*

U.S. President **Grover Cleveland,** whose wife invited Duse to the White House for tea during her American tour. She shocked Washington, D.C. society by treating her substantially better than the "average actress" would have fared in an era when "painted ladies and actresses" were held in scandalized contempt.

Here, Cleveland appears as painted by one of the Gilded Age's most famous portraitists, Anders Zorn

volved with a young actress, Emma Gramatica, and later, with singer Yvette Guilbert. As her years grew to a close, Duse developed a love relationship with the British-born American stage actress, Eva Le Gallienne, who was also sexually and emotionally involved with Mercedes de Acosta.

During the final months of Duse's life, when she was sixty-five years old, Mercedes entered into a sexual relationship with her.

Mercedes had gone backstage in Washington after Duse's performance in *The Swan*, ostensibly to interview her for the *Boston Evening Transcript*. Duse was mesmerized by the young Spanish beauty. She became even more so after learning that Mercedes had written a play for her, with the firm understanding that its lead could only be interpreted by Duse herself. It was entitled *The Mother of Christ*.

In her presence, Duse read the play and pronounced it brilliant. According to Mercedes, "Miss Duse adored my play and told me that she would tour the world with it before her final retirement."

Mercedes was thrilled, although that world tour was never to happen. Duse was already touring America in a play called *La Porta Chiusa*.

Suffering from asthma, she set out from Washington, facing dust storms in Arizona, blizzards in Detroit. Finally, in Pittsburgh, she got soaked in icy rain and took to bed, where she developed pneumonia, dying on April 21, 1924.

For four days, her body, which had been shipped from Pittsburgh to New York City, lay in state as mourners passed by. After the body was forwarded back to her native Italy, thousands of mourners passed by to pay their final respects.

Months before her death, Duse had become the first woman (and the first Italian) to be featured on the cover of the nascent magazine known as *Time*.

Mercedes later wrote of becoming enthralled by the "white flame passion" Duse had ignited in her. "There was a sort of mystic magic about her."

Her first sighting of Duse had occurred when Mercedes was only eight

For a woman who was proficient in the over-the-top, elaborately overblown theatrical styles of her era, **Eleonora Duse** could be remarkbably straightforward, direct, and without artifice. Here she is, displaying the "artful simplicity" for which she was revered.

The photo above is a still from the only movie she ever filmed, **Cenere** *(Ashes;* 1916). Silent and deeply evocative, it sent fans into tears when Duse, as a selfless (grown up) mother of the child she was forced to abandon years ago in a village in Sardinia, kills herself as a means of causing him no more trouble.

years old in Venice, and each of their gondolas almost collided.

According to Mercedes, the setting sun shone down on her famous face whose body was dressed all in black. "I looked at a strikingly tragic face. For a second, I was almost close enough to touch her when our eyes met, and she smiled at me."

Mercedes' gondolier, who recognized her, immediately proclaimed, "La Duse! La grande attrice!"

From then on, Mercedes admitted to an obsession with Duse, which finally morphed into a sexual encounter in a Washington, D.C. hotel suite.

In 1924, at the age of 31, Mercedes went down to the pier in New York, where she stood and watched a dark ship moving out of dock and toward the sea. It carried the body of Eleanora Duse, to be buried in her native soil.

In 1947, director Fillippo Walter Ratti made *Eleonore Duse*, a movie based on the incredible life of Italy's greatest actress. It starred Elisa Cegai as Eleonora, with Rossano Brazzi as Arrigo Boito.

When the movie was released internationally, Brazzi was the only actor known to world audiences. The 90-minute film was inspired by the novel, *La grande tragica* by Nino Bolla.

The intense and spectacularly avant-garde writer/journalist/musician **Arrigo Boito** (1842-1918; left figure in photo) wrote the *libretti* for two of **Giuseppe Verdi's** operas.

In ways equivalent to the romantic poet, Gabrielle d'Annunzio (another of Duse's lovers), he fought under in the 1866 war against Austria, as a result of which Venice was ceded to Italy.

The photo above shows Boito with Verdi in the late 1880s, probably discussing their fiery collaboration on what are considered two of Verdi's ate masterpieces

Between 1887 and 1894, Boito sustained an *amitié amoureuse* with Duse, leaving behind a voluminous correspondence with endless insights into the mores and manners of Europe's late 19th-century gilded age.

Boita and Duse remained on good terms until his death.

Although she detested the comparison, Eleanora Duse was often defined as "the Italian version of the (French) actress, **Sarah Bernhardt,** who's depicted above.

More than any French icon since Madame Recamier, Bernhardt taught affluent women of the Romantic 19th Century how to recline.

Rossano Brazzi (above), perhaps the most handsome Italian of his generation, portrayed Arrigo Boito, Duse's lover, in the 1947 Italian-language biopic dedicated to her life as Italy's most evocative and celebrated actress.

Although **Duse** lived in an age when photography was new and remarkable (see center image of her, above), her fame resulted in a number of portraits being made of her by important painters.

Duse portraits to the left and right, immediately above, are by **Giovanni Boldini** and **Franz von Lenbach**, respectively. Each of them labored, obviously, to capture the nuances of her emotional projection and power.

CHAPTER FOUR
THE GODDESS OF MODERN DANCE

ISADORA DUNCAN
DANCE AS A REVOLUTIONARY CELEBRATION OF LIFE

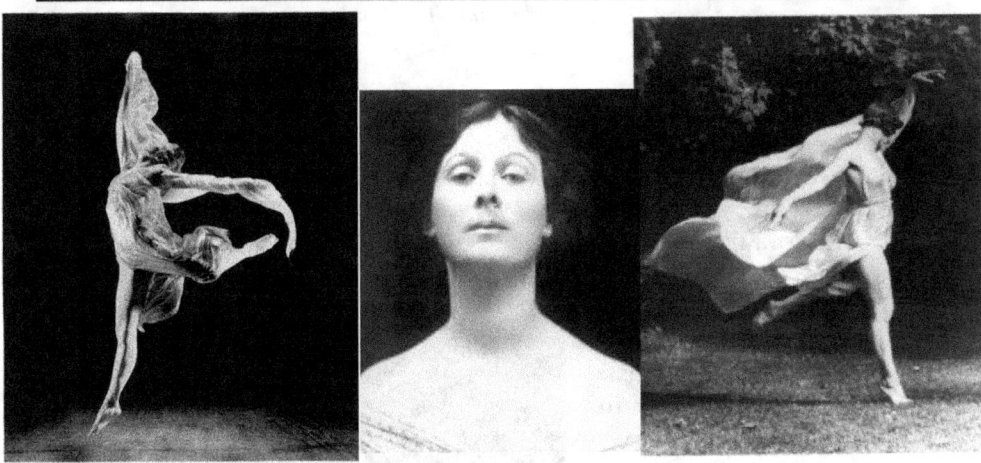

Views of **Isadora Duncan,** whose artful simplicity reflected the values and presuppositions of radical chic during the *Belle Epoque*.

WHAT CRITICS SAID ABOUT ISADORA DUNCAN DURING THE PRUDISH YEARS OF HER HEYDAY

"What mattered in Isadora's Hellenic dances was not the Greek themes or the gauzy costumes, but the uninhibited vitality, the sense of a glorious nakedness."

— Lewis Mumford, Cultural Critic, 1905

"Isadora Duncan creates, she poses, she dances. But not like anyone else. Oh, no! She would be a revelation to the star ballet dancer; she is no high kicker, or toe acrobat. She employs no illusions, no cunningly arranged mirrors, no beautifully multicolored lime-lights. Never was there anything less sensational than her work; it is severe in its simplicity."

— St. Louis Sunday Gazette, December 26, 1902

Isadora Duncan (1877-1927), was the world's greatest modern dancer. Two months before her tragic death, Mercedes de Acosta wrote an erotic poem about her. In part, it read:

Two sprouting breasts
Round and sweet
Invite my hungry mouth to eat
From whence two nipples firm and pink
Persuade my thirsty soul to drink.

***

The first time Mercedes saw Isadora, she fell in love with her from a distance. It occurred at a party (circa 1913) hosted by Princess Violette Murat.

"Isadora was there, walking about with Nijinsky and holding him by the hand," Mercedes said. "The orchestra played 'The Blue Danube.' They rose to dance, Isadora clasped her hands behind her head, forcing Nijinsky to lead her by placing his hands around her waist. She became oblivious, lost in the beat of the waltz. With her eyes closed, she allowed Nijinsky to guide her in and out among the other waltzing couples. Gradually, everyone stopped dancing to watch."

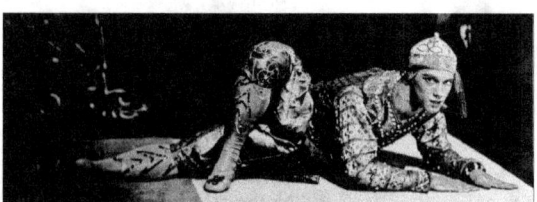

Nijinski, the toast of the dance world just before Isadora Duncan's heyday, reclines artfully, onstage..

A native of San Francisco, Isadora Duncan would grow up to become a legend, known for her innovative techniques in modern dance, but also as a temperamental, headline-generating bohemian and advocate of "free love."

Even as a teenager, she announced she was devoting her life to the pursuit of art and beauty...and love.

She appeared first on

The great modern dancer, **Isadora Duncan,** glides more gracefully than a swan against the backdrop of a surging ocean.

the stage in 1896, billed as "Peppy Dora" at a rowdy music hall revue in Chicago. That same year found her in Manhattan, a member of Augustin Daly's theatrical troupe. But she felt the group's dancing was too restrictive "for a free soul like me" and she dropped out. With money she'd saved, she headed for England.

In London, inspired by Greek vases and bas-reliefs in the British Museum, she created a new style of dance. It focused on natural movement in contrast to the rigidity of classic ballet. She traveled to Paris and later toured both Europe and the United States, showcasing her unique interpretation of dance. Many critics, preferring a more traditional form, came down hard on her free-flowing style. To answer the attacks, she said, "My aim is to create beauty on the stage."

Left photo: **Paul Poiret**, the most sucessful designer of the Belle Epoque, fits a dress on a model in his Parisian showrooms. Isadora, impersonating an orgiastic "Bacchanale," danced at one of his receptions.

Right photo: Two of his designs, including (left) harem pants and (right) a "sultana" skirt.

When not peforming, she taught dance to the young. In 1904, she was found in Berlin, operating a dance school where a group of devotees, known as the "Isadorables," perpetuated her legacy.

A highlight of her career occurred in 1911, when the fabled fashion designer, Paul Poiret, threw a lavish party to recreate a Bacchanalia as it might have been hosted by Louis XIV at Versailles. As champagne flowed, Duncan, in a Greek gown, danced on tables for 300 elite guests.

Many of her statements confounded critics when she described her vision of dance, defining it as "the force of progress change, abstraction, and liberation."

Mercedes De Acosta encouraged Isadora, by now a pale, impoverished shadow of her former charismatic glory, to write her autobiography. Here's the cover of the resulting book she produced.

By 1914, at the outbreak for World War I, she fled back to Manhattan where she operated a school on Gramercy Park.

She narrowly missed being a passenger aboard the ill-fated 1915 sinking of the RMS *Lusitania*, which was attacked by German U-boats and sank.

Three years after World War I, her Leftist sympathies took her to Moscow, where she founded a dance school, but the Soviet government failed to honor the commitments it had made to her. "Dancing is about skipping, running, jumping, leaping, and tossing," she told her would-be backers in Moscow. "I want to link emotion and movement."

She later said,"I don't think those Communists had a clue as to what dance was about."

Despite her legions of critics, she enjoyed an array of devotees, who were soon hailing her as "the creator of modern dance."

On a personal level, she flouted tradition and lived openly as a bisexual and atheist.

In spite of her initial disillusionment with her would-be communist backers in Moscow, Isadora remained committed to the world movement throughout an extended U.S. tour in 1922 and 1923. She ended her performances by baring her breasts and waving a red scarf. "This scarf is red and so am I!"

In 1923, she returned to Moscow, where she fell in love with the poet, Sergei Essenin, in spite of a language barrier. He was blonde, well-muscled, rather studly, and eighteen years her junior.

In May of 1923, they were married. She proclaimed, "I don't speak Russian, but we speak the language of love."

In reference to their brief time together, she later told friends, "I spent most of my marriage with him in bed on top of me. Talk about multiple orgasms!"

On December 28, 1925, he was found dead, an apparent suicide, in his room at the Hotel Angleterre in St. Petersburg.

Isadora, with her children, Deirdre and Patrick, in 1913. Both of them died, along with their nanny, when the car they were in plunged into the River Seine in Paris.

Chic, stylish, avant-garde, and famous: cult icons **Isadora Duncan with her paramour, Paris Singer**, the most flamboyant of the many heirs of the sewing machine fortune, and father of her two children.

***

Mercedes de Acosta and Isadora Duncan began their affair long before Duncan's marriage to the Russian poet .

Mercedes first met Isadora in 1917 at Amagansett on New York's Long

Island. "I was bewitched by this dark, intense, adoringly lovely woman," Mercedes said. "She came toward me on the beach, with her arms outstretched. She moved with quick, spontaneous gestures, as if we had known each other all our lives."

Isadora recalled, "Mercedes came into my life like an archangel, offering her slender body, so soft, so white, for my delight."

Isadora with her husband, the suicidal Russian poet, **Sergei Essenin**

Mercedes was fleeing from the ardent pursuit of Paris Singer, heir to the Singer sewing machine fortune. She was eager to begin an affair with Isadora, who was sixteen years older.

"On cool summer evenings, Isadora danced just for me," Mercedes said. "Once, she danced during the entire recording of Richard Wagner's Parsifal."

When Mercedes had to return to Manhattan, Isadora wrote Mercedes a love note:

"Lead me with your strong hands, and I will follow you to the top of the mountain, to the end of the world, wherever you wish."

What music was in vogue during Isadora's choreographic frenzy?

Among others, the grandiose, stirring music of **Richard Wagner,** depicted above with his complicated, ambitious, and fiercely Teutonic wife, **Cosima.**

A long separation followed, as both women moved on to other affairs. But in 1925, Mercedes once again encountered Isadora, finding her slipping into alcoholism and living in a seedy hotel on the Left Bank of Paris. She was broke and in despair.

Mercedes lent her money and urged her to write her autobiography, for which Mercedes felt she could get a New York publisher to offer her a substantial adance.

Mercedes was convinced that Isadora had never recovered from the loss of her two children, who had drowned when their car had plunged into the Seine.

Isadora's autobiography was published in 1927, a critic calling it "a life-enriching masterpiece."

Yet after that, she seemed to drift even more into alcoholism and despair. Along the French Riviera, she checked in and out of hotels, fleeing with unpaid bills. A biographer of hers referred to this period of her life as "extravagant waywardness."

On that fateful late afternoon of September 14, 1927, Isadora, wearing a long red scarf, got into the front seat of an open automobile driven by Benoit Falchetto, a French-Italian mechanic and sometimes race car driver.

They took off with her long, free-flowing scarf blowing in the wind. Her final words to her friends were, "Adieu, mes amis! Je vais à la gloire!" ("Farewell, my friends! I go to glory!")

Her long silk scarf became entangled in the open-spoked wheels and rear axle, pulling her from the open car and breaking her neck. By the time she was rushed to a hospital, she was pronounced dead.

When the sad and horrifying news reached Mercedes, she said, "Somehow, the world seems to have grown darker."

***

The English actress, Vanessa Redgrave, was nominated for a Best Actress Oscar when she starred in the 1968 movie, *Isadora (aka The Loves of Isadora)*.

Her co-stars included James Fox, cast as Gordon Craig, a young stage designer she meets in Berlin. He already has a wife but impregnates her, leading to the birth of a daughter.

Jason Robards played Paris Singer (the sewing machine heir), who lavishes gifts on her and fathers a son with her.

Bored with the quiet life, she deserts him and goes to the Soviet Union, where she has a passionate affair with Sergei Essenin (Ivan Tchenko).

Made for $1.7 million, Isadora generated $1.25 million at the box office in the U.S. and Canada.

One critic wrote, "Redgrave could not convey the élan of the dancer, though she danced semi-nude sometimes, she seemed more sensual than aesthetic. She stressed the elements of female liberation in the role."

Three views of **Vanessa Redgrave as Isadora Duncan** in her big-screen impersonation of the dancer's life, released in 1968. The film depicted her tragic death when her long scarf got entangled in the open-spoked wheels of her driver, Benoit Falchetto, breaking her neck, crushing her larnx, and almost ripping her head from her shoulders.

CHAPTER FIVE
LONELY ARE THE BRAVE

EVA LE GALLIENNE

ONE OF BROADWAY'S MOST ADMIRED GRANDE DAMES, AMERICA'S ANSWER TO SARAH BERNHARDT

The theatrical career of **Eva Le Gallienne** spanned tumultuous decades. She vied with Helen Hayes, Katharine Cornell, and Lynn Fontanne for the title of First Lady of the American Theater. "As an actress, I was a step ahead of my century," she proclaimed.

She tranlsated works of Chekhov and Ibsen, and lived a notorious private life, going through defeats and triumphs, joy, pain, and sometimes, love. Presidents Gerald Ford and Ronald Reagan hailed her as "a national treasure."

She appeared in some of the most classic works of Shakespeare, Molière, and Euripedes, but also could delve into experimental theater. "In a great play or a half-born drama, I gave it my all," she said.

"Will I be remembered when my admirers die out?" she asked. "Will they know me in the next century? I doubt it. Maybe someone forty years from now will be looking in an old theater book of Broadway stars and see me playing Hedda Gabler."

"The path of every vaguely closeted lesbian who ever made it on Broadway and in Hollywood during the 1920s, '30s, and 40s seemed to erotically coincide with the seductive charms of Mercedes de Acosta."

—Arts industry socialite & author,
Stanley Mills Haggart

One weekend at Magnolia House, Mercedes de Acosta told Darwin Porter, "If you write my life story one day—and I suspect you might—you'll need a chapter devoted to my love affair with Eva Le Gallienne. We were madly in love, our affair lasting for five tumultuous, argumentative, jealous years. Yes, we 'strayed' and fell into the arms of other lovers, but we always returned to each other for comfort, solace, understanding, and a grand and fiery passion."

A figure of diminishing fame in the 21st Century, Eva Le Gallienne (1899-1991) was a towering cultural icon in her heyday. Born in London in the closing year of the 19th Century, she became America's theatrical an-

Derived from a prosperous, cosmopolitan, and avant-garde home, Eva was raised by brainy, progressive parents in France, Denmark, England, and the U.S. The inset photo above shows **her** dilettantish **father**, evocative to some of Oscar Wilde, next to a mother-daughter portrait of **Julie,** Ava's ferociously feminist mother, posing with her pride and joy, **Baby Eva.**

LE GALLIENNE: They called her an American *tragedienne* worthy of the grand tradition of Sarah Bernhardt:

Photo above shows **Eva Le Gallienne** on Broadway in 1938 as Marie Antoinette in the well-reviewed costume drama and crowd-pleaser, *Madame Capet*.

swer to France's Sarah Bernhardt. She also vied—some say "obsessively"—with Helen Hayes, Lynn Fontanne, and Katharine Cornell for the title of "First Lady of the American Theatre."

A producer, director, translator, author, and actress, she excelled in many fields, both on and off the stage and screen.

Her parents separated when Eva was four years old. Her mother, Julie Nørregaard, a Danish journalist with financial means of her own, promptly sought a change of air and moved with her daughter to Paris, spending the next several years shuttling back and forth between London and the French capital. As Eva grew older and began expressing an interest in the theater, Julie invited her to some of Bernhardt's theatrical performances in Paris.

Julie escorted her mesmerized daughter backstage, where Eva told the seasoned diva, "In a few years I'll be on the stage performing like you. You're good—in fact, very, very good. But I'll be better."

Bernhardt laughed and hugged her to her bosom. "So you will, *ma petite fleur*. But you've got to blossom first."

EVA'S ROLE MODEL, SARAH BERNHARDT, "THE TOAST OF BELLE ÉPOQUE EUROPE"

Eva operated in a theatrical climate infused with very grand drama, indeed. Photo above shows her role model, the French thespian, **Sarah Bernhardt,** artfully reclining "like no one else ever could."

More views of Eva's role model, **Sarah Bernhardt,** an actress whose stage presence no one ever seemed to forget.

As a star-struck early teen, Eva lacked tact during her first backstage encounter with Bernhardt, the toast of theatrical Europe. But much to her credit, the *Überdiva* was bemused, supportive, and kind.

Eva made her stage debut, a walk-on in the 1914 stage production of

Maurice Maeterlinck's *Moona Vanna* (a then avant-garde play celebrating the concept of emancipated, rejuvenated women) when she was fifteen.

In 1916, dreaming of Eva's success on the Broadway stage and enamored with visions of America and its bold approaches to the theater, Eva and Julie sailed from Paris to New York, where Eva would suffer a series of depressing failures and an unpromising debut. One director fired her from the cast of a troupe experimenting with an out-of-town "tryout." That was followed with a gig in summer stock and a return to Paris.

A few months later, she returned to "conquer Broadway," in a successful run of Arthur Richman's nostalgic *Not So Long Ago*, which depicted New York in the 1870s. After try-outs in Boston, it opened in New York on May 4, 1920 at the Booth Theatre.

In reference to that performance, critics from *The New York Times* praised Eva, defining her as "appealingly beautiful."

To some degree, she was guided to her success by a mentor, Lee Shubert, the oldest brother from the renowned theatrical family. A Lithuanian, Lee was born in 1871 in territory that was part of the Russian Empire, the oldest of the seven siblings of the theatrical Shubert family.

Impresario and entertainment-industry mogul **Lee Shubert** ("Mr. Casting Couch"), who took a strong (some say obsessive) interest in Eva Le Gallienne's career. Was it lust? Was it love? In reference to the lousy maintenance backstage at his theaters, Eva, years later, quipped that she had personally repaired every broken toilet in every dressing room she'd ever used within a Shubert Theater.

He was only eleven when his family emigrated to the United States. In time, the Shubert Brothers became the most successful operators of theaters in New York, eventually presiding over the largest theater empire of the 20th Century.

[Lee persuaded the great actress Sarah Bernhardt to perform in New York in 1905. He was also responsible for introducing the "campy" Portuguese/Brazilian entertainer Carmen Miranda to American audiences in 1939.]

Early in her career, Eva signed a binding contract with Lee, who really wanted to put her on the casting couch. She continued to resist him, even though he plied her with expensive gifts like leather purses and French perfumes. Although he hired directors who'd show her in her best light, he soon learned that Eva liked to direct herself.

It was around this time that Ethel Barrymore, one of the reigning and most temperamental divas in the American theater, spotted Le Gallienne and "sensed a great talent here. She has a chance to become a formidable figure in the theater."

Thus, the great Miss Barrymore became a mentor to Eva Le Gallienne.

For an eighteen-month gig beginning in 1918 (the year that marked the end of World War I), Eva performed with Miss Barrymore on Broadway, cast as her daughter in two separate plays, *The Off Chance*, and *Belinda*. "Ethel virtually taught me how to act by letting me watch how she did it," Eva recalled.

Born in 1879 in Philadelphia, Ethel was a member of the famous Barrymore family of actors, which included both John and Lionel, in a career spanning six decades. She, in discreet but ferocious competition with a few other entertainers, was sometimes defined as "First Lady of the American Theater."

Ethel Barrymore, the ultimate (some said "ultimately terrifying") *Grande Dame* of the American Theater.

She "adopted" Eva as her *protégée*.

Ethel Barrymore's string of hit Broadway plays and movie roles would merit a separate book.

In 1926, she scored one of her greatest hits as the wise and worldly wife of a philandering husband in W. Somerset Maugham's comedy, *The Constant Wife*. The author himself attended a performance, later telling Ethel, "I have fallen madly in love with you." [*Actually, what might have attracted him even more than a live interpretation of his play was the sight of her brother, John Barrymore, wearing those revealing green tights he often wore on stage.*]

On tour with Eva, Miss Barrymore confided some startling details about her life during those unguarded moments after the curtain fell. She claimed that in 1900, when she was performing in England, a young Winston Churchill had proposed marriage to her.

[*Eva never got to see all three Barrymores in the film,* National Red Cross Pageant *(1917), which is now lost in the dust bin of Hollywood history, but she did go see Ethel perform with her brothers in* Rasputin and the Empress *(1932).*]

After several months of friendship, rumors spread in theatrical circles that Eva and Ethel were engaged in a lesbian affair, which both actresses ferociously denied.

***

The "historic" first meeting of Mercedes de Acosta with Eva Le Gallienne occurred on April 20, 1921 in Manhattan after Mercedes attended a presentation of the Theater Guild's Broadway production of *Liliom*. In the role of Julie, Eva was lauded by critics. One writer asserted that "She was not poetic—She was poetry."

Having migrated backstage, Mercedes invited Eva for lunch the next day at Manhattan's Ritz Hotel. Much of the talk over lunch was of their mutual admiration for Eleonora Duse.

[In the early '70s, about twenty years before her death, Eva wrote The Mystic in the Theatre: Eleanora Duse, promoting her as a philosopher and spiritualist, and her biography as a self-help book devoted to awakening the mystical aspects of Duse's legacy. Critics reviewed it as a fascinating glimpse into both herself and the tired, fading great actress whom Eva adored.]

The luncheon with Ethel went so successfully, with such bonding and sexual attraction that Mercedes invited Eva back to her Manhattan apartment. Mercedes later admitted, "We spent the rest of the afternoon making love before she had to head back to the theater. Our affair had begun."

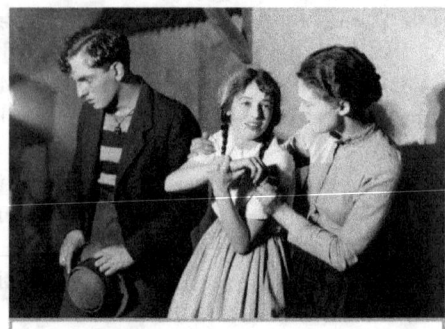

This photograph shows what Mercedes de Acosta witnessed from a seat in the audience the first time she ever saw Eva Le Gallienne on stage, just before inaugurating their affair.

Left to right, **Joseph Schildkraut** (as Liliom), **Evelyn Chard** (as Louise) and **Eva Le Gallienne** (as Julie) in the Theatre Guild production of *Liliom* (1921), a play that launched her as an American icon.

***

Eva's future biographer, Robert A Schanke, described Mercedes' appearance: "She was almost reptilian in looks, with her pale white face, black hair, and thin red lips. She had met Toscanini and Caruso and had a thirst for knowledge and a love of theater. She made a statement with her mannish pants, pointed shoes, trimmed with big buckles, a tricorn hat, and cape."

Mercedes, as she later revealed, was overwhelmed by the charm and beauty of the actress. Many people who met Eva were turned off by her strong ego and sense of independence, but Mercedes interpreted that as one of her most attractive qualities, eventually telling Eva, "I think most men treat women like a pet dog who follows its master around., Not me. I want to chart my own course in life, like I heard that you do. Our mutual friend, Nazimova, has talked so much about you that I think I know you already."

Picture of **Mercedes de Acosta,** by her then-husband, society portraitist Abram Poole.

Some say it evokes a severe, macho, self-entitled Iberian *grandée* in the mannerist style of El Greco.

Mercedes and Abram? Perhaps they were (briefly) in love...once.

[*In 1918, in Hollywood, Eva had sustained a short affair with Alla Nazimova. At that time, Nazimova was at the height of her fame on the silent screen, ruling over MGM as its Queen. Too much jealousy eventually ended that affair.*

Eva was also involved with three other famous actresses of that era: Beatrice Lillie, Tallulah Bankhead, and Laurette Taylor. Eva, however, seemed frequently ambivalent about her lesbianism, at times seeming to flaunt it, but at other (usually depressed) periods taking pains to conceal it.]

Mercedes entered Eva's life when she was particularly vulnerable. One night when she remained late within her dressing room, long after the cast, crew, and audience had fled, a burly stage hand appeared unannounced, held her down, and raped her. That experience made her loathe the idea of sex with men all the more. The next day, the manager of the theater fired the stagehand.

Soon, Eva and Mercedes were dating, attending Bob Chanlet's avant-garde parties on East 19th Street in New York that attracted everyone from vagabonds to visiting Euro-

Mercedes de Acosta (left) with her then-lover, **Eva Le Gallienne**, on holiday together in Europe in 1922.

According to Mercedes, "That summer, Eva and I walked through Brittany like a pair of tramps and bunked with fishermen and their families. Back in Paris, we watched Mata Hari dance in the nude at a private party for a coven of American lesbian expatriates."

Three gender-bending stage manifestations of Eva Le Gallienne: Left: Eva as the Duke of Reichstadt, Napoleon's exiled don, in *L'Aiglon* (1934). Center, Eva in *The Swan* (1923), wearing a silver-threaded couture by Molyneux, the most fashionable designer of his era. Right, as the (according to her interpretation) ruthless and "way over-the-top macho" female protagonist (Hilda) of Henrik Ibsen's *The Master Builder*.

peans with titles. They were also seen together at dives in Harlem or at chic restaurants.

One night "from out of nowhere," (Eva's words), Mercedes delivered an unexpected shock to her newly minted lover. She announced she was sailing to France the next morning with her new husband, Abram Poole, a Russian-born painter and sculptor. Mercedes was twenty-seven at the time, and he was thirty-seven. Eva had assumed that Mercedes was a lesbian, not bisexual.

"I'll write every day," Mercedes promised. "Abram will make almost no demands on me. I'm saving all my love for you."

"By then, I was too far gone into my relationship with Mercedes that I didn't break off with her," Eva later said. "She and I would be lovers, but not necessarily faithful."

Since they were often apart, each of the women sustained affairs with other bisexuals or lesbians, which ignited jealous feuds.

Tallulah Bankhead inducted Eva into the Algonquin Round Table, from whose ranks they developed lunchtime friendships with Estelle Winwood and Blyth Daly. *[Daly was the least known of this infamous quartet, although she had appeared on stage and in silent films. She was notorious for her*

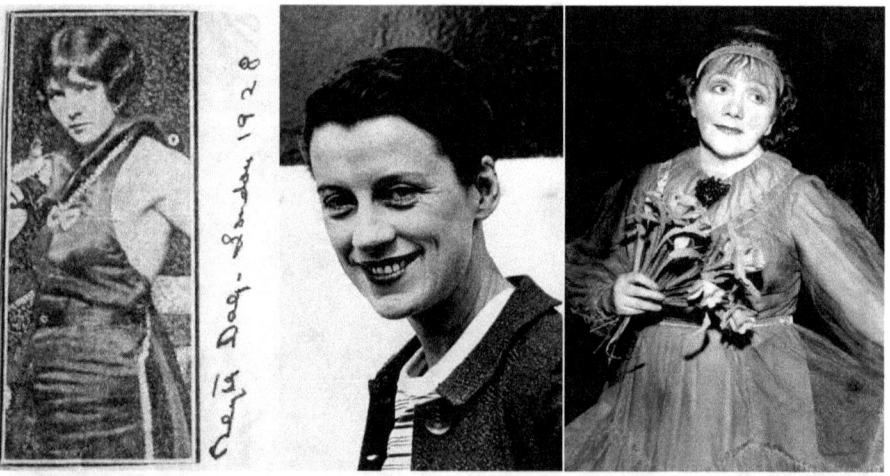

Three famous lesbians, each a consummate and--to the public, at least, closeted--entertainer of the first order:

Left: **Blyth Daly,** snapped in London in 1928. "Tallulah Bankhead, Eva, Estelle Winwood, and I were dubbed 'The Four Horsemen of the Apocalyse'...I mean, 'of the Algonquin.'"

Middle: **Beatrice Lillie**. She once confessed to "The Girls" that she'd had an affair with Vivien Leigh.

Right: **Laurette Taylor.** She led a tragic life on and off the stage, battling alcoholism. Here, she appears in her most memorable stage role as "mother from hell" (Amanda) in Tennessee Williams' *The Glass Menagerie*.

friendships within the "lesbian underground" of New York. Her career never took off, but she was always seen in the company of famous persons, ranging from novelists Edna Ferber to comedian Harpo Marx.]

***

With Mercedes away on her honeymoon with Poole, Eva moved in a circle of the theatrical elite, showing up at parties with big stars like Laurette Taylor, Alfred Lunt, and Lynn Fontanne.

"One night I danced with a drunken John Barrymore, who felt my breast as we moved about the floor," Eva later confessed to Mercedes. "Even though intoxicated, he had a serious, very intense side to him. I had the feeling he was laughing at all the other fools in the room. I turned down his invitation to go home with him. When I did, he took my hand and placed it on his crotch. He told me to feel it, and he said he despised the rumors going around Broadway that he stuffed his crotch with a sock whenever he came on stage in green tights."

"It's real," he said. "I'm all man...and then some."

"Even though it was impressive, I rejected him, stating that I did not like to go to bed with men."

"I don't like to go to bed with men, either, unless I'm too drunk to say no," Barrymore told her.

Once, after one of their knock-down arguments, Eva admitted to Mercedes, "At parties, don't get jealous if you see me flirting with men. I don't like to have sex with them, but I often play the role of a *femme fatale*, since I adore being adored. My wonderful, vivacious mother, Julie, advised me to follow my own inclinations and to be a free soul. She told me when I was only thirteen that she never expected me to adhere to a boring, stifling, restraining sense of bourgeois morality."

Eva once attended a party that Douglas Fairbanks, Jr. hosted at the Algonquin for his stepmother, Mary Pickford. "I found Fairbanks handsome and dashing, a real charmer, and he flirted with me outrageously."

She would continue to see the young Fairbanks over the years. "He was forever after me," Eva said. "He kept pursuing me although I noticed that Tallulah Bankhead

John Barrymore, "The Great Profile" as *Hamlet*. A deeply entrenched alcoholic, he claimed to never remember his often embarrassing sexual overtures the morning after his drunken binges.

He attended a dinner at Blood Moon's headquarters, **Magnolia House**, hosted by Senator Howard Bayne, during the filming on Staten Island of *The Amateur Cracksman* (1917).

and Marlene Dietrich, not to mention Loretta Young, were not immune to his seductive power, either."

"Douglas and I became friends, and I noticed men were attracted to him as much as women," Eva said., "One night at a party, Noël Coward told me he'd written his hit song, 'Mad About the Boy,' with Doug in mind."

Eccentric Hollywood Royals: **Douglas Fairbanks, Jr.,** (left) with his stepmother, Hollywood megastar, **Mary Pickford** (right). "Mary played a little girl on the screen long after her expiration date," Doug claimed.

"Despite acting frequently like a gentleman, Doug could also be a cad," Eva said. "One night at a party, when he was still married to Joan Crawford, he came up to Bette Davis and quickly thrust his hand into her bra, feeling her tits. When he withdrew, he told her she should use ice cubes on her nipples, like his wife does. 'It makes them stand out better,' he told her. Davis, of course, was appalled at such outrageous behavior."

***

Mercedes returned to New York after a honeymoon she called "boring," and spent the following night in Eva's arms.

Eva told Mercedes, "The thought of you satisfying the sexual desires of Abram Poole is just the same as if you'd stabbed me in the heart with a sword. Other than my work, of course, you have become my sole reason for living."

Using Poole's money, Mercedes pursued Eva after her return from her honeymoon, buying her expensive presents. During the weeks that followed, when Eva and Mercedes were separated, they wrote passionate letters to each other. In one of them, Eva proclaimed, "I have an agonizing ache for you, and long for your sweet lips on my breasts."

In one letter, she vowed eternal devotion, claiming "I will love you until the end of time. My only fear is that you are a pirate. You have already committed an act of piracy by stealing my heart. My greatest fear is that you will steal my soul."

***

In the spring of 1922, "overwrought and emotionally devastated," Eva decided to go on a vacation in Europe. Mercedes was already in Paris with Poole.

Boarding the *Mauretania* at the Port of New York, Eva sailed to Southampton, where she took a train to London. There, she had a long overdue reunion with her Danish-born mother, Julie.

Julie, it was reported, was shocked by her daughter's appearance. Frail and given to fits of trembling, Eva was on the verge of a nervous breakdown.

On her first night in London, she wrote to Mercedes in France, "My longing for your love is like an all-consuming madness., You will have to marry me—or else I might kill myself."

In London, as Eva later revealed to Mercedes, "When I showed my mother a picture of you, she thought you were a man. For a moment, I planned to tell her that you were my husband."

At long last, Eva and Mercedes were reunited in Paris at Mercedes' furnished apartment in the Hotel Foyot *[33 rue de Tournon, Paris 6e]*. Poole had left the previous night to return to New York to accept a commission for a sculpture.

"It was a night of fiery passion and the outpouring of love like I had rarely experienced before," Mercedes later confessed to Darwin years after that night had passed.

The following evening, they enjoyed the cuisine and the belle époque décor of Maxim's, later patronizing a lesbian bar on the Left Bank.

After a week in Paris, they took the train to Rouen where Joan of Arc had been burned at the stake in 1431. It was in that ancient city that Mercedes revealed to Eva that she was considering writing a play for her to star in as the martyred French saint and nationalist.

That was followed by a romantic weekend in Venice where, in the moonlight, Eva and Mercedes were cuddled in each other's arms as a gondolier glided them smoothly along the moonlit

Eva is depicted (right) in a 1919 vaudeville schtick as a French coquette accepting an invitation to dance from **Elsie Janis**, cross-dressing as an amorous (male) soldier. Gender confusion was a then-widely prevalent bit of stagecraft that Eva, as a talented actress with a then-nascent lesbian streak, fit into with assurance and style.

Joan of Arc (Jehanne d'Arc), as conceived by Emmanuel Frémiet (1824-1910), in the Place des Pyramides, Paris 1er.

Grand Canal.

After riding by train to Budapest, the Hungarian playwright Ferenc Molnár awaited them with banners, a brass band, and flowers. Eva had previously starred in his play, *Liliom*, on Broadway.

After a festive time in Hungary, Eva and Mercedes had to part once again, although Mercedes begged her to accompany her onward and into Turkey.

When Eva declined, Mercedes took the Orient Express alone to Constantinople. *[That city's name wasn't officially changed to Istanbul until 1930.]* Eva returned to New York to rehearse an upcoming play.

In Constantinople, in the lobby of the very posh Pera Palace Hotel, Mercedes spotted a stunning Nordic beauty, who had walked so regally, she thought the beautiful young woman must be a Russian princess. She was distinguished, elegant, and aristocratic.

At the hotel's reception desk, Mercedes asked the clerk who this mysterious woman was. He told her she was an actress from Sweden in Turkey with her director, Maurice Stiller.

It was months later that Mercedes learned that the enigmatic enchantress had been the future movie star, Greta Garbo, who would change her life forever.

During her separation from Mercedes, Eva bombarded her with love letters. In one, she wrote, "I am afraid I'm losing my independence, as I am turning my life over to you. I hope soon to be kissing your feet and your crotch. I want us to run naked in the moonlight, shouting our love all the way to the stars."

***

When not making love to Eva, or just being in her presence, Mercedes was at work on a play, *Sandro Botticelli*. It was named after the Renaissance painter (1445-1510) known for his deep, saturated colors, linear rhythms, and vivid imagined compositions, as reflected in his most celebrated paintings, *The Birth of Venus* and *La Primavera*.

The play centered on Simonette Vespucci, hailed as "the most beautiful woman in Florence." Her stunning look was compared to that of an "exquisitely sharp knife…the hilt may be jeweled but if one comes too close, the blade draws blood."

According to its plot, to entice Botticelli into making love to her, Simonette visits his studio naked except for a black cloak. When she removes it, the artist wants to paint her instead of making love to her. At the end, she runs off naked into the cold Florentine night, only to catch pneumonia and die.

In an attempt to attract financial backers, with dreams of an opening on Broadway, the play was previewed at the Provincetown Theatre in 1923, with almost 200 people in the audience, including critics. Long before its opening, Eva feared that both the play and its previews would end disastrously, although she concealed her opinion from Mercedes.

The set included an overscale reproduction of Botticelli's *Birth of Venus*, which, ironically, had been painted by none other than Abram Poole, the husband of Mercedes.

Critics sharpened their knives, attacking both the playwright and the star. "Miss Gallienne conveys none of the sparkle, the seductive tone, or the passion to bring the character of the nude model alive," wrote one reviewer.

One critic denounced Mercedes as a "yearning society amateur," while another found the play "as florid as a flower seed catalogue."

That night, Mercedes threatened to give up playwrighting forever, but Eva pleaded with her to learn from her mistakes and to grow as a writer, producing another work.

Detail from Sandro Botticelli's Renaissance fantasy, **Birth of Venus.**

The play crafted by Mercedes de Acosta, as inspired by this painting, generated lacerating reviews of its star, Eva Le Gallienne.

Back in New York, Mercedes was morbidly depressed, almost suicidal, and since Poole was on the road, moving frequently between Chicago and Los Angeles working on commissions, Eva moved in with her.

Eventually, Mercedes started writing again, forming and shaping her long-delayed Joan of Arc play, which she'd entitled *Jehanne d'Arc*.

To recuperate from stress, both Mercedes and Eva sailed to Europe once again, vacationing in Paris before Eva continued on, alone, to London. There, she had the life-changing (for her) experience of watching Eleonora Duse perform in *Così Sia* at the Oxford Theatre.

"For the first time, I saw and understood the meaning of true beauty," Eva wrote to Mercedes in Paris. She sent flowers to Duse backstage, claiming, "You have given me the strength and faith to live."

Back in New York, Eva stayed with Mercedes—while her husband was away in Chicago—at her home at 134 East 47th Street. During her stay, an offer arrived for Eva to co-star with Basil Rathbone in *The Swan*, set in a mythical European kingdom.

Before going on tour, the play opened on Broadway on October 23, 1923, attended by Mercedes.

The Swan was a hit, her reviews sublime.

Beginning with a ten-week run in Chicago, *The Swan* drew Rathbone and Eva closer together every day. Somewhere along the way, she began an affair with him. It survived until the end of *The Swan's* tour.

When she told him she was pregnant [as it happened, it turned out to be a false pregnancy], he fled.

Of course, Rathbone would go on to greater fame on the screen, first as an all-around villain and later as Sherlock Holmes. Memorable film roles included starring opposite Greta Garbo in *Anna Karenina* (1935), and later, in the "sword fighting on the staircase" scene with Errol Flynn in *The Adventures of Robin Hood* (1938).

Her biographer, Robert Schanke, presented a portrait of Eva as having terrible anxieties about her sexual preference in an era of rampant homophobia. She told one of her female co-stars, "If you have any thoughts about becoming a lesbian, don't go there. Your life will be nothing but tragedy."

Basil Rathbone and Eva Le Gallienne in *The Swan* (1923).

"I had an affair with him only because he had the most beautiful legs in the world," Eva confessed to Mercedes.

Helen Sheehy, author of *The Girls*, presents a different scenario: Eva told Mary Sarton, her close friend, "People hate what they don't understand and try to destroy it. Only try to keep yourself clean and don't allow that destructive force to spoil something that to you is simple, natural, and beautiful."

Eva told another friend, Eloise Armen, that "Love between two women is the most beautiful thing in the world."

***

When The Theater Guild offered Eva the role of Joan of Arc in George Bernard Shaw's play, *Saint Joan,* Eva turned it down, telling the directors, "This play should have been renamed *Saint Shaw.*"

Mercedes also tackled the redaction of a stage play about the legendary French warrior icon, polishing her avant-garde bio-play, *Jehanne d'Arc.* In contrast to Shaw, Eva found Mercedes' portrait of the saint "human and sincere, a simple woman whose great spiritual forces and powers ultimately deserted her."

Eva and Mercedes tried to produce *Jehanne d'Arc* in Paris but encountered one disaster (mostly financial) after another. The play opened on June 12, 1925, and the critics pounced on it, one of them calling it "a great show for the eyes, but nothing at all for the brain and spirit."

During their "post Joan of Arc" transit back to New York, Eva and Mercedes—their affair nearing its end—became visibly depressed. Noël Coward, a friend to both women, noticed that, "They were mired in gloom and doom for most of the voyage, and always, but always, darling, dressed in black like two black widows."

As their ship neared the Port of New York, their dream of bringing Mercedes' *Jehanne d'Arc* to the stage (any stage) faded and grew bitter.

In New York, Eva met with Joseph Kennedy, whom she'd known before, having been introduced to the producer/bootlegger by his mistress, Gloria Swanson. Eva solicited his financial support for *Jehanne d'Arc*, but, as she told Mercedes, "All I got from that shit was his hand up my dress and his attempt to force his little Irish dick into me."

[Although he struck out with Eva, the future ambassador to the Court of St. James's fared better with Greta Garbo, Marlene Dietrich, Constance Bennett, Nancy Carroll, Evelyn Brent, and Clare Booth Luce.]

Word reached Mercedes that Eva was having an affair with Rathbone. Mercedes confronted her with the accusation, "I wouldn't call it an affair, exactly. After the tenth night, I became bored with him. I did not love him."

The first production Eva staged at the Civic Repertory was Benavente's *Saturday Night*. Attending the premiere was Noël Coward, who later wrote, "The production was hideous, the writing lousy, and Miss Le Gallienne, although I adore her, was a ghastly failure."

For its next production, the company bounced back with the first English language production of Anton Chekhov's *The Three Sisters*, which became a major success.

An aspiring young actress, Bette Davis, tried to join the repertory company, but Eva rejected her, calling her "frivolous and insincere."

By now, the tensions simmering between Eva Le Gallienne and Mercedes de Acosta surged out of control. One night, Eva told her, "I have this insane desire for freedom, to gain my independence once again and to call an end to this relationship. It's like a fire burning within me."

Thus, their once-consuming love affair ended. Poole had returned to New York and Mercedes continued along in her loveless marriage, all the way to 1935, when she finally filed for divorce.

Philandering patriarch & Hollywood investor **Joe Kennedy, Sr., with his wife, Rose**, in 1940.

Eva Le Gallienne did not appreciate his roaming hands, wandering fingers, and aimless manipulations regarding the influence he could have on her career. .

***

Confronted with the difficulty of finding suitable roles

and fascinated by the concept of the theater as a "holy temple," Eva began devoting herself to what she termed "the art of the theater." She founded, and for an entire decade (1926-1936), ran New York City's Civic Repertory Theater, a 1,100-seat arena popularly known as Manhattan's 14th Street Theatre. [The battered neoclassical building that contained it was demolished in 1938.]

In her constant search for operating funds, she migrated unsuccessfully from one prospective backer to another, suffering thousands of disappointments.

Finally, Eva found what in show business is called "an angel." One of her lovers, Alice De Lamar, a Colorado gold mine heiress, came through with the funds to open the theater.

As an heiress with ten million dollars, De Lamar was frequently pursued by fortune hunters. She moved into the elite of social circles and was befriended by everyone from conductor Leopold Stokowski to designer Hubert de Givenchy.

During its history, the Civic Repertory mounted thirty-seven plays, most of them successful. Eva had to close the company, bowing to the financial pains brought on by the stock market collapse of 1929.

***

Rejected and disliked: Young **Bette Davis**. Her sultry charms and often bitchy wit were not appreciated by Eva Le Gallienne and her entourage.

Two views of Eva's benefactor and investor, **Alice De Lamar.** The photo on the left, from 1925, shows her looking like a rich, couture-clad bohemian. The photo on the right dates from two years later (1927), presumably after she'd accepted her "butch' persona and cared less about *haute* fashion.

In 1918, De Lamar had inherited a family fortune assessed at $10 million, the equivalent of $169 million in 2020 currency, prompting newspaper editors to call her "The richest bachelor girl in the United States." When she died in 1983, she left a quarter (then valued at $1 million) of her estate that remained to her friend and lover, Eva Le Gallienne.

Even though she'd ended her affair with Eva, Mercedes continued to follow her career as she delivered one spectacular performance after another throughout the 1920s, '30s, '40s, and beyond.

Some of her more memorable performances were interpretations of Henrik Ibsen's *The Master Builder,* presented in 1925 and again in 1926. Cast as Hilda Wangel, Eva portrayed the radical, aggressive, rather masculine heroine of the play. *The New York Times* claimed she gave "a luminous portrait."

In 1928, Eva starred in another Ibsen play, *Hedda Gabler,* which her former lover, Nazimova, had executed so brilliantly in 1907. Hedda is newly married and already bored with both her husband and her life. She sets out to change it.

Over the course of her career, Eva maintained a long association with this play, which remained her favorite., She starred in the role in New York six times and took it on two coast-to-coast tours through America. In one production, she updated the play from its 1890s setting to the 1920s, with Hedda smoking cigarettes, having her hair bobbed, and wearing short dress styles of the Roaring Twenties.

In 1928, she also opened in Anton Chekhov's *The Cherry Orchard.* It revolved around an aristocratic Russian landowner who returns to her family estate just before it is auctioned off to pay the mortgage. Eva and Alla Nazimova united in "acting in the Russian technique" to bring this classic drama back once again to the stage. There was a great demand for tickets.

After *The Cherry Orchard,* Eva took on a very different role, that of Sir James Barrie's *Peter Pan* (1928). Critics defined her interpretation of the role as "mercurial, muscular, and agile." She made a stunning appearance in blue leotards and a small pointed hat in a vibrant violet color.

In 1929, she returned to Chekhov, starring in *The Seagull* as Masha and later hailed as her greatest part in a decade. The audience loved her por-

Eva Le Gallienne was lionized and spectacularly famous in her day.

On November 25, 1929, perhaps as a distraction from the horrors of the stock market crash that had occurred a month before *[October 24-29 of the same year]*, she graced the front cover of *Time* magazine.

Eva was at her most beautiful in 1931 when she appeared onstage as the tragic heroine of *Camille* at the Billy Rose Theatre in Manhattan.

trayal so much that on opening night, they gave her a five-minute standing ovation.

In 1931, in her stage performances of *Camille*, Eva starred as *La Dame aux Caméllias*, based on the novel, first published in 1848, by Alexandre Dumas fils. The character she portrayed, Marguerite Gautier, was based on Marie Duplessis, Dumas' real-life lover.

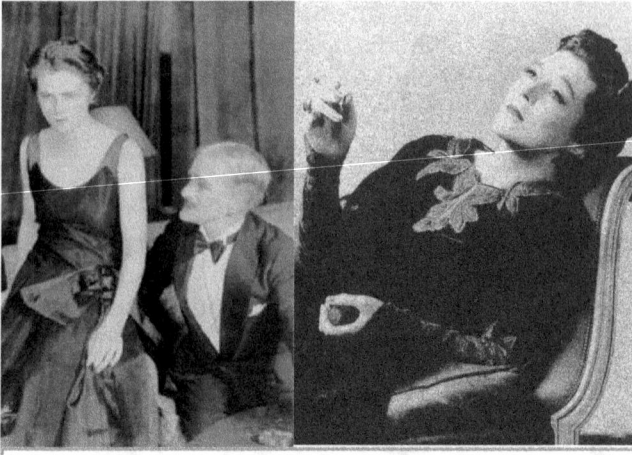

Two views of Eva Le Gallienne as Hedda Gabler. Left photo: with with Sayre Crawley as Judge Brack in Henrik Ibsen's classic in 1926, and again (same role) in 1948.

Eva's former lover, Nazimova, had brought *Camille* to the silent screen in 1921 alongside Rudolph Valentino, who played her lover. In an odd coincidence, Lillian Gish, also in 1931, also opened in New York in the same play. Critics rushed to attend both stage versions so that they could compare the two fabled actresses. Whereas the Gish version opened and closed quickly, Eva's interpretation lasted until the end of the season.

Three years later, the lover of Mercedes de Acosta, Greta Garbo, would bring *Camille* to the screen, starring opposite Robert Taylor as her young lover.

Eva as a crowd pleaser in *Alice in Wonderland* (1932).

In 1932, Eva brought *Alice in Wonderland* to the stage. *[In 1982, in New York, she'd reprise it as her life's final performance on stage.]* Eva had a lot of fun adapting the Lewis Carroll classic, playing with such characters as The Queen of Hearts and White Rabbit, succeeding at making the play popular with both adults and children.

Her most daring role was that of the lead role in *Hamlet* in 1937, following in the footsteps of Sarah Bernhardt in an interpretation of that male role. Eva—as part of an effort to be more convincing with her small, boyish body—decided to play Hamlet as a youth. One critic defined her as a performance as a rival to Bernhardt's. Many others, however, panned her, citing her lack of passion in the role and suggesting that it was a production that might have been staged by the drama department of a local high school.

[Ironically, history's most famous interpretations of Peter Pan were played by a quartet of lesbian actresses, Eva Le Gallienne, Maude Adams, Jean Arthur, and Mary Martin.]

***

Margaret Webster would re-enter Eva's life in 1938 as her lover and remained so for a tumultuous decade, including the war years of the 1940s. Nicknamed "Peggy," Margaret was the daughter of two famous British actors, Dame Mae Witty and Ben Webster. Her mother gave birth to her in New York, which made Peggy a U.S. citizen.

Her face aging, and with brilliance and understated panache, **Eva starred as Queen Marguerite** in *Exit the King* (1968).

During his performance on Broadway in a play by Shakespeare, her father announced her birth from the stage.

Eva and Peggy first met when they were schoolgirls in England, both of them boarders at Queen Anne's School in Caversham. She remembered Peggy as a "small, rather plump girl with big blue eyes made rounder by large, lensed glasses."

Peggy would remember the summer of 1913 as "the end of the Edwardian era."

As a girl, Peggy had appeared on stage with Ellen Terry, England's greatest actress, and she had made her professional debut in London's West End theatre district starring opposite John Barrymore in *Hamlet*.

She later appeared as Masha in Chekhov's *The Seagull* with Alfred Lunt and his wife, Lynn Fontanne, and later opposite Helen Hayes in *Twelfth Night*. The press dubbed Peggy "the girlfriend of The Bard."

In 1929 and 1930, she worked with her fellow actors at London's Old Vic. But by 1937, she was back in New York, directing Maurice Evans in the title role of Shakespeare's *Richard II*. Both the director and the star got sensational reviews.

[Born in 1901 in England, Evans made Shakespeare his forte. Before his triumph on Broadway, Evans had appeared in a handful of British movies in the 1930s, including White Cargo *and* Raise the Roof, *both released in 1930.]*

Evans and Peggy formed a partnership that lasted until 1942 when he joined the Army. In 1941, she directed Evans and Judith Anderson in *Macbeth* on Broadway, along with *Twelfth Night* and *Henry IV, Part I*.

Peggy also staged Shakespeare's Comedy of Errors, *A Midsummer Night's Dream*, and *As You Like It*. Critic George Nathan hailed her as "the best director of Shakespeare we have."

Back in 1938, Peggy and Eva came together, recalling their days as schoolgirls. Both women found the more mature versions of each other far more enticing and so began a love affair that would last a decade.

Eva later wrote, "Peggy has a lot of her mother's wit, but without her mother's wickedness," referring to Dame May Witty. "Time has greatly altered her looks, and she has emerged as a handsome, intelligent, and appealing woman at the age of thirty-three, no longer that awkward schoolgirl."

Soon, Eva and Peggy were spending summers together on Martha's Vineyard in a rustic cottage. On Broadway, they soon became known as "that lesbian couple."

The first time Peggy ever directed Eva in an adaptation of Zola's *Thérèse Raquin* (1945), starring veteran actor Victor Jory (*Gone With the Wind*) and Peggy's mother, Dame May Witty. Most critics denounced the play as "sedate and superficial."

Through the war years, Peggy continued to earn critical acclaim, helming a big hit, *Othello* (1943), starring Paul Robeson in the title role and José Ferrer as Iago. It ran for nearly 300 performances, the longest run on Broadway of any play by Shakespeare. Peggy also helmed Eva in *The Cherry Orchard* in 1944.

Their biggest achievements in the theater occurred in the immediate aftermath of World War II.

Two views of Margaret ("Peggy") Webster, one of the nation's premier authorities on the staging of Shakepearan plays.

The upper photo was snapped in 1944. At the time, she was sleeping with Eva and also said to have become very intimate and perhaps obsessed with The Bard himself——or at least with his texts and theatrical nuances.

***

Three formidable women, Eva Le Gallienne, Margaret (Peggy) Webster, and Cheryl Crawford, each a lesbian, came together in an attempt to launch a repertory company in New York. They had a dream, and that was to turn their new theatrical company into the American version of London's Old Vic.

The trio would always be plagued with money problems during the short life of the company. They solicited donations through the phones, eventually finding backers in such personages as Fredric March, Helen Hayes, Raymond Massey, Katharine Cornell, and others, many others. Contributions would never be enough, however.

Nonetheless, this trio forged ahead, and each of them spoke the same language, knew many of the same people, and, according to Eva, "ignited fire in each other." Of course, with such highly volatile and artistic people, the usual disagreements emerged.

Day by day, Eva got to know Crawford. "She helped me combat the ten thousand devils who lurked within me," Eva claimed.

She introduced Eva and Peggy to her lover, Ruth Norman, with whom she'd begun an affair in 1944.

Born in Akron, Ohio, in 1902, Crawford later studied at Smith College. Upon graduation, she headed for Manhattan, enrolling in the Theatre Guild. She didn't want to be an actress, preferring instead to work behind the scenes in production.

Soon, two figures entered her life, Harold Clurman and Lee Strasberg, and months later, they launched the Group Theater, inviting young actors to join.

In 1948, Crawford founded the Actors Studio with Lee Strasberg, Robert Lewis, and Elia Kazan. The studio soon became famous across the country, linked to such future stars as Marilyn Monroe, Paul Newman, Montgomery Clift, James Dean, Marlon Brando, Shelley Winters, Carroll Baker, Jane Fonda, Robert De Niro, Jack Nicholson, Al Pacino, and Dustin Hoffman.

As a producer, Crawford would play a major role in the careers of Ingrid Bergman, Tallulah Bankhead, Helen Hayes, Ethel Barrymore, and two African Americans, Bojangles Robinson and Paul Robeson.

In time, Crawford would produce such Broadway hits as *Brigadoon* in 1947 and *Paint Your Wagon* in 1951. She also produced two plays by Tennessee Williams, which were later made into movies—*The Rose Tattoo* in 1951 and *Sweet Bird of Youth* in 1959.

[By 1979, Crawford would be inducted into the Theatre Hall of Fame. She died in October of 1986.]

***

In 1946, Eva joined her lover, Margaret ("Peggy") Webster and a fellow lesbian, Cheryl Crawford, in the launch of another acting troupe, the American Repertory Theatre.

They founded it with a profound sense of idealism, and valiantly carried on for two years. During its two-year lifetime, they encountered great difficulties, most them associated with a lack of money. There was never enough of it. They faced "assaults" from critics, inept technicians, endless trouble with the unions, and mistreatment based on their genders and their sexual preferences.

During the peak of their travails, it became obvious that they needed fresh new plays and charismatic stars to make them come alive. Early in his career, Marlon Brando was asked to play leading roles in both Shakespeare's *Hamlet* and in Ibsen's *Ghosts*, but he rejected both parts.

Then Peggy set her eyes on John Gielgud, persuading him to visit her home in Connecticut, and enrolling the sexual services of a handsome chauffeur, a gay-for pay driver whose bedtime skills might help clinch a commitment from the distinguished British stage star. But although Gielgud took advantage of her hospitality and repeatedly visited the bed of the driver she'd hired, he ultimately rejected her offer and retreated from the idea of appearing in any of her revivals of Shakespeare's classics.

A titanic force like **Cheryl Crawford** faced financial horrors trying to launch a repertory theater in New York City.

When she offered a prospective role to Marlon Brando, based on its low salary, he fled.

There was also dissension within their administrative trio. Eva often rejected Crawford's suggestions, including when Crawford wanted to hire Mary Martin as the female lead in George Bernard Shaw's *Anthony and Cleopatra*. Eva brusquely responded, "You're joking, of course."

Then it was suggested, perhaps with a touch of desperate whimsy, that Mercedes be contacted to reach out to Garbo to see if she'd appear as the female lead in Shaw's *Saint Joan*.

Then Crawford discovered a talented playwright, Arthur Miller, who had written *The Sign of the Arches*, which she wanted to stage at the American Repertory. However, when both Peggy and Eva read the script, they found it "dull and boring." *[Months later, Elia Kazan produced it as a mainstream Broadway hit retitled* All My Sons.*]*

Even when the three women agreed on the desirability of any particular actor, most of them declined after learning of the very low salaries associated with their involvements. They included Vincent Price, Montgomery Clift, Geraldine Fitzgerald, Greer Garson, José Ferrer, and Barbara Bel Geddes.

Even Katharine Hepburn briefly considered appearing, claiming, "I would do the right play for my love of the theater." But after thinking it over, she, too, bowed out.

Ruefully, Peggy later commented, "New York is the worst place in the world to try to start a new theater—there's too much competition from commercial theater."

Although the trio of ladies who controlled the theater never managed to secure any really big names, they did attract an array of known actors, including the husband-and-wife team of Anne Jackson and Eli Wallach, even the amazingly talented Julie Harris.

Their first season opened with Shakespeare's *Henry VIII,* with Victor Jory as the king and with Eva Le Gallienne portraying his wife, Katherine. That was followed with Barrie's *What Every Woman Knows*; Ibsen's *John Gabriel Borkman*, and Shaw's *Androcles and the Lion.* Even though attendance was good, profits were chronically low.

Familiar classics were also presented, including *Hedda Gabler,* as well as Ibsen's *Ghosts.* Eva revived her long-standing favorite, *Alice in Wonderland,* with Peggy appearing as the Queen of Hearts, Julie Harris as the White Rabbit, and Eva as the White Queen.

Critical reaction to the plays were mixed. Brooks Atkinson of *The New York Times* defined the troupe as "a brilliant group of performers who act like a living work of art."

But George Nathan, one of the leading critics of his day, had always come down hard on Eva as an actress. It began when he attacked her performance in *Madame Capet* in 1938. "She wants to soar like an eagle but has only a pair of cuckoo wings at her command."

The dream ended in the summer of 1948, and the American Repertory closed its doors. "I wanted it to succeed so very much," Eva said." But we failed. Life is going by me as if I never lived. But I must carry on."

And so she did.

***

Eva continued to work on and off in the years to come, not just on the stage but in films. Lured by the Shuberts, she returned to Broadway in January of 1954 to star in *The Starcross Story* by Diana Morgan. Eva played Lady Starcross, the widow of Christian Starcross, who set out on an expedition in the Arctic that cost the lives of himself and his men. He was revealed to have been an unscrupulous adventurer, who recklessly endangered not only his own life but those of his brave but foolish men.

In a summer tryout at the Westport Playhouse, Eva co-starred with Faye Emerson, but for the Broadway opening, she was replaced by Mary Astor.

Its Broadway opening was a gala event, with Mercedes de Acosta showing up on the arm of Tallulah Bankhead. Katharine Hepburn came with the actress and (very famous) acting coach, 75-year-old Constance Collier, who had played a major role in her development as an actress.,

Eva later wrote, "How incredibly 'New England' Kate Hepburn is, her face scrubbed so clean with all those cold showers she takes. It is still a good face but getting a little gnarled. My god, did you see her with Bogie in *The African Queen*?"

Based on fear of litigation, the play ran for only one performance. Stanley Kauffmann, editor of Ballantine Books, threatened legal action, claiming that *The Starcross Story* was an act of plagiarism, lifted from his novel, *The Hidden Hero.*

***

In 1957, Eva bounced back with great success Off-Broadway. She played Queen Elizabeth I in Schiller's *Mary Stuart*. Its director was Tyrone Guthrie, and Irene Worth starred as Mary.

The producers felt they were taking a chance on Eva at this point in her career. One of them, Norris Houghton, said, "Le Gallienne was no longer a star, her heyday long past. Her name was pretty dreary at this time."

Nonetheless, critics praised her performance, using words like "electric," "commanding," "grand style acting," and "vigorous." Her triumph was a great incentive to her ego and waning career.

In 1958, she co-starred with such actors as Hume Cronyn, Boris Karloff, Franchot Tone, and Judith Anderson in such made-for-TV movies as *The Bridge of San Luis Rey, Bitter Heritage,* and *The Shadow of a Genius.*

Late in her life, when she was in her early 80s, Eva triumphed again in the 1980 movie *Resurrection,* starring opposite Ellen Burstyn in the story of a woman who returns to life from the brink of death with amazing healing powers. For her efforts, she won a Best Supporting Actress Oscar nomination, becoming at that time the oldest such nominee in the history of the Academy.

***

Upon the publication of Mercedes' indiscreet autobiography, *Here Lies the Heart,* Eva denied their lesbian link, but Mercedes had saved her passionate letters filled with purple prose that trumpeted her love for the Spanish beauty. In them, Eva had defined her love for Mercedes as "a light before the altar." In another letter, she wrote, "You came to me with the scent of acacia blossoms—and it is to you I say I love you!"

Critic Walter Kerr claimed that Eva was "the epitome of stardom." By 1977, President Gerald Ford, who had replaced Richard Nixon after he resigned over the Watergate scandal, hailed her for the "excellence of her achievement."

Yet another President, Ronald Reagan, awarded her the National Medal of the Arts.

Lee Strasberg at Actors Studio told his pupils that Eva was "the best example of what American actors are capable of being. She could play every role from Peter Pan to Hamlet."

Death came to this distinguished actress on June 3, 1991 when she was 92 years old. She died of natural causes and asked that her ashes be scattered over her property in Weston, Connecticut.

Shortly before her death, she commented on her work in the theater. "I feel in my more experimental work that I was born a century before my time."

***

In her biography of Eleonora Duse, *The Mystic in the Theatre,* Eva wrote, "Miss Duse saw the theater as a great force capable of spreading beauty and understanding, whose function was to quicken in the minds and hearts of the people and appreciation of the nobility of suffering, to awaken in them a sense of the sublime, to rouse them from their torpor and through a heightening of the emotions make them aware of the mystery and wonder of the human spirit."

Although she meant that to describe Duse, it eerily resounds like something that applies, like an epitaph, to Eva herself.

POSTSCRIPT

Producer Lucille Lortel was hailed as the Queen of Off Broadway, after having launched a seven-year run of *The Threepenny Opera* at her Theatre de Lys in Greenwich Village. She also operated the White Barn Theatre in Westport, Connecticut, where she presenteed both experimental works by unknown playwrights or else the classics, often with well-known stars.

She had long admired the acting techniques of Eva Le Gallienne, and the two formidable ladies of the theater formed a working relationship in the summer of 1955.

Lucille entered into an agreement with Eva to teach acting at the White Barn, offering her a salary plus a percentage of the tuition collected from aspirant actors., Eva turned out to be a brilliant teacher, performing roles from plays by Shakespeare, Ibsen, and Chekhov, her longtime favorites. Then she'd sit down in the theater and watch as her students performed the same scenes.

Eva made a grand entrance to every class she taught. Her biographer, Robert A. Schanke, described her: "With her wispy, grayfish-colored hair and translucent skin, she dressed always in cashmere sweaters of lavender or blue, with gored tweed skirts and wedge-heeled shoes. To the family at the

Eva Le Gallienne, left, in a publicity photo for *Resurrection* (1980), with **Ellen Burstyn.**

White Barn, she was something of a spirit mother."

Eva told the press, "The White Barn is one of the very few places in the country where people—actors, directors, singers, dancers, and scenic designers—are given an opportunity to experiment in a congenial atmosphere and on a perfectly equipped stage, unhampered by the restrictions of Broadway."

On September 10 and 11, 1955, Eva and her students entertained audiences with a fascinating evening of memorable *Scenes from Shakespeare, Ibsen, and Chekhov.*

Years later, when Darwin Porter got to know Eva, she spoke fondly of her role as a teacher. "I loved working with those students, who reminded me so much of myself when I was starting out, all nervous and awkward. To new pupils I always performed my favorite scenes from *Hedda Gabler,* a role to which I was forever identified."

Sometimes, Eva asked Darwin to accompany her to a social event.

According to Darwin, "I felt she was apprehensive about going out with a woman. In the past, she had some unfortunate experiences…Attacks on her lesbianism. Oddly enough, she relayed a story about how—when she was dining with a group of other lesbians at a restaurant in Ridgefield, New Jersey—a woman at a nearby table kept giving her coven of lesbians a disapproving glare. That woman turned out to be Jacqueline Kennedy Onassis."

Philanthropist and stage producer **Lucille Lortel** was hailed as "the Queen of Off Broadway." She's shown here with **Eva Le Gallienne** (center) and **Audrey Wood** at her White Barn Theater in the late 1950s.

Wood was one of the leading literary agents of New York, famous for helping launch a new young playwright, Tennessee Williams.

Lortel presented **Eva Le Gallienne** in performances both at her White Barn Theatre in Connecticut and at her Theatre de Lys in Manhattan's Greenwich Village.

"I've followed Eva's career since the Stone Age," Lucille told her friend and frequent escort, Darwin Porter.

Sometimes, Darwin would take all three of these formidable ladies out to various gala events in New York.

"On any evening, we might, for example," he said, "entertain Laurence Olivier, Helen Hayes, Mary Martin, Ethel Merman, or Jessica Tandy. It was the Golden Age of Off-Broadway, and Lucille was one of its lynchpins."

"When I met Eva Le Gallienne, she had recognized many of her career mistakes as errors, and had, after years of self-flagellations and regrets, moved on to the point where she had forgiven herself, and come to terms with them," Darwin told Danforth Prince during the compilation of this book.

Eva soon evolved into more than an acting coach for students at the White Barn: Lucille Lortel booked her on occasion as a performer there, too.

On January 22, 1957, as part of her *ANTA Matinee Series* in Greenwich Village, Eva presented *An Afternoon with Oscar Wilde*. She gave a dramatic reading of two of the gay playwright's children's stories, *The Birthday of the Infants* and *The Happy Prince*. She had memorized the stories and, instead of reading them, she acted them out. *[She had first presented this same show at the White Barn on the night of July 17, 1955.]*

At the White Barn on August 4 and 5, 1956, Eva returned to her familiar role in *Ghosts*, starring with such actors as Roger Plowden and Dalton Dearborn. She had previously starred in this play in Manhattan back in 1948.

On August 29 and 31, 1975, Eva delivered one of her memorable performances in Barbara Wersbe's *The Dream Watcher*. Her supporting players featured David Jay, Doug Rowe, Carol Heil, and Margaret Barker, among other talented actors.

Eva Le Gallienne lived to be ninety-two, dying on June 3, 1991. "I'm not afraid of dying," she said.

"I am not a believer, so I don't have to fear the damnation of hell. I'll just go to sleep and close my eyes forever, as the curtain goes down on my incredible life."

The drama was based on a juvenile novel of the same name. A lonely misfit, Albert Scully, is a teenage boy who is befriended by Orpha Woodfin, an eccentric elderly lady who tells him that she was once a celebrated actress on the stage.

As Eva told Darwin, "I was playing myself." She was seventy-three years old at the time.

She received rave reviews for her performance in *The Dream Watcher*, *Variety* evaluating her performance as "flawless." Actress June Havoc claimed, "*The Dream Watcher* is Eva's lovely jewel to us. It is her crown of superlative achievements."

***

One night in Greenwich Village, Eva learned that Darwin had been a friend of Mercedes de Acosta, her long-ago lover. She was still bitter over what Mercedes had written about her in her confessional autobiography, *Here Lies the Heart*.

"In the original manuscript, which I learned about, she had actually published word for word two of my most impassioned letters to her. I wrote those at the time I was in a fit of white passion. They were for her eyes only, not for the public. I felt a sense of betrayal. Fortunately, through my lawyer, I got the letters suppressed. But even so, Mercedes made it damn clear that we'd been lovers."

"I understand how you feel," Darwin said. "It was definitely a violation of your trust. But Mercedes was desperate at the time. She was coming to an end of her life and in ill health. She needed money. I know that doesn't excuse her behavior, but I know how hard she was fighting to survive. The world had grown cold for this once celebrated beauty. She didn't want pity, as she told me so many times, but I could not help but feel sorry for her."

"You are so kind, and perhaps I shouldn't judge her too harshly," Eva said. "Who knows what I will have to do as I face the end of my own life."

REST IN PEACE
EVA LE GALLIENNE
(1899-1991)

CHAPTER SIX
SELF-ENCHANTED, IMPERIAL, & UNFORGETTABLE

NAZIMOVA

EMPRESS OF SILENT FILMS & QUEEN OF METRO

"Nazimova! We will never see the likes of her again. She was unique—a force of nature on stage and screen. Once, briefly, I was her passion—and she was mine."

"When the fiery love between us faded, we threw another log into the blaze and kept alive our friendship until her end. We saw each other's lovers come and go. Often we each had affairs with the same beautiful women, as in the case of Eva (Le Gallienne) and Ona (Munson)."

—**Mercedes De Acosta to Darwin Porter,**
late one summer night before she died

***

Her stage name, Alla Nazimova, was a combination of Alla (a diminutive of Adelaida) and the surname of Nadezhda Nazimova, the heroine of the Russian novel, *Children of the Streets*.

Who was Alla Nazimova, known professionally only by her last name? She became a legend on stage in the early part of the 20th Century and had a brief reign in the film world as Queen of Metro in the 1920s.

When scholars encountered her name as the godmother of the future First Lady, Nancy Reagan, they had to research the by-then-faded Nazimova for identification.

Gavin Lambert, Nazimova's biographer, wrote: "To have been famous for forty years, then forgotten for fifty years, is better than simply being famous for fifteen minutes. But fame as intense and prolonged as Nazimova's is rarely followed by total eclipse. Acclaimed as 'The New Duse' and the first truly 'modern' actress in the American theater, she became merely the last of the Old World giants for theater and film historians after her death."

One night in 1947 at Manhattan's Algonquin Hotel, Tallulah Bankhead, who had had a brief fling with Nazimova, said, "She was not only the godmother of that silly little fellatio queen, Nancy Davis (later Reagan). Nazimova was the godmother of all of us—and not just yours truly, but of Lynn Fontanne, Katharine Cornell, and most definitely, Marlene Dietrich and Greta Garbo, too."

"Nazimova," Tallulah continued, "was also the lesbian lover of Mercedes de Acosta (*and who hasn't had HER, dah-ling?*). And she seduced Mildred Harris—you know, Charlie Chaplin's wife—when she was sweet sixteen. She also accomplished something that Rudolph Valentino never did: She enjoyed sexual intimacies with both of his wives—Jean Acker and Natacha Rambova."

A legend on stage and screen during the first two decades of the 20th Century, Nazimova introduced the plays of Chekhov and Stanislavsky to the American theater. She also became a movie goddess at the age of forty, something that in her wake, only Mae West in the 1930s could accomplish.

In Key West, Tennessee Williams told Darwin Porter, "The first time I saw Nazimova on the stage, she was so shatteringly powerful, I couldn't stay in my seat but stood up and loudly clapped."

In 1916, **Nazimova**—in a way that evokes a self-enchanted star throwing a bone to a starstruck fan—inscribed this photo of herself to Mercedes de Acosta, who was desperately in love with her at the time.

As Mercedes recorded in her memoirs and as she revealed during her dialogues with Darwin, Nazimova seemed to appreciate the younger woman's adulation and lovemaking at the time.

Playwright Eugene O'Neill claimed, "Nazimova gave me my first conception of modern theater."

While touring America from 1907 to 1910 in such plays as *Hedda Gabler*, *The Master Builder*, and *A Doll's House*, she earned theater owners around five million dollars, a staggering sum in those days.

A writer at the time described Nazimova as being known for her "bold, highly stylized acting, which was most idiosyncratic, not to say downright bizarre. Her personality was distant, aloof."

***

Born Marem-Ides Leventon on June 3, 1879, this future Russian-American actress came into the world at Yalta, part of the Imperial Russian Empire.

For three years, the future actress, Nazimova, lived in a small apartment over her father's chemist shop. Thus, her fabled life began in this Crimean resort at the edge of the Black Sea.

Her family was dysfunctional. Her mother and father fought daily, often ending with him beating her severely. Soon after their family's move to Switzerland, he divorced her. Consequently, as her mother engaged in dalliances with other men, Nazimova came to maturity in boarding schools and foster homes.

In time, she became one of the most graceful actresses to appear on stage, but she admitted that as a little girl, she was "a bit fat, dull, and always bumping into the furniture." Since her parents were Jewish, Nazimova faced a lot of anti-Semitism, her schoolmates labeling her "The Little Turnip."

This little chub, as the years went by, morphed into an international beauty. By 1912, *Vanity Fair* profiled her looks: "Her lips are full and richly red. Her eyes are great black coals of intensity. Her forehead is high, a wide expanse of intellect. Her throat is a long, sensuous expression of sensuality. Her long, lithe, and supple body is even more serpentine in movement or repose than the sugges-

Young **Tallulah Bankhead**, around the time of her most intimate involvement with Nazimova.

LESBIAN CHIC: **Nazimova** dolled up and ready for a closeup in an era when her entourage—at least to *cognoscenti*, progressives, and insiders—was lavender, ferociously feminist, and very gay, indeed.

tion of her clinging, reptilian garment."

She showed an early interest in the theater and enrolled at the Academy of Acting in Moscow and studied music at the St. Petersburg Conservatory. Already an accomplished violinist, she made her stage debut in Moscow at the age of nineteen. Under the direction of Konstantin Stanislavsky, she auditioned for, and got, some of the lead roles at the Moscow Art Theatre.

By 1903, she'd become a major star in both Moscow and St. Petersburg. She emerged as such a hit that she was invited to appear in plays in both Berlin and London.

In 1906, the American producer, Henry Miller, assigned her her first Broadway role as the title character in *Hedda Gabler*. One of the leading critics and writers of the time, Dorothy Parker, claimed she was "the finest *Hedda Gabler* I have ever seen."

Nazimova's fame spread quickly and helped her succeed in importing the plays of Ibsen, Chekhov, and Turgenev to American audiences.

The Shubert Brothers renamed a theater in her honor, calling it "Nazimova's 39th Street Theatre." They were well aware of her lesbian streak, and her affairs with such distinguished actresses as Laurette Taylor and Constance Collier.

They were less impressed with Mercedes de Acosta. Lee Shubert suggested that she shave off her slightly mannish mustache, but she protested: "I could never do that. It gives women such pleasure."

Nazimova, as she looked playing the title role of *Hedda Gabler*, the play by Henrik Ibsen about a well-bred wife who is trapped in a marriage and a house that she does not want. Critics consider it one of the quintessential dramatic roles in the history of late 19th-century theater.

No one from classical antiquity could have posed more gracefully, or portrayed the role with such a simmering sense of repressed hysteria.

NAZIMOVA'S HUSBANDS
FICTITIOUS BUT USEFUL PROPS WHO NEVER EXISTED

Although primarily a lesbian, Nazimova—during her early years on the stage in Moscow—had once been (dysfunctionally) married. In 1899, she'd wed Sergei Golovin, a young actor pursuing some of the same goals she was. Their friends dubbed them, "the odd couple."

He was a penniless drama student, the son of an impoverished countess. He later claimed, "The moment I saw Nazimova, I fell hopelessly in love with her." Three weeks after meeting her, he proposed marriage, not expecting her to accept his offer. Yet she did.

For their bizarre wedding ceremony, they exchanged vows in a small, austere chapel, the centerpiece for the cemetery that contained it. *[It was usually a venue for funerals.]* Attended by a few of their fellow drama students, it was followed with champagne and caviar.

Slightly drunk, Golovin escorted Nazimova back to the entrance to her hotel room, where she confronted him in the hallway, barring his entrance to her chamber. "There will be no wedding night," she told him. "You will need to find a room at the little inn about three blocks away."

[Rejected as his married life began on this bizarre note, he staggered off into the night.]

Traumatized, Nazimova had nearly fainted during her wedding ceremony in the funeral chapel. She was later medically diagnosed as having "a hysterical condition of the heart."

She always maintained a shroud around information associated with her first husband. She later told Mercedes, "I never loved him. But at the time, I was hopelessly in love with Alexander Sanin, an actor who was a special aide to the great Stanislavsky."

Asserting that Sanin never reciprocated her affection, she confessed, "I got married to spite Sanin." She went on to assert that when he eventually saw the light and began pursuing her, she spurned him "for having arrived too late."

Mercedes admitted to Darwin that she had trouble interpreting Nazimova's descriptions of her early "affairs of the heart," since the actress consistently delivered a distorted picture of what really happened. According to Mercedes, Nazimova claimed to have been "young and confused. You couldn't say I was torn between two lovers, because neither of them had made love to me. And frankly, I never wanted to have sex either with my husband or with Sanin."

"I was having sex with an actress from the Moscow Art Theatre," Nazimova continued. "I met her when I made my stage debut as a peasant girl in the play *Tsar Fyodor* in 1899, the same year I married my first husband. Sergei professed love for me, but he was really deeply in love, I found out, with a handsome young actor who had arrived in Moscow from St. Petersburg. I think the young man had a Finnish mother."

Finally, Nazimova and her new (unconsummated) husband, Sergei, had a confrontation. By then, each had recognized that their hasty marriage had been a mistake. She pleaded with him not to divorce her, fearing a scandal and willing to use their marriage as a shield to conceal her affairs with women.

Although they separated, they didn't file for divorce until years later, delaying that unpleasant legality until 1923, almost a quarter-century later. In the interim, she managed to keep her marriage

Husbands: A necessary hindrance: **Here's Nazimova** with **Sergei Golovin** a few days after their wedding.

Somewhere, in the mysterious and deliberately distorted fog of Nazimova's personal history, there might have been an (aborted) romantic link with **Alexander Sanin** (1869-1956), a founding member of the Moscow Art Theatre who collaborated frequently with Stanislavsky.

But with every retelling, the links grew more confused and murky, all part of the carefully orchestrated myths Nazimova cultivated about her background and origins.

to Golovin a secret from the Hollywood press corps.

At the peak of her fame, during Nazimova's billing as the Queen of Metro, her fans were somehow made to believe that she was married to Charles Bryant, a British-born actor (1879-1948), who was frequently cast as her leading man. But even if she had been married to Bryant (and there was a lot of gossipy confusion about whether a ceremony had transpired, and if it had, whether it was ever consummated), their union was interpreted by Hollywood insiders as a lavender marriage between players who otherwise pursued their own (usually homosexual) affairs.

***

Bryant had been born in Cheshire, England, in 1879. He dropped out of Ardingly College in Sussex when he was fourteen to pursue a career onstage. Within three years, he sailed to America and began working on Broadway, starring in *The First Born* in 1887.

Nazimova with her conveniently homosexual, conveniently British, and conveniently respectable husband, **Charles Bryant,** who absolutely never outshone or eclipsed her on the stage or screen.

It was Nazimova, during the era when they aggressively maintained their status as husband-and-wife, who elevated him into a leading man in silent pictures

Before meeting her, Bryant sustained many affairs. In reference to the year (1902) spent touring America in a play starring Mrs. Patrick Campbell, Bryant colorfully boasted, "I managed to knock off a piece in every town in which Mrs. Pat and I toured."

[*The English actress, Mrs. Patrick Campbell was one of the most sought-after celebrities of the late Victorian age. Born in 1865— the same year the United States concluded, disastrously, its brutal Civil War—she was christened "Beatrice Stella Tanner."*

She married Patrick Campbell in 1884, an unhappy, absentee union that lasted until his death in South Africa's Boer War in 1900. Short of funds, and following a prim Victorian tradition, she used her married name as her stage billing.

Cultivating fans and links to impresarios in both London and New York, she became a hit on Broadway in role after role. In 1914, she portrayed Eliza Doolittle in the original West End production of Pygmalion, *a role which George Bernard Shaw (who, it's said, became deeply infatuated with her) wrote specifically with her in mind.*

In 1914, she married George Cornwallis-West, a union that lasted until their deaths in 1940. A British soldier and writer, he had previously been married to Jennie Jerome, the American-born mother of Sir Winston Churchill.

Despite her second (reportedly, rather happy) marriage, she continued to bill herself as Mrs. Patrick Campbell in stage performances in New York as late as 1933.

What was "Mrs. Pat's" most famous quote? Before meeting Mercedes de Acosta, "Mrs. Pat" was informed that Mercedes was a lesbian. She was aware

of her co-star (Bryant's) male assignations, too. Her reaction? (even though it has also been attributed to others): "My dear, I don't care what they do, so long as they don't do it in the street and frighten the horses."]

Bryant entered Nazimova's life in 1911, when she was rehearsing for the play *Bella Donna*, whose theme involved a dying husband, a murderous wife, and a suspicious doctor. They bonded almost immediately, even though they came from radically different backgrounds and had divergent interests. Soon after their first encounter, she nicknamed him "Chumps."

It was reported that once, early in their relationship, they had attempted sex. She reported, "It was horrible, a disaster. We will never try that again."

To the press, for public consumption, she presented Bryant as her husband, a pretense that began in 1912 and lasted until his eventual (*bona fide*) marriage in 1925 to another woman.

Throughout the duration of this deception, Nazimova was still married, technically, at least, to Sergei Golovin.

Friends of Nazimova reported that whereas she did not want a husband, she craved a strong male figure in her life, and that Bryant and Nazimova maneuvered together like a father and his daughter. Gossips maintained that the durability of their association derived from the need to deflect rumors about their respective same-sex affairs, news of which would have destroyed either of their careers.

For Bryant's cooperation in this ruse, Nazimova cast him as her leading man in film after film, even though critics found him "wooden" as an actor. [*Actually it's likely that she didn't want a strong leading man who would deflect attention away from her as a film star. This became painfully obvious during her co-starring performance with Rudolph Valentino in* Camille *(1922).*]

Mercedes de Acosta once asked Nazimova if she had ever loved Bryant: "No, that's not part of the deal. I do not love him and never did. It's a pretend marriage, and he provides a cover for me and keeps me from getting involved

What's another favorite quote from the quick-witted actress, **Mrs. Patrick Campbell**, who's depicted here as a then-very-much-in-vogue Pre-Raphaelite beauty.?

"Moses probably said to himself, 'I must stop or I shall be getting silly.'"

Nazimova's premises shocked (and delighted) Edwardian audiences. Above, she appears in the 1912 Broadway stage version of *Bella Donna* with a (male) lover defined as "Egyptian" and a dress (of her own design) whose train she described as "inspired by serpents."

in scandal. Another reason I formed a liaison with him is to improve my English, so I can be stronger in my stage and screen performances in America. Frankly, my dear, you've met Chumps. Unlike you, he's a total bore."

"Besides, he takes delight in spending my money, a lot of it going to his wardrobe and three fancy cars. That makes him very, very content. Of course, he is free to seduce other women on the side, providing he is discreet."

"Chumps recently bought me (with my money) an antique double bed imported from England. I told him he would never sleep in it. Imagine having such a big lout of a man beside you in bed, snoring, farting, and growing a grisly beard overnight, waking up in need of a shave. Men can be so very repulsive, whereas women are delicate and beautiful at all times. Chumps has hair on his chest. Man is truly descended from apes. Unless we're working, we spend very little time together."

The fiction associated with Nazimova's sham marriage to Charles Bryant began around 1912 and endured until 1925, when reporters revealed that he impulsively married a 23-year-old socialite, Marjorie Gilhooley, in Connecticut. (Their marriage lasted until 1936.)

News of his marriage to Gilhooley came as an unpleasant surprise to both Nazimova and her fans. When accusations of bigamy arose, it was revealed that he had never actually married Nazimova, and the interconnected scandals damaged her career.

In 1929, Nazimova met the love of her life, Glesca Marshall (1907-1987), a hopeful young actress. Their deep friendship and association would last until Nazimova's death in 1945.

The changing fortunes of Alla Nazimova's life are symbolized in this photo of the (financially disastrous) transformation of her former (luxurious and private) home into a resort hotel in the years following the summits she reached as a money-making actress for Metro.

Significantly, the blonde in the center is believed to be Nazimova's long-time companion, **Glesca Marshall.** The bashful-looking male on the left is unidentified, and the brunette on the right is believed to be **Nazimova** herself.

***

In 1914, Nazimova was offered a starring role as "Joan" in a Broadway-bound "playlet," *War Brides,* a 35-minute pacifist drama that opened on January 25, 1915 at Manhattan's Palace Theatre just after Europe became embroiled in World War I.

[*At the time, although most of the U.S. sympathized with England and opposed Germany's Kaiser, America still remained officially neutral.*

Since the "playlet" was so short, Nazimova shared the bill with a troupe of acrobats, a trained chimp, some jugglers from Hong Kong, a stand-up comedian, and a minstrel group from Dublin singing "Danny Boy."]

In reference to War Brides, in an interview at the time with a leading newspaper (*the New York American*), she announced, "I am not merely appearing as an actress in a play. I'm doing something for the womanhood of the world with an anti-war message. The play is an indictment of the miseries and brutalities that subject women to—not to mention the husbands and sons slain on battlefields."

Charles Bryant appeared in the play as her character's husband before he's killed, along with two of her brothers, in the trenches of Europe during World War I.

The king of the (unnamed) nation in which this drama unfolds orders its women to produce more children to fight in future wars. Nazimova (as Joan) protests, but when she's threatened with imprisonment if she doesn't conform, she commits suicide.

Commercially, War Brides was a hit, enjoying the longest run on Broadway's Palace Theatre of any play in the theater's history to that point, except for a production with Sarah Bernhardt when she had starred there in 1905.

In War Brides' most stirring *tableaux*, Nazimova appeared as a uniformed Cossack, waving the Czarist flag, her thick black hair standing out from her scalp as if in electric shock.

For her performance, Nazimova was heralded as a champion of women's rights and a darling of the fast-emerging Suffragettes. The play itself was reviewed as "The Magna Carta of Women."

In the audience on opening night sat a thirteen-year-old Tallulah Bankhead, who had skipped school that day to see Nazimova perform.

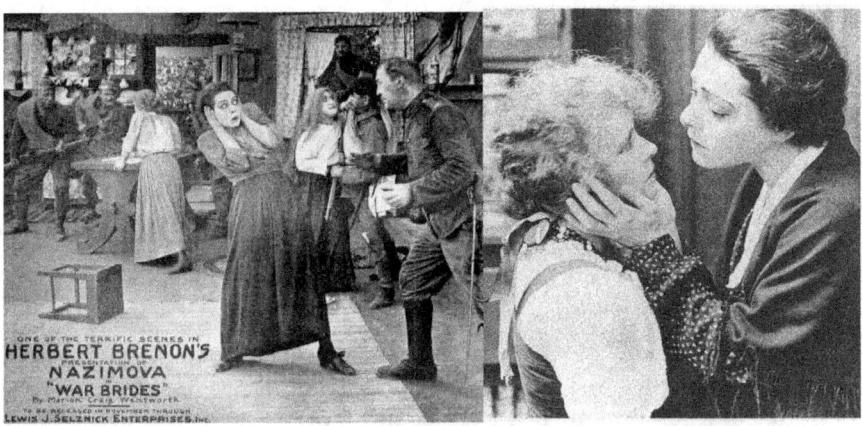

With the clear understanding that its pacifist intentions were noble and uplifting, hipsters instantly recognized the lesbian eroticism that permeated some scenes of Nazimova's short anti-war love drama, War Brides (1916) The first of Nazimova's films, and defined as "lost" to modern viewers, it was a deeply emotional vehicle that taught her many ways to improve her later films.

The photo above shows **Nazimova** emoting, perhaps with nuances of love, with **Nila Mae**, her co-star, an attractive *ingenue*.

Also in the audience was Mercedes de Acosta, who later promoted Nazimova as "a great artist and an even greater soul."

After its theatrical debut in Manhattan, Nazimova toured the country with *War Brides* as part of a six-month road show on the vaudeville circuit. She was highly paid, drawing $2,500 a week, a tidy sum back then.

In Boston, a newspaper headline greeted her arrival in the city with "NAZIMOVA WORKS TO END THE WAR."

Eventually, as America became increasingly preoccupied with "The Great War," film producer Lewis Selznick invited Nazimova to star in a film adaptation of *War Brides*. Released in 1916, it paid Nazimova $1,000 a day for her performance. The film would mark the beginning of her transition to movies.

***

A few months before the film's release, on May 7, 1915, a German submarine 11 miles off the coast of Ireland—following the Kaiser's orders to attack British ships in the Atlantic—torpedoed and sank the British ocean liner, *RMS Lusitania,* en route from New York to Liverpool with more than a hundred Americans on board at the time.

Mercedes at the beach, probably around 1910 as an impressionable teenager on the verge of leaving the sheltered confines of the aristocratic Gilded Age for the wild imbroglios and pansexual scenes of the Jazz Age.

It was around the time of her first exposure to the plays, films, and lesbian contexts of Nazimova.

[Historical note: Many historians have noted the "grey zone" in which the Lusitania was being operated by the British at the time. Britain had mined the entrances to Germany's ports on the North Sea, and in addition to its role as a passenger ship, the Lusitania was transporting weapons and arms at the time of its sinking.

After that and several other incidents, the mood of (till then, aggressively pacifist) America shifted toward armed intervention. Within two years, the U.S. declared war on Germany.]

After it had relayed its message, and after its flood of inaugural publicity had ended, Selznick withdrew *War Brides* from circulation as the tides of public opinion became less pacifist and more in favor of war. So far as it is known, no copy of it exists today.

***

When she was twenty-two, Mercedes de Acosta was introduced to Nazimova, not backstage after any of her performances, but at a charity event at Madison Square Garden. Nazimova, dressed as a Cossack representing Imperial Russia, made a dramatic entrance into the arena. She ran around the arena waving the Russian flag. Every minute or so, she took a leap into the air.

Alert to the allure of Nazimova, Mercedes had pleaded with her friend, Elisabeth ("Bessie") Marbury, to arrange an introduction.

[Marbury, who was one of Nazimova's financial backers, was in charge of fundraising for the Madison Square Garden charity event. Marbury, "the Doyenne of Sapphic Broadway," delighted in orchestrating "matchmaking arrangements" between women. She was also a major fundraiser for the Democratic Party, and one of the earliest backers of a young Franklin D. Roosevelt.]

After the show, Mercedes met Nazimova in her dressing room, as she was removing her large fur hat. At first, the younger woman was shocked at how short she was. In *Hedda Gabler* and *Bella Donna*, Nazimova had worn a long train, which had somehow made her look taller.

As Mercedes recalled, "Nazimova had the only truly purple eyes I have ever seen. Her lashes were black and thick. She held out both hands to me and told me she had heard so much about me from Bessie. Here before me in flat Russian boots, she seemed tiny and more like a naughty boy. I felt completely at ease, as if we'd always known each other."

"Almost from the beginning we became soulmates," Mercedes claimed. "I was going through my Russian period at the time, reading voraciously of that country's literature. We talked of Pushkin and Chekhov. Later that night she confessed that men did not fulfill her heart's desire. She felt that only a woman could do that. You might say that I liberated Nazimova. She soon became one of the theater's grandest lesbians."

Elisabeth ("Bessie") Marbury (left) with her long-time companion and beneficiary of her will, **Elsie de Wolfe ("Lady Mendl")** at the home they shared in 1923.

A prominent agent and theatrical impresario, Marbury helped define the upper echelon of the arts community—especially the business end of Broadway—and helped maneuver her lover, Lady Mendl, into a spectacularly career as an interior decorator and social arbiter of the Gilded Age.

It was these two formidable lionesses of the theater and NYC social scene who helped introduce, perhaps a part of a romantic matchmaking attempt, the young Mercedes de Acosta to their associate and business client, Nazimova.

Nazimova is said to have coined the term "A Sewing Circle," to describe a coven of lesbians. Her seductions of legendary stage and film actresses became legendary: Eva Le Gallienne; both of Valentino's wives; Dolly Wilde, the niece of Oscar Wilde; and Dorothy Arzner, a leading female film director of silent-era and early-Talkie Hollywood.

[A relatively forgotten name today, Arzner—pejoratively nicknamed "Little Miss Mouse Fart"—helmed seventeen films over the course of a decade, beginning in 1927. She became the best-known woman director in Hollywood, guiding such stars as Clara Bow, Katharine Hepburn, Claudette Colbert, Rosalind Russell, and

Joan Crawford, whom she seduced. She died in 1979 at the age of 78, a dim figure of the Golden Age.]

Despite never having visited it, but based on her reading of its literature, Mercedes told Nazimova that "Russia is in my soul." After hearing this, Nazimova invited her to escort her back to her apartment where a late night candlelit dinner had been prepared by her housekeeper.

That led to a night of passion, which was duplicated in the days that followed. "Nazimova found her *forte* in lovemaking," Mercedes claimed. "A beautiful woman was what her heart desired."

Eventually, Mercedes and Nazimova arranged a holiday in Paris together, checking into the Hotel Montalembert on the Left Bank. According to Mercedes, "We were in love in the City of Love, holding hands as we walked along the Seine, attending the theater and patronizing bars where women like us gathered at night to meet kindred spirits. Many of them shared the same forbidden desires that consumed our very souls."

"Nazimova knew our love affair wasn't meant to be eternal." Mercedes confessed, years later. "There would be other lovers, perhaps even greater passions. But we bonded into an everlasting friendship and engaged in an 'eternal embrace.' In 1916, Nazimova moved on to Hollywood and soon became Metro's biggest star, moving into the orbits of Rudolph Valentino and his wife, Natacha Rambova."

The bonds between Mercedes and Nazimova weren't always harmonious. Mercedes gave Nazimova a copy of her play, *Jehanne d'Arc*, telling her she saw it as a vehicle for Eva Le Gallienne, an actress who had been a lover to each of them.

Then Nazimova delivered a blisteringly candid opinion: "This play is not worthy of either your writing talent or the acting talent of Eva."

Later, when Nazimova's opinion reached Eva, she consoled and soothed Mercedes' ruffled feathers with, "Nazimova is behaving like a thorough cad. Don't pay attention to her, darling. She's been wrong about many other theatrical roles, too."

In New York, prior to her first encounter with Nazimova, Mercedes had continued her stalking of celebrities. An invitation to one of her "kitchen suppers" was highly regarded. On any given evening at around midnight, at Mercedes' apartment, a visitor might thrill to the collective presence of Tallulah Bankhead, Nazimova, Katharine Cornell, Alfred Lunt, Lynn Fontanne, Beatrice Lillie, Laurette Taylor, Constance Collier, Jeanne Eagels, Noël Coward, and/or Clifton Webb.

Eva Le Gallienne at NYC's Civic Theater, around the time she was comforting her then-lover, Mercedes de Acosta, from the critical ravages of Nazimova.

In the years to come, Mercedes continued to enter and exit at regular intervals from Nazimova's life, sometimes showing up unexpectedly. In 1927, after Nazimova had completed a long and arduous tour of America, Mercedes was waiting for her at Grand Central Station, greeting her with a large WELCOME HOME sign.

When Nazimova appeared in London as the heroine of an Ibsen play, Mercedes came backstage to greet her, inviting her for late-night champagne and caviar at the Savoy Hotel. At that supper, Nazimova was introduced to W. Somerset Maugham.

The last letter from Nazimova to Mercedes read:

Darling,
Keep busy and I hope you are happier than when I last saw you. Take the advice of an old lady. Find happiness and purpose within yourself. Don't rely on others to bring it to you. It does not work that way, and you will ultimately be disappointed in people., Sounds trite, but I have found it to be true.
Love,
Alla

***

ALTHOUGH THERE WAS NEVER A CAMELOT, ONCE UPON A TIME, THERE WAS A GARDEN OF ALLA

In 1919, with the extravagant salary Nazimova was drawing from Metro, she leased a Spanish-inspired mansion at 8080 Sunset Blvd. in West Hollywood. *[Back then, that was a rural area.]* The following year, she bought it for $65,000. It stood on a 2.5-acre estate called "Hayvenhurst." *[The spelling was later changed to "Havenhurst."]*

The property had been built by real estate developer William H. Hays. It contained a dozen bedrooms, each with furnishings crafted from Circassian walnut, which he'd purchased during a trip to the Philippines. In 1912, Nazimova had to sink another $30,000 into the building for alterations, repairs, and landscaping.

She christened her estate "The Garden of Alla" after her first name. *[Its name was not, as some assumed, based on the title of the best-selling 1905 novel,* The Garden of Allah, *by the British author, Robert S. Hichens. Marlene Dietrich, later a resident of the hotel, appeared in a film adaptation of the novel in 1936.]*

Nazimova ordered the construction of a swimming pool whose shape was vaguely influenced by the outline of the Black Sea she'd known as a little girl. It became the site of some of the most notorious pool parties in Hollywood, with many stars, both male and female, disrobing, in public, before jumping nude into the water.

Nazimova occupied the most elaborately decorated bedroom of her newly renovated mansion, assigning her so-called husband, Charles Bryant, a bedroom down the hall.

After World War I, Nazimova was hailed as "The First Lady of the Silent Screen." *[At the same time, Mary Pickford—her rival, known for a radically different and more wholesome style—was frequently described as "America's Sweetheart."]*

Behind closed doors, Nazimova was also hailed as "The Hollywood Queen of Lesbians." She told actress Bebe Daniels, "I betray women just like men have betrayed them down through the ages."

Nazimova's sometimes lesbian lover, silent screen star Dagmar Godowsky, had famously appeared opposite Rudolph Valentino in A *Sainted Devil* (1924). She told a reporter, "Nazimova moves through your life like the moon, lighting your way through the darkness of the night. But, like the moon itself, she often disappears behind a cloud. She continues to write the story of her life, adding another chapter every month. It reads like a movie script. We are reduced to mere supporting players because she is the reigning star supreme. You might call me her lady-in-waiting. Indeed, I played an attendant when I starred with her in *Stronger than Death* (1919). In it, she performed an Indian temple dance."

Nazimova embraces **Charles Bryant**, her "perhaps" real-life husband, in the namesake gardens she developed around their ostentatious and widely publicized new home, Havenhurst.

Later, in the mid-1920s, when Nazimova was on the verge of drowning in financial difficulties, she took out a mortgage and commissioned the construction of 25 villas, scattered artfully across and within the verdant trees and shrubberies of her estate.

Front entrance, during its Nazimova-controlled heyday, of **Havenhurst**, perhaps the most widely publicized, and most pansexually decadent, home in L.A.

To help publicize the adaptation of her home into the Garden of Alla, she hosted an opening night party on January 9, 1927. Soon, the stylish new hotel and watering hole became the choice address for movie stars, who knew their privacy would be protected by the armada of security guards who patrolled the property.

To earn extra money, many of the guards rented themselves to homosexuals who frequented the hotel.

Checking in and out were Tallulah Bankhead and John Barrymore, sharing the same room; Lauren Bacall, Barbara Stanwyck, Ginger Rogers, Orson Welles, the Marx Brothers, David Niven, Laurence Olivier, Greta Garbo, Ernest Hemingway, Charles Laughton, Humphrey Bogart, Clara Bow, Ronald Colman, and Joan Crawford.

One night in the late 1930s, a drunken Ronald Reagan checked in. As related in Bill O'Reilly's biography, *Killing Reagan,* Reagan had reached bottom when he woke up one morning at the Garden of Alla and did not know the name of the nude woman lying next to him.

The Garden of Allah *[around this time, an additional "h" was added to its name]* attracted the attention of novelists and journalists for years after its heyday. Author Herman Wouk referred to the Garden of Allah as "Rainbow's End" in his best-selling novel, *Youngblood Hawke*.

Columnist Sheilah Graham wrote, "There is no place like the Garden of Allah that, for one brief moment, was Camelot. It was inevitable that Hollywood, as we knew it, and its satellite, Alla's Garden, should disappear together." Later, she expanded her observations into book form (*The Garden of Allah*), which recalled the hotel in its Golden Age heyday.

One of the silent era's most spectacularly self-enchanted film stars was **Dagmar Godowsky,** Nazimova's part time/sometimes lover.

Sandford Dody, the ghost-writer of her memoir, wrote: "Dagmar lived in a perpetual state of self-adoration and would accept nothing less from others. Her need for constant proof of this adoration kept her on a merry-go-round, whirling to the screeching calliope."

Graham's very famous lover, the jazz-age novelist F. Scott Fitzgerald, lived at the Garden of Allah for several months in 1937 and '38. From within its premises, he wrote himself a postcard: "Dear Scott, How are you? Have been meaning to come in and see you. I am living at the Garden of Allah. Yours, Scott Fitzgerald."

Nazimova's "Black Sea Hotel Pool" was the scene night after night of debauchery without gender preference. Its participants included many of the very famous movie stars of that era, each confident that their antics would not be reported in the press. Stripped down, John Barrymore and Tallulah Bankhead didn't bother with swimsuits. Neither did Gary Cooper, whose nudity earned him a reputation as "The Montana Mule." Forrest Tucker liked to display his heavy endowment there, an appendage he referred to as "The Chief." And frequently, Errol Flynn was on display in his naked glory. As it happened, just before its closing in 1957, he was one of the hotel's last and final overnight guests.

In the Garden's dying days, two "gay-for-pay" hustlers checked in. They were James Dean *[Star of* East of Eden *(1955)* and Rebel Without a Cause *(also 1955)]* and Nick Adams *[doomed star of the TV series,* The Rebel *(1959-1961)]*. Both were aspirant actors, looking for adventure, sex, and drama. At the time, they earned their living by hustling gay men from the sidewalks along Santa Monica Boulevard.

Nazimova knew nothing about running a hotel, and her financial partners took advantage of her. Finding herself bankrupt in 1928, she sold her remaining interest in the property and auctioned off her furniture and household goods. She returned to the Broadway stage in 1930 at the dawn of the talkies.

An ill woman, Nazimova returned to the Garden in 1938, renting Villa #24, where she lived until her death in 1945.

Francis X. Bushman, the legendary star of the silent screen in such pictures as *Ben-Hur* (1925), had attended the opening party of the Garden of Alla in 1927. More than thirty years later, on August 22, 1959, he showed up for its farewell party, Many of the guests came costumed, some of them in drag, as the legendary stars of yesterday: Gloria Swanson, "The Vamp" Theda Bara, Valentino, or cowpoke William S. Hart.

Ultimately, the Garden of Allah ceased to exist. In 1959, Bart Lytton, President of the Lytton Savings and Loan, purchased the hotel for $755,000 with the intention of demolishing it and using its site as the location for the headquarters of his bank. Demolition permits were issued, and on November 2, the Garden of Allah faded into history.

***

In the waning years of her life, Nazimova became almost delusional, like a crazed Norma Desmond in *Sunset Blvd.* (1950). According to her, "Years from now, when film historians probe the stars of the Silver Screen, the name of Nazimova will be there at the top of the list. I was the bright, glittering light of the era, bringing glamour, glitz, and passion to the flickers—in fact, I put the gold into the Golden Age."

***

Soon after her arrival in Hollywood in 1917, Nazimova signed a contract with Metro Pictures (later, MGM) for the then-staggering salary of $13,000 a week. *[At the time, America's Sweetheart, Mary Pickford, made only $10,000 a week.]*

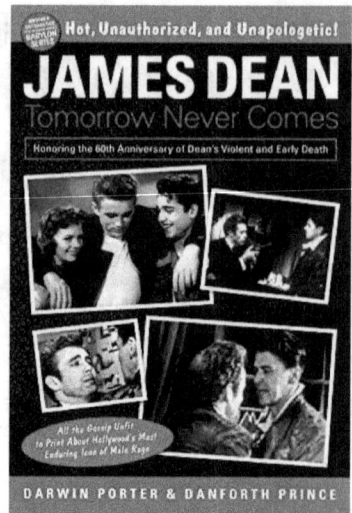

In 2016, the authors of this biography of Mercedes de Acosta penned the publishing industry's most unvarnished, least apologetic overview of **James Dean**, the brilliant but unlikely "live fast, die young" actor who changed the face of Hollywood forever.

It describes, among multitudes of other shockers, how he made a living, early in his nihilistic career, of hustling johns around the legendary pool of the Garden of Allah in the months before its demolition in the late 1950s.

Nazimova was the first movie star to become a screen goddess—not just a character actress, but a seductress—at the age of 40. That success would later be matched only by Mae West, who managed to succeed with her characterization of a screen siren after she'd passed the age of forty, too.

Nazimova also became known as "the foreign sophisticate," paving the way for Greta Garbo, Marlene Dietrich, and Pola Negri.

***

Nazimova's first film for Metro was *Revelation* (1918), shot mainly in New Orleans. The historic Vieux Carré in that city had to pass for the Latin Quarter of Paris.

Nazimova's "husband," Charles Bryant, was cast as her leading man, and he would go on to play equivalent roles in nine of her eleven films for Metro.

Directed by George D. Baker, *Revelation* (1918), according to a movie

Here's **Nazimova** make-believing that the man she married, **Charles Bryant,** portraying a painter, is actually her husband. The scene is from a press and publicity photo from the silent drama *Revelation* (1918) in which Joline, an artists' model, becomes virtuous through a revelation that instructs her to care for the "wounded in action" soldier (Bryant) she loves.

magazine, is the story of Joline, a cabaret entertainer (read that as "prostitute"). She attracts the attention of a young artist, Paul Granville (Bryant), and goes to his studio, where she poses for him as Cleopatra, Salome, and Sappho. When he is commissioned to paint a picture of the Madonna, he asks her to pose for that portrait, too. He paints her beside a rose bush in a monastery.

Pretending to be the Madonna leads to a spiritual revelation for Joline. She decides to devote the rest of her life to "good causes." The artist and his model separate, but the coming of World War I reunites him. The artist, by then enlisted in the army, is a soldier wounded in battle. As a Red Cross nurse, Joline tends to his wounds.

One critic claimed that in *Revelation,* "Nazimova runs the gamut from vice to virtue." No copy of Nazimova's first movie is known to exist.

The same fate has befallen her second movie for Metro, *Toys of Fate,* in which she was cast in the dual roles of Zorah (a gypsy) and her daughter (Hagah).

Both films, released within three months of each other, were hits at the box office. Nazimova was on her way to becoming a major movie star.

***

Her next film was *L'Occident* (later retitled *Eye for Eye* (1918), which brought together Nazimova with scriptwriter June Mathis, who became a major scriptwriter for the early silents. Rather overweight and plain-looking, Mathis seemed to have a gift for writing scripts with glamourous screen characters. A former child star in vaudeville, she hit Hollywood like a storm, and would play a major role in the careers of both Nazimova and Rudolph Valentino.

In *Eye for Eye,* Nazimova was cast as Hassouna, the daughter of an Arab sheik who falls in love with an officer of the Foreign Legion (Bryant again). At one point, after being left to die in the desert, she's captured by Bedouins who sell her into slavery. Escaping from bondage, she makes her way to Tangier, Morocco, and later to Marseilles, where she becomes a café dancer and circus worker.

Motion Picture Classic lauded her performance in *Eye for Eye:* "In Alla Nazimova, we have beauty, we have a depth of emotionalism never depicted before, and we have art with such touches of finesse that she unconsciously stands alone."

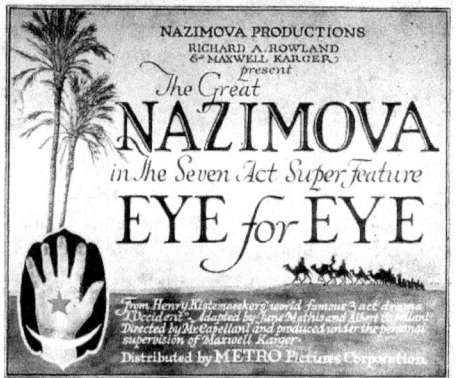

***

Nazimova's next film, *Out of the Fog,* featured her in a dual role, that of both a mother (Faith) and her daughter (Eve). Faith is the sister of a lighthouse keeper. She is impregnated by a sailor who abandons her. She gives birth to Eve before throwing herself into the sea to drown.

As a sixteen-year-old, the film reveals Eve sensually emerging from the same sea where her mother, Faith, had thrown herself to drown. Daring for its time, the lighthouse keeper seems to have a sexual desire for his sister.

> In *Eye for an Eye* (1918), **Nazimova,** playing a well-bred rich girl who just graduated from a convent school, is led off, on a camel, into a life of slavery and degrading sex.
>
> Except for whatever background music was provided by the theater, the action proceeds silently and stirringly, but with such high-strung emotion that some viewers insisted they could smell the spices in the nearby bazaar.
>
> To the Edwardian-era audiences who screened it, it was riveting entertainment, and to some, absolutely terrifying.

***

Mathis also penned the script for *The Red Lantern* (1919), a film that was notable for marking the debut of Anna May Wong. Set in Peking at the time of the Boxer Rebellion *The Red Lantern* again found Nazimova playing dual roles that included the part of Mahlee, a half-Chinese, half white woman who's an outcast from both of those societies, and the role of Blanche Sackville, Mahlee's half-sister. The plot gets complicated when both of them fall in love with the same man.

Wallace Beery played the leader of the insurgents fomenting the Boxer Rebellion.

Filming of *The Red Lantern* took place during the worldwide flu pandemic that killed millions around the globe, causing jittery nerves across the set.

***

As her scriptwriter, Mathis came up with another scenario for Nazimova called *The Brat,* which was directed by Herbert Blache and released by Metro. It was based on Maude Fulton's hit Broadway play (1917) and would later be remade as a talkie in 1931 with Sally O'Neil in the lead. Alas, the silent version of *The Brat* is believed to have been lost.

Nazimova plays the lead, a chorus girl (not named) who is fired from her job at "The Summer Garden" when she rejects the sexual advances of her boss, Stephen Forrester (Darrell Foss).

She gets into trouble and goes to court where she is rescued by MacMillan (as portrayed by Bryant Forrester, brother of the better-known Stephen Forrester). He is in search of an underworld character on which to base his next novel. From there, the drama unfolds with a lot of complications.

Nazimova performed two musical numbers, including a classical Greek dance and a "rabbit dance," during which she wore a furry costume.

One critic asked, "What is Nazimova attempting to do? Become another Mary Pickford? One Mary is enough."

"THEN (DURING THE SILENTS) WE HAD FACES!"

That was what Gloria Swanson, portraying a silent film star (Norma Desmond) in *Sunset Blvd.* (1950), raged to William Holden about the decline in emotive standards since movies became "talkies."

Depicted above is **Nazimova,** buttressing Norma Desmond's claim.

***

In 1920, Nazimova led off with another film, *Stronger Than Death,* the first of four movies she shot that year. This film was directed by Herbert Blache with Bryant as her leading man.

Nazimova played Sigrid Fersen, a dancer and *femme fatale* who attracts his attention. He is fighting the cholera epidemic in the distant city of Bjura, and she agrees to follow him there. Her most memorable line is, "I am afraid of nothing in word or deed—except ugliness."

At the end of the film, an exhausted Nazimova decides (through the film's subtitles) "to live for the love that is *Stronger than Death.*"

The film was memorable for Nazimova in that she fell for the rather butch script girl and launched a brief affair with her. The younger woman would soon become famous as Dorothy Arzner, the leading female director of the 1920s and '30s.

Arzner was the daughter of Louis Arzner, a well-known restaurant owner in Los Angeles.

In *Stronger Than Death,* Nazimova faced criticism for what was called "self-parody," a comment on her exaggerated style of acting.

***

In *The Heart of a Child* (1920), Nazimova played Sally Snape, a Cockney girl from the slums of London's East End. She sleeps and schemes her way to success, eventually marrying an English aristocrat, a role again portrayed by Bryant.

The film did not do well at the box office, signaling a downward spiral in Nazimova's movie career. One critic wrote, "The story is not only unconvincing but preposterous."

On a personal note, the film was notable in that a nineteen-year-old, Sam Zimbalist, a projectionist, began an affair with Nazimova.

***

In *Madame Peacock* (1920), Nazimova once again was cast in dual roles, playing both Jane Goring and Gloria Cromwell. She was not only the writer of the scenario, but its producer and star, too. She hired Ray C. Smallwood as its director.

Her portrayal of Goring, an imperial actress of the stage, is cold, cruel, and uncompromising. In contrast, Cromwell is the antithesis of that.

In the plot, Goring leaves her small town, deserting both her husband and her daughter. She becomes a big star on Broadway, until she is threatened by the emergence of a younger, better actress. Naturally, as the audience might have guessed, the younger actress is the daughter she abandoned so long ago.

Latter-day critics might have seen some shades of *All About Eve* (1950) in this early version, the film that gave Bette Davis and Anne Baxter their best roles.,

Madame Peacock continued Nazimova's fall from grace at the box office, as she went from Number Four to Number Twenty.

***

Smallwood, who had directed Nazimova in *Madame Peacock*, was called back to helm *Billions* (also 1920). Once again, Bryant was her leading man, and both of them worked on the scenario, based on a French play *L'Homme riche*. She portrays a Russian princess, Triloff, who falls for an American poet, Krakerfeller (Bryant). She tries to dissuade him from abandoning his self-identity as a poet when he inherits a fortune.

Motion Picture Magazine denounced the story as "impossible and Nazimova for playing it impossible."

For the past, she had gotten away with playing younger roles, but her age was attacked in *Billions*, one critic suggesting she should only be filmed in long shots so "we don't have to see what Father Time has done to her face."

When *Billions* failed at the box office, Metro called Nazimova in for a showdown. Executives suggested that Bryant as a leading man was lackluster and that she should drop him. She was told that she should appear opposite a rising and dashing young star in future pictures. He was named Rudolph Valentino.

***

Nazimova left Metro late that afternoon knowing she needed a comeback picture. That night, she decided to star as *La Dame aux Caméllias*, commonly known in English as *Camille* and released in 1921. It was based on a novel by Alexandre Dumas, *fils*, which he published in 1848 to instant success. The title character of Marguerite Gautier was based on Marie Duplessis, the real life love of Dumas, *fils*.

Many actresses had played *Camille* on stage, including Sarah Bernhardt, Eleonore Duse, Ethel Barrymore, and Eva Le Gallienne. In silent films, both Norma Talmadge and Pola Negri had already starred as *Camille*.

Nazimova decided to take Metro's advice and cast Valentino as her film lover, Armand Duval. *Camille* was in pre-production two weeks before the Manhattan premiere of *Four Horsemen of the Apocalypse* (1921), the movie that made Valentino a star.

At the time, June Mathis was aggressively promoting Valentino, and a special screening of *Four Horsemen* was arranged for Nazimova to see. Eventually, she agreed to let him portray Armand, despite her (fully justified) fears that "he might steal my thunder."

He was **Valentino**, a neophyte, a newcomer, a bisexual, and a foreigner to the culture and values of decadent Hollywood during the Silent Era in which he eventually thrived.

His ardor translated into quickening pulses and breathing and to many sexually repressed, some said "hysterical" women of the jazz age, roaring surges of sexual fantasies.

Hollywood publicists had a field day, promoting him, as shown on the poster displayed above, as "The Greatest Lover of the Shadow Stage."

No slouch to the value of publicity, **Nazimova** moved fast to ensure that her billing was equally lush, demanding that she be described as "Incomparable...The (Sarah) Bernhardt of the Screen."

Her entrance at the beginning of *Camille* was the most dramatic of any of her movies. She stands at the top of a stairway and descends slowly, her face covered with white powder, her lips "bee stung," and her head capped with a black, curly wig. Her gown was stunning. Patterned with camellias, it was set off with a fur train that was "darker than midnight."

Valentino was hired as her on-screen counterpart for the relatively modest fee of $350 a week. At the time, he was sharing an apartment with his lover, Paul Ivano, a screen photographer who later became Nazimova's lover, too. A photographer for the French Signal Corps during World War I, he immigrated to America at war's end. Here, he became caught and entangled in the life of the rising bisexual Italian star, Valentino.

Ivano was only twenty when he became Nazimova's lover. *[At the time, Valentino was falling in love and preoccupied with Natacha Rambova, the designer of Camille's elaborate sets.]*

Camille drew mixed reviews and became only a moderate success at the box office. Many critics, while applauding Valentino, made it a point to attack Nazimova, which in-

 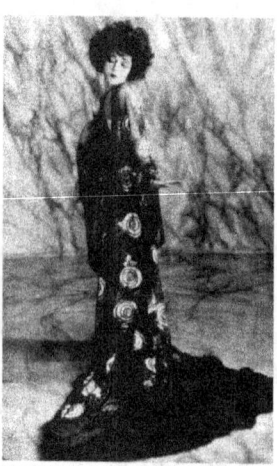

LET'S TALK ABOUT
ERTÉ, ART DECO, AND NAZIMOVA
AS A LIVING INCARNATION OF HIS AESTHETIC:

Romain de Tirtoff (1892-1990) was a Russian-born French designer who identified himself as **Erté,** based on the French pronunciation (AIR TAY) of his initials . His set designs and fashion illustrations became hugely *à la mode* in Paris in the 1970s, when sophisticated investors rushed to acquire them for their decorative values, exquisite details, and brilliant transitions between the best aspects of Art Nouveau and Art Deco.

In Paris, during its Jazz Age, he hung out with the White Russian aristocracy, worked with the era's most important couturier (Paul Poiret) and launched an association with *Harper's Bazaar* magazine that included designing costumes and stage sets. He designed costumes for the real-life Mata Hari; illustrated many editions of *Cosmopolitan, Ladies' Home Journal,* and *Vogue*; designed stage costumes for the then very famous French dancer, Gaby Deslys, and crafted set designs for the Folies Bergére and the Lido.

In 1925, Louis B. Mayer brought him to Hollywood to design sets and costumes for the silent films *Paris, Ben-Hur, The Mystic, Time, The Comedian, Dance Madness,* and *The Restless Sex* starring Marion Davies and financed by William Randolph Hearst. Today, Erté's designs are featured in the collections of museums worldwide. One of them, left photo, above, was used on the cover of the February, 1916 issue of *Harper's Bazaar*.

Nazimova, in her designs for some of her own costumes, was acutely aware of the aesthetic genius of Erté, as shown (right) in this photo of her from *Camille* as a *tragedienne* draped in fabric splashed with images of (guess what?) camellias.

furiated her.

Picture Play magazine wrote, "The Camille and Armand of tradition are forgotten in this film. It is lost in the potent allure of modern characterizations brought to the screen by Nazimova and Valentino. Bizarre, ephemeral, at moments and at others, frenzied, their version promises a haunting succession of mesmeric pictures. It does not aim to present the *Camille* that generations have applauded."

Carl Sandburg, writing in the *Chicago Daily News*, applauded Nazimova for her best screen performance. The *New York Mirror* stated that she was "direct and without affectation." *Photoplay*, the leading movie magazine of its day, asked, "What has happened to this great actress, the splendid genius, the incomparable *artiste?*"

When the box office receipts came in, Metro executives fired her, claiming they could no longer tolerate her temperamental outbursts and changing moods—and also her "impossible demands" that included insisting they produce a screen version of *A Doll's House*. [Actually, only three of Nazimova's movies had ever lost money for Metro.]

When it became obvious that Valentino was being better received than Nazimova, "Metro delivered its final betrayal of me," according to Nazimova. They gave Valentino star billing in large letters on its posters and reduced the size of the fonts spelling out her name.

From that day forth, Nazimova was on her own, plotting her own course.

Years later, in her own appraisal of *Camille*, gossip maven Louella Parsons wrote: "Nazimova's torrid love scenes with Rudy Valentino pioneered sex and glamour on screen, and I might say 'incubated' the possibility of censorship on all future film scenarios."

***

Photoplay had once written that Nazimova wore "too many hats" in all her films, maneuvering to supervise the script, the directions, the costumes, and her preferred choice of elaborate sets, most of them designed by Natacha Rambova.

For her 1922 screen adaptation of *A Doll's House*, she wrote the scenario, based on the Ibsen play, but decided to use a pseudonym, designating herself as "Peter M. Winters."

Filming began at the seedy Brunto Studios on Melrose Avenue. For the role of the husband, Torvald Helmer, she hired veteran actor Wallace Beery. This Kansas City native, born in 1885, was called "the most unlikely superstar of Hollywood's Golden Age." He had a gravelly voice and an ugly face noted for its "jowly look." Later, during the early days of the Talkies, he tried to come across as a lovable lug, comfortable in starring roles with Marie Dressler in *Min and Bill* (1930) and with Jean Harlow in *Dinner at Eight* (1933).

After just one week of shooting on *A Doll's House*, Beery realized that the psychologically complicated part was not for him, and he bowed out before any more footage was shot.

For his replacement, he recommended his friend and fellow actor, Alan Hale, a beefy, imposing guy with a bushy mustache and a sturdy bass voice. Although he had originally intended to become an opera singer, he was known as an actor who could play both a villain or a jovial type. He'd made his screen debut in 1911 in *The Cowboy and the Lady*.

He would survive silent pictures and find himself a star in the talkies too, appearing in such movies as *Susan Lennox (Her Fall and Rise)* in 1931 in which he attempted to rape Greta Garbo.

Metro had long refused to allow Nazimova to make a film of Ibsen's *A Doll's House*, which she had performed so successfully on the stage. Now fired by Metro, she went from studio to studio to obtain financing, but to no avail. Finally, she decided to put up the money for the movie herself in spite of her limited resources.

When she finally managed to accumulate $300,000 in a bank, she spent all of it on the production of a film version of her stage classic and then borrowed an additional $100,000 in the form of a mortgage.

Hiring stars and staff, she moved ahead, deciding to hire Charles Bryant once again, except this time she would make him the director and not her leading man.

She was never good at handling money, as noted by *Vanity Fair* in a profile in its February 1923 issue. The periodical referred to her as an "irresponsible child lashed by extravagancies. She seeks physical relief in the unchecked range of artistic expressions. Physical spending and nervous tension are inevitable."

At this point in her life, Nazimova was far too old to play Nora *[the heroine of* A Doll's House*]*, but she was saved by the brilliant camerawork of Charles Van Enger, who took at least a decade off her age, making her look no more than thirty. He would soon become famously associated with the films of rising director Ernst Lubitsch.

Nazimova was delighted when she sat with Bryant and watched the rushes. "I feel *A Doll's House* will put me back on my throne in Hollywood once again. I'm in a time-tested role. I'm being photographed beautifully, and I know the picture will have them lined up at the box office."

Regrettably, the world will never get to see Nazimova as Nora unless they were around for its showing in 1922. It is another of her films lost to history.

The movie opened that February with Nazimova, though middle-aged, playing a "child-wife" in the opening scenes. *The New York Times* characterized her movements as equivalent to a "jumping jack."

Photoplay praised her for controlling her extravagant acting style, which she had demonstrated in *Camille*.

Samuel Greenson, a reporter for *Photoplay*, visited her at the Garden of Alla soon after the picture opened. He found her bitter about "my last days at Metro," where she felt she had suffered unfair attacks on her work.

He wrote, "She's a misunderstood actress who desperately wants to be understood." He described her appearance as "boyish, with her hair in an Eton crop enhanced by a white Eton collar and wearing a midnight blue blouse and a Scottish plaid skirt. She came into her living room in flat-heeled brogues. She looked like anything but a flapper of the 1920s."

In spite of all the publicity hovering over the picture, Nazimova's screen treatment of *A Doll's House* bombed at the box office.

***

In one of those accidental coincidences, through another of his associates, Stanley Mills Haggart, Darwin Porter formed a close friendship with Philippe De Lacy, who had been hailed in the 1920s as "the most beautiful boy in pictures." Both Darwin and De Lacy worked for a time for J. Walter

Thompson, a leading advertising agency.

Way back during De Lacy's early teens, Nazimova had cast De Lacy as Ivar, Nora's young son, alongside her in *A Doll's House*.

Born in Nancy, France, in 1917, De Lacy became a war orphan and was rescued by a Red Cross nurse, Edith de Lacy. In the aftermath of the war, Nazimova brought him to America, where—stunning and very photogenic—he was spotted by a photographer and talent agent.

After working with Nazimova, De Lacy went on to play Mary Pickford's brother in *Rosita* (1925). She tried unsuccessfully to adopt him. After that, he portrayed Neil Hamilton's child in *Beau Geste* (1926) and John Barrymore as a child in *Don Juan* (1926).

The movie that immortalized him was *Love* (1927) in which he played Greta Garbo's son, based on Tolstoy's *Anna Karenina*. "Greta and I, as mother and son, practically made love to each other on the screen," De Lacy told Darwin one night at his residence over dinner. "One critic referred to our scenes together as incestuous."

He revealed marvelous behind-the-scenes stories of his star days, working with such fabled directors as John Ford, Victor Fleming, and Ernst Lubitsch.

His best friend at the time was Stanley Mills Haggart, who was seven years older than him.

"Stanley visited me on the set every day, and between scenes, we would play games with Greta," De Lacy said. "She was so young then, and so full of fun, unlike her later goddess image. All of us were so young in those days, but time took its toll."

Two views of child star **Philippe De Lacy**, celebrated at the time as the most beautiful boy in the world.

In the lower photo, he's the about-to-be-abandoned son of Anna Karenina (**Greta Garbo**) in *Love (1927)*

"I sensed great tension between our director, Bryant, and Nazimova when we made *A Doll's House*. I don't think they were really married. He had another girlfriend, and so did she."

"She blew up one afternoon and fired a script girl who had made a flippant comment about how she'd been fired from Metro," De Lacy said.

"I was not fired, damn you," Nazimova shouted at her in front of the cast and crew. "I walked out of the studio. They were begging me to stay."

De Lacy also told painful stories of how he'd been molested as a child. "I learned soon enough that a lot of men who worked in the film industry had this thing for little boys. If they did, they tended to gravitate to me. As

I aged, I lost my looks, but back then, I was hot stuff."

"That old geezer, Wallace Beery, on his third day on the set, beckoned me to him and asked me to sit on his lap. I couldn't believe it—he felt me up. He also asked me, 'Is that little thing of yours starting to grow?' The guy gave me the creeps. I escaped his clutches. Gloria Swanson was once married to him, and she told me awful tales about what a pervert he was."

De Lacy said he lamented the loss of all the prints of Nazimova's version of *A Doll's House*. "Back in those days, we were just turning out one picture after another. Film preservation was not even heard of then."

***

In her book, *Sappho Goes to Hollywood—The Girls*, Diana McLellan wrote: "Nazimova's next picture, *Salome,* was 'a hothouse orchid of decadent passion.' She decided to finance, produce, write, direct, and star in Oscar Wilde's *Salome*. Bryant was credited wherever possible This one, she decided, would be a homosexual manifesto. She would pay homage to Wilde, the brilliant Dublin-born writer jailed in England in 1895 for sodomy and indecent behavior. It would be America's first all-gay production for a mass audience."

Wilde himself had said, "I am writing a play about a woman dancing in her bare feet in the blood of a man she craved for and slayed."

Nazimova's lover at the

At the age of forty-two, **Nazimova** dared to play a teenage Salome, depending heavily on Van Enger's 1922 camera to make her look like a juvenile seductress.

For her *Dance of the Seven Veils,* Nazimove, wearing a platinum blonde wig, was inspired by the dancing of Isadora Duncan.

Salome does not show the beheading of John the Baptist, although the exectuioner appears onscreen with a large sword.

"As I heard the axe fall off screen, I tried to make my eyes orgasm," Nazimova said.

When the severed head is brought before her, Salome covers it with her cape before uttering a line from Oscar Wilde: "Thou wouldnt not suffer me to kiss thy mouth, Jokanaan. Well, I will kiss it now!"

Cultish, cryptic, avant garde, and self-consciously "aesthetic and artsy," **Salome** (1923) showcased an image of **Nazimova** as a primeaval and pagan goddess, despite its roots in the Biblical tale of King Herod and the 14-year-old virgin he pined for.

Depicted above is one of many scenes that evoke Nazimova's fervent and deeply emotional replications of Old Testament (pagan) life as a Silent Film Freudian might have analysed it.

time, Natacha Rambova (later to marry Rudolph Valentino) designed the costumes and sets for this loose adaptation of the Wilde play in its retelling of the Biblical story of King Herod and his execution of John the Baptist at the request of Herod's stepdaughter, Salome.

[For more details of Natacha's set designs and costumes, see the next chapter.]

One critic wrote, "*Salome* is called one of the first art films to be made in the United States. The highly stylized costumes, exaggerated acting, minimal sets, and absence of all but the most necessary props make for a screen image much more focused on atmosphere and on conveying a sense of the characters' individual heightened desires than on conventional plot development."

Nazimova did much to publicize the film, even before shooting it. She rented space at a seedy studio on Melrose Avenue. She also announced that in the future, she would be starring only in "vehicles of artistic merit."

Adela Rogers St. Johns was the most popular columnist of her day, entertaining readers with backlot stories of Hollywood before Louella Parsons and Hedda Hopper took over. Nazimova told her, "I want something so different, so fanciful, so artistic, that it would take the taste right out of my mouth."

Wilde was proficient in French, and he'd originally written the play in that language, seeing it as a stage vehicle for the great Sarah Bernhardt. With this play, he was hoping to be admitted to the *Académie française*. His play was called "a sordid twist on the Biblical epic, given a moody *fin-de-siècle* symbolism and decadence."

Bernhardt never got to star in *Salome* in London because it had been banned by the Lord Chamberlain.

In 1919, Hollywood had made *Salome* into a film starring the original vamp, Theda Bara. But many States in America refused to allow any movie house to show it.

Nazimova raised $350,000 to film *Salome,* and Rambova convinced her to allow her to design sets and costumes based on the illustrations originally created by Aubrey Beardsley in the printed edition of Wilde's play. *[It led to conflict: The publisher of the play had originally rejected some of Beardsley's illustrations, defining them as obscene.]*

In *Salome,* although it seemed ridiculous to Hollywood insiders, Nazimova, at the age of

Latter-day scholars have defined Nazimova's *Salome* as a then very avant-garde homosexual manifesto. Its producer (Nazimova herself) insisted on an all-gay cast, and defiantly dedicated it to the acerbic wit of the Anglo-Irish "toast of London's West End," **Oscar Wilde.**

Once the most celebrated playwright in London, Wilde's fortunes came crashing down in 1895 after a widely publicized court case sentenced him to two years of hard labor for his romantic links to the arrogant, entitled, shallow, and very spoiled **Lord Alfred Douglas (Bosie)**, the right-hand figure in the photo above.

Bankruptcy, social ostracizations, endless humiliations, and an early death, at the age of 46, followed soonafter.

forty-four, cast herself as a fourteen-year-old girl. This challenged her favorite photographer, Charles Van Enger, who had shot *A Doll's House* with her looking younger. "I know that Charles was the only photographer in Hollywood who could make me look like a teenager," Nazimova said.

"Salome is about forbidden love," she told the photographer. "Anything about forbidden love excites me, because it has been the passion of my life."

Even before its release, word spread that Nazimova was making a "blue movie."

She countered by telling the press, "*Salome* is the one pure creature in Herod's court, where sin was abundant. Yet the young girl remains uncontaminated by all the evil she sees around her. She is like an innocent flower growing in evil soil. The first time she loves, she asks all, since she is eager and willing to give all."

One of the highlights of the film was the Dance of the Seven Veils. For Nazimova, in this scene, Rambova designed a sheathlike tunic of white satin, which clung to the star's body like a sausage casing. Then, she capped Nazimova's head with a towering platinum wig.

In homage to its playwright, Oscar Wilde, both Nazimova and Rambova insisted that all the members of its cast be homosexual, or at least bisexual. Homosexual dwarfs were hired to perform in harem pants and plumed helmets., For the female roles, Rambova dressed men in drag, some of them looking as if they had recently emerged from the court of Marie Antoinette.

The costumes used material only from the very upscale Maison Lewis in Paris, including real silver *lamé* loincloths worn by the prison guards. These skimpy "*cache-sexes*" initially attracted bands of American homosexuals intrigued by the near-naked actors.

Nazimova and Bryant struggled to release the film and held advance previews, which, for the most part, drew favorable comments. The reviewer at the *Seattle Post-Intelligence* claimed that Nazimova was great in the role of Salome. Most critics hailed it as a triumph within the genre of an "artsy" picture.

Ultimately, *Salome* failed at the box office, to some degree because of its limited access. Some theaters wouldn't show it, and some states banned it completely.

> Ultra-artsy, sexually flamboyant, and allegorical.
>
> **I AM WOMAN: Nazimova, in Salome**, appears here on the verge of enslaving and sacrificing a satyr.

Of course, as expected, Nazimova also received her share of bricks thrown at her, one critic defining her as "a petulant little princess with a Freudian complex."

The New Republic labeled the film "degrading and unintelligent. Nazimova flits hither and thither with the mincing step of a toe-dancer. She has the figure of a boy, and her satin bathing suit is like that of Old Tetarch's cup-bearer. Try as she will, she just can't be seductive. She tosses her head impudently, grimaces repeatedly, and rolls her eyes with a vitreous stare. The effect is comic."

The deadly lure of sex, which haunts the Wilde drama like a subtle poison, is dispelled the instant one beholds the puerile and boyish form of Nazimova.

Screenland described *Salome* as "a painting deftly stroked upon the silversheet. Poets and dreamers will find imaginative delights in the weird setting and the still more weird acting, depressing at times to ordinary folks. And it is worth something to watch Nazimova balance her Christmas headdress."

A final poster was rushed into print advertising Nazimova as "THE DECADE LUSTS OF THE AGES."

But by now, it was too late to attract movie-goers.

In spite of her many efforts, Nazimova ended up broke.

***

Nazimova referred to her next role of Mary Carlson in *Madonna of the Streets* (1924) as "The Quintessential Queen of Movie Whores."

Directed by Edwin Carewe, it was based on the novel, *The Ragged Messenger*, by W.B. Maxwell, who had little talent when it came to devising a title.

First Nation agreed to both finance and distribute it, offering Nazimova a fee of $23,000 to shoot the entire picture, a figure in stark contrast to her former compensation of $13,000 a week.

At the age of forty-five, she once again was cast as a young girl, this time a streetwalker from the slums of London's Limehouse district.

Eventually, she marries a pastor, who in time inherits a lot of money. But when he distributes his fortune among the poor people of the slums, she abandons him for bestowing the money on those "wretched people" and not spending it on her.

Salome: The tragedy of the characters she portrayed seem to distill its way into the fabric of Nazimova's life.

Years later, in a chance meeting, she encounters her former husband. This time, the whoring sinner finds redemption.

Wallace Beery, who had dropped out of *A Doll's House,* agreed to appear with Nazimova, taking the minor fifth lead. Forgotten names like Milton Sills, Claude Gallingwater, and Courtenay Foote had the other male roles.

Reviews were bad. So was box office. One critic called Nazimova's performance "demeaning, cheap sentiment."

In 1925, Nazimova starred in *The Redeeming Sin* for Vitagraph. Based on a short story of the same name by L.V. Jefferson, it co-starred Lou Tellegen as her leading man. In spite of her fading allure at the box office, director J. Stuart Blackton still insisted on running her name above the title on movie posters.

The New York Times wrote, "The story requires a less heavy hand, but Nazimova redeems the picture. The fact is, the picture would be a sin without her."

The story was refilmed in 1929, this time starring Dolores Costello, after Warners purchased Vitagraph and acquired rights to all of its films.

Nazimova ended her silent film career when she made one final movie, *My Son* (1925), a drama directed by Edwin Carewe, and produced by First National. The brother of Mary Pickford, the gay actor, Jack Pickford, played her son, a character called Tony. As Ana Silva, Nazimova is a fisherman's widow.

Her son becomes infatuated with a "flapper," portrayed by the then relatively unknown blonde beauty, Constance Bennett, who appears seductively in a black satin bathing suit. The sister of the movie star, Joan Bennett, Constance would go on to become one of the reigning beauty queens of the 1930s as pictures learned to talk.

The setting of *My Son* was supposed to be a fishing village in New England, but it was actually filmed in a village in northern California.

During the shoot, Carewe made several promises to Nazimova about how he would try to resurrect her declining film career. But one fateful day, he met Dolores Del Rio, the Mexican beauty with the porcelain skin.

It was goodbye Nazimova, hello Dolores.

***

After Nazimova's long-delayed reunion with Tallulah Bankhead in New York in 1940, both women reflected on the ironies of fame. Although legendary in their heyday, each of them expected to be forgotten by a fickle public.

Both of them had appeared in only a limited amount of film work, as their greatest roles had been on the stage. Memory of that fades as generations come and go.

In her diary, Nazimova wrote: "I admit it…I am vain. When I die, there will be so little left to remember me by. A stage actress is completely dead when the last person to see her perform dies. I know that will be my inevitable fate when the last person to see me perform passes on."

"Perhaps some theatrical or film historian will discover me and bring life to my long-faded career. If Jesus Christ can pull off a Resurrection, surely the Great Alla Nazimova can, too. In my heyday, I was viewed as a goddess, not a mere mortal. Please, please, God, don't let me be forgotten like those silent screen stars like Mae Murray or Laura La Plante."

Nazimova, summoning her best energies after the failure of *Salome*, portrayed the female lead in *Madonna of the Streets*.

Her performance was rewarded with a new nickname: Queen of the Movie Whores.

***

After the commercial failures of *Salome* and *A Doll's House,* as well as a trio of lackluster silents, Nazimova fled from Hollywood, heading for the stage once again.

As she departed, she was painfully aware that other movie goddesses had begun occupying the lofty position she once had. Emerging as the screen vamps of the 1920s were Pola Negri, Gloria Swanson, Mae Murray, and, as of late, the Swedish actress, Greta Garbo.

"There is nothing left for me in California," Nazimova said, mournfully, as she boarded an Eastbound train.

"Before my 50th birthday, I was back on stage performing in plays by Mr. Ibsen," she said. "In the 1930s, I had my ups and down, more downs than ups. But there were triumphs along the way. A critic hailed my 1935 performance in *Ghosts* as the greatest performance she'd ever seen on the American stage."

Fifteen years would pass before Nazimova returned to Hollywood, occupying Villa #24 at the Garden of Allah, over which she had presided—during the glory days of silent pictures— as its Queen.

A bisexual, she would find herself cast in two movies, each starring the two leading bisexual movie stars of the early 1940s, Robert Taylor and Tyrone Power.

A figure from her distant past, Mercedes de Acosta, learned that Nazimova was back in Los Angeles and phoned her for a luncheon date at the Brown Derby. Arriving on time, Nazimova sat there for an hour, fearing that she had been stood up by Mercedes.

Finally, she arrived, apologizing for being late. "My darling Marlene kept me on the phone for an hour." Of course, she was referring to her ongoing affair with the screen goddess Marlene Dietrich.

Back in Hollywood on a Monday morning, Nazimova reported to the sound stages of MGM, the very studios over which she had reigned as Queen in 1920. That day was long gone. Now she was just a supporting player.

Originally, *Escape* (1940) was set to be directed by George Cukor, but at the last minute, MGM replaced him with Mervyn LeRoy, who was in the throes of launching a new screen goddess, the sultry, blonde-haired beauty, Lana Turner. *Escape,* a best-selling novel by Ethel Vance, had been acquired for $50,000 by MGM.

Its stars included Norma Shearer, who had reigned as MGM's queen in the 1930s, but was at the twilight of her career; and one of the hottest actors in Hollywood at the time, Robert Taylor, who greeted her. At the time, he was wed to Barbara Stanwyck in a sort of "lavender marriage."

The supporting cast included Conrad Veidt, who soon would be starring in one of the greatest movies ever made, *Casablanca* (1942), co-starring Humphrey Bogart and Ingrid Bergman.

Escape told the story of an American, Mark Preysing (Taylor), staying in pre-World War II Nazi Germany. There, he discovers that his mother, a famous German actress, Emmy Ritter (Nazimova), is being held in a Nazi concentration camp awaiting execution. He sets out to do whatever he can to help her escape death.

Norma Shearer was cast in *Escape's* lead role of Countess Ruby von Treck, an American-born widow. She is backed up by such stars as Philip Dorn, Bonita Granville, and Blanche Yurka.

[*Before the beginning of shooting, Nazimova learned that Yurka had lobbied to get*

When Nazimova returned to Hollywood, she met and worked with the new matinee idols of the late 1930s and '40s.

None were sexier than **Robert Taylor** (left) and **Tyrone Power** (right).

Taylor told her, "I'm a red-blooded man, and I resent people calling me pretty." Power said, "For anyone truly interested in the theater, like me, it's a tragedy to be born so handsome."

her role but had to settle instead for the smaller part of a nurse in a concentration camp.]

The studio would reteam Taylor with Shearer in her final picture, *Her Cardboard Lover*, in 1942. *[After sitting through the final cut of that classic, Shearer decided to bid her farewell to the screen, drifting into retirement.]*

When *Escape* was released, some critics attacked the performance of Nazimova "for acting like the star she was in silent pictures. What Miss Nazimova doesn't seem to realize is that the movies have learned to talk since her heyday."

Escape (1940) was a movie based on springing Robert Taylor's mother, portrayed by the aging **Nazimova** (right) from a concentration camp. The scheme was assisted by a demure and mature American-born Countess, played by a mature **Norma Shearer** (left), whose career was, like Nazimova's, on its last legs.

Before the war, Germany had been one of the most lucrative markets for Hollywood films. Hitler himself was an avid movie fan, but after demanding, receiving, and then screening a copy of *Escape* in Berlin, he ordered it banned throughout the Third Reich.

***

One of Nazimova's favorite silent screen flickers had been *Blood and Sand*, the 1922 film that had starred Valentino as the bullfighter, Juan Gallardo, the greatest matador of Spain. His leading ladies were sirens from the silents, Lila Lee and Nita Naldi. The plot was based on the best-selling novel by Vicente Ibáñez. This, the film's 1941 version (yet another would follow in 1989) would be directed by Rouben Mamoulian.

It came as a surprise when Director Mamoulian phoned Nazimova and offered her the role of the bullfighter's mother, with the understanding that it would be filmed and produced at 20th Century Fox, with Tyrone Power as a bullfighter, Juan Gallardo, alongside two rising stars of the 1940s, Rita Hayworth and Linda Darnell. A strong supporting cast had already been signed when Nazimova reported to work to meet John Carradine, J. Carrol Naish, Laird Cregar, Lynn Bari, and a future major star, Anthony Quinn. *[The Mexican actor bluntly told Nazimova, "You may be getting on in years, but if you want to sample what drives the girls crazy, call on me."]*

The film would be the fourth and last of the screen team of Darnell and Power, following *Daytime Wife* (1939), *Brigham Young (1940)*, and *The Mark of Zorro* (also 1940).

During its filming, Nazimova befriended Rita Hayworth, to whom she was physically attracted. Hayworth learned that Zanuck had wanted his mistress, Carole Landis, to play her role of Doña Sol des Muire, but Landis refused to dye her blonde hair. Before Hayworth got the role, it was also offered to Gene Tierney and to Dorothy Lamour.

Nazimova congratulated Mamoulian on his sets, which he told her were inspired by the paintings of El Greco, Goya, and Velázquez.

Although she'd played the two most glamourous figures of the silent screen—the title roles of both *Camille* and *Salome*—Nazimova was cast in *Blood and Sand* as a peasant scrubwoman, Señora Augustias.

Blood and Sand was a hit, but Nazimova knew its success had nothing to do with any box office appeal from her. On the dawn of America's entry into World War II, most of the people who flocked to see it had never seen Nazimova before in the movies.

***

At night, Nazimova returned to her villa at the Garden of Allah, and Mercedes became a frequent visitor, dropping in for a late afternoon "tea and a wafer."

Nazimova met her next-door neighbor, a young singer from Hoboken, New Jersey. She could hear Frank Sinatra practicing his singing from a nearby villa during the early morning hours.

"Hollywood has its peaks and valleys," **Nazimova** told her director Rouben Mamoulian when she reported to work on the remake of *Blood and Sand* (1941).

"Once I was a siren, the Queen of Metro. Now I'm reduced to a peasant scrubwoman whose son becomes a famous matador."

When she wasn't working, Nazimova attempted—but ultimately failed to produce—an autobiography of her fabled life.

For her next movie role, *In Our Time* (1944), Vincent Sherman, the lover of Bette Davis, asked her to appear in a new picture for producer Jerry Wald. Warners had already cast Ida Lupino and Paul Henreid in the leads.

Once again, Nazimova was cast as a matriarch, Zofia Onwid, the mother of Henreid, who played a Polish aristocrat, Count Stefan Orwid.

He meets, falls in love with, and marries Jenny Whittredge. He takes her home to meet his mother and other noble Polish relatives, who do not immediately welcome her, this English commoner.

The Polish story within the greater plot takes place when that country was entering its darkest hour: The invading forces of Nazi Germany were about to bomb Warsaw.

Nazimova thought so little of her role and her performance that she didn't bother to see it when it opened in Los Angeles.

***

Before leaving the screen forever, Nazimova would make two more films, both of them in 1944, when she took delight that Americans were winning the war against Imperial Japan and Nazi Germany. Director Rowland V. Lee offered her the role of the Marquesa, Doña Maria, in *The Bridge of San Luís Rey*.

A United Artists release, the script had been adapted from the famous novel written by Thornton Wilder. It starred two B picture actors, Lynn Bari and Frances Lederer, with Dimitri Tiomkin providing the musical score. Blanche Yurka, a rival actress of Nazimova, was also in the film, cast as "The Abbess."

Published as a novel in 1927, *The Bridge of San Luís* tells the saga of number of interrelated people who die in the collapse of an Inca rope bridge in Peru. It also details the events that foreshadowed their crossing of that bridge in its final moments. A witness to the disaster, Brother Juniper (Donald Woods) travels to Lima to seek cosmic answers about why those victims were chosen for such violent deaths.

The Wilder novel won the Pulitzer Prize in 1928 and became the best-selling novel of that year.

The Bridge of San Luís Rey had been made into a part talking film in 1929, starring Lili Damita, a French-born actress who would later marry Errol Flynn.

***

Nazimova's *adieu* to the screen was in *Since You Went Away* (1944), taking place in a setting on the homefront. It became one of the most popular movies released during the waning years of World War II.

Producer David O. Selznick had acquired the rights to film this popular novel. He hired John Cromwell to direct an all-star cast—and what a cast: Claudette Colbert, Jennifer Jones, Joseph Cotten, Shirley Temple, Monty Woolley, Lionel Barrymore, Robert Walker, Hattie McDaniel, Agnes Moorehead, Keenan Wynn, Craig Stevens, Dorothy Dandridge, and John Derek. The film introduced Guy Madison as a very appealing sailor. "The swoons could be heard in the balcony," wrote one reporter. From that point forward, Madison was launched as a movie star.

The film also introduced Rhonda Fleming in an uncredited role as "girl at a dance." In the 1950s, she would reign as "The Queen of Technicolor," appearing with such stars as Ronald Reagan.

Nazimova, cast as Zofia Koslowska, a working class immigrant employed in a shipyard, appeared on the screen for only six minutes.

She told Colbert, "I've been having dizzy spells. My clock is ticking. I fear I don't have much time left."

> The degree to which America and its Entertainment Industry had changed was screamingly apparent to Nazimova during the filming of her final movie, a romance based on "social distancing" during World War II.
>
> Each of her co-stars was hugely more sought-after by now than she was—and the sense of having been left behind was epic, indeed.

***

Hearing that Nazimova might be ill, her goddaughter, the starlet named Nancy Davis, came to visit her at the Garden of Allah. She was shocked and dismayed to see her living in reduced circumstances.

[Most of the world does not know that Nazimova was the godmother of Nancy Davis Reagan. It all began back in 1921, when Nazimova met and befriended her mother, Edith Luckett.]

Way back in 1921, while touring in the play, *Captain Shoals*, Nazimova formed a close relationship with Edith, a high school dropout who left school to become a stage actress. She had been cast in a small role as a passenger in a motorboat. Edith's father was a railroad clerk, and her mother ran a small boarding house in Washington, D.C.

Nazimova had been a long-ago pal and perhaps lover of *ingénue* **Edith Luckett** (left photo), who became the mother of starlette **Nancy Davis** (right photo.)

As First Lady of the United States, she faced roles more profound and influential than anything she ever confronted in Hollywood.

Edith eventually married Kenneth Robbins, an insurance salesman, but almost from the beginning, their union didn't work well. It did, however, produce a daughter, Anne Frances Robbins.

Edith eventually escaped with her daughter and soon became romantically involved with Nazimova, according to other cast members who starred with them in *Captain Shoals*.

Later, Edith married Dr. Loyal Davis, a neurosurgeon, who officially adopted (and gave his name to) young Nancy.

Soon after Nancy's reunion with her godmother in Hollywood, she invited Nazimova to meet her new beau, James Platt White, Jr., who was on leave from aircraft duty. Before he was introduced, Nancy said, "He's marvelous, the most wonderful man…and bright, too. After the war is over, he's going into politics. Maybe run for Congress from California, even governor. His eventual plan is to seek the presidency of the United States. Just think: You may be staring at your goddaughter, who will one day be First Lady of the United States."

Despite his engagement to Nancy, White dumped her three months later for another woman.

That did not destroy Nancy's dream of becoming First Lady.

She went on to marry a failing actor nearing the end of a lackluster film career. His name was Ronald Reagan.

***

On July 13, 1945, the great Nazimova, exotic star of yesteryear, died of coronary thrombosis at the age of sixty-six at the Good Samaritan Hospital in Los Angeles. Her ashes, according to her will, were interred at the Forest Lawn Memorial Park Cemetery in Glendale.

Today, pedestrians from all over the world walk on her star on the Hollywood Walk of Fame without a clue as to who she was.

***

To a new generation, the name of Nazimova came alive in the 1977 film *Valentino*. Directed by Ken Russell and starring ballet dancer Rudolf Nureyev as Valentino, the movie also starred Michelle Phillips as Natacha Rambova (Valentino's second wife), and Carol Kane as Jean Acker (his first wife). Nazimova was portrayed by Leslie Caron.

The film was such a failure that Russell called it "the biggest mistake of my career." Even seeing Nureyev almost completely naked did not attract the audience its backers had anticipated, although it did develop a mostly gay cult following.

In a gross caricature of Nazimova, Caron makes a spectacular entrance at Valentino's funeral. Impersonating her in mourning, Caron parades into a theatrical setting loaded with flowers. She carefully stage-manages her entrance, acting, in the words of one writer, like "a heroic tragedy-queen, her twenty-foot train of white camelias carried by a bevy of starlets. As they drape her train over the coffin, she — with stylized drama and theatricality — sinks down upon it. Then, after being informed that the photographers didn't get the shots they wanted, she repeats her dramatic scene, with equivalent *faux* pathos, again."

According to Nazimova, "There will never be another Valentino. There will never be another remotely like him. He was a god."

POSTSCRIPT

[As regards the film named Valentino *(1977), in real life, it was not Nazimova who staged the film's farcical mourning at the funeral home that prepared Valentino's body for burial. It was another screen vamp of the 1920s silent era, Pola Negri, a rival of Gloria Swanson.*

With the intention of greeting Valentino's funeral cortège, she had already staged a well-publicized arrival at Manhattan's Grand Central Station, where she encountered a coven of eager photographers and reporters.

Later, in Hollywood, with the intention of delivering a final farewell to his corpse she'd had a designer craft a stunning black dress for the then-staggering cost of $3,000. Then, even though she'd never married Valentino, the press incorrectly defined her costume as her "widow's weeds."

In addition to give the appearance of mourning Valentino's death, Negri simultaneously promoted her upcoming film, Hotel Imperial *(1927), in which she played a chambermaid who becomes the unwilling love object of an obnoxious general.*

From a florist, Negri had ordered a 12' x 6' blanket of scarlet roses, upon which she had garishly embedded her name, POLA in clusters of white carnations.

Later, her assistants draped the casket with this blanket of flowers. At the time and for years later, she was mocked for morphing Valentino's funeral into a farce and using it to promote herself.]

ALIA NASIMOFF, AKA ALLA NAZIMOVA, AKA

NAZIMOVA

(1879-1945)
ONCE THE HIGHEST-PAID ACTRESS IN SILENT FILMS

REST IN PEACE

CHAPTER SEVEN
MERCEDES' SEDUCTIONS OF VALENTINO'S WIVES

JEAN ACKER & NATACHA RAMBOVA

How "The Sheik of Araby" Got Cuckolded, by a Woman, Twice

DYSFUNCTIONAL TRIO
(LEFT TO RIGHT, JEAN ACKER, RUDOLPH VALENTINO, & NATACHA RAMBOVA)
MARITAL BLISS WAS NEVER AN OPTION

Valentino's marriage to starlet and part-time lesbian Jean Acker was one of the most bizarre in Hollywood history. It didn't even survive the wedding night. The Acker/Valentino wedding took place on November 5, 1919. Later that night, she slammed the bedroom door in his face.

On May 12, 1922, Valentino took Natacha Rambova as his second wife. He told a reporter, "No other woman ever made me touch ecstasy. All the rest were stuffed with sawdust."

Unfortunately, his divorce from Acker had not come through, so bigamy charges were filed. Not only that, but Natacha made it clear that conjugal relations would not be part of the deal. "Our love will be of the mind, not the body," she cautioned him.

It was just a chance meeting, but two of the most glamourous and enigmatic cultural figures of the 1920s were about to get launched into the celebrity-studded life of Mercedes de Acosta. They included Rudolph Valentino, the newly christened "Sex Symbol of the Silver Screen," and Natacha Rambova, a self-styled "goddess" and star of her own fabulous myth.

It was a cold February night in Manhattan in 1923, and the glittering pair—stars for a benefit of Actors Equity—had just appeared on stage to enchant a rapturous audience of devotees in the ballroom of the Hotel Astor. When Mercedes appeared in front of the dazzling couple, backstage, the evening's master of ceremonies, Charlie Towne, introduced her to them.

Mercedes had sat in the ballroom's front row, spellbound as they danced a tango. Valentino was dressed in the costume of Julio Nesnoyers, the character he'd played in *The Four Horsemen of the Apocalypse* (1921). As the newly crowned King of Hollywood, he would have a short but forever memorable reign before his tragic life came to an end.

Rambova, a costume designer,

Relentlessly avant garde, relentlessly stylish, and relentlessly unhappy together: In the upper photo, dressed as tango dancers, **Rudy and Natacha** made personal appearance tours across America. They launched a seventeen-week promotional tour of forty cities, for which they earned $7,000 a week.

She designed their costumes: A gaucho outfit for Rudy, evoking his role in *The Four Horsemen of the Apocalypse;* and she in Spanish attire crafted from black velvet and silk taffeta.

among other talents, was clad in a chic Andalusian-inspired dress crafted from velvet and black taffeta.

When they were introduced to Mercedes, the entertainers merely shook her hand before they were called back for an encore bow on stage. By then, the audience had risen to its feet as the clapping reached a crescendo.

Weeks went by before Mercedes encountered them again. She'd have been stunned if she'd known that in different ways, each would enter a chamber of her heart—Valentino as a dear friend and Rambova as her lover.

Mercedes had been so enthralled by them that she set about learning whatever she could about this romantic but mysterious pair, especially Rambova.

It would take Nazimova to bring Mercedes together with both of them upon their return to Hollywood.

***

When Mercedes published her autobiography, *Here Lies the Heart,* in 1960, it did not include the material that described her deep involvements with Rambova. Rambova, who was still alive at the time, had legally blocked its publication.

It was around this time when Darwin Porter entered Mercedes' life. Recognizing a kindred spirit in this fellow writer, she shared those written but unpublished chapters with him, as she did with others of her friends, too.

In 2001, rephrased and fully credited material, along with material culled from their many conversations, reappeared in his "non-fiction novel," *Hollywood's Silent Closet.*

What follows is a preview of the tantalizing secrets that Mercedes was not allowed to reveal to the world: i.e., details about Mercedes' love affair with Natacha Rambova and Valentino's first wife, Jean Acker.

The memories began with Acker's dramatic entrance into Mercedes' tumultuous, celebrity-studded life.

***

In Manhattan, in September of 1919, Nazimova became immediately intrigued with an attractive young woman she'd recently met, a former dancer in vaudeville. After a weekend together in Nazimova's hotel suite, she invited her to ride the train with her across the country and back to Hollywood. When they got there, Nazimova promised, she'd make her a star.

Her name later became Jean Acker. She entered movie history as the

Cast as **The Sheik** in 1920 (see poster), Valentino became the biggest star in Hollywood. Rambova violently opposed his taking the role, but women across America swooned to him as a swarthy Arab seducer in an erotic film about sex in a desert tent with super machismo.

In the lower photo, **Valentino** starred with **Vilma Banky** in the sequel,. *The Son of the Sheik* was the last film he made before his death that year. Despite their divorce, he continued to wear the slave bracelet Rambova had given him.

first wife of Rudolph Valentino, whom she would marry later that year.

Photoplay announced Nazimova's discovery: "Nazimova has brought back a new brand of perfumed cigarettes, together with a *protégée* who used to be known as Jeanne Acker, but who now prefers to call herself Jeanne Mendoza."

[The ambitious and budding starlet would later be billed as Jean Acker.]

Part Cherokee, the young beauty was twenty-six years old. During some of the previous summers, she had toured through North America with a summer stock troupe. Movie star Patsy Ruth Miller, a friend of both Valentino and Nazimova, thought that Acker looked mannish, often dressed in rigorously tailored suits more appropriate for a man of that day.

Installing her in a room at the Hollywood Hotel—not at her Garden of Alla—Nazimova used her star power to persuade MGM to offer her newest *protégée* a contract at MGM for $200 a week. It was very high pay for that day.

Then, with Nazimova's approval, MGM endeavored to change her image, posing her in shorts with a striped blouse and a Louise Brooks bullet-shaped hair bob.

The impressionable young starlet found herself at parties at the Garden of Alla, moving within a circle of the rich and very famous. Members included blonde-haired Mae Murray, already a movie queen; director George Cukor; screenwriter June Mathis, who would help Valentino morph into a superstar; actresses Patsy Ruth Miller and Dagmar Godowsky; and two of the era's most visible silent stars, sisters Constance and Norma Talmadge.

Amid this glittering assemblage, Acker felt out of place and sometimes sat in a far corner of the patio, speaking to no one.

Soon, another evening at another gathering, a lonely figure, Valentino, approached her, and

In a costume she designed for herself, **Natacha Rambova** performs one of her celebrated pantomimes.

Her terpsichorean talents were not star material, but she made up for it by presenting a striking figure on the stage, fascinating audiences with her attire and clever movements. She was less successful as a solo performer, having achieved far greater fame when she danced a *pas de deux* with Theodore Kosloff when he was her lover. Critics cited their "Sensuous exoticism."

Cameraman **Paul Ivano**—part of a tangled web of gender-bending Hollywood homo-intrigue.

He seemed an unlikely physical specimen, but he drifted between the boudoirs of both **Nazimova** and **Valentino**, infinitely preferring the love-making of "The Sheik."

they began to talk, opening up to each other. At the time, he was filming a movie called *Eyes of Youth* (1919).

Around the same time, she also met Grace Darmond, a minor actress appearing in B pictures. Acker was soon sleeping with Darmond, but continued to rendezvous with Valentino for "compassionate talks."

In the meantime, Nazimova conducted an on-again, off-again affair with Acker, working her in between other romantic entanglements.

For his sex life at the time, Valentino was living with cameraman Paul Ivano, who would later, at the ago of nineteen, also become the lover of Nazimova.

As the gay actor Clifton Webb said, "Hollywood was a tangled web of intrigue in those days. Changing partners and cheating spouses were all the rage."

As a struggling starlet, **Jean Acker** was asked to pose inspired by Louise Brooks, showing off her "gams" and with her hair styled into Brooks' trademark bullet-shaped bob.

At the time, Brooks—rivaled only by Clara Bow—was the flapper supreme of the 1920s. She became a symbol of the emerging sexual freedom for women and wanton Jazz Age caprice.

In the intensely competitive and erratic pecking order of silent-era Hollywood, Acker just didn't make the grade.

Screen vamp **Gloria Swanson and Rudolph Valentino** emote in the 1922 film *Beyond the Rocks*. She looked fantastic in a beaded gown that became a style setter, and Valentino was convincing, (scandalously) declaring his love for a married woman.

One critic defined their screen pairing as a "glamourous, clothes-and-jewel-bedrenched love story which set off their mutual electric chemistry."

To Nazimova's dismay (some described it as "horror"), Acker announced that she was going to marry Valentino. Long before he appeared as her romantic co-star in *Camille*, Nazimova had denounced him as a "dago gigolo."

"It wasn't just jealousy," Mercedes said. "Nazimova felt that Acker and Valentino were not the marrying kind, despite the fact that she, too, was engaged in a lavender marriage to Charles Bryant. Valentino seemed to want the same arrangement that Acker and Nazimova had with her 'husband.'"

Paul Ivano said that "Rudi married Acker in November of 1919 because he thought she was well connected and might advance his film career. He told me later that he did not know she was a lesbian, but that was a lie. Actually, Rudi wanted a cover for his homosexual activities, which were rampant at the time—not just with me, but with some of Hollywood's leading matinée idols."

In one of the most famous stories of that year, Acker was said to have locked Valentino out of her room on their wedding night.

According to Ivano, "She never planned to consummate the marriage, preferring it as 'only an arrangement,'" Ivano said. "Rudi spent his wedding night with me in my bed, but there was no sex. There may have been another reason Acker locked him out: Shortly after their wedding ceremony, he confessed to his new bride that he had gonorrhea. After that, he was off-limits to all of us until he was cured."

"Nazimova was no longer sleeping with Acker," Mercedes told Darwin Porter years later. "But I was, only occasionally. She was still living with Darmond, but those two actresses fought a lot. Personally, I thought neither of them had the charisma to become a real star in silent pictures. There were at least fifty major divas at the time, each of them competing ferociously for roles, each of them far more charismatic and photogenic than either Darmond or Acker. Frankly, neither of them seemed to have any real sex appeal for men, although Hollywood lesbians found Acker appealing. She was good in bed, giving freely of herself."

That December, Acker got her first job on a film called *The Roundup*, co-starring the ill-fated Fatty Arbuckle, who was on the verge of a major-league sex scandal that would destroy his career.

Thus, married life, if it could be called that, began disastrously for Valentino and Acker. She told him, "I not only don't want you in the same

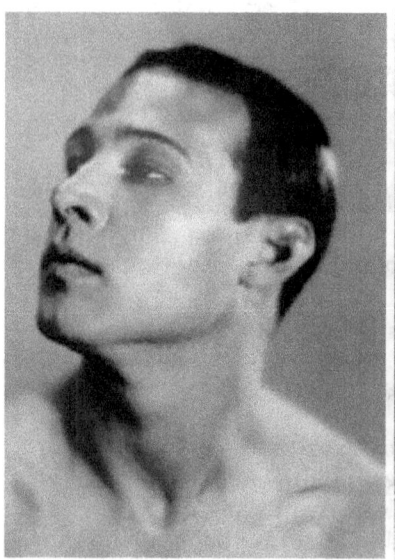
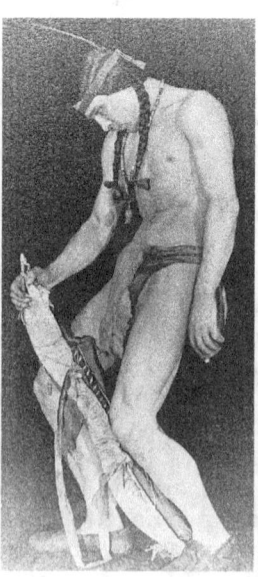
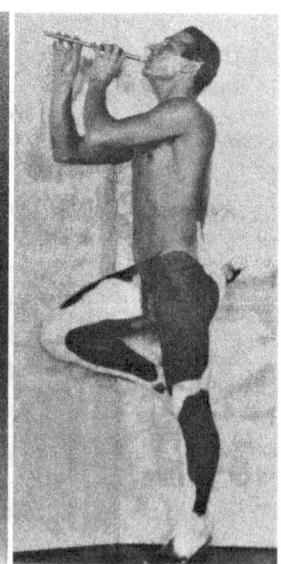

Valentino's fans were clamoring for publicity stills of him, preferably ones that showed off his body as much as was allowed. On the left, he appears shirtless, in the middle, almost nude as Black Feather, an Indian Brave; and on the right, seductively playing a flute, he pauses half-dressed in an enchanted forest as a faun.

room with me, but I don't want you in the same building with me."

Acker went on to say, "The best thing I ever did for Rudi was to urge him to quit having himself billed with that stupid name 'Rodolfo di Valentina' and change it to 'Rudolph Valentino.'"

After recovering from his venereal disease, Valentino embarked on one of the most promiscuous periods of his life. "I couldn't believe it," Ivano said. "He was seducing all these leading men in those days of silent pictures, even though many of them were married. Somehow, perhaps based on his sheer magnetism, he managed to intrigue and arouse sexual passion in them. He began drifting away from Acker the day he married her. They no longer had those soul-searching talks that they'd had at the beginning of their friendship.

"My affair with Acker was very limited," Mercedes said. "She wanted a lesbian relationship with someone who would also go horseback and motorcycle riding. That's not for me. I'm a parlor and boudoir lesbian."

When Valentino's breakup with Acker finally happened, and divorce was inevitable, both Mercedes and Nazimova agreed that their getting rid of each other was "not a loss for either of them."

A POSTSCRIPT

Mercedes never saw Jean Acker again after her divorce from Valentino. Acker found work in minor roles, sometimes as an uncredited extra, in films of the 1920s. By the advent of talkies, she was reduced to walk-ons, also uncredited. Her last appearance on the screen was in *How To Be Very, Very Popular* (1955), starring Betty Grable, whose own career was grinding to a halt.

Following her divorce from Valentino, Acker sued him for the right to bill herself as "Mrs. Rudolph Valentino," and won.

After they feuded for years, they made up shortly before his death in 1926. She wrote a popular song about him called "We Will Meet at the End of the Trail."

To his ardent fans, the image **Valentino** tried to convey was that of a red-blooded, All-American guy with a sense of playful fun.

Through it all, **Mercedes de Acosta**, depicted here in a grainy snapshot from the 1920s, did her best to navigate the rocky, sometimes steamy shores of a friendship with Valentino AND with each of his two (very difficult and demanding) wives.

After her breakup with Grace Darmond, Acker was said to have become involved with the Marquis de Bezan y Sandoval of Spain, but that didn't work out. Neither did her affair with Rahmin Bay or with William Delahanty, a married politician. She sued him, claiming that he had agreed to pay her $18,500 a year if she gave up her career and became his full-time mistress. He denied her accusations, though admitting he'd spent thousands of dollars on her.

After that scandal, she met and bonded with Chloë Carter, a former Ziegfeld Follies dancer, the first wife of film composer Harry Ruby.

Acker lost all her money in the Wall Street Crash of 1929, but she and Carter recovered and bought a small apartment building in Beverly Hills, which provided them with an income for life.

She and Carter remained a couple until Acker's death on August 16, 1978 at the age of 84. She is buried next to Carter in the Holy Cross Cemetery in Culver City, California.

Forgotten today, but a very big deal when Silents reigned.

Here's **Grace Darmond**, Jean Acker's comfort zone after her breakup from THE SHEIK.

***

A new woman, Natacha Rambova, far more ravishing than Jean Acker, was about to enter the lives of both Mercedes and Nazimova, soon becoming a part-time lesbian lover to each of them. *[Natacha Rambova, some said, managed to be more intimidating and formidable than both of them, combined. She was as different from Jean Acker as Elizabeth Taylor was from Lauren Bacall.]*

Rambova, despite her self-proclaimed associations with the romance and drama of Old Russia, originated as Winifred Kimball Shaughnessy in January of 1897 in Salt Lake City. She was the thoroughly American daughter of a Federal Marshal charged with the enforcement of anti-polygamy laws in the Mormon enclaves of Utah.

She was reared in San Francisco. Her parents eventually divorced, and she was sent to live with her lesbian aunt, Elsie de Wolfe, a flamboyant socialite credited as the mother of modern interior decorating.

Educated in England, Rambova trained as a dancer, eventually shacking up with Theodore Kosloff, the noted Russian ballet virtuoso and choreographer. She joined his ballet troupe, which toured America on the vaudeville circuit. When she was nineteen, she migrated to Hollywood, where she was hired by Cecil B. De Mille as both a costume designer and a performer. Impressed with his muscular grace, the director cast Kosloff in his movie, *The Woman God Forgot* (1917).

Tensions arose when Kosloff was hired to design a movie set and persuaded Rambova to do the sketches. Passing them off as his own, he presented them to De Mille.

Rambova became disillusioned with him, especially when she came home early one afternoon and found him in bed with two ten-year-old girls.

Kosloff sent Rambova to the Garden of Alla to present some sketches to Nazimova. The great star was so impressed with how quickly she made alterations that she hired her as her art director and costume designer, paying her $5,000 per picture, the equivalent of $65,000 in 2020 currency.

Powerfully attracted to this Utah beauty, who looked both foreign and exotic, Nazimova quickly moved in with her, inducting her into lesbian love. She put her to work at once on her latest film, *Billions* (1910), all copies of which are believed to have been lost.

Rambova attended one of the notorious outdoor parties at the Garden of Alla hosted by Nazimova. It was here, one hot night, that she met Mercedes de Acosta, who would eventually become her lover.

In addition to working for Nazimova, Rambova also designed two films for De Mille, *Why Change Your Wife?* (1919) and *Something to Think About* (1920).

In 1921, she was credited as the art director for the De Mille Epic, *Forbidden Fruit*, for which she designed an elaborate costume for a Cinderella-inspired fantasy sequence for screen diva Agnes Ayres.

Natacha also began work on the elaborate sets and costumes for *Aphrodite,* a movie that was never made. She decided to end her tumultuous relationship, packed her luggage, and began moving out of Kosloff's home.

Rambova with **Theodore Kosloff** in "Aztec Dance"

Natacha Rambova was not the only wildly flamboyant costume designer of her era. Depicted above is Russian dancer **Theodore Kosloff** as "The Spirit of Electricity" in Cecil B. De Mille's *Madam Satan*. Released during the early, most frantic year (1930) of the Depression, it was reviewed as "a delightfully bizarre mélange of song, dance, bedroom farce and airship disaster."

Learning of her impending departure, he roared into his living room with a hunting rifle and fired at her, wounding her above her left knee. Flesh, bone, and blood exploded as she screamed in agony, convinced that she'd been fatally wounded.

Rushed to the hospital in an ambulance, she spent a week there, recovering. Mercedes and Nazimova visited regularly, as she vowed never to see Kosloff again. She did not press charges.

Her reputation as a designer grew as she favored, in the words of one reporter, "bright colors (even though the films she worked on were in black and white), baubles, bangles, shimmering draped fabrics, and foreign effects in both costume and stage design."

After watching how beautifully Valentino emoted in *The Four Horsemen of the Apocalypse* (1921), Nazimova changed her mind about him and cast him opposite her in *Camille* (also 1921). Based on Alexander Dumas *fils*, romantic novel, *La dame aux Camélias*, it was interpreted as a thorough "modern" reinterpretation of that classic, tear jerking heart breaker.

To their collective disappointment, *Camille* bombed at the box office, leading to the firing of Nazimova. Still locked into a sham marriage to Jean Acker, Valentino drew closer and closer to Rambova.

Both of them were spiritualists, and they frequently visited psychics and took part in *séances* that focused on "automatic writing" sessions which, in theory, at least, allowed communications with the dead. Sometimes, they invited Mercedes along, since she, too, was interested in the occult.

It was during the production of *Camille* that Rambova and Valentino became involved, sometime near the "tail end" of Mercedes' sexual affair with Rambova.

The newly forged romantic pair (Valentino and Rambova) slowly began to bond and form

Agnes Ayres, wearing a costume designed by Natacha Rambova, in Cecil B. De Mille's 1921 costume drama, *Forbidden Fruit*.

The drama ran high, and the couture was very *haute*, indeed.

a friendship. Nazimova thought he brought out a maternal instinct in Natacha, as she had sympathy for this "sad, lonely, foreigner," who spoke both French and Italian and was far, far away from home in a strange land. Both had been either reared in or spent significant time in England and/or Europe, and they exchanged stories of their experiences there, all of them radically different from the norm in Hollywood.

As the best cook of the lot, Valentino prepared Italian dinners for Paul Ivano (his lover), Nazimova, screenwriter June Mathis, and, on occasion, Mercedes.

In 1922, Natacha designed the costumes for *Beyond the Rocks*, a drama directed by Sam Wood in which Valentino co-starred with Gloria Swanson, based on a story by Elinor Glyn.

This was a glamourous clothes-and-jewelry-drenched love melodrama. In it, Swanson plays a society girl who marries a rich and much older man to please her father. She is saved by a handsome English lord, who prevents her from tumbling down the side of an Alp and then falls madly in love with her.

Swanson appears in glittering costumes, and Valentino is an elegant dandy. One critic reviewed the costumes designed by Rambova as "ridiculously overblown and even outrageous attire, fantasy designs out of control."

In *The Young Rajah* (1922), Natacha, through her costumes, seriously compromised Valentino's image as a Latin Lover. In his most memorable scene, he is virtually nude except for jewels, pompons, and a skimpy loincloth much smaller than the one Tarzan made famous. An even more provocative scene had him carrying a boat over his head. The outline of his penis is clearly visible through his shorts.

Confronted with scenes they considered unacceptable, many censors controlling film distribution in their respective states refused to allow *The Young Rajah* to be exhibited.

"Natacha and I were never in love, but I was attracted to her both physically and spiritually," Mercedes said. "But with Valentino, it was a purely spiritual link. All three of us were intrigued by ancient religions. In time, Natacha taught us both yoga and astrology. She was also a specialist in Egyptology."

"Had Natacha wished, she could have successfully pursued a social or artistic life," Mercedes said, "But she chose a more difficult path of the mind. It was the way that all sincere seekers of The Truth must see, sooner or later, and follow The Way toward anonymity and seclusion."

One night, Natacha shocked Mercedes by arrogantly announcing that she'd "recreate Valentino into an image of her choice."

"I can mold him like a figure of clay into this godlike being on the screen, a leading man like no other the world has ever seen," Natacha boasted. "The raw material is there. I must refine it."

Much of the success of *The Young Rajah* was based on Rambova's provocative costumes. **Valentino** appears above in a loincloth to which was attached jewels, pompons, and several strings of pearls wrapped around his thighs and legs.

Valentino and Rambova lived together throughout most of his legally binding but unconsummated marriage to Jean Acker. Their relationship was based on friendship and shared interests, not on sexual attraction. Mercedes and Nazimova each warned Natacha not to marry Valentino, and Nazimova made her skepticism about the duration of the union clear, warning Valentino that Natacha would "swallow him like a boa constrictor."

"I told Natacha that she and Valentino should remain as spiritual friends, not even attempting to bring it to a physical level," Mercedes said. "He had Paul Ivano for lovemaking, plus some of Hollywood's finest leading men. I knew that if they got married, divorce would be inevitable, and he hadn't officially divorced Acker yet. Frankly, she was convinced that he was going to become a big star, and that if she could ride on his coattails as 'Madame Valentino,' she could become a big star, too."

An early attempt to legalize their union transpired, disastrously, on May 13, 1922 in Mexicali, Mexico. California law required that a year must pass before Valentino would be free to remarry after his divorce from Acker. After the ceremony, when he returned to Los Angeles, he was jailed for bigamy, having to be bailed out by friends.

Nine months later, on March 14, 1923, after the requisite waiting period had ended, Valentino and Rambova were married in a ceremony that authorities accepted as legal. It was conducted in Crown Point, Indiana.

***

Unwilling to "out" himself in public, Valentino rejected a role as the male lead in Nazimova's *Salome* (1923), since

Rambova and Valentino pose for their wedding photo in front of the home of the mayor of Mexicali. His Honor booked a string quartet and a military band to entertain guests at the ceremony. Natacha looks grim.

Valentino (right) as the dashing hero—the Duc de Chartres/Beaucaire—in the 1924 silent film, *Monsieur Beaucaire*.

Although Natacha designed the costumes with spectacularly crafted references to the *ancien regime* of 18th-century France, audiences most clearly remembered scenes (see above) where costumes didn't seem to matter.

The setting is the court of Louis XV. Bebe Daniels, cast as Princess Henriette, was his leading lady.

Natacha was blamed for Valentino's appearance as "less than manly, in heavy make-up, frilly attire, and overly feminized mannerisms."

every player in the cast had been proudly predefined to the press as gay, in homage to Oscar Wilde.

Natacha's involvement as its set and costume designer provided a platform from which she could be as exotic, outrageous, and flamboyant as she wanted.

In the words of one critic, "*Salome* reflects a homogeneity among players, and the décor is evocative of French expressionist cinema, but with unusual elegance. She stunningly combined the straight silhouettes of Art Deco *haute couture* with ancient Asian and European curves and florets, using shimmering silvers, whites, and blacks, all of them memorably interpreted Aubrey Beardsley drawings."

Natacha was at her most outrageous when she signed to design her husband's costumes as showcased in *Monsieur Beaucaire* (1924). Besotten with conflicts, it eventually emerged as the most high camp movie of the 1920s.

As biographer David Bret wrote, "No role could have been better set for critical lampooning, 'The World's Greatest Lover' appearing on screen in silken breeches, powdered wigs, and sporting twin heart-shaped beauty spots while his limp-wristed courtiers minced around him, one of whom pouts at the camera before fixing his lipstick and plucking his eyebrows! Rudy is seen perched on a balustrade, plucking a ridiculously long, phallic-shaped lute, which in an early scene in the film he does, admittedly held provocatively."

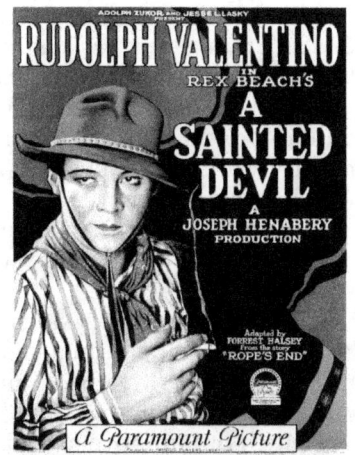

Valentino with Helena d'Algy in *A Sainted Devil* (1924). Rambova objected to the script, but Valentino defied her. In it, he played a drunkard who sails down to the jungles of South America to rescue his wife from bandits.

Valentino, in heavy makeup and frilly attire, acted with arch mannerisms and a feminized movements. Natacha was blamed by his male fans for making him appear effeminate and fey in the movie, accusing her of "de-masculizing" him." At this point in her career, she was known as "the most disliked woman in 1920s Hollywood."

In *A Sainted Devil* (1924), Natacha did not like Valentino's role as Dom Alonzo Castro, a drunkard who rushes to a South American jungle to save his wife from bandits. When she showed up, early in the filming, with designs for her husband's costumes, his co-star, Jetta Goudal, the exotic French actress, mocked them: "Your costumes were designed for an effeminate male or else for a deformed woman."

[In retaliation, Rambova flexed her muscles as Valentino's manager by having Goudal fired the next day and replaced with Dagmar Godowsky, the actress who had introduced Valentino to Nazimova.]

When Valentino signed with United Artists in 1925, it was contingent on Rambova's removal and banishment from his professional life. This public humiliation damaged her career and contributed to their divorce, which was granted in 1925.

The world mourned when Valentino died on August 23, 1926. After registering the news, some women in America and England committed suicide.

Long after their passions faded, Mercedes continued following Rambova's career. She influenced designers such as Adrian, whom she had hired for his first feature film, and she greatly inspired the attitude and output of the photographer, Cecil Beaton.

Much of Rambova's work has been lost. Although she had divorced Valentino, she was shocked by his early death at the age of 31 the following year.

***

In the early 1950s, Rambova developed schleroderma, adversely affecting her throat and damaging her ability to speak and to swallow. It led to severe malnutrition. As the years went by, she also became delusional, believing that one of Valentino's lovers had returned from the grave and was plotting to poison her.

On September 29, 1965, it was reported that she had gone berserk in a hotel elevator in Manhattan and had to be admitted to Lenox Hill Hospital. She was diagnosed with "paranoid psychosis" that was aggravated by her ongoing malnutrition.

At the age of 69, on June 5, 1966, Natacha Rambova *[aka "Madame Valentino"]* died.

Her body was cremated, her ashes, according to her will, scattered within a dense forest in northern Arizona.

In an irony of fame, she had been largely forgotten by the entertainment industry and the world in general.

Mercedes de Acosta would survive her by only two years.

A late-in-life photo of **Natacha Rambova.** Still relentlessly preoccupied with aesthetics, her outrageous glamour and flamboyant costumes belonged to another day. Much subdued and demoralized, at this stage of her life, she evoked a mousey secretary.

REST IN PEACE

Rudolph Valentino (1895-1926);
Natacha Rambova (1897-1966);
Jean Acker (1893-1978)

In retrospective, **Valentino**, in part because of the makeup and costume effects of his imperious and demanding wife, **Natacha Rambova**, was one of the most daring ambisexual symbols in of the silent era.

Counterclockwise from upper left, he appears 1) as a surfer in *The Young Rajah*; 2) in beautiful, partially undressed proximity to Natacha herself; 3) as a darkly symbolic icon of raw male sexuality (i.e., a desert sheik); 4) as a foppish dandy at Versailles in *Monsieur Beaucaire (*in a costume for which he was mercidlessly mocked); and 5) as a pansexual object of beauty in a pose rarely, if ever, adopted by other male sex symbols of his era.

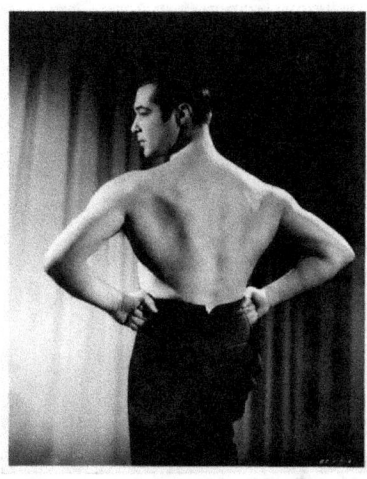

Rudolph Valentino, His Wives, & Mercedes de Acosta

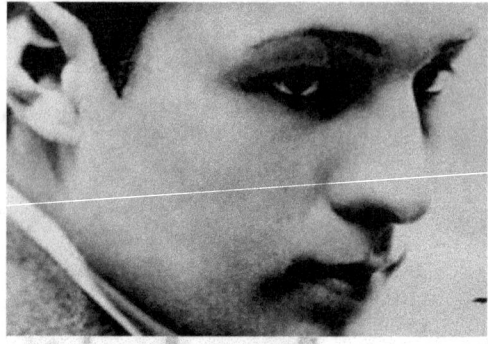

Partly to combat the ridicule he confronted for the "out there" sexuality that made him a lust and love object for fans throughout America, **Valentino** aggressively pursued boxing, his favorite sport.

Here he's seen in an exhibition fight with Gene Delmont at the Los Angeles Sports Club. The referee is the former world's heavyweight boxing champion Jack Dempsy. The photo was snapped just six weeks before Valentino's death in New York.

WANNA KNOW MORE ABOUT WHO WAS DOING WHAT TO WHOM IN THE PANSEXUAL FRENZY OF PRE-CODE HOLLYWOOD?

In 2001, **Darwin Porter** wrote and **The Georgia Literary Association** published an unvarnished overview of the *brouhahas* behind the über-dramas of silent-era Hollywood.

Drawn from eyewitness accounts from then-elderly players in the "anything goes" years when everyone knew everyone in La-La land, and widely reviewed by the LGBT press at the time of its publication, it is available everywhere, online, now.

HOLLYWOOD'S SILENT CLOSET

THE LUSTY SAGA OF AMERICA'S FIRST STAR-F*^%CKER

by Darwin Porter
ISBN 978-0-966803-02-0

The real story of Sessue Hayakawa, Thomas Ince, Marion Davies, Charlie Chaplin, Tom Mix, John Barrymore, Douglas Fairbanks, Sr., Wallace Reid, Theda Bara, Mary Pickford, William Boyd, and many other "soaked in scandal" household names.

CHAPTER EIGHT
Les Desmoiselles de la rue de Fleurus

GERTRUDE STEIN & ALICE B. TOKLAS
Mercedes' Affair with The World's Most Celebrated Lesbian Couple

Alice B. Toklas and **Gertrude Stein** pose against a backdrop of ivy and ancient masonry in 1934 in Chamborg, France. They were visiting the villa where Jean-Jacques Rousseau (1712-1778) lived with his mistress, Mme. de Warens, for a decade beginning in 1731.

[This writer, of course is not to be confused with their friend, Henri Rousseau (also known as Le Douanier), the French artist (1844-1910), known for his richly colored paintings of jungles and wild beasts.]

Center photo: **Toklas** (left) and **Stein** descend onto the tarmac in Chicago after their first airplane flight during an American lecture tour that same year.

Gertrude Stein and Alice B. Toklas were the most famous lesbian couple of the 20th Century, enjoying their heyday in Paris with what Gertrude defined as "The Lost Generation."

Stein was a giant of literature, an American novelist, poet, playwright, and fabled art collector. In 1933, she published a quasi-memoir of her Paris years, *The Autobiography of Alice B. Toklas.* Although written by Stein, it was in the voice of her lifetime companion, Miss Toklas.

The book became a bestseller and vaulted Gertrude from the relative obscurity of cult literature into the glare of mainstream acclaim. Even to people who had never read her, she was a literary lion and legend. Her most famous quotation was "a rose is a rose is a rose." Critics dubbed her "The Third Rose."

The ever-faithful Alice, not a world class beauty, was a woman of intellect and charm. She was defined and made famous by her relationship with Gertrude, which lasted for almost forty years until Stein's death in 1946.

Gertrude Stein, the youngest of five children, was born on February 3, 1874 in Allegheny Pennsylvania, a community which later merged with Pittsburgh. Her parents were Jewish, her father a well-to-do realtor.

As a young girl, Gertrude learned English and German. For a while, her parents lived abroad in both Vienna and Paris.

She lost her parents when she was young, and her beloved brother, Leo, became like a surrogate father to her.

She attended Radcliffe College from 1893 to 1897, later enrolling in Johns Hopkins School of Medicine for four years, though she seemed to have little interest in becoming a doctor. She finally dropped out, citing boredom.

"Besides, men dominate the field of medicine," she said. "I was struggling to find an identity of my own."

It was at Johns Hopkins that she realized she was a lesbian, getting involved with a fellow student, Mabel Haynes., Stein called it, "my erotic awakening."

In 1902, her brother, Leo, told her he was leaving for London, and she uprooted herself and followed him. Within a year, the brother and sister settled in Paris, which was to become her permanent home.

It was while installed at 27 rue de Fleurus in the city's 6th *arrondissement* that they began to collect art and to meet up-and-coming artists such as Paul Cézanne. Among the early paintings they acquired were two Renoirs, Gauguin's *Sunflowers,* and Cézanne's *The Bathers.*

[They also purchased Cézanne's Portrait of Mme Cézanne, Delacroix's *Perseus and Andromeda,* and—two of their finest acquisitions—Picasso's Young Girl with a Basket of Flowers and Matisse's Woman with a Hat. Other artists whose work was acquired included Pierre

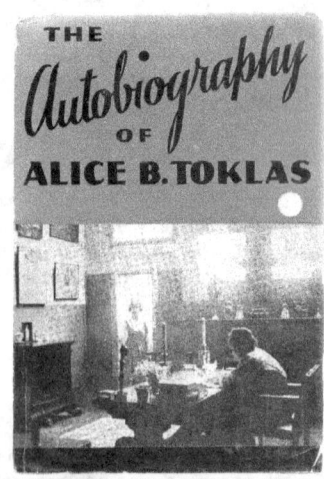

Cover art of its first edition, published in 1933 by Harcourt, Brace & Co. with a shot of the relentlessly avant-garde Stein-Toklas apartment at **27 rue de Fleurus, Paris 6.**

Bonnard, Honoré Daumier, Henri Manguin, and Toulouse-Lautrec.]

Leo and Gertrude began to amass one of Paris' greatest collections of modern art. They seemed to have a radar about which artists, such as Matisse or Picasso, would one day become celebrated. Their collection grew and grew until it lined the walls of their apartment in tiers, trailing many feet to the (very high) ceilings.

As the 1930s moved on, and after her 1914 split with Leo, Gertrude turned to other artists such as Juan Gris, Sir Francis Rose, and André Masson. The Spanish painter, Francisco Riba Rovira, did her portrait.

In the winter of 1905 and 1906, Gertrude posed for Picasso when he created the most celebrated of all literary portraits. It would take eighty sittings. Day after day, she trudged over to the Right Bank and entered his ramshackle Bateau Lavoir studio. Warmth was provided by a potbellied stove.

***

Alice B. Toklas was born in 1877 to Polish Jewish parents living in San Francisco. She was educated at the University of Washington. After the devastating earthquake that destroyed San Francisco in 1906, Toklas moved to Paris. On her second day in the city, September 8, 1907, she was introduced to Gertrude Stein. Her life would be changed for all time.

The day after Alice was introduced to Gertrude, the older woman called her and invited her for a walk in the Luxembourg Gardens. It was while looking at birds drinking from a fountain that Gertrude asked, "Will you be my bride? I want you for my wife. I'll make a fine and proud husband for you."

Alice said "yes" and received the first of thousands of kisses from her

Perhaps because she was a revered collector or their art, and perhaps because they were genuinely intrigued by her pervasive aura of masculine authority and aplomb, artists seemed to compete in renderings of **Gertrude Stein**'s portrait. Left, above, is a depiction of Stein by Pablo Picasso; right above is by Felix Valloton.

matronly looking spouse-to-be.

"Stein was vastly overweight, with closely cropped hair," Zelda Fitzgerald asserted, "She dressed like a German scrubwoman, but when she spoke, she created a spell of rhapsody around her. You were drawn to her words like a moth to a flame."

The dowdy-looking Stein was a woman of mystery, known as "the most obscure, yet the most famous, female writer in the English language."

"She was a literary lioness," Picasso said, "though she would have preferred to be known as a literary lion."

As Alice remembered Gertrude: "She was a golden brown presence, burned by the sun and with a golden glint in her warm brown hair. She often wore a brown corduroy suit and a large, round, coral brooch. When she talked, I thought her voice came from that brooch. It was unlike anyone else's voice—deep, full, velvety like a great contralto, like two voices. She was large and heavy, with delicate small hands and a beautifully modeled and unique head."

Within a week of their bonding, the two women developed nicknames for each other—"Lovie" for Gertrude and "Pussy" for Alice.

As a couple, Gertrude and Alice hosted a fashionable literary salon at 27 rue de Fleurus, "bringing together confluences of talent and thinking that helped define modernism in literature and art," as one of their guests phrased it.

Dedicated attendees included Paul and Jane Bowles (a gay/lesbian Anglo-American couple), Ernest Hemingway, F. Scott and Zelda Fitzgerald, Matisse, Picasso, Thornton Wilder, Ezra Pound, Sherwood Anderson, Georges Braque, Max Jacob, Henri Rousseau, Guillaume Apollinaire, Cecil Beaton, Jean-Paul Sartre, Jean Cocteau, columnist Janet Flanner, Edith Sitwell, and Carl Van Vechten.

A critic for the *New York Sun* wrote: "Gertrude Stein collected geniuses rather than masterpieces. She spotted them a mile away."

While Gertrude talked to the giants of literature and art, Alice shopped for fresh food, did some gardening out back, walked the dogs in the Luxembourg Gardens, knitted gloves and blankets, and embroidered "a rose is a rose is a rose" on handkerchiefs, which she gave to everybody from Zelda Fitzgerald to columnist Janet Flanner.

She also poured tea and sat with the wives of geniuses. They included Hem-

Stein and Toklas documented their travels from their base in Paris to other parts of Europe in ways that are interpreted today as nostalgic odes to ways of life long gone with the wind.

Although their travels in the late 1920s through fast-changing Spain ("See Spain now, before it's gone forever") this photo was snapped in 1908 in Venice, where the "desmoiselles" were two of hundreds of well-upholstered women of means looking for art and meaning beyond the immediate circumstances of their station and wealth.

ingway's wife, Hadley; Elisabeth de Gramont, Mildred Aldrich, Jane Peterson, and Fernande Olivier, the mistress of Picasso. Alice paid special attention to the painter, Marie Laurencin, the mistress of Apollinaire. Jane Bowles, the emotionally unstable lesbian and American wife of English-born Paul Bowles, evolved into a particular favorite of Alice.

"Oh, those glorious days in Paris!" author Anaïs Nin told Darwin Porter. "In the 1920s, Paris was a haven for lovers of all persuasions, and it oozed a kind of lesbian chic. We danced in the clubs. We patronized the cafés and bars. We moved into the orbit of such figures as Violet Trefusis, and Vita Sackville-West. F. Scott Fitzgerald and Ernest Hemingway were in town often. The first time I met Picasso, he invited me into his boudoir where, later, he asked to paint me."

In addition to being Gertrude's lover, Alice was also a cook, secretary, muse, editor, critic, and general organizer of the life of Gertrude Stein. She was also a writer herself.

Poet James Merrill visited Stein in Paris. "Before meeting her, I knew about her tiny stature, the sandals, the mustache, the eyes., But one did not anticipate the enchantment of her speaking voice—like a viola at dusk."

In a memoir, W.G. Rogers wrote:

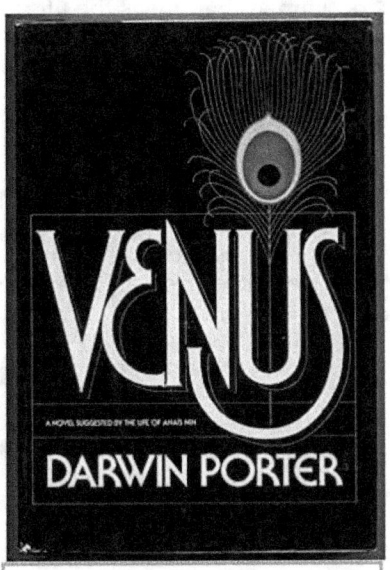

Darwin Porter's frenemy and inspiration, **Anaïs Nin.** "Would you like to read my pornography?" she asked him. "I wrote it when I was young, in Pairs and was paid two dollars a page."

In 1982, Darwin released **Venus**, a novel suggested by the life of the feminist literary icon, **Anaïs Nin**. For decades, he'd been captivated by stories of her years in Paris in the 1920s, moving within the inner circles of Henry Miller, Gertrude Stein, and Alice B. Toklas.

Darwin agreed with the assessment of author Erica Jong: "Anaïs left so many trails of clues about her several lives that she could have confounded Sherlock Holmes himself."

Feminists and literary scholars from academia and pop culture flocked to meet her at Darwin's home (Magnolia House) to learn more about her scandal-soaked and very competitive life and travails.

Les Demoiselles de la rue de Fleurus: Toklas & Stein

"She gives the appearance, in short, not of a drudge, but of a poor relation someone invited to the wedding but not the wedding feast."

***

Alice said, "I learned about life and all its pain and all its glories by typing and editing the manuscripts of Gertrude. When reading her copy, I knew I was in the presence of a genius of modern literature."

Arthur Nigel Cawthorne wrote: "A dedicated modernist, much of the work of Gertrude Stein is so inaccessible that it is unreadable. Her defenders claimed that it was the literary equivalent of cubism. The Hearst press asked in exasperation: 'Is Gertrude Stein not Gertrude Stein but somebody else living and talking in the same body?' More recent, and more partisan, commentators suggest that her elliptical tongue is motivated by a desire to unleash the lesbian tongue—surely it could be put to better use?"

Gertrude once admitted to Hemingway that she might be the only person in the world other than Alice who understood the exact meaning of her words. She said, "The central theme of the novel is that they were glad to see each other."

In reference to that, a critic asked, "Just what in hell does that mean?"

Over the course of Gertrude's life, she wrote novels, plays, libretti, and poems in what a critic called "a highly idiosyncratic, playful, repetitive, and humorous style."

In writing of her home in Oakland, she said, "There is no there there." One of her most famous literary remarks was, "Sugar is not a vegetable." One especially enigmatic quote was widely reprinted: "The change of color is likely and a difference a very little difference is prepared."

The published writings of Gertrude Stein were evaluated by one critic as "Stream-of-consciousness experiments, rhythmical essays or 'portraits' designed to evoke the excitingness of pure being. It is literature's answer to visual art styles and forms such as Cubism."

Only the most avant-garde press praised her works. The mainstream press either ignored her or, if writing about her works, failed to interpret her meaning.

Eccentric, ideosyncratic, odd, and at the center of the Lost Generation's artistic cross-currents stood **Toklas** (left) and **Stein.**

"The first time I met Stein, and spent some time with her, she stood up after three hours and told me it was time to go, our talk to be resumed tomorrow," Mercedes said. "In departing, Miss Stein found herself intensely kissed on her eyes and on her succulent mouth."

Even so, Gertrude became a noted figure in the 1920s, mainly for her personality. She and Alice, hailed as "the odd couple," were widely photographed. She was also written about because of her fabulous art collection and her friends, who included both Picasso and Hemingway. Of course, it was her lesbian notoriety that generated speculation and comment, much of it presented as caricature.

One reviewer made this claim: "Social judgment is absent in the writing of Miss Stein, so the reader is empowered to decide how to think and feel about her writing. Anxiety, fear, and anger are so absent in her works, which are harmonic and integrative."

English teachers often suggest to students who want to explore the writings of Gertude to begin with *Three Lives,* which she wrote in the spring of 1905 and finished the following year. It is not a novel, but three short stories, each a psychological portrait of two impassive German women and a young black woman.

She made the claim that her work was influenced by the portrait Cézanne had painted of his wife. During her writing sessions, she sat in a chair under the portrait of Madame Cézanne, creating her characters drawn from women she'd known.

Her most monumental work was *The Making of Americans,* which she wrote from 1902 to 1911. She compared her work to that of *Ulysses* by James Joyce and *In Search of Lost Time (A la recherche du temps perdu)* by Marcel Proust. She kept the manuscript locked away until 1924 when, at the urging of Hemingway and others, she began to publish part of it. *[The full version of this monumental work was not released until 1966.]*

The book was called a "queer psychological experiment with more ambition than insight." Even though it was denounced by critics, she considered it her masterpiece.

Her biographer, James R. Mellow, wrote, "Her writing style is slow and ponderous. The simplest ideas and observations are introduced and worried over endlessly. The pace of the novel is elephantine; the plot, such as it is, lumbers forward, foraging in strange jungles of psychological observation."

Her only bestseller was *The Autobiography of Alice B. Toklas,* published in 1933. No other work lifted her from a literary cult into celebrity across America. *[Of course, it was not a real autobiography: Its title was adopted as a literary conceit.]*

It was eventually reviewed by the distinguished poet, John Malcolm Brinnin, who wrote, "Some of the book's whimsical preferences in food, landscape, and literature belong to the book's nominal subject, some of its speech rhythms, and most of its personal peccadilloes. But the impulsive egotism that gives zest to the book and the four-square glory it celebrates are wholly Gertrude Stein, and so are its wise-child style, its self-centered recalls, and its maternal murmur."

***

Mercedes' sister, Rita Lina Hernández de Alba, was already socially connected in Paris, moving in the world of such lesbian hostesses as Natalie Barney and the American painter, Romaine Brooks. Sunday lunches were at the villa in Versailles of Elisabeth Marbury and Elsie de Wolfe (aka Lady Mendl). One afternoon, Rita escorted her sister, Mercedes, to a Sunday luncheon at the apartment of Gertrude and Alice.

For Mercedes, it was the beginning of a long-enduring friendship with these two famous and formidable lesbians, who presided over an array of artistic and literary personages.

"The following night was fabulous," Mercedes said. "Not just the food but the conversation. Gertrude didn't do all the talking, and Alice chimed in, revealing herself as a woman of wit and charm, not just an echo of Gertrude."

"Both of these women understand me and my goals both as a lover of women and as a struggling figure trying to make a statement as a writer."

"I knew that an invitation for a communal sleepover was coming, and, to be frank, I wasn't looking forward to that, since neither woman was physically attractive to me."

"Instead of pursuing goddesses, I was their goddess to be worshipped. It was a different experience for me, and I was willing to surrender my body for the sake of this burgeoning friendship with two great women, who in time would immortalize themselves and their era."

"Although my basic friendship was with Alice," Mercedes said, "I admired Gertrude's mind for her views on art and literature."

Gertrude gave Mercedes some advice: "To judge by your wardrobe, you spend a lot of money on clothes. I go around in my old sloppy attire. You see, I spend my money on buying paintings by artists I know will be famous one day. Their works will sell for millions of dollars. I suggest you spend less on clothes and invest in paintings, instead."

"During the lean years of my latter days," Mercedes confessed to Darwin, "I wish I had followed her advice."

***

During the months when Mercedes was becoming an intimate friend of Alice and Gertrude, Stein was also involved in a meaningful and sometimes combative relationship with a budding American novelist, Ernest Hemingway, who was

Hemingway marries Hadley in 1921.

In Paris together, they met "Gertrude and Alice" in 1922. He was twenty-two, and Stein was forty-eight. He wrote, "She had beautiful eyes and a strong German-Jewish face that also could have been Friulano. She evoked a northern Italian peasant woman with alive immigrant hair."

"Alice had small, sharp features and a Joan of Arc haircut.," Hemingway continued. "Both Hadley and I found her frightening."

married at the time to Hadley.

Hemingway urged Gertrude and Alice to explore Spain, a fabled land of bullfights, paella, Don Quixote, and *ferias*, the most fascinating, exotic, and mystical of which was celebrated every year in Seville.

A trip to Spain would also offer views of original works by such towering figures in the art world as Goya, Velázquez, and El Greco. A Spaniard himself, Picasso also urged the pair to visit his homeland, giving them specific addresses and contacts in Barcelona and Málaga.

One afternoon, they invited Mercedes to join them on their trip to Spain, and she eagerly accepted.

In fact, the first night that Mercedes was introduced to Darwin at a small party, he had just returned from an in-depth research trip for the Frommer Travel Guides, to every major city and site of touristic interest on the Iberian peninsula.

Mercedes said to him, "The last time I visited Spain was in the company of Gertrude Stein and Alice B. Toklas."

"Who could ever top that?" Darwin said. "It was 'the ultimate name drop." He was eager to learn any details she wanted to share, since he was a long-time admirer of both Stein and Toklas and was the only person among his friends who had actually read Gertrude's literary *oeuvre*.

"We talked until four in the morning, and I agreed to spend Sunday afternoon with her," Darwin said. "It was the beginning of a friendship which lasted until her death."

"She knew I was a devotee of cultural figures of the 20th Century," he said, "and I was virtually starved for inside information. In time, she spoke of

As a translator, facilitator, bed mate, and "tour guide" for Stein and Toklas during their long sojourn in Spain, **Mercedes de Acosta** wore many hats, making herself useful. allowing herself to be "worshipped," and soaking up the last vestiges of "Old Spain" before it disappeared into the jaws of its Civil War.

Also, as the rigor of her Cuban/Iberian roots in the upper photo shows, she became better versed in the severe and fascinating aesthetics of Spain.

"Sexually," Mercedes told Darwin Porter, "Gertrude was the alpha male of our *ménage*."

Les Demoiselles de la rue de Fleurus: Toklas & Stein

all the great beauties she'd loved and seduced, especially Marlene Dietrich and Greta Garbo. She also made friends with legendary men, too, even John Barrymore."

Mercedes spoke of the trip which began on the Costa Brava on the northeastern corner of Spain. In Barcelona, they explored the medieval city and met with several of Picasso's friends. After that, they headed to Valencia, where Alice was more interested in learning "the true secrets" of making paella.

It was on to Málaga and its associations with Picasso. They met many of his boyhood friends, who shared memories of the great artist.

After exploring Granada, they drove to Seville, enjoying "a city of fairs and Andalusian beauties, each a rival of Carmen," Mercedes said.

Then they headed north to Toledo to pay homage to El Greco before descending on Madrid, a capital which all three of them found dull and boring except for the artistic wonders of the Prado.

Their motor trip returned to Paris through the Basque Country and along the Atlantic (i.e., western) coast of France.

"I don't want to sound too confessional," Mercedes said, "but I did sleep with Alice and Gertrude. I treasured their friendship, but they did not arouse my erotic desires. I preferred goddesses of the screen or theater. But I was willing to go along with some of their desires because I found them the most stimulating lesbian couple I would ever encounter in my life."

Toklas: No beauty, but beloved.

"I didn't look forward to Hemingway's visits with Gertrude," Toklas said. "He met homosexuals at our home, many of whom were masculine, intelligent, and talented. When they didn't dovetail with his locker-room stereotypes, he was befuddled."

"During stopovers in Spain, I shared their bed," Mercedes said. "Gertrude was definitely the alpha male of our trio, as you might have guessed."

"It is unlikely that the world will ever see a dynamic pair like those two again. They were no great beauties, but they enchanted their generation, including me."

***

One afternoon when Alice went shopping for ingredients for the evening's dinner, Gertrude invited Mercedes to join her on a visit to Picasso's studio.

"We were ushered in by an assistant, and I was introduced to the great man himself," Mercedes said. "He was standing stark naked, painting on a canvas. He was hardly embarrassed to be without clothes in front of us, as the nude body, male or female, did not embarrass him at all. He once stated he believed in painting the male or female nude in all its beauty and ugliness."

"I was a bit horrified by the dingy studio itself," she said. "Dirty dishes, empty wine bottles, trash scattered about, and an army of roaches devouring stale bread on his kitchen table."

"In all those ugly surroundings, he created beauty...well, art. He offered us some wine, and Gertrude went to pour it. Finding none, she came back and said she'd go out and buy a couple of bottles."

"After she'd gone, Picasso said that on several occasions, he had asked Alice to pose for him, but she had constantly refused.

"She has a large cyst between her eyebrows, and she combs her hair forward to conceal this monstrosity," he said. "But I want to paint it. I'll make her look like a unicorn with the object projecting from her face. Of course, I'll exaggerate it and make it six inches long, if not longer. Such a portrait might one day hang in the Louvre."

"She is a small, shadowy figure, always walking behind Gertrude so that approaching this lady of girth, you wouldn't at first know that Alice was trailing behind. Since she lives in the shadow of a great woman of girth, I would have to paint her shrouded in black like all shadows."

"Before Gertrude returned," Mercedes said, "Picasso asked me to come to his studio Saturday afternoon. He told me he wanted to paint me in the nude and then make love to me."

"Fool that I was, I rejected his offer," she said. "I told him I preferred the love of a woman."

"Then we have something in common," he answered. "So do I."

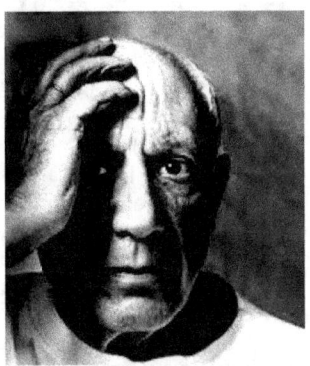

***

Gertrude and a young American novelist, Hemingway, had bonded and formed a friendship in the Lost Generation Paris of expatriates in the 1920s.

Frequently, he visited the apartment she shared with Alice, and was sometimes accompanied by his wife, Hadley. While Hemingway and Gertrude sat in her salon in front, Alice entertained Hadley in the kitchen.

"It was a case of a macho male meeting a macho woman unlike any Hemingway had ever known," Mercedes recalled, revealing to Darwin what Gertrude had told her about her friendship with Hemingway.

He compared Gertrude's looks to that of a Roman emperor. "That is fine if you like your women looking like a Roman emperor who's dreaming of engaging with five catamites that night."

At first, in spite of their differences, the friendship had been so intense that he asked

Picasso: Brooding, brilliant and egomaniacal.

Stein met the budding Picasso late in 1905 when he had decided to settle permanently in Paris.

"He was becoming a key player in a motley cast of vagabond artists, writers, dilettantes, and characters whom only Toulouse-Lautrec could capture on canvas," Stein said.

"They patronized the cafes and bistros of Montmartre. They were drawn together and united on some front, which they had not defined, yet. Perhaps it should be called 'modern art.'"

Gertrude if she'd become the godmother of his child.

"Ernest had the most primitive view of homosexuals that I have ever known," Gertrude said. "His opinion belonged to the Dark Ages."

He told her that because of homosexuals, he carried a sharp knife wherever he went. "In case one approaches me, and demands sex, my answer will be to stab him, preferably aiming for his heart," he told her.

"As a young boy growing up, I started carrying a knife with me because several men from time to time approached me with their sickening, perverted propositions. If one of them had tried to force sex on me, I would have stabbed him to death, a fate he would deserve for harboring such unnatural desires."

Gertrude confessed to Mercedes that her friendship with the novelist ended "the night I confronted him to the reality of who he really was."

She told him, "You are a homosexual and can't admit that to yourself. Not only that, but you're in love with F. Scott Fitzgerald. You just can't face your own desires."

After that charge, Hemingway stormed out of her apartment, never to return.

Although Gertrude attacked Hemingway for his view of male homosexuals, she, too, was not very enlightened," Mercedes told Darwin.

"She was, of course, tolerant of all forms of sexual diversion, depending on one's desire," Mercedes said. "But on a deeply personal level, she was offended by how men made love."

"I can't help myself," she told Mercedes. "But the thought of one man sodomizing another man is ugly and repugnant to me. After committing that horrid act, a homosexual is consumed with guilt, which drives him to consume inordinate amounts of alcohol and drugs. They flit from one sexual encounter to another, never forming lasting relationships, but experiencing a life of wild promiscuity, searching for the love that Alice and I have, but one that eludes them."

"In contrast," Gertrude continued, "sex between women is the most beautiful thing on earth. It is about loving, giving, being generous, being kind, finding fulfillment unknown to the male homosexual. How unlike the male experience with their stabbing penetrations of each other, which must cause agony racing through their bodies. It is a violation."

"I was horrified the night I left Gertrude's apartment," Mercedes said. "I expected those views from some redneck in Georgia, not from a sophisticated woman of the world like Gertrude Stein, the world's most famous lesbian. Homosexuals are among my dearest friends, and sex between them can be beautiful and fulfilling, especially when they form life-long partnerships."

"I never challenged Gertrude on her ill-informed opinions, because I valued my friendship with Alice. I never wanted to learn what caused her to have such an unenlightened view about male homosexuality, because in all other aspects, I viewed her as the Queen of Enlightenment in the artistic and literary world of the 1920s."

***

In October of 1934, Gertrude and Alice returned to America for a nationwide lecture tour.

Even though most Americans had never read anything by Gertrude, her fame—and news of her lesbian links to Alice B. Toklas—had spread across the country.

When the *Champlain* sailed into New York Harbor, a coven of reporters and photographers arrived aboard a Coast Guard cutter to interview Gertrude in advance of the ship's docking. It marked the beginning of a six-month nationwide tour that criss-crossed twenty-three states and 37 cities.

With her luggage packed, and ready to disembark, Gertrude, holding Alice's hand, stood on the ship's upper deck, surveying the New York skyline. The tall towers of Rockefeller Center were still under construction.

Before she arrived back in her homeland, Gertrude had been labeled "the Sibyl of Montparnasse" and the "Matron Saint of Paris Art."

Reporters found the two women dressed in a bizarre fashion. Gertrude's hat was described as "headwear for Robin Hood" and "a deer stalker's cap."

Stein in 1935, around the time of her American tour, reveling, as the flag suggests, in her American origins.

Alice's headgear was described as "something a Cossack would wear."

Several members of the press described Alice as "a frail little thing, hovering in the background and looking very, very nervous."

Their dear friends, Carl Van Vechten and the publisher, Bennett Cerf, were on hand to welcome them and escort them to their three-room suite at the Algonquin Hotel.

Newspapers heralded their arrival with frontpage headlines. *The Sun* mocked Gertrude's writing style in its headline—GERTY GERTY STEIN STEIN IS BACK HOME HOME BACK.

Later that evening, they strolled through Times Square, as the Times Building flashed the news—GERTRUDE STEIN HAS ARRIVED IN NEW YORK.

Celebrities turned up to greet them, including Mary Pickford, who was past her prime as America's Sweetheart in silent films. When asked to pose for a picture with Gertrude, "Mary just melted away," in the words of a photographer.

Sometimes, fans were overzealous, as demonstrated by an eighteen-year-old student from Columbia. He bowed to the ground, kissing the hem of Gertrude's corduroy dress.

Mostly, she had nothing but praise for America, except for its drugstores, which she found to be "filthy." She also lamented that in the five-and-ten-cent stores, there was not one item available for sale at that price.

Arriving in Chicago, she expressed regret that she had never had the chance to meet Baby Face Nelson.

In Baltimore, they had a reunion with F. Scott Fitzgerald, who sadly informed them that he had had to commit Zelda to a mental institution.

Fitzgerald told the press, "I equated a visit from Miss Stein to be the equal of a visit from Jesus Christ himself."

On December 30 of that same year (1934), both Gertrude and Alice were invited to tea at the White House by Eleanor Roosevelt. Later,

Gertrude referred to the First Lady as "our fellow lesbian-in-arms."

In city after city, Gertrude lectured to packed houses from Ohio to Minnesota. In Wisconsin, she quipped, "I hear you have a lot of cows. Now you have one more," referring to her massive girth.

In Detroit, an anonymous call came in for the city's police chief. It threatened to "assassinate those two disgusting lesbians." He assigned two of his officers to safeguard them.

Gertrude's spirits picked up as she and Alice were driven to Ann Arbor. She even praised "the poetry" of the Burma-Shave billboard advertising.

As a fabled art collector, she was asked to comment on the American art she'd seen exhibited in galleries: "The paintings are like any learnt paintings, good painting enough not awfully good painting as painting but good painting enough. However, I don't think the Louvre will be acquiring any of their works."

From Oklahoma to Dallas, Houston, and Fort Worth, Gertrude and Alice finally made it to Los Angeles. Mercedes de Acosta, in the throes of her romance with Greta Garbo, was waiting with roses.

The two expatriates from Paris seemed eager to be with Mercedes and to share memories.

It was inside a movie studio that Gertrude was shown newsreel footage of her arrival in New York City with Alice.

As a speaker on tour, Gertrude drew a mixed press, some claiming that many in her audiences did not understand her points of view. Psychologists maintained that she suffered from a speech disorder, causing her "to stutter over words and phrases."

On one point, many of her listeners seemed to agree. Yet despite that, she was a commanding presence on stage and an intriguing personality who could hold listeners spellbound with the musicality of her tongue.

The Hollywood elite turned out to welcome the visitors, most notably, Charlie Chaplin, who was accompanied by the actress, Paulette Goddard, whom Alice found "incredibly beautiful and an *enfant terrible.*"

Gertrude had seen three of Chaplin's films. "He was a gentle soul like any Spanish gypsy bullfighter. He is very like my favorite Gallo, who could not kill a bull, but could make him more better than anyone ever could."

Anita Loos met Gertrude, informing her that she'd written *Gentlemen Prefer Blondes*. Gertrude's response? "Not this gentleman."

Lillian Hellman showed up with Dashiell Hammett, "The only writer I wanted to meet in all of California," Gertrude said.

In May of 1935, the traveling duo returned to New York, their point of departure for their ocean crossing back to France, once again aboard the *Champlain*. Her final words before embarking aboard the ship were, "Here Alice and I stand, most reluctant to say goodbye to our native land."

Back in Paris, Gertrude told reporters, "I found America a fascinating place filled with beauty spots, all except California, which brought back painful memories of my childhood. My favorite state was Texas. Some day I might return to these shores, but some day I might not."

Later, also in Paris, Gertrude claimed, "I am already homesick for America. I never knew it was so beautiful. I was like a bachelor who goes along fine for twenty-five years, then decides to wed. That's the way I feel—I mean, about America."

After her departure, the *Chicago Daily Tribune* wrote: "No writer in years has been so widely discussed, so much caricatured, so passionately championed."

***

In 1939, Mercedes had written to Gertrude and Alice, urging them to return to America because war clouds loomed over Europe. She was told that they planned to remain in France. Mercedes feared for their safety because both of them were Jews, and the Nazis were either killing or imprisoning Jews in concentration camps—the equivalent of a death sentence for most of them.

Fearing a German occupation, Alice had hoarded supplies such as dried fruits and chicory for coffee. The most difficult years were 1941 and 1942, as they were chronically short of meat, milk, and eggs.

They lived in constant fear as they were classified as "American enemy nationals."

Gertrude knew the Vichy leader Marshal Henri Pétain, and believed that he had been right in surrendering France, as it was not equipped, militarily, to oppose the Nazi invasion.

Alice and Gertrude became especially concerned for their safety after the Japanese attack on Pearl Harbor and America's entry into the conflict.

During this horror, she began writing *Wars I Have Seen*.

In 1944, she and Alice were impatiently awaiting the American Liberation of France. She used a *cliché* to describe her feelings: "It is darkest before the dawn." She later characterized the era as "The Liberation of Gertrude Stein."

Having survived the Nazi occupation of France, Gertrude died on July 27, 1946, age 72, in the Parisian suburb of Neuilly-sur-Seine. Upon her death, she was hailed as "a giant of literature."

***

"In the years to come, Alice and I kept in touch through letters," Mercedes said. "I knew that the years after Gertrude's death were lonely ones. She wrote sensitive, insightful letters to me. They looked like they were written with the eyelash of a fly."

In 1951, after years of separation, Alice boarded a bus in Paris and found Mercedes aboard the same bus. According to Alice, "Mercedes was wearing the most beautiful yellow gloves I had ever seen. She looked bourgeois and middle-aged, not the Spanish beauty of yesterday when she'd gone with Gertrude and me to Spain."

Mercedes told Alice she had visited 27 rue de Fleurus the previous evening to visit her, since she didn't have her phone number. "I was with Cecil Beaton and Greta Garbo, both of whom were looking forward to seeing you."

Alice responded with an invitation to visit her later that evening. In July of 1948, she wrote to her friend, Samuel Steward, "I heard that Garbo and Cecil are going to get married, but I could not believe that Garbo would be that crass."

For both Mercedes and Alice, the years seemed to rush by. Mercedes noted with amusement that Alice achieved a certain notoriety with the younger generation in 1954 when she published *The Alice B. Toklas Cookbook*, filled with recipes and reminiscences.

One of its recipes, contributed to the book by Brion Gysin, was for "Haschick Fudge," a mélange of fruit, nuts, spices, and marijuana. Later, her name was associated with a wide range of cannabis concoctions, one of which came to be known as "Alice B. Toklas Brownies."

In September of 1953, Mercedes sent Alice a copy of the Kinsey Report, a survey of American sex habits. Alice wrote back: "These reports are hopelessly dull. As you say so rightly, American sex is the most banal point from which to study our compatriots—it is so small a part of their character—and completely lacking in subtlety and complexity."

When Alice heard that Mercedes was penning her memoirs, *Here Lies the Heart*, for a release in 1960, she wrote to her with a request: "In honor of the memory of my beloved Gertrude, please, for the sake of privacy, exclude us from the list of your loved ones."

Mercedes later sent her a copy of her memoir. Alice responded, "To those who have looked at it, it makes us come alive. It is a fascinating book of rare beauty."

In 1963, Alice published her own memoir, *What Is Remembered*. Its narrative ended with Gertrude's death.

"When her mate died, Alice had been willed Gertrude's multi-million dollar art collection," Mercedes claimed. "But once, when she went away on vacation, members of the Stein family broke into her apartment and stole every single painting. I urged Alice to sue for grand theft, but she never did. She spent the rest of her life struggling financially when she could have had millions in the bank through the sale of just one of those paintings. What an outrageous shame!"

On March 7, 1967, Alice died in Paris at the age of 89, following years of ill health and financial woes. She was buried at Père Lachaise Cemetery, next to the grave of her one true love, Gertrude Stein.

In 1973, a book was published, *Staying On Alone: Letters of Alice B. Toklas*. Critic Edward Burns wrote: "Though the famous bell within Alice rang for the genius of Gertrude Stein and others, she had her own genius, revealed in these chatty, fascinating letters, written during the twenty years after Stein's death in 1946."

Depicted above is a plaque honoring the Stein-Toklas home and literary/arts salon at 27 rue de Fleurus in Paris.

REST IN PEACE

ALICE (1877-1967) &
GERTRUDE (1874-1946)

CHAPTER NINE
The Venus's Flytrap from Alabama

TALLULAH BANKHEAD & HOPE WILLIAMS
Darlings & She-Devils

Few other American actresses developed as frantic a coterie of gay male fans as **Tallulah**, but even those who slavishly followed her tabloid-generating ambisexual scandals never really understood the degree of her fame on the London stage during the silent-screen cinematic heyday of Nazimova and Rudolph Valentino.

Truth is, the theatrical personality that her fans adored had already developed an impossibly famous public image in the U.K. long before she became widely known in Hollywood.

In the upper left corner is her name in lights in downtown Chicago during a U.S. tour of one of her news-generating plays.

On the right is Tallulah getting bourbon-soaked and cozy with what looks lke an (unknown but hot-to trot) lesbian acolyte.

In the lower center is Tallulah portraying a decadent American flapper on the stage in London, more overblown and hysterically dramatic than anything ever mustered by Nazimova or Gloria Swanson.

And at the bottom left is Tallulah, bored and chain-smoking (she was estimated to have smoked 150 cigarettes a day every day for decades), accompanied at a stylish nightspot by a handsome young man who faded into oblivion, like many of Tallulah's stage performances. It proves, however, a quip from one of her frenemies about **how "Tallulah was always well-accompanied."**

TATTLING ABOUT TALLULAH: WHAT OTHERS SAID

"Tallulah has a warm heart, but it beats in the wrong places."
—Estelle Winwood

"Tallulah burns the candle at all ends."
—Cecil Beaton

"A day away from Tallulah is like a week in the country."
—Lyricist Howard Dietz

"I suppose you could say that Tallulah is a tramp, but only in the most elegant sense."
—Tennessee Williams

"She chose never to disappoint anyone. She wanted to be remembered since she could not be loved."
—Dennis Brian

"She was great fun to be with and had more glamour than almost anybody alive."
—Lord Laurence Olivier

"She was a woman without inhibitions."
—Alfred Hitchcock

"Listening to her constant talk was like Chinese torture."
—Walter Slezak

WHAT TALLULAH SAID ABOUT RECREATIONAL DRUGS, GENDER PREFERENCE, & SEXUAL PROMISCUITY

"My Daddy [the stern three-term U.S. Senator from Alabama, 1907-1920, and one of the most powerful politicians in the South] *warned me about men and booze. But he never said a word about women and cocaine."*

"Cocaine isn't habit-forming. I should know. I've been using it for years."

"I don't know what I am. I've tried several varieties of sex. The conventional position makes me claustrophobic, and all the others give me a stiff neck or lockjaw."

"I went to Hollywood for only one reason—and that was to fuck that divine Gary Cooper, the Montana Mule."

"Say It for Shock Value" Tallulah

Naughty Tallu: What She Said to Lillian Gish, Ingénue Star of the Silent Screen, After Years of Separation

"Dear Lillian: Here we are, still surviving after all these years, you with your face lifted and your vagina dropped, and me my vagina lifted and my face dropped."

***

"You don't have to be in love to make love to a woman."
—Mercedes de Acosta

"America's Other Sweetheart of the silent screen," **Lillian Gish**, the rival of Mary Pickford.

The sexual trysts of Mercedes de Acosta with actresses Hope Williams and Tallulah Bankhead took place between 1917 and 1920. After that, the "unholy trio," as they were once known, met only sporadically, their youthful passions gone with the winds of summer. But although Tallulah sometimes mocked Mercedes behind her back, all three of them turned their relationships into lasting friendships.

Mercedes began her affair with Hope the night she met her, during World War I at the lavish home of Mrs. John Jacob Astor on Fifth Avenue.

Across a crowded room at the Astor party, Mercedes spotted Hope and was instantly intrigued. She asked her friend, Thornton Wilder, "Who is that woman?"

"A rich socialite, Hope Williams," he answered.

As Mercedes later wrote, "She had a charmingly shaped head, and I was amused by her delicate and turned-up nose. She was lovely looking, and even at that early age, she had a strong personality. When we were introduced, we clicked."

"That very night, Hope went home with Mercedes, where she learned that Hope wanted to go on the stage, in defiance of the adamant intentions of her socially connected family.

In time, many of their mutual friends became aware of their love affair, most of them predicting it would survive only as long as the life of a plucked wildflower.

Noël Coward described Hope as "having a charming speaking voice with a sort of beguiling tonelessness. She is slangy without being vulgar, modern without being brash, and her *gaucheries* of movement have a particular grace."

Born in Manhattan in August of 1897, Hope

Madeleine Astor, a survivor, in 1912, of the *RMS Titanic*, the second wife and widow of Gilded Age robber baron John Jacob Astor IV.

In semi-retirement from the social scene after the trauma of the liner's demise, she hosted a party in 1920 where Mercedes de Acosta met one of the loves of her young life, Hope Williams and the very "in vogue' star of London's 1920s stage, Tallulah Bankhead.

was the daughter of a prominent physician and had grown up into a world of privilege. She attended the best schools and was highly educated. In college, she had appeared in several plays.

At sixteen, she was launched into society as a debutante, despite her boyish body, clipped blonde hair, and rather comical walk.

As her career as an actress progressed, she had success in the Philip Barry comedy, *Paris Bound* in 1927.

A year later (1928) she had even greater success as a rebellious socialite in *Holiday*, a classic comedy of manners, also written by Barry. Katharine Hepburn was her understudy in the Broadway production of that play. *[In 1938, Hepburn would star in a movie adaptation, also named* Holiday, *opposite Cary Grant.]*

Hepburn told the *Hollywood Reporter*, "I stole a great deal from Hope Williams. She was a fascinating stage personality from 1929 to 1932, although America wasn't ready for her. She was a woman who blossomed with a little more than she was supposed to."

In *The New York Times*, Brooks Atkinson wrote, "Miss Williams is one of the most clear-headed *comediennes* we have. She plays quietly with a sort of comic incandescence that is one of the superlative dialogues of the season. In the play, *Holiday*,

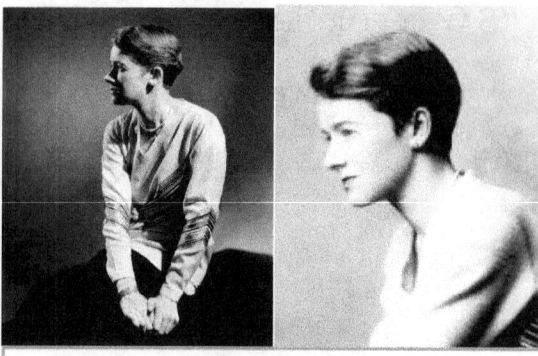

Two views of **Hope Williams**, a boyish-looking, deeply emotional truth-teller who never, absolutely never, fitted into the high-society world of Mrs. Astor's debutante receptions. Mercedes and to some degree, Talllulah Bankhead, found her irresistible.

Hope Williams, a socially connected heiress trained from birth to behave with perfect manners in Mrs. Astor's drawing room, appears here on stage in *Holiday* in 1928.

Katharine Hepburn was her new-to-the-stage and insecure understudy, soaking up every nuance about how rich, classy socialities speak, walk, and emote.

Hepburn, despite a classy family background and firm intellectual buttressing, assimilated so much stage technique from Hope Williams that she pulled off playing rich socialite roles throughout the rest of her career. In the upper right photo, Hepburn appears in the 1938 film adaptation of *Holiday* with Cary Grant.

she remains very much herself, boyishly awkward but quick and sparkling."

During the second week of their affair, Mercedes claimed that she wanted to write the perfect play for Hope, although that didn't work out.

Hope did get to see a performance of a play that Mercedes had written, *Sandro Botticelli,* and later referred to it as "a beautiful work." The critics did not think so, however, and attacked Mercedes for it savagely. Mercedes later told Hope, "I'm disillusioned with Broadway."

"Aren't we all, darling?" Hope answered.

Hope did not have to work as an actress. She had married Dr. R. Bartow Read in 1922, and he was rather wealthy. After she divorced him after six years of marriage, he died in a plane crash in 1931. He had never changed his will, and Hope was the sole beneficiary. Financially, she was secure for the rest of her life.

In 1939, Hope appeared as the careless governess, Miss Prism, in the 1939 revival of Oscar Wilde's *The Importance of Being Earnest.*

After that, she retired, spending the rest of her life moving between her 1,000-acre dude ranch in Cody, Wyoming, and her deluxe apartment in Manhattan. Mercedes once visited her ranch, but decided, "Wyoming is not for me."

Cecil Beaton escorted Mercedes to a 1930 Broadway play to see Hope star in the premiere of Donald Ogden Stewart's *Rebound* at the Plymouth Theatre.

"A lot of the opening night audience stared at us," Beaton later told Noël Coward. "In Broadway circles, Mercedes is called a star-fucker, devouring some of the most fabled ladies of the day. There are those who call her a perverse psychopath, but that is a bridge too far. I find she has great taste in women, preferring those with legendary reputations, including the star of that night, Hope Williams, herself."

A biographer wrote, "Williams boasted a mannish beauty, a tomboyish charm, a lovely voice, and a sufficient amount of acting ability, as evidenced by her roles in Philip Barry plays. Her success on the stage brought about a *rapprochement* between New York high society and the entertainment business."

As the years went by, Hope and Mercedes—mostly through letters and from afar—continued their friendship. Whenever Hope learned of another break-up between Mercedes and her current lesbian love, she often sent her a letter of condolence.

Years later, when Hope heard that Mercedes had fallen on bad days in New York, she wired her money with the message, "For old times' sake, darling."

Mercedes wasn't the only actress who pursued Hope during her early days. She was soon introduced to Tallulah Bankhead, who was outrageous, outspoken, and uninhibited.

This snapshot from 1929 shows a prosperous, expensively dressed and well-connected **Mercedes de Acosta**, left figure, carrying recent acquisitions with an unidentified female companion, probably her sister, **Aida**.

THE FORMIDABLE TALLULAH BANKHEAD

Infuriatingly unpredictable, and often cruel in her mockeries, Tallulah Bankhead was at times kind and gallant. She had a reckless spirit, often mired in alcohol and drugs, and a lonely and wandering soul in search of the love she never found. One of the most dynamic personalities of the 20th Century, she become a legend, mainly because of her stage work, her wit, and her brilliant talent for being outrageous.

As an actress, she made many disastrous choices, yet she also had many memorable moments in such plays as *The Little Foxes, The Skin of Our Teeth,* and Noël Coward's *Private Lives,* in which she toured endlessly. The one film that immortalized her screen presence was Alfred Hitchcock's *Lifeboat,* released in 1944.

Although she was never called The First Lady of the Theater, she was always credited as a member of the coven that included such other divas as Eva Le Gallienne, Helen Hayes, Lynn Fontanne, Ethel Barrymore, and Katharine Cornell.

Since she never remembered names very well, she called everybody "*dah-ling,*" even people she hated.

She also became known for her tempestuous sexual adventures, some of them inter-racial, with both men and women. "I never wanted to discriminate because of color," she told playwright James Leo Herlihy when she toured with his play, *Crazy October,* in 1958. "I went to bed with both Billie Holiday and Hattie McDaniel."

She would later recall, "I went home to Alabama not long ago and located some of my relatives. To my horror, I found them to be racists...*still!* Even though we're related, I loathe them."

"From the very beginning, I fucked across color lines, both men and women. In the 1960s, I could find only black men from Harlem to royally screw me. My assistant—I called him my caddy—was the '*oh, so gay*' Ted Hook. For a hundred dollars, he picked up black studs in Harlem and brought them to me, where they fucked me. After that, he slipped them another fifty if they would do the same for him. I think he embezzled his stud fees by looting the money I gave him for groceries."

Tallulah was sexually intimate with a greater variety of men

It's been argued that Tallulah Bankhead never fit into either her era or the social landscape of Alabama, feeling infinitely more comfortable in the rarefied show-biz circles of London, New York, and Los Angeles.

Above are women of color she enjoyed lesbian flings with, jazz singer **Billie Holiday** (left) and Oscar-winning actress **Hattie McDaniel.**. In Alabama, around the time of Tallulah's birth, such a dalliance might have led to disinheritance and a casting out for the white woman, and possible lynching for the black one.

than almost any other stage personality. They included Marlon Brando, with whom she co-starred in 1946 in Jean Cocteau's *The Eagle Has Two Heads,* and Sir Winston Churchill when she was the toast of London in the 1920s, starring in plays in the West End.

"When it came to the Barrymores, I could never decide," she said. "Was I more in love with John than I was with Ethel? Count Lionel out, although Clark Gable once told me that Lionel was one of the best cocksuckers in Hollywood. *[Lionel and Clark had co-starred together in* A Free Soul *(1931) with Norma Shearer.]*

"As an actress on Broadway, I took on the usual suspects," Tallulah claimed. "Naturally, they included Mercedes de Acosta, as it seems that nearly all the lady stars had her. There was also my always reliable Patsy Kelly, and even Beatrice Lillie when she was in town. When she wasn't murdering one of her husbands, singer Libby Holman and I shared a bed. When they were younger and before they turned into old crones, Estelle Winwood and Constance Collier did the honors with me, too. And if Lilyan Tashman were in from the coast, she drifted my way, too. Would you also believe Lillian Gish? (That was only one night and she never called for an encore.) It seems I left out Laurette Taylor. Forgive me, Laurette. Perhaps I'm still mad that I didn't get to play Amanda in the stage version of *The Glass Menagerie."*

Tallulah sustained an affair with the notorious torch singer and alleged murderess, **Libby Holman** (photo above).

In Tallulah's later years, she simply could not resist tormenting Holman whenever she saw her in, say, a crowded elevator: "What, between murders, *dah-ling*?" she said to her one day.

Almost instantly, that anecdote became widely bruited through New York and London.

***

Symbolically, at least, a tornado swept over Alabama on January 31, 1902, the night Tallulah Bankhead was born. She was named after her paternal grandmother, who in turn had been named after Tallulah Falls in North Georgia.

Born into a prominent Southern political family, she was the daughter of William B. Bankhead, the Speaker of the U.S. House of Representatives from 1936 to 1940.

"My daddy wanted me to grow up to become the first woman President of the United States," Tallulah told Darwin Porter one night in Key West. "He thought I had the balls for it, although he would never use such a vulgar expression, since he was a true Southern gent."

The year before Tallulah came into the world, her parents had another girl, Eugenia, born on January 24, 1901. Their mother, Mississippi-born Adelaide Eugenia Sledge, died from blood poisoning three weeks after giving birth to Tallulah.

As Eugenia and Tallulah grew up, whereas the older sister was praised for her youth and beauty, Tallulah, who was "extremely homely and plump," (her words) languished in the background.

To attract attention, Tallulah, as a young girl, learned to do cartwheels, a feat she continued to perform well into her thirties. "I prefer to do them without panties because men find it more interesting. I you want to know, *dah-ling*, it's ginger-colored, although gray hairs are creeping in. What to do? Pick them out, one by one."

"By the way, *dah-ling*," she continued telling Darwin. "If you ever write about me one day, and I know you will, please don't say I have a husky voice. Call me a mezzo-soprano. Bette Davis did a poor imitation of my voice in *All About Eve* (1950). I should have sued the bitch for impersonation."

"While I was in kindergarten, I won First Prize in an acting contest. The judges were two brothers, Orville and Wilbur Wright—you know, those 'come fly with me' boys."

"My Daddy couldn't control me, so he sent Eugenia and me to a convent in Manhattanville, New York. Two of the sisters there tried to seduce me when I was only ten. My Gawd, they liked 'em young."

Tallulah at fourteen, the expensively brought-up and indulgently reared (i.e., uncontrollable) daughter of the most important politician in Alabama.

"Eugenia got married when she was only sixteen. Not me! I didn't want to put myself in bondage to some man. Other than with those horny nuns, my first sexual experimentation was with Zelda Sayre. Of course, she became a hell of a lot better known after she married F. Scott Fitzgerald. When I asked her about how her marriage was going, she complained that his cock was too small. But later, she found a Navy pilot who didn't have that problem."

As a teenager, Tallulah arrived in New York "on my Daddy's money," and moved into the Algonquin Hotel, the retreat of the literary and artistic elite.

She claimed that the first man who took her virginity was Robert Benchley, a distinguished member of the "Algonquin Round Table."

"I'm fully aware that later, I claimed that it was Lord Alington in London during my heyday there," she said. "I lied. The reason I didn't cite Benchley was because I didn't want him to get arrested on a morals charge for seducing a teenager."

It was during her residency at the Algonquin that Tallulah met Mercedes de Acosta. "She went for me right away," she told Darwin. "I mean, the first night. Like a hungry fox, she gravitated to my room and spent the weekend. She was a ravenous beast, and seemingly could not get enough of me. She had obviously had a lot of experience before getting around to me in the glory of my youth and beauty. I felt I was a special treat for her. At least that's what she kept telling me."

"Mercedes told me on rare occasions, she had sex with men. After all, *dah-ling*, she was married to one. She felt that sex with men was something that a woman had to endure. It certainly was not pleasurable for her. In contrast, she felt sex with a woman was erotic, beautiful, and most satisfying, perhaps the best thing ever invented on Planet Earth. Frankly, I'm not sure I buy that."

Mercedes later admitted to Darwin, "Tallulah and I had a brief fling that stretched on and off, mostly off, between 1917 and 1920. We were never in love—far from it. But we enjoyed the sex, and I loved being around her. Tallulah was the single most fascinating woman I ever met in the theater or in Hollywood, either, for that matter. In contrast, Garbo could be boring."

According to Mercedes, "Soon, Hope Williams, Tallulah, and I could be seen making the rounds in Manhattan. Rumors were rampant that we were a *ménage à trois*, but I'm not going to go into that. Whatever we did, Tallulah was the ringleader, the Alpha Male of our trio."

"At the age of nineteen, Tallulah was hosting wild parties at the Algonquin. Even Mercedes was shocked that on occasion, she opened the door of her suite at the Algonquin to party guests stark naked.

"I remember one night, Tallulah got into an argument with Ethel Barrymore, the actress she most admired on stage. Ethel was demanding that Tallulah change her name to Barbara Bankhead, claiming it would look more dignified on Broadway marquees."

Years later, Tallulah told Darwin, "I'm glad I stood up to the formidable Miss Barrymore and stuck with the name my daddy gave me at birth. Today, Tallulah is known on two continents. In my heyday as the toast of London in the 1920s, I could get mail delivered to me if it were only addressed to 'SHE, LONDON.'"

Vanity Fair once stated, "Tallulah Bankhead is the only actress on both sides of the Atlantic to be recognized by her first name only."

***

At the age of sixteen, in 1918, Tallulah made her stage debut on Broadway at the Bijou Theater in *The Squab Farm*. It starred Lowell Sherman as a film director seeking a suitable candidate for the portrayal of Eve. The play was a send-up of the "lunacy" of Hollywood.

Tallulah joined three other young girls onstage in what *The New York Times* would define as "a garish travesty of life in the movies, all in bad taste."

Sherman, a native of San Francisco, became known for

Even though it was Tallulah's first-time-ever appearance on stage, in *The Squab Farm*, she refused to collaborate with the instructions of the photographer to face relentlessly forward in this detail from a much larger photo with other starlettes in the show.

She posed sideways because the great Barrymore himself, famous for his profile, suggested that Tallulah might have some of his genes, and therefore, a very fine profile, as she's showing off in this photo. He was insinuating that his father might have been her biological father through some past sexual indiscretion in Alabama.

Years later, **Tallulah** (right) compared her getup and the style of the film to something which might have starred **Theda Bara** (left photo)

screen villainy, appearing in D.W. Griffith's classic, *Way Down East* (1920), in which he impregnates Lillian Gish and later abandons her and her unwanted child. Sherman had made his screen debut in *Behind the Scenes* (1924) with Mary Pickford and James Kirkwood, Sr. *[At the time, they were secret lovers, offscreen.]*

As a movie star, Sherman became known as "The Wickedest Villain on the Silver Screen." *[His career was endangered, at least temporarily, when the movie-going public learned that he'd been at a party in that San Francisco hotel room where Fatty Arbuckle was accused of raping Virginia Rappe, causing her death. He managed to bounce back in such pictures that included* Morning Glory *(1932) with Katharine Hepburn and* She Done Him Wrong *(1933) with Mae West.]*

Although, in rapid succession, Sherman had married and divorced actress Pauline Garon and then Helen Costello, he was also alleged to have had a secret life as a homosexual, seducing some of Hollywood's most notable leading men before they became famous.

During rehearsals for *The Squab Farm*, Tallulah was chastised for whistling in the communal dressing room, unknowingly breaking one of the theater's oldest superstitions about the bad luck it allegedly brings.

"For my first entrance, I was nervous as hell, dressed up like a garish Theda Bara, the reigning screen vamp of the day. I'd later describe my role as that of a mute child in a flophouse."

Although it never mentioned her name, Tallulah got her first newspaper review: "There are three or four young girls in the company, who might be better back in the care of their mothers." Then, although her role amounted to nothing but a walk-on, another newspaper headlined her in their feature story as: "SOCIETY GIRL GOES ON THE STAGE," a reference to her father's illustrious political machine.

Another critic described her as "exquisite of feature, dainty of form, deliciously feminine, with a pair of large eyes expressing all their emotions in a glance. She has supercharged energy."

"After that, everyone in the cast, especially the leading actors, treated me like I was Typhoid Mary, hogging all the publicity," she said.

In the audience on opening night was a movie director shooting "silent flickers" in New York. Backstage, he offered Tallulah a supporting role in the first of her many screen roles. It was a silent film entitled *When Men Betray* (1918).

It detailed the plight of a young woman who falls in love with and marries a glib con artist, who abandons her on their wedding night without any money. Tallulah, cast in the supporting role of Alice, also has man troubles. Her sister's *fiancé*, portrayed by Jack McLean, falls for Tallulah's character. Trouble ahead.

She later quipped, *"When Men Betray* was as trifling as it was silent."

When it premiered in New York, Harriet Underhill of the New York *Tribune* wrote: "Miss Tallulah Bankhead is new to the screen, and she proves the truth of the theory that brains are better than experience."

Tallulah later said, "This verdict thrilled and confused me. My elation at being cited by a motion picture critic was tempered by my conviction that brains were the monopoly of schoolteachers and politicians. Why hadn't she said anything about my beauty? Only by indirection did Miss Underhill hint that I could act. Why hadn't she talked about my rhythm and style and sense of mockery?"

"Then Samuel Goldfish *[he later changed his name to Goldwyn]* entered my life, but didn't enter ME," Tallulah said. "He wasn't my type. He asked me to appear in a movie, *Thirty a Week*."

Directed by Harry Beaumont, it starred Tom Moore, Alec B. Francis, and Brenda Fowler. Tallulah was still sixteen when she made this appearance in 1918.

Moore, an Irish American actor and director, made 186 films between 1908 and 1954, frequently cast as a romantic lead. At the time he seduced Tallulah, he was married to the silent screen star Alice Joyce. His brother, Owen Moore, also an actor, had once been married to Mary Pickford.

[*Every copy of* Thirty a Week *is believed to have been lost. However, a still photograph of Moore with Tallulah can be viewed in* Daniel Plum's Pictorial History of Silent Film, *published in 1953.*]

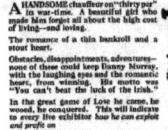 

Tallulah was cast in another film, *The Trap* (1919), released in the U.K. as *A Woman's Love*. A drama, it was based on a 1915 Broadway play, the story of a schoolteacher (portrayed by Olive Tell) in Alaska who is pursued by two men. She had a small supporting role, the character of Helen Carson.

In the same film, also in a supporting role, that of Doc Sloan, Rod La Rocque, was on the dawn of becoming a dashing matinee idol. "I went for him big time, but found he was having a torrid affair with another soon-to-become famous star, an Italian who blazed to glory on the screen as Rudolph Valentino."

[*La Rocque later entered into a lavender marriage with another big silent screen star, Vilma Bánky.*]

Tallulah in *Thirty a Week* with **Tom Moore**. "During the shoot, I seduced Tom. He did not seduce me," Tallulah said. "By the time we had completed this dim-witted movie, I had drained him dry."

***

Tallulah told her friend and fellow actress, Estelle Winwood, "I detest working in films. From now on, it's the stage for me."

In the summer of 1919, she was heavily in debt. Her family had been providing her with fifty dollars a week, but she usually spent it the day she received it. One afternoon, the manager of the Algonquin pounded on her door, demanding immediate payment. She had to borrow money from Winwood.

Tallulah auditioned for a play, *39 East*, written by Rachel Crothers, and was cast in it. Its title referred to the address of a boarding house in which struggling actors lived. Its stars were Henry Hull and Constance Binney. Tallulah's character is abducted in Central Park, and eventually rescued.

[Born in Kentucky, Henry Hull was a Southerner like herself. He'd worked as a miner before making his stage debut in 1911. By 1917, he was also appearing in films. On the screen, he would play practical oldsters and crotchety seniors. In 1933, he virtually immortalized himself through his portrayal of Jester Lester in Tobacco Road, one of the longest-running of all Broadway hits.

Cast as Penelope Penn, Binney shot to stardom. 39 East ran for 160 performances on Broadway and subsequently toured America. Critic Edward Wagenknecht called it "a homey sort of play—real comedy, not farce—about the daughter of a minister who is not a very good preacher but a perfectly darling man."

Two views of closeted homosexual matinee idol, **Rod La Rocque**. In right photo he's romancing **Dolores del Rio**.

La Rocque once proposed marriage to Gloria Swanson, who responded by laughing in his face. He attracted world attention by playing Richard Dix's brother in De Mille's The Ten Commandments.

"Rod and Dick," Mercedes said. "Phallic-sounding names were all the rage for male stars in Hollywood."

After than, Binney was lured to Hollywood, where she co-starred with John Barrymore in The Test of Honor (1919), for which she was hailed as the screen's most exciting new ingénue. Known for her "dancing eyes," she made fourteen feature films until 1924, when she was evaluated as "more earthy than ethereal."

She retired from the screen and in time, and in succession, married three rich businessmen as her fame faded in the dust. Nearly all her films are lost today.]

During rehearsals, Tallulah worked with Sidney Blackmer, another Southerner, a native of North Carolina, who had returned to America after fighting in Europe during World War I. "He reminded me of Teddy Roosevelt," Tallulah said, "and in several films, he would indeed play the president."

He'd made his screen debut in the popular serial, The Perils of Pauline, in 1914. His biggest stage triumph would not come until 1950, when he won a Tony for Come Back, Little Sheba. However, he lost the role in the film adaptation to Burt Lancaster.

Between rehearsals and performances, Tallulah studied ballet, French, and diction.

Her ability to fascinate observers was not lost on the playwright Zoë Akins. As a means of closely studying her character, Akins attended nearly every rehearsal of 39 East because Tallulah fascinated her. Later, Akins claimed that she used Tallulah as inspiration for her character of Eva Lovelace, a budding actress, in her play, Morning Glory. [Katharine Hepburn brought it to the screen in 1933 and was awarded with her first Oscar. The role called for an aspiring actress to be "half-mad with ambition."]

Tallulah had met Akins when both of them were living at the Algonquin. At 2AM early one morning, there was a loud pounding on Tallulah's door. Staggering to open it, she confronted a distraught Akins, who—clad only in her underwear—looked battered.

"I've been raped," she said. "Do you have a douche bag?"

Tallulah didn't, but gave her an enema bag instead.

***

For the 1919 production of *Footloose*, a noted producer, George Tyler, persuaded Akins to update a popular melodrama from the 1880s called *Forget Me Not*.

Playwright **Zoë Atkins**. As a character study, she found Tallulah fascinating.

"One day, I'll write a play based on Tallulah."

In this updated version, its star was Emily Stevens, cast as a predatory adventuress. Tallulah played her daughter. "All I remember is that I had to cry a lot," she said. The play opened at the Greenwich Village Theatre before moving uptown.

Tallulah was reviewed in *The New York Times*, a newspaper that would often be highly critical of her later stage work: "If there is an individual success scored in *Footloose*, it goes to Tallulah Bankhead. She plays with considerable power and sustains a difficult role with real skill."

With much-needed money coming in, Tallulah moved out of the Algonquin and into an apartment at 686 Madison Avenue. Mercedes de Acosta, Laurette Taylor, and Estelle Winwood, among others, were frequent visitors.

Tallulah's next play was *Nice People*, which premiered at Manhattan's Klaw Theatre in March of 1921. A comedy in four acts, it was written and staged by Rachel Crothers and starred Tallulah with Francine Larrimore. Crothers had been impressed with Tallulah's acting style since she'd worked with her on *39 East*. She had written *Nice People* expressly for her.

As a beautiful flapper, Tallulah contrasted with the mannish-looking Larrimore, "who came out in workman's overalls and looked like a very butchy lesbian," Tallulah said.

 [A THEATRICAL FOOTNOTE: Nice People marked Katharine Cornell's Broadway debut in the role of Eileen Baxter-Jones. Cornell would become a 40-year contender for the title of First Lady of the American Theatre. During the run of that play, rumors spread that Tallulah and Cornell were having an affair. At the same time, Mercedes de Acosta was having a fling with Cornell, too.]

Cornell left the cast of *Nice People* to star in the new Clemence Dane play, *A Bill of Divorcement*. RKO executives saw the play and acquired the film rights. But instead of Cornell, they cast Katharine Hepburn as the female lead, marking her film debut.

In that film, Hepburn played the daughter of John Barrymore. "The play might have been called *Incest*," Hepburn later quipped. "On screen, he was my father; off-screen he was my horndog."

When Tallulah later ran into Hepburn back in New York, she bluntly asked her, "Did you and Mr. Barrymore do the dirty deed?"

"Not at all!" Hepburn answered. "I went to his dressing room to rehearse. He asked me to take off my clothes and lie on his sofa. When I refused, he said, "I see. Let's just go over our lines, then."

"That's not what happened with me," Tallulah said. "One night he asked me, 'Do you think that if I screwed you, you'd leave me alone?'"

"I said that I would, but I lied," Tallulah said. "After I spent a night with him, I knocked on his door night after night until he told me to give him some rest. I said to him, 'You're an actor. All actors are supposed to like an encore performance.'"

***

Rachel Crothers then wrote another play called *Everyday* expressly for Tallulah. The playwright told the press, "I am very impressed with the new generation, especially Tallulah Bankhead." In many respects, the play evoked the Sinclair Lewis classic, *Main Street*.

Cast as Phyllis Noland, Tallulah returns home to a dreary small town in the Middle West, where her father, a judge, has already selected a husband for her.

Everyday opened on November 16, 1921, at the Bijou Theatre in Manhattan, but ran for only three weeks. *Variety* thought Tallulah looked "ravishing," but the New York *Morning Post* criticized her diction.

In April of 1922, Tallulah—on the verge of a nervous breakdown after the loss of her grandmother—went into rehearsals for a starring role in an upcoming Broadway comedy, *Her Temporary Husband*. She bowed out of the production and was quickly replaced with another actress. The movie rights for a silent screen version were sold, and the resulting film starred Owen Moore.

Tallulah's last play in New York before heading back to London was *The Exciters*. Martin Brown, a former actor and dancer, had switched to writing plays. He was instrumental in getting Tallulah cast as Ronnie Rand, a "wild and reckless woman with a gun tucked into her garter belt." The play, which critics defined as both a drawing room comedy and a crime adventure, opened at the Times Square Theatre on September 12, 1922.

By now, in addition to her fans in London, Tallulah had developed a cult following in America, too. On opening night, her fans, who had booked most of the front-row seats, stood and applauded her entrance for five minutes before she could deliver her first line.

One reviewer defined Tallulah as "ripe and gorgeous," predicting that she would go far in the theater. But others attacked her "silly friends who scream wildly and applaud 'TALLU! TALLU!' before she utters one word."

One critic of *The Exciters* noted that "success is weighing heavily on

John Barrymore, snap-shotted from the deck of his yacht.

Almost everyone in the theater had seen him clothed and emoting as, among others, *Hamlet*, but only some of them, (including Tallulah) had seen him naked.

It's believed that the loincloth he appears to be wearing in this shot was added as a technical afterthought.

her, and she looks tired and a bit fed up with her work."

Tallulah herself defined the play as "the unfunniest thing I've ever done."

A writer for *Vanity Fair* hailed her as "the world's most subtly amusing imitator of Ethel Barrymore."

For some time, Estelle Winwood had been urging her to try her luck on the London stage. "They have a dearth of beautiful women there, and you would fit in perfectly, especially in all those roles that call for an American girl."

Then, quite coincidentally, an offer appeared involving Tallulah's relocation to England.

***

As the first cold winds of October blew down from Canada, Tallulah and Estelle Winwood put on their overcoats to attend a party on Fifth Avenue for the theatrical elite.

Tallulah was already on her third drink when Winwood gently took her arm and guided her across the room to meet Charles Cochran, a British impresario who was visiting New York from London. He came to Manhattan every year to see the latest shows on Broadway and to be on the lookout for actors who might fit into plays in the West End, particularly if the role called for an American, as so many of them did.

Born in Sussex, England, he first came to New York at the age of eighteen, when he wanted to become an actor. But soon, he realized that his talent lay in management rather than acting.

In the 1920s and '30s, he became known for producing musical revues and plays, particularly the works of Noël Coward. He was influential in the careers of Beatrice Lillie, Gertrude Lawrence, Elizabeth Bergner, Eleonora Duse, Anna Neagle, and the Dolly Sisters, among many others. He also produced the Ballets Russes and managed London's Royal Albert Hall for twelve years.

He told Tallulah that he was in town "property hunting," and that he thought she'd be wonderful cast as the waif in *Seventh Heaven* or as the prostitute, Sadie Thompson, in W. Somerset Maugham's *Rain*. Regrettably, he claimed, the rights to both of those plays had already been sold to other producers.

Back in London, he talked to Sir Gerard du Maurier, the pre-eminent actor and director in the West End, trying to persuade him to cast Tallulah in his latest play, *The Dancers*.

When Tallulah got wind of this, she told her family and her friends at the Algonquin that she was on the verge of

It was in the 1920s when **Tallulah** got photographed a lot, usually clad in clingy, low-cut satins and invariably with a cigarette. There's a coterie of collectors who insist that some of her repertoire included artfully arranged nudes, too, one of which allegedly appears on the left, above.

sailing to London to star opposite Du Maurier. But three days later, another telegram arrived, informing her that Du Maurier had decided to cast Dorothy Dix into the role instead.

Du Maurier told Cochran, "I don't dare take a chance on this untried thespian."

Having already announced her casting, Tallulah found herself in an embarrassing position "because I've bragged to everybody that the role is mine."

Winwood urged her to go to London anyway, thinking that once Du Maurier saw her again, he might change his mind—or that some other role might become available for her.

Borrowing $1,000, she set sail for the U.K. and then—even though she couldn't afford it—checked into London's Ritz Hotel. "One needs to put up a good front," she said.

With Dix in the role, rehearsals had already begun. At the time, Du Maurier was appearing for the final week's run of *Bulldog Drummond* before joining the cast rehearsing *The Dancers*. Cochran escorted Tallulah to see this popular detective mystery, then led her backstage to meet Du Maurier.

His fame had certainly traveled to Broadway. Born in Hampstead in 1873, he was the father of Daphne du Maurier, who was destined to become one of the most famous English novelists of her era. [*Her best known work would be* Rebecca. *In 1940, it would be adapted into a hit film starring Laurence Olivier and Joan Fontaine.*]

When Tallulah met him, he had just been knighted. [*Beginning in 1917 with the film* Justice, *he'd also become a movie actor, although his filmography was neither long nor impressive.*]

At their introduction, Du Maurier did not seem impressed with Tallulah. "Why did you come over here? I was told you were sent a telegram telling you that the role had already been cast with someone else. You've wasted your trip."

This publicity photo of **Tallulah Bankhead**—snapped by photographer-Ira Hill—is the one carried by Charles Cochran from New York to London as a means of "selling" the British theatrical producer Sir Gerald du Maurier on the theatrical (and other) charms of the Alabama bombshell.

Daphne du Maurier was the lesbian (and very butch) daughter of Sir Gerard de Maurier, a theatrical agent whose endorsement was coveted by Tallulah.

When Daphne—later famous as the author of the (subliminally lesbian) Gothic novel, *Rebecca*—met Tallulah, she told her father that she was the most beautiful girl she'd ever seen.

She expressed her regret and disappointment later that evening, when Cochran escorted her to a late-night supper at the Savoy Grill.

According to Tallulah, "Charles took Du Maurier's rejection of me as a personal defeat and came up with another plan. He wanted me to show up the following evening with him in a sexy evening gown, looking like a flapper with her hair let down—no hat."

This time in Du Maurier's dressing room, Tallulah met his soon-to-be-celebrated teenaged daughter, Daphne. She and Tallulah chatted while her father removed his stage makeup.

In time, Daphne became a well-known English lesbian who was visibly attracted to Tallulah. They agreed to meet the following day for lunch. After Tallulah and Cochran disappeared together into the night, Daphne told her father, "That is the most beautiful girl I've ever seen."

On the third night, after an intimate lunch with Daphne, Tallulah showed up alone to visit Du Maurier, *père*. On this, the night of his final appearance in *Bulldog Drummond,* Du Maurier was far more amicable and invited her to a late night supper, after which she spent the night with him. Later, she told Winwood, "He didn't force me onto the casting couch. I forced him. The next morning, he paid off Dix and announced that Tallulah Bankhead would be cast as the female lead of *The Dancers.*"

Her casting in what evolved into a second-rate melodrama would lead to her "eight-year gig" in London. "I played a waif trapped by circumstances in a dance hall in British Columbia. As the part unfolds, I capture the carnal eye of a young Englishman. Although I start out as a Pocahontas in an elaborate feathery headdress, I end up as a ballerina in Paris."

At the premiere, Tallulah was "nervous as hell. I got through the first act and retreated to my dressing room." She had performed a tender scene, but as she left the stage, she heard nothing except the roar of the crowd.

In tears, she confronted her gruesome fear that she had flopped. "I had been booed and disgraced."

Only later did she learn that the screams and yells were of approval. Her career in London was launched, an instant success. While appearing in *The Dancers,* she developed a cult following that would stick with her through all her performances. Working class girls—secretaries, waitresses, department store clerks—formed a cult labeled "The Gallery Girls," a reference to their booking of the cheapest seats.

A Tallulah craze swept through London, as these women began to walk, talk, and look like Tallulah. When she appeared on stage, a chant arose—"TALLULAH! TALLULAH! TALLULAH!"

"That always made my co-stars furious," she said. "It became mandatory for me to strip down in every play, showing off my expensive lingerie."

"I saw my name in lights," she said. "It was the most obscene thing I had ever seen in my life. I was on my way."

But then "it" happened. She appeared in a disaster called *Conchita,* a florid melodrama set in Cuba during the dying days of Spain's rule over that Caribbean nation.

"When the curtain went down on *Conchita,* the boos would have rocked the Walls of Jericho," Tallulah said. "It lasted a week."

Rehearsals for *Conchita* had started well, with Basil Dean directing. This Londoner was an actor, writer, and film producer. In World War I, he'd led ENSA, a government-sponsored organization bringing live entertainment to Allied troops "Even such an august personage couldn't save

Conchita," Tallulah claimed.

In the play, she started out as a serving girl in a rowdy sailors' bar. "I did my best impersonation of Lupe Velez."

On opening night, Tallulah came out with a monkey which, the moment she walked with it into public view, went berserk. "He snatched my black wig from my head, leaped from my arms, and scampered down to the footlights. There, he paused, peered out at the audience, then waved my wig over his head. The audience had been giggling at the absurd plot before this simian had at me. Now, it became hysterical."

What did Tallulah do in this crisis? "I turned a cartwheel. The audience roared. After the monkey business, I was afraid they might boo me. Instead, I received an ovation."

***

Tallulah had high hopes for her third play, *This Marriage,* in that she'd be co-starring with two of London's best stage actors, Herbert Marshall and Cathleen Nisbett.

A Londoner, Marshall had lost a leg during World War I, but he walked so well that one would not know that. It would be in Hollywood where Marshall would achieve international fame in such movies as *The Letter* (1940) with Bette Davis, and in *The Little Foxes* (1941), also with Davis. Other prestigious pictures would include *The Razor's Edge* with Tyrone Power. Over the years, his leading ladies would include Greta Garbo and Marlene Dietrich.

A native of Cheshire, Nesbitt was both a stage and film actress. She had made her stage debut in 1910, appearing in countless plays after that.

By 1912, she'd become the lover of Rupert Poole, the English poet, who wrote love sonnets to her. Engaged to be married to her, he died during World War II.

She had been John Barrymore's leading lady in his first dramatic stage role.,

Nesbitt's first Hollywood film would not come until 1954, when she was a supporting player in *Three Coins in the Fountain.* She also starred as Mrs. Higgins in the 1964 film adaptation of *Pygmalion, My Fair Lady* starring Rex Harrison. In time, she would play both the mother of Richard Burton and the grandmother of Cary Grant.

"I was in distinguished company," Tallulah said in reference to her role in *This Marriage.*

Tallulah "*a l'Espanol,*" as Conchita, evoking Carmen in all her Sevillana finery, replete with a fan and a very black wig.

Imitating a fiery Spanish dancer, despite her many previous successes on the London stage, she was almost booed off the stage.

What did quick-witted Tallu do, as an "informal modern American" to rescue the moment?

She performed—impromptu and out of context, and wearing underpanties—a cartwheel on stage to break the tension

Whereas the audience and critics continued to relentlessly destroy the play, they gave Tallulah herself a standing ovation.

The play was about a sort of *ménage à trois* as Tallulah goes after Marshall, whose character was wed to Nesbitt's. As the *Christian Science Monitor* phrased it, "Vera Farrington (Nisbett) has outspoken views upon which the Victorian girl was presumed to be ignorant."

After four years of marriage, Vera's union with Christopher (Marshall) is growing stale. Yvonne (Tallulah) sets out to seduce him. Vera suggests that they share her husband.

Some critics praised Tallulah for her acting, one suggesting that Christopher had no more chance of escaping from her clutches than a rabbit does from a snake. The play lasted for only three weeks. Tallulah announced to Nesbitt and Marshall, "It's my fault. I surely must be the lousiest actress in London."

Quintessential British humor in a consummate British actress: **Cathleen Nesbitt**, later in her life, around the time she portrayed Rex Harrison's mother in the film version of *My Fair Lady*.

***

After many of her performances, Tallulah retired to her dressing room and then emerged in a seductive gown for an evening on the town. After carousing at a dance club, her party often retired to one or another of the late-night "after hours" dives of Soho or to an "anything goes" private party in Mayfair.

In affair after affair, she seemed to be searching for that elusive thing called love. "I'm always changing the objects of my objections. More frequently, it's the objects who fall out of love with me."

The actress with the unusual billing, "Mrs. Patrick Campbell," claimed, "Bankhead, during her stay in London, had abortions the way most women have permanent wave. She was rumored to have aborted the child of the Prince of Wales."

Tallulah responded to that by making an outrageous revelation to Noël Coward. "The Prince's penis is so small I didn't know it was capable of penetration."

"Tell me something I don't already know," Coward shot back.

"Speaking of abortions, there's one doctor in Limehouse I'll never patronize again," she said. "He uses rusty nails and antique razor blades."

Both the Prince of Wales and Tallulah were teenagers when they first met at a reception in Washington. He was in the U.S. as part of a state visit, and Tallulah's grandmother

Two views of a British actor **Herbert Marshall**: left with **Tallulah Bankhead** in a London production of the "very racy for its time," *This Marriage*, and (right) with **Joan Crawford** in the MGM's 1941 romance, *When Ladies Meet*.

insisted she come with her. In preparation for the event, she taught her granddaughter how to curtsy. "There is a correct way to genuflect," she said, demonstrating how to do it before a very young Tallulah, who protested, "I'm supposed to bow before that little boy, my nose touching the rug? I'll look like a damn fool."

Nonetheless, she curtsied in style before Prince Charming, and he remembered her when she arrived in London. One night at the theater, he came backstage to invite her dining and dancing. Since he was viewed as the most desirable man in all the British Empire, she eagerly accepted.

In 1923, a periodical in Manhattan ran an item about him: "According to gossip, the heir to the throne of Great Britain is paying marked attention to Tallulah Bankhead, a beauteous young American actress now the toast of the West End."

During her first months in London, they were seen dining at her favorite restaurant, the Savoy Grill, before moving on for dancing at a club in Mayfair.

"I think the Prince was infatuated with her, really smitten," Cathleen Nisbitt said. "Let's face it: She was a hell of a lot prettier and much more fun than the American *divorcée* and slut, Wallis Warfield. Warfield, so I heard, could bring the Prince's little thing to life by a feather trick she learned in the brothels of Shanghai."

Tallulah misinterpreted the Prince's infatuation, writing back home that she fully expected to be married in Westminster Abbey and would become the Princess of Wales and the future Queen of England. "I guess that will also make me Empress of India."

The **Prince of Wales** (later King Edward VIII) dated Tallulah in London and had a brief affair with her.

He then fell in love with the American divorcee, **Wallis Warfield Simpson**, and gave up his throne for "the woman I love."

Mrs. Patrick Campbell as Electra.

She made it clear that she did NOT approve of what she described as Tallulah's easy propensity for having abortions.

***

Her next play, *The Creaking Chair* (1924), was a murder mystery which she claimed was "a tired old melodrama fished from the East India docks in Limehouse."

She was cast as the enigmatic spouse of an Egyptologist confined to a wheelchair. The potboiler gave her a chance to work with the distinguished actor, C. Aubrey Smith, and another talented thespian, Nigel Bruce.

"Aubrey was as much a symbol of the British Empire as the British lion," Tallulah said. "The play was ghastly, and on opening night the author was booed. Since it was a lousy script, Aubrey decided to play it for the pure farce of it all."

"I was scandalous in my performance, inventing my own lines. I was so popular that I attracted Prince George (later the Duke of Kent). He fell madly in love with me, and he packed a pistol two or three times bigger than the Prince of Wales."

"By caricaturing the dumb play, we made it a hit, and it played for thirty weeks to packed houses."

[Aubrey was born in 1863, and was an "English test" cricketer, perhaps the finest in the Empire. He tried to explain the game to Tallulah, "but I didn't get it. He told me that in 1888, he'd gone to South Africa to prospect for gold."

According to Aubrey, "In Africa, all I got was pneumonia, and I was pronounced dead, but before they buried me, I woke up, and called them quacks."

In 1932, he went to Hollywood to make movies. There, he founded The Cricket Club, attracting such members as Nigel Bruce, Leslie Howard, Boris Karloff, Laurence Olivier, and David Niven. He became a familiar figure to American filmgoers, thanks in part to his bushy eyebrows, beady eyes, and handlebar mustache.

Actors who appeared with him in some of his films included Gary Cooper, Maurice Chevalier, Vivien Leigh, Clark Gable, and Ronald Colman.

"Aubrey told me if I had been alive in 1883, I would have experienced one of the biggest thrills of my life," Tallulah said. "He claimed that in one 24-hour period, he blasted off ten times."

During the run of *The Creaking Chair*, actor **C. Aubrey Smith** became a father figure to Tallulah.

"Time and time again, she came to me in tears when the press was cruel to her."

She threatened *London Evening Standard* with a libel suit when the caricaturist, Tom Till, drew her as a "cottage-loaf wavering on spindly legs."

***

It was during her appearance in *The Creaking Chair* that Basil Dean, the British theatrical impresario, came backstage to meet with Tallulah in her dressing room. He had just returned from one of his trips to America, where he'd seen the charismatic actress Jeanne Eagels in her stage performance of *Rain*, a drama by W. Somerset Maugham which featured her as the decade's most memorable prostitute, Sadie Thompson.

"When the play opens in England, I think you'd be great as the whore," he told Tallulah.

"But I never charge, *dah-ling*," she protested, although intrigued with the idea.

Dean suggested she return to the United States and catch one of Eagel's performances. Tallulah took his advice.

Even before Tallulah left for America, there was much speculation in the London press as to which actress would play Sadie Thompson. The

Prince George, Duke of Kent, according to Tallulah, "knew what to do in the boudoir, unlike the Prince of Wales."

Prince George was known to have had numerous affairs without gender preference.

entertainment editor for the London *Times* wrote, "The American Actress, Tallulah Bankhead, would be ideal as Sadie Thompson. She has a certain dynamic quality with smouldering looks and a husky voice. She could come out on stage dressed as a whore to rival any tart in Soho."

As the curtain fell on *The Creaking Chair*, Tallulah packed her luggage and took the train to Southampton. She had reserved a suite aboard the *SS Berengaria*, at the time the pride of the Cunard fleet.

During her Atlantic crossing, she danced every night with the captain and his officers. "One good looker in his uniform was a darling. He was from Liverpool. But he was also jealous. He later told the press that during the crossing, I must have gone to bed with at least eight officers on board. What slander! I went to bed with only seven!"

SS Berengaria, with Tallulah aboard, arrived at the Port of New York on February 24, 1923. Her sister, Eugenia, was waiting on the pier to welcome her.

After their reunion, Tallulah boarded the train to Pittsburgh, where Eagels was appearing on stage in a road tour of *Rain*.

Tallulah was mesmerized seeing Eagels perform. After the curtain fell, she went backstage to congratulate her. "You're magnificent," Tallulah said, bowing before her and kissing her hand. "I'm in the presence of greatness."

"Cut the shit, Tallu," Eagels said. "Let's you and I go out and get drunk. I've got an idea. I'll wear my Sadie Thompson whorish drag, and I'll dress you in one of my garish outfits. We'll pretend to be whores and pick up some steel workers or soldiers."

Tallulah thought that would be "a swell idea." That night, they failed to pick up any "blokes," but ended up in bed together in a hotel suite. "We were drunk, but we could still explore each other's nether regions," Tallulah said. "Thank Gawd she was double-gaited. She entertained me both on the stage and in bed."

After Tallulah's return to New York, she learned that Basil Dean, W. Somerset Maugham, and herself had each reserved space aboard the same ship to Southampton. Then Dean virtually ordered her to cancel her reservation because Maugham did not like being pestered by actresses seeking roles in his plays. *[Maugham, because of his prestige as a playwright, had retained the power of casting the right actress for the role of Sadie.]*

Sir Gerald Kelly's portait of a foppish-looking **W. Somerset Maugham** as a young man. As a frequently toxic and mean-spirited critic, he terrorized actresses stronger than Tallulah with his sometimes vitriolic reviews of their stage work.

Tallulah in a publicity shot for *The Creaking Chair*. That's a LOT of cleavage....

The gay playwright, Emlyn Williams, attended a performance and later said:

"Tallulah's voice had a timbre steeped as deep in sex as the human voice can do without drowning."

"Don't worry," Dean told her. "At the right time, I'll set up a tryout where you'll perform in two or three scenes as Sadie Thompson."

Eventually—after many protests—she acquiesced to Dean's wishes and canceled her booking aboard the *SS Berengaria*. The ship that followed in its wake was a grubby-looking cattle boat. "The transatlantic crossing was a nightmare," she lamented. "Horrible food. Grotesque passengers. In the cabin next to mine was the corpse of an Englishman who had died during a visit to his family in Brooklyn. I decided to remain in my cabin for most of the trip, during which I memorized the script of *Rain* from my lips to my toenails."

When she finally got to London, she told Dean, "I can play Sadie Thompson, that hussy, even though I'm a lady."

After several late-night sessions on his own with her, Dean later said to his assistant, "Tallulah can definitely play a hussy. She's had vast experience in the role."

A stoic Maugham eventually sat through two auditions of Tallulah as Sadie. As she remembered it, "I'm a great imitator., I think I impersonated Eagels in the role."

Then Dean met with her and delivered the bad news: "Maugham has rejected you. He claims you have no personality. He's assigned the role to Olga Lindo."

"Losing the role devastated me," Tallulah said. "I was on the verge of suicide."

She stopped off in a pub and had an inordinate amount of alcohol before staggering back to her apartment at 44 Curzon Street. There, she put on one of Sadie's costumes and swallowed a bottle of aspirin. Then she wrote a suicide note that included the line "It ain't gonna *Rain* no more, no more."

Sometime in the middle of the night, she rushed to her apartment's toilet and "vomited violently" into the bowl.

At 8AM after her botched suicide attempt, her phone rang. On its other end was Noël Coward: "Our star has dropped out of my latest play, *Fallen Angels*. I want you for the lead. We open in a week. You've got only days to learn the part. Are you on board?"

"I'm your number one passenger," she said. "I'll be there as soon as I put on my lace drawers."

With Olga Lindo in the lead, the London production of *Rain* survived for five months. Dean claimed, "With Tallulah as Sadie, we would have run for more than a year."

She was later somewhat gratified to learn that Maugham, at his villa on the French Riviera, told Noël Coward, "The biggest mistake in my experience in the theater was rejecting Tallulah Bankhead for the role of Sadie."

[Ironically, in 1935, Tallulah would play Sadie Thompson in New York in a revival of Rain at the Music Box Theatre. In the opening night audience sat Gary Cooper, Noël Coward, Bebe Daniels, and Beatrice Lillie, among other distinguished playgoers.]

***

After ending her phone conversation with Coward, Tallulah pulled herself together and rushed to the London theater where *Fallen Angels* was being rehearsed. There, she learned that *Fallen Angels* contained roles for only two characters and that Margaret Bannerman, its original star, had had a nervous breakdown. Tallulah was introduced to Edna Best, her co-star. She had only one week to learn her part. The role paid one-hundred pounds a week.

According to the script, both women had been in love with a Lothario with a roving eye, who is returning to London.

Conveniently, each of their husbands is temporarily absent on a golfing trip, leaving both women alone and "unsupervised." The question was, will either of them, or both of them, fall once again for this wandering Romeo?

In a 1937 memoir, *Present Indicative,* Coward described how quickly Tallulah learned her role. "She had a remarkable vitality. She tore off her hat, tossed her fur, kissed everybody on the mouth, and then hurled herself into the role and pulled it off."

As the curtain fell after the production's opening night, Best and Tallulah received standing ovations that continued for ten minutes. During the performance, some advocates of public morality had risen from their seats and stormed out. One of them told the press, "This is the worst filth ever presented in London since the days of the Bard."

Another remarked, "Drunken women! How disgusting!" Noël Coward should be ashamed."

A critic described *Fallen Angels* as "vulgar, disgusting, shocking, nauseating, vile, obscene, and degenerate."

Despite those damning reviews, *Fallen Angels* opened at The Globe on April 21, 1925 and ran for 158 performances.

It was during the run of the play, owing in part to Noël Coward's homosexual following, that gay men (they weren't called that back then) began showing up in numbers that rivaled those of The Gallery Girls. Tallulah soon dubbed them "The Gallery Boys."

Until her final days and beyond, Tallulah would become *"the dah-ling"* of the gay set. The adulation of her devoted following would endure much longer than the approval of her Gallery Girls, who eventually settled down into staid mar-

Tallulah in the revival of *Rain* as Sadie Thompson.

Theater critic Percy Hammond wrote, "In her turbulent impersonation of the sad joy-girl of Pago-Pago, Tallulah Bankhead swaggers into Trader Horn's in the South Seas, swinging her rounded shanks in the wanton manner of Miss Mae West. As she laid her big eyes on a handsome leatherneck and dropped husky wisecracks from her full lips, the resemblance to West grew terrifying."

Rich, self-indulgent, married, spoiled, and unreliable. **Napier, Lord Alington**. "I had no difficulty luring Naps from his male lovers," Tallulah said. "He was big where it mattered. Take it from me, *dah-ling*, size does matter. That divine man also knew how to use his lips."

ried lives, when Tallulah became just a faded memory of their younger days.

A devoted admirer of *Fallen Angels* was Sir Winston Churchill, who came to see it five times, visiting Tallulah backstage on every occasion. According to rumors, he did more than visit. Although they left the theater in separate cars, they were said to have met later at an apartment of one of his deputies in Mayfair.

Sir Winston told her he had fallen in love with Ethel Barrymore and that he had once proposed marriage to her. According to Tallulah—and not confirmed—the statesman also confessed that he had seduced Miss Barrymore, too.

***

During Tallulah's years in the British Isles, a far more serious romance unfolded with Napier, Lord Alington, who she nicknamed "Naps."

She had first met Naps in York's Greenwich Village during the era he was in New York "to master the banking business." As a house guest of Mrs. Cornelius Vanderbilt, he had become bored with her society friends.

Invited to a party downtown, he arrived in an overcoat thrown over his pajamas, with a bottle of gin in his pocket. There, he met nineteen-year-old Tallulah. His first question to her was, "Are you still a virgin?"

Whether true or not, she told him, "the glories of penetration have eluded me."

Lord Beaverbrook, the British press baron, was often "the beard" who concealed the affair between Tallulah and his best friend, **Sir Winston Churchill.**

The statesman attended five performances of Tallulah's stage productions, sometimes disappearing with her after the curtain went down.

On two occasions, Churchill invited Tallulah to have lunch with him at the House of Commons.

During World War II, Tallulah wrote to FDR, requesting that "for patriotic purposes" he issue a postage stamp showing her with Churchill on her right, the President on her left.

Although the then-president rejected the idea, he suggested that she work with Eleanor Roosevelt to raise money for the war effort, which she did.

"I would like to remedy the situation, becoming the first of what I know will be many beaux. I want to be your hymen buster."

She rejected his offer that evening, but when she met him a second time, she retreated to a hotel room with him. After a week of nightly encounters, he proposed marriage.

She later wrote, "I was irked by his nonchalance, his cynicism, his flashes of cruelty. Away from him, I found those flaws attracted me."

She spent most of the nights of December 1921 and January of 1922 in his arms. They were sometimes accompanied by what she called "a frustrated young Englishman, Noël Coward, who wanted Naps for himself."

After an absence, Tallulah hooked up with him again when she returned to London. She was attracted to his charm and wit, although admitting, "He wasn't good looking and had an almost repulsive mouth. He was known for practicing the art of living recklessly."

He was born in November of 1896 as Napier Sturt, 3rd Baron Alington. He would eventually marry Lady Mary Sibell Ashley-Cooper, daughter of the 9th Earl of Shaftesbury, in 1928, but before that, he was far better known as the lover of Tallulah during her years in London.

One author said, "He was well cultivated, a notorious bisexual with sensuous, meaty lips, a distant antic charm, a history of mysterious disappearances, and a streak of cruelty."

When not with a woman, he seduced most of the guards at Buckingham Palace. "They were underpaid and earned extra money hustling homosexuals." He once told Tallulah, "Many of them are quite studly and have already serviced the Prince of Wales *[later King Edward VIII, and after his abdication, the Duke of Windsor]*, that 'lady-in-waiting' who'll take over the throne."

During World War I, he was a captain in the Royal Air Force, telling Tallulah, "Away from their wives or girlfriends, I had to become the wife or girlfriend. I did it for love of country."

"Or for the love of something else," she answered. She never criticized Naps for his bisexuality, since she was a "part-time lesbian myself."

Tallulah openly confessed to both loving and resenting Naps, calling him "unpredictable, irresponsible, and never having an appointment he didn't skip."

During their affair, he often fled from London for months at a time, never telling her when he was leaving or when he'd return. But she always welcomed him back with open arms.

In Paris, Tallulah found herself in the awkward position of competing with **Jean Cocteau** for the love-making of Naps.

Nicknamed "The Frivolous Prince" he was a poet, dramatist, novelist, and filmmaker. In his early twenties, he was "hanging out" with Marcel Proust and André Gide.

Unlike most men of his era, he never hid his homosexuality, famously authoring the homoerotic and semi-autobiographical *Le livre blanc (The White Paper)*.

She once told a friend, "I loved Sir Winston as much as I hated Somerset Maugham." Lord Beaverbrook once drove her to Churchill's country home, which stood in apple orchards and hop fields in Kent, southeast of London. When they pulled up in front of Chartwell, they discovered him laying bricks for a garden wall.

Even after she left England, she and Churchill stayed in touch. In time, Tallulah became a close friend of Eleanor Roosevelt and sometimes she'd brag, "Do you know who called me the other night?" she asked Eleanor. "Sir Winston himself."

"I'm sure he needed advice on how to hold onto the British Empire," the First Lady said.

***

Edward Molyneux was a leading British fashion designer. Sometimes based in Paris, he was known for an "impeccably refined simplicity" favored by screen stars and European royalty, As articulated by historian

Caroline Milbank, "Molyneux was the designer to whom a fashionable woman would turn if she wanted to be absolutely right without being utterly predictable in the Twenties and Thirties."

A close friend of Noël Coward, Molyneux was designing the clothes for *The Gold Diggers,* Tallulah's next play. She was in Paris to be fitted by him.

In a stylish neighborhood in Paris, in front of the Hotel de Crillon, she ran into Naps, who invited her to dinner at Jean Cocteau's night club, Le Boeuf sur le Toit, which drew a large homosexual patronage.

"Cocteau and I spend our nights together smoking opium," Naps told her. "He's marvelous. So is smoking opium. The other night, he introduced me to André Gide. They both wanted to do me."

At midnight, he introduced her to Cocteau before the two of them headed off into the night, leaving Tallulah alone.

She saw him occasionally before she finally left London for New York. "Some of the fire had gone out of our relationship," she said. "I think it was time I moved on. Then he told me he'd be in Switzerland for a while," she said. "He didn't know when he'd return."

"We'll meet again someday," he told her. "Another rendezvous, perhaps. Life is so unpredictable."

Back in America, still maneuvering for a fling at a movie career in Hollywood and success on the Broadway stage, Tallulah thought of Naps on occasion. "He still occupied a place in my heart, but, as the years passed, the memory grew dimmer," she told Darwin Porter one night at her townhouse in Manhattan.

She was saddened to learn of his death in September of 1940 at the age of thirty-three. In Cairo, he came down with a fatal attack of pneumonia and was buried in Egypt.

He left no male heir, so his title (Lord Alington) became extinct. His estate, including his massively impressive homestead in Dorset (Crichel House), was passed to his eleven-year-old daughter.

***

Some critics wrote that Michael Arlen's best-selling novel of the 1920s, *The Green Hat,* was actually inspired by Tallulah's love affair with Naps. Its lead character was Napier Harpendon, a scion of landed gentry.

Born in Bulgaria in 1895, Arlen eventually fled to England, where he was educated. In time, he became a British essayist, short story writer, novelist, scriptwriter, and playwright. When Tallulah met him, just before she was cast as the female lead in the stage adaptation of *The Green Hat,* he was enjoying success for his satirical romances set in Eng-

Michael Arlen persuaded some of his era's greatest divas (Greta Garbo, Katharine Cornell, and Tallulah Bankhead) to portray his heroine, Iris March in stage and screen versions of his hit play *The Green Hat.*

Time magazine put him on its cover, portraying him as a noble outcast and *demi-mondaine.* A critic wrote: "*The Green Hat* exposed the hypocrisy and rottenness of the decent, society that had cast Iris March out."

lish smart society.

Published in 1924, *The Green Hat* narrates the short life and violent death of Iris Storm, a dashing widow, *femme fatale*, and owner of a yellow Hispano-Suiza, as well as the green hat which inspired the title of Arlen's novel.

He had adapted his own novel into the stage play, which was initially a hit on Broadway, starring Katharine Cornell and Leslie Howard. Eventually, with Tallulah, it became successful in London, too.

The Green Hat was later adapted into a film, *A Woman of Affairs* (1929), co-starring Greta Garbo and her then lover, the matinée idol, John Gilbert. American censors demanded that its references to homosexuality and venereal disease be removed before they'd allow it to be distributed.

[After the talkies came into vogue, The Green Hat *was adapted for the screen once again, in 1934. Entitled* Outcast Lady, *it co-starred Herbert Marshall and Constance Bennett.*

Others of Arlen's works became the inspiration for such pictures as The Golden Arrow *(1936) with Bette Davis, and* The Heavenly Body *(1944) with William Powell and Hedy Lamarr.]*

Tallulah's friend, actress Gladys Cooper, was originally offered the London stage role of Iris, but rejected it because of the play's "immorality." Nonetheless, she showed up at its premiere to watch Tallulah as Iris.

On looking back, Tallulah was critical of much of its writing, finding it "too full of lyrical lines. The dialogue seemed out of place for actors in modern clothes to utter—lines such as 'Boy died of purity.' Who talks like that? I grew to hate appearing every night in *The Green Hat*."

"No wonder the play was a bigger hit in New York than in London," Tallulah said. "In London, I had to deliver such lines as 'I despise our England. We are shams, with patrician faces and peasant minds. You want to buy me with your traditions. May God forgive you for the sins committed in your name and me for ever having believed in them. You've got Union Jacks instead of hearts.'"

One reviewer wrote, "Iris Storm is intriguing. Although she has acquired the reputation of a shameless, shameful woman, she is actually a tragic figure—lonely, misunderstood, slandered, and trying to forget the past. She says, 'I have lit many fires to quench one large fire.' Iris could be seen as a woman before her time. In a man's world, she tries to play as a man—and loses tragically."

Hannen Swaffer, nicknamed "The Pope of Fleet Street," wrote: "Tallulah Bankhead is the most modern actress England has. She belongs to the semi-exclusive set of whom Michael Arlen writes in *The Green Hat*. She has beauty and a shimmering sense of theater."

Word of Tallulah's appearance in *The Green Hat* reached Broadway and Katharine Cornell. It was a play with which Cornell had had much success. In an interview with *The New York Times*, the great stage diva said, "I had to do a lot of work to envelope myself into the aura of Iris March. For Tallulah Bankhead, it was almost autobiography."

***

In January of 1926, Tallulah appeared in *Scotch Mist*, a play by Sir Patrick Hastings.

In Ramsay MacDonald's Labour government (1924 and 1929-31), Hastings had been his attorney general. As Mary Denvers, Tallulah played the indiscreet wife of a cabinet minister.

[An Irish actress, Mary Malone, who was married at the time to Tallulah's co-star, Geoffrey Tearle, showed up every day during rehearsals. "Miss Bankhead's reputation has preceded her, and I want to make sure she doesn't dig those red claws of hers into my Geoffrey."

On opening night, Malone sat in the front row. "My husband was supposed to have a love scene with Bankhead. Nothing in the script called for her to rape him."]

"The Gallery Girls" turned out *en masse* to see Tallulah emote in *Scotch Mist*. From her first scene to her curtain call, they cheered her on. "With fans like this," she told the press, "I'm going to stay on the London stage until I'm old and gray."

She claimed that she'd signed a ninety-year lease on a charming "Mews House" in Mayfair at 1 Farm Street, off Berkeley Square. Her first house guest was Ethel Barrymore, with whom she used to be in love, a definite one-way crush. As Tallulah told Basil Dean, "Sir Winston never got Ethel to marry him. Neither did I."

Dean said, "We were loudly denounced for *Scotch Mist*, especially by the Bishop of London. Thank god we were. Our critics kept it running far longer than the play deserved."

Tallulah later delivered her verdict: "Instead of *Scotch Mist*, the play should have been called *Marriage on the Rocks*."

A latter day critic, who sat through a college revival, said, "*Scotch Mist* was a forerunner of Edward Albee's *Who's Afraid of Virginia Wolff?*"

***

Tallulah's best role in London came in the 1924 Sidney Howard play, *They Knew What They Wanted*. In America, it had won the Pulitzer Prize, with a cast that starred Richard Bennett, Pauline Lord, and Glenn Anders.

Basil Dean had acquired the rights for a London production, and he once again asked Tallulah to play the lead, and she accepted. Its playwright objected to the director's choice, but he was overruled since he did not have cast approval.

It opened at St. Martin's Theatre in the West End. Its male stars included Sam Livesy as Tony and Glenn Anders reprising the part of Joe.

Tony was an aging Italian wine grower in California's Napa Valley. By letter, he proposes to Amy, who had waited on him in a spaghetti joint at the beginning of the play. Fearing that she will find him too old for consideration as a husband, he encloses a photo of Joe, his young hired hand. Thinking that it is Joe who wants to marry her, Amy accepts and journeys to the wine country to meet her future husband. There, she is horribly disappointed in Tony but falls in love with Joe. Preoccupied with affairs of the heart, it was a radical departure from the racy performances some critics had previously condemned as "sex plays."

[Howard's script later morphed into a trio of movies, beginning with Secret House *(1928), with Jean Hersholt and, later, a talkie,* A Lady to Love *(1930), featuring Edward G. Robinson and Vilma Banky. In 1940, Garson Kanin was behind its reaching the screen again, this time as* They Knew What They Wanted, *the title of the play that had inspired it.]*

What seemed like a squadron of Tallulah's loyal Gallery Girls showed up but did not applaud her when she first appeared in the drab costume of a spaghetti waitress.

They Knew What They Wanted opened in London in May of 1926 and for the most part, Tallulah received praise from the critics, many of whom had attacked her previous performances. "Miss Bankhead acted brilliantly," proclaimed the London *News*.

During the run of the play, Tallulah fell for Anders (playing Joe), "a big lug of a stud with shoulders so broad they stretched to New York. His shoulders weren't the only thing big about him."

One late night, after their performances, he took her dancing, ending up at the Embassy Club, where she spotted the Prince of Wales sitting alone in the corner. He wasn't alone for long. A guard from Buckingham Palace soon showed up after work to join him.

They Knew What They Wanted marked the pinnacle of Tallulah's stage career in London. "My only disappointment was that my Gallery Girls did not give me a standing ovation."

***

Tallulah's devoted coterie of Gallery Girls, however, turned out in full force to welcome her on opening night of her next play, *The Gold Diggers* (1926), a comedic *tour de force* about how showgirls "capture" sugar daddies. Ina Claire had already made it a hit on Broadway in 1919. In London, Tallulah starred in it four months after the close of *They Knew What They Wanted*.

Before its opening, the London press was running reports that Tallulah would soon announce her engagement to Prince Nicholas of Romania, who was lavishing expensive gifts, even diamonds, on her. She jokingly said, "I was merely rehearsing for my stage role as a gold digger."

Cast as Jerry Lamarr, a chorus girl, Tallulah actually falls in love with her rich catch—and not just for his money. As the highlight of the evening, Tallulah did a giddy Charleston and a cartwheel, wearing gold pajamas. It proved so popular she did it again and again. Adele Astaire, the sister of Fred Astaire, was in the audience on opening night. Later, she told Tallulah, "I have never seen a better dance. The only thing that will ever equal it would be Katharine Cornell swinging from a trapeze."

A dance critic said that although Tallulah performed a bad French cancan, her Charleston was better than what "that flapper," Joan Crawford had performed during her early Hollywood silents.

The Gold Diggers ran for five months. Although it eventually spawned at least three Hollywood films (*Gold Diggers of 1935*, *Gold Diggers of 1937*, and *Gold Diggers in Paris*), none of them was directly based on Tallulah's play.

***

Tallulah's next play, *The Garden of Eden,* by Avery Hopwood, was one of her most controversial. It wasn't about Adam and Eve. Hopwood had adapted it from an original work by two German playwrights, both with the first name of Rudolph: Bernauer and Osterreicher. One London critic later denounced the work as "something only a German mind could create."

The Garden of Eden opened at the Lyric Theater in London in 1927 and ran for 232 performances. Cast as Toni Le Brun, Tallulah played a dance hall girl in a seedy café, a clip joint named le Palais de Paris.

Provocative for its day, Toni resists the sexual overtures of her boss, Madame Grand, who wants more than just persuading her to wear a skimpy costume. Toni is rescued by a wealthy Moroccan playboy who falls in love with her and wants to marry her. Despite the objections of his father, the wedding is about to take place.

Then, in a fit of pique against her groom's father, Toni, dramatically poised at the top of a flight of stairs, rips off her wedding dress. With arms akimbo, she strips down to a skimpy version of what lingerie experts at the time called "camiknickers," shocking some members of the audience. As she 'liberated" herself, the Gallery Girls screamed in hysterical unison, delivering a standing ovation that interrupted the flow of the play.

Critics attacked the play for its lesbian overtones and for Tallulah's striptease. It was reviewed as "disgusting and oppressively vulgar." One critic attacked her for her "slouch walk" and her "habit of tossing her head back."

On Broadway, it was announced that Jeanne Eagels would star in a New York production of the play, but the role of Toni was eventually assigned to Miriam Hopkins instead.

In 1928, Hollywood adapted the play into a movie that starred Corinne Griffith, known at the time as "The Orchid Lady of the Silver Screen" and the most beautiful woman of the silent era. Tallulah saw the film, later defensively asking Estelle Winwood, "Tell me the truth, *dah-ling*: Am I not more beautiful that this Corrine bitch?"

Tallulah, a jazz age "*piéce de la résistance.*"

Never again in her long career did Tallulah receive the hysterical shouts and screams of approval—and what some witnesses described as the theatre's longest ovation—as she did during her stint in the provocative *The Gold Rush*.

The New York Times' London correspondent, Charles Morgan, commented on opening night:

"Cheers began some time before her first entrance. When she entered, they became deafening, mechanical, and persistent. There seemed to be a reasonable possibility that the play would be prevented from proceeding further. Greetings of stars is, in any case, an objectionable practice that destroys the theater's illusion, but tradition does offer some excuse for it when it is done in moderation. When it is exaggerated, as at the first night of *The Gold Diggers*, it becomes oppressive and disgusting."

Before her next play, *The Sphere,* a magazine published on Fleet Street named the ten most popular women in London. Tallulah got more votes than even the Queen of England. Also on the winners list were Claire Sheridan, Edith Sitwell, Lady Diana Cooper, Lady Astor, and the Duchess of Hamilton.

***

Tallulah found herself mired in controversy when she accepted the lead role in her next play, *Blackmail,* written by Charles Bennett. Directed by the famed actor, Raymond Massey, it was the story of a young woman who is blackmailed after fatally stabbing the lecherous man attempting to rape her.

Tallulah found the playwright "just divine, most charming." They concluded that their producer, A.H. Woods, had a condition known as "wall-eye."

"When talking to him, you never knew who he was looking at," she said.

During rehearsals for the play, Tallulah was negotiating to star in a film version of *The Green Hat*, the role eventually going to Blanche Sweet.

Before *Blackmail* opened, Tallulah battled with her producer (Woods), demanding rewrites he would not grant.

Bennett, its playwright, appeared weekly at Tallulah's residence on Farm Street, where she threw parties, inviting the elite of the British theatre, including such personages as Dame Sybil Thorndyke.

"One night I introduced Bennett to Sir John Gielgud. When he went to shake his hand, Sir John reached for his crotch instead. Sir John was supposed to have impeccable manners, but not that night. Of course, could you blame him? Bennett had a notable crotch to feel."

Blackmail opened at the Globe on February 28, 1927 but closed shortly thereafter. The ever-faithful Gallery Girls, now including young men, had screamed, yelled, and applauded, but many in the auditorium booed the play.

One critic attacked Tallulah for her diction: "The audience understood only half of what this American actress from Alabama had to say."

She shot back with, "Why do London newspapers hire only morons?"

An up-and-coming English director, Alfred Hitchcock, rescued *Blackmail* (the play) from oblivion, turning it into an exciting movie (also entitled *Blackmail*), the first successful European talkie. A silent version was also issued since most theaters at the time were not wired for sound.

It was voted the best British film of 1929.

***

Tallulah followed her involvement with the theatrical version of *Blackmail* with *Mud and Treacle*, "a real clunker" in her words. It opened with the death of her character, the rest of the play focusing on what led to her demise. Before opening night, she told her director, Basil Dean, "I'm about to go on that damn stage in the worst play ever to fog the footlights."

This would be the fourth and final time Dean would direct her onstage.

Tallulah played Polly Andrews, the daughter of landed gentry, Solomon Jacks (Nicholas Hanne), a middle-aged socialist. Onstage, he expounded on his theory of love: "It's like jumping into a river whose current is compounded of mud on the one hand and treacle on the other."

Benn Levy, its 28-year-old playwright, seemed confused when asked to describe his play:

It is said that the British Prime Minister, **James Ramsay MacDonald** (1866-1937), always remembered his one-night stand with Tallulah. The British politician was a leader of the Labour Party.

"It's a comedy, perhaps a tragedy, or a murder mystery, even a shameless tract in three acts, perhaps a post-dated prologue."

One critic claimed, "Tallulah Bankhead plays a Noël Coward type heroine, or at least someone moving in that direction."

Mud and Treacle held its premiere at The Globe on the night of May 9, 1928. In equal measure, critics attacked both its playwright and Tallulah. "This American actress should be tarred, feathered, and shipped back to Alabama," wrote one critic.

The Era, a London periodical, had kinder words: "The brilliant dialogue between mother and daughter is very witty."

The wild stories about Tallulah's private life were growing more scandalous by the week. One rumor floating around the West End asserted that she had seduced eight Eton teenagers in one night in her bedroom on Farm Street.

In spite of this notoriety, James Ramsay MacDonald came to see her perform. After the show, he enjoyed a bottle of champagne in her dressing room before both of them strolled out of the theater together. "What a glorious adventure, parading down Piccadilly with the PM," She told Dean the next day. "He took me back to my humble abode on Farm Street."

"Did you invite him in for some parlor games?" he asked.

"Don't be a silly fool, *dah-ling,*" she said. "Of course I did. He left at three that morning."

"What was it like?" he asked.

"On a scale of one to ten, I'd give him a six and a half," she said. "Churchill was much better…and much bigger."

***

Before involving herself in another play in the West End, Tallulah rushed to Paris for what she called "a quickie…that's quickie as in 'vacation,' *dah-ling.*"

She agreed to a rendezvous with actor Clifton Webb, also vacationing in Paris at the time. "I'd define the purpose of his sojourn there as 'cruising,'" she said. "Miss Priss had an insatiable appetite for well-hung young men."

She arrived at the designated rendezvous ten minutes before Webb and sat at a café table near the front of the bar. From there, she made eye contact with a tall, blonde, well-built young man wearing an Austrian military outfit.

Just as she was about to signal him over, Webb pranced into the bar. "His greedy eyes targeted the stud immediately," she said. "Completely ignoring me, he rushed out the door and returned with an entire pushcart of flowers." *[He had bought all the flowers it contained as well as the pushcart itself.]* "He wheeled it over and began dropping one flower after another at the feet of this Viennese gift from God."

Not to be upstaged by Webb, Tallulah rushed out onto the Parisian street, found a rival

In Clifton Webb's **"la bataille des fleurs,"** Tallulah won.

pushcart-based flower seller, bought everything it contained (and the pushcart, too), and wheeled it into the bar. Then she, too, began to drop flowers in front of what she later defined as "this divine gift package to all horny women and greedy cocksuckers."

After a few minutes of this "flower duel" with Webb, the soldier gravitated toward Tallulah and took her arm to escort her out of the bar. "Before he did that, this generous soul, as an apology to Webb, gave him a passionate, wet-lipped kiss with a foot of tongue."

The next day, when she lunched with Webb, he wanted to know all the anatomical details.

"Now I know why all those rumors about Austro-Hungarian officers have spread across Europe."

***

Tallulah had announced to the press, "Although I don't want to disappoint my Gallery Girls, I'm not doing any more sex plays."

Yet she accepted the lead in London production of *Her Cardboard Lover*, slated to open in August of 1928 in the West End at the Lyric Theatre, where it would run for 173 performances before going on tour and re-opening in Glasgow.

Her co-star was Leslie Howard, whose cultivated sensitivity on the stage was said to belong to a bygone era.

Two views of **Tallulah**, "the American Goddess" in *Her Cardboard Lover*.

Lower photo is with **Leslie Howard**, who called himself "a ladies' man."

["He was multi-talented," Tallulah said. "You name it, he could play it—soap opera, drawing room comedy, melodrama, Shakespeare. He fucked me only eighteen times during rehearsals and run of the play."

Years later, she said: "Had it not been for that bastard, David O. Selznick, I would have been playing Scarlett O'Hara lusting after Ashley Wilkes, played by Howard, in *Gone With the Wind*."]

In the United States, both Jeanne Eagels and Laurette Taylor, were assigned roles in *Her Cardboard Lover*.

Act One takes place in France in the resort of St-Jean-de-Luz. Simone Lagore, Tallulah's character, is a rich young *divorcée*. A young man, André Sallicel, loses ten thousand francs to her at a gaming table. When it's revealed that he doesn't have the money to pay her, she suggests he work it out by becoming her cardboard lover—that is, pretending to be her lover when, in fact, he'll be working innocuously as her secretary.

It's all a ruse to make another beau jealous. As might be expected, Tallulah's character falls for her cardboard lover.

Reviews were mixed. One London critic suggested that Tallulah, at last, had discarded the exaggerated mannerisms of characters she'd played in previous plays.

James Agee, writing in London's *Sunday Times*, called Tallulah "the mistress of the world," and the Gallery Girls and Boys continued their worshipful adulation of the "American goddess."

Another critic objected to all this adulation from her fans, writing, "Scotland Yard should go after this American actress, Miss Tallulah Bankhead. The charge? If only one-tenth of the rumors are true, it would mean lifetime imprisonment."

In 1928, in Hollywood, Cosmopolitan Productions released *Her Cardboard Lover* as a silent romantic comedy starring Marion Davies, the mistress of press baron William Randolph Hearst.

In 1932, it was remade as a talkie entitled *The Passionate Plumber*.

In 1942, *Her Cardboard Lover*, starred Norma Shearer and Robert Taylor. When Shearer, the former Queen of MGM, saw the final cut, she retired from the screen.

***

For one of her final plays on the London stage, Tallulah choose to revive a stage version of Alexander Dumas *fils'* 1849 novel, *La dame aux Camélias* (1930), more popularly known as *Camille*.

Over the course of many decades, many international stars, including Sarah Barnhardt, had played the then-shocking role of the love-smitten courtesan. In its 1936 film version, Greta Garbo starred as Marguerite Gautier, the courtesan who takes a young lover, Armand.

At first, Tallulah's co-starring stage counterpart was designated as a young Laurence Olivier, but he rejected the role, claiming, "Miss Bankhead will do anything, turn a cartwheel, whatever, to upstage me."

Tallulah later claimed, "I felt stifled in the play. The damn director wouldn't even let me smoke a cigarette on stage. I detest period pieces."

Eventually, Glen Byam Shaw, "even better looking than Olivier" (her words), played Armand. "Of course, *dah-ling*, I had to 'audition' him to make our love scenes more effective."

The reviews displeased Tallulah, especially the one in the *Times* of London, which referred to the rhythm of her lines as "wearisome." They went on to assert that she was "Horrible at delivering antique lines and was more suited to modern melodrama."

When the first reviews came in, Tallulah was completely demoralized, and the director found her crying in her dressing room.

***

Tallulah's reign as the toast of London was nearing its end when she signed to star in *Let Us Be Gay*. *[The meaning of that phrase was different from what it would have implied now.]* After an opening at the Lyric Theatre, it ran for 128 performances. It was written and produced by Rachel Crothers, who had worked with Tallulah before. Her co-stars included Helen Haye *[no, not Helen Hayes]*, Joan Matheson, and Bellenden Powell.

A cinematic adaptation of *Let Us Be Gay* was released the same year (1930). Distributed by MGM, it starred the studio's queen, Norma Shearer. Many critics who saw both the play and movie in London preferred the stage version with Tallulah.

[Shearer's film co-star was Rod La Rocque, who visited London around the same time. Tallulah pursued him, finding the six-footer so sexy she nicknamed him

"Rod Le Cock." But to her dismay, he was still a promiscuous homosexual despite his longtime lavender marriage to screen star Vilma Banky.]

In *Let Us Be Gay*, a romantic melodrama, Tallulah played both a *divorcée* and a mother, Kitty Brown, a witty and sophisticated "modern woman." Portrayed as a designer of fashionable clothing, she was made up with carmine-colored lipstick and inch-long eyelashes.

One critic stated that she "revealed moods of passion and emotion not explored before in her stage appearances." Another said that she "romped through this boomerang with enough spirit for six plays."

***

During her appearance in *Let Us Be Gay*, executives from Paramount flew in from Hollywood. Each of them told her that their studio wanted her to be "The Next Garbo," competing with films turned out by the MGM goddess.

She was offered the most money she'd been offered to that point—$3,000 a week at the beginning of the gig, increasing to $8,000 a week if the studio decided to pick up her option, depending on the box office reception of her first pictures.

Early in 1930, as she departed from England through the port of Southampton, mobs of Gallery Girls and Boys cheered her on her way. She'd been in England for eight years and had starred in sixteen plays and gone—based on her own estimate—through thirty-eight lovers, both male and female. It was time to go.

As she departed, the marquee lights were being systematically switched off at key points within the West End as a Great Depression settled over the land.

***

The *SS Acquitania* arrived at the Port of New York on January 13, 1931. Tallulah disembarked to see a country in crisis after the Wall Street crash of October, 1929. Waiting for her at the pier were two family members she hadn't seen since 1925: William B. Bankhead, her father, and her stepmother, Florence.

She checked into the Elysée Hotel on East 45th Street, where she had rented a suite for herself, her secretary, Edie Smith, and her dresser, Elizabeth Locke.

That afternoon, she met the press, telling them she had grown bored with the stage and that she was eager to try her luck in films, which had recently "graduated" to sound. "I want to entertain movie audiences with this voice of mine."

It was clearly understood that she'd have to sing in the roles she hoped to nab. To that effect, she stayed with her friend, America's leading torch singer, Libby Holman, at her elaborate estate at Sands Point, on the north shore of Long Island. Critic Brooks Atkinson

Haute dudgeon and lesbian love from a spectacularly disgraced long-ago torch singer, **Libby Holman**

had called Holman "a dark and purple flame."

Her lesbian lovers had included actress Jeanne Eagels and Josephine Baker, the African American dancer. In time, Holman would become notorious for the alleged murder of her young (and some say, *naif*) husband, tobacco heir Zachory Smith Reynolds.

Years before, Tallulah and Holman had had a brief fling during Tallulah's residency at the Algonquin Hotel. At Sands Point, they resumed their affair.

***

After dining with her parents on the evening of the day of her arrival in New York, Tallulah received her first visitor, Mercedes de Acosta, during the late morning of the following day. The women spent a gossipy three hours catching up on each other's latest conquests.

Within a few days, Tallulah reported to work at Paramount's East Studio in Astoria, Queens. Although it had been closed since 1926, it had reopened with the advent of sound. More and more Broadway stage actors were being lured into films "since they had voices." Meanwhile, many seasoned veterans of the silent screen saw their careers turn to ashes as they failed to adapt to changing times.

When Tallulah heard a recording of her voice, for the first time, she was horrified. "I sound more British than Queen Mary. I've been abroad too long. No Belle of Alabama like me should talk like that."

The governor from her home state then sent her a wire: "All the eyes of Alabama are trained on you, watching our favorite daughter become a movie star."

For an long-expatriated American who had built a formidable stage career in faraway London, **Tarnished Lady** was Tallulah's American film debut

Three separate film scripts were in pre-production for her. She met with a rising young director, the gay visionary, George Cukor. "He didn't like me, and I certainly didn't like him," she said. *[Later, however, in Hollywood, they became dear friends.]*

"It seemed that Paramount saw me as rather smoky and languid, a creature with a lurid past, lacking in humor and torn between two lovers. I was to be dressed in slinky gowns no respectable lady would wear."

Produced by Walter Wanger, and written by Donald Ogden Stewart, *Tarnished Lady* (1931) was a Pre-Code drama which Paramount hoped would introduce Tallulah as serious competition for Marlene Dietrich. "In contrast, Dietrich had Josef von Sternberg, and here I was out in Queens on Long Island with this George Cukor on his first solo venture as a film director."

Tallulah's leading man was Clive Brook, a Londoner, who had already made the transition from silent films to talkies. She referred to his style of acting as "deadpan lockjaw." He had been chosen to play Sherlock Holmes twice on the screen. After working with Tallulah, he was assigned a role as co-star to Dietrich in *Shanghai Express* (1932). In it, the German-born star would play an overdressed "Shanghai Lil," a *femme fatale* riding the rails in war-torn China.

During the day, Holman rehearsed Tallulah in her songs, trying to make her convincing as a cabaret entertainer. They spent weekends together in Tallulah's hotel suite. Dressed in mannish attire of the type made popular by Marlene Dietrich, the women visited the nightlife dives of Harlem.

When a picture of Tallulah dancing with a black man appeared in the newspapers, her relatives, especially her father, were horrified.

Noël Coward often accompanied Holman and Tallulah to the seedy clubs of Harlem because he had developed "a taste for black stallions," as he colorfully phrased it.

It was in the dives of Harlem that Tallulah developed her life-long passion for cocaine, which she would snort regularly until the end of her life. *[In fact, her last words in a hospital were, "COCAINE! BOURBON!"]*

It was at Harlem's Club Hotcha that Tallulah first met the fabulous singer, Billie Holiday, with whom she began a fling. This Belle of Alabama had no trouble at all crossing the color line when it came to bedtime partners, and she and Noël Coward sometimes shared the same studs.

The third lead in *Tarnished Lady* was played by Phoebe Foster, who soon would be cast opposite Greta Garbo in *Anna Karenina* (1935).

Tallulah and Cukor clashed during the first days of the shoot. "When he wasn't trying to direct me, he was seducing the more studly members of the crew," she claimed. "He preferred rough trade."

In *Tarnished Lady*, Tallulah was cast as Nancy Courtney, a young woman who marries for money to save her mother from the poor house.

When the rushes were shipped to Hollywood, studio chief Adolph Zukor said he was disappointed. "She's no Garbo and certainly no Dietrich."

Nonetheless, Paramount's publicity staff heralded her appearance as "The Second Coming" (Tallulah's words).

Back at Paramount in California, Zukor was banking on his other stars, already discounting the commercial appeal of Tallulah. Her competitors at the time included Miriam Hopkins, Kay Francis, Clara Bow, Claudette Colbert, and an over-40 Mae West, who had been imported from Broadway to save Paramount from bankruptcy.

Upon the release of *Tarnished Lady,* a poster in Times Square announced, "The producers who brought you Dietrich bring you another woman-thrill! TALLULAH BANKHEAD! She enthralled a nation! England's adored beauty on the screen! Get within range of her radiance! Feel the rapturous thrill of her voice, her person!"

Yet another poster advertised a quote reported to have been uttered by her, but in fact, it came from Paramount's publicity department. "Men are pleasant and as exciting to me as the lavish gowns I adore! I drink the sparkling cup of love, for I know my heart will never betray me! I am Tallulah the Modern!"

The reviews of *Tarnished Lady* were negative, the critic for the *New Yorker* agreeing with Zukor: "In *Tarnished Lady*, Tallulah Bankhead fails to establish any sort of celebrity of her own. Forget about her being the new Dietrich or, for heaven's sake, no Garbo!"

The New York Times claimed, "Bankhead acquits herself with considerable distinction, but the vehicle to which she lends her talent is not a masterpiece—far from it."

Variety issued its own verdict: "*Tarnished Lady* is a weepy and rugged melodrama that has little outside its cast to recommend it. Clive Brook suffers from having to utter silly dialogue."

Yet another critic wrote, "Tallulah Bankhead gives a credible impersonation of Marlene Dietrich singing in a cabaret."

***

Tallulah's next two films, *My Sin* and *The Cheat* (both released in 1931), would be directed by George Abbott, whose first command was, "I want you to play the part as smoky-languid." She had wanted a more experienced film director. Signed by the studio in 1929, he was in at the dawn of the talkies. He was also an actor and writer, and he openly admitted to Tallulah, "Films are not my medium."

"*My Sin* smelled like a bad perfume," **Tallulah** said. **"Fredric March** was as sexy as Calvin Coolidge. And I detested his wife, the god damn stuck-up and patronizing bitch, Florence Eldridge."

For reasons known only to herself, she wanted the cast to think that she and Abbott were lovers, perhaps aping Marlene Dietrich and Josef von Sternberg. Privately, she told him, "You are safe with me. As a man, you're too solid and reliable. I prefer a man who is a rogue, not dependable at all, just like my divine Lord Alington back in London."

My Sin was a Pre-Code movie where Tallulah got star billing over her leading man, Fredric March.

He had been born in Racine, Wisconsin, in 1897, and became one of the most reliable of Hollywood's leading men. "But he was no Clark Gable," Tallulah said. "Not the kind of man women swoon over. I saw many of his films in the years to come, and he always looked a bit stodgy on the screen."

"However, in private, he was rather lascivious in spite of his long marriage to actress Florence Eldridge. He liked to visit women's dressing rooms and try to put his hands up their dress. Katharine Hepburn once worked with him and heard of his reputation. She strapped on a dildo. When March reached for the honeypot, he made contact with a big, hard object and quickly withdrew."

Filming of *My Sin* also took place in Astoria in Queens, although the setting was supposed to be Panama. As the hostess of a seedy nightclub, Carlotta (Tallulah) kills a man who tries to assault her sexually. Her defense lawyer is Dick Grady (March), who is on the road to becoming an alcoholic. He proves Carlotta's innocence and also saves her from committing suicide.

Film Daily wrote, "Adapted from the play, *Her Past*, *My Sin* offers the latest evidence that Tallulah Bankhead is first-rate starring material."

"Film-goers stayed away from *My Sin* as if there were a skunk running loose in the theater. I told myself, 'Tallulah, *dah-ling*, press on!'"

Her final film, also shot in Astoria, was *The Cheat*, yet another Pre-Code melodrama directed by Abbott with Harvey Stephens as her lackluster leading man. *The Cheat* was a remake of the 1915 silent film directed by Cecil B. De Mille.

Tallulah was cast as Else Carlyle, a compulsive gambler and spendthrift who is overly concerned with her social standing and appearance. There is blackmail, there is a fatal shooting, and there is a trial. What was missing was an audience for this clunker.

The Cheat opened in Manhattan, receiving mixed reviews. One critic wrote, "Except for Tallulah Bankhead, the rest of the cast is talented but relatively unknown. Tallulah needs a leading man like Gary Cooper to be her co-star. With one of Paramount's studly actors, perhaps one like Cooper with his stunning good looks, she might make it as a star. She needs a backup, someone to make us feel that the man could actually arouse passion in her."

Another reviewer wrote, "John Gilbert and Garbo were hot lovers on the screen, enough so that many of their scenes ended up on the cutting room floor."

"Who does poor Tallulah get? Clive Brook, Fredric March, and Harvey Stephens. Give the Alabama Belle a break. He's at the wrong studio, but a picture with Tallulah and Clark Gable would have them lined up around the block to get in to see a dynamic duo like that emote on the screen."

After the failure of *Tarnished Lady*, *My Sin*, and *The Cheat*, Tallulah fully ex-

Tallulah: She's back in America, and she's got herself a gun!

In *The Cheat*, she starred as Elsa Carlyle, a Long Island matron with an uncontrollable urge to live on the razor's edge.

Joan Crawford and Douglas Fairbanks, Jr., married each other, but Tallulah Bankhead, among others, claimed that the two of them spent more time in bed with other stars than with each other.

Noël Coward developed a powerful crush on the young Fairbanks, and wrote a song, "Mad About the Boy," using him as his inspiration.

pected to be dropped by Paramount, especially since they now had the sensational Mae West, "who made me look like a prim Sunday school marm."

But instead of firing her, Zukor and Walter Wanger increased her salary to $6,000 a week and ordered her aboard the next train to Hollywood.

She told the press, "I'm on my way to Hollywood to make my next picture. Actually, the real reason I'm going is to fuck that divine Gary Cooper."

Of course, the press could not print that remark.

***

Aboard the westbound train, Tallulah dined nightly with her fellow passengers, Douglas Fairbanks, Jr., and his wife, Joan Crawford. She had long known Fairbanks but was meeting Crawford for the first time. Her introductory remark stunned Crawford: "I've had your husband, *dah-ling*. You're next!"

Tallulah needed a place to live, and Crawford informed her that the home of her best friend, William Haines, was available to rent.

Haines, at the time, was the leading box office star in Hollywood, but his movie career would soon be dashed by Louis B. Mayer. The studio chief had demanded that he abandon his male lover, which he refused to do. When Haines became the target of Mayer's revenge and ire, he left the screen forever and became Hollywood's leading interior decorator.

In Hollywood, Tallulah met the real estate agent in charge of renting Haines' house. She shocked him by saying, *"Dahling,* I just have to sleep in the bedroom where Haines used to suck off Clark Gable when he was getting his start in pictures."

After that, she went on to say, "California itself is far, far from civilization, and by civilization, I mean New York, the only city big enough to hold me., What is there for me out here? To become the leading lady of a cowpoke like William S. Hart or to play love scenes with Francis X. Bushman?"

Tallulah rented Haines' home at 1712 Stanley Street (now 1712 North Stanley Avenue) in Hollywood. She billed herself as "the hostess with the mostest" and began to throw what became the most notorious venue for parties in Tinseltown. "Most of her guests seemed to indulge in sex without gender preference," remarked director George Cukor.

Years later, she reflected on those days in the early 1930s in Hollywood," speaking to James Leo Herlihy, her director and playwright during the 1958 nationwide tour of his play, *Crazy October.*

William Haines was a leading man in silent films, but was fired by Louis B. Mayer for refusing to give up his male lover.

He became the leading interior decorator in Hollywood, hired by Joan Crawford (his best friend), Jack Warner, U.S. ambassador Walter H. Annenberg, and, ultimately, Ronald Reagan and Nancy Davis.

"Of all my male Hollywood seductions, the best was Tarzan—that is, Johnny Weissmuller. Talk about a penetration of the deep. He also had the longest foreskin in town. He was far better sex than Dame Sybil Thorndyke."

"Larry Olivier came to two of my parties with his wife, Jill Esmond," Tallulah claimed. "He's a fine actor and an attractive man, but I was more turned on by Jill. He'd married a lesbian. One night, I had her while Larry wandered off into the garden with Douglas Fairbanks, Jr."

Sometimes, Doug showed up with his wife, Joan Crawford. "I didn't mind it when Tallulah bedded my husband, Doug," Crawford said. "It gave me a chance to slip away and spend the night with Clark Gable."

"Doug had picked up a lot of tricks from his slutty wife," Tallulah said. "I think Joan began having sex when she was five, perhaps forced on her by her brother. She did porno in the 20s."

According to Crawford, "All of us adored Tallulah. We were fascinated by her, yet scared to death of her, too. I think she was one of the most exciting actresses who ever lived."

Olivier defined Tallulah as "great fun to be with. She had more glamour than almost anybody alive."

Burgess Meredith said, "She was way ahead of her time. Hedonistic is the word that applies to her."

Marlene Dietrich said: "She was without inhibitions and would do anything—and I mean *anything*—that came into her head at any given moment. She desperately sought attention, and she got it. When a party started to get stiff and boring, she would take off all her clothes."

"Both Carole Lombard and Tallulah had this party game they often played," Dietrich claimed. "They would come up to a man, unbutton his pants, and take out his cock for display."

The gay actor and the gay director, Clifton Webb and George Cukor, would show up with their latest tricks. A madame in downtown Los Angeles supplied them and other homosexual actors with a stream of hustlers.

Sometimes, Crawford arrived with William Haines, who was still a box office attraction.

All of Tallulah's parties lasted until dawn was breaking over California. Then, the hostess and at least some of her guests would rush to their respective studios and into makeup, hoping to conceal the ravages of the previous night.

During the filming of **Thunder Below**, its director, Richard Wallace, told **Tallulah** that her nose was not photogenic.

"What about Marlene Dietrich? She too, has a broad and inelegant nose. Have you sniffed at the noses of Ginger Rogers, Carole Lombard, and Claudette Colbert? I'll stack up my nose against any of those broads."

***

Tallulah's first Hollywood movie was *Thunder Below* (1932), yet another Pre-Code drama, this one directed by Richard Wallace. Her leading men were two of the most talented actors in films, Charles Bickford and Paul Lukas. "I admired their talent, *dah-ling*. I told Wallace, 'But even lavender lips Billy Haines wouldn't suck off those blokes.' That's a word I learned in London."

"As filming began on *Thunder Below*, I was reading my screen obits in the papers," Tallulah lamented. She was referring to *Silver Screen's* description of her as a "eulogy."

"Tallulah Bankhead on the stage was the toast of London, a West End dynamo, but in Hollywood, she has almost been shown the door even before she walked in."

The London press missed Tallulah since she always made hot copy. *Picturegoer Weekly* said, "It would have been better if Miss Bankhead had never left our shores. Unlike we British, the Americans don't seem to know what to do with its native daughter."

Her director, Wallace, soon discovered that whereas Garbo was said to have "no bad angles," Tallulah was not photogenic if shot from the wrong angle,

Her first director and dubious friend, George Cukor, told the press, "Unlike Dietrich and Garbo, even Norma Shearer, Tallulah does not have a good screen presence. Her eyes photograph dead and cold. Instead of succulent lips, her mouth sometimes seems a bit grotesque when she smiles. She's a beautiful woman, but the camera is not her friend. She always looks better on stage."

Tallulah might have agreed, more or less, with Cukor's latter-day assessment. Dorothy Spensley, who wrote for *Variety*, interviewed her and quipped. "I found her frank in self-appraisal."

"I don't think I will ever rank among the screen goddesses," Tallulah said. "Until I started my movie career, I had a face. Now I wonder. I seem without grace on camera, appearing awkward, even unnatural in some scenes. I have good eyes in spite of what some say, but that nose of mine. It needs work. *Dah-ling*, I think I sometimes look ghastly, absolutely ghastly. Up there with my face magnified a hundred times on the screen in a close-up."

Sidney Buchman and Josephine Lovett adapted *Thunder Below* from a novel by Thomas Rourke. One critic found some of the sequences in the book obscene.

In her role of Susan, a "tropical wife"

It was rumored that Tallulah might get a choice role as the star in **Blonde Venus** (1932), but ultimately, the script went to her chief rival, Marlene Dietrich.

Tallulah had heard that **Dietrich**, as a stage and film prop, regularly sprinkled gold dust in her hair.

At a scandalous party, Tallulah suddenley appeared nude at the top of the stairs. As she slowly and theatrically descended the steps, it became obvious that her vagina and pubic hair had been liberally sprinkled with gold dust.

"Guess where I've been?" she announced raucously to her guests.

married to a man in the oilfields of Central America, Tallulah once again is torn between two lovers, with Charles Bickford as her spouse and Paul Lukas as her lover. Lukas, incidentally, was supposed to be the "best friend" of Bickford, which brings betrayal into the "stew plot."

At the end, the adulterous Susan leaps to her death for a maudlin fade-out.

"Wallace was a dear boy but not really a film director," Tallulah said. "He once worked in a morgue—in fact, during the shoot, he took me to a morgue to view dead bodies., "They are so peaceful, even though they may have led wretched lives," he told her.

Eugene Pallette, "one of the most grotesque bundles of fat" (Tallulah's words) in the movies, was also one of its most talented. In *Thunder Below*, he provided comic relief "and, by Gawd, we needed it in this ponderous melodrama."

"I think it was as if we made the movie just to drive the people away from the box office," she said. "One critic attacked me as banal. No one, not even a critic, had ever called me that before."

She preferred her characterization in Paramount's advertising—"One woman desired and desiring, in a village of lonely men below the equator where civilization's barriers swiftly burn away."

The best praise, if it could be called that, came from London, where the *Times* called her acting "steady and extravagant."

The *New York World-Telegram* conceded that "Miss Bankhead has her moments." One critic wrote that Tallulah plays Susan as "a woman who's hot to trot."

Variety claimed: "In spite of the ballyhoo and provocative advertising, Tallulah Bankhead has failed to find a base among Hollywood fans. In fact, she is rapidly becoming Hollywood's box office poison."

"Since I had proclaimed that I had come to Hollywood just to fuck **Gary Cooper**, I had to live up to my boast, so the press wouldn't make a liar out of me," **Tallulah** said.

"He wasn't the most talkative actor in Hollywood, but once you got his pants off, he lived up to his reputation as the Montana Mule. He had great staying power. What a man!"

***

Tallulah got top billing in her next film, *Devil and the Deep*, with Gary

Cooper—at long last—cast as her co-star. Below the title, Charles Laughton, in his American film debut, was listed with Cary Grant as fourth in the billing. Directed by Marion Gering, this Paramount deep-sea adventure was released in August of 1932.

"I made bitter enemies of Grant and Laughton, who had been taking turns giving Gary blow-jobs—one at ten in the morning, the other at three in the afternoon. It angered them when I moved in on their territory."

"Laughton got his revenge," she said. "In one scene, he had to slap me, and did he ever! He hit me so hard I was thrown out of camera range. In the movie, he was my husband, and I played an unfulfilled woman, bored, unhappy, and depressed. Just what I would be in real life married to a monstrosity like Laughton. I don't know how Gary could get it up for this creature. Eventually, Laughton became typecast after portraying *The Hunchback of Notre Dame* (1939)."

In *Devil and the Deep*, Laughton was cast as a naval commander who abuses his wife, Diana (Tallulah), and makes life unbearable for her. She wanders off and meets Lieutenant Sempter (Cooper).

After sitting through the final director's cut, Tallulah stood up and gave her opinion: "*Devil and the Deep* never surfaced."

Reviews were mixed. David Fairweather of *Theater World* claimed, "This picture, in my opinion, is the best dramatic talkie we have yet seen. It is unabashed melodrama at times, but Laughton's acting disarms criticism of the more violently sensational incidents. Tallulah Bankhead has better opportunities than of late as the distant wife, but she is overshadowed by Laughton's amazing performance."

After the film was released, rumors of an affair between Tallulah and Cooper reached London. Reuters sent her a telegram—CONFIRM ENGAGEMENT TO GARY COOPER.

***

Since every movie Tallulah made for Paramount flopped at the box office, the studio released her to MGM for the final picture she made in Hollywood before returning to New York. Directed by Harry Beaumont, *Faithless* (1932) starred Tallulah opposite Robert Montgomery. He would soon be a staple at MGM, appearing opposite its leading ladies: Joan Crawford and Greta Garbo.

In *Faithless*, Tallulah was cast as a New York socialite, Carol Morgan, who romps through the Depression living a lavish lifestyle until she loses all her money. The

"**Faithless** was an apt title for my private life," **Tallulah** recalled. During its filming, Louis B. Mayer called her in for a stern lecture about rumors of her lesbian adventures.

"He threatened me with exposure if I didn't clean up my act."

"I retaliated, telling him I'd had affairs with any number of leading female stars—Barbara Stanwyck, Joan Crawford, Jobyna Howland...and others"

"Realizing how big this scandal could get, he withdrew his threat."

same fate awaits her boyfriend and later, husband, Bill Wade (Montgomery).

He, too, loses his job as an advertising executive the same day her attorneys tell her she's gone through all her money.

He finally gets a job as a truck driver but is seriously injured in a wreck., She must take care of him, as medical bills and living expenses come in with no money to pay them. In desperation, she walks the streets as a prostitute.

The New York Times called the movie a "lumbering species of drama," and *Variety* thought that Tallulah's talent was wasted in "this heavy-handed and depressing story."

Film Daily agreed, finding the picture "excessively gloomy and a poor vehicle for showcasing Tallulah's talents." The *Motion Picture Herald* disagreed, claiming that Tallulah's performance was more vivid than her past movies."

***

When a depressed and dejected Tallulah arrived back in Manhattan at Grand Central Station, Mercedes de Acosta was no longer waiting with flowers. She'd left for Hollywood herself.

As the 1930s moved on in Hollywood, Tallulah kept hearing periodic reports on Mercedes' latest lesbian conquests.

Ironically, they included Tallulah's most formidable competitors—Marlene Dietrich and Greta Garbo.

Bankhead adrift with **John Hodiak** in *Lifeboat* (1944)

Estelle Winwood, Tallulah Bankhead, and **Joan Blondell** in the road show rumpus known as *Crazy October*

Wanna know more about the final days of **Tallulah Bankhead,** and her role as a "frenemy" of Darwin Porter?

If knowing more about Tallu appeals to you, check out Chapter Seven of Volume Two of Blood Moon's Magnolia House series, **GLAMOUR, GLITZ, AND GOSSIP AT HISTORIC MAGNOLIA HOUSE,** now available everywhere online.

Tallulah 223

Tallulah Bankhead catalyzed more fascinating, oft-repeated gossip than all but a handful of other personalities of the 20th Century.

Farewell, Tallu, with affection, amusement, and respect from your legions of fans who will remember you forever.

TALLULAH BANKHEAD
(1902-1968)

THE VENUS'S FLYTRAP FROM ALABAMA
&
THE TOAST OF LONDON

REST IN PEACE

CHAPTER TEN
Eagles Fly High

JEANNE EAGELS
Beautiful, Doomed, and Uninhibited,
An Actress of Myth & Legend

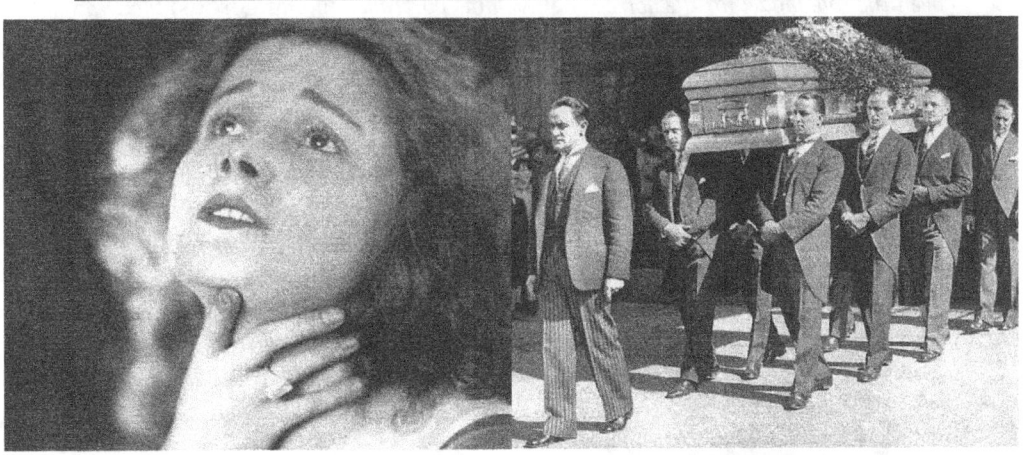

Upper left: In a tender and evocative moment, **Jeanne Eagels** appears as a tear-inducing Liane de Merode in the 1918 silent screen version of *The Cross Bearer*, which ran for only fifty minutes.

Upper right: In Manhattan, pallbearers carry her still-young body out of **Campbell's Funeral Home** at 65th Street and Broadway. Funeral services were later repeated at St. Vincent de Paul Catholic Church in Kansas City, Missouri.

It was estimated that she earned more than two million dollars during the course of her stage and film career and did not save a penny of it.

The Roaring Twenties, in which she played a key role, abruptly ended only three weeks after her death, when the Wall Street Crash collapsed the economy of America.

Eagels, with the energy and wistful beauty that made her fans want to throw themselves at her feet—and many of them did.

Jeanne Eagels

Once upon a time in Hollywood, there lived a blonde and fragile beauty of charm and grace. Although she's a relatively forgotten name today, with talent, luck, hard work, and grit, she triumphed as both a Broadway goddess and a silent screen diva. Her greatest fame derived from her portrayal of a prostitute, Sadie Thompson, the creation of the gay author, W. Somerset Maugham.

Her personal life was said to evoke the tragic saga of a latter-day Marilyn Monroe, and in many ways, Jeanne was a precursor of the tempestuous screen divas, Barbara Stanwyck and Bette Davis. *[Jeanne was said to have been the role model for the actress Bette Davis portrayed in* Dangerous, *the 1935 picture that brought her an Oscar.]*

The drama of Jeanne's life topped any role she ever played on the stage or screen. Emerging from the bowels of the Middle West, she seemed to live on a roller-coaster, roaring between ill-fated romances, with two disastrous marriages thrown in.

She desperately wanted love but found only torrid sexual liaisons with both men and women. Rising to lofty heights, and widely adored, she descended the ladder rung by rung, a victim of drugs, ambition, emotional instability, and alcohol.

Like a true legend, she died young and tragically at the age of 39 in 1929, but she lives on in theatrical lore. George B. Best, a newsman for *The Boston Post*, summed up her legacy: "The thing that made Miss Eagels great, that perhaps made her the greatest emotional actress of her day, was her eventual ruin."

***

So who was this mysterious actress who once enchanted much of the world with her charm and beauty?

Born Eugenia Eagles, she later changed her first name and the spelling of her last name, too. "I didn't want any bird comparisons," she said. She emerged with the revised name of "Jeanne Eagels."

She falsely claimed that she was born in Boston, the daughter of a Spanish architect, in 1894.

Despite those assertions, she'd actually been born on June 26, 1890, the

When even the Silents were young: Two early publicity photos (1915 and 1917) of **Jeanne Eagels**. Each conveys what critics later defined as her "naturalism" and "authenticity."

daughter of a carpenter, the second of six children. Her father, Edward, was of German and French Huguenot descent, and her mother, Julie Sullivan, was Irish. Jeanne's place of birth was near the smelly stockyards of Kansas City, Missouri.

Called "Gee-Gee" by her parents, she was a sickly, frail child, suffering from respiratory illnesses. At seven, she fell out of a tree, breaking her right arm. The doctor, whom she later referred to as a quack, did not set her arm properly, and she suffered acute pain from it for the rest of her life.

At St. Joseph's Catholic School, she appeared in school plays, including Shakespeare's *A Midsummer Night's Dream*, cast as the mischievous Puck. In years to come, she would see Mickey Rooney play the same role in the 1935 film version. "I was also in another play by The Bard," she claimed. "I was a gravedigger in *Hamlet*."

Her biggest chance to show off her emerging talent was when she was cast as Little Eva, the dying daughter of a plantation owner in *Uncle Tom's Cabin*, a play based on the abolitionist novel by Harriet Beecher Stowe. The play was later adapted into a silent movie (1927).

After the curtain went down on Jeanne as Little Eva, she told her parents, "I've found my calling in life."

"The stage is a wicked place for a young girl," her father warned her. "I've heard awful tales of what happens to girls who go to New York."

"I was a very good dancer," she recalled. "No one in Kansas City could toe dance like I could. But I didn't want to end up in the chorus line on Broadway. I wanted to be a dramatic actress."

She had not been particularly attractive until she entered her teens. "My bosom began to swell, and I got the eye from a lot of boys. My hair was the color of a wren; one day I planned to dye it blonde. My chin was dimpled and my nose was called 'pert.' I was proud of my porcelain skin, and I dreamed one day of becoming such a beauty I would enchant the world."

At the age of thirteen, she dropped out of school.

She was hired as a "cash girl" at a local department store, turning over her five dollars a week salary to help pay household expenses. During her lunch break, she went to a nearby theater to see the billboards announcing what acting troupe was in town. Some nights, she'd come home late because she'd slip into a theater after the box office closed for the night to see the final act of a play.

She, too, wanted to perform on the stage, "The sooner, the better."

In time, Jeanne would join the ranks of other legendary stars who also emerged from Kansas City: Wallace Beery, Ginger Rogers, William Powell, Jean Harlow, and Walt Disney.

"My daddy was ill and couldn't work most of the time, and my mother kept having kids my family could ill afford," Jeanne recalled. "At one point, I realized it was time for me to flee Cow Town, or, as the expression goes, 'get out of Dodge.'"

At the age of fifteen, she ran away from home and got a gig touring the country with the Dubinsky Brothers' traveling troupe, migrating from one little town after another. It was during an era when locals were "starved" for entertainment.

At first, she was hired as a dancer, but she was soon "elevated" into a position as the troupe's "repertory actress," appearing in dramas and comedies staged by "The Dubinsky Brothers."

As she matured into a late teenager, she dated Morris Dubinsky, a manager who doubled as an actor whenever a performance called for a villain, as many of their performances did.

"Life on the road was rough," she said. "Seedy hotels, horrible food, uncomfortable train travel, kerosene lamps lighting the stage in a barn, a toilet for a dressing room. I traveled through such hot spots as Nebraska."

One night, Morris came into my room at this $1.50-a-night hotel and told me he was going to make a woman out of me. I didn't understand all his talk about the pleasures of sex. It was like stabbing pain."

She may have married Morris while still a teenager. She was also said to have had a son with him, and that she and Morris gave the child away for adoption when they separated. Other rumors suggested that she gave birth to a stillborn.

Not bothering to tell her husband Morris goodbye—if indeed he were her husband—she slipped out of their hotel and rode the train to Chicago, using money she'd stolen from his pants.

There, she dyed her hair blonde, "which made me look ravishing" (her words), and she honed her skill with acting lessons from a retired actress, Beverley Sitgreaves.

In Chicago, during her audition for an upcoming play, *Jumping Jupiter*, she met Richard Carle, its director and male lead. *[Widely respected as a stage actor, he would, in less than five years, star in silent films that included* Madame X *(1929).]*

Carle cast Jeanne as Miss Renault in a play that starred the well-known actresses, Ina Claire and Helen Broderick. Each of them would remain Jeanne's friends for years to come.

A chorus girl in the Follies of 1907, Helen became widely known for her comic roles, especially as a wisecracking sidekick to other, more famous stars. In the 1930s, she starred in such revues as As Thousands Cheer *and* The Band Wagon, *and she appeared on the screen with Fred Astaire and Ginger Rogers in* Top Hat *(1935) and* Swing Time *(1936).*

Helen was also the mother of screen actor Broderick Crawford, who would win a Best Actor Oscar for the character he played in All the King's Men *(1949).*

Ina Claire, a stage and film actress, launched her career in vaudeville and later became identified in the high comedies of S.N. Behrman, creating the leads in three of his films such as End of Summer *in 1936. She'd made her film debut in Cecil B. De Mille's* The Wild Goose Chase *(1915).*

 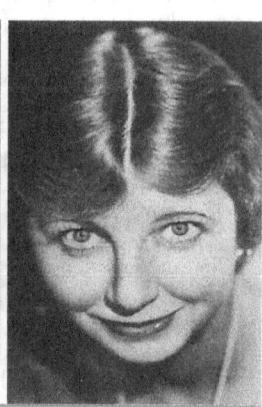

Despite ferocious competition for screen roles, both **Ina Claire** (left) and **Helen Broderick** remained friends with Jeanne Eagels and with each other.

In the year Eagels died (1929), Claire was honeymooning with screen heartthrob John Gilbert, the top male sex symbol of the decade.

By the late 1920s, Broderick was playing leads and featured roles, most notably in *Fifty Million Frenchmen*.

She is best remembered today for playing Grand Duchess Swana in the romantic comedy Ninotchka *(1939), directed by Ernst Lubitsch.*
  Billboards promoted it with the slogan GARBO LAUGHS.
  There was a certain irony associated with Claire teamed alongside Garbo. In the late 1920s, Garbo, with John Gilbert, had electrified audiences with their on-screen lovemaking and their off-screen romance. A wedding was announced, but Garbo didn't show up. (At least, according to legend, that is the story, although it has been much disputed.) When Gilbert recovered, he married Claire on the rebound, but it didn't work, and he divorced her in 1931, as his screen career faded with the advent of the talkies.]

Jumping Jupiter went over well in Chicago, the *Chicago Examiner* claiming, "It jumps all over the place." The play was praised for its "rollicking nonsense" and its wit and skillful acting.

But when it opened in New York, playing to more sophisticated audiences, it lasted for only a dozen performances, garnering lukewarm applause at the Knickerbocker Theatre.

The New York Times claimed, "The play doesn't jump, it limps," as the *New York Press* reviewed it as "offensively stupid and tedious."

Jeanne soon found herself out of a job in a city filled with hundreds of unemployed showgirls. Flooding the theater district's casting offices, they all seemed to be auditioning for the latest shows.

***

In the next few weeks, Jeanne was seen around town with a number of well-dressed married men. *[In those days, they were known as "stage door Johnnies."]* They introduced Jeanne to the chic restaurants and "watering holes" of Manhattan. The last thing she seemed to want in her life was to be married again.

Both Helen Broderick and Ina Claire lent Jeanne money until she got another job in the theater. That came when she joined the cast of *The Pink Lady,* an Edwardian musical comedy that opened at Manhattan's New Amsterdam Theatre, running for 312 performances beginning in March of 1911. It would later go on a road tour.

Jeanne was cast as Gabrielle, a chorus girl. The musical introduced such songs as "My Beautiful Lady," and its costumes became so popular that they inspired ladies'

As a newcomer to show-biz, Jeanne's most ferocious competition came from **Hazel Dawn**, subject of both photos above.

It's tough to compete with skin, pearls, and the American flag all embodied in one beautiful stage star....but it's what Jeanne Eagels faced when she was cast in a Hazel Dawn production as a chorine.

fashions of that day. A reviewer described the costume of Jean *(sic)* Eagels as "a gown of pal green faille veiled in flesh mousseline soie."

She had been hired by the producing team of "Klaw and Erlanger," an entertainment management production company based in New York from 1888 through 1919. They were key players in the Theatrical Syndicate, the booking monopoly for first class legitimate theaters.

[They made a star not of Jeanne, but of nineteen-year-old Hazel Dawn. Born to a Mormon family in Utah, she sang and played the violin and became so popular that bartenders introduced a new drink, "The Pink Lady," in her honor.

An original chorus line cutie in the Ziegfeld Follies of 1907, she starred in feature films beginning in 1914. Jeanne envied her rise to stardom.

Actress Ruth Gordon cited Dawn as an inspiration for her becoming an actress. Only fourteen at the time, Adele Astaire, sister of Fred, saw The Pink Lady *and pronounced Dawn as "the loveliest and most graceful creature" she'd ever seen on any stage.]*

***

Jeanne shared her dressing room with a fellow chorine, Cecil Cunningham, a chorus line charmer at the age of eighteen, although she'd trained to be an opera singer. She remembered Jeanne as "young, charming, and gracious."

On tour, the two young starlets met the novelist Booth Tarkington in Indiana. *[In 1919 he would win the Pulitzer Prize for his authorship of* The Magnificent Ambersons.

Cunningham herself would go on to greater glory. She eventually appeared alongside Carole Lombard in the 1937 film, Swing High, Swing Low.*]*

***

In September of 1912, producer Charles Frohman cast Jeanne as "Olga Cook" in his latest play, *The Mind-the-Paint Girl*. It opened at Manhattan's Lyceum Theatre in September of 1912.

The Ohio-born Frohman had

Two views of **Billie Burke**, an actress famous for marrying Flo Ziegfeld at the time, and famous today for her falsetto voice as Dorothy's benefactor, Glinda the Good Witch of the North, in *The Wizard of Oz*.

begun producing plays in 1889 and would discover many stars during the course of his career. He was one of the first to spot the emerging talent of Jeanne. He produced J. M. Barrie's *Peter Pan* and was a force in the stage career of the great Maude Adams. He produced 700 shows before his death in May of 1915. Then at the peak of his career, he went down with the *RM Lusitania* after it was torpedoed off the southern coast of Ireland by the Kaiser's navy in World War I.

The plot of *The Mind-the-Paint Girl* centered on a rising starlet discovered by a musical director who yells, "Mind the paint, girl!" The play included a song by Jerome Kern. Its star was the celebrated actress, Billie Burke.

Jeanne was assigned eight lines of dialogue with Burke. A review in the New York *World-Telegram* said, "Jeanne Eagels has a brief walk-on where she comes out in red high heels, and she is a personality to watch."

Born in 1884, Burke became an actress on Broadway in both silent pictures and in talkies. She was also known as the wife of Flo Ziegfeld, Jr., the producer and impresario known for his *Ziegfeld Follies,* first presented in 1914.

One of the great secrets of vaudeville was that Burke was bisexual. She allowed her husband, Flo Ziegfeld, to seduce Ziegfeld girls because she, too, had a fondness for ladies of the chorus. Eagels later asserted that Burke had made lesbian advances to her, but did not provide details such as, "Did she accept?"

[Of course, Burke would immortalize herself as Glinda, the Good Witch of the North in the classic The Wizard of Oz (1939), *starring Judy Garland as Dorothy.]*

In her first memoir, Burke described Jeanne as "lovely to look at." She was so struck by her beauty that she urged her husband to sign her to a contract for $100 a week in *Follies,* but Jeanne declined.

[Excelling in the portrayal of dim-witted society ladies Burke had a high-pitched, wavering, aristocratic voice. It became her trademark. Such was the case in 1933 when she played a scatterbrained society matron in Dinner at Eight *(1933). George Cukor directed her, alongside Lionel Barrymore, Marie Dressler, Jean Harlow, John Barrymore, and Wallace Beery.*

Burke lost out on a chance to portray herself in the 1936 biopic of her husband, The Great Ziegfeld. *It won a Best Actress Oscar for Luise Rainer, who was cast as Ziegfeld's common law wife, Anna Held. The role of Burke went to Myrna Loy, with William*

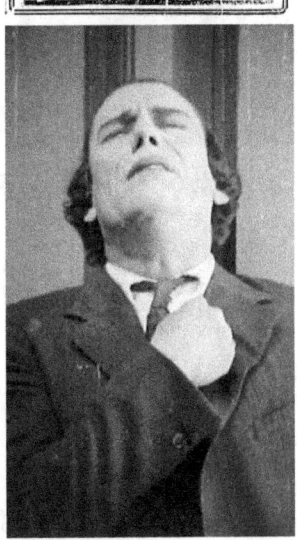

Lon Chaney in *Ace of Hearts*

"I was hardly noticed in my first appearance on the screen in *Ace of Hearts,*" Jeanne said. "Lon Chaney, the star, ate up the scenery. John Gilbert's first wife, Leatrice Joy, was the female lead."

Powell cast as Flo Ziegfeld, the film's protagonist.

In 1938, Billie was nominated for a Best Supporting Actress Oscar for Merrily We Live, starring Constance Bennett.

During the brief time that George Cukor directed Gone With the Wind (1939), he offered the role of Aunt Pittypat to Burke, but she rejected it, something for which Laura Hope Crews would be forever grateful.]

As the weeks passed and no stage roles were forthcoming, Jeanne signed to appear in silent films. At the time, many were being shot in and around New York City at locations that included New Jersey, Staten Island, and Long Island through studios with names such as Edison, Essanay, and Biograph before most of them moved to California.

The emerging Ryno Film Company offered Jeanne her first role. It was in a film called *Ace of Hearts*, a short shot in 1913. She was billed simply as "The Girl."

She and another girl play a prank on a soldier who's asleep at his guard post. They delicately place an ace of hearts in his shirt. Later, in a poker game, the card falls out of his shirt, and he's accused of cheating. After contemplating suicide, he falls for Jeanne before the end of the film. All copies of this film are believed to have been lost.

Ryno liked her work enough to cast her in a second short, *The Bride of the Sea*, in 1913. In this short, she was once again billed as "The Girl." Director John Noble was able to take advantage of a real life sinking of the *John D. Wilson* steamer as it departed from Brooklyn Pier. In a dramatic scene, Jeanne is rescued from the deep and, as its heroine, she was cited for her acting and Noble was praised for his direction.

Still in 1914, Jeanne led the cast in *A Lesson in Bridge*, released by the Reliance Motion Picture Corporation. She was cast as "Mrs. Willis," the wife of a Wall Street clerk. She gambles away the household budget. Reliance hyped the short as "a tale of trumps and trickery." The movie sent out a warning to housewives addicted to card games.

Blanche Sweet had the lead in D.W. Griffith's first feature-length film, *Judith of Bethulia*, made for the pioneering Biograph.

Her city is under siege by the Assyrians. A widow, she disguises herself as a harem girl and goes to the camp of the enemy. There, she seduces Holofernes (Henry Walthall), a general of King Nebuchadnezzar. She gets him drunk and beheads him with a saber, returning to her besieged city as a heroine.

***

232

Jeanne's next film role came when D.W. Griffith tapped her for his 1914 *Judith of Bethulia,* the first feature length film (61 minutes) of the pioneering film company, Biograph. The script was written in part by Griffith himself, and was based on the Deuterocanonical Book of Judith, an apocryphal tale set against the siege of the Jewish city of Bethulia by the Assyrians. A widow named Judith (Blanche Sweet) activates a plan to stop the war and save her city.

Griffith assembled a huge cast, including the Gish sisters (Dorothy and Lillian) and even Lionel Barrymore (as an extra). Chicago-born Sweet became a major star in silents, and by 1910, she'd become the rival of Mary Pickford. She later starred in vehicles shot by Cecil B. De Mille and Marshall Neiland, with whom she had an affair. Although she starred in the first film version of *Anna Christie* (1923), with the advent of sound, her career faltered.

Hailing from New Mexico and "discovered" by Griffith, Mae Marsh played the second lead, launching a career that would span half a century. During her heyday in silents, she sometimes made eight films per year, working with directors like Mack Sennett. She was a star in two of Griffith's most famous movies, *The Birth of a Nation* (1915), and *Intolerance* (1916).

She continued to work when talkies supplanted the silents, starring with Shirley Temple in *Rebecca of Sunnybrook Farm* (1932) and in John Ford's *The Grapes of Wrath* (1940), with Henry Fonda.

Flanked with all that star power, Jeanne ended up uncredited along with a handsome newcomer from Madrid, Antonio Moreno. During the shoot, she had an affair with him. He would go on to become a matinee idol and heartthrob in the 1920s, a rival of Rudolph Valentino. Moreno rose to stardom opposite Norma Talmadge, but also worked with Gloria Swanson, Pola Negri, and was typecast in his early films as a Latin Lover, like Ramon Novarro. Some of his most memorable roles were opposite

Mae Marsh in the now-notorious *Birth of a Nation* (1915) a few years after performing with Jeanne Eagels.

In one of the film's most racially charged scenes, she leaps to her death rather than submit to the lustful advances of Gus, the so-called "Renegade Negro," who later is killed by the KKK.

Madrid-born **Antonio Moreno** was only an extra in *Judith of Bethulia,* but he soon rose to stardom, challenging Rudolph Valentino and Ramon Novarro as the leading Latin Lover of silent pictures. On the set, Jeanne Eagels got to sample his manly charms, as did many leading ladies—"and a few gents, too."

Greta Garbo in *This Temptress* (1926) and Clara Bow in *It* (1927).

***

Jeanne returned to Broadway in 1915, co-starring in *The Governor's Boss*. Penned by J.S. Barcus, a former senator from Indiana, it revolved around the 1913 impeachment of former New York State governor, William Sulzer.

In the three-act play, Jeanne played Ruth, the daughter of the beleaguered governor. The governor tangles with Boss Tally, the crooked party leader. When he defies him, the dictator plots to remove him from office. The governor is framed, and his daughter fights hopelessly to save him.,

It opened at the Garrick Theatre in Manhattan on August 13 but closed after only sixteen performances. A critic for *The New York Times* called it "as poor and uninteresting a play as might possibly be imagined."

***

Disappointed by its failure, and with money saved, Jeanne sailed to Europe to forget her woes.

On board during the crossing, she began a lifelong friendship with the prissy actor, Clifton Webb, a native son of Indiana who always went everywhere with his mother, Mabelle. She referred to her homosexual son as "my beloved Little Webb."

Who you were likely to have met on a transatlantic crossing in 1923: **Clifton and Mabelle Webb**, in her case, wearing the *ne plus ultra* of matronly Jazz Age fashion.

The homosexual actor lived with his domineering mother until her death at the age of ninety-one in 1960.

Noël Coward remarked, "It must be terrible for poor Clifton to be orphaned at seventy-one."

As a late teenager, Webb became a professional ballroom dancer, first appearing with the overdressed and "decorative" star, dancer Bonnie Glass, who replaced him on her dance card with Rudolph Valentino.

Despite his rather effeminate manner, Webb rose quickly as an actor, dancer, and singer on Broadway, appearing with such stars as Al Jolson, Will Rogers, and young Humphrey Bogart (who had to fight off Webb's sexual overtures.). The future silent movie star, Richard Barthelmess, allowed Webb, according to rivers of local gossip, "to enjoy me but only below the belt."

Like Jeanne, Webb also appeared in silent films. He formed a close bond with the homosexual playwright, Noël Coward, appearing in his plays such as *Blithe Spirit*.

Webb had reached his mid-fifties before he became the most unlikely of movie stars. The press labeled him "everyone's favorite prissy snot. He could be counted on to toss off a witty *bon mot* or an insult like the sting of a wasp."

Otto Preminger insisted that Webb be cast in Fox's classic, *Laura* (1944), a brooding *film noir* starring Gene Tierney and Dana Andrews. Webb played Waldo Lydecker, despite the objections of Darryl F. Zanuck, who interpreted Webb as "too much of a sissy boy." For his performance, he received an Oscar nomination for Best Supporting Actor.

Webb's success with *Laura* prompted Fox to sign him to a long-term contract. During its run, he co-starred with Gene Tierney again, playing the elitist Elliott Templeton in *The Razor's Edge* (1946), for which he received another Oscar nomination.

During its filming, Webb chased after its handsome star, Tyrone Power, who allowed Webb "only to service me," the same privilege he'd granted to the "beastly ugly" Charles Laughton. When he wasn't with Webb, Power got involved in a torrid romance with Lana Turner.

As Mr. Belvedere in *Sitting Pretty* (1948), Webb achieved major stardom as a snide, know-it-all babysitter. It was a big hit, and once again, he got an Oscar nomination, this time for Best Actor in a Leading Role, losing to Laurence Olivier in *Hamlet*.

Always with his mother on his arm, Webb explored the high spots of Paris with Jeanne. Both of them were seen at the glittering party for the legendary actress Gaby Desly. Jeanne returned to her hotel later that night to find her room had been looted, her jewelry stolen. Nonetheless, she was seen the next night with Webb and Mabelle at the

The matinee idol **Tyrone Power** and the sex symbol known for years as "The Sweater Girl," **Lana Turner,** were caught by surprise when a photographer snapped their picture at the Cocoanut Grove in Los Angeles in the 1940s at the peak of their torrid affair.

The bisexual actor had numerous affairs—not only with Lana, but with Robert Taylor, Errol Flynn, Howard Hughes, Judy Garland, Rita Hayworth, Marlene Dietrich, Joan Crawford, and Rock Hudson, to name only a few.

LUSCIOUS LANA, READ ALL ABOUT IT: Lots that you never knew about **Lana TURNER** appears in this 2017 overview of The Sweater Girl and what became of her. Configured as a well-reviewed insight into how Hollywood affected the sometimes bizarre course of the American Experience and the outcome of World War II, it's available on websites everywhere.

Moulin Rouge.

From Liverpool, Jeanne boarded the *Lusitania,* which, a few years later (in 1915) would meet its doom in the cold waters off the southern coast of Ireland. She had just lured the famous tenor, Paul Draper, away from his wife. The two of them had booked a suite for a voyage to the port of New York.

Draper had given a concert in London. He was famed in the music world for appearing as a soloist with both the Boston and Chicago Symphony Orchestras. He specialized in the music of Brahms and Bach and was hailed as the best singer of German *Lieder,* a musical form well suited to his vocal powers.

His romance with Jeanne, however, lasted only for the duration of their ocean crossing. By the time they spotted the Statue of Liberty, the lovebirds had called it quits and separated.

Like Jeanne herself, Draper would have a short life, dying on February 15, 1925, of heart disease at the age of thirty-eight.

***

Back in America, Jeanne's next gig was an oddity, co-starring in *The Crinoline Girl* with Julian Eltinge, America's most famous female impersonator. He despised that label, preferring to identify himself as "a male actress."

He was also known as "Mr. Lillian Russell," named after the fabled stage beauty.

Julian Eltinge (1881-1941) was America's most famous female impersonator, the quirky star of plays and silent pictures.

On the left, he appears as the star of *The Crinoline Girl* (1914) opposite Jeanne Eagels. In the center, he's wearing men's street clothes, a rarity for him. On the right, he toured the country for years in the lead role of *The Fascinating Widow.*

At the age of ten, Julian had first appeared on stage dressed as a girl, which led to a beating that night from his father.

In spite of that, he went on to appear frequently in drag, making his Broadway debut in 1904. He later toured in vaudeville in both America and Europe, even giving a command performance in London before King Edward VII. His Majesty was so impressed, he presented Julian with a white bulldog.

Comedian Milton Berle, who worked with Julian in vaudeville, later told his friend, Bob Hope, "Julian is the only cocksucker on Broadway who can deep throat my pole."

There was confusion about Eltinge's sexual orientation, actress Ruth Gordon calling him "as virile as anybody virile." However, Dorothy Parker created a new term for him: "ambisextrous."

Eltinge had worked on the script of *The Crinoline Girl,* which, according to the plot, has him dress in drag to capture a gang of thieves, hoping that by doing so, he would win the hand of a rich girl he wants to marry.

His original female co-star was the actress Helen Luttrell. He got rave notices, but she did not, and he blamed her for the dwindling audiences for whom they performed. After a disappointing box office, the play closed after only six weeks.

He remained convinced that *The Crinoline Girl* could be rescued. At this time, producer A.H. Woods introduced him to Jeanne, and Julian thought she would be ideal as his leading lady. The revamped play embarked on a successful nationwide tour, critics hailing Jeanne as "charming," "bewitching," and "a blonde attraction."

In 1914, he starred in a silent screen version of *The Crinoline Girl.* By 1917, he was living in Hollywood, where he made films for several months. He soon became one of the entertainment industry's highest paid actors, both in vaudeville and in pictures.

In 1920, Eltinge bought a lavish mansion, Villa Capistrano in Los Angeles. He starred that year with Rudolph Valentino in *An Adventuress,* released in the United States as *The Isle of Love.*

A rumor spread that Julian and the bisexual Valentino had an affair.

Also in the movie was starlet Virginia Rappe, a wild party girl, who would soon meet her death in a San Francisco hotel room. Fatty Arbuckle was charged with rape and murder.

Arbuckle was later acquitted, but his career was forever damaged. He died in June of 1933.

"In *The House of Fear,* **Arnold Daly** got all the best notices," Jeanne recalled.

"The film by Pathé Exchange was released in November of 1915. I was hardly thrilled by one review, a critic writing, "Mr. Daly is supported by Jennie Sagels (*sic*)."

***

For Jeanne, 1915 was not an especially prolific year. She was cast in only one film, a five-reeler called *The House of Fear*, produced by Pathé Exchange and directed by John Ince. Her co-stars were Arnold Daly and Sheldon Lewis, with her accepting third billing in a minor role.

Brooklyn-born Daly was the father of the actress Blyth Daly, a friend of Jeanne's and the sometimes lover of Tallulah Bankhead.

Jeanne, according to her roommate, Helen Broderick, had an affair with Daly (born in 1875). He once held a reputation as a bad boy, having been expelled from four public schools. Since 1892, he'd been a handsome and talented actor appearing on the stage.

In theatrical circles, he was known for introducing some of the plays of George Bernard Shaw, including *You Can Never Tell* and *Candida*. He starred in *Mrs. Warren's Profession,* but authorities shut it down right after its premiere because Mrs. Warren's profession was that of a prostitute.

At the time Jeanne met him, he had become a matinee idol in silent pictures, starring as detective Craig Kennedy in a trio of Pearl White serials.

House of Fear with Jeanne was the third and final film in the Ashton-Kirk Investigator series, produced by Daly himself and distributed by Pathé,

Its plot centers around a Mexican gang of thieves who have stolen currency printing plates. Our hero captures the bandits and destroys the plates that had been churning out bogus U.S. currency.

Jeanne did not like her minor role as Grace Camp. She never saw Daly after filming ended but was saddened by news of his death in January of 1927. He was burned alive in his Manhattan apartment after it had caught fire. Police found his charred corpse just a few steps from an open window overlooking a rooftop. Perhaps he could have escaped were it not for a serious head injury he'd sustained two months before the fire. He was only fifty-one years old.

***

The producing team of Klaw & Erlanger hired Jeanne for a third time for their latest play, *Outcast,* which ran from October of 1915 to January of 1916 before setting out on a nationwide tour. It was written by Hubert Henry Davis, a leading British playwright of the early 20th Century. Jeanne met him right before he left for England, where he

SEX, THE PROFIT MOTIVE, AND SHAME

Outcast was first presented on Broadway in 1914, and Jeanne Eagels toured with it from October of 1915 to January of 1916. Later that year, she would star in the silent screen version under a new title: *The World and the Woman.*

As noted in the poster above, Elsie Ferguson made her own silent version of *Outcast* that was released by Paramount in 1922. Censors demanded that the producer cut three gambling scenes and remove the line that read, "I was driven to the streets. I had no choice."

Then, in 1928, it was once again filmed as *Outcast* with Corinne Griffith and Edmund Lowe in a Vitaphone version.

Finally, it inspired the plot of *The Girl from 10th Avenue* (1935) starring Bette Davis.

volunteered his services as a hospital orderly, since he was too old to fight as a soldier. [He was born in 1869.]

After seeing all those men suffering from their battle wounds, he had a nervous breakdown. He returned to England to live at Robin Hood's Bay, in Yorkshire, but was so traumatized that he died in 1917 before the end of World War I.

The star of *Outcast* was Elsie Ferguson, a Manhattan-born beauty (born 1885) who was both a stage and film actress, often billed as "The Aristocrat of the Silver Screen," and "The Most Beautiful Woman Ever to Set Foot on the Stage."

Ferguson was cast into the role of Miriam, a streetwalker in a story of tormented love and redemption.

Jeanne was quite envious of Ferguson and lobbied to play Miriam during its tour of the Southern states. She began to reshape her image and wardrobe to parallel that of Ferguson's. On the road, many fans asked for her autograph, thinking she was the fabled actress. She signed programs with "Love, Elsie."

She got rave reviews after hitting the boards across the South. She was especially popular in Atlanta. After returning to New York, she starred in Brooklyn's Standard Theatre, where producer Joseph Brooks saw her opening night performance.

Joseph Brooks offered Jeanne the *ingénue* role of Kate Merryweather in his new Broadway-bound play *The Idler*. [Its name was later changed to *The Great Pursuit*. It was a revival of C. Haddson Chambers' play that had premiered in 1891.]

Jeanne was surprised to find herself the only American in the cast, alongside some of the best-known thespians in the British Empire.

The heroic female lead was assigned to Phyllis Neilson-Terry, a third-generation member of the British theatrical dynasty, the Terry family. She had made a name for herself portraying Shakespearean heroines which included Juliet in *Romeo & Juliet*; Desdemona in *Othello*; and Portia in *The Merchant of Venice*, all in 1912. From 1914 until the end of the decade, she worked in the United States, usually in lightweight presentations such as her role opposite Jeanne in *The Great Pursuit*.

Another Londoner in the cast, Marie Tempest, was hailed as "The Queen of Her

After a stint in Hollywood, **Phyllis Neilson-Terry,** the third-generation descendent of the most famous acting dynasty in England, returned to the U.K., where she pursued a varied career—cabaret, pantomime, and variety, as well as many stage adaptations of Shakespeare.

She won praise for her performance as the female lead in *Romeo and Juliet* with actor Vernon Steele, who hailed from Santiago, Chile.

Profession," becoming the most famous soprano in Victorian light opera and Edwardian musical comedies. Her career spanned fifty-five years, during which she toured extensively in the United States and Canada. On Broadway, she was hailed as "the only serious rival to Lillian Russell," the great diva of that era. Critics cited Tempest as "that other *prima donna* on the English-speaking stage."

During rehearsals, Tempest's temper flared, and she fought with both the director and with her fellow actors, including Jeanne.

Before working with Jeanne, she had starred in the title role of J.M. Barrie's *Rosalind*. The author of *Peter Pan* praised her ability "to both laugh and cry, creating a masterpiece of letting those two emotions melt one into the other."

Also performing in a major role in *The Great Pursuit* was the English stage, screen, and vaudeville actor, Montagu Love. He had made his Broadway debut in *The Second in Command* (1913), and from there, moving into silent movies, he was usually cast as a heartless villain.

He survived the silents and worked in talking pictures, notably twice with Errol Flynn in *The Prince and the Pauper* (1937) and *The Adventures of Robin Hood* (1938).

The Great Pursuit opened in Manhattan's Shubert Theatre on March 20, 1916. Despite of its stellar cast, it ran for only twenty-nine performances,

Two views, in two eras of fashion, of **Marie Tempest**, who worked with Jeanne Eagels in *The Great Pursuit*. Born in 1864, she had a long and distinguished career, which led to her being named a Dame Commander of the Order of the British Empire in 1937.

She survived the Blitz of London in 1940 but lost her home and possessions.

She said, "Hitler has taken nearly everything from me but my life, but you can't live on regret." She died two years later at the age of seventy-eight.

One of the leading roles in *The Great Pursuit* went to **Montagu Love**, an English screen, stage, and vaudeville actor. He was often cast as a villain in silent films.

In the 1920s his roles included playing opposite Valentino in *The Son of Sheik;* opposite John Barrymore in *Don Juan;* and opposite Lillian Gish in *The Wind*.

In talking pictures, he starred opposite Errol Flynn, Tyrone Power, and Cary Grant.

drawing critical attack as a "hopelessly aged" English drawing room comedy. However, the *New York Clipper* hailed Jeanne as "a firmly established Broadway favorite."

In spite of the play's failure, Brooks announced that he would star Jeanne in his next play, *Somebody's Luggage,* but she was dismissed and another actress went on instead.

***

Brooks hired Jeanne again for his roadshow production of *What's Your Husband Doing?* In 1916, it would be presented in both the Valentine Theater in Toledo, Ohio, and in the Blackstone Theatre in Chicago.

Cast as Beatrice, Jeanne played a young wife with a devoted husband. But she spends a lot of time imagining he is a roving Lothario pursuing other women. Before the end of the play, it's revealed that all her neuroses and fears were imaginary.

Her co-stars were Thomas Ross and Macklyn Arbuckle, a cousin of the comedian, Fatty Arbuckle. A native of San Antonio (Texas), Macklyn often co-starred in movies with Marion Davies, the mistress of William Randolph Hearst.

Because of what he described as his "failing health," Brooks abruptly shut down the play, even though it was playing to packed houses. A report soon reached Jeanne that he had tried to cut his throat. Two months later, on November 16, 1917, Brooks jumped from the eighth floor of his apartment on West 79th Street in Manhattan.

In 1920, the stage version of *What's Your Husband Doing?* was adapted into a silent comedy produced by Thomas Ince, directed by Lloyd Ingraham, and released by Paramount. It co-starred Douglas MacLean and Doris May. *[Jeanne had desperately wanted the female lead.]*

[Thomas Ince, the "Father of the Western," was one of the most influential and gossiped-about figures in Silent-Age Hollywood. In 1915, he had formed Triangle, the forerunner of United Artists, in partnership with D.W. Griffith and Mack

A shroud of mystery still lingers over the sinister death of producer **Thomas Ince**, who died on November 15, 1924 aboard a yacht owned by William Randolph Hearst, *The Oneida.*

Two views of Hearst's mistress, actress **Marion Davies**. On the left, she's seen welcoming Thomas Ince aboard *The Oneida* for the cruise wherein he died.

On the right, she's pictured with **Charlie Chaplin**, her secret lover. It was rumored that in a jealous rage, Hearst fired at Chaplin with his diamond-studded revolver. The bullet missed Chaplin and strayed, exiting out through a porthole and striking Ince on the forehead while he was strolling on deck.

Sennett. Ince became the principal backer of the screen's first major Western hero, the stoic William S. Hart.

Ince's death in 1924 remains one of the great mysteries of 1920s Hollywood. He went sailing with Hearst and his mistress aboard Hearst's yacht, Oneida. The party also included a young Louella Parsons, Charlie Chaplin, and screenwriter Elinor Glyn.

Ince's body was taken off the yacht in San Diego. His doctor announced that his death had resulted from heart failure, but for many years, rumors circulated that Hearst had shot Ince for making a pass at his mistress. It was also rumored that Parsons used that knowledge as a means of forcing Hearst into elevating her into the gossip queen of the Hearst newspaper empire.]

Press baron **William Randolph Hearst** went to his grave without ever revealing who shot Ince. Did he fire the fatal bullet?

***

Almost immediately after the shutdown of *What's Your Husband Doing?*, Jeanne went to work on her next film, *The World and the Woman*, in which she was cast as "A Woman of the Streets"—read that prostitute. She later said, "I think I was rehearsing for the major role of my life—that of Sadie Thompson in *Rain*. The co-author of the script was William de Mille, the brother of director Cecil B. De Mille. [They spelled their names differently.] Released on November 19, 1916, the film had co-directors, Frank Lloyd and Eugene Moore, with Edwin Thanhouser, the chief honcho of Thanhouser Film Corporation, as the producer.

Born in the closing year of the Civil War, Thanhouser, a native son of Baltimore, would cast Jeanne in her next two films. His company became one of the first motion picture studios, pioneering in their first commercial releases as early as 1910.

In *The World and the Woman*, Jeanne was cast as Mary, who went from streetwalker to faith healer, playing opposite two "forgotten actors," Boyd Marshall and Thomas A Curran.

The World and the Woman: **Jeanne Eagels,** by now, seemed indelibly associated with roles whose theme was "fallen women" and/or "good girls gone bad."

Filming took place at the studio's lot in New Rochelle, New York. Nitrate was used in these early films, and most of Jeanne's work is lost to history—that is, except for *The World and the Woman*, a copy of which was discovered at the George Eastman Kodak Film Archives in fairly good condition.

Most critics claimed that the movie represented Jeanne's finest performance to date. *Motion Picture News* called her "a real actress and a real beauty."

***

Jeanne's next two films for Thanhouser—*The Fires of Youth* and *Under False Colors*—were both directed by Emile Chautard. In addition to Jeanne, both of them co-starred Frederick Warde.

On the screen, he had starred in silent films based on Shakespeare's *Richard III* and *King Lear*. *[Whereas the first of these is believed to have been lost, a copy of Warde's* King Lear *still exists.]* Another of his lost films was *A Lover's Oath* (1921), in which he starred as Omar Khayyam opposite Ramon Novarro.

Born in 1851, Warde was the right age to be cast in *The Fires of Youth,* in which he played an evil, aging industrialist who forces his employees to work in unsanitary and unsafe conditions until he "sees the light." Cast as one of his factory workers, an *ingénue* named Rose, Jeanne is in love with a young man who also slaves for Warde.

Jeanne Eagels, still looking wholesome despite ALL those fallen woman themes.

The *Syracuse Daily Journal* called Jeanne "a movie find," predicting a major Hollywood career for her.

Warde and Jeanne also co-starred in *Under False Colors* (1917). Thanhouser once again was the producer. He hired Emile Chautard again to helm this feature. This time, Jeanne was cast as the Countess Olga in a drama set in Russia during the dethronement of the Czar. In the film, she assumes the identity of a simple Polish girl and flees from Russia to America. Before its premiere, Thanhouser ordered his studio publicist to promote Jeanne as "The Most Charming Woman on the American Stage."

The *Exhibitors Trade Review* wrote, "Miss Eagels has never been seen in a role where her pleasing personality was so pronounced."

As for Warde, Jeanne's so-much-older leading man, he lived until the age of eighty-three, dying in 1935.

***

In 1917, Jeanne returned to Broadway, starring in three plays, each as co-star to the aging character actor George Arliss.

After meeting and interviewing Jeanne, the distinguished English actor took her under his protective wing and soon made her his *protégée*. She met his wife, Florence, an actress herself. Born in London, she'd married Arliss in 1899. In time, she would play his wife in such films as *Disraeli* (1921), *The Millionaire* (1931), and *The House of Rothschild* (1933). The latter two films were Talkies.

Born in London in 1868, Arliss was no beauty, and on both the stage and screen, he was noted for his austere, long, and bony face, sometimes wearing a monacle. He'd made his debut on the London stage in 1890, appearing rather aristocratic, florid, and commanding.

Amazingly, Arliss was sixty-one when he became a film star, soon to be famous for playing historical figures, notably Disraeli.

[Benjamin Disraeli was a Conservative British politician who, under Queen Victoria, twice served as Prime Minister (1868 and again from 1774-1880) of the United Kingdom.]

He was far more than a co-star to Jeanne, since he also supervised her diction, her makeup, and her wardrobe. She respected him as an actor and religiously followed his advice, although privately, she told Ethel Barrymore, "Mr. Arliss has never quite escaped traces of being a stage actor from the 1890s."

Arriving in the United States, he had first worked in the troupe of actors hired by the woman who kept billing herself as Mrs. Patrick Campbell, a consciously old-fashioned style of billing.

On stage, Arliss cast Jeanne in one of his weaker plays, *The Professor's Love Story*, which ran on Broadway at the Knickerbocker Theatre from February to April of 1917.

In it, he played an absent-minded professor. *Variety* claimed he "looked like a tortoise without its protective shell."

He becomes enchanted with his lovely secretary, Lucy White. The role originally went to actress Margret Maude, who dropped out to accept another part.

In search of a replacement, Jeanne came into his orbit.

The script was by J.M. Barrie, who would have far more success with *Peter Pan*.

In addition to Arliss' wife, Florence, Reginald Denny, another English actor, had the second male lead. Born in 1891, he had been the amateur boxing champion of Great Britain. Attracted to his good looks and muscular body, Jeanne flirted outrageously with him, even though he'd married Irene Haisman in 1913. "He can throw me a punch any time," she told Florence. "I never saw why married men should not make themselves available to a gorgeous woman who might come along. I think adultery can add spice to a man's life, making him a better husband."

The second night after meeting him, Denny was seen entering Jeanne's hotel room

Of her co-star, the English actor **Reginald Denny, Jeanne Eagels** said, "He is my idea of a real man."

Denny, once the amateur boxing champion of Britain, had been born into a theatrical family. He was a very close friend of John Barrymore, co-starring with him in *Hamlet* (1933).

A stunt pilot in the 1920s, and a gunner during World War I, Denny later developed his remote-controlled "radioplane" for military use. Denny and his partner manufactured 15,000 of these radio-controlled drones for the U.S. Army during World War II.

at ten o'clock, not departing until three that morning. Their liaison continued for the duration of the play.

When he wasn't seducing her, Denny shared stories of his life, revealing that he had first appeared on stage in *The Merry Widow,* later joining an opera company for a tour of colonial India. Like Jeanne, he, too, had begun a career in silent films in 1915.

In time, he would form a close bond with John Barrymore—some gossips called it "more than being mere friends." They co-starred together on Broadway in Shakespeare's *Richard III* in 1920.

Long after his romance with Jeanne lost its bloom, in the decades that followed, as his male beauty receded, Denny became known to American audiences as a character actor.

His most memorable roles included *The Little Minister* (1934) with Katharine Hepburn; *Anna Karenina* (1935) with Greta Garbo; and Alfred Hitchcock's *Rebecca* (1940) with Laurence Olivier and Joan Fontaine. One of his last parts was opposite Frank Sinatra in the crime caper, *Assault on a Queen* (1966).

Jeanne Eagels, lovely in satin and lace, playing an English aristocrat in *Disraeli.*

She'd come a long way from the back alleys of Kansas City.

Arliss liked working with Jeanne so much, he cast her in his next play, *Disraeli* which also played at the Knickerbocker in April and May of 1917. This biographical play by the British writer, Louis N. Parker, had first been staged in 1911. It became Arliss' signature role. It focused on the Prime Minister's role in attempting to gain control of the Suez Canal and secrete Britain's sea route to India.

Disraeli was also depicted as Queen Victoria's confidant and the most famous Jew in England.

To add spice to the life of *Disraeli*—or at least to the stage version—Parker created some fictional parts, including Jeanne's role of Lady Clarissa Pevensey. Most critics found Jeanne "enchanting" in her impersonation of a British aristocrat.

For five years, Arliss would make the lead in the stage version of *Disraeli* his signature role. In 1921, Hollywood called, and he turned *Disraeli* into a silent film. Actually, another actor beat him to the silver screen portrayal. In 1916, the stage actor Dennis Eadie was the first to bring this famous Victorian to the screen in a silent film. When critics compared the two different screen portrayals, Arliss emerged as the star favorite.

Arliss had managed to acquire the rights to the play for just $3,000. In 1929, with the advent of sound, he made *Disraeli* as a talkie, starring his wife, Florence, and the emerging screen star, Joan Bennett, a sultry brunette and the sister of screen legend, the blonde-haired Constance Bennett.

In an amazing coincidence in the 1929 sweepstakes for Best Actor at the Academy Awards, Arliss competed with himself, since he had also been nominated for *The Green Goddess.* He was competing against two other actors, who also had been double nominated: Maurice Chevalier for *The Big*

Pond and *The Love Parade*, as well as Ronald Colman for *Bulldog Drummond* and also for *Condemned*.

Arliss lives on in film history for being the "sparkplug" who ignited the faltering career of a young starlet, Bette Davis, by casting her opposite him in The Man Who Played God *(1932)*.

Jeanne's final stage appearance with Arliss was also in 1917 when she was cast as Mrs. Maria Reynolds in the play *Hamilton*, which co-starred his wife, Florence. Carl Anthony played Thomas Jefferson and Hardee Kirkland was cast as James Monroe.

Once again, the Knickerbocker was the venue for *Hamilton*. It ran from November of 1917 until April of 1918.

The real-life Alexander Hamilton, known to yesteryears' generations of American school kids, was Secretary of Treasury during the presidency of George Washington. Jeanne was cast as Hamilton's mistress, which led to the secretary being blackmailed by Jeanne's stage husband, James Reynolds (played by Pell Trenton).

Reynolds would later blackmail Hamilton for having an adulterous affair with his wife. That would so outrage Mrs. Reynolds, as played by Jeanne, that she filed for divorce from her husband, finding him "a rogue and a professional con man."

Aaron Burr, in 1804, would kill Hamilton in a duel.

The critics praised *Hamilton*, the *New York Post* saying, "It is a real play with real men and real women in it, containing an appeal not only to popular taste, but to the attention of the intelligent theatergoer."

The New York Times cited Jeanne's "great charm and very considerable subtlety and humor."

***

For her next film, *The Cross Bearer*, produced by World Film Corporation in 1918, Jeanne was reteamed with Montagu Love from *The Great Pursuit*. *The Cross Bearer* revolves around Cardinal Mercier, who protects his flock when the Kaiser's troops invade his Belgian town during World War I.

Cast as Liane de Merode, Jeanne played the young ward of the cardinal. She gets to perform a passionate love scene with Anthony Merlo, cast as her lover, Maurice Lambeaux. She told Love, "Every night, Tony feeds me a foot of tongue."

MONTAGU LOVE
justly renowned for his master character impersonations — brilliant as he was in "Rasputin," "The Awakening," "The Brand of Satan," etc., reaches the highest of dramatic art as
"CARDINAL MERCIER"

Jeanne's next picture, **The Cross Bearer,** was originally advertised as **Cardinal Mercier,** the title role played by Montagu Love. World Film shot the picture in New York and Fort Lee, New Jersey. It was directed by George Archainbaud.

She received little publicity except in the *Motion Picture Studio Directory*, which wrote: "**Jeanne Eagels** has blonde hair and a blonde complexion. She enjoys horseback riding and swimming. She stands five feet four inches and weighs 120 pounds. Her natural hair color is brown but for much of her career, she bleaches it blonde. Her eyes are blue."

The magazine *Motion Picture* wrote: "The world of Jeanne Eagels as the charming Liane de Merode entitles her to rank with the best leading women on the screen."

***

Jeanne continued to alternate between stage and screen roles. Producer David Belasco got in touch with her, asking if she'd play the female lead opposite George Abbott in his latest production of the play, *Daddies*. It had been scripted by John L. Hobble and told the story of three confirmed bachelors who make a wager that each of them will stay unmarried. Along the way, each of them decides to adopt an orphan from World War I.

As Ruth Atkins, Jeanne arrives on the scene as an innocent sixteen-year-old English girl. Complications follow, including love.

After a week of rehearsals, Jeanne knew she was miscast, and so did Belasco, but he kept her in the role, admitting, "The part is not suited for her particular talent."

Until she got to know him better, Jeanne was thrilled to be working with Abbott, a virtual renaissance man (director, playwright, screenwriter, and producer) of the theater. Born in 1887, he'd made his Broadway debut in 1913, playing in *The Misleading Lady*. His first big hit came in 1926 when he starred in the play *Broadway*, which ran for 603 performances. In the years that followed, it was unusual for him not to have a hit every year on Broadway.

Mr. Showman, **George Abbott,** had a reputation as a "show doctor," called in to save a production with drastic last-minute changes before it opened on Broadway. He referred to it as "rejiggering."

He would live to the astonishing age of 107, dying in Miami Beach on January 31, 1995. When he was born, Grover Cleveland was president, and when he died, Bill Clinton sat in the Oval Office.

Called "The Bishop of Broadway," because of his priest-like wardrobe, Abbott told the press that Jeanne was "the fourth jewel in his theatrical crown," taking her place alongside such hugely popular actresses as Ina Claire.

He was known along The Great White Way for having the most used casting couch, and he later admitted that he fell in love with nearly all of his leading ladies. Next to his office was a bedroom with a four-poster. "I recall the only actress who ever rejected me was Laurette Taylor."

Did that mean he seduced Jeanne? She neither confirmed nor denied it.

Even at the age of sixty-five, Abbott was boasting "I'm still a stallion."

In a memoir, he described Jeanne as "a girl who showed up in shabby clothes, with the air of Eleonora Duse, the voice of a duke's daughter — perhaps an earl — and the mien of a starved little alley cat."

Opening in 1918, *Daddies* ran for 304 performances, a big hit.

Over the course of his long career, Abbott played a key role in the careers of not only Jeanne, but other theatrical personalities such as John Kander, Jule Styne, Betty Comden, Elaine Stritch, Carol Burnett, Bob Fosse,

Leonard Bernstein, Stephen Sondheim, Jerome Robbins, and Liza Minnelli.

***

Jeanne's next role was also on Broadway, where she was cast in *A Young Man's Fancy*, which ran for thirteen performances at the Liberty Theatre in Manhattan. She co-starred with Frank Allworth and Harry Barfoot, playing the role of "Mary Darling."

It was the story of a young poet who strolls about at night, falling in love with a beautiful mannequin in a department store window display.

Lynn Fontanne and Alfred Lunt originated the roles at the National Theatre in Washington.

Jeanne played both the mannequin and a real live girl., The play encompassed a number of fantasy scenes. One reviewer suggested that she was "as artificial as only a mannekin can be."

Her leading man, Allworth, a native of Ontario, became one of many actors who died while onstage, although not in any production directly associated with Jeanne.

[In 1935, Allworth collapsed during the second act of Portuguese Gal, *a rowdy comedy, at the Broad Street Theatre in Philadelphia. Since he was playing a drunken policeman, the audience laughed hysterically, thinking it was part of the script. After about a minute, his leading lady, Lenore Ulrick, realized he'd had a heart attack and called for the curtain to be pulled down. Within a few hours of entering the hospital, on September 2, 1935, Allworth was dead.]*

***

In the autumn of 1919, Jeanne sustained a brief affair with a prominent, socially connected Manhattan attorney, Thomas L. Chadbourne, who was about twenty years her senior. She could be seen arriving at rehearsals and performances of her latest play, *The Wonderful Thing*, in his chauffeured limousine.

A drama in four acts, it was based on a story by Lillian Trimble Bradle and Forrest Halsey. Jeanne played the daughter of a well-to-do rancher who falls for the oldest son of a snobbish but financially strapped English family. He marries her for her money.

Her husband-to-be was portrayed by Gordon Ash, an English actor born in 1877. He often showed up for rehearsals drunk. Ironically, both he and Jeanne would die in the same year (1929), in his case by acute alcoholism.

Critics attacked the tired old melodrama, suggesting it was "flimsy and jerrybuilt." But for the most part, Jeanne was cited for saving the night with her acting and charm.

For its 1921 film adaptation, *The Wonderful Thing*, Norma Talmadge purchased the screen rights to star in Jeanne's role opposite Harrison Ford. (No, not that one.)

***

A dry spell of seven years was coming up for Jeanne as a screen actress. She made one more short film before her long furlough. For a 1920 release for the Stage Women's War Relief Fund, she agreed to star in *The Madonna of the Slums.*

Her co-star was Amelita Galli-Curci, an opera diva coloratura and soprano from Milan. She'd made her debut in 1906 in Giuseppe Verdi's *Rigoletto,* and soon was acclaimed throughout Italy, even performing with Enrico Caruso. Her arrival in the United States was in 1916.

Today, the film, made with Jeanne, is believed to have been lost.

Both women received critical praise for their co-starring roles in "this little drama which both Madame Galli-Curci and Jeanne Eagels carried to a pleasing finale."

***

Jeanne's next play, *In the Night Watch,* had already been a hit in London's West End before the Shubert Brothers, Lee and J.J., brought it to Broadway. It opened at the Century Theatre in January of 1921 and ran for 111 performances.

It was directed by Frederick Stanhope with a script by Michael Morton. It was set almost entirely on a French warship at the dawn of World War I. Robert Warwick was cast as Captain Corlaix, a commander in the French Navy, with Jeanne (cast as Yvonne) portraying his wife.

According to the plot, Jeanne is also romantically involved with Lieutenant Bramboure, as portrayed by Cyril Scott.

She arranges a shipboard dinner for officers of the cruiser, but the vessel is attacked and sunk by a German U-Boat. Both the captain and Yvonne survive, but he faces a court martial before the Admiralty.

Born in Sacramento in 1878, Warwick was a handsome stage and film matinee idol with a booming voice. Originally, he wanted to be an opera singer—that is, until he

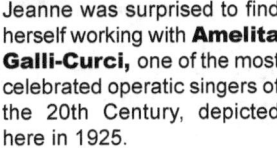

Jeanne was surprised to find herself working with **Amelita Galli-Curci,** one of the most celebrated operatic singers of the 20th Century, depicted here in 1925.

She'd arrived in the United States in the fall of 1916 as an unknown, but in time, became famous as a recording star.

In 1921, she made her debut at the Metropolitan Opera in Manhattan in *La Traviata*. There, she remained for nine years until her retirement.

A Broadway play, *In the Night Watch*, cast Jeanne in the female lead opposite handsome **Robert Warwick.** When it was sold to the movies, its title was shortened to *The Night Watch* and Jeanne lost out on the film role.

There is strong evidence that Jeanne and Warwick became lovers, although he was married at the time. She told him she could not decide which medium she preferred, the stage or screen. "Do both," he advised. "Follow in my footsteps. Let's face it: More people will see us in the flickers than on the stage."

met another charismatic young actor, John Barrymore. Both of them made their debut on Broadway in 1903. When they co-starred in *Glad of It*.

Beginning in 1914, Warwick became a romantic hero in silent films, his first movies shot at Fort Lee, New Jersey.

As time went by and his looks faded, he became a character actor in talking pictures, including *The Little Colonel* with Shirley Temple; *The Adventures of Robin Hood* (1938) with Errol Flynn; and several Preston Sturges films such as *Sullivan's Travels* (1941) co-starring Joel McCrea and Veronica Lake.

Warwick was stiff competition, but Jeanne garnered the better reviews. *Variety* cited her "sincerity that goes directly over the footlights."

During the run of *In the Night Watch*, rumors were spread that Jeanne was having affairs with both of its good-looking male actors. Those reports were more probable than rumors that appeared in the press stating that she was set to marry the blatantly homosexual actor, Clifton Webb.

When his involvement in *In the Night Watch* ended, Cyril Scott faced a personal tragedy. He returned home to find that his wife of twenty years had committed suicide by hanging herself from the second-story balcony of their home. According to gossip, she was motivated by reports that her husband was having an affair with Jeanne.

First National purchased the film rights to *In the Night Watch* for a 1928 release directed by Alexander Korda and starring Billie Dove and Paul Lukas.

***

[In November of 1922, Jeanne was under the management of Sam H. Harris at Maxine Elliott's Theatre in Manhattan. To wild acclaim, she enjoyed a smashing success in the role of a prostitute, Sadie Thompson, the focal character in W. Somerset Maugham's play, Rain.

For more details about the history of that play, and her era's fascination with "good girls who get degraded," turn to Chapter Eleven. It's devoted to Jeanne's performance

Cyril Scott, British actor and alleged lover of Jeanne Eagels whose wife committed suicide, allegedly out of desperation from her husband's alleged infidelity.

For the 1928 movie version of *The Night Watch*, **Billie Dove** took over the Jeanne Eagels' role of Yvonne. As a teenager, she had been hired as a chorus girl in the *Ziegfeld Follies*. She quickly evolved into a popular screen actress starring in such hits as *The Black Pirate* (1926) opposite swashbuckler Douglas Fairbanks, Sr.

In spite of three unhappy marriages, she sustained a legion of male lovers, none more persistent than the billionaire aviator and film mogul, Howard Hughes.

in the role of the prostitute, and to the other legendary actresses who interpreted it in later productions of Rain *on the stage and in film.]*

***

At long last, love came to Jeanne. It took the form of Ted Coy (aka Edward Harris), who was born in 1888 in Andover, Massachusetts.

With his blue eyes and blonde hair, he was powerfully built, a football hero standing six feet tall and weighing 195 pounds. He had been selected as a first-team All America three years (1907, 1908, and 1909) in a row. He was later designated as the fullback on Walter Camp's all-time, all-America team, and he also served as Yale's head football coach beginning in 1910.

Sportswriter George Trevor described Coy as "a leonine figure with a pug nose and a shock of yellow hair like a Gloucester fish girl. He ran with high-knee action."

Sports writers in the locker room after the game privately said, "When Ted pulls off his jockstrap and heads for the shower, he gives all the other players penis envy."

Coy was an early hero of the novelist F. Scott Fitzgerald, and he is mentioned in Fitzgerald's first novel, *This Side of Paradise* (1920). As the writer's boyhood hero, he was also featured as the character "Ted Fay" in his 1928 short story, *The Freshest Boy*.

Ernest Hemingway told Fitzgerald, "I think you're in love with this jock."

Flocks of women and a few homosexuals, including a Wall Street banker, pursued Coy, but in 1913, he married Sophia Meldrim of Savannah. It was not a happy marriage, and frequently punctuated with evidence of his infidelity. But he was with his wife long enough to father two sons, both of whom he expected to mature into football stars.

His parents left him an inheritance of $300,000 and a home at 863 Park Avenue in Manhattan.

One of his football buddies from Yale attended a performance with Coy to

Ted Coy is seen as a Yale undergraduate. Sports writers hailed him as one of the greatest football players in the history of the game. It became a familiar sight when he would burst through the opposing team's defenses, his long blonde hair held in place with a white sweatband. He later had his locks cut, as the photo above reveals.

In 1925, he secretly married **Jeanne Eagels**. In the lower photo, the happy couple is seen the day after their wedding at her farm.

watch Jeanne performing as Sadie Thompson in *Rain*. "The moment Jeanne came on stage, Ted nudged me and whispered, 'I've got to have her.'"

Later, they went backstage. "She ignored me and flirted with him," Coy's buddy said. "She was hot for him, and he was burning up like a firecracker. From what he told me, their affair began the night after we saw *Rain*."

In December of 1924, Sophia filed for divorce, citing Jeanne as the woman who ruined her marriage.

Clifton Webb, Jeanne's best friend, remembered it differently, asserting that Coy met Jeanne in January of 1923, but didn't begin to date her then since he was heading for Europe for a sojourn of eighteen months. After that, he returned to New York to find his stage idol performing "as that whore, Sadie."

Webb later told Noël Coward, "I was overcome with this jock's sex appeal. He was dynamite. Of course, I knew I didn't have a chance. At least I could one day take him to a Turkish bath where I could look but not touch."

Long before his divorce was final, Coy proposed marriage to Jeanne. Their wedding finally took place in August of 1925 at the home of Jeanne's best female friend, the actress Fay Bainter (Mrs. Reginald Venable), Mayapple Farm in Stamford, Connecticut. He was thirty-seven years old, and on her marriage license, she had listed her age as "twenty-seven."

[Jeanne did not live to see Fay Bainter's breakthrough in movies. She appeared in It Happened One Night *(1934) the romance that brought Oscars to its stars, Claudette Colbert and Clark Gable.*

Four years later, Bainter made Oscar history in 1938 when she was nominated for two separate awards. They included a Best Actress nod for her performance in White Banners, *and a Best Supporting Actress nod for her performance in* Jezebel *with Bette Davis.]*

Many of her friends thought Jeanne would retire after her marriage to Coy, but she was forced to work since she'd become the breadwinner of the family. He'd lost most of his money in his divorce, having been ordered by the court to make a huge settlement on his spurned spouse.

After a honeymoon that had been idyllic, the couple returned to New York, where Clifton Webb and Noël Coward threw a party for them, inviting the theatrical elite, including Ethel Barrymore and Lynn Fontanne.

Back on the road again with *Rain*, Jeanne was overstressed and "worn to a frazzle." She began to drink heavily, and somehow managed to find a drug dealer in whichever town she played in, including Salt Lake City.

Out of work, Coy maneuvered to become her manager, but she rejected his offer, even though he still handled many of her affairs. When her drinking increased, he returned to New York, seeing her rarely.

Webb became Coy's drinking buddy, listening to his marriage woes. He often suggested they head to the steam room together to sweat things out.

On the road, Jeanne was becoming more temperamental, often arguing with the cast and crew members. Once, in a discussion with Bainter, she said, "I should never have married Ted. It was the mistake of my life."

When she told Webb that her marriage was falling apart, he said jokingly, "Will you give him to me?"

Although she laughed, Webb's offer wasn't really uttered in jest.

When Webb asked Coy what was going wrong in the marriage, he said, "I could fulfill her physical desires, but not her emotional needs."

As the couple drifted apart, Jeanne was rumored to have renewed her relationship with Whitney Warren, Jr., and reports of an affair reached Coy in New York.,

Webb's crush on Coy never faded. He claimed, "Jeanne was far too demanding a personality for the poor, dear boy. He was not the type to carry around her baggage, or to follow a star from one train station to the next. He was so very handsome, so very masculine, that he should have been the man of his house. One moment, Jeanne would be a saint, the next minute a tigress. She could turn at the snap of a finger."

"I think Ted was only relaxed when he was on my massage table," Webb continued. "My skilled hands could bring him relief."

Webb told Noël Coward, "I let the dear boy know he was welcome to put his shoes under my bed at any time of the day or night."

Webb claimed, "Sometimes, he'd show up on my doorstep, broke and begging for a loan. He got it, but not before he sang for his supper."

Tired of Coy and living apart, Jeanne filed for divorce in 1928, alleging extreme cruelty. "My husband often assaulted me, and once, he broke my jaw. He threatened to destroy my beautiful face so I could never work on the stage again."

In his final years, Coy moved to El Paso. In the year of his divorce, he, at the age of 47, married the 21-year-old Lottie Bruhn.

Seven years later, in September of 1935, Coy was found dead in El Paso.

A few months later, his widow was seen at a pawnbroker, trying to sell her wedding ring and some gold medals he'd won in football. She claimed that she had not eaten in five days.

As the months in her own life dwindled to a precious few, Jeanne's life was about to change.

Mercedes de Acosta became a fixture, trying to take over her career and wean her from drugs and alcohol.

***

Mercedes had been mesmerized when she went to see Jeanne Eagels perform as Sadie Thompson in W. Somerset Maugham's *Rain*. She later urged her friends to go and see it. "As far as I'm concerned, Miss Eagels has entered the Pantheon of Eleanora Duse, Nazimova, and my dear Eva Le Gallienne."

Mercedes wanted to become involved in the life of Jeanne as soon as possible, and she asked her new friend, John Colton, co-author of stage adaptation of *Rain*, to arrange an introduction as soon as he could. She told Colton, "I think Jeanne, to

Mercedes de Acosta, of sublime appeal and almost unlimited understanding of the sense of isolation shared by many lesbians then (and now).

judge from the play, has a husky voice the equal of Tallulah Bankhead or Garbo."

In the previous few months, Mercedes had developed a close bond with Colton and had been lured into his turbulent, troubled world.

One night, she told Darwin Porter, "John had a preference for what homosexuals call 'rough trade.' I would get a desperate call from him in the middle of the night, begging me to come to his rescue, and often to bring emergency cash to bail him out of some horrible thing."

"Once, I had to retrieve him from an alleyway in Brooklyn, where he had been badly beaten. He had picked up these two dockworkers for rough sex, but instead of that, they had beaten him up and robbed him. He was so badly injured I had to call an ambulance and take him to the hospital. Regrettably, that night would be just one of many other evenings like it. I think he had a death wish."

She later wrote in her memoir, "I walked where angels feared to tread, and sometimes, I had to argue with gangsters to let me take John home."

Colton didn't have to arrange an introduction between Jeanne and Mercedes as they met accidentally one night.

Mercedes' introduction to Jeanne came about when she accepted Colton's invitation to go with her to a speakeasy.

As they were sitting having a drink and chatting, Jeanne made an entrance into the room on the arm of her friend, Sonny Whitney. The star and Whitney joined Colton and Mercedes at table.

During the course of the evening, Mercedes told Jeanne about a play she'd written, claiming it would be an ideal vehicle for her to star in after *Rain*. As she described it, Jeanne was intrigued and agreed to meet with Mercedes that Sunday afternoon.

"Suddenly, she and Scotty were gone," Mercedes said. "Although she was playing a whore on Broadway, I thought I had met a woman of angelic beauty."

"I spoke at length about her to John," she said. "Although hardly a prostitute like Sadie, she did have some of the elements of one, a sense of her own doom, a violent recklessness, a daredevil character. I was overcome with emotion, since I'm a very sensitive spiritual person. I sensed from our short meeting that her life would end tragically. There was an aura of doom about her."

Jeanne and Mercedes met that Sunday, and she was startled when Mercedes read her play to her. She was surprised that Mercedes had envisioned her as the lead in her play, *The Mother of Christ*.

"To go from Sadie Thompson to the Virgin Mary is a bit of a stretch," she said. "But I want the challenge." She told Mercedes that she was a religious person and came from a Catholic background and had once played a faith healer in *The World and the Woman*.

Mercedes did not tell Jeanne that she'd originally written the play for Eleonora Duse. In the first act, Mary goes to Pontius Pilate and offers to give up her own life if he will spare Jesus.

"You will not only be the Mother of Jesus, but the Mother of all people suffering around the world. It will be your most heroic role and your greatest performance."

During the next few weeks, Mercedes went to every possible backer, ranging from Sam Harris to Joseph P. Kennedy, facing rejection from all of them.

A staunch Catholic, Kennedy told her that "the public will not accept

Eagels as the Mother of Jesus because she's too identified with playing a prostitute."

In spite of the rejection of financial backers, Jeanne and Mercedes bonded as lovers, and she became a major fixture in the star's life during her final months.

Mercedes spent weekends at Jeanne's home at Ossining-on-the-Hudson in New York State. "I became aware of Jeanne hitting the bottle, as you Americans say, and she was also heavily into drug use."

She spoke of the long walks the two took into the countryside, where she urged Jeanne not to be so dependent on stimulants. "Time and time again, she promised me she'd wean herself from both drugs and liquor, but she never kept that vow. We made mad, passionate love, and every day, I fell more in love with her. I was also on a mission to save her life."

Back in Manhattan, facing the pressures of stardom, Jeanne resumed her drug use and heavy drinking.

"Intoxicated or not, she pulled herself together and delivered a magnificent performance of Sadie every night," Mercedes said. "Audiences were never disappointed. Frankly, I don't know how she did it in her weakened condition."

An executive from Paramount Pictures offered Mercedes and Jeanne a contract for a silent screen adaptation for *The Mother of Christ*, but they turned it down, claiming they wanted to present it on the stage first. Both of them later regretted their refusal.

***

Mercedes attended every performance she could of Jeanne's last major starring role on the stage, *Her Cardboard Lover*. Before going on tour, it had opened in Manhattan at the Empire Theatre on March 21, 1927, running until August, a total of 152 performances. As Simone Lagorce, Jeanne was cast opposite the English actor, Leslie Howard, playing André Dallicel.

In the plot, Jeanne was a liberated Parisian, who employs a penniless young man as her secretary and has him masquerade as her lover to make her estranged husband jealous.

The director was a young and inexperienced George Cukor, who would go on to greater glory as the leading "woman's director" in Hollywood. Before helming Jeanne, Cukor had gotten good notices for a stage version of *The Great Gatsby*, based on the acclaimed novel by F. Scott Fitzgerald.

Cukor was hired by producers A.H. Woods and Gilbert Miller, who wanted Laurette Taylor in the lead. During tryouts in Washington and Atlantic City, Cukor realized that she was miscast, and the star often showed up intoxicated.

"She was the most neurotic actress I ever directed," he later said. "Except for Vivien Leigh whom I directed in *Gone With the Wind* until Selznick fired me."

Taylor was later removed from the role and threatened a lawsuit. That led to arbitration with Actors Equity which awarded her $4,000.

Cukor then offered the role to Katharine Cornell, who was touring at the time in *The Green Hat*. Although Cornell wanted to accept, she was still tied up in the closing weeks of *The Green Hat* and would not be available for rehearsals.

Cukor then sent the script for *Her Cardboard Lover* to Ossining, where

Jeanne read it to Mercedes, who thought it "will be an amusing vehicle for you."

A few days later, in a meeting with Cukor and the producers, Jeanne accepted the role.

Cukor later evaluated the onstage dynamic of the Broadway version of *Her Cardboard Lover:* "As co-stars, Leslie Howard and Jeanne Eagels were a match made in hell, feuding through every onstage performance," Cukor said. "She frequently upstaged him. For example, she would suddenly demand that he fetch her a glass of water, which had nothing to do with the plot. Once, onstage during a live performance in a boudoir scene, she just left the stage and was gone for four minutes, leaving him to improvise."

Born in London in 1893, and long before his appearance as Ashley Wilkes in *Gone With the Wind,* Howard was a virtual Renaissance man of the theater. He was a matinee idol, a Shakespearean actor, writer, director, and producer.

Leslie Ruth Howard, the star's daughter, wrote, "Never was a play more fraught with friction and dogged by difficulties. Leslie wondered why he had ever become involved. He longed to get out of the whole thing. He had had more than enough of temperamental female stars, recasting, rewriting, and repetition. He was appallingly bored with the entire performance."

Upper photo: **Jeanne Eagels** with **Leslie Howard** in *Her Cardboard Lover*, and (lower photo) as they were caricatured by Covarrubias in 1927 in arts reviews at the time.

On opening night and the nights to follow, Jeanne was mortified at the play's end. She'd go out on stage looking stunning in gold and pink. But as she took her bows, the audience kept yelling, "HOWARD! HOWARD! HOWARD!"

Further humiliation awaited her, as he got better reviews that she did. Brooks Atkinson, in *The New York Times* wrote: "Jeanne Eagels was not happily cast. On the other hand, Mr. Howard as a blind young fool plays boyishly with droll flourishes and a sustaining sardonic intelligence."

Alexander Woollcott commented on Jeanne's "almost fey charm and delicacy as she plunged into the romp of comedy with true comedic spirit."

"The critic for *Time* magazine was supportive of Jeanne, describing a feline quality to her role. "Peculiarly herself, she glides from slouch to crouch as a tawny lioness playing with catnip. Yet so nimbly does she manage, especially in the second act bed-to-telephone scene, that the audience takes her kitten-face value, almost missing the sinister suggestion of claws."

After the play closed, Howard bid Jeanne "*adieu* forever." He sailed to London, where he opened *Her Cardboard Lover* in the West End. It co-starred Tallulah Bankhead, who boasted, "I had them lined up at the box office."

In June of 1943, Howard flew from neutral Lisbon to war-torn London. *En route*, six Luftwaffe planes fired on his aircraft. It went down in flames, with all its crew and passengers, into the ocean's depths.

[During the run of the Jeanne's stage version of Her Cardboard Lover, *film offers were coming in from Hollywood. Louis B. Mayer wondered if Jeanne might be able to appear in* Love—*based on Tolstoy's* Anna Karenina—*with John Gilbert. Garbo had co-starred with Gilbert (and had also become his off-screen lover) in* Flesh and the Devil, *but she was threatening to return to Sweden if Mayer didn't meet her salary demands. As it turned out, Mayer capitulated, so the deal to cast Jeanne as the female lead in* Love *fell through.*]

The peak of **Leslie Howard**'s American fame lay in his not-too-distant future, when, in 1939, he interacted, as Ashley Wilkes, with Scarlett O'Hara (**Vivien Leigh**) in *Gone With the Wind*.

***

During the run of the New York stage production of *Her Cardboard Lover,* Mercedes invited the leading women stars of Broadway to the Manhattan townhouse she shared with her husband, Abram Poole, who never seemed to be there.

The guest of honor was Jeanne Eagels. Also attending were Estelle Winwood, Mrs. Patrick Campbell, Helen Hayes, Constance Collier, Elsie Ferguson, Katharine Cornell, Doris Keane, Nazimova, and Helen Menken, wife of Humphrey Bogart.

"What a cat party," Mercedes confessed to John Colton the next day. "Never again. All those big stars in the same room, vying for attention and competing with each other for the same roles. From now on, only one big star at a time at a party. That way, she'll

Ironically, after directing it on Broadway, George Cukor would also be hired to direct the 1942 screen adaptation of **Her Cardboard Lover**. It starred Robert Taylor and Norma Shearer in her last film role.

Bosley Crowther of *The New York Times* reviewed it like this: "The years have not been kind to *Her Cardboard Lover.* It may have been a charming bit of nonsense fifteen years ago when Leslie Howard and Jeanne Eagels did it, but not today with the world at war."

be the center of attention."

Jeanne often asked Mercedes to take her to Tomaso's Speakeasy, a dive on 45th Street that was a virtual legend among the "in" theater crowd.

When he was in town, Charlie Chaplin with a "belle du jour" would show up and might be seen chatting with John Barrymore (even Ethel on occasion).

The club catered to both black and white patrons. Ethel Waters might be there talking to Paul Robeson and Tallulah Bankhead.

On some nights, Cornell showed up with some aspiring young Broadway starlet, with whom she was romantically involved. Her husband, Guthrie McClintic, might be making a date later that night with the handsome black bartender from Harlem.

***

Because Jeanne had been consistently late or else didn't show up at all for her stage role in *Her Cardboard Lover*, she was suspended from working on Broadway for eight months by Actors Equity.

However, that didn't mean she could not work in silent films. She asked Mercedes to go with her as a kind of personal assistant to California, where she was to report to work on the latest John Gilbert film, *Man, Woman, and Sin*. It was shot in the summer of 1926.

She had no desire to work in films, referring to movie work as "stupid." Yet she was intrigued with her co-star, John Gilbert, finding him "dashing, handsome, and a wild swashbuckling figure on screen."

To welcome Jeanne to Hollywood, Gilbert threw a lavish party in her honor at his home. She showed up with Mercedes, an uninvited guest, where they mingled with Ethel Barrymore, Beatrice Lillie, and Mae Busch.

The party ended late Saturday night, and by Sunday morning, Mercedes and Jeanne studied the script of *Man, Woman, and Sin*. Throughout that ordeal, Jeanne was shaking and nervous, constantly asking Mercedes to pour her a stiff drink, which she refused to do.

At five o'clock Monday morning, their mutual friend, John Colton, pulled into their driveway to take them to Culver City. He was one of the co-authors of the screenplay, which was to be directed by Monta Bell.

In a nutshell, Mercedes summed up Colton's plot during their drive to MGM: "It's the story of a kept woman and a naïve young reporter."

Albert Whitcomb, the character played by Gilbert, is devoted to his mother, Mrs. Whitcomb (Gladys Brockell). Then he becomes romantically involved with the jaded, worldly wise society editor, Vera (as played by Jeanne Eagels). What the young reporter doesn't know is that she is the mistress of his boss at the newspaper, Mr. Bancroft (Marc McDermott).

[Their director, Monta Bell, had worked, early in his career, as a news editor in Washington, and he had long wanted to direct a film with the newspaper theme. After he migrated to Hollywood, he was employed for Charlie Chaplin as his story editor and assistant. His big break had come when he was allowed to direct Garbo in her first Hollywood film, Torrent *(1926).]*

During the filming of *Man, Woman, and Sin,* Mercedes had to return to New York. Left on her own, Jeanne began consuming greater and greater amounts of alcohol and drugs. Once, she completely disappeared for two weeks. *[She was eventually discovered wandering around Santa Barbara.]*

Frilly and fluffy, with enough *voile* and lace to keep male hearts a'flutter, **Jeanne Eagels** here appears off-screen with **John Gilbert.**

During Jeanne's long, unexplained absence, Bell pleaded with Louis B. Mayer to replace her with rising starlet Joan Crawford, who was finishing *The Understanding Heart* (1927) with Francis X. Bushman. Mayer didn't allow that, but he became intrigued with the idea of casting Gilbert with Crawford, which he did in the upcoming *Twelve Miles Out.*

Gilbert told Mercedes that he was displeased with his weak role in *Man, Woman, and Sin,* suggesting it should have gone to one of MGM's homosexual actors instead, perhaps Ramon Novarro or William Haines.

During its filming, both Jeanne and Gilbert received some distinguished visitors on the set. They included the fabled aviator Charles Lindbergh and the press baron, William Randolph Hearst.

Man, Woman, and Sin ended with the characters facing heartbreak, tragedy, and disillusionment. Gladys Brockwell, who played the male protagonist's mother, died in a car crash soon after the movie was wrapped.

Writing for *Life* magazine, Robert E. Sherwood found Jeanne "obviously ill at ease and inclined to blink in quieter moments." Norman Lusk of the *Los Angeles Times* claimed that "Jeanne is a figure of amazing interest and a certain strangeness, quite unlike anything else on the screen today."

Jeanne was particularly offended by a reviewer from *Photoplay*, who wrote, "John Gilbert does well, but Jeanne Eagels is no Garbo."

***

During the winter of 1928, Mercedes often rode in a limousine to Astoria—with Jeanne at her side—for the filming of a Pre-Code drama, *The Letter.* Distributed by Paramount, it was based on a play by W. Somerset Maugham, the original creator of the Sadie Thompson saga.

It relayed the story of a married woman who fatally shoots the man she loves. She is brought to trial but lies her way out of a murder conviction by claiming the victim broke in and tried to rape her.

Jeanne was cast as Leslie Crosby, who is married to Robert Crosby, played by Reginald Owen, the owner of a rubber plantation near Singapore. She is in love with Geoffrey Hammond (Herbert Marshall).

When Marshall (as Hammond) tells her he has fallen in love with his Chinese mistress, Li-Ti (cast with Lady Tsen Mei), Jeanne (portraying Leslie) kills him. She's brought to trial but is acquitted. Then, however, the dead man's mistress blackmails her because of an indiscreet letter she'd written him when he was alive.

After the trial, and despite her acquittal, she confesses the truth to her husband, speaking the most famous line of the drama: "I am still in love with the man I killed." She ends up living out her life on this dreary plantation with a husband she no longer loves.

Paramount publicists were busy writing ad copy: "Blinded by the fury of passion, by the despair of lost love—she had not reckoned with THE LETTER."

Jeanne Eagels appears on camera in a tense moment with **Herbert Marshall** in the first screen version of *The Letter*. Ironically, he would also be the co-star with Bette Davis in its remake.

[Marshall's role differed in the project's second version. In the original, he was cast as the murdered lover. In the second, Bette Davis version, he was her husband.]

Years later, Mercedes told Darwin Porter, "I had nothing but disappointment as a playwright. But as I watched Jeanne appearing on set in her first talkie, I was mesmerized. At last the movie-going public would hear her enchanting voice. I became intrigued with movie making—the cameras, the lighting, the microphones. I began to wonder if there were a future for me in Hollywood—perhaps selling scripts to the movie studios. Also, maybe I'd get to meet either Greta Garbo or Marlene Dietrich—perhaps both."

The Letter's producer was Monta Bell, who had previously helmed Jeanne in *Man, Woman, and Sin* with John Gilbert. Jean de Limur was its director, although in Mercedes' judgment, Bell was doing most of the work. The real boss was Walter Wanger, head of Paramount's production on the East Coast.

Wanger tangled on several occasions with Jeanne, denouncing her as "a temperamental bitch." Sometimes she would lock herself in her dressing room after storming off the set. Wanger would summon Mercedes to lure her back.

"Jeanne was one of the marked children of nature," Mercedes said. "Marked for tragedy by a kind of genius, a violence of character. With gentle coaxing, I could get her to return to the set to finish a day's work."

The Letter was the first full sound feature shot at the studio in Astoria, although a silent version was made too, because most movie houses in America were not equipped to show talkies.

The Letter opened at Manhattan's Criterion Theatre on March 2, 1929 to good reviews.

The *New York Journal-American* claimed that Jeanne's role was "one of the most gorgeous portrayals ever caught upon the Silver Screen."

The *Galveston Daily News* gave Jeanne a rave: "As the faithless, lying wife of the Maugham play, Jeanne Eagels offers what is assuredly the most moving, honest, and thoroughly exciting portrayal that talking pictures ever provided."

Jeanne was dead before Oscar night, but she was nominated for a Best Actress Academy Award, losing to Mary Pickford for *Coquette*. Many Hollywood insiders felt that Pickford used her carloads of influence within the industry to walk off with the gold that should have been presented posthumously to Jeanne.

Jeanne is often cited among the top ten losers who should have been winners at the Oscar presentations. The most famous loser of all time was Judy Garland for *A Star Is Born* (1954). Instead, Grace Kelly walked away with the honor for her performance in *The Country Girl*.

By 1940, Warner Brothers purchased the rights to make yet another talking version of *The Letter*, this time featuring its most powerful star, Bette Davis. [*Incidentally, she'd wanted to play Sadie Thompson in the 1932 film version of* Rain, *losing the role to her all-time rival, Joan Crawford.*]

HAVE GUN, WILL SHOOT: Posters and scenes from two different versions of *The Letter* draw a contrast between the great **Jeanne Eagels** (in 1929) and the great **Bette Davis** (in 1940).

Paramount released the first version; Warners the second. Warners paid $25,000 for the film rights.

Also considered for the role of Leslie Crosby in the second version were Barbara Stanwyck, Merle Oberon, Joan Crawford, Claudette Colbert, Vivien Leigh, Katharine Hepburn, Greer Garson, Frances Farmer, and Marlene Dietrich.

Like Jeanne herself, Davis was nominated for an Oscar for her performance as Leslie Crosbie but lost to Ginger Rogers for *Kitty Foyle* (1940).

***

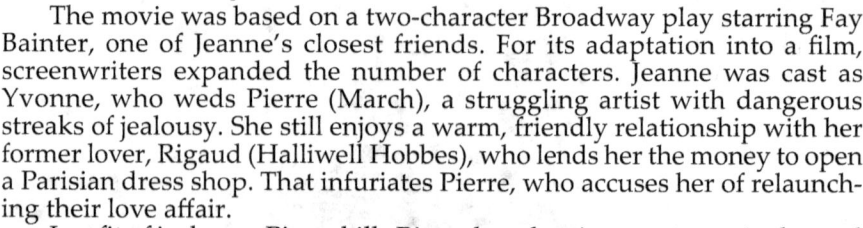

Released in 1929, the year she died, *Jealousy* would be Jeanne's last film. Based on a French play, *Monsieur Lamberthier*, by Louis Verneuil, it was another pre-Code talkie, and once again, Jean de Limur was her director. Its final cut, released by Paramount, ran for sixty-six minutes

In its early stages, Anthony Bushell, the British actor, was designated as Jeanne's leading man, but he was replaced with Fredric March. *[Jeanne had preferred John Gilbert or John Barrymore, but neither was available.]*

The movie was based on a two-character Broadway play starring Fay Bainter, one of Jeanne's closest friends. For its adaptation into a film, screenwriters expanded the number of characters. Jeanne was cast as Yvonne, who weds Pierre (March), a struggling artist with dangerous streaks of jealousy. She still enjoys a warm, friendly relationship with her former lover, Rigaud (Halliwell Hobbes), who lends her the money to open a Parisian dress shop. That infuriates Pierre, who accuses her of relaunching their love affair.

In a fit of jealousy, Pierre kills Rigaud, and an innocent man is charged with the crime. Pierre does nothing until he is exposed as the murderer. He confesses to the killing and awaits his fate.

At its opening, the film was heavily criticized, the recipient of mediocre reviews. *Film Daily* defined it as "a sophisticated story of Paris, carrying a dramatic punch. Jeanne Eagels makes it more important than it is."

New Movie Magazine claimed "the emotionalism never catches fire with Eagels as the young woman. Halliwell Hobbes is the best cast as the mellow old spider who gets what he wants."

Months later, March delivered his own critique, "Jeanne Eagels is a great actress, but our film stunk."

Thus, Jeanne's last appearance as an actress ended with a whimper.

***

October 1929 was marked by the Wall Street Crash, hurtling America into its worst depression. It also was the worst period of Jeanne's life, as her days dwindled down to a precious few. Recovering from eye surgery, she was also hovering on the brink of a total nervous breakdown. She was drinking heavily and taking heroin. Her medical treatments were supervised by Dr. Spencer E. Cowles at his Park Avenue office.

On October 3, as darkness blanketed Manhattan, she had swallowed an inordinate amount of chloral hydrate, a powerful sedative. She began to complain to her housemaid that her head was spinning, and her body was convulsed by sharp, stabbing pains.

The maid managed to get her out of the house and into a taxi, where they headed for the office of Dr. Cowles. There, a nurse, Jennie Hogulund, told her that the doctor was examining another patient, but would be with her soon.

Jeanne could not wait. Within minutes, she went into convulsions, collapsed, and died. She was thirty-nine years old.

After an autopsy, the chief medical examiner, Dr. Thomas A Gonzales, declared that she had died of "alcoholic psychosis." The results were later altered to report it as death from an overdose of chloral hydrate.

News of Jeanne's untimely death flashed from coast to coast. She was mourned by family, friends, and fans. Encased in a silver casket, her body was placed inside the train, the Twentieth Century, for shipment to her home town of Kansas City. There, a private memorial service for family members was conducted before a hearse hauled her body to its burial site at the Calvary Cemetery, seven miles away.

Her former husband, Ted Coy, told the press, "Jeanne was a magnificent person and America's greatest actress. Our different temperaments drove us apart, to my everlasting regret."

Alexander Woollcott, who had written frequently about her in the press, said, "Jeanne Eagels knew pain, she knew heartbreak, and she knew despair. Yet she could pull herself together and appear as a glorified presence on stages or on the Silver Screen. Her early demise was the death of the trapped. She was defiant in life and also courageous."

In Memory of & With Admiration for
JEANNE EAGELS
(1890-1929)

A Controversial & Ground-Breaking American Actress
Rest in Peace

How the Legacy of Jeanne Eagels Thrived in Films Inspired by Her Life in the Decades that Followed Her Death

For any number of valid reasons—including her recurrent theme of an ingénue maiden gone bad—the movie-going public continued its fascination for Jeanne Eagels for decades after her death.

Hollywood rushed to take advantage of this, churning out films inspired by her life. A brief rundown is inserted below.

DANGEROUS (1935): Inspired by the experiences of Jeanne Eagels, its plot was based on Laird Doyle's *Hard Luck Dame*. It starred the tempestuous Bette Davis in her first Oscar-winning role. *[Eagels had been one of Bette Davis' role models and idols.]* Her co-stars included Franchot Tone and Margaret Lindsay. At first, Davis had rejected the role, but the film's production chief Hal B. Wallis—later famous for producing *Casablanca* (1942)—persuaded her the she could turn this script into a star vehicle. Bette's character of Joyce Heath was clearly inspired by Eagels' tragic life.

Perc Westmore, the leading hairdresser of Hollywood, was called in, and he gave Davis a bob cut which she would favor for the rest of her life.

Fresh from the set of *Mutiny on the Bounty* (1935), in which he had co-starred with Clark Gable, Franchot Tone—engaged at the time to Joan Crawford—was introduced to Davis. Davis fell for him in ways that culminated in a torrid off-screen affair. Word reached Crawford, marking the beginning of Hollywood's most famous feud between the rival divas, both on and off the screen.

Variety, in its review of *Dangerous*, stated that "Doyle's dialogue is adult, intelligent, and has a rhythmic beat. On the whole,

Even though it became one of her most famous screen roles, **Bette Davis** did not like the script of *Dangerous*.

"It was maudlin and mawkish with a pretense at quality, which in scripts, as in home furnishings, is often worse than punk."

Davis' performance is fine, despite a few imperfect moments. When called upon to reach an intense dramatic pitch without the hysterics, she is capable of turning the trick. Yet there are moments in *Dangerous* where a lighter acting mood would be opportune."

"That Bette Davis has been unable to match the grim standard she set as Mildred in *Of Human Bondage* is not to her discredit," *Variety* continued. "In *Dangerous*, she tries again. Except for a few sequences where the tension is convincing as well as deadly, she fails. Say this for Miss Davis: she seldom lets down."

Margaret Lindsay, in the third lead of *Dangerous* as the beautiful and wealthy Gail Armitage, is engaged to the Tone character when the film begins. Her performance largely fails. For the most part, *Dangerous* remains worthy of screening today because of Miss Davis, who delivers lines that evoked the cruelty of a character she played in 1934, the self-centered, shallow, and cruel Mildred in *Of Human Bondage*:

BETTE TO HER BESOTTED, SPURNED LOVER IN DANGEROUS:
"Oh, you cheap, petty bookkeeper, you! Every time I think that those soft, sticky hands of yours ever touched me makes me sick. Sick, do you hear? You're everything that's repulsive to me. your wife! I've never been a wife to you, you poor, simpering fool!"

In regard to Bette's delivery of that line, one critic wrote: "Jeanne Eagels tonight is turning over in her grave."

OF HUMAN BONDAGE (1934):

Although she was eventually rewarded with an Oscar for her performance (see above) in *Dangerous*, Bette Davis went to her grave believing that she should have also won an Oscar for her earlier interpretation of "that bitch Mildred" in RKO's 1934 film adaptation of W. Somerset Maugham's *Of Human Bondage*. Released a year before *Dangerous*, it had made her a star. Directed by John Cromwell, it co-starred Leslie Howard and Francis Dee.

The role she played in *Bondage* was exceptionally challenging for her. She had to speak in a Cockney accent to a cast of British actors, and Leslie Howard, her English co-star, obviously despised her. Yet despite her difficulties with the film's logistics and the character she played, *Life* magazine defined her performance as "the finest ever given on the screen."

Years later, reflecting on her loss, Davis ungallantly phrased it like this: "The Oscar that year went to that dyke Claudette Colbert for *It Happened One Night*."

[Davis was not alone in interpreting the unattractive character of Mildred as a difficult one: Before Davis accepted it, several other actresses had pointedly rejected the role, including Katharine Hepburn, Irene Dunne, and Ann Harding.]

***

Of Human Bondage reached the screen again in 1946, this time a more sanitized version that featured Paul Henreid as the club-footed failed artist, and Eleanor Parker as the horid Mildred.

Bosley Crowther in *The New York Times* found this remake "pretty much of a thorough-going bore, a pale and pedestrian repeat. The role of Philip Carey is performed by Henreid in a highly self-conscious and completely unconvincing style. Parker giggles and whines so elaborately in the role of the licentious waitress that her manner seems almost in jest."

Author Ed Sikov wrote: "When **Bette Davis** cuts loose in the film's climatic scene, it's scenery chomping—loud, attention grabbing, histrionic. She gives Mildred the feral rage of a cornered animal, and the scene is justifiably famous."

***

Hollywood brought the by-now-tired *Of Human Bondage* back for an *adieu* in 1964, this time through MGM and starring Kim Novak and Laurence Harvey. In this last and final version, Mildred, in the advanced stages of syphilis, dies in the arms of her spurned lover.

Time magazine asserted, "As portrayed by Novak, Mildred giggles and speaks Cockney like a girl who learned the sound of Bow Bells from somewhere in South Chicago."

This final version of *Of Human Bondage* was condemned by the National Legion of Decency for what they called blatant sexual content and masochism.

***

[How did Bette Davis refer to and interact with W. Somerset Maugham in the aftermath of her 1934 interpretation of his play? According to many witnesses, she remained forever grateful for his authorship of Of Human Bondage. Its screen adaptation had made her a star.

To Davis' everlasting regret, she never got to portray two other roles that Maugham had created and that she wanted: Sadie Thompson in Rain and the female lead in Cakes and Ale.

Davis didn't meet Maugham until 1941 when she was starring in The Letter, a film also adapted from one of his works.

She was shocked to learn he had a bad stutter. "When he gave Philip a club foot in Of Human Bondage, that was the equivalent of his stutter," Davis claimed. "He would sometimes go on for five minutes, trying to get his tongue around the words. You'd just sit there and pray to God that he didn't think you noticed it. I'll always remember his comment about Hollywood: 'If your scripts were as great as your sets, what a town this would be.'"

Maugham lived to the advanced age of ninety-one, dying in 1965 in a world remarkably different from the one he had entered in 1874.]

DECEPTION (1946):

Even as late as 1946, Jeanne Eagels had not disappeared from the life or career dreams of Bette Davis. Warners asked her to star in a film noir, *Deception*, with Paul Henreid, her co-star in *Now, Voyager* (1942), and with Claude Rains, her favorite actor and her co-star in *Mr. Skeffington* (1944).

Deception was a remake of Eagel's last motion picture, *Jealousy*, which had been shot at Paramount in 1929. In it, she had co-starred with Fredric March.

Jealousy had originated as a play, *Monsieur Lamberthier*, by Louis Verneuil, first presented in Paris in 1927.

In one of her most memorable roles, Davis is a suffering pianist torn between Rains and Henreid, her true love. This was one of the most entrtaining of Davis' soaps, although Rains challenged her every step of the way for acting honors.

Deception was the first picrture Davis made for Warners that lost money. The studio promoted it with an aggressive ad campaign, the billboards touted the slogan SHE DECEIVED WITH ALL HER CUNNING SO SHE COULD LOVE WITH ALL HER HEART.

Davis was greatly disappointed, even though most reviews were favorable. *Deception* did not attract her usual fan base. She had hoped for a Best Actress Oscar nomination.

Actually, her once spectacular career at Warners was winding down. It would come to an end with the 1949 release of *Beyond the Forest*, a dud at the box office.

In that picture, in which she co-starred with Joseph Cotten, she uttered one of her most iconic lines—WHAT A DUMP!

Beyond the Forest was condemned by the Legion of Decency. An aggressive promotion didn't work. The studio's press department hailed the character she played as "A Midnight Girl in a Nine O'Clock Town."

Also, an ad read, "Nobody's as Good as Bette When She's Bad—in a Good Picture."

She received the worst reviews of her career. Hedda Hoper claimed, "If Bette had deliberately set out to wreck her career, she couldn't have picked a more appropriate vehicle than her role of Rosa Moline, which called for a much younger actress."

> Warner Brothers originally offered the lead role in *Deception* to Barbara Stanwyck, but ended up giving it to **Bette Davis,** cast opposite **Paul Henreid.**
>
> In *The Letter*, she had proven that she could look magnificent while firing a pistol at the man she's loved.
>
> Davis later complained, "The film was ruined by censorship."

THE LEGEND OF LYLAH CLARE (1964):

At MGM in 1968, Kim Novak portrayed yet another blonde goddess, Lylah Clare, in a film directed and produced by Robert Aldrich. Her co-stars were Peter Finch and Ernest Borgnine. Aldrich had enjoyed big box office with *What Ever Happened to Baby Jane? (1962)* co-starring Bette Davis and Joan Crawford. A few years later, he'd also produce *The Dirty Dozen (1967)*.

Although *Lylah Clare* was not specifically identified as the story of Jeanne Eagels, many reviewers felt that Eagels had been its inspiration.

The script called for an untalented neophyte to play the tempestuous but fictitious actress Lylah Clare, who had mysteriously died (according to the script) twenty years ago.

Originally, it was announced that the French actress, Jeanne Moreau, in what would have been her American film debut, would portray Lylah, but that deal fell through.

Novak, then in a slump of her career, hadn't worked in three years when she signed on to portray her.

[Novak herself, like the character she played in the film, had been beset with personal problems. She still suffered the painful after-effects of a riding accident she'd received on the set of Eye of the Devil *(1966); she'd been divorced and also involved in two car crashes. Not only that, but she'd recently lost her home in a California mud slide.]*

Finch commented on the film to the press: "It is a Hollywood melodrama with bitter irony, right on the edge of being too much. I play Lewis Zarkan, one of those Tinseltown monsters who can charm people. He's passé, yet you have a sneaking admiration for him. Let's say Ernest (Borgnine), Kim (Novak), and I are a seedy lot in the picture. It's black mahogany Gothic horror."

The Legend of Lylah Clare flopped at the box office, but in the decades since, it has developed a small cult reputation, especially among gay males.

Newsweek claimed "*Lylah Clare* fights clichés with clichés." Critic Pauline Kael claimed, "There are groans of dejection at *The Legend of Lylah Clare* with, now and then, a desperate little titter."

In *The Legend of Lylah Clare*, **Kim Novak** starred opposite **Peter Finch**, who said, "The girl was not ashamed to show off one of her best assets, her knockers, in a brassiere. I didn't make it with her like I did with Vivien Leigh. But I knew plenty of other dollybirds—a Sabena airline stewardess, a Prussian princess, a professor of Greek, the daughter of an African chieftain, and tons of prostitutes, starlets, and socialites. A high libido and a sense of life's absurdities can breed queer bedfellows."

Another critic, Roger Ebert, claimed that *Lylah Clare* "is awful but fairly enjoyable."

Life's Richard Schickel predicted that it would develop a cult following because *Lylah Clare* is not merely awful. It is grandly, toweringly, amazingly so. I laughed myself silly, and if you're in just the right mood, you may, too."

Journalist Averill Harrison wrote, "I went to see the movie thinking it was another aspect of the Jeanne Eagels story... But it wasn't. Yet it was worth the ticket price just to see Coral Browne as a malicious columnist (read that Louella Parsons) eat up the scenery. I dug Lylah's acting coach Rosella (played by Rossella Falk) with all its lesbian overtones."

More than a decade later, in 1977, Aldrich defined Novak as "the most underrated actress in Hollywood. She was badly served by me, her director. But take a look at her work in *Middle of the Night* (1959): She was brilliant. I could never understand why, after *Picnic* (1955) with William Holden, she was put in so much garbage."

In reference to *Lylah Clare,* Novak said, "It was a weird movie. It didn't have to be that bad. I was very upset when I learned tht Aldrich had Hildegard Knef dub some of my lines in a deep German-accented voice. He didn't warn me. I thought I'd die when I saw the final cut. God, it was so humiliating."

***

THE BIOPIC STARRING KIM NOVAK ENTITLED
JEANNE EAGELS (1957):

Over the years, many stars were challenged with the task of bringing the Jeanne Eagels saga, as a biopic, to the screen, but the project always died. If such a film had been made in the 1930s, the female lead might have gone to the platinum blonde, Jean Harlow.

One morning, Hollywood players turned within whatever newspaper they were reading to Louella Parson's syndicated column appeared. Surprising many of her readers, she asserted that Columbia's studio chief, Harry Cohn, was moving ahead to cast Rita Hayworth in *The Jeanne Eagels Story.*

Rita was back, after a long absence, and working in films.

Soon, however, Cohn had second thoughts, telling his associates, "I think Rita is getting near her expiration date. I've decided to cast our lavender blonde, Kim Novak, instead. Besides, she's the star in Hollywood who most resembles Eagels."

As her leading man, he selected the bisexual actor, Jeff Chandler, who was engaged at the time in two affairs—one with Esther Williams; the other with Rock Hudson.

Iron jawed and muscular, Chandler sometimes secretly dressed in drag. Despite his prematurely grey hair, critics often called him "the epitome of 1950s virility."

Set for a 1957 release, production on *Jeanne Eagels* moved ahead, casting Charles Drake as the ex-footballer who marries Eagels. Both of them end up as sodden, malfunctioning alcoholics.

Agnes Moorehead, involved in a long-running lesbian affair at the time with Debbie Reynolds, was cast as Eagels' formidable acting coach.

The fictionalized script of *Jeanne Eagels* did not actually depict the real story of the doomed actress. One of its most memorable (and hottest) scenes appears at the beginning of the film, with Novak in a skimpy costume performing a provacative hoochy-koochy dance.

The depiction of Jeanne Eagels as a druggie and alcoholic infuriated the Eagels family, who sued for libel after the picture's release. That was an ill-informed move, since only living people can be libeled, and Eagels had died in 1929. The film was not particularly successful at the box office.

Like Eagels herself, Chandler was doomed for an early death. he died tragically on June 17, 1961 in the hospital, suffering from blood poisoning.

CHAPTER ELEVEN: AMERICA'S OBSESSION WITH GIRLS YOU'D NEVER BRING HOME TO MOTHER

RAIN

IT'S A HIT! STAGE AND FILM PORTRAYALS OF AMERICA'S MOST NOTORIOUS PROSTITUTE

SADIE THOMPSON

JEANNE EAGELS, GLORIA SWANSON, JOAN CRAWFORD, TALLULAH BANKHEAD, & RITA HAYWORTH

WHO PORTRAYED THE MOST CONVINCING SLUT?

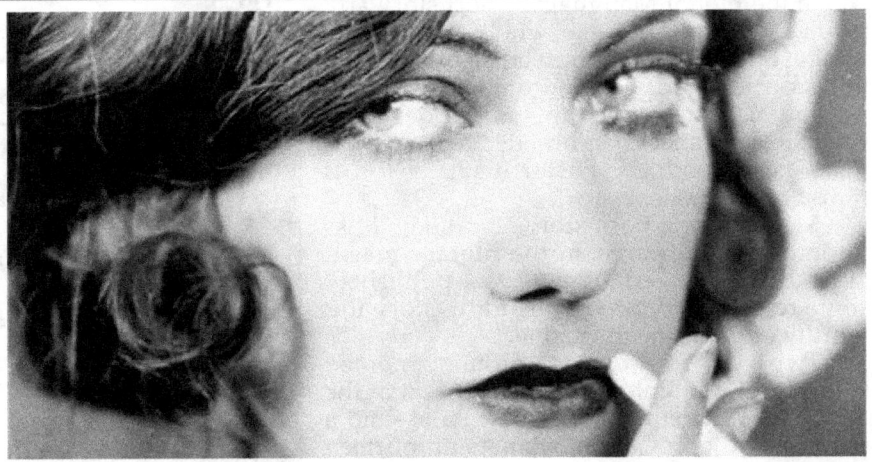

In the sexually neurotic early 20th Century, producers and filmmakers raced to find vehicles that would artfully, and with box-office appeal, showcase bad girls with good hearts.

Rain, the story of Sadie Thompson, a liberated, well-intentioned prostitute who knew how to show sailors and marines a good time, and how to dress down religous bigots too, emerged as the most consistently profitable winner.

Here's a closup of **Gloria Swanson** —one of a famous half-dozen actresses who maneuvered to portray Miss Thompson in many different productions, in the title role of the silent film version, Sadie Thompson, released in 1928.

RAIN, a eulogy to the fictitious prostitute, Miss Sadie Thompson

W. Somerset Maugham, the then very famous gay English author, had based his most famous fictional character, the prostitute, Sadie Thompson, on a real person.

"Miss Thompson" evolved directly from notes that the author penned during his waterborne transit from Hawaii to Tahiti.

According to Samuel J. Rogal in his tome *W. Somerset Maugham Anthology,* "They lodged at a seedy boarding house in Pago Pago during the rainy season for a quarantine inspection."

The real-life Miss Thompson who inspired Maugham had fled from the police in San Francisco for some unknown crime. Prior to their meeting in Pago Pago, she had worked in Honolulu's Red Light district.

Maugham said, "Sadie had a cabin next to mine, and she played a damn gramophone day and night while she serviced her Samoan clients. Those rusty bedsprings could be heard creaking until well after midnight."

In the plot of Maugham's short story appears a fanatical preacher who's hellbent on wiping out sin, even though he lusts for Sadie in his carnal heart. He is accompanied by his puritanical wife who wants Sadie deported back to San Francisco to be jailed.

Near its end, the pastor lustfully forces himself onto Sadie.

Maugham's short story, entitled "Miss Thompson," appeared in the literary magazine, *The Smart Set.* After it was published, some readers protested "this filthy story unworthy of your fine magazine."

Two writers, one a woman named Clemence Randolph—a former student at the American Academy of Dramatic Arts—and a playwright, John Colton, who spent fourteen years in Japan, combined their talents and created a play from the short story. They entitled it *Rain,* since it rains throughout most of the play.

Launching it as a Broadway play proved difficult. It often went unread after certain submissions. Then, after a producer or a member of his or her staff actually read it, it was frequently denounced. Maugham eventually agreed to sell the rights, but informed the playwrights, "I don't think it'll go over as a play."

Finally, it landed in the office of producer Samuel Harris, who had Jeanne under contract. He saw it as a vehicle for her and agreed to produce it.

As Sadie Thompson, prostitute *extraordinaire*, **Jeanne Eagels** is charming and fetching, and far more beautiful than any real-life, down-to-earth hooker a lonely marine might encounter south of Pago Pago.

In full Edwardian drag, she braves the hot, muggy climate of the South Pacific, selling sex to love-starved military men.

When she read it, she told Harris, "I've lived Sadie a thousand times. I know how to bring her alive on stage."

At the time she endorsed it, she could not have known that *Rain* would become her signature stage role for the next four years. *[Ironically because of censorship issues in Hollywood at the time, she never performed in any subsequent film version.]*

The play opened on Broadway at the Maxine Elliott Theater on November 7, 1922 and ran for 256 performances. It was an immediate hit, even though the tryouts in Philadelphia had gotten bad reviews.

Jeanne would perform in *Rain* across the country, in cities that included Washington, St. Louis, Kansas City, Cincinnati, Boston, Detroit, San Francisco, Salt Lake City, and Los Angeles.

After its opening in Manhattan, Dorothy Parker, who had attacked Jeanne before, wrote, "At last Miss Eagels has found a role worthy of her talent." Even the staid *Wall Street Journal* claimed that her performance "touched on greatness."

Life magazine wrote, "Seldom have we experienced a more powerful night in the theater."

Variety claimed, "Producers don't make stars, audiences do, as in the case of Miss Jeanne Eagels."

She told the press, "I've become a bigger star than I've ever dreamed of becoming—and it frightens the hell out of me."

Since he was traveling when the play opened, Maugham did not get to see Jeanne's performance until five months later. Having previously seen her onstage in other roles, he thought she was wrong for the role, telling friends, "She has this willowy frame and a blonde mop, making her ideal as *Peter Pan*."

But after he saw the play in New York, he told the press, "She has made my fiction come alive, a living, breathing Sadie Thompson with all her flaws but with something of her heart, too."

Now that she was a Broadway star, Jeanne's personal life had become the subject of lurid gossip. Little was known about what she did at night after the curtain fell. She was rumored to be bisexual, engaging with both men and women with equal ardor.

One romance that made the press was her affair with Whitney Warren, Jr., born into a wealthy family, a member of Manhattan's Social Four Hundred.

As would be expected, the young man's father opposed the budding romance and made plans to squelch any talk of marriage to "that whorish tramp." Within a few months, he had shipped his son off on a long sojourn in Europe.

Lee Shubert, the theater impresario, was said to still be in love with Jeanne, although she didn't have the same emotional ardor about him.

She played Sadie Thompson nearly 700 times, missing only seven performances over the many months of the run of the play. She was constantly asked what producer Sam Harris had in store for her after that.

"We haven't decided yet," she said. "But I can assure you of one thing: It will be set in a dry climate like Death Valley. I've had it with rain, some 10,000 gallons of the stuff, dumped on stage every night. Even if I have a parched throat in my next play, I won't call for a glass of water."

CARRYING A TORCH THROUGH THE RAIN

AFTER JEANNE EAGELS, A HALF-DOZEN OTHER ACTRESSES INTERPRET THE QUIRKS, CHARACTER, AND VULGARITY QUOTIENT OF SADIE THOMPSON, UPDATING HER PRIORITIES (AND COSTUMES) FOR NEW GENERATIONS OF THEATER AND MOVIE AUDIENCES.

GLORIA SWANSON
LOVE FOR SALE

Although Jeanne Eagels was dead, the character she developed, Sadie Thompson, lived on. Months before she succumbed to a heart attack, Jeanne told Mercedes, "My dream is to immortalize myself as Sadie on the screen. When a generation passes, my stage performances will disappear from memory, but on film, I can be seen two centuries from now."

Jeanne was disappointed and to some degree, enraged, when Gloria Swanson announced her intention of bringing Sadie to the screen for a 1928 release of a silent version entitled *Sadie Thompson*. Produced by Gloria Swanson Productions, it was eventually released and distributed by United Artists.

Years before, Jeanne herself had tried to star in the movie version, but Will Hays, a refugee from "Gothic America" and head of the censorship board, denounced the script as obscene. He'd labeled the film version of *Rain* as "a leper and threat to the morality of America."

Somehow, Swanson met with him and convinced him to allow the project to go through. "I will clean up the script," she promised. "I'll make a moral fable of a girl who goes wrong but finds redemption in the love of an American soldier, who puts her on the right path again."

Raoul Walsh was the silent film's leading actor and director. He cast Lionel Barrymore as the fanatical minister who maneuvers Sadie into a reform of her evil ways. Later, near the end of the film, he rapes her and commits suicide.

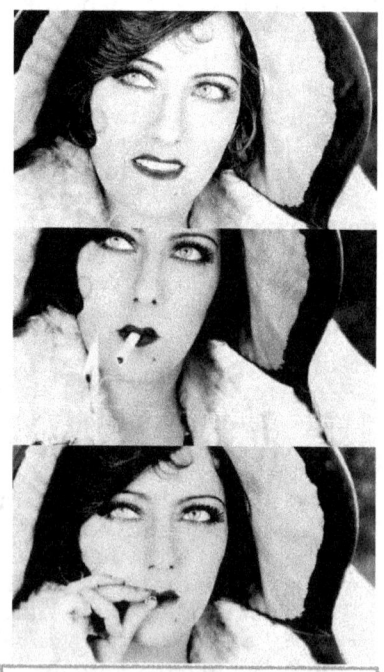

Jazz Age audiences were shocked, and flocked to see it in droves: Three views of **Gloria Swanson** chain smoking and emotiong as a cheap tart, **Sadie Thompson**.

Blanche Frederick played Barrymore's puritanical wife, who thinks Sadie should be deported back to San Francisco to stand trial for some unnamed offense.

Before the beginning of filming, Douglas Fairbanks, Jr., age seventeen, visited Swanson and pleaded with her to be her leading man. "He was certainly handsome enough, but I rejected him because he was just too young. I would look like a child molester."

Sadie Thompson was the last film in which Raoul Walsh would act, because he'd soon have an accident and lose his sight in one eye, forcing him to wear a black patch for the rest of his life.

Jeanne heard reports that Swanson's company was running out of money, and that she might be forced to sell her country estate at Croton-on-Hudson. At the last minute, producer Joseph Schenck provided cash to keep production going.

Swanson as Sadie in a "foreplay" flirt with her co-star, **Raoul Walsh**, before the loss of his eye and his transition to full-time movie director.

The movie would become Swanson's greatest financial success, and she'd be nominated for an Academy Award. However, she lost to Janet Gaynor, the twenty-two-year old actress who'd made *Seventh Heaven, Street Angel,* and *Sunrise.* In those days, Oscars were awarded on the basis of an actor's yearly output—and not just for one movie.

[In the early days of the Academy Awards, Swanson had opposed the prizes, claiming that comparing movie performances of different actresses in different films was like comparing apples to oranges.]

For years, Gloria Swanson's silent version of Sadie Thompson was thought to be lost, but a copy of it was later found in Mary Pickford's personal archives.

JOAN CRAWFORD
ENTERTAINING MARINES IN PAGO PAGO

Four years later, Joan Crawford invited unfavorable reviews and comparisons to both Jeanne Eagels and Gloria Swanson when she starred in the first talkie that brought Sadie Thompson (1932) to the screen again.

Entitled *Rain*, it co-starred Walter Huston and Beulah Bondi as the fanatical missionaries. Its director, Lewis Milestone, hired William Gargan to play Sergeant O'Hara, the U.S. soldier who falls in love with Sadie.

From the beginning, the mostly stage-trained cast members insulted Crawford. On the first day of shooting, after a scene with her, Huston said, "I guess it takes a real tramp to play one on the screen."

Gargan told her, "I have never seen one of your films, and I don't plan to."

Infuriated, she told Milestone, "I can't imagine Sadie wanting to fuck Gargan. Why didn't you cast Clark Gable in the role? He's a real man."

During filming, Crawford discovered that she was pregnant, and began making plans to slip away after the shoot for an abortion in Mexico.

"I don't know if the kid belongs to Gable or to Doug," she told Milestone.

[At the time, she was married to Douglas Fairbanks, Jr., although her union with him was on the rocks and would soon be heading for the divorce court.]

Milestone answered, "Yes, I'm sure it could be either Doug or Clark...perhaps any of a dozen other men, too."

Fairbanks had wanted to visit Catalina Island, where the movie was being shot, but she put him off, claiming she did not want to be distracted from her role. "I'm tired of Doug," she told Milestone, "but also unsure if I'll have a future with Gable."

By the third week of filming, Crawford learned that Milestone had wanted Jean Harlow to play Sadie instead of her.

Reviews were harsh on Crawford, some critics suggesting she was made up to look like a drag queen.

Newlyweds **Joan Crawford** and **Douglas Fairbanks, Jr**., are snapped on their honeymoon. His stepmother, Mary Pickford, had previously asked, "Why are you marrying that cheap whore?"

Sadie Thompson in *Rain* was the first famous role **Joan Crawford** had ever been offered. She feared unfavorable comparisons to Jeanne Eagels and Gloria Swanson.

In reference to *Rain* as an emotionally charged cinematic venue, her best friend, the gay actor, William Haines, warned her: "You couldn't find a sharper razor to cut your throat with."

Film critic Alexander Walker described Crawford's get-up as Sadie Thompson: "She has developed the high, protruding bosom, tight waist, accentuated hips and ramrod straightness more commonly associated with her later career. She gives a superbly controlled impression of a woman battered by life to the point where she cannot be hurt by more knocks. Her entrance is done in graphic, staccato close-ups of her gaudy appearance—a bangled arm, a be-ringed hand, white high-heeled shoes almost stamping defiance at convention, and, suddenly, there she is, giving a rakish salute to the marines, lolling against the doorway with the casual, negligently provocative posture of a woman thoroughly sure of what men want from her."

Variety claimed, "It was a mistake to have assigned the role of Sadie Thompson to Miss Crawford. It shows her off unfavorably. The dramatic significance of it all is beyond her range. Her get-up as a 'light lady' is extremely bizarre. Pavement pounders don't quite trick themselves up as fantastically as all that."

Joan Crawford's interpretation of *Rain* was not successful, losing about a quarter of a million dollars. "*Rain* was an ordeal for me," she recalled. "I thought it was my worst performance so far. Because of my motion picture background, all the Broadway actors treated me like I *was* really Sadie Thompson. I didn't know any of them, and I was made to feel like I was in quarantine. Just like Sadie. But looking back years later, I'm proud of my Sadie Thompson."

KAY FRANCIS
"What is Shirley Temple Doing in a Movie About a Prostitute?"

Director Michael Curtiz was eager to make a drama centered on "a woman of ill repute" like Sadie Thompson in *Rain*.

His Pre-Code result, *Mandalay*, based on a short story by Paul Harvey Fox, was released in 1934 before the censors moved in.

Originally, its female lead was offered to the husband-and-wife team of Ruth Chatterton and George Brent. Fearing getting "typecast," Chatterton rejected it because she had recently played a prostitute in another film. Gallantly, Brent bowed out, too. Curtiz then offered the lead to Kay Francis.

Born in the Oklahoma Territory, Francis starred on Broadway but would achieve her greatest success in talkies, which she made from 1930 to 1936. She rose to become the number one female star at Warners, and the highest paid actress. She had a slight rhotacism, pronouncing the letter "r" as "w." That gave rise to her nickname, "Wavishing Kay Fwancis."

In *Mandalay*, she co-starred with Ricardo Cortez, Warner Oland, and Lyle Talbot, alongside featured players Ruth Donnelly and Reginald Owen.

Its story centers on a world-weary woman—read that as "prostitute"—who works at a local brothel-bar. Her name is Tanya Borodoff, but she answers to the nickname of

Kay Francis, the star of *Mandalay*, threw a fit, yelling, "I'm not a star! I'm a woman! I want to get fucked!"

Many men heeded her calls: Maurice Chevalier, George Brent, Leslie Howard, Herbert Marshall, William Powell, and Prince Alex Mdivani, among others.

"Spot White."

In a casting oddity, little Shirley Temple, soon to become (from 1935 to 1938) one of Hollywood's number one box office attractions, was cast as the daughter of Donnelly. Later, as a major league star, she tried to get her short sequence removed from the by-then scandalous *Mandalay*.

Temple had begun her film career at the age of three in 1931. Her first appearances were in *Baby Burlesks*, ten-minute shorts that featured children as they satirized recent films.

In *Glad Rags to Riches,* Shirley delivered a parody of Mae West's performance in *She Done Him Wrong. [In it, Shirley starred as a* wunderkind *saloon singer.] Baby Burlesks* and films like it became favorites of child molesters, whose libidos were aroused by these tots provocatively imitating grown-ups.

Eventually, Bette Davis—during her reign as Queen of Warner Brothers—would eclipse Kay Francis. In 1938, Francis was (arbitrarily, unfairly, and irresponsibly, and to some degree as a publicity stunt) designated as "Box Office Poison" by the Independent Theatre Owners Association. She was in good company: Greta Garbo, Joan Crawford, Fred Astaire, Mae West, and Katharine Hepburn were designated as "Poison" in the same way.

Francis was mocked as a "fag hag," since she was regularly seen with a coven of homosexual men who included Anderson Lawler, the wealthy tobacco heir who sustained a long affair with the new rage of Hollywood, Gary Cooper—that is, when he wasn't seducing Lupe Velez, Clara Bow, or Marlene Dietrich.

In *Mandalay*, **Kay Francis** dressed like a millionairess and played the piano like a concert pianist—a VERY accomplished (and sanitized) prostitute, indeed.

Kay Francis in *Mandalay*: A well-dressed hooker, seemingly on the verge of intimacies with an officer in uniform.

Francis was a secret lesbian, but also seduced a string of men who included George Brent, Leslie Howard, and William Powell. She married four times on record, but may have been involved in as many as three other marriages which were never revealed.

In her private diaries, she wrote, "As long as they pay me my salary, they can give me a broom and I'll sweep the damn stage. I want the money. When I die, I want to be cremated so that no sign of my existence is left on earth. I can't wait to be forgotten."

***

TALLULAH BANKHEAD
"Me, play a whore, dah-ling?" she asked. "What is this? Type casting?"

Playwright W. Somerset Maugham had long overcome his objections to Tallulah Bankhead playing Sadie Thompson in *Rain*. Producer Samuel Harris wanted to cast her in a Broadway revival set to open at Manhattan's Music Box Theatre on February 12, 1935. Upon signing to do the role, Tallulah said, "I wanted Sadie Thompson to be my first all-out hussy."

Years before, she had seen Jeanne Eagels perform the role on stage. At first, she had tried to imitate the great star, but eventually worked up her own interpretation of the role.

Although Tallulah had high hopes for a big, long-running hit, she was disappointed on opening night. "The limited applause I received was mostly from a coven of young homosexual men, who always adored me regardless of what turkey I was appearing in. On the second night, when the butterflies fluttered away, so did the loud applause. The show folded after forty-seven performances. On its final night, the auditorium was only half full."

Some critics thought Tallulah was very effective in the role and blamed the play's failure on the changing attitudes of the public since 1920. Columnist Mark Barron wrote, "Broadway is no longer shocked or outraged to see the collapse of a pious man when tempted by a woman of dubious reputation."

James Axwell of the New

Picture hats, high-button shoes, and peekaboo lace: **Tallulah Bankhead** throwing her own slurred, cynical, and jaded coquettishness into the character of Sadie Thompson.

Before she opened on Broadway, she met with a reporter from *The New York Times*:

"I'm in a bit of a jam. One minute I'm thrilled to be playing Sadie Thompson. Then a chill descends. Am I out of my mind? I go to sleep but wake up in a cold sweat. The role of Sadie Thompson is different from other parts I have played. Of course, I've played so-called bad girls before, but they were always ladies in their hearts. But now...Let's face it, *dah-ling*: Sadie Thompson is a cheap little floozie who has been run out of San Francisco by the police."

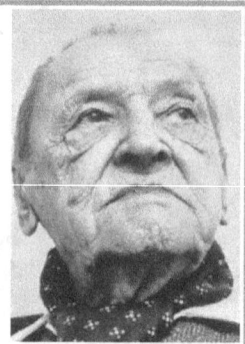

TALLULAH AND THE STAMMERING AGNOSTIC, W. SOMERSET MAUGHAM

Tallulah had a tense relationship with the sometimes imperious and very well paid gay author, **W. Somerset Maugham,** who had vetoed her as a candidate for the role of Sadie Thompson in the original version of *Rain* presented on the London stage.

Later, she signed on for a revival of the role on Broadway, mainly to show him how wrong he was in rejecting her for the part.

At a tryout in Philadelphia of what later evolved into a full-blown Broadway production, Tallulah addressed the audience, her eyes teary:

"I am daring to play this part where *Rain* was first presented by the great, late Jeanne Eagels. You must think I'm the bravest or else the most conceited actress on the planet. Neither is true. I have the greatest respect for Jeanne Eagels and thrilled at her stage presences. I come here tonight to honor her where ever she is. If you're looking down on us, especially me, Jeanne, please be kind."

York *Morning Herald* wrote: "Tallulah Bankhead played Sadie Thompson just about as well as Jeanne Eagels, but Tallulah, whose offstage life is colorful enough, does not bring to the role the obscure chemistry of the crazy, don't care bravado of Eagels. Nonetheless, Bankhead did amazingly well, and I see no reason why a younger generation should not get a kick out of her, despite the fact they are no longer as shocked as the "ancients' of the 1920s."

"Some critics suggested that my voice was a combination of a Texas cowgirl and an Alabama Southern belle," Tallulah said.

"Of course, in some quarters," Tallulah continued, "there were unfavorable comparisons to Jeanne Eagels, and I expected that from the bastards. At least Marlene Dietrich on opening night clapped the loudest and came backstage to bestow endless kisses on me, telling me she had experienced the thrill of her life, second only to having been fucked by Gary Cooper, an experience I had also thrilled to. I invited Marlene home with me, and she licked my pussy until three o'clock that morning."

Let It Rain: A poster advertising Bankhead's pre-Broadway "tryout" in Philadelphia.

MAE WEST
INSTEAD OF A SETTING IN THE SOUTH SEAS, A CHARACTER SIMILAR TO SADIE THOMPSON HEADS FOR THE FROZEN NORTH.

Director Raoul Walsh, who had co-starred as an actor with Gloria Swanson in the 1928 silent version of *Rain,* had been designated as director of Mae West's latest picture, *Klondike Annie* (1936).

The movie was based on her 1921 play, *Frisco Kate.* In this latest version, she portrays a kept woman named Rose Carlton, a.k.a. "The Frisco Doll."

In self-defense, she murders her keeper, Chan Lo (Harold Hubert), and escapes aboard a steamer headed to Nome, Alaska.

She is joined mid-voyage by Sister Annie Adlen (Helen Jerome Eddy), a Salvation Army missionary. The sister dies *en route,* and West assumes her identity as a means of avoiding arrest on a murder charge. As the plot unfolds, West is romanced by the ship's blustering, crazy captain, Bull Bracket (Victor McLaglen) and the handsome young sheriff Jack Forrest (Philip Reed).

Eight minutes of the film were deleted, as many censors objected to the veiled connection of the (*risqué,* some said whorish) Sister Annie, as portrayed by Mae. Those cuts made the post-censored version of the film choppy.

Press baron William Randolph Hearst vowed never to have West's name printed in any of his newspapers. It was odd that he took such a strong moral position on this, as he was "living in sin" with his mistress, actress Marion Davies.

Critic Graham Greene said the movie was harmless fun and not a satire on religion.

Another critic commented on the censored scene. "A spicy gumbo has been turned into a film closer to chicken noodle soup."

Full-figured, curvy, and voluptuous, vaudevillian **Mae West** appears here with then-megastar **Victor McLaglen.**

It was the "cold weather adaptation" of Sadie Thompson's Pago Pago in **Klondike Annie**

MARLENE DIETRICH
HER SUBTLE SPOOF OF THE SADIE THOMPSON HOOKERS WHO HUSTLED SAILORS IN THE SOUTH SEAS

In one of Marlene Dietrich's best pictures, *Seven Sinners* (1940), the Sadie Thompson character returns to the South Seas. Run out of San Francisco and kicked out of every other gin joint in the Pacific, she's more notorious than in previous incarnations. Armed with a *mitteleuropäische* (central European) accent, she's more exotic than ever.

Dietrich had just made her "comeback" picture in *Destry Rides Again* with lanky, long-legged James Stewart. Stewart had made her pregnant, so she had to have an abortion before shooting began.

As her leading man, she selected John Wayne. . As she was having lunch with producer Joe Pasternak in the commissary at Universal, she spotted the tall, handsome star. She leaned over to Pasternak and purred, "Mommy wants that for Christmas."

Her affair with Wayne began on the first day of shooting. Wayne later told Ward Bond, his close buddy and frequent co-star, "The best sex I ever had. She's the mistress of fellatio and every other sex act, too."

As Bijou Blanche, Dietrich drifts from port to port with two traveling companions, navy deserter Edward Patrick (Little Ned) Finnegan, played by Broderick Crawford. a lovable, empty-headed sailor. Her other companion is Sascha Mencken (Mischa Auer), a part-magician and part-time pickpocket, who can't keep his hands out of other men's pockets.

Deported once again, Bijou (Dietrich) boards another battered steamer, this one heading for yet another island. The ship's doctor (played by Albert Decker) falls for her. As she sings "I've Been in Love Before," a young lady, Dorothy Henserson (Anna Lee) tosses her a coin, humiliating her. A blonde, Lee told the press that

Gender-bending, very sophisticated views of the sublimely glam **Marlene Dietrich** in *Seven Sinners*.

The upper photo shows her as a "dress military white and female" version of John Wayne. The middle photo shows her alluring penchant for "ridiculous glamour," the likes of which will never come again.

The lower photo shows her with a poignantly youthful John Wayne before anyone called him "The Duke."

Dietrich had pressured her to dye her hair brown so as not to compete with her visually, on screen.

Another romantic interlude follows as Bijou encounters Lt. Dan Brent (John Wayne), a strapping naval officer. She meets him upon her arrival in "Boni-Komba." Later, he escorts her on a tour of the U.S. Naval Base and to a party at the governor's mansion.

In their throaty voice, Dietrich sings "The Man's in the Navy."

The New York Herald Tribune's critic, Howard Barnes, wrote, "In *Seven Sinners*, you wil find the tough, glamourous eloquent *demi-mondaine of The Blue Angel*. If anything, she is even better than she was in her original triumph in that German picture for director Josef von Sternberg. She cuts loose in *Seven Sinners* with a perfect impersonation of a high-class slattern."

For *The New York Times* Bosley Crowther, a sometimes critic of Miss Dietrich, viewed *Seven Sinners* as a triumph for her. "Miss Dietrich's Frenchy in *Destry Rides Again* was an Arno sketch of countless sultry Western barroom belles. Her Bijou Blanche in *Seven Sinners* (sometimes called *Cafe of the Seven Sinners*) is a delightfully subtle spoof of all the Singapore Sals who had stirred the hot blood of cool customers south and east of Manila Bay. If Miss Dietrich and her comedies were just both a little broader, Mae West would be in the shade."

BRENDA MARSHALL
INTERPRETS ANOTHER "EAST-OF-SUEZ" PROSTITUTE EVOCATIVE OF SADIE THOMPSON IN *RAIN*

Director Jean Negulesco hired Brenda Marshall as Vicki Moore in a drama called *Singapore Woman* (1941), a quickie B-picture programmer. Like W. Somerset Maugham's *Rain* or *The Letter*, it re-creates the world of gin joints, rubber plantations, monsoons, and the colonial South Seas. One of the settings used in the film, Singapore's Raffles Hotel, even has rickshaws.

For his efforts, Negulesco got good reviews. One critic wrote, "Early in his career, Negulesco was largely confined to Big Band shorts. But in *Singapore Woman* he digs into this exotically seasoned stew with gusto. he makes every minute

count and makes the movie look good, too."

What the reviewer left out was that the director was fired halfway through the film's production. During the course of his career, Negulesco was often assigned to direct film adaptations of trashy sentimental novels. But he had some highlights, including *The Mask of Dimitrios* (1944), that Eric Ambler thriller starring Sydney Greenstreet and Peter Lorre. That same year, he filmed *The Conspirators* with Hedy Lamarr and Paul Henreid. He also shot *Humoresque* with Joan Crawford and John Garfield.

The following year was the highlight of his career as he helmed Jane Wyman in her Oscar-Winning role of the deaf-mute in *Johnny Belinda*. He also directed *Road House* with Ida Lupino and Richard Widmark. She was brilliant as a sultry *chanteuse* thrilling unruly audiences with her laconic delivery of moody torch songs.

For extra thrills in *Singapore Woman,* expect thundrous monsoons, crocodile attacks, and barroom brawls.

In this atmospheric B-picture, Brenda Marshall, cast as the boozy Vicki Moore, is resuced by a farmer, David Ritchie (David Bruce), who accepted the role only after another actor, Jeffrey Lynn, went on suspension for turning it down.

After meeting Vicki (Brenda Marshall), the gin-soaked floozie, he takes her to his rubber plantation to sober her up. As might be expected, he falls in love with her.

But there are two problems: David already has a *fiancée*, a blonde, rich, spoiled temptress, Claire Weston (Virginia Field).

Long presumed dead, Vicki's husband, Jim North (played by Jerome Cowan) mysteriously shows up.

Two views of **Brenda Marshall.** Upper photo: with her husband, William Holden. "If only he knew how to be faithful," she lamented.

Born in the the city of Negros in The Philippines, Brenda Marshall (also known as Ardis Ankerson (her name assigned at birth by her Swedish parents) became famous for marrying William Holden in 1941.

She was Matron of Honor (her husband was Best Man) at the 1952 wedding of Ronald Reagan to starlet Nancy Davis.

Marshall had a popular success in *The Constant Nymph* in 1943, but she virtually retired after marrying Holden.

One of her last pictures was in 1946: *Whispering Smith*. It starred Alan Ladd. Her previous co-stars had included Errol Flynn and George Raft.

She divorced the philandering and increasingly alcoholic Holden in 1971, and lived to the age of seventy-six, dying in Palm Springs in 1992.

JUNE HAVOC
"WHEREAS SHE COULD GIVE A MARINE A HARD-ON, ETHEL MERMAN COULD NOT"
—Director Rouben Mamoulian

In 1944, Allied armies in the Pacific were advancing island by island on the long, bloody road to Japan. In Europe, the Allied armies embarked on the final months of the world's most horrific battles, which would lead to the overthrow of Hitler's Third Reich.

It was at this terrible time that director Rouben Mamoulian decided it was time to bring *Rain,* featuring the prostitute, Sadie Thompson, back to Broadway.

There was a suggestion that he should update the original W. Somerset Maugham story, which had been set in Pago Pago, to a location on an island the Allies had already invaded and taken from the Japanese. But he decided to keep the setting as defined in the 1920 original.

Paramount invested $50,000 into the musical with lyrics by Howard Dietz. If the musical were a hit, the studio wanted to hold the movie rights, perhaps as a vehicle for Betty Grable.

Mamoulian needed a star, and he came up with an unlikely choice, Mary Martin. "Not for me, baby," she said.

He then offered it to Marlene Dietrich, thinking that she would be more convincing as a prostitute. She, too, turned it down.

He went next to Joan Crawford, who had starred in the movie version. She told him "Once as Sadie was enough." Later, Joan Blondell rejected the script, too.

"Then, in a 'fit of madness' (Mamoulian's words), I decided on an unconventional casting. 'Old Leather Lungs' herself, Ethel Merman."

Merman later admitted that she accepted the role of Sadie because her career was at a low point, as was her personal life. She'd just experienced a miscarriage.

She had not had a hit on Broadway since she'd starred in *Panama Hattie* in 1940, playing a nightclub singer. She also felt she was getting older and less attractive. With her stage career in jeopardy, she needed a hit, and felt that Sadie Thompson might do it for her.

Rehearsals began in September of 1944. From the beginning, Merman didn't understand the lyrics. "What is Mal Maison lipstick?" she asked the director.

Stage star and "professional belter,." **Ethel Merman** tried for, but didn't get, the role of Sadie in a 1944 Broadway revival of *Rain,* when the Pacific theater of World War II was on everybody's mind.

But would anyone believe that even a very horny G.I. would REALLY want to f*** Ethel Merman?

Biographer Geoffrey Mark wrote: "For the first time, Ethel was uncomfortable with the material. It wasn't just one song she didn't care for—she didn't like any of them. Merm felt that the lyrics were too precious and over the head of the average Merman theatergoer. After ten days of rehearsals that were more of a battle, Merman delivered one of her famous ultimatums. Either they changed the lyrics to suit her, or they could find themselves another star."

She was told they preferred to recast it. She stormed out of the theater. Before the end of the following day, June Havoc, the sister of the famous stripper, Gypsy Rose Lee, was signed to replace her in the role of Sadie.

Two views of **June Havoc** as Sadie Thompson in the 1944 Broadway stage revival of *Rain*. In the right-hand photo, **Lansing Hatfield** plays the vindictive Reverend.

Born in British Columbia, Havoc was a vivacious blonde who had emigrated to the United States. Over the course of her career, she would be not only an actress but a dancer, writer, and stage director, too.

She got her start in vaudeville and later starred on and Off Broadway. One of her most memorable film roles was in *Gentleman's Agreement* (1947), the Oscar-winning adaptation of Laura Z. Hobson's novel, in which Havoc played Peck's self-loathing secretary.

Havoc's biggest Broadway hit was Rodgers and Hart's *Pal Joey*.

Later, although she didn't like how she was characterized, she was immortalized as the real-life model for "Baby June" in the classic Broadway musical *Gypsy,*.

A dishy "top tomato" of her era, here's **June Havoc** looking fabulous as a midwar pinup in *Hi Diddle Diddle* (1943)

In semi-retirement at Cannon Crossing, her home in Wilton, Connecticut, she told Darwin Porter, "Would you believe it, I turned down *Carousel* to star as Sadie Thompson? Big mistake. I thought I had a hit on my hands."

The show opened at the Alvin Theatre on Broadway on November 16, 1944 and closed on January 6, 1945.

Critic Charles P. Driscoll wrote, "I saw Jeanne Eagels do the part of Sadie Thompson in its original run. I saw Tallulah Bankhead do the 1935 revival. June Havoc is far better than either of them. Of course, she has the advantage of superior staging, perfect scenery, and the artistic support of a choral ensemble, about everything a star could ask for. The lyrics of Howard Dietz and the music of Vernon Duke bring a refreshing breath of originality to the plagiaristic atmosphere of Broadway."

In 1949, producer Jerry Wald pitched the idea of reviving the play *Rain*, this time starring Barbara Stanwyck. She told him, "I've played whores before," but the deal fell through.

The following year at RKO, Howard Hughes considered casting Jane Russell, the brunette beauty with the big bosom, as Sadie. That film never got made.

However, Russell did get to play a prostitute in *The Revolt of Mamie Stover*, a film released in 1955 (see below).

FRANCINE EVERETT
SADIE GETS TRANSFORMED INTO "THE MOST BEAUTIFUL WOMAN IN HARLEM"

The Sadie Thompson character was sometimes presented at theaters catering to black audiences. Some 600 such stage and movie houses existed in the 1950s.

In 1946, a film was made called *Dirty Gertie from Harlem, U.S.A.* It was inspired by but not directly adapted from the actual W. Somerset Maugham drama.

Actress Francine Everett played Gertie La Rue, nicknamed "Dirty Gertie" because of her callous treatment of men. Fleeing Harlem and her lover, she arrives on the fictional island of "Rinidad," to star as the headliner of a cabaret revue.

On the island, she attracts the attention of, among others, a soldier and a sailor, whom she nicknames "Tight Pants" and "High Pockets."

Then her obsessive former boyfriend from Harlem tracks her down and fatally shoots her, all the while proclaiming, "I still love her."

Dirty Gertie was the last starring role for Everett, who once proclaimed, "The most beautiful woman in Harlem."

Filmmaker William Greaves said, "She would have been a superstar in Hollywood were it not for the apartheid climate in the movie in-

Dirty Gertie from Harlem, U.S.A., a 1946 race film, was a big hit in black theaters across the United States.

It was an unauthorized adaption of the 1921 W. Somerset Maugham short story, *Rain*, but no charges were ever filed.

The adaptation changed the names of the characters and switched the location from the Tropical Pacific to the Caribbean.

Shown above is the film's cheerful heroine, **Francine Everett**.

Producer **Spencer Williams** in 1958. During military service in World War I, Williams was General Pershing's bugler in Mexico.

Working in Hollywood, he created *The Melancholy Dame* in 1929, the first black talkie.

He appeared in a small role in *The Public Enemy* (1931), the gangster film starring James Cagney, and in other films where he portrayed racial stereotypes with grammatically mangled dialogue.

Earlier, he had been hired to cast African Americans in Gloria Swanson's unfinished *Queen Kelly*, a silent film, in 1928.

dustry at the time."

Everett's most notable film was not *Dirty Gertie*, but *Ebony on Parade* (1947), made a year later, with an all-star cast that included Dorothy Dandridge, Cab Calloway, and Count Basie.

Spencer Williams, a native of Vidalia, Louisiana, was a leading African American producer of his day, although most of his movies are lost. He was better known for playing Andy on TV's *Amos and Andy Show.* He also directed the 1941 race film, *The Blood of Jesus*, hailed as "possibly the most successful race film ever made."

Williams' films have also been the subject of criticism. Richard Corliss, writing in *Time* magazine, stated: "Aesthetically, much of Williams' work vacillates between inert and abysmal. The rural comedy of Juke Joint is logy, as if the heat had gotten to the movie; even the musical scenes, featuring North Texas jazzman Red Calhoun, move at the turtle tempo of Hollywood's favorite black of the period, Stepin Fetchit. And there were technical gaffes galore: in a late-night scene in *Dirty Gertie*, actress Francine Everett clicks on a bedside lamp and the screen actually darkens for a moment before full lights finally come up. Yet at least one Williams film, his debut *The Blood of Jesus* (1941), has a naïve grandeur to match its subject. It should also be realized that Williams often worked on a very meager budget. *The Blood of Jesus* was filmed for a cost of $5,000; most black films of that era had budgets of double and triple that amount."

SHELLEY WINTERS
As a Sadie-Like Bombshell, She Sizzles, Erupts, & Crackles, but Ultimately Fizzles

In 1950, Marlene Dietrich's *Seven Sinners* was disastrously remade, this time with Shelley Winters cast as a prostitute inspired by Sadie Thompson. Her name was "Coral," a promiscuous woman of ill repute. The plot of this so-called adventure film centers on a cafe owner on a

South Sea island who plays a dangerous game of blackmail with a fugitive from justice.

During filming, the project's title was *East of Java*. Its director, H. Bruce Humerstone, borrowed Macdonald Carey from Paramount as the lead, "Jake Davis. " He and Shelley were backed up by a strong supporting cast whose talents were utterly wasted in what critics referred to as a "stinker." Luther Adler played "Cognac," Frank Lovejoy "Doc," and Helena Carter was Margaret Landis.

The film deserves a very tiny footnote in Hollywood history in that it marked the cinematic debut of the campy Liberace in a very small role.

In his only scene with Shelley, Liberace plays the piano which she sits on top of it, showing off her figure. "He looked at me only once: He was too nervous to take his eyes off the keys. Of course, a sexy woman like me was not his cuppa."

During filming, Shelley admitted that she was "nervous and tired," having made three films in five months. She launched several temperamental outbursts during the shoot, most notably with Carter.

"I sang several songs," Shelley said, "but the dialogue was phoney, real crappy. All that was required of me was to pose on banisters and pianos and look sexy. I was down to 118 pounds, and Orry-Kelly, that fluttery gown designer and former lover of Cary Grant, designed twenty sensational costumes for me. 'Lucky' Humberstone, our director, would sometimes have me change costumes in the middle of a scene for any ridiculous reason, just to get them all in. I sometiems felt I was part of the scenery."

"As for Macdonald Carey, he and I had about as much sexual chemistry as Wallace Beery and Marie Dressler. His acting range went from uninspired to merely adequate."

"During the shoot, I desperately needed to get fucked,

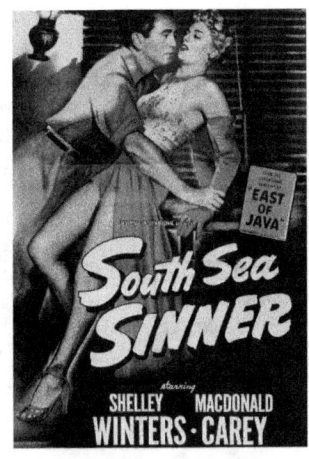

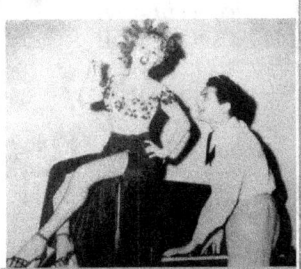

Shelley Winters with **Liberace** in *South Seas Woman*.

In private, she asked, "What would this piano player know what to do with a woman?"

but I was out of luck," she said. "With Carey and Liberace in the act, it was hopeless. I'd gone through some of the leading men in Hollywood—William Holden, Robert De Niro, John Ireland ("what a whopper"), Errol Flynn, Clark Gable, Marlon Brando, John Garfield, Lawrence Tierney, Sean Connery, Albert Finney, Farley Granger ("Yes, he tried a girl for a change"), Anthony Quinn, and Howard ("strictly oral") Hughes.

"As for Frank Sinatra, he called me 'a bowlegged bitch of a Brooklyn broad.' I shot back, telling him he was a 'skinny, no-talented, stupid Hoboken bastard.'"

Upon the release of *South Sea Sinner, The New York Times* summed it up. "It is a ridiculously romance-soggy film which has about as much South Sea flavor as a roadside papaya bar."

BETTE DAVIS
"I Can Play It Cheap & Vulgar"

Gene Ringold wrote, "Since Jeanne Eagels starred in *Rain*, Sadie Thompson has been impersonated by budding, aspiring, inspiring, exasperating, popular, has-been, unheard-of, good, and merely adequate actresses in stage revivals on Broadway, in summer stock,, with touring road companies, with theatrical workshop groups, and by amateurs in semi-professional productions. Sadie has even been lampooned in a musical revue starring Bette Davis."

[*He was referring to* Two's Company, *the 1952 Broadway revue in which a singing, dancing, self-deprecating Davis sang* "Roll Along Sadie," *a takeoff on Sadie Thompson. She also imitated Tallulah Bankhead watching Bette Davis imitate Bankhead from a theater box.*]

Two views of **Bette Davis** as a "way over-the-top," and slightly psychotic Sadie Thompson clone in *Two's Company*.

RITA HAYWORTH
In Her Sanitized Interpretation of Sadie, Rita is Still a Bawdy, Shady Lady

Sadie, the bar girl prostitute, came alive again, perhaps in her most vibrant reincarnation, when Rita Hayworth signed to star in *Miss Sadie Thompson,* set for release in 1953—in Technicolor and 3D, no less. Produced by Jerry Wald and directed by Curtis Bernhardt, it co-starred José Ferrer. Fresh from having to testify before the House Un-American Activities Committee, he played the religious zealot who eventually attacks her.

Most critics defined Aldo Ray, cast as the U.S. soldier who falls for Sadie, as the best of the lot.

He and Rita became confidants. He told her that he had to "service both director George Cukor and co-star Spencer Tracy when he was getting started in the business, appearing in *Pat and Mike* (1952), which also starred Katharine Hepburn. "My God," he told Rita. "I think Kate, our other co-star, gets more pussy than I do."

Rita, still glamourous after her long exile when married to Prince Aly Khan, "kicks out" (in the words of one critic) several songs, including the Oscar-nominated "Blue Pacific

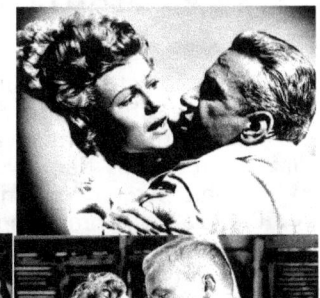

| Rita, as Sadie Thompson, is seen swaggering though a coven of sweaty, salivating soldiers in her role as the number one shady lady of the South Seas. Critics carped about her performance, but Maugham said, "I can think of no better actress than Miss Hayworth to play my Sadie." | Lovely **Rita** as Miss Sadie Thompson, dysfunctionally matched with (upper photo) **José Ferrer**, and (lower photo) **Aldo Ray** |

Blues."

She told the press, "I want to give the tired old tramp a new slant."

During the shoot, Rita—the pre-eminent princess and love goddess of the 1940s—launched an affair with the "Argentine heartthrob," singer Dick Haymes, who concluded that she could advance his career and help him financially.

Rita's portrayal of Sadie got mixed reviews. *Variety* claimed, "Rita Hayworth catches the feel of the title character well, even braving completely deglamourizing makeup, costuming, and photography to fit her physical appearance to that of the bawdy, shady character of Sadie Thompson."

Bosley Crowther of *The New York Times*, wrote, "The character of Sadie is drained of considerable point by the prudence of the producers, and Miss Hayworth is left with a role in which she is able to inject very little outside of her own particular brand of appeal."

The Hollywood Reporter declared that Rita played the role "with fire and conviction." Jesse Zunset of *Cue Magazine* said, "I never thought I'd see the day when Rita Hayworth could steal acting honors from José Ferrer." Other reviewers thought Sadie Thompson had been "overly sanitized" as a means of getting past the censors of the Hays Office.

In spite of that, some cities banned the film. The head of the Memphis Board of Censors called the movie "filthy because of a torrid, vulgar musical number when Miss Hayworth sings 'The Heat is On.'"

JANE RUSSELL
Buxom, Ready, Willing, and Artfully Whorish

W. Somerset Maugham's short story about Sadie Thompson set off an avalanche of other scripts devoted to a whorish character as its lading lady.

One example of this was the 1956 romantic drama, *The Revolt of Mamie Stover*, directed by Raoul Walsh, who had starred opposite Gloria Swanson in the silent screen version (see above) way back in 1928.

Like Sadie Thompson in the original version, prostitute Mamie Stover is pressured to leave San Francisco. Her character was first created in the 1951 novel by William Bradford Hule.

Walsh cast the ruggedly handsome Richard Egan as Russell's leading man, with supporting roles filled by Joan Leslie and Agnes Moorehead.

Howard Hughes, who had cast Russell in *The Outlaw (1943)*, an act which had made her a star, could hardly compete with her breasts blown up in CinemaScope.

In Honolulu, Mamie (aka "Flaming Mamie') becomes the chief draw—accessorized with a red wig—at a notorious strip club.

After the attack on Pearl Harbor in December of 1941, Mamie makes a fortune as she buys up cheap real estate as hundreds of local residents sell their property and flee to the U.S. mainland. Mamie and her (licensed) pin-up photos also become popular with the troops.

Twentieth Century Fox (Marilyn Monroe's studio) had originally purchased the screen rights to *Mamie Stover* for its major star (Marilyn), but she was feuding with them and had "gone on strike."

Although ultimately, the movie would barely recoup its original two million dollar investment, Fox had high hopes for the film since the paperback had sold a staggering three million copies.

After Monroe dropped out of consideration as its female lead, Walsh did not immediately approach Russell, but talked over the role with both Lana Turner and Susan Hayward.

As a Hollywood footnote, this was Joan Leslie's last film appearance before fading into oblivion.

It opened to critical attacks, mostly centered on how the original novel had been "sanitized." One headline read: MAMIE STOVER'S REVOLT SUPPRESSED BY CENSORS.

Bosley Crowther in *The New York Times* commented on the ad campaign which asked, "Why Did Mamie Stover Leave San Francisco?"

He wrote: "If you must know why Mamie Stover had to leave San Francisco, you'll have to ask someone other than this reviewer, who did not get the answer from the film."

Surprisingly, as the years have gone by, latter-day critics have been kinder. For its DVD release, Gary Tooze wrote: *"The Revolt of Mamie Stover* has adult themes, female empowerment, war, and romance. It offers an impressive, tough girl performance from Jane Russell. I love the film's exotic look, extravagant costumes, and mixed genres."

Filmmaker Peter Bogdanovich wrote in 1965: "Very good...fascinating, ambiguously told story of a tough, flamboyant prostitute, her expulsion from San Francisco, her affair with a 'respectable' writer, her rise to wealth during the war in Hawaii. Very cleverly writen and directed with typical Walshian vigor and spirit; an amusing and devastating character study, with Russell staring at camera in the beginning, defying the viewer to judge her."

Italian film historian Ermanno Comuzio wrote in 1982, "The story of this 'rebellious woman' is 'explosive.' Jane Russell perfectly incarnates an unusual female character with her fighter's broad shoulders. She is the female equivalent of the implacable and conquering hero who wants to take the world in her fist. *The Revolt of Mamie Stover* is an unconventional film, typical of Walsh's last period, when he had even less patience with red tape and was more explicit in his speech, more focused on his filming, as well as the dismantling of the internal mechanisms of the more typical and standardised Hollywood filmmaking, and so of his own cinema."

The novel had described **Mamie Stover** as a blonde, evoking the screen actress Lizabeth Scott. But the producer of the film adaptation, Buddy Adler, feared that movie audiences might not accept **Jane Russell** as a blonde, since she was the most famous brunette in Hollywood.

A compromise was therefore necessary, so she wore a long red wig and dyed her eyebrows auburn before she was flown to Honolulu to begin filming.

MARILYN MONROE
HER SADIE THOMPSON NEVER REACHED THE SCREEN

Sadie Thompson almost came to life again in the early 1960s when Marilyn Monroe lobbied to be cast in a franker, more unvarnished version than the Rita Hayworth version. "I've always wanted to play a whore," she said.

She told the press, whether it was true or not, that W. Somerset Maugham had endorsed the casting of her in the role. "What I like about Sadie is that she can be gay even though she's sad."

The film went into pre-production in the spring of 1961, with veteran actor Fredric March cast as the zealous bigot of a minister. *[Coincidentally, March had been the co-star of Jeanne Eagels in her last screen performance in* Jealousy *(1929).]*

At some point, he dropped out, and the role was then offered to Richard Burton. Either jokingly or otherwise, he said he would agree to it only if he would be allowed to actually penetrate Marilyn during a love scene. In that scene, he played a U.S. soldier infatuated with Sadie.

"I'm sure Marilyn would go for it," the Welsh actor said. "I know you can't depict our genitals, but the love scene will look a hell of a lot more authentic if you allow me to poke her. She'll love it, I assure you, if for no other reason than to have one up on Elizabeth Taylor."

This new version of Sadie Thompson, as projected, would have marked Marilyn's first starring role on televison, and it would mean working with the most widely recognized writer in America, Rod Serling.

The offer came for Marilyn to appear in a ninety-minute adaptation of *Rain* for NBC-TV. She was offered $100,000 for the role.

On June 15, 1961, he met with Marilyn in Manhattan after she'd flown in from Los Angeles. Although jet-lagged, their conversation lasted until 4AM. As was revealed in that conversation, she'd seen only two versions of *Rain*, one with Joan Crawford, the other with Rita Hayworth. She'd also seen her former roommate, Shelley Winters, strut her stuff in a distantly related spinoff, *South Sea Sinner*.

Serling had already written two drafts of a TV version specifically tailored to Marilyn, but he was "severely disappointed" when he learned that she favored the original "Jeanne Eagels" version by John Colton and Clemence Randolph.

"I was outraged," he recalled. "I had no interest in writing a script that was a total lift from the original. I took on the assign-

Marilyn Monroe never brought Sadie Thompson to life on the screen, but she'd amply demonstrated that she already knew how to play a slut in her career-making performance in *Niagara*, in which she portrayed the errant wife of Joseph Cotten.

ment when I was assured that the producers wanted a completely new and updated Sadie. I thought that a repetition of the original would be pointless."

Somehow, no agreement was reached, so when Marilyn was admitted to a hospital for a gall bladder operation, the plan was abandoned.

Keith Badmann, author of *The Final Years of Marilyn Monroe—The Shocking True Story*, claimed, "There was probably more than one reason why the project was finally scrapped. Rumorsd within the industry suggested Monroe's drama coach, Lee Strasberg, was partly to blame as a dispute between him and *Rain's* director, George Roy Hill, had arisen, causing the director to threaten to quit if Strasberg continued to interfere with the directing of Monroe. Reports about her unstable mental health and her visit to a psychiatric clinic were also rife and thus her illness most likely contributed to the final decision."

"Had *Rain* been made," surmises Badmann, "it would have shown Monroe's capabilities as a serious actress. *The Misfits* had demonstrated this; *Rain* would have cemented it, especially in the television format. Serling described the tragic sex goddess as 'a warm, friendly, beautiful, but odd girl.'"

The Monroe version of *Rain* was shelved, never to be produced. The tragic star who had so desperately wanted the part was found dead in August of 1962.

Rod Serling's introduction to
The Twilight Zone

"You're traveling through another dimension, a dimension not only of sight and sound but of mind ... a journey into a wondrous land whose boundaries are that of imagination—your next stop, *The Twilight Zone*."

On loan from CBS-TV, **Serling,** one of the best-known writers in America, was offered $25,000 to concoct a script for "a new look at Sadie."

In 2012, Blood Moon published a biography of Marilyn that one critic defined as "the best bio of MM ever written."

Look for it **(Marilyn at Rainbow's End)** as a reprinted revised edition sometime in 2021.

SADIE COMES.... AND SADIE GOES.

The April, 1921 cover of *Smart Set* Magazine, which promoted the then-ragingly successful short novel, **Miss Thompson,** by W. Somerset Maugham as "The Most Brilliant Short Novel of the Year."

By the time **Gloria Swanson** and **Raoul Walsh** got around to their silent film adaptation seven years later, Miss Thompson was a lot less "smart set' and a lot more steamy.

Sadie Thompson's name (if not her story) has become relentlessly famous:

Here's a view of the guest house (now **"The Sadie Thompson Inn"**) on American Samoa where, beginning in December 1916, W. Somerset Maugham lived for six weeks.

THEY SHOULD GET AN AWARD: In 1953, as part of the marketing campaign for **Rita Hayworth**'s interpretation of the by-now most famous (fictional) prostitute (Sadie) in modern history, a team of movie marketers created slogans for this pair of inspired photos: **"Sadie Comes"** (left photo), and **"And Sadie Goes"** (right photo.)

CHAPTER TWELVE
"The Happiest Married Homosexual Couple of the Theater World"

KATHARINE CORNELL & GUTHRIE McCLINTIC

Mercedes & Tallulah Seduce their Beloved "Kit" as McClintic Falls for a Young Actor Named

KIRK DOUGLAS

Katharine Cornell was hailed as "The First Lady of the Theatre" by critic Alexander Woollcott. She was noted for her major Broadway roles in serious dramas often directed by her husband, **Guthrie McClintic**. As a couple, they were the most famous "lavender marriage" in the theater.

Their greatest successes on stage came in productions of *Romeo & Juliet, Candida, Antony & Cleopatra, No Time for Comedy, Antigone, St. Joan, The Doctor's Dilemma, Three Sisters,* and *The Constant Wife*.

In March of 1921, during the run of a play, *Nice People*, at the Kraw Theater in New York, Tallulah Bankhead, one of its stars, introduced the play's other star, Katharine Cornell, to Mercedes de Acosta.

Almost the entire cast of *Nice People*, which was written and directed by Rachel Crothers, were either gay or lesbian. Other actors included Francine Larrimore, Henry Hull, and—before he became a matinee idol in Hollywood of the 1920s— Rod La Roque.

"I met Katharine (aka "Kit") when we were young," Mercedes said. "She and I were born within months of each other. The first night I went out with Tallulah and Kit, I could tell they were having an affair. I envied Tallulah. And although I was also having an affair with the Belle of Alabama, I greedily wanted Kit for myself. It got complicated."

Cornell came from a background radically different from Mercedes'. Born in Berlin to American parents, she grew up in the cold winters of Buffalo, New York, a city to which she would forever be returning to perform, although never living there again.

When Tallulah was involved with her other friends, Mercedes and Cornell—secretly and without telling Tallulah—began to date. "It wasn't love. Instead, it was sex that brought us together," Mercedes told Darwin Porter. "Besides, Tallulah had other girlfriends, including Laurette Taylor, Beatrice Lillie, and Dame Sybil Thorndike."

"I can never figure Tallulah out," Cornell told Mercedes. "One night, she took me to Harlem, where I discovered she was having an affair with the 300-pound Gladys Bentley, Harlem's answer to Mae West. Heavy-set and black, she wrote and performed really dirty songs in front of wild, raucous audiences. Tallulah was fascinated by her."

Unknown to Cornell, Hattie McDaniel loomed in Tallulah's future, too.

Although attracted to Cornell, Mercedes never considered her a raving beauty. "She was refined, with a romantic aura on stage, an understated seductive quality."

One critic wrote, "Miss Cornell does not have a robust romanticism. It tends toward dark but delicate tints, and the emotion she conveys most aptly is that of an aspiring girlishness, which has always been subject to theatrical influences."

One night, Cornell spoke to Mercedes, confiding in her that as a young girl in Buffalo, she had a "burning ambition to become a stage actress. Like so many others, I found the road to stardom a rough one. No one wanted to extend a

Gladys Bentley. Still relatively young, still relatively thin from the 300 pound "stage amazon and raunchy earth mother" she became.

helping hand., I wandered the streets of Broadway feeling lonely and desolate., I went from audition to audition, fearing I faced an uncertain future as an actress. The heartbreaks were inevitable. I kept hoping to see my name in marquee lights one day."

She once spoke to group of aspiring actresses: "First of all, there must be a fierce determination, a deep conviction that acting is the thing one must do, then there must be a carefully planned series of assaults on a fortress—the commercial theater—that is none too easy to storm. Mere physical beauty isn't everything, but it is one barrier less to climb if you possess it. Intelligence, awareness, sensitivity, self-effacement, industry—all these are necessary in greater or lesser degree. I plunged into the theater back in 1916."

In Manhattan, she joined the Washington Square Players and soon became known as one of its most promising actresses. A series of forgettable roles in theater companies followed. A highlight of her early career derived from her performances in a London production of *Little Women* (1919), based on Louisa May Alcott's novel.

***

Back in America, Cornell's life was about to change forever. She had not only begun her life as a lesbian with Tallulah and Mercedes, but the man who would forever influence her career entered the picture.

He was Guthrie McClintic, who in time would become a successful theatre director and producer, though he had started out as an actor.,

Born in Seattle, he decided, at the age of twelve, to become an actor after watching Laurette Taylor, at the age of eighteen, perform in a local theater as the star of *Stolen by Gypsies*.

"I wanted to be up there on the stage emoting with Laurette," he said. "A certain magic seemed to hover over her head like a halo. The acting bug bit me that night. But it would take my conservative Southern parents five years before they allowed me to go to Manhattan and enroll in the Academy of Dramatic Arts."

Cornell on the London Stage in 1919 in *Little Women*.

Fifteen producers had rejected Marian de Forest's stage adaptation of Louisa May Alcott's classic novel. But finally, thanks in part to Cornell, it became a hit, luring *blasé* New Yorkers and Londoners into the theater to both laugh and weep.

Some scholars contest that in *Little Women*, the semi-autobiographical story of the March sisters, Alcott articulated an early example of "the All-American girl" whose personality traits are embodied in one or another of young, on-the-verge-of-womanhood characters.

Cornell, incidentally, portrayed the most macho and tomboyish of the quartet of March sisters: Jo.

"My first night in town, I checked into the YMCA and headed for the lights of Broadway. I walked up and down, marveling at the brightly glowing marquees."

Ironically, in the years to come, he would be directing some of the stars whose names he saw lit up on the marquee.

On a Sunday night in January of 1919, McClintic went with a friend to a gathering of the Washington Square Players. She was Noel Haddson, who had played Helen of Troy in Philip Moeller's one-act play, *Helena's Husband*.

In a far corner, his eyes feasted on Cornell. He asked his friend, Noel, about her. She told him that Cornell had been awarded a starring role in *The Man Who Came Back,* a production being presented at multiple sites in and around New York City.

"I had seen her from a distance before," McClintic said. "But this night was different. She was sitting by herself, and she had the same mystic aura about her that I had seen on the stage, a curious, haunting luminosity."

They didn't meet that night, but a few weeks later, he was introduced to her and identified as the casting director who reported to Winthrop Ames, a major Broadway producer of the time. They started talking and ignored the rest of the party, sharing their stage-related dreams and aspirations.

He escorted her from the party back to her residence, and kissed her on the cheek, inviting her for dinner the following night.

The next evening marked the beginning of a relationship that would stretch across the decades and would end only at his death.

McClintic had been married once before, in his case to the eccentric, pencil-thin Estelle Winwood, who was Tallulah's best friend. He had met her in 1916 when she was appearing in an English play called *Hush*. A graduate from the Liverpool Repertory Company, she was "an extraordinary artist on the stage," he said. "Unerring and right in all she did."

No one will ever know what drove Cor-

Cornell's most celebrated role was Catherine Barrett (Browning) in the Rudolf Besier play *The Barretts of Wimpole Street*, which she first presented on Broadway in 1931.

In the drama, poet Robert Browning has read her character's poetry and comes to meet her. Their attraction is immediate.

Before McClintic became enchanted by the play, it was rejected by twenty-seven Broadway producers.

Cornell in the early 1920s, around the time she was spotted by the discerning (directorial) eye of Guthrie McClintic.

nell and McClintic into a lavender marriage, although it was theorized that it was, to some degree, to conceal each of their respective homosexualities. At any rate, the couple were married on September 8, 1921 at her aunt's house in Cobourg, Ontario.

When a drunken Tallulah heard of McClintic's marriage, she said, "That darling Guthrie only marries women he doesn't have to fuck, including that dear soul, Estelle, and my beloved Kit. Fortunately, he has me to take care of those ladies for him."

After a brief honeymoon in Canada, from a base in New York, this newly established but powerful couple formed their own production team, the M.C. & Company. It became the legal entity that would produce plays, often starring her, for the rest of his life.

They would have their failures, but more famously, they'd become known for their successes, including *The Barretts of Wimpole Street, Romeo and Juliet, Candida, Antony and Cleopatra, No Time for Comedy, Antigone, St. Joan, The Letter, The Doctor's Dilemma, Three Sisters, There Shall Be No Night,* and *The Constant Wife.*,

Robert Sherwood compared Cornell's view of acting to "a vestal virgin guarding a sacred flame."

"Kit and Guthrie," as they were known, "imported" Shakespearean actors and awarded them with prominent Broadway roles. They included Ralph Richardson, Maurice Evans, John Gielgud, and Laurence Olivier. Eventually, McClintic sustained affairs with both Gielgud and Olivier.

Cornell and McClintic jointly bought what became a gathering place for the theatrical elite of Broadway—a townhouse at 23 Beekman Place in Manhattan. Mercedes was a frequent guest, sometimes showing up with Tallulah.

It was at this address that Gielgud delivered his stunning first reading of *Hamlet* before retiring for the night with McClintic to his upstairs bedroom.

It was in this same parlor that George Gershwin played his new "Rhapsody in Blue."

As a theatrical couple, Cornell and McClintic rivaled the fame of the even more famous Alfred Lunt and Lynn Fontanne. (There was a lot of

Young, rail-thin, British, and one of the "smart young things," here's **Estelle Winwood** before she got pigeonholed as a character actress with a gift for portraying eccentrics.

McClintic's first marriage was to Winwood, who later claimed, "Never once did he ever come to my bedroom."

Young **John Gielgud** as *Hamlet*. McClintic had an affair with this talented thespian, but found his rival, Laurence Olivier, a far better lover.

competitive jealousy among this quartet.)

Noël Coward called Lunt and Fontanne "the happiest married couple I know." Privately, he referred to the union of Cornell with McClintic as "the happiest homosexual couple I know."

Although Cornell and McClintic maintained a surface friendship with Lunt and Fontanne, Cornell in private could be sarcastic. "Of course, darling, they're great on stage. They rehearse in bed."

Cornell and McClintic were not always harmonious. Their backstage brawls became so frequent that they were said to be the inspiration for the musical *Kiss Me, Kate*.

One night, on stage with McClintic, Cornell walked off three minutes before the descent of the final curtain, leaving him to improvise as best he could to bring the performance to some sort of conclusion.

***

In 1921, the year of her marriage, Cornell was assigned her first Broadway role, playing Sydney Fairfield in *A Bill of Divorcement*. It ran for 173 performances. *The New York Times* defined her performance as "one of memorable understanding and beauty." A series of other long-forgotten plays followed.

The theatrical version of *A Bill of Divorcement* was adapted into a movie that starred another lesbian, Katharine Hepburn, who made her screen debut opposite John Barrymore.

The question was often raised: "Why didn't an actress as talented as Cornell star in some of the movie versions of her plays?"

In response, she expressed doubt about "how my broad face would appear on the screen." She did write to George Cukor, telling him that if he would find the right script, and agree to direct it, she would make her screen debut. He did not respond.

In 1924, Cornell achieved major stardom in George Bernard Shaw's play, *Candida*. It was a role she would reprise many times in the years to come. Her reviews were ecstatic as she played to packed houses. Shaw

Alfred Lunt and Lynn Fontanne were even more famous as a Broadway theatrical couple than Katharine Cornell and Guthrie McClintic. Although very competitive, they maintained an uneasy surface relationship—no saber-rattling.

Cornell on Broadway with **Allan Pollack** in *A Bill of Divorcement* (1921).

He was a Scot and most of the time wore a kilt, walking with a swagger and wearing no underwear.

"For the role of Sydney," he said, "I want that American girl who played Jo in *Little Women*. What was the kid's name again? Oh, yes... **Katharine Cornell.**"

himself wrote her, claiming, "You have created an ideal British Candida."

The following year, she tackled another most daring and controversial role, playing Iris March in *The Green Hat* (1925), a romance by Michael Arlen that dealt with such themes as syphilis and "loose morals."

She later said, "Whereas Tallulah was already there, I had to work into the role of Iris." *[She was referring to that star's performances of The Green Hat in London.]*

On Broadway, Cornell emoted with the very talented Leslie Howard, who would go on to greater glory playing Ashley Wilkes in *Gone With the Wind* (1939).

Ashton Stevens, a drama critic in Chicago, gave the most daring review. "*The Green Hat* should die at every performance of its melodramatics, its rouge and rhinestones, its preposterous third act. Already, I am beginning to forget its imperfections and remember only its charm. Its chief charm is Katharine Cornell, who sent tiny bells up and down my unpurchasable vertebrae."

In 1928, Greta Garbo starred in the silent movie adaptation, its title changed to *A Woman of Affairs*. Her co-stars were Lewis Stone and John Gilbert, who at the time was known as "the matinee idol of the flappers."

W. Somerset Maugham personally suggested that Cornell reprise the character on Broadway, a character whose most famous line is "I've killed the man I love," in Maugham's play, *The Letter*. Although critics were not impressed, Cornell's loyal fans turned out to see it. It ran for 107 performances during the autumn and winter of 1927-'28. Around the same time, Gladys Cooper appeared in a production of the same play onstage in London

With the advent of sound, Paramount purchased the rights to adapt the play into a talking picture. Released in the spring of 1929, it starred Jeanne Eagles in the year of her death.

[A decade later, in 1939, for yet another talking version remake, Warner's purchased its film rights for $25,000 as a star vehicle for Bette Davis.

In case she backed out (which she didn't), Claudette Colbert, Joan Crawford, Barbara Stanwyck, Katharine Hepburn, Marlene Dietrich, and Vivien Leigh were

Katharine Hepburn with David Manners in the film version of *A Bill of Divorcement*.

After seeing Hepburn emote in the film, McClintic told a reporter, "Kit would have been so much better on the screen."

Cornell as the Countess in Edith Wharton's *The Age of Innocence*.

Gladys Malvern, who wrote about the theater, said, "Flappers with their flimsy, knee-length skirts crowded into New York's Empire Theatre to see Katharine Cornell in trains, bustles, and velvets."

all standing by.]

In 1928, Cornell played Countess Ellen Olenska in the stage adaptation of Edith Wharton's *The Age of Innocence*. It opened in New York at the Empire Theatre and got mostly positive reviews. [*Cornell was following in the footsteps of other actresses who had tackled the role, including Maude Adams, Billie Burke, Ethel Barrymore, Ellen Terry, and Nazimova. In 1993, Michelle Pfeiffer tackled the role, too, in a film version.*]

Cornell followed that with *The Dishonored Lady*, a role originally intended for Miss Barrymore. This true-life drama about a murder in Glasgow was labeled "fifth rate claptrap" by one critic. Despite negative reviews, Cornell's faithful fan base kept it going for a moderate run, as *The New York Times* called her "sure-fire box office."

Mercedes claimed that in 1929, Cornell was furious when she came in sixth in a *Theatre Guild Magazine* poll of the most outstanding stage actors in America. Ranking before her were Alfred Lunt, Lynn Fontanne, Eva Le Gallienne, Helen Hayes, and Dudley Diggs.

Both McClintic and Cornell were also angered when the Theatre Guild praised Lunt and Fontanne as a company with the most accomplished actors in the country.

McClintic cited actors he had hired: Leslie Howard, Orson Welles, Burgess Meredith, Ruth Gordon, Ralph Richardson, Dame Edith Evans, Mildred Natwick, Basil Rathbone, Franchot Tone, and Laurence Olivier.

Cornell eventually found the role she felt she was "destined to play," that of Elizabeth Barrett Browning in *The Barretts of Wimpole Street*. Her husband endorsed the idea and knocked on the doors of twenty-seven producers before deciding they should produce it themselves.

Everyone on Broadway said, "No one reads Elizabeth Barrett Browning any more—she's *passée*. You'll lose your shirts with this one."

Nevertheless, they went to England in search of an actor to play Robert Browning. Laurence Olivier was an obvious choice, but they chose Brian Aherne instead, despite warnings that "No one in New York will know who he is."

On a cold night in January of 1931, *The Barretts of Wimpole Street* opened at the Empire Theatre and was an overnight success. Dorothy Parker claimed, "I paid it the tribute of tears." It ran for 370 performances, but Cornell rejected any involvement in its movie adaptation of 1934, the part going to Norma Shearer.

In spite of her advancing age, Cornell decided she wanted to star in *Romeo and Juliet* for an opening on Broadway in De-

Cornell as Juliet with **Basil Rathbone** as Romeo in a 1934 road show revival in Detroit.

In reference to their performances, a theater critic wrote, "For the first time, the carnal desires, the youthful romanticism, and the earthiness of the language are given equal importance."

cember of 1934. Orson Welles made his Broadway debut as Tybalt, with Basil Rathbone as Romeo and with Brian Aherne as Mercutio. Dame Edith Evans was the nurse. Reviews were glowing, and Cornell was hailed "as the greatest Juliet of her time."

***

As the years went by, Mercedes and Cornell grew apart, but in Mercedes' words, "The wonderful memories lingered on."

McClintic died in October of 1961 of a lung hemorrhage, shortly after he and Cornell celebrated their 40th wedding anniversary. She retired from the stage, dying of pneumonia in June of 1974 in Tisbury, Massachusetts.

KIRK DOUGLAS
More Was Never Enough.
And When It Came to Kit Cornell & Guthrie McClintic, Who Was Hustling Whom?

Kirk Douglas, then a struggling young newcomer in the theater world, played a part in the orbit of Katharine Cornell and Guthrie McClintic. In Blood Moon's pioneering biography *Kirk Douglas, More is Never Enough* (2019), his interactions with them were detailed for the first time. In some ways, his story was typical of dozens of other actors who were hired by McClintic, although Kirk wasn't as "cooperative" as some in satisfying McClintic's libido.

An excerpt from that biography has been replicated in the pages that follow:

***

After his college graduation, Kirk (Douglas) haunted the New York offices of Broadway talent agencies. Many were quite seedy looking, with upholsteries long past their expiration dates. He was also an avid reader of *Actor's Cue*, listing which upcoming plays were being cast.

At every office, he got nothing but rejections. "A couple of agents wanted to audition me all right, and one asked me to strip so that he could better see what parts I might be suited for. But I wasn't interested in that kind of audition."

"I learned early in life that an aspirant actor has to live with rejection. Even big movie stars get rejected time and again. Many roles I wanted to sink my teeth into went to Burt Lancaster, Charlton Heston, Richard Widmark—and most definitely, Robert Mitchum. Those guys just ripped the parts from my jaws."

Confronted with no work on Broadway, he signed for summer stock at the Nuangola Playhouse, located in a forest in the Poconos, near Scranton, Pennsylvania.

Although beginning as a stagehand, he was persistent, demanding and getting small parts. Before the end of the season, he was cast as the lead in five different plays. "They were coming at me so fast, with so much dialogue to learn, that I got confused about which lines belonged to which plays."

His meatiest role was in a play called *Broadway*, the 1926 work of the notoriously hated producer Jed Harris and playwright George Abbott. In 1929, Universal adapted it into its first talking picture.

"I liked the play and my role in it because I could use street slang in a hard-boiled realistic background," Kirk said. "I would later remember the play when I made another realistic New York drama, *Detective Story* (1951), one of my most famous movies."

By late September of that year, he was working at Schrafft's, waiting tables and gobbling down those half-eaten sandwiches. "For fifteen cents, at breakfast, I had a glass of OJ and a doughnut at Nedick's. On many occasions, I splurged on a coke at Walgreen's on Broadway at 44th Street, where out-of-work actors hung out—and there were plenty of those guys like me."

One day, he read that Katharine Cornell—hailed as the greatest stage actress on Broadway at the time—in collaboration with her husband, Guthrie McClintic, were producing *Spring Again*, set for a Broadway opening in November 1941 at the Booth Theatre. He still remembered Cornell's magnificent performance in *The Barrett's of Wimpole Street*, which he'd seen during its tour through New York State.

He went to Cornell's office at Radio City, where he was told by her assistant, Stanley Gilkey, to go to the Booth Theatre, where auditions were being held that very day.

With dreams that Cornell might pluck him out of the lineup as her new leading man, he arrived with hope but also with the fear of rejection. He immediately learned that although

Darwin Porter and Danforth Prince were amazed that, until a few months before his death, no one had ever penned a comprehensive overview of the life of mega-league actor **Kirk Douglas**.

That changed in 2019 when they released this well-received biography. Kirk, as it reveals, and the Hollywood niche he occupied, was amazing in many different ways. Read about it here.

One of **Kirk Douglas'** ultimate triumphs, to some degree because of his many upsetting months "in training" in the orbit of Cornell and McClintic, was his portrayal of Vincent van Gogh in *Lust for Life* (1956).

her husband, McClintic, would be directing it, Cornell would not be starring or even appearing in it.

That afternoon, McClintic was nowhere to be seen, having delegated the audition to his assistants. Kirk waited two hours before being called by the stage manager, who gave him lines associated with the character he might be playing: That of a telegram boy from Western Union. He was to sing his lines to the tune of "Yankee Doodle."

To his surprise, he got the part.

The next day, he met the two stars of the upcoming production, Grace George and C. Aubrey Smith. George was married to the famous theatrical producer, William Brady, who had been instrumental in launching the career of Humphrey Bogart.

A darling of theatrical critics, Miss George had gone from one triumph to another. They had included George Bernard Shaw's *Major Barbara, The School for Scandal,* and *Kind Lady.* And although he had developed a reputation for discovering and then nurturing young talent, "All I could do for her," Kirk later said ruefully, "was bring her a glass of coke before the curtain went up. She told me the drink made her 'high.'"

Born in 1863, C. Aubrey Smith was a distinguished English actor and—during his youth—a famous cricketer. He'd appeared in such films as *The Prisoner of Zenda* (1937) and had recently completed a secondary role in Alfred Hitchcock's *Rebecca* (1941) a film that had starred Laurence Olivier and Joan Fontaine.

To denizens of the theater world, **McClintic and Cornell** (imaged at different periods of their careers, above) were almost messianic at the time...a faraway dream for then-destitute Broadway hopefuls like Kirk Douglas.

When Kirk finally met McClintic, the director was most impressed with him. "He even made me his assistant stage manager and gave me more money," Kirk said. "He wanted me by his side all the time. I brought him his coffee. I lit his cigarettes. And I shared his daily lunch of a chocolate milkshake for him and one for me, too."

"Even though I was only a bit player, he gave me a private dressing room.

He had my messenger boy outfit tailor made, and saw that it fitted real tight, feeling around my legs and butt a little too closely for comfort."

Kirk feared that McClintic was a homosexual and talked it over one afternoon with Smith. "Of course he is, and his wife, Miss Cornell, is a lesbian. You could advance your career by lying on McClintic's casting couch. I'm an old relic today, but when I was a young man, a studly cricketer, I was highly desired by homosexuals. I took advantage and launched myself in the English theater, which, as you know, is filled with stately homos such as Laurence Olivier and John Gielgud, among countless others."

"I'm not sure I'm cut out for the casting couch," Kirk protested.

"That's a choice every young man has to make for himself," Smith said. "Guthrie and Katharine have the ideal working relationship: a 'lavender marriage.'"

In his memoirs, in an abbreviated way, Kirk did at least refer to McClintic's homosexual interest in him. Alone with the director at his private home, he claimed that McClintic's "hands started to wander. Frightened, I bolted for the door."

Cast members during the run of *Spring Again* just assumed that Kirk was McClintic's "boy." It was common gossip. "I, for one, urged Kirk to give Guthrie what he wanted," Smith said. "I didn't see it as any great sacrifice on his part."

The scenic designer, Donald Oenslager, said, "It was obvious to all of us that Guthrie had the hots for young Kirk. When they went on the road with our play, Guthrie insisted that Kirk share his hotel rooms, and so he did in Massachusetts and Connecticut. Surely, something must have happened on those cold nights in New England. No one can be sure what happened, and Kirk, of course, to maintain

C. Aubrey Smith offered kind, worldly advice to Kirk Douglas about obstacles he'd encounter on the road to his horizons.

He warned about—and ultimately recommended—the casting couch.

Young, athletic, hot, virile, and fresh out of the Navy and the Pacific Theater, **Kirk Douglas** is depicted on the left with **Katharine Cornell** and **Guthrie McClintic** in one of the salons at 23 Beekman Place, oozing the kind of charm and male flash that made him a movie star.

Who could resist?

Certainly not McClintic, who promoted young Kirk into "my boy."

his macho image, had to deny it."

That Thanksgiving, shortly after the play opened, Kirk received a coveted invitation from Cornell to a lavish dinner at her elegant home at 23 Beekman Place. Its garden terrace opened onto a view of the East River. Photos of Cornell in her greatest roles lined the walls of a house filled with theatrical memorabilia.

She greeted Kirk and was overheard thanking him "for being so nice and helpful to my husband. He just adores you, talks about you all the time, and thinks you'll become one of the truly big stars on the stage, perhaps even having a Hollywood career."

The guest of honor that night was the formidable Tallulah Bankhead, the Southern belle from Alabama. A bisexual, her affairs were the most diverse of any stage or film actress.

Although Kirk gave Tallulah almost no mention in his memoirs, she was far more gossipy, at least in private and after some drinks:

While she was touring in *Crazy October* in 1958, she described to its author, James Leo Herlihy, her version of what happened that evening with Kirk in the home of Katharine Cornell:

"*Dahling*, I was full of fish eggs (caviar) that dear Kit [i.e., Katharine] served, and tanked up on champagne. I followed this dashing boy, Kirk Douglas, into the bathroom. Since it was Thanksgiving, I fellated him."

As Herlihy related later, "Tallu, she admitted herself, was a grand Southern lady. She always said that she never let the truth get in the way of a good yarn."

"To my knowledge," Herlihy continued, "Kirk never admitted he had sex with either McClintic or Tallu. But it's been pretty well documented that she seduced Marlon Brando, James Dean, and Rock Hudson. And if she could seduce those gay or bi-guys, I don't see why she couldn't have conquered Kirk."

"If given half the chance," Herlihy continued, "I'd have gone after Kirk myself.

As a consolation prize, I got Paul Newman, who wanted to play the Joe Buck character from my novel, *Midnight Cowboy*. Let's face it: Those Jewish guys, Douglas and Newman, are two of the sexiest men in films."

Although not widely remembered today, **Katharine Cornell** was a household name, remaining in the public imagagination partly because of her frequent appearance on the cover of arts-oriented and theatrical magazines, such as the ones replicated above.

***

The December 7, 1941 Japanese attack on the U.S. Naval Fleet at Pearl Harbor sent shock waves through Kirk and millions of other Americans. Up to then, he hadn't given the war in Europe too much consideration, except for the horrifying reports reaching America's shores about the attempts by Hitler and Himmler to exterminate European Jews.

Now, war had come to America. There was a sudden fear of invasion, especially along its Pacific coasts. In the general confusion and consternation, many Californians began hastily evacuating their beach homes.

Kirk felt it was his patriotic duty to sign up for military service, preferably as a pilot in the U.S. Air Force. He'd have to put his acting career, such as it was, on hold.

At a recruiting station in Manhattan, as part of his application for entry into the Air Force, he was subjected to a battery of tests, both physical and psychological. He was twenty-five years old and was told by a recruiting officer, "You're a bit too old. We like to train much younger pilots."

He was shocked to learn that he'd flunked the psychological evaluation. "You seem too methodical. The Air Force needs young pilots who can make split-second decisions. Their own life, and those of fellow airmen, could depend on their ability to make accurate but quick decisions. You seem to like to mull things over."

After he was rejected, as he had been for roles on the stage, he turned to the recruiting officer and said, "You're losing a good man. Who knows? I might have become the first pilot to bomb Tokyo."

***

Feeling rejected and disappointed, Kirk turned his attention once again to making it as a stage actor. He learned that McClintic was casting a serious drama, Anton Chekhov's *The Three Sisters* with Cornell as the lead. She would be backed up by two distinguished actresses, Ruth Gordon and Judith Anderson. The minor roles were still being cast.

Ever since Kirk had finally turned down McClintic's sexual overtures, there had been tension between them. There were two roles for Russian soldiers, and Kirk—who reminded McClintic that he had Russian blood flowing through his veins—wanted to be cast as one of them.

McClintic seemed more distant from him than ever, but he eventually agreed to let Kirk play one of the soldiers.

The leading roles for three other male characters had already been cast with actors Alexander Knox, Dennis King, and Edmund Gwenn.

The plot revolved around the dismal story of the frustration and futility engulfing upperclass Russians before the revolution.

Kirk felt there was a lot he could learn about acting by watching this formidable array of talent during their rehearsals. He set about to ingratiate himself with all six of the leads.

Born in South Australia of English parents, Anderson was already a renowned stage star, and had been nominated for a Best Supporting Actress Oscar for her performance in *Rebecca* (1941).

Ruth Gordon was being courted at the time by the playwright, Garson Kanin, and Kirk admired her talent, especially her nasal voice and distinct personality. "She was very standoffish, with no time for a little unknown like me."

A Canadian, Alexander Knox had just appeared with great success in the Broadway production of *The Sea Wolf* (1941) and was just months away from filming his best-known movie, *Wilson* (1944).

An English actor, Dennis King, not only performed Shakespeare, but also starred in musicals, introducing such famous songs as "Rose-Marie" and "Indian Love Call."

Since Kirk had stopped being "cooperative," McClintic suddenly took the role of the more prominent Russian soldier from Kirk and awarded it to a more accommodating young man, whom Kirk found "effeminate."

Instead, Kirk was assigned the thankless role of a lesser soldier carrying a samovar and following veteran actor Gwenn across the stage. The Londoner is best remembered today for his iconic role of Kris Kringle in *Miracle on 34th Street* (1947). Gwenn cautioned him, "Just follow me onto the stage. No need to act like Julius Caesar invading Gaul."

Cornell, too, made it clear that she thought Kirk was overplaying the scene, telling him, "As a Russian peasant soldier, you're supposed to place the samovar on a table and leave. The way you're entering will make the audience feel you have something to say, which you do not."

"I was humiliated, but followed her advice until that day I, too, would have my shining hour on the stage."

Opening on December 21, 1942, at the Ethel Barrymore Theater, *The Three Sisters* ran for 122 performances.

"At the end, I decided to take off that peasant makeup and put my stage uniform into mothballs. I was going to join the military and put on a real uniform and go kill some Nazis or perhaps a few Japs. If the Air Force wouldn't take me, there was always the Navy."

Cover of *Time* Magazine from the darkest months (December, 1942) of World War II, when America needed some diversion. Left to right on the cover are **Katharine Cornell, Judith Anderson**, and Ruth Gordon as Anton Chekhov's *Three Sisters*.

Kirk Douglas, hot, untested, green, and very ready, willing, and enthusiastic, spent long months portraying a messenger with just a few lines to deliver—entirely at the grace and pleasure of Guthrie McClintic.

As Douglas later admitted years later, "I finally dropped trou and gave Guthrie what he had wanted for so long."

THIS CHAPTER IS DEDICATED
TO THE ARRANGEMENTS NAVIGATED AND SUSTAINED BY

KATHARINE CORNELL & GUTHRIE McCLINTIC

IN THE DEVELOPMENT OF THEIR ENDURING CAREERS IN THE PERFORMING ARTS

REST IN PEACE,
ENTREPRENEURIAL GIANTS OF AMERICAN ENTERTAINMENT

GUTHRIE McCLINTIC (1893-1961) &
KATHARINE CORNELL (1893-1974)

CHAPTER THIRTEEN
"Star Crazed" Before Anyone Called It by That Name

MERCEDES' MANIA FOR CELEBRITY CHASING

Diaghilev, Nijinsky, & Stravinsky;
Jean Cocteau (France's *Enfant Terrible*);
Ethel (High Priestess of the American Theater) Barrymore;
John Barrymore & His Wife, Michael Strange;
Aldous ("Brave New World") Huxley;
Cult Singer Yvonne George & Socialist Robert Desnos;
The Great Russian Ballerina, Tamara Karasavina;

Plus the Hindu Mystics
Meher Baba & Jiddu Krishnamurti

Mercedes' passion for conversation and her ongoing immersion in the avant-garde continued long after the fires of her sexual appetites diminished. Here are three views of her as a deeply well-informed member of the *cognoscenti*, capable of sustaining long intellectual and artistic dialogues about whatever was new and in vogue among "The Smart Set" of her era. Perhaps it was her early immersion into "polite society" as a child... but in any event, she became widely respected as a booster and catalyst to the creative output of dozens of news-making writers, musicians, philosophers, and painters. Keep reading to find out what we're talking about.

Despite her many flaws, including her status as a failed writer, Mercedes must have had something going for her. Some of the greatest names in the world of dance, of letters, and of the theater gravitated to her, in some cases forming life-long friendships.

SERGEI DIAGHILEV & VASLAV NIJINSKY

"Many world class dancers gravitated to me for reasons I don't truly understand," Mercedes de Acosta told Darwin Porter one night at his home. "I was never that close to Nijinsky, although I adored his talent. But Sergei Diaghilev found me mildly intriguing. He was the ballet impresario who founded Les Ballets Russes in Paris, from which the era's most famous dancers and choreographers would emerge."

"One of my greatest experiences as a young woman in Paris was to be introduced to Vaslav Nijinsky. In person, he was shy and introverted, and we didn't have a lot to say to each other. He reserved his magic for the

Mercedes' passion: Russia-born British ballerina **Tamara Karasavina**.

"Even though I knew Tamara in London, her soul was still in Russia," Mercedes claimed. "She once told me, 'I have never lost the attachment to the country of my birth, though I realized I would now feel a stranger in it.'"

Serge Diaghilev, as perceived in 1904 by portraitist Valentin Serov.

The communist leaders of the Russian Revolution attacked him as "an insidious example of bourgeois decadence."

stage."

"Wherever he danced, I was in the front row," she said. "Everybody in the damn world knew that Nijinsky and Diaghilev were lovers, although it may have been in the context of what latter-day Hollywood players call 'the casting couch.'"

"During the years I followed the Ballets Russes, I met the most incredible people—and not just Picasso. In addition to my friend, Igor Stravinsky, Diaghilev commissioned such composers as Claude Debussy and Sergei Prokofiev; artists such as Vasily Kandinsky, Henri Matisse, and Alexandre Benois; and costume designers such as Coco Chanel and Léon Bakst."

"I got to see the great Anna Pavlova dance," Mercedes claimed. "But to me, Tamara Karasavina was just as good. She became my lover."

"During the years I knew Diaghilev, I also got to meet a string of his male lovers—and not just Nijinsky, but Serge Lifar and Léonide Massine, who replaced Nijinsky after he married Romola de Pulszky, a Hungarian. That led to an enormous emotional break with Diaghilev."

[Ironically, Diaghilev's last lover was Igor Markevitch, the Ukraine-born composer and conductor. He would one day marry Kyra Nijinsky, the daughter of Vaslav Nijinsky. The parents named their son, Vaslav, after Kyra's father.]

Nijinsky came to a sad end in April of 1950. After 1920, he was mostly confined to asylums. He was buried in the Montparnasse Cemetery in Paris.

His memoirs were translated into English in 1936. His wife deleted most references to sex and homosexuality, suggesting his relationship with Diaghilev was "involuntary homosexuality."

Mercedes did not confine her friendships and love affairs to members of the dance world. Significant in her life were John Barrymore (her friend) and his second wife (her lover), who went by the odd name of "Michael Strange."

Nijinsky with **Karasavina** (left) in Diaghilev's *Le Spectre de la Rose* (1911).

"I fell in love with Karasavina when I saw this performance," Mercedes said. "She was a revelation of harmony between the spirit and the body."

JOHN & ETHEL BARRYMORE

Even as a schoolgirl, and especially after moving to New York City, Mercedes was a devotee of the theater. Her favorite stars were a brother/sister team, Ethel and John Barrymore. It would be beyond her wildest dreams that she would one day become their friend.

Born in 1879, Ethel vied with Helen Hayes for the title of "First Lady of the American Theater," joining other claimants.

Ethel's career would span six decades. At the age of fifteen, she'd made her professional debut, starring with her uncle, John Drew.

In 1901, she appeared for the first time on Broadway in a play, *Captain Jinks of the Horse Marines*. By 1915, she was starring in silent pictures, beginning with *The Nightingale*. In 1917 alone, she was featured in six silent films, including *The Eternal Mother*.

She always returned to the stage, however, defining Broadway as "my natural home."

Through Ethel, Mercedes met her charismatic younger brother, John. Like Ethel, he had been born in Philadelphia—in his case, in 1882. A reckless youth, he was appearing on Broadway with his actor father, Maurice, and about a year later, acting onstage with Ethel.

By the time he'd performed in *Richard III* (1920) and *Hamlet* (1922), he was hailed as "The Greatest *tragedien* in America."

In 1925, he abandoned the stage to become a full-fledged movie star, hailed onscreen as "The Great Profile." In *Dr. Jekyll and Mr. Hyde* (1920), he played the famous transformation scene from doctor to savage beast without makeup. He followed that with such titles as *Sherlock Holmes* (1922) and *The Sea Beast* (1926). The success of *Beau Brummel* (1924) won him a contract with Warner Brothers.

Ethel Barrymore in 1901. She's depicted in one of the costumes she wore in *Captain Jinks of the Horse Marines*.

In September of 1910, he married socialite Katherine Harris, though later referring to their union as "a bus accident." After only a week of marriage, Katherine complained to friends, "I almost never see my husband."

Morose because of his failed marriage, he began to drink even more heavily than before, lamenting, "Unhappiness increases the drink and drink increases the unhappiness." His entire marriage would be characterized by a series of adulterous affairs.

Barrymore and Mercedes had a mutual friend, Edward ("Ned") Sheldon, a noted playwright of his day. It was at his home that she was introduced to Barrymore, beginning a life-long friendship sparked by chaos and turmoil. "John turned to me on occasion for advice and comfort," she said. "Then he'd go for years without calling on me until one night at some ungodly hour, he would show up, tossing a rock at my second-floor bedroom window, often breaking the glass pane. I would invite him in. Long after dawn came, he would still be pouring out his woes to me."

Two views of **John Barrymore**. Famous for having no sense about handling money, he married and divorced four times and once declared bankruptcy.

In his later years as an actor, he began to self-parody, often portraying a drunken has-been, a caricature of his former grandeur. Before that, he was "perhaps the most influential and idolized actor of his day," in the words of Martin Norden, his biographer.

"Of the dozens and dozens of actors I met over the decades, I found John the most compelling, and I avidly followed his career."

After meeting Barrymore for the first time, Mercedes concluded, "He and Ned were as close as two men could ever be. To an increasing degree, he became John's artistic conscious."

When she met him, Barrymore was appearing in a play called *Princess Zim-Zim*. To Mercedes' surprise, he told her that Sheldon had arranged for him to take voice lessons from a woman coach who was hailed as the best in her profession.

His vocal coaching evolved after Barrymore's uncle, John Drew, an actor himself, said, "Jack has a shoddy accent, which is an embarrassment to the Barrymore family. I'll never know where he picked it up, perhaps from sleeping with those Coney Island barkers, all of whom are homosexuals."

Edward (Ned) Sheldon was Barrymore's best friend, mentor, and occasional lover. He trusted him completely, and often turned to him for advice.

Four years younger than Barrymore, Sheldon had received critical praise for his first play, *Salvation Hall,* which he'd written while still a student at Harvard. His friendship with Barrymore began in 1914 and lasted a lifetime.

Sheldon usually downplayed his role in Barrymore's career. "He bubbled over with talent," the playwright said. "He is responsible for his own success—not me."

As Mercedes put it, "Sheldon unbound Prometheus."

"The two men toured Italy together, finding Venice their favorite and most romantic city," Mercedes said. "On those moonlit nights, sailing along the Grand Canal, Ned told me he fell in love with Jack, who was not a homosexual."

An acting dynasty, **the Barrymores, John, Ethel, and Lionel**, in 1904. Acting was in their blood.

Ethel was the aunt of John Drew Barrymore, and the great aunt of actress Drew Barrymore. She was also the granddaughter of actress and theater manager Louisa Lane (Mrs. John Drew) and she was the niece of Broadway matinee idol, John Drew, Jr., and also the niece of Sidney Drew, the early Vitagraph silent screen star.

One night, as she became better acquainted with Barrymore, he explained his sexual intimacies with Sheldon. "Why not give my dear friend what he desperately needs? It feels good, and I enjoy it. I feel wonderful knowing that I am giving something to the man to whom I owe so much. If that is the price of our friendship, it's such a little offering to pay."

Later, and tragically, Sheldon began to grow paralyzed. Both Mercedes and Barrymore continued to visit him as the years went by. "His speaking voice was clear even if he couldn't move his body," she said. "His mind was sharp as a bell, and he continued to help artists with their plays—and not just Jack. He also worked on such productions as *Lulu Bells* with Charles McCarthy, the husband of Helen Hayes."

One night, Sheldon told her, "I live for the nights Jack comes to visit me. I hang on to his every word. He is completely aware of how much I worship him. Everything he says and does. When I am with him, the rest of the world does not exist for me. Much of my life has been spent in his orbit. He is the Prince of Players, a Godlike man who accepts my total idolization of him."

"Ned continued to worship John throughout the course of his life," Mercedes said. "To him, the sun rose and set in Jack. He would walk in the door, and Ned's eyes would brighten with joy."

"Without a doubt, Jack was the love of Ned's life. Jack was also the cause of the suffering and emotional frustrations that eventually erupted into Ned's illness, at least in my view."

Mercedes' Affair with
MICHAEL STRANGE

Long before Barrymore divorced his first wife, he became romantically involved with Blanche Marie Louise Oelrichs, a poet, playwright, and actress. Born in Newport, Rhode Island, she grew up among the Astors and the Vanderbilts, a spoiled rich girl with a talent for writing poetry.

Some of it had an erotic content. Since she didn't want to embarrass her parents, she began associating it with her fabricated *nom de plume* of "Michael Strange." Eventually, her poetry went over so well that, for the rest of her life, she opted to use that macho-sounding name in public and among friends.

Michael had been married before, in her case to Leonard Moorehead Thomas, son of a prominent Philadelphia banker, from 1910 to 1919. With him, she had two sons, Leonard Jr. and Robin.

After the collapse of her first marriage, and before her widely publicized 1920 wedding to "The Great Profile," she became pregnant with the future Diana Barrymore. Born in 1921, she went on to become a famous stage and screen actress herself. *[Lana Turner brilliantly portrayed a character vaguely patterned after Diana in* The Bad and the Beautiful, *released in 1952.*

Although Barrymore might have expected a doting wife, he quickly learned that she was ferociously independent, an activist in woman's suffrage.

She attracted many admirers, both men and women. The French portrait artist, Paul Helleu, hailed her as "the most beautiful woman in America."

"With her olive skin, Michael reminded me of a pretty Arab boy," Mercedes said. "She had a beautiful face resting under brown hair, and her glistening eyes seemed to devour you. She was healthy, vibrant, seductive, and very much alive. In her affair with Jack, I felt she was the one cracking the whip."

Two views of the odd couple, **John Barrymore** with **Michael Strange**. (lower photo) on a transatlantic crossing aboard the *Mauretania*.

When Mercedes learned that Michael planned to marry Barrymore, she advised her not to: "It will be a case of which of you kills the other first."

"But I'm pregnant," Michael protested.

"I can arrange an abortion," Mercedes told her.

Michael answered: "Thank you, but no. I want to have Fig's child." *[The couple had taken to calling each other 'Fig.']*

"Against my advice, Michael and Barrymore got married," Mercedes said. "It was a case of loving each other too much and hating each other even more."

"Being married to Jack is like setting up light housekeeping inside the crater of Mount Vesuvius, right before it erupts to destroy Pompeii," Michael told Mercedes.

"Every time I saw them, they were always fighting about something before making up, which meant a sexual assault from him."

When his daughter Diana was born, Barrymore said, "I'm glad it's a girl. If it had been a boy, I'm sure he would have picked up all my bad habits."

James Kotsilibas-Davis, author of *The Barrymores*, wrote: "Jack's ardor of Michael was laced with jealousy and drink. He affected maniacal rages when she displayed interest in other men or women. She matched his tantrums. They continually threatened suicide, filed separation agreements, then reconciled."

Barrymore told Mercedes, "I didn't marry Michael. She married me. Marriage to me is a potted plant. I can't stand seeing a plant trapped in a pot. It's like caging a bird who should fly free."

As for his marriage, he said, "To keep the grand passion of our love flaming, we often have to indulge in flagellation. Our soliloquies clash with our odes. We can never be compatible because each of use realizes we can never possess the other."

"As I got to know Jack as the months went by, I found him a troubled and deeply conflicted man," Mercedes told Darwin Porter one night before one of his fireplaces. "He was afraid of his own desires, and he was always falling in love, perhaps with the likes of Mary Astor, or just some script girl. But the illusion, perhaps delusion, came and went quickly. He would pour out troubles to me. He was the supreme egotist, and I don't remember he ever asked me how my own life was going."

"On the stage, he is the personification of masculine virility," Mercedes said. "He told me his greatest dream would be to play Hamlet in the nude, so that all the world could feast on his manly glory. Yet, aside from the physical, there was an overpowering feminine streak in him. He wanted to be dominated by a woman. He was filled with inner conflict as the manly side of him battled with the woman who lived inside."

"I think this conflict was partially the cause of his heavy drinking. He confessed that he went to bed on occasion with a handsome young actor who was in awe of him."

"These young men might think I'm taking them to bed to fuck them, but they soon find that I'm the one who wants to get plowed."

One Friday night, Michael called Mercedes, extending an invitation to the Barrymore home for a candlelit dinner. She fully expected that it would be a dinner for three.

Yet when she got there, she learned that Jack had already stormed out of their house and had not returned.

"I not only stayed for dinner but spent the night and most of the weekend in Michael's arms," Mercedes said. "When I met her, and based on her mannish attire, I just assumed she needed the love of a woman—not a man—to satisfy her deepest needs."

Michael's dress was unusual for its day. Mercedes found it had been inspired by such French icons as Geôrges Sand and Alfred de Musset, "but always with a wide-open collar like Walt Whitman wore."

John Barrymore with **Greta Garbo** in *Grand Hotel*. Embedded within an all-star cast, Garbo plays a melancholic ballerina who "*vants to be alone.*" Barrymore is a debonair jewel thief who romances her.

"She never wore a woman's hat," Mercedes said. "Always borrowing one from Jack. Sometimes the two of us had lunch with Ethel, who was always tolerant of such things and tended to overlook someone's sexual preference. I learned from a friend that Ethel suspected that Michael, Jack, and I were having a *ménage à trois*. She may have been right about that, but it was something I planned to leave out of my memoirs."

One day, a distraught Michael phoned Mercedes and asked her to come over. When Mercedes was ushered into her living room, she found Michael perturbed over her younger son, Robin, from her first marriage. "The boy is only six years old, and he insists he wants to be raised as a girl. When he goes to school, he wants to wear a dress and be treated like a little princess. He spends most of the day with his dolls."

"You cannot change him," Mercedes cautioned. "When I was a little girl, I wanted to be a boy. I can understand what he's going through. It's traumatic, and you'll need to be loving and understanding."

"I'm prepared to do that, but Jack is carrying it to extremes," Michael said. "You know from your frequent visits that Jack at home walks around naked most of the time. He has no shame at all. Robin is fascinated by his stepfather's penis. Jack has even let him play with it as if it were a damn toy. He believes, and he's sincere about this, that getting to play with his penis will encourage Robin to grow up and become a man and have a penis himself. What do you have to say about that?"

Mercedes sighed. "Robin is such a pretty boy, so delicate. For all we know, he'll be wanting to play with the penis of some man for the rest of his life, and there is nothing you can do about it except let him grow up and follow the desires of his heart."

***

Mercedes became a frequent visitor at the Barrymore home, She was particularly helpful to Michael, who was writing a play called *Claire de lune*. Starring both Ethel and John Barrymore, it opened on Broadway in 1921, having been based on Victor Hugo's *L'Homme qui rit (The Man Who Laughs)*.

"I attended opening night and thought it was a memorable night in the theater," Mercedes said. "Jack was all right until the reviews came in, and then he became hysterical, getting roaringly drunk. He was particularly upset over attacks from Alexander Woollcott."

Michael spoke to Mercedes about Barrymore's reaction. "Alexander and the other critics brought out all their heavy artillery to assault a butterfly. They descended on Jack like he was everyone from Benedict Arnold to the Anti-Christ. He was devastated and locked himself into his study, drinking day and night, not eating anything. The press also suggested that the play would never have opened on Broadway were it not for my links to Ethel and Jack."

Years later, Barrymore himself evaluated the play written by his then-wife, Michael Strange: "It was a genuinely charming Kansas outhouse graced with chandeliers and a doorman from the Ritz."

***

Two views, two different eras, of **Blanche Oelrichs (aka Michael Strange).**

One night, she wrote an ode to Mercedes: "Your hands are beautiful—magnetic. I feel your hands peeling pale fresh almonds under plea of limpid— myriad eyes—by a wall near the city of Masques."

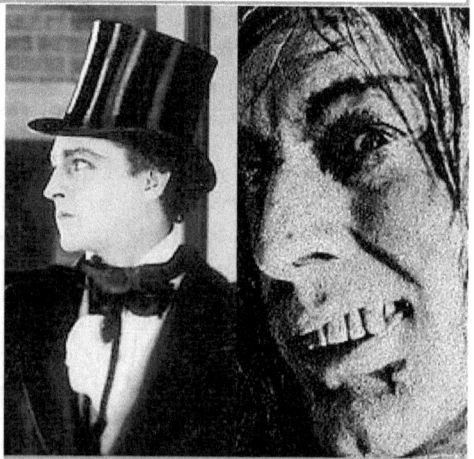

In his 1920 film, *Dr. Jekyll and Mr. Hyde*, **John Barrymore** appeared (left) as Dr. Jekyll before making his schizophrenic shift into (right) the monstrous and terrifying Mr. Hyde—just as he would that fateful night with Mercedes at Honfleur.

When Alla Nazimova and Mercedes were staying together at a hotel on the Left Bank of Paris, they received an invitation to visit John Barrymore and his wife, Michael, at their vacation rental near the town of Honfleur in Normandy. *[Rich in literary traditions, Honfleur, in Normandy, had been the town where Flaubert had written many of his novels.]* Whereas Nazimova had to return to New York, Mercedes traveled alone to Honfleur where Barrymore met her at the railway station.

She found him living in domestic bliss with his wife, Michael, in a small cottage with a little garden. They had no help, so all of them joined in cooking dinner. "To my amazement, Jack was sober," Mercedes recalled.

All of them retired at around one that morning after many stimulating conversations. At that point, Barrymore had resumed his drinking and was getting rather belligerent toward Michael. Mercedes discreetly excused herself and headed for the guest bedroom, which was in the rear of the house, near the kitchen.

At around 3AM, Mercedes heard Michael screaming for help. The sound came from the upstairs master bedroom. Throwing on a robe, Mercedes bounded up the steps to find the bedroom door open. She rushed inside to discover Michael and John rolling around on the floor. He had a butcher knife in his hand and was threatening to cut her throat.

Since he was intoxicated and in a weakened condition, Mercedes was able to pull him off her and force him to drop the knife.

Angered, he rose from the floor and headed for a nightstand, where he picked up an unlit kerosene lamp and threw it in the direction of the women. It hit Michael directly in the face before bouncing off her and splintering into sharp-edged fragments. One of them hit Mercedes in the face, and she began to bleed.

Seeing what he had done, Barrymore seemed to sober up and rushed into the bathroom to retrieve a bandage. With Michael, he helped Mercedes to stop the bleeding and to bandage her. Then, murmuring her regrets, she retreated downstairs and back into her bedroom for the remainder of the night.

No more sounds came from upstairs. When she rose later that morning, both Barrymore and Michael, each ignoring the incident of the night before, were in the kitchen preparing breakfast for her. Over their morning meal, each of them affectionately called each other by their shared nickname of "Fig." They even came up with a nickname for Mercedes, referring to her as "Winged Meadow Lark."

Later, they drove her to the train station for her trip back to Paris. She waved to them from her window seat as they blew her kisses.

1928: **Dolores Costello** marries **John "The Profile" Barrymore.**

The daughter of actor Maurice Costello, Dolores was a delicately pretty blonde actress of silent pictures. Her son became John Barrymore, Jr., and her granddaughter is the actress Drew Barrymore.

***

Back in New York months later, Mercedes ended her affair with Michael when she learned that she was engaged in a tryst with her girlfriend at the time, Eva Le Gallienne.

"I never made love to Michael again," she confessed to Darwin. "That part of our relationship ended on a sour note of betrayal, but, in time, we recovered from that, and our friendship remained intact for the rest of her life."

After Barrymore divorced Michael in 1925, he visited Mercedes, discussing the divorce, in which he had agreed to pay her $18,000 annually in child support for their daughter, Diana.

"Alimony is the most exorbitant of all stud fees," he said. "The worst aspect of it is that you have to shell out all that money retroactively."

"As the years went by, I saw him only periodically," Mercedes said. "Sometimes, we'd go for years without seeing each other, and then, one night, he'd just show up unannounced."

One time, he drove over to her home completely intoxicated and hardly in any condition to pilot a vehicle. She ushered him into her kitchen for some black coffee.

"With Fig, I could never satisfy her Sapphic desires," he said. "I'm a man with her. I felt like a soufflé that had been placed straight from the oven onto the doorstep of a cold, wintry night."

In time, Barrymore married and divorced the actress, Dolores Costello, his co-star in The Sea Beast (1926), based on the legend of Moby Dick.

There would be one more marriage after that: to one Elaine Jacobs, a Hunter College student who came to interview him for her school paper.

It was to be Barrymore's final marriage, and, as Mercedes anticipated, it did not work out.

He spent the final years of his life in Hollywood, living with Errol Flynn.

As Mercedes phrased it, "That's a story for another day. I know so much about the relationship of those two horndogs, I could write a five-act play."

Michael Strange would have one more marriage, wedding Harrison

Like Barrymore, **Errol Flynn** was a drug-and-alcohol-abusing swashbuckler noted for sexual intimacies with everybody.

He's pictured above with **Eleanor Parker** in *Never Say Goodbye*.

A late in life photo of **John Barrymore**, jowly but still with a profile, drunk and soggy with **Errol Flynn**.

Tweed in 1929. He was a prominent New York attorney, who would in time become chairman of Sarah Lawrence College.

In 1940, she met "the love of my life," as she once confessed to Mercedes. She launched a long-term relationship with Margaret Wise Brown, an author of children's books.

In 1942, Michael divorced Tweed.

In the years ahead, Mercedes sometimes visited the two women, Michael and Margaret, at their home at 10 Gracie Square in Manhattan.

She was saddened to learn of Michael's death from leukemia in Boston in 1950.

Heartbroken, Margaret lived for two more years. In 1960, Diana Barrymore died at the age of thirty-eight, suffering from drug and alcohol addiction.

Mercedes' Affair with the Legendary French Chanteuse
YVONNE GEORGE
AND FROM THERE, HER LINKS TO ROBERT DESNOS

Before her affair with Jeanne Eagels, Mercedes became involved with yet another female lover, whose life would end early because of her addiction to drugs.

In Paris in the early 1920s, she fell in love with Yvonne George, a singer born in Belgium, who became a cult favorite in Paris, attracting the *literati* and the theatrical élite for her nightly renditions of Mercedes' favorite song, "Paris."

Paul Franck, director of Paris' Olympia Theater, had first spotted Yvonne singing in a café in her native Brussels. He was intrigued by her sultry looks, her seductive voice, and exotic beauty. He aspired to transform her into Belgium's answer to France's Edith Piaf.

By 1922, under his baton, she was singing at the Olympia, where she developed a devoted following. Chief among them was France's pre-eminent gadabout and arbiter of style, the very brilliant actor, director, and producer Jean Cocteau. As her gig at the Olympia worked through its paces, Cocteau brought an array of his

"With a lover like **Yvonne George**, and with the heady company we were keeping, names in films, the art world, theater, cabaret performers, the *literati*, it was a heady time to be in Paris." Mercedes said.

"Perhaps nothing in the future will ever equal Paris in the 1920s."

"*crème de la crème*" Parisian friends: Jean-Paul Sartre; Jean Genet, Léonide Massine, and Antonin Artaud, who often appeared with his mistress, the novelist and very controversial diarist, Anaïs Nin.

Yvonne became famous for two songs which were requested nightly: "Nous irons à Valparaiso" ("We'll Go to Valparaiso"); and "Goodbye and Farewell." Europe's intellectual and artistic élite delighted in her performance, which epitomized the principles of what was known at the time as "the French realist song."

"Yvonne's voice was tremulous, broken, and troubled," Mercedes said. "She was also a progressive voice for the emancipation of French women between the wars."

On the second week that Mercedes knew her, Yvonne invited her to spend a weekend at her ground floor apartment in Neuilly, where she received many artists and men of letters. "We made love every day, sometimes more than twice a day. I was falling madly in love," Mercedes said. "She made me forget other lovers I had known. I wanted to devote my life to her. Of course, that fantasy would soon run its course."

Jean Cocteau became so fascinated with her that he cast her as the nurse in his production of *Romeo and Juliet*. He told Mercedes, "I am not that familiar with the English language. But as much as I can make out, I read in Shakespeare that *Romeo and Juliet* is the story of doomed children. Their purity is not able to survive outside their playground, where love is pure."

After Yvonne's gig at the Olympia, Mercedes went on weekends to hear her sing at the cabaret, Chez Fischer, on the Left Bank. It attracted painters, writers, and chic lesbians dressed as men.

"Although Yvonne was attracted to men, I fulfilled her need for the love of a woman," Mercedes claimed. "In some ways, she reminded me of the doomed life of Zelda, the tormented wife of F. Scott Fitzgerald. I welcomed Yvonne into my arms, offering her love and comfort."

When Yvonne was invited to perform in New York, Mercedes went with her. She had signed with Lee Shubert of the famous theatrical family. Perhaps nervous and stressed out, she was drinking heavily late at night.

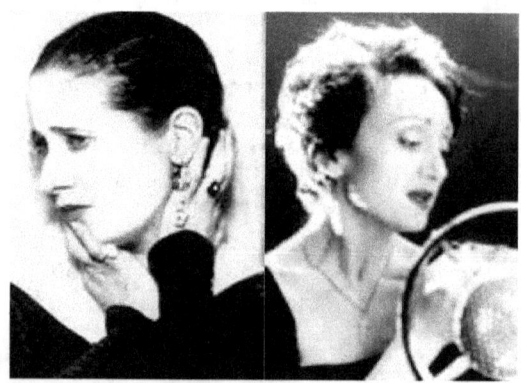

Although **Yvonne George** (left) was authentic, poetic, evocative, and styliish, ratcheting the emotion quotient high and higher in front of audiences in Paris, she never reached the wild success of her competitor, **Editih Piaf** (right) onstage with audiences in New York.

And when it comes to all things Piaf, it's important to note that the authors of this book are still, years after her death, wildly, frenetically, weepily, and spectacularly emotional fans.

"At two in the afternoon, I tried to get her ready for the night's show, giving her a warm bath and massaging her. In spite of my attempts to prevent it, she was slipping around and taking drugs. I felt that if she didn't stop, her addiction would lead to an early grave. Although she missed some performances—and sometimes she couldn't make it—she was always inspired on stage," Mercedes said. "But for Shubert, not to show up on time for a performance was unforgivable."

Yvonne—like Edith Piaf—didn't find the same acceptance in America as she did in Paris. In Paris, her fans (more like "devotees of her cult") always forgave her when she didn't show up, and returned for her show the following night. In Manhattan however, she was quickly blacklisted and defined as unreliable.

Back in Paris, after the collapse of Yvonne's show-biz ambitions in America, Mercedes joined Cocteau at table. It was autumn and he sometimes showed up wearing a trench coat that concealed (at least when he was outside on the street) his harlequin costume. His friends and fans surmised that to some degree, he wore it in honor of Picasso, who was fascinated by harlequins, as shown in some of his cubistic paintings.

To Mercedes' regret, Cocteau lured Yvonne into many of his "opium nights." [*Opium was a drug to which Cocteau was fa-*

 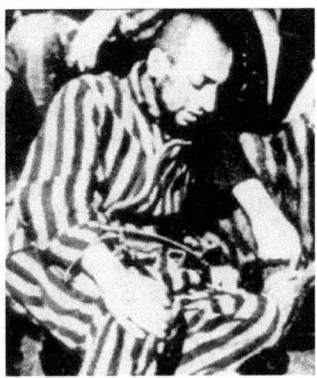

Left photo: **Robert Desnos** in Paris 1940. Right photo: **Robert Desnos** after the liberation of Theresienstadt concentration camp. Having already survived imprisonment in other camps, he died of typhus a few days after the liberation of this third and final prison.

His manic, sometimes charismatic behavior inside Theresienstadt was described, years later, by the feminist poet, Susan Griffin:

"One day Desnos and others were taken away from their barracks. The prisoners rode on the back of a flatbed truck; they knew the truck was going to the gas chamber; no one spoke. Soon they arrived and the guards ordered them off the truck. When they began to move toward the gas chamber, suddenly Desnos jumped out of line and grabbed the hand of the woman in front of him. He was animated and he began to read her palm. The forecast was good: a long life, many grandchildren, abundant joy. A person nearby offered his palm to Desnos. Here, too, Desnos foresaw a long life filled with happiness and success. The other prisoners came to life, eagerly thrusting their palms toward Desnos and, in each case, he foresaw long and joyous lives."

"The guards became visibly disoriented. Minutes before they were on a routine mission the outcome of which seemed inevitable, but now they became tentative in their movements. Desnos was so effective in creating a new reality that the guards were unable to go through with the executions. They ordered the prisoners back onto the truck and took them back to the barracks. Desnos never was executed. Through the power of imagination, he saved his own life and the lives of others."

mously addicted.]

After her return to Paris with Yvonne, Mercedes learned, to her regret, that the singer was more heterosexual than she had originally believed. She launched an affair with a native Parisian, the avant-garde poet, Robert Desnos. Born in 1900, he would play a key role in the Surrealist movement of his day.

After he finished school, he worked for a while as a literary columnist of the newspaper *Paris-Soir*.

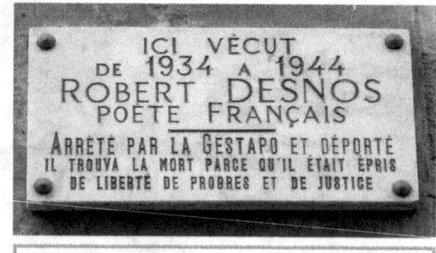

Here is the "landmark plaque" at 19 rue Mazarine, Paris 6e, honoring **Robert Desnos** as a vocal, articulate, and "trouble making" member of the French Resistance.

His first poems appeared in print in 1917 in a volume called *La Tribune des Jeunes (Platform for Youth)*. In 1919, he published his first book *Rose Sélavy*, a collection of surrealistic aphorisms. Then he wrote a controversial novel, *La Liberté l'amour* (1927). Later, Desnos wrote poems declaring his love for Yvonne.

In some quarters, his *oeuvre* was branded as obscene, the same fate the American author, Henry Miller, had met with his *Tropic of Cancer*. Critic Ray Keenoy asserted that Desnos' vision was "literary and lyrical in its outpouring of sexual delirium."

Whereas Mercedes avoided them, Desnos joined Cocteau and Yvonne on their opium highs.

By 1932, based to some degree on his reputation as a literary radical, Desnos became friends with Picasso, Ernest Hemingway, and John Dos Passos.

When war came to France, Desnos joined the French Resistance, but the Gestapo caught up with him in February of 1944, and he was arrested and sent by "cattle car" to Buchenwald in occupied Poland.

In 1945, during the closing months of World War II, he was transferred to Terezin in occupied Czechoslovakia. About a month after Allied soldiers liberated the camp, at the age of forty-five, he contracted typhoid, from which he never recovered. His body was shipped to Paris, where he was buried at the cemetery in Montparnasse.

In April of 1930, no longer involved with Mercedes, fifteen years before Desnos' death at the hands of the Nazis, Yvonne's drug addiction caught up with her. She fell ill with tuberculosis, from which, despite many treatments, she never recovered. She was dead at the age of thirty-three, her body found in a hotel near the port of Genoa in Italy.

Mercedes' Amitié-Amoureuse with
JEAN COCTEAU

Appearing here in robustly good health, for a change, is the most widely publicized *enfant terrible* of his era, **Jean Cocteau.**

Darwin Porter managed to acquire a set of Louis XIV chairs, formerly part of the decor from Cocteau's home at Milly-la-Forêt, that he sold during a moment of penury during the Great Depression.

Through Yvonne George, it was inevitable that Mercedes would meet that singer's most devoted fan in Paris.

Born in 1889, Jean Cocteau was already a legend, acclaimed as a French poet, playwright, novelist, designer, filmmaker, and visual artist. Spectacularly flamboyant, and once a friend of Marcel Proust, he was nicknamed "The Frivolous Prince" and a genuine *"enfant terrible."*

Cocteau and Mercedes immediately became friends. Although a homosexual, he had lost his virginity to the legendary Mistinguett of music hall fame.

"He appeared like a vision before me, enchanting and gracious, yet a supreme egotist," Mercedes said. She would surely have agreed with Frederick Brown's latter-day description: "Cocteau was luminously intelligent, and he knew it, but he was also what the French call *un joli garçon*, with his long renard nose, his delicate lips, (the upper one immobile while the lower parted slightly to emit an endless stream of conceits), his thickish eyebrows sweeping out from the bridge of his nose like bird's wings, his alert, dark eyes compared to a nightingale's, and his hair combed young-Hugo style. He had a thin, patrician face and long hands, which never ceased gesturing."

Novelist Edith Wharton described Cocteau as a man "to whom every great line of poetry was a sunrise, every sunset the foundation of the Heavenly City."

A friend of Proust, André Gide, and Maurice Barrès, Cocteau searched not only for beauty, but for love and acceptance, too. One writer said he "adopted the opinions, mannerisms, almost the personae of some of the most outstanding figures in 20th Century art, music, and letters."

During World War I, he drove an ambu-

Two of a set of four 18th-century Louis XIV chairs, formerly part of *enfant terrible* Jean Cocteau's home at Milly-la-Forêt, an hour's drive south of Paris.

Sold by Cocteau in the 1930s to the American artist & socialite Woody Parrish-Martin (who was sustaining an affair with Cocteau at the time), and later bequeathed to Stanley Mills Haggart, a long-time associate of Darwin Porter, they now "reside" with the authors of this book at Historic Magnolia House in Staten Island.

lance for the Red Cross, and it was during this period that he met and befriended the poet Guillaume Apollinaire and artists who included Modigliani and many other painters and writers with whom he would collaborate after the war.

[*Cocteau met Picasso during the autumn of 1915 and got to know him between expeditions to the Front in his ambulance. (As a citizen of Spain, Picasso was never drafted.) At first, Cocteau was surprised to find that he had no concern for the war, calling it "a stupid embroilment."*

"I prefer insulation from the world at war," he told Cocteau.]

Cocteau's sometimes lover, French actor **Jean Marais**, in an artfully narcissistic scene from Cocteau's ultra-avant garde film, *Orpheus* (1950).

Sergei Diaghilev persuaded Cocteau to write a scenario for a ballet, which resulted in *Parade* (1917). It was produced by Diaghilev with sets by Picasso and the libretto by Apollinaire. Later, it was turned into a full opera of dubious merits.

Cocteau later said, "If it had not been for Apollinaire in uniform, with his skull shaved, the scar on his temple and the bandage around his head, women would have gouged our eyes out with hairpins."

Cocteau once confessed to both Mercedes and his long-time lover, the French actor, Jean Marais, that on a rare occasion, Picasso let himself be fellated. Cocteau began a love affair with Marais, the handsome French actor, in 1938, the relationship lasting until 1963.

In 1928, Cocteau gave Mercedes a copy of his mildly homoerotic and semi-autobiographical *Le livre blanc (The White Paper)*. He'd had it published anonymously.

In it, he wrote, "As far back as I can remember, and even at an age when the mind does not yet influence the senses, I find traces of my love of boys. I have always loved the strong sex that I find legitimate to call the fair sex. My misfortunes came from a society that condemns the rare as a crime and forces us to reform our inclinations."

Since they lived in different parts of the world, Mercedes would go for years without seeing Cocteau. However, when he heard that she was living with Greta Garbo in Hollywood, he contacted her.

Mercedes wrote: "Cocteau begged me to intercede for him. He wanted to write a picture for Greta, and also direct it. To all entreaties of this kind, I have been entirely indifferent, just because I have seen her suffer too much in pictures."

In later years, Mercedes strongly disagreed with Cocteau's right-leaning positions during the Nazi occupation of France. "He viewed Hitler as a pacifist (of all things) and a patron of the arts."

[*"Hitler has France's best interest at heart," he is alleged to have said.*

In his diary, Cocteau accused France of disrespect toward the Führer and attacked the speculation about Hitler's sexuality, especially the homosexual rumors.

In 1945, Cocteau was accused of collaboration with the enemy, though he was later cleared of any wrongdoing.]

Today, Cocteau is best remembered for his novel, *Les Enfants terribles* (1929), and for his films such as the so-called *Orphic Trilogy*, beginning with Orpheus in 1949.

Cocteau died in October of 1963 at his house in Milly-le-Forêt, 45 miles south of Paris, at the age of seventy-four.

His friend, the great French singer, Edith Piaf, had died the day before. It was said that he died of a heart attack on hearing news of the death of his beloved friend.

Earlier, he claimed that his doctors have "torn me from death without bringing me back to life."

At the time of his death, he was working on his unpublished memoirs, *Le Passé défini (The Historical Past)*.

News of his death was broadcast over French National Radio. Flowers arrived from all over France. Maurice Chevalier sent the largest bouquet with this note: "TO THE ONE AND ONLY."

How Mercedes Worshipped at the Temple of
IGOR STRAVINSKY

It was during Mercedes' sojourn in Paris that she was introduced to Igor Stravinsky, the Russian-born (1882) composer, pianist, and conductor, one of the most influential composers of the 20th Century.

He was known for his stylistic diversity, first achieving world fame for three ballets commissioned by the impresario Sergei Diaghilev and performed in Paris by the Ballets Russes: *The Firebird* (1910), *Petrushka* (1911), and *The Rite of Spring* (1913), the latter becoming Mercedes' favorite.

In time, he would also collaborate with Picasso on *Pulcinella*, performed in Paris by the Ballets Russes in May of 1920. Picasso would, in December of that year, do a famous drawing of Stravinsky.

Things did not go well when Mercedes first met Stravinsky. She found him "conceited and ungracious." How-

Igor Stravinsky before his emigration to Los Angeles.

Mercedes asked him if he'd write the music for her play *The Mother of Christ*. But they had artistic differences, and the project never materialized.

Whereas Merdedes wanted the Virgin Mary to be played by a real woman, Stravinsky preferred that She be manifested as some form of radiant light as a symbol and suggestion of her presence.

ever, as she later admitted, "I came to love him and his wife, Vera, when they moved to Hollywood during the war years."

[After an "Exile" in neutral Switzerland, the composer moved to California in September of 1939, a few weeks after France and England declared war on Nazi Germany. By the age of fifty-seven, he was living in West Hollywood. He became a naturalized citizen of the United States at the end of the war.]

At first, he feared that California would be a cultural wasteland, but soon found himself enjoying long evenings, often talking until dawn, with some

Must **The Rite of Spring** be seen as well as heard to be fully understood? YES, emphatically yes.

Here's a photo of the *Tanztheater Wuppertal*, as choreographed by Pina Bausch, performing the fecund, erotically charged ballet that, even in a more decorous presentation in Paris at its opening in 1913 caused fistfights, riots, and screams of outrage.

Stravinsky's *The Rite of Spring* became one of Mercedes' most passionately defended expressions of "music with movement."

of the most talented artists, writers, conductors, and composers, who, like herself, had fled from their homelands in Europe to escape from the invading Nazi armies.

On any given evening at Stravinsky's home, a gathering might include Thomas Mann, Otto Klemperer, Frank Werfel, Arthur Rubenstein, and George Balanchine. A number of British writers also moved into his orbit, notably W.H. Auden, Dylan Thomas, and Christopher Isherwood. The night Mercedes met Aldous Huxley, she found him speaking in French with Stravinsky.

"In Los Angeles during the war, it was my good fortune to meet and get to know some of the leading cultural figures of my era," Mercedes said. "Igor and Vera became like a second family to me. I knew I was in the presence of greatness. The subject I avoided with Igor was politics."

Stravinsky had been an early supporter of Mussolini. In 1930, he had informed the press, "I don't believe that anyone venerates Mussolini more than I do. He is the savior of Italy."

However, by the end of World War II, he played a radically different tune. Having become more or less Americanized, he asserted, "Give me Harry S Truman any day, and I'll be satisfied."

Although he had a lovely wife, the composer also had a roving eye, and he had a reputation as a philanderer, enjoying affairs with a number of notable women, including the fashion designer, Coco Chanel.

Their affair became the inspiration for the novel *Coco and Igor* in 2002, and the movie, *Coco Chanel and Igor Stravinsky* (2009).

As the years moved on, Mercedes saw less and less of the composer. Eventually, he outlived her, dying in April of 1971.

How Mercedes "Danced" with
TAMARA KARASAVINA

While in Paris for a prolonged stay, Mercedes fell in love (from a distance) with the stage presence of Tamara Karasavina (1885-1978), a Russian prima ballerina noted for her beauty.

Mercedes first saw her perform in *L'Oiseau du feu (The Firebird)* and was enraptured by her. "She was a revelation combining the spirit with the body. I was haunted by her artistry and her supreme beauty. She could soar away in the air, leaving her earthly body, floating on the wings of an angel. It was like she was flinging a woman's love into the circus of life. More than any ballerina I ever saw, she made the dance the music of the body with her very soul on display."

After leaving her native Russia, where she had faced many hardships, Tamara—formerly a principal dancer for the Imperial Russian Ballet—arrived in Paris. In time, she became the prima ballerina of the Ballets Russes of Sergei Diaghilev.

She was celebrated for such roles as Lisa in *La Fille mal gardée*, and Tsar Maiden in *The Little Humpbacked Horse*. In 1915, she had famously, and to wide acclaim, performed *Le Corsaire pas de deux*, solidifying her international reputation as a dancer.

By 1910, she was dancing for Diaghilev. Her most famous roles were in the ballets of choreographer Mikhail Fokine, including *Le Spectre de la rose*.

Mercedes never got to meet Tamara in Paris, but then she arrived in New York with a letter of introduction from one of Mercedes' best friends. The letter was from Prince Agoutinsky, a rich Russian aristocrat,

Ballerina **Tamara Karasavina's** greated triumph occurred in 1911, when she danced with Vaslav Nijinsky in *The Firebird*. The production was staged by one of the greatest (and most flamboyant) choreographers of his era, Michel Fokine, who fell in love with her and proposed marriage, but she turned him down.

After that, other than delivering instructions as her choreographer, Fokine never spoke to her again.

who had fled Russia in the immediate aftermath of the Russian Revolution.

Tamara arrived at Mercedes' apartment in New York for a one-night stopover *en route* to Chicago, where she'd been scheduled to dance with Peter Vladimirov in the ballet troupe of Adolf Bolm. According to Mercedes, "From the moment we met, I was charmed by her, and we hugged and embraced as if we were longtime friends coming together."

The champagne flowed that afternoon, but their bonding did not become intimate at the time of their first meeting. Also living at Mercedes' home at the time was her husband, Abram Poole, and her lover, Eva Le Gallienne.

Karasavina with Nijinsky in *Giselle* (1910) as directed by Diaghilev.

Tamara and Mercedes agreed to get together more privately on her return to Manhattan. Mercedes eagerly looked forward to that occasion.

Back in New York, Tamara performed with Vladimirov at the Manhattan Opera House. She invited Mercedes to stand in the wings to watch them perform. She later described that night in her memoirs, commenting on the virile dance style of her partner and Tamara's own exquisite beauty—extreme grace like a swan gliding by, and artistry with which she wooed the audience.

After the performance, Mercedes invited Tamara to her favorite bistro, the Russian Eagle, a gathering place for Russian expatriates.

They were greeted by Max Reinhard and Konstantin Stanislawsky. At one point, Maria Ouspenskaya joined them with a pitcher of Scotch (not vodka). On empty stomachs, Tamara and Mercedes downed too much. They left the restaurant intoxicated, heading for Tamara's suite at the Plaza Hotel.

"After we recovered a bit and ordered black coffee from room service, we made love," Mercedes confessed to Darwin Porter. "It was heavenly. Rarely are two bodies in

Two views of **Karasavina,** each from around 1911.

Upper photo: in *Scheherazade*; lower photo: in the kind of poignantly alluring street clothes that would have sent Mercedes, lesbian-at-large within the arts community, into orbit.

such harmony. Although I'm sure many men had made love to her, she also needed a woman's love and devotion. Before I left her suite at 8AM, we agreed to meet wherever we were, Manhattan, London, Paris, to continue our secret rendezvous with each other, away from the prying eyes of the world."

Tamara survived two marriages, one to civil servant Vasili Mukhin in 1907, a union that lasted a decade, and later to British diplomat Henry James Bruce, whom she wed in 1918. Two years before her wedding to Bruce, she had given birth to their son, Nikita.

Later in life, Tamara moved to London, where she became a major figurehead of British ballet, assisting in the establishment of the Royal Ballet and the Royal Academy of Dance. She occasionally taught ballet, too, her most famous pupils being Rudolf Nureyev and Margot Fonteyn.

Tamara would outlive Mercedes, dying in Buckinghamshire, England, at the age of 93 in May of 1978.

Mercedes always remembered her final nostalgia-soaked rendezvous with Tamara, which occurred very late at night in Paris.

"We sat at a little café in Montmartre once patronized by Picasso and his mistress of the moment," Mercedes said. "We talked until dawn broke across Paris. It was a sad, nostalgic time. Diaghilev had just died in Venice. That August (1929) Nijinsky was in an insane asylum in Switzerland, where Tamara had made a special trip to see him in his sad, tormented condition. She told me he did not know her. When she spoke of Diaghilev, he did not recognize the name of his former mentor and lover either."

As the sun rose, the former lovers kissed each other on the lips.

As she stood at the edge of a square just coming to life, Tamara looked at her woefully and said: "Those glorious days are over. Everything has been taken from us."

"We will always have Paris," Mercedes responded.

[Ironically, that very line was made famous when delivered by Humphrey Bogart to Ingrid Bergman during the closing reel of Casablanca *(1942).]*

Mercedes Jousts with
ALDOUS HUXLEY

Igor Stravinsky, from his home in Hollywood, had introduced Mercedes to Aldous Huxley (1894-1963), the English author and philosopher, who wrote some fifty books. The composer would dedicate his last orchestral composition to Huxley.

Penning his first novel at the age of seventeen, Huxley had his greatest triumph with *Brave New World* in 1932. He would be nominated for the Nobel Prize for Literature seven times.

Long before meeting him, Mercedes had read *Brave New World*. Set in dystopian London, the novel pictured a universe operating on the principles of mass production and Pavlovian conditioning. As Mercedes got to know the author, she was surprised that he resented the success of this one book, feeling that it distracted from the value of other works that he liked equally as well, including *Point Counter Point* (1928).

During her co-habitation with Greta Garbo in Hollywood in the 1930s, Mercedes befriended Huxley, who lived a few houses away. "He was the most intelligent man I ever knew, a walking encyclopedia of world knowledge on almost any subject that came up. I went for long walks with him in the afternoon and sought out his opinions on virtually anything—homosexuality, literature, music, art, and politics."

Huxley, with his wife Maria, whom he'd wed in 1919, had moved to Hollywood in 1937 and remained there until his death at the age of sixty-nine in 1963.

"His Belgian wife, Maria, was a frail little thing, but full of charm and grace," Mercedes said. "She, too, had a quick mind, although nothing to equal her husband's."

"I was somewhat surprised that this learned man turned into a Hollywood movie writer," Mercedes said. "His fellow Englishman, Christopher Isherwood, had lured him into the business. The money was good—$3,000 a week, fancy pay in those days."

Much of the money Huxley earned went to help Jewish refugees flee from Nazi Germany.

Among the film projects he'd worked on was *Madame Curie* (1943), which was envisioned as a comeback vehicle for Greta Garbo, who had retired after the release of *Two-Faced Woman* in 1941. It had bombed at the box office, and the title role of Madame Curie was eventually awarded to Greer Garson instead.

Before that, Huxley had worked on the script for *Pride and Prejudice* (1940). Starring Laurence Olivier and Joan Fontaine, it had been based on the novel by Jane Austen about five husband-hunting sisters.

Huxley also worked on the script for *Jane Eyre* (1944), starring Orson Welles and Fontaine. This was one of Elizabeth Taylor's early movies.

Mercedes said that to define Huxley as a "deep thinker" would be "to damn him with faint praise. He was a humanist and a pacifist, with a growing interest in philosophical mysticism and universalism. *The Doors of Perceptions* (1954) interprets his own psychedelic experiments with mescaline."

Huxley with **Maria Van Nys**, around 1921 lower photo: His labyrinthine intellect was among the most far-reaching and avant-garde and original than anyone else's at the time.

How Mercedes Got Calm & Clairvoyant with the Most Famous Hindu Mystics of Her Era:

MEHER BABA & JIDDU KRISHNAMURTI

"I was a spiritual person but not as deeply intrigued by it as Huxley," Mercedes said. In the 1930s, she became intrigued by Hinduism and sought out the Indian guru, Meher Baba, during his visit to Hollywood. To learn more about his teachings, she was introduced to yoga and meditation.

By 1938, she'd taken up with Ram Gopal, the Hindu dancer, in Hollywood, which marked the beginning of a lifelong friendship. They would later journey to India together to sit at the feet of Ramana Maharshi, the great spiritual leader.

Both Huxley and Mercedes became involved in the teachings of Jiddu Krishnamurti (1895-1986), who was born in Madras when it was still part of British India.

He became famous as a philosopher, public speaker, and writer. When he came to California, he held his lectures while standing under a tree.

One biographical description of Krishnamurti noted, "His interests in-

Left to right, **Meher Baba, Ram Gopal,** and **Jiddu Kirshnamurti**

According to Norina Matchibelli, the socialite who had introduced them, the first time she met Meher Baba, Mercedes felt an overwhelming warmth radiating from him. She rushed into his embrace and asked, "Who are you?" Baba, who had adopted a strict regimen of silence at the time, gestured, "I am you." Then suddenly he spelled out on his board, "Go and bring me your revolver." Mercedes was amazed, for she had told no one about the gun in her car. She went to her car and returned with the revolver, handing it to Baba. He took the bullets out one by one and handed the gun back to her.

Baba then consoled her, "Suicide is not the solution. It only entails rebirth with the same problems all over again. The only solution is God-Realization – to see God in everything. Everything is easy then. Promise me that you will put this revolver away and never again think of suicide."

cluded psychological revolution, the nature of the mind, meditation, inquiry, human relationships, and bringing about a change in society."

Sometimes, Mercedes and Huxley spent long evenings with him, listening as he stressed the need "for a revolution of the psyche in every human being." He claimed that such a revolution could not be brought about by any external entity, be it religious, political, or social.

"Krishnamurti told me I was too evolved to be trying to peddle movie scripts, and he gave Huxley the same advice," she said. "Neither of us heeded his wisdom."

"Movies are a commercial thing, and therefore a bad thing," he told them. "The film world will taint both of your souls."

"Jiddu was dynamic—no, more than that," she said. "He was atomic. As scientists split the atom on the physical plane, he split the core of thought on a spiritual plane."

In some circles, Krishnamurti came to be regarded as the Second Coming of Jesus Christ. *[Meanwhile, his detractors defined him as the Anti-Christ.]*

Even if she didn't follow the guru's advice about her career, she respected and admired him greatly. Although she promoted many of his spiritual beliefs, she set out on a different type of conquest—i.e., to become deeply involved in the lives of, and in some instances, to seduce, some of the 20th Century's greatest female stage and film stars.

***

"I will always remember, with respect and admiration, Mercedes de Acosta," Darwin said, "for reasons that go way beyond the astonishing variety of her affairs. With style, empathy, and verve, she conversed with many of the great intellects of the mid-20th Century. And despite her many failures and disappointments, did her best to respect and perpetuate their legacies."

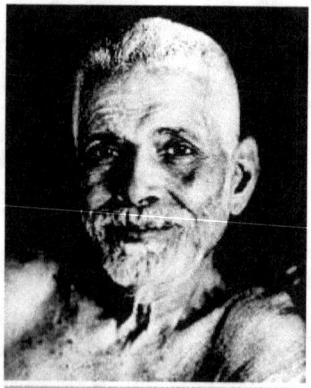

Ramana Maharshi...Mercedes made a journey to India just to sit at his feet.

Socialite **Norina Matchabelli** with **Mercedes de Acosta** and the **Meher Baba** in California, January, 1935.

CHAPTER FOURTEEN
"The Face of the 20th Century"

GARBO THE DIVINE

Shrouded in Mystery, She Reigned as a Goddess of the Moviegoing Public

Her Legend Never Dies

Although the paparazzi salivated at any opportunity to capture Greta Garbo at unguarded private moments, as they did in the photo above, the sight of **Greta Garbo** (right figure in photo above) with her lover, **Mercedes de Acosta** (left) sauntering along Hollywood Boulevard was by then an everyday occurrence to jaded Los Angelenos.

Decades after their passion had died, the details that Mercedes recorded (and later published) about their romantic trysts shocked "ordinary mortals" and absolutely horrified Garbo, who furiously denounced and rejected Mercedes after their publication in 1960.

Although Mercedes' memoir (photo, right) revealed indiscretions about many other bisexual women in Hollywood, too, they focused more extensively on Garbo than on anyone else. Garbo's reaction, according to sources at the time, was "litigious and volcanic."

Garbo

"I have known and seduced some of the most famous and glamourous goddesses of the 20th Century, including Marlene Dietrich. But Greta Garbo is in a class by herself. Her unique allure, her legend, her fabled beauty will live forever. Her fame was—and is—the equal of Cleopatra."

—**Mercedes de Acosta**

"Maybe it was like the dreams you have when someone you have seen in the cinema comes to your bed at night and is so kind and lovely. He could remember Garbo still. Maybe it was like those dreams the night before the attack on Pozoblanco, and Garbo was wearing a soft silky wool sweater when he put his arms around her, and when she leaned forward, and her hair swept forward and over his face, and she said why he had never told her that he loved her when she had loved him all the time...and it was true as though it had happened."

—**Ernest Hemingway**, in For Whom the Bell Tolls (1940), perhaps the only erotic reference to a movie star he ever made

For aficionados, the bisexual actress, Greta Garbo, remains a passionate obsession, a subject of adoration, speculation, and intrigue—elusive, exotic, and ethereal beauty. Almost a century after her heyday, she reigns as a cult figure for the ages, an enigmatic woman, a mysterious goddess who enthralled the embittered members of "The Lost Generation" who flocked to see her in, among others, *Flesh and the Devil* (1927) and *Love* (1927).

With a seductive image that combined the spiritual with the sensual, her mystique appealed to women in ways that were just as compelling as her allure to men.

Although her most enduring lesbian relationship was with Mercedes de Acosta, other same-sex interludes were documented with Marlene Dietrich and Louise Brooks. Among the men who (at least temporarily) adored her, her most publicized love affair was with John Gilbert, the reigning matinee idol of the silent screen, followed by, Joseph P. Kennedy and Robert Taylor, her handsome co-star in *Camille* (1936).

Part of her image (and a gnawing and

Greta Garbo as she looked in her native Stockholm in 1925. Her magic and mystery live on into the 21st Century, even in the minds of people who have never seen one of her films. In this photograph, she is already a svelte and alluring creature.

persistent aspect of her personality) was restlessness and a chronic lack of fulfillment: In reference to her illustrious roll call of lovers, she proclaimed, "I have .tried everything at various times of my life, but my body and thoughts were never satisfied."

She emerged from Viking ancestors to become the most charismatic actress to grace the silver screen. In picture after picture, from silent to talkies, she mesmerized audiences who flocked to see her in *Mata Hari, Grand Hotel, Queen Christina, Anna Karenina, Camille,* and *Ninotchka.*

Early in World War II, when audiences in England, France, and Germany were denied access to her films, she abandoned moviemaking altogether. Despite numerous, often frantic and potentially lucrative offers, she relegated her contribution to the art form to films she'd already made. She spent the rest of her life running from the press, trying to shield her face from photographers, some of whom began referring to her as "The Swedish Sphinx."

For the luminous quality of her power on the screen, she also became forever labeled as "The Divine Garbo," a woman of incomparable beauty.

Who was she—and how did it begin?

A Swedish Working-Class Maiden Meets Her Svengali

For a woman of the world who would later enjoy some of its greatest luxuries (including sailing aboard Aristotle Onassis' yacht), Greta Lovisa Gustafsson was born on September 18, 1905 in a seedy coldwater flat on the fourth floor of a tenement building.

She came into the world in Södermalm, a working class district of Stockholm. Her early childhood was described as "Dickensian and Stringbergian." She was born with the help of a midwife in an apartment that was freezing cold in winter, where she would huddle up in bed with her older sister. The overworked toilet for all the occupants of the building was located in a smelly corner of its garbage-strewn courtyard.

Her alcoholic father, Karl Alfred Gustafsson (1871-1920), was often unemployed, suffering from frequent illnesses, including nephritis (severe inflammation of the kidneys). When he was willing and able, he found occasional part-time work as a butcher's assistant, factory worker, night watchman,

Garbo, an icon of glamour,. had tough, cold, working-class origins in a grimy, coldwater flat. Pictured above, 2nd from right, is her father, **Karl Alfred Gustafsson,** hard at work in a late 19th century slaughterhouse.

grocery clerk, and street cleaner.

Her mother, Anna Lovisa (1872-1944), was a course, fat woman who earned money at various odd shops, once working as a cleaning lady in a jam factory, and also taking in sewing. Greta had an older brother, Sven Alfred, and an older sister, Alva Maria, who died young in 1926, just as Greta was breaking into world fame in Hollywood as a star of silent pictures.

"I was the youngest of my siblings," Greta said, "but I was treated like I was the oldest. No one ever thought of me as a little girl."

When money was lean, or unavailable, the Gustafsson family often ate at a local soup kitchen maintained by the Salvation Army.

With almost no interest in schoolwork, Greta harbored a dream of becoming an actress on the stage. She never attended high school, and although she later wined and dined with some of the most illustrious men and women on the planet—including Sir Winston Churchill and icons from the world of theater, film, and music—she was always sensitive about her very limited formal education. As a teenager, she found work as a "lather

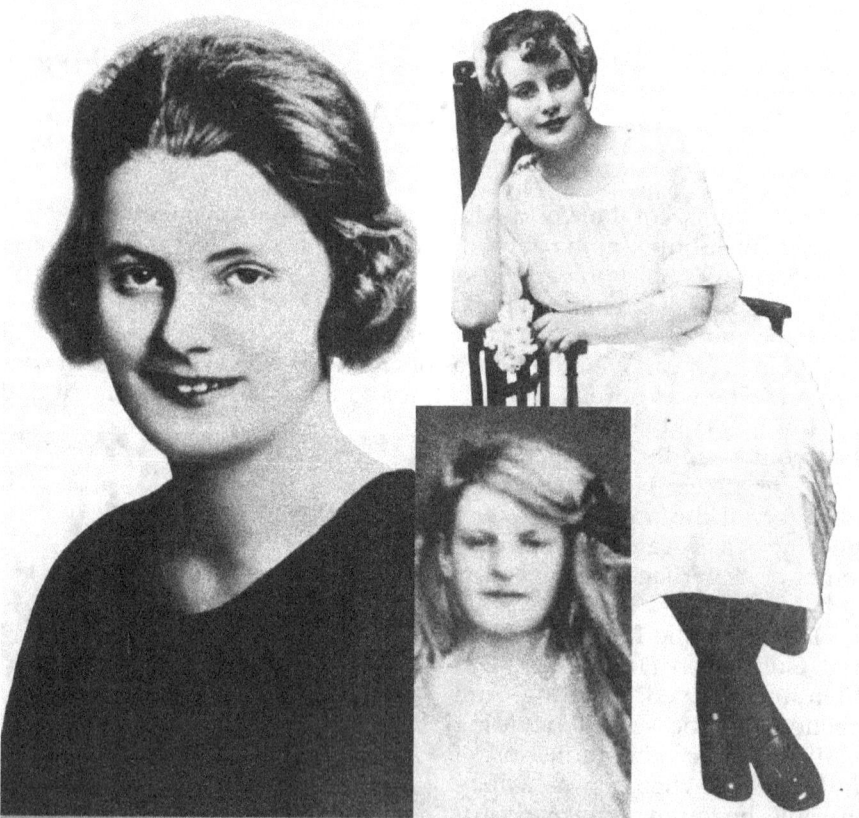

Three views of young **Greta Garbo**, a far cry from the formidably glamourous icon she became. Snapped on the left at age seventeen, she said, "When I am left to myself, I long so dreadfully for the theater."

girl" in a local barbershop, a job she loathed.

The fragile state of her father's health worsened when the "Spanish flu" pandemic hit Stockholm in 1918, the final year of World War I. Greta walked with him once a week to a local hospital for treatment. In 1920, two months before her fifteenth birthday, Karl died at the age of forty-eight.

Greta eventually found a job in the millinery department of the PUB department store, where she was paid the equivalent of twenty-five dollars a month to model hats for their 1921 spring catalog. It marked the beginning of her career posing for cameras.

Sometimes at night, if she could afford it, she'd buy one of cheapest tickets (sometimes for "standing room") tickets to productions at various theaters. A stage-struck teenager, she maintained a ferocious grip on her dream of becoming a stage actress.

It was around this time that she developed an unusual menstrual cycle, generating bleeding and discharge at least once a week. A gynecologist told her that her (rare and unusual) condition was "incurable" and that there was nothing she could do about it. As a remedy, he recommended long walks and "natural foods."

When she became romantically involved with Mercedes de Acosta in the 1930s, she confessed that she masturbated a great deal while looking at photographs of her favorite movie stars. She also admitted that she'd had her first sexual experience when she was fourteen. It was with her older sister during one of their summer camping trip.

She lost her virginity to a male in an interlude with Max Gumpel, a 31-year-old construction engineer. He came into the photographer's studio to see his nephew, who was modeling men's spring fashions at the same time

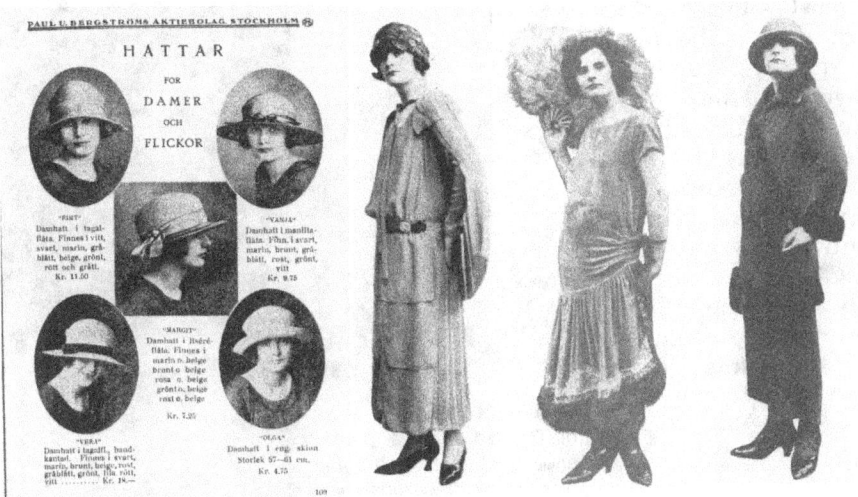

Pre-Hollywood **Greta Garbo** modeling five different styles of hats (left) and dresses, each the height of turn-of-the-20th-century chic, for Stockholm's PUB Department store, and developing the 'camera sense" for which she later became famous.

that Greta was showcasing hats for PUB department store.

Gumpel was taken with her beauty and flirted with her, perhaps the first man to ever do so. She found herself attracted to him and accepted his invitation to visit his home after she got off from work. As she later revealed, she was introduced to three new things before the night ended: a bubble bath; a globe artichoke at dinner, and a man's penis.

LUFFAR-PETTER
(AKA, PETER THE TRAMP; 1922)

SWEDISH TEENAGER FALLS DESPERATELY (AND SCANDALOUSLY) FOR A SOLDIER

Her modeling gig for PUB led to Greta being cast in her first film role, *Peter the Tramp* (*Luffar-Petter* in Swedish) released in 1922. The producer-writer Erik A. Petschler spotted a photo in which Greta had modeled and cast her as one of the daughters of the town's mayor, who gets involved with a soldier stationed in her town. The film called for her to appear in a bathing suit with two other girls in the Swedish countryside. Petschler cast himself as the film's male lead, Peter.

The film had obviously been inspired by those comedies being turned out in Hollywood at the time by Mack Sennett. The first review Greta Gustafsson ever got read, "She may perhaps become a Swedish film star. Reason: Her Anglo-Saxon appearance."

In closeup, she appears rather plump, and in need of that MGM dentist in Hollywood, who, in the near future, would get her crooked teeth straightened.

Luffar-Petter: Two views of **Garbo** and a poster showing her as a bathing beauty in a decorously unrevealing one-piece bathing suit.

THE SAGA OF GÖSTA BERLING (1924)
A CINEMATIC RENDERING OF A SWEDISH GIGOLO AND WOMAN WHOSE LOVE SET HIM STRAIGHT

A year would go by before Mauritz Stiller, the "King of Swedish Cinema," entered her life—and changed it forever.

For his next picture, *The Story of Gösta Berling* (1924), he was looking for a female lead to star as Selma Lagerlöf's heroine. The romantic drama was based on her debut novel, published in 1891, for which she would win the Nobel Prize for literature.

As a young girl, Greta had "devoured" the novel, the saga of a defrocked Lutheran vicar who is sacked because of his "inappropriate lifestyle." He operates as a male hustler to a rich woman until he meets and falls madly in love with Elizabeth Dohna (Greta). They run away and start a new life together.

At the time, Greta was enrolled in the *Dramatens Teaterns Elevskola*, Sweden's Royal Academy of the Theater Arts. Her acting had impressed its director, Gustaf Mohlander. When Stiller approached him for advice about any of his "unknowns" who might perform believably in his upcoming film, the director recommended Greta. A meeting as arranged for the following day at his apartment.

As an avid patron of her era's films, Greta was already familiar with his name, as he had shot forty-four movies in Swedish.

An effete homosexual, he had been born in 1883 in Helsinki, the Duchy of Finland, then part of the Russian Empire. His early life had been marked with tragedy. He had lost both of his Jewish parents when he was only four years old, forcing him to be raised in a foster home.

Left photo: With **Mauritz Stiller** (second figure from left), imperiously directing, and with a support staff that looks something like an ambulance corps during World War I, **Greta** appears on the far right emoting with her co-star, **Lars Hanson.**

Right photo, **Greta** as the female lead in the film adaptation of the potboiler that everyone was reading, *The Saga of Gosta Berling*.

When he was notified of his imminent induction into the Czarist Army, he fled from Finland and moved to Sweden, where he quickly mastered its language. In 1912, he worked in that country's film industry and quickly rose through its ranks. In 1921, he became a citizen of Sweden.

When he met Greta, he was forty years old, and she was only seventeen. Although he found her "a tad chubby," he was immediately impressed with her. First, he told her, "Greta is a fine marquee name, but there are already too many people in Sweden named Gustafsson. Your last name must be changed. How about Gabor? Greta Gabor....No, not that...From now on, your name will be Greta Garbo. I will see to it that your name one day—sooner than later—will be celebrated worldwide."

He thus became her mentor, teaching her how to talk, how to walk, how to act, and how to dress.

To her, at least, Stiller was rather strange. Standing more than six feet tall, he had hands and feet so large as to almost be deformed. His face was adorned with a mustache, and brooding gray eyes. His tailored Savile Row suits from London prompted his detractors to refer to him as "the Grand Duke." Diamonds studded his shirt, and he was always seen in a sunflowery yellow overcoat that descended to a point only three inches above the floor.

Demanding, imperious, and remembered in film history as the mentor who launched The Divine Garbo, Finno-Swedish director, **Mauritz Stiller**. Upper photo: with young **Greta Garbo**.

A Garbo biographer, John Bainbridge, wrote, "[Stiller's] manner was attractive, though his temperament mercurial. He was intense, talented, ambitious, noisy, egotistical, troubled, and brutally outspoken."

Garbo adapted herself to the fact that he wore so much perfume that it was "most intoxicating to be too close to him."

Tragedy struck on New Year's Day of 1923 when Axel Esbensen, the set decorator for *Gösta Berling*, committed suicide after Stiller announced he was breaking up with him.

Stiller had abandoned and replaced him with Lars Hanson, who was introduced to Garbo as her leading man. Hanson (1886-1965) was known as a handsome blonde with "porcelain hands" and an exquisite profile similar to that of John Barrymore.

Hanson first became well-known as a Shakespearean actor starring in

Swedish-language interpretations of both *Hamlet* and *Othello*. In 1915, Stiller cast him in the film *Dolken*. After that, his popularity grew until he became one of his country's most famous actors. Like Garbo, he was shipped off to Hollywood, this time at the request of Lillian Gish. He was also engaged in a "lavender marriage" to the Swedish screen actress, Karin Molander.

[Hanson became known as a master of disguise for whatever role he was assigned, "accessorizing" himself with padding to make himself look bigger or smaller, starving himself or bulking himself up with overeating, deliberately bruising his face, and altering key aspects of his appearance, sometimes to the point that fellow actors who had known him for years sometimes didn't recognize him backstage.]

Although Garbo got good reviews, Selma Lagerlöf (the author of the novel the film was based on) detested its screen adaptation. The film met an even better reception and generated bigger box office in Germany. In September of 1924, Stiller was invited to Berlin for its German premiere, and he asked Garbo to accompany him for the Weimar Republic's equivalent of a press and promotional tour.

Even though **Lars Hanson**, pictured above, lay almost nightly on Stiller's casting couch, the director did not hold him in high regard.

Stiller put him through scenes where he suffered cuts and bruises. Once, in a fire scene, Hanson screamed, "I'm burning!" Help! I'm on fire!"

"Burn a little longer," Stiller shouted back at him." At least until I finish this shot!"

Grande Dame of Swedish letters, novelist **Selma Lagerlof.**

She wrote *Gösta Berling* while teaching school in her native Värmland. In time, Bosley Crowther of *The New York Times* would label her as "The Bard of Sweden."

ODALISQUE FROM SMOLNEY
(NEVER RELEASED)
THINLY DISGUISED EROTICISM WITHIN A CONTEXT OF SLAVERY, DEGRADATION AND SHAME

Gösta Berling was such a big hit in Germany that Stiller was offered directorship of a film that involved location shooting in Turkey. Two separate film enterprises (one German, one Swedish) advanced funds for him to shoot *Odalisque from Smolney* in Constantinople (later Istanbul). It was the titillating but tear-jerking "morality tale" of a young girl who flees from the (Smolney) convent in St. Petersburg and ends up, ruined, in a Turkish harem. Garbo was enrolled as the aristocratic Russian beauty who's sold into slavery.

It was in Constantinople that Mercedes de Acosta first laid eyes on Garbo, mistaking her for a Russian princess. "One day in the lobby of the *[historic, posh, and very expensive]* Pera Palace Hotel, where I was staying, I saw one of the most hauntingly beautiful women I have ever beheld."

Extravagant and spendthrift, Stiller proceeded to waste a huge part of his film budget before any scenes had been filmed. The backers in Berlin pulled the plug during a corruption and political scandal associated with the Weimar Republic's government, and the movie was never made.

Temporarily defeated, Stiller and Garbo returned to Berlin, using the rest of the film's budget to live in luxury at the Esplanade Hotel. "Something will turn up, I just know it," he said.

How right he was.

Garbo, right, with an unidentified companion, left, in Constantinople (now Istanbul) in 1924.

Three good-looking Swedes, wide-eyed and footloose amid the decadence of Weimar Berlin in 1924.

Left to right, actress **Gerda Lundquist**, director **Mauritz Stiller**, and **Greta Garbo**.

"What?" you might ask, "is an odalisque?" **François Boucher** (1703-1770, perhaps the finest painter and decorative artist of the French 18th Centuery, envisioned one like this in his *Portrait of an Odalisque*

DIE FREUDLOSE GASSE
(THE STREET OF SORROW; 1925)
WHEN BAD GIRLS SUFFER AND DIE, GOOD GIRLS GET REWARDED AND GO TO HEAVEN

Garbo's next film offer came not from her long-time mentor, Mauritz Stiller, but from G.W. Pabst, the Austrian movie director and screenwriter.

[Although he was a relative newcomer to film-making, in time, he'd be known for his discoveries of major stars, not only Greta Garbo (he and Stiller fought for that honor), but Asta Nielsen, Louise Brooks (Pandora's Box; 1929), and the spectacularly infamous Leni Riefenstahl, who later produced and directed propaganda films for the Third Reich. In time, Pabst would be acclaimed for his direction of the 1931 musical film version of Die 3 Groschen-Oper (The Threepenny Opera), *starring Lotte Lenya and created by Bertolt Brecht and Kurt Weill.]*

Bruised from her previous role as a Russian "odalisque" in a film deal that had failed, Greta—now directed by the young, still-green Pabst—was assigned a role as Greta Rumfort, the second female lead in a film that was eventually distributed with a trio of names. In the German-speaking world, it was *Die freudlose Gasse* (1925); in the UK it was distributed as *The Joyless Street;* and in the U.S. it was called *The Street of Sorrow.* In it, Greta's character would suffer for her (accidental) fall from grace, and eventually be rewarded for her virtues.

Greta portrays a dutiful daughter to an ailing father, members of a struggling Viennese family impoverished by World War I. She is saved from having to prostitute herself in a bordello by the romantic and dashing Lieutenant Davis, portrayed by Einar Hanson, a handsome Swedish actor who was Stiller's lover at the time. *[Einar Hanson (1899-1927) is not to be confused with the previously mentioned Lars Hanson (1886-1965), who was no longer emotionally involved with Stiller.]* Stiller had de-

Top: **Einar Hanson**; middle: **Greta Garbo**, where she's about to become a desperate woman of ill repute; and bottom, a poster for *The Street of Sorrow*.

manded that Pabst cast Einar Hanson as *Die freudlose Gasse's* romantic hero, making it contingent on his securing (or not securing) the participation of Greta.

[Ironically, in a complicated "rondelay" of thwarted mentorships and romantic ambitions, Stiller—in a fit of jealous rag—accused Garbo, his protégée, of having a "casting couch affair" with Pabst as a means of securing her role in Freudlose Gasse. According to gossipy rumors at the time, as a means of wreaking revenge, Stiller "pimped" a deal with a syphilitic prostitute to snare Pabst into bed, with the vengeful hope that he'd contract a venereal disease.]

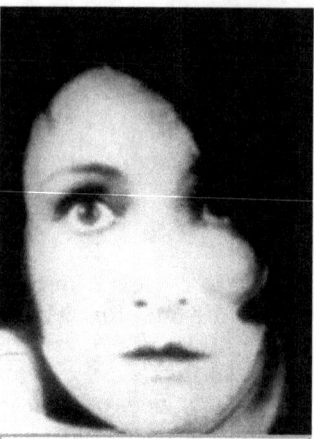

A tight closeup of **Marlene Dietrich** in an uncredited part in *Die Freudlose Gasse*.

She and Garbo had an affair.

Top billing in *Freudlose Gasse* went to the Danish star, Asta Nielsen. Cast as the female lead, Maria Lechner, she was known for her large, dark eyes, inscrutable, mask-like face, and boyish figure. Although relatively unknown in America, where her films were demeaned as "too erotic," she was one of the first silent film stars to become internationally famous in Europe.

Cast as Metzger von Melchiorstrasse, the local butcher, Werner Krauss was a famous German stage and screen actor, and the most politically notorious figure Greta would ever work with. He had played the demonic title role of Dr. Caligari in Robert Wiene's then very *avant-garde* film, *The Cabinet of Dr. Caligari* (1920), screened in film studies courses today as a milestone in German Expressionism.

However, it is for his work with Josef Goebbels, the Nazi Propaganda Minister, for which Krauss would be forever associated and condemned. During the opening years of World War II, in his officially designated capacity as a cultural ambassador of Nazi Germany (for which he was exempt from military service), Krauss pejoratively portrayed six "stereotypically Jewish" *[his words]* characters in the most anti-Semitic movie ever filmed, the vulgar hate-mongering *Jud Süss* (1940).

***

Although both Marlene Dietrich and Greta Garbo denied for decades that they had ever known each other, they appeared in their one and only film together in *Die freudlose Gasse*.

In an unbilled role, Dietrich comes to the aid of Greta, the film's second lead, when she faints from starvation in a line of shoppers waiting for hours to buy meat from a butcher.

The two aspirant actresses bonded at once, each powerfully attracted to the other. Soonafter, they began a passionate affair, and were seen together at the White Mouse Cabaret, then hailed as the most notorious lesbian bar in Berlin, and cuddled together at the Eldorado Club, a drag venue in that (then very permissive) city. *[The Eldorado was said to have provided inspiration for one of Christopher Isherwood's* Berlin Stories, *later adapted into the musical* Cabaret *(1972), Liza Minnelli's most famous movie.]*

When *Street Without Joy* was released in the U.S., *Variety* wrote: "The picture's only commercial value is the presence in the cast of Greta Garbo, although her role is a poor one, that of a furtive and bedraggled heroine."

The English critic Paul Rotha compared Garbo's frail beauty to that of an ice flower warmed by the sun.

THE TORRENT (1926)
A ROMANTIC ODE TO LOST LOVE AS A SPANISH MILKMAID (HOLLYWOOD'S NEWEST VAMP!) ILLUMINATES THE STAGES OF PARIS

As a highlight of his European tour in search of emerging screen talent for MGM, Louis B. Mayer arrived in Berlin on November 26, 1924. He had been informed that Mauritz Stiller, a director of Swedish films, was a possible talent who should be interviewed.

The next day, Stiller was ushered into Mayer's suite at the *[very posh]* Adlon Hotel. A translator accompanied him. Mayer was informed that the German-language version of his film, *The Story of Gösta Berling,* was scoring big at the box office, and he invited Mayer to go see it.

Two days later, after Mayer had seen the film with his daughters, he met again with Stiller. Stiller said he'd welcome signing a contract with MGM, but he also requested a contract for the newly emerging Greta Garbo, then nineteen years old. Whereas Mayer had been intrigued with Stiller's direction of the picture, he was fascinated by Garbo's screen *persona*. In advance of any signature, however, he clearly warned Stiller, "She'll have to lose weight. American men don't like fat women."

The next day, Garbo herself was ushered into Mayer's suite at the Adlon. He found her "very nervous. Insecure, but quite sensual."

Before departing from Berlin, Stiller and Garbo signed MGM contracts which went into effect on January 30, 1925. The deal included their passage to California. She would be paid a starting salary of $400 a week with periodic raises.

As it turned out, it wasn't until July 7 that Stiller and Garbo sailed into the

MGM publicity photo: **Garbo** and **Stiller,** in transit from Sweden via Germany and on their way to Hollywood, arrive at the Port of New York.

Port of New York aboard the Swedish liner *SS Drottningholm*.

After a whirlwind tour of New York City, taking in Broadway shows, both of them arrived in Los Angeles. When they reported to work at Culver City, they found no film assignments. Stiller had envisioned directing Garbo in her first Hollywood motion picture. Each of them would need translators fluent in Swedish.

It had already been established that their point of contact would not be Mayer, but a young Irving Thalberg, the "Boy Wonder" of MGM. Stiller and Thalberg came into conflict during their

MGM publicity cameras were there to record the arrival of **Garbo and Stiller** in Los Angeles after their cross-continental train ride.

first-ever meeting, when Thalberg demanded that Garbo submit to a screen test. She hadn't known that she'd be subjected to that, but she went through with it. When Thalberg saw it, he told Stiller, "We've got to send her to our MGM dentist and do something about those teeth. And, oh my god, that hair....I hope our best hairdresser can do something with it."

Awaiting an assignment, Garbo had checked into the Miramar Hotel in Santa Monica. Stiller lived nearby in a rented beach house. As the weeks went by, they made friends with the Swedish expatriates working in the film industry, most of whom they already knew, including Lars Hanson, Greta's co-star in *Gösta Berling* and Stiller's former lover. They also bonded with Victor Seastrom (Sjöström).

***

Finally, after many neurotic weeks had passed, a film assignment was directed at Garbo. Norma Shearer had rejected the lead role in *The Torrent*, eventually released in 1926. It was based on a novel, *The Four Horsemen of the Apocalypse* by Vicente Blasco Ibáñez. Its 1921 film adaptation had made a star out of Rudolph Valentino.

The title (*The Torrent*) derived from a poetic interpretation of the feelings of its protagonists: "A torrent as furious and relentless as the passion in the hearts of the ill-fated lovers.'

Stiller was deeply disappointed that he had not been designated as its director. Instead, the post was assigned to the producer and screenwriter Monta Bell, a former reporter from Washington, D.C. Refusing to abandon his involvement in Garbo's "training," Stiller demanded that she let him "direct and transform" her at night, prepping her for the next day's shooting.

Before Garbo's research for her first day of filming at MGM, she assumed that her leading man, Ricardo Cortez, was Mexican. To her surprise, she learned that he had been born to Jewish parents in New York City, and that he'd changed his name from Jacob Krantz to Ricardo Cortez in an attempt to capitalize on the Latin Lover craze then sweeping through Hollywood. Its beneficiaries had included the late Rudolph Valentino, Ramon Novarro, and Antonio Moreno.

In the year that *The Torrent* was released, Cortez would enter into a lavender marriage to the heroin-addicted Alma Rubens as a means of concealing his homosexuality. His lover, a young actor who was never formally introduced to Garbo, hung around awkwardly on the set every day.

The plot called for Garbo to play a Spanish peasant, Leonora Moreno, who falls in love with Don Rafael (Cortez). Don Rafael has been born into wealth, and his domineering matriarch Doña Bernarda Brull (Martha Mattox) stridently opposes her son's marriage to Leonora.

Aching with unrequited love, the spurned bride abandons her sleepy village and moves to Paris, where she becomes a singing sensation known as "La Brunna." Rich noblemen besotted with love literally throw themselves at her feet.

In time, jaded and world-weary, she returns to her humble Spanish town, finding that Don Rafael's passion for her is still on fire, despite his (newest) commitment to marry Remedios Matías (Gertrude Olmstead).

This picture of **Garbo** and **Ricardo Cortez** in *The Torrent* was misleading.

On screen, they were lovers; off screen they hated each other, Cortez referring to her as "Miss Dumb Bitch."

Right in front of him, she said, "If only Rudolph Valentino were alive to star opposit me. Rudy and I could have electrified the screen."

Sadder but wiser, Leonora returns to Paris as a sophisticated rouée, lamenting her lost love.

Throughout the shoot, Garbo conflicted with both her co-star (Cortez) and her director (Bell). As she told Stiller, "Cortez is most disagreeable, very rude, and difficult to work with. I find playing love scenes with him revolting. Bell attacks me all the time, and Cortez calls me 'Big Foot.' When I was a few minutes late on the set, Bell yelled through his megaphone, 'Will someone go and get that fat woman?'"

Cameraman Williams Daniels became her favorite film technician. No one would ever take greater care in photographing Garbo. "I found her best features and emphasized them. Her eyes were magnificent. Those long lashes were real, not artificial. In certain moods, I could throw the light from quite high, and show the shadows of the eyelashes coming down on her cheeks. It became a sort of trademark for her."

Because of language difficulties, Thalberg hired a "Viking god," a

Swedish wannabe actor named Hugo Borg, as Garbo's translator. He became much more than that, and an affair ensued with this "Body Beautiful" (Garbo's words). According to Stiller, she defined Borg as "My love slave."

Well educated, he spoke perfect English, remaining at Garbo's side throughout the day and in her bed at night. In time, he impregnated her, but the MGM abortion doctor took care of that.

Borg later told Stiller, "Our son, if he'd been allowed to live, would have been a stunning beauty. Me, the father, Garbo, the mother. He would have become the matinee idol of the world. But even though she absolutely adores children, Garbo opted to end his life. Thalberg didn't want a scandal to wreck her career before it was launched."

One scene in *The Torrent* called for Garbo to sit astride a horse, with the understanding that the animal had to slide through a sea of mud. As her stunt double, a fourteen-year-old boy, Joel McCrea, an aspirant actor, was hired for this dangerous feat. In the years to come, be became one of the biggest stars of Golden Age Hollywood.

After sitting through a screening, Mayer declared that Garbo was "an electrifying presence on the screen. She'll go over big with our (profitable) European market, as perhaps she's too sophisticated for our American audiences."

Garbo with her translator, **Sven Hugo Borg**, on the set of *The Torrent*. Here is how Wikipedia describes him:

"Sven Hugo Borg was born in Vinslöv, Skåne, Sweden. Early in his career, Borg was a secretary with the Swedish Consulate in Los Angeles. While working at the consulate he met the actress Greta Garbo who had recently arrived in Hollywood. Garbo asked Borg to be her interpreter for an upcoming movie to which he readily agreed. He served as her interpreter from 1925 to 1929. After interpreting for Greta, Borg decided to pursue acting as a career. He had done some dramatic work on the Swedish stage. He continued to remain with the consulate until the late 1930s.

"Borg became much in demand during World War II Hollywood films, playing both Nazi officers and Scandinavian resistance fighters. Throughout his acting career, Borg was an actor who portrayed a wide range of many different characters, e.g. Sverre—King of Norway in *The Crusades*. He died in 1981 at the age of 84 in Los Angeles."

Thalberg asserted, "In Garbo, we've found our vamp, MGM's answer to Paramount's Gloria Swanson and Pola Negri."

Variety hailed Garbo as "a girl who has everything—looks, acting ability, and personality." Richard Watts Jr. in the *New York Herald Tribune*, stressed Garbo's evocation of Gloria Swanson, referring to her as "Gloria (sic) Garbo, puffing languidly on a cigarette."

Motion Picture found her "pretty, wistful, and intensely feminine, suggesting a composite picture of our best-known stars."

Mercedes de Acosta told her lesbian friends, "It was sitting through

The Torrent that I fell in love with Greta Garbo. Her looks have been compared to Norma Talmadge, but Norma can't carry Garbo's makeup kit. She is the new enchantress of the Silver Screen, a goddess, really. I have always had this great intuition. I predict that Garbo will become the greatest of all screen actresses. Her unique personality and startling beauty will enchant the world. But, first, I've got to meet her."

THE TEMPTRESS (1926)
VAMPINESS, CAMPINESS, UNEXPRESSED LUST, & UNREQUITED LOVE

In the 1926 silent melodrama of jealousy and degradation, *The Temptress*, Greta Garbo (a bisexual) played opposite the mostly homosexual Latin heartthrob, Antonio Moreno. Reverberations of Stoker's vampirism were audible in a toast "to the temptress, who asks for nothing, but takes everything a man can give . . . and more!"

Although Garbo's mentor, Mauritz Stiller, had been hired to direct his *protégée*, on the first day of shooting, he clashed with Moreno, the film's male lead. Stiller had demanded that Moreno shave off his (trademark) mustache. Next, he insisted that Moreno wear larger (clumsier) shoes as a means of making Garbo's feet look smaller.

From there, morale on the set went steadily downhill until MGM fired Stiller after only 10 days. Garbo wanted to walk off the picture in protest, but at Stiller's urging, she stayed on until the bitter end, even though she detested Moreno and evaluated love scenes with him as "disgusting."

As a replacement for Stiller, Fred Niblo, who had "saved" MGM's *Ben Hur* the year before, was called in to direct. Consistent with her increasing reputation as a difficult-to-direct diva,

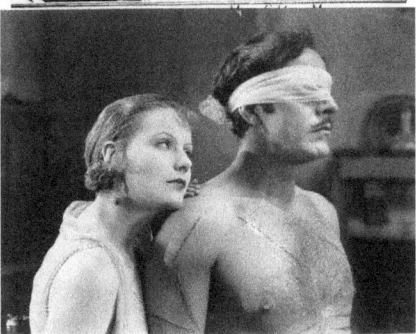

Campy, vampy, and spectacularly over the top, **Garbo** with whipped, scarred, and blindfolded **Antonio Moreno.**

Garbo found him "less than inspiring. He seems to think I'm a horse in his damn chariot race."

The plot was set in Paris and Argentina. The Paris scenes are most effective, the scenes in Argentina less so. Garbo plays Elena, the Marquess of Torre Blanca. At a masked ball in Paris, she meets Manuel Robledo (Moreno), a young and handsome Argentine architect who becomes enthralled with her, even though she's married to an effete dilettante, "The Marquis," portrayed by Marc MacDermott. He doesn't mind "lending" his wife to a banker who's about to extend an important loan.

Learning that she's married, Manuel returns to his native Argentina where he's hired to direct the construction of a dam. Elena follows him there.

The most dramatic scene in the film — sadists will take delight — takes place in Argentina. The villain of the piece, the rather ridiculous Roy D'Arcy, is challenged to a bola fight (i.e., a whip duel). D'Arcy has been harassing Elena, and Manuel sets out to defend her honor.

The whip duel is long and vicious, both men suffering cuts and lashes on their naked chests. Of course, thug D'Arcy is vanquished. At the end of the duel, Elena gratefully kisses and licks the blood from her hero's chest, a bit kinky for the easily shocked audiences of 1926.

D'Arcy added to the closeted "queer quotient" of the cast. He was a boyfriend of Ramon Novarro, Hollywood most notorious homosexual of the late 20s.

Upper photo: **Garbo** as *The Temptress*,

Lower photo: **Garbo** and **Antonio Moreno** as the Argentinean architect who adores her.

In this dramatic scene, she rushes to comfort him, his bare chest showing the bloody scars resulting from a whip duel that had also momentarily blinded him.

What are our favorite lines of subtitled "dialogue" from this silent film?

MORENO: Men have died and killed and been destroyed for you.
ELENA: Not for me, but for my body. Not for my happiness, but theirs.

As a Latin man, Moreno's amorous character is seeking the Madonna, and he definitely wants a virgin. That the Marquess is not. As one reviewer quipped: "Moreno wants retroactive rights to her body as well as universal rights to her soul."

Predictably, Garbo's Elena will fall on bad days. In some ways she foreshadows Tennessee Williams' doomed Blanche DuBois in *A Streetcar Named Desire*. In the final reel she's back in Paris sitting in a café, sodden with wine, half out of her mind and diseased, pursuing the lower end of a trade that's been called "the world's oldest profession."

That was the sad ending. MGM also filmed an alternative "happy" ending, and exhibitors were given a choice.

Some reviewers have suggested that although *The Temptress* has many flaws, the seeds of Garbo's future greatness are planted here. Yet despite the film's provocative title and its heavy breathing, Garbo does not evoke the devil's daughter. She even comes across as somewhat passive, looking supremely gorgeous as silly, infatuated, lovesick men throw their hearts away like discarding a pit from an overripe plum. And it's not without hyperbole: the character played by Lionel Barrymore, a closeted gay in real life, is driven to jealous murder at the mere sight of Elena.

Garbo as *The Temptress*.

It was hard for audiences to believe she was only nineteen.

One reviewer noted that Garbo wanders through *The Temptress* "like a world traveler without a passport, renting her body out to many men but pledging her love to only one. To her, sex is a pleasant time-killer, marriage a nonbinding contract, but love is a sacred vow."

Garbo was only nineteen when she vamped her way through Blasco-Ibáñez's soapy melodrama, her second film shot in America. Being Garbo, she appears far more worldly and sophisticated than any teenager we've known. Even so, this is hardly vintage Garbo of the incandescent soul. Many of her gestures seem painted on like Pinocchio's smile. When she rolls her eyes back and forth, it comes across as mechanical, like something you'd expect from Betty Boop.

Not all critics of that era agreed. Even at such an early stage, Garbo had already begun to weave her magic spell.

Dorothy Herzog of the *New York Mirror* penned her reviews as if she were in love with Garbo: "Greta Garbo vitalizes the name part of this picture. She is The Temptress. Her tall, swaying figure moves Cleopatra-ishly from delirious Paris to the virile Argentine. Her alluring mouth and volcanic, slumberous eyes entice men to such passion that friendships collapse."

Garbo and Moreno were an uneasy couple. During filming of *The Temptress* they had many fights, and playing a convincing love scene was most difficult. Fred Niblo always claimed he knew the reason for their feud: One hot afternoon, when tension between Garbo and Moreno had reached a breaking point, Moreno insultingly retorted: "You're not the only one John Gilbert fucks."

[In addition to moments of periodic intimacy with Gilbert, Moreno also "bottomed" for some of the leading lights of the silent screen, including "the great lover" himself, Rudolph Valentino.]

FLESH AND THE DEVIL (1927)
GARBO'S HOMOEROTIC LOVE TRIANGLE

In a 113-minute silent made in 1927, MGM teamed Garbo (as Felicitas) with her off-screen lover, John Gilbert, cast as Leo von Harden. The third member of this love triangle was Lars Hanson (who had been Garbo's leading man in *Gösta Berling*), playing the role of Ulrich von Eltz.

In *Flesh and the Devil,* directed by Clarence Brown, Leo and Ulrich are presented as a good, virtuous couple (not only best pals, but perhaps boyhood lovers), and Felicitas (Garbo) as an evil interloper. The characters portrayed by Garbo and Gilbert (as Leo) fall in love at a military ball. *[There was always a ball in these films.]* The plot thickens: Despite his declarations of love for her, Felicitas neglects to tell Leo that she's married to a no-count count, Count von Rhaden (Marc MacDermott).

Leo and the Count fight a duel and the Count is killed. As punishment, Leo is ordered to a military outpost in Africa for five years. He asks Ulrich, who remains behind, to take care of the widowed Felicitas in his absence.

Unaware of her long-running affair with Leo, Ulrich in time marries Felicitas. After three years, Leo gets a pardon, returning home hoping to reclaim Felicitas. But once he's back in Austria, he learns that his lady love has married his best friend, Ulrich.

Leo tries to avoid Felicitas but "The Flesh" is too weak to resist "The Devil." He returns as a lover, creating a deadly triangle involving his childhood friend.

The pace of the soapy melodrama quickens. Felicitas, not wanting Leo killed, runs across an ice-packed river but falls through and drowns. Leo wounds Ulrich in a duel, but nurses him back to health. The two become bosom buddies once again, and, at least in the eyes of gay fans, "lovers for life," although this movie hardly

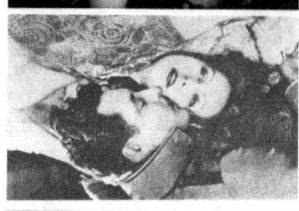

In Flesh and the Devil, **Greta Garbo** and **John Gilbert** emote both on and off the screen.

He wrote: "She is marvelous, the most alluring creature I have ever seen. Capricious as the devil, whimsical, temperamental, fascinating. What appeal! What a woman!"

spells out that possibility.

Clarence Brown has Gilbert as Leo simultaneously carrying on two very different love affairs—and two very different kinds of love—in this flicker. He's in love with both Ulrich and Felicitas, and at least insofar as this script is concerned, his two loves seemingly can't coexist.

The film's director was fully aware of the homoerotic nature of the material. At one point he asked, "How do you have the woman die and the two men embrace without making them look like a couple of fairies?"

Flesh and the Devil was a box office hit, establishing Gilbert and Garbo as an on-screen team. *The New York Times* pronounced Garbo as "undeniably alluring in a compelling piece of work."

Variety predicted that Garbo would become the "next Theda Bara." That critic went on to say, "There are love scenes in *Flesh and the Devil* that will make anyone fidget in their seat."

Photoplay evaluated the Gilbert/Garbo love scenes as "smoulderingly fervent."

***

During the filming of *Flesh and the Devil*, Garbo's leading man, John Gilbert, fell madly and hysterically in love with her.

Ever since her arrival at MGM, Garbo had heard ongoing gossip and anecdotes about Gilbert. It seemed that everyone she met had an opinion about him.

Screenwriter Ben Hecht claimed, "Gilbert drank with carpenters, danced with waitresses, and made love to whores and movie queens."

In the scenes above, **Lars Hanson** (left) and **John Gilbert** are clearly in love with each other as they co-starred in *Flesh and the Devil*.

Relatively innocent audiences didn't get it, but latter-day critics interpreted the scenes as "homoerotic."

In this ruined "bromance" *[a latter-day term]*, **Lars Hanson** (left), **Greta**, and **Gilbert** are embroiled in a love triangle, a key element within *Flesh and the Devil*.

Garbo 359

If the star of Garbo's previous film, *The Temptress*, Antonio Moreno, is to be believed, Gilbert, like Greta, was bisexual, in spite of his billing as "the screen's perfect lover."

From 1918 to 1921, Gilbert had been married to a little-known actress, Olivia Burwell, but he'd left her early in their marriage after entering the U.S. Army during World War I. He later described his stint in the army as "the worst time of my life."

In 1922, he married another actress, Leatrice Joy, with whom he produced a daughter. He was never faithful to her. In her divorce petition, she cited his adulterous involvements with screen legends who included Barbara LaMarr, Bebe Daniels, and Lila Lee (Valentino's leading lady).

Actress Eleanor Boardman claimed, "John Gilbert was the type of man who turned to the bottle after every disappointment." She seemed aware of his numerous affairs with megastars who included Jeanne Eagels, Miriam Hopkins, Beatrice Lillie (usually a lesbian), Lupe Velez, Laurette Taylor, and writers Dorothy Parker and Adela Rogers St. Johns. He was also one of the best customers at the exclusive (usually heterosexual) bordello operated by Lee Francis in Beverly Hills.

During the initial stages of "Getting to know Gilbert," Garbo was tiring of her interpreter and fellow Swede, Hugo Borg, who occupied a front-row seat to the burgeoning romance between Garbo and her newest co-star. "It was instant chemistry between those two," Borg claimed. "Whenever they looked into each other's eyes, a solar flash seemed to pass between them. When they played their first love scene on camera, no one else existed. I knew my time with Greta was coming to an end."

By the summer of 1926, millions of movie-goers worldwide knew about their burgeoning and photogenic romance.

When Garbo met Gilbert, she knew nothing of his background, except that his fame by then was equal to that of the recently deceased Rudolph Valentino.

Born in Utah in 1895, the child of vaudeville actors, Gilbert was a decade older than Garbo. He'd struggled through a childhood of abuse and neglect before drifting to Hollywood as a teenager.

First, he found work as an extra in the Thomas Ince Studios, and soon became a favorite of producer Maurice Tourneur, who hired him to write the scripts for several films.

Eventually, he got cast as an actor, appearing in such films as *Heart o' the Hills*

Greta Garbo and **John Gilbert** became one of the greatest pairings and teams in the history of silent pictures.

Critic Alexander Walker claimed, "A woman who could sin and suffer simultaneously was a god-send in a censor's world where moral misdeed had to be balanced by statutory repentence or inevitable destruction."

(1919) with Mary Pickford.

In 1921, he signed a contract with Fox as a romantic leading man in such films as *The Count of Monte Cristo* (1922). Two notable movies in 1923 included *Cameo Kirby* with Jean Arthur and *The Wolf Man* with Norma Shearer.

He did not "arrive at the Pearly Gates" (his words) until 1924 when he signed with MGM. His biggest break came when he danced with Mae Murray in *The Merry Widow* (1925), directed by the tyrannical Erich von Stroheim.

Gilbert became "An immortal of the Silver Screen" when he starred in the war epic, *The Big Parade* (1925). It became the second highest-grossing film of all time to that point.

The following year, he was cast in *Flesh and the Devil* (1926) with Garbo. Within the first week of filming, she moved into his home on Tower Grove Drive in Beverly Hills. He was known for his Sunday brunches, to which he invited the elite of the film industry.

Soon the still shy Garbo was introduced to Norma Shearer, Ronald Colman, Adela Rogers St. Johns, Mae Murray, Irving Thalberg, Paul Bern, Anita Loos, and a host of other bigwigs in the film industry.

One Sunday afternoon, Eleanor Boardman noted that "Garbo, like a true Swede, was casual about nudity. I saw her jump nude into Gilbert's swimming pool."

One of the most famous incidents, and the most widely publicized, may never have happened. On September 8, 1926, Boardman was set to marry director King Vidor. The elite of MGM, including Louis B. Mayer, arrived for the ceremony at the home of Marion Davies, the mistress of the fabulously wealthy press baron, William Randolph Hearst. It was envisioned as a dual wedding that included the marriage vows of Gilbert and Garbo.

Garbo, however, never showed up. Extremely agitated, Mayer was said to have encountered Gilbert in a bathroom, finding him extremely agitated, too. "Why marry her?" Mayer is alleged to have asked. "Why not settle for just fucking her?"

It was alleged that Gilbert hauled off and slugged Mayer in the face, breaking his glasses.

Mayer was said to have responded, "For that, I'll destroy you, even if it costs me a million dollars."

Many biographers claimed that this legendary encounter never happened.

At the time of the alleged incident, Gilbert was MGM's biggest star. He went on to film nine profit-making movies with Metro during the silent era.

Although he did propose to Greta on several occasions, she held him off.

Finally, the last time Gilbert proposed to Garbo, she signaled to him her true sexuality. "John, you don't want to marry one of the fellows, do you?"

The so-called "love affair of the century" may have lasted for only four months. It soon dissolved into "friendship only."

LOVE (1927)

THE SILENT FILM ADAPTATION OF TOLSTOY'S ROMANTIC TRAGEDY, *ANNA KARENINA*, IT SPINS DESPERATE AND DOOMED AFFAIRS BOTH ON AND OFF THE SCREEN

Once again, Mayer teamed Garbo and Gilbert in the 1927 movie *Love*, a screen adaptation of Leo Tolstoy's *Anna Karenina*. Greta would remake yet another adaptation of that epic novel as a talkie in 1935.

She demanded—and got—William Daniels as her photographer. "No one can make me more beautiful than Bill."

Edmund Goulding, also an actor, directed *Love*. [He would later helm Garbo in one of her most famous talking pictures, *Grand Hotel (1932).*]

In an obvious reference to the Garbo/Gilbert romance, and as a tagline that advertised its release, MGM publicized it as GILBERT & GARBO IN LOVE.

Originally, Ricardo Cortez, Garbo's former co-star, was to have been her leading man. But after about a week, Irving Thalberg fired him and hired Gilbert based on the rave reviews generated by *Flesh and the Devil*.

Garbo (as Anna Karenina) is married to a prosperous, easy-to-dislike husband during the Czarist era in St. Petersburg. The role was cast with Brandon Hurst, whom one critic described as "a husband with deadened eyes and sewn-on scowls."

A handsome, dashing, and charming Russian count, Alexis Vronsky (Gilbert), an *aide-de-camp* to the Grand Duke, falls in love with Anna. Finding him "vibrant and impulsive, although selfish," she succumbs to his romantic and sexual advances.

Her husband will not give her a divorce, so defiantly, and against her better instincts, she deserts him to live with her lover. That means she'll lose

GRETA GARBO   JOHN GILBERT

> Before being reunited with **John Gilbert** on the screen in *Love*, **Garbo** had made a long disappearance. There was speculation that she'd either had an abortion or a miscarriage.
>
> *Motion Picture* magazine wrote that "Lovers of Tolstoy will be disappointed by this movie. Those who like to study the Gilbert-Garbo embraces will also be disappointed."

her son, played by the beautiful ten-year-old actor, the French-born Philippe de Lacy.

In one love scene with her son, Garbo and the ten-year-old sparked more electricity than Gilbert ever did with her. Some critics found the scene vaguely incestuous.

Critic Richard Corliss wrote, "De Lacy projects a Pre-Raphaelite sensuality that made him the perfect love object for a repressed and doting mother."

When Mayer saw the scene, he at first wanted to have it cut from the film as "too erotic. My God," he told Thalberg. "The way our Swede plays that scene, she'll give our boy a hard-on." As it seemed vital to the plot, and memorable, the scene remained in the final cut.

As time goes by, Vronsky deserts Anna, returns to military life, and leaves her with a sense of abandonment. With her son taken from her and her lover deserting her, she feels she has nothing to live for, and throws herself in front of a moving train.

Joan Crawford, who co-starred with Gilbert in *Twelve Miles Out* (also 1927), said, "Gilbert was still in love with Garbo, but, to me, judging from a distance, she seemed self-enchanted. Gilbert told me she hated Hollywood and sometimes for days on the set, she would not speak to him except on camera. He said she wanted to buy lots and lots of land in Montana and raise wheat and children."

Ruefully, Garbo told Mauritz Stiller, "Jack is in love with the goddess I project on the screen. He would be bored with Greta Gustafsson."

Upon the release of *Love,* Variety predicted that the pairing of Garbo with Gilbert would become the biggest box office mating in Hollywood history. *Motion Picture* recommended the movie for "those wishing to see what Garbo could do without any help from the script, the director, and John Gilbert." *The New York Times* called her "The Screen's Mona Lisa."

Mercedes de Acosta rushed to see the movie with a coven of girlfriends, each of them enthralled with Garbo, and each critical of Gilbert. Most of them found him "quite silly, even effeminate at times."

"When I saw Gilbert making love to Garbo, I envied the bastard," Mercedes said. "I wanted to be the one making love to her. In some ways, Gilbert evoked that little man on top of a wedding cake."

In the year that Garbo made *Love,* the film career of Mauritz Stiller was winding down. After he was booted from MGM, he'd gone over to Para-

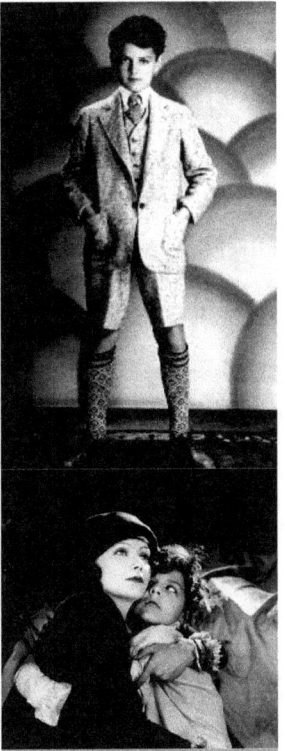

As a child star, **Philippe de Lacy** was hailed as "the most beautiful boy of the silent screen."

Garbo and **De Lacy's** mother-son scenes in *Love* shocked audiences. One critic wrote, "Never in the history of motion pictures has a mother of twenty-two and her ten-year-old son been depicted in such a 'sexy' scene."

mount, where he'd directed the hugely successful *Hotel Imperial* (1927) a World War I drama co-starring the Polish vamp, Pola Negri.

He followed that with two movies that flopped, including *The Woman on Trial* (also 1927). It, too, starred Negri.

Stiller's swan song to Hollywood was his direction of *The Street of Sin*, co-starring Fay Wray and Emil Jannings. After that "turkey," his career virtually ended.

As he was telling Garbo goodbye, he admitted that his greatest failure in Hollywood had involved not getting to direct her in any film. As she kissed him goodbye, she told him that she, too, would be leaving Hollywood soon and that she'd join him again, soon, in Stockholm.

They were never to see each other again.

Back in Sweden, and suffering from pleurisy, Stiller died in November of 1928 at the age of forty-five.

When Louis B. Mayer at MGM sat through *Love* with **Greta** and **John Gilbert,** he wanted to change its title to *Sacred and Profane Love*, but was talked out of it.

THE DIVINE WOMAN (1928)
GARBO PLAYS A YOUNG AND TEMPERAMENTAL SARAH BERNHARDT

Louis B. Mayer and Irving Thalberg decided that the time had come to give Garbo star billing without referencing the allure of any leading man like John Gilbert.

The property they selected was a Broadway play first produced in 1925, *Starlight*. Authored by Gladys Unger it had starred Doris Keane, a major-league stage star in her heyday.

The plot was loosely based on the early life of the great French actress, Sarah Bernhardt (1844-1923). She was the illegitimate and convent-raised daughter of a Jewish prostitute.

Throughout her life, "The Divine Sarah," as she was called, had numerous affairs without gender preference, and she became known for strange habits such as preferring to sleep in a coffin. She continued her stage career even after a 1915 accident forced her to have a leg amputated.

Mauritz Stiller had wanted to direct Garbo in the picture, but his fellow Swede, Victor Sjöström, was assigned as director instead. Born in Värmland in Western Sweden, he was taken to Brooklyn when he was only one year old. But his mother died when he was seven, and he was repatriated back to Sweden. There, he grew up, becoming a player in his country's growing film industry.

He and Stiller became friends, and Stiller helmed him in his first movie, shot in 1912. In time, Sjöström would direct forty-one movies in his native country, having his most success adapting into films the novels of the Nobel Prize-winning author, Selma Lagerlöf.

By 1923, he'd arrived in Hollywood, where in time, as a director, he would helm such stars as John Gilbert, Lillian Gish, Norma Shearer, and Lon Chaney.

For Garbo's leading man, Sjöström signed a fellow Swede, Lars Hanson, who had previously co-starred with Garbo in the *Gösta Berling* saga, and also co-starred with her (and Gilbert) in *Flesh and the Devil*.

Every month, Garbo was improving her English, but she noted that Hanson spoke his limited English with a very pronounced Swedish accent, which would doom his American film career with the advent of talking pictures the very next year.

The second male lead went to Lowell Sherman, a native son of San Francisco, who began his film career as a child actor.

Greta Garbo's eighth movie, a silent picture, would mark the last time she co-starred with Lars Hanson. He never learned to speak English well enough to survive a transition to Talkies.

In the lower photo, impersonating Sarah Bernhardt, **Garbo** wants to be narcissistically alone.

By 1915, D.W. Griffin had cast him in that classic, *Way Down East* (1920), starring Lillian Gish. In 1923, he was back on Broadway, co-starring with Katharine Cornell in *Casanova*.

As a director, Sjöstrom survived and later, thrived, when talking pictures came in. In 1933, he helmed Mae West in her film debut in *She Done Him Wrong* and Katharine Hepburn in her Oscar-winning performance in *Morning Glory* (also 1933)..

A secondary role in *The Divine Woman* went to Johnny Mack Brown, an extremely handsome former football star from Alabama. Garbo learned two new English words that were often used to describe him—"stud" and "heartthrob."

Throughout the months it took to film, Brown's photo adorned the shelves of grocery stores throughout the nation, advertising the breakfast cereal, Wheaties.

After working with Garbo, he became the love interest of Mary Pickford in *Coquette* (1929), which brought her an Oscar.

Brown would go on to appear with such stars as Clark Gable, Joan Crawford, Jean Harlow, and Wallace Beery before his career declined to the point where he appeared in low-budget Westerns as "The Cowboy King of the Bs." He retired, embittered, after making 160 movies.

In *The Divine Woman*, Garbo is depicted as an impoverished French peasant girl. Migrating to Paris, she rises in fame as a dramatic actress. She is torn between two lovers, Lucien (Hanson), a poor but passionate soldier, and Henry Legrand (Sherman), a rich, middle-aged producer of stylishly naughty stage events in Paris.

This is the front cover of a fan mag in 1928 reviewing the life story—and entrenching the reputation—of Hollywood's most famous Swede.

Problem? It doesn't look like Garbo.

Today, *The Divine Woman* is defined as "Garbo's Lost Film," all known copies having been destroyed in 1965 in a vault fire at MGM.

After the movie was reported as lost, one reporter claimed that "In years to come, *The Divine Woman* will become like Elvis and the Loch Ness Monster, often sighted but never actually found."

After seeing *The Divine Woman*, many members of Sweden's (unimpressed) expatriate community living in Hollywood predicted: "Garbo's film career in America is over." Yet although it received mixed and/or uneven reviews, it was a huge hit at the box office. *The New York Times* reviewed it with, "We are not sure that Miss Garbo is beautiful. It seems to be a soul, rather than prettiness, that makes her face attractive."

Screenland went negative, defining it as "a major disappointment. Here is Garbo, who flutters and mugs. This interestingly reserved lady goes completely Hollywood, all at once."

Motion Picture found her "something more than a vamp, quite capable."

In a latter-day appraisal, film historian David Robinson claimed, "If Garbo's silent films weren't novelette rubbish to begin with, they ended up that way after Metro's script department had done their stuff. But Garbo gave them a little of her own divinity."

MYSTERIOUS LADY (1928)
PASSION AS A FORM OF TRAGIC DEPRESSION

Refusing to wear a brassiere, and in some scenes "artfully undraped" in ways that barely scraped past the era's censors, Garbo—in this, her sixth American film—portrays Tania Fedorova, a "dream princess of eternity, the knockout of the ages," in the words of a writer from *Life* magazine who might have gotten carried away with the character's temptress charms. For aficionados of Greta Garbo, *Mysterious Lady* showed her as a consummate actress who could convey passion even in scenes in which she appears alone.

Fred Niblo directed the story of this complicated "throw everything away for love" woman, a spy who—dominated by her reckless passions—shoots her supervisor as a means of protecting the man she loves. *[The man she loves, alas, is a highly effective fighter for an enemy nation.]*

At this point in her career, Garbo had not yet been paired with superstar Clark Gable, and the actor who was designated as her romantic counterpart was the less-than-compelling Conrad Nagel, a stoic blonde who usually isn't included in the list of "heartthrob heroes" of the silent screen.

Seductively beautiful and illuminating the screen with fire—and arousingly showcasing the outline of her nipples through her silky and clinging garment—Garbo is cast opposite the silly Gustav von Seyfferitz, playing her boss, General Boris Alexandroff. He is of the 1885 acting

No one liked the working title (*The Glorious Sinner*) of Garbo's latest movie, released in 1928, just as Hollywood was learning to talk. Some insiders thought talkies would end Garbo's film career.

"Boy Wonder" Irving Thalberg offered a fifty-dollar bonus to any studio worker who could devise a better title.

The studio eventually settled on *The Mysterious Lady*, an apt description of Garbo herself.

Garbo's leading man, **Conrad Nagel,** was "pleasant enough" for **Garbo,** but secretly, she told her director, "Nagel is the dullest co-star so far."

Reviewers seemed to agree. "Garbo and Nagel are not Garbo and Gilbert," one critic said. "As lovers, they just don't gel."

school of exaggerated mannerisms. Off screen he asked (the deeply offended) Garbo why she didn't wear a brassiere. After that, both in private and in public, Garbo mockingly referred to Von Seyfferitz as "Safer Tits."

The plot of Mysterious Lady starts spinning when Nagel—portraying an Austrian military commander, Karl von Raden—attends a performance at the opera. There, he meets Tania (Garbo), a formidable undercover spy who—against her instincts and her training—is swept away with love for him at first sight. The captain has been commissioned to deliver some important military secrets to Berlin.

Before boarding his train, he learns she's a Russian spy. She comes to see him aboard that train, admitting that she set up their rendezvous as a vehicle for tricking him. She goes on to insist that she truly has fallen for him and that she's desperately in love. When he rebuffs her coldly, she steals his classified secrets. That leads to his court martial and imprisonment. His influential uncle is able to provide him with one last chance to clear his name.

Captain Von Raden flees to Russia where he learns that Tania really does love him. To prove her devotion, she double crosses her "espionage supervisor," Von Seyfferitz. When her boss learns of her deception, she is forced to shoot him. To trick his bodyguards a few moments after shooting him, she deceptively plays a love scene with his corpse. Somewhat unrealistically (but that's the magic of Garbo), she and Captain Karl (Nagel) flee from Russia to Austria to clear his name and to start a new life as lovers.

A reviewer for the *New York Morning Telegraph* wrote, "This Garbo girl seems to develop just a little more of that intangible 'it' with each picture, and the love scenes between her and Nagel are what might be termed burning. There are love scenes by the score, many of which are in close-ups, with the famous La Garbo kiss given full sway as well as full camera focus."

Its rival, the New York *Evening Graphic* claimed, "Miss Garbo takes to a close-up like no other star in Hollywood. She overcomes the handicap of an atrocious wardrobe, big feet, and widening hips with a facility of expression and charm which still keep her in a class by herself."

This is a lobby card from 1928 for *The Mysterious Lady* in which **Garbo** appears bra-less and with hints of S&M. Her co-star was the stern and scary-looking, German-born **Gustav von Seyfferitz** (1862-1943).

Marketed, accurately or not, as "A True Hollywood Aristocrat," he was known for having five wives and "more mistresses than I can count."

A WOMAN OF AFFAIRS (1928)
BRIGHT YOUNG THINGS OF THE LOST GENERATION

Michael Arlen's novel, *The Green Hat,* created a sensation when it was adapted for the stage. In London, Tallulah Bankhead starred in it, and on Broadway, Katharine Cornell played the lead.

In Hollywood, Irving Thalberg paid $50,000 for the film rights, changing its title to *A Woman of Affairs.*

As the film went into production, many studios, such as Warner Brothers, were switching to sound. But Thalberg wanted to keep Garbo in silents for as long as he could because he was nervous about how her voice would go over with American audiences. He ordered her to take daily lessons from MGM's vocal coach.

Clarence Brown was hired to direct the picture. In time, this New Englander would helm Garbo in seven films and Joan Crawford in six. He never won an Oscar, although he was nominated six times, holding a record for the most nominations for a director without a win.

The picture marked the reunion of Garbo and John Gilbert, once again designated as her leading man. However convincing (or not convincing, according to the reviewer) their onscreen lovemaking appeared, their torrid passion belonged to another day, as both of them were having affairs with others at the time they shot this film.

The Green Hat had dealt with abortion, venereal disease, adultery, and a hint of homosexuality. Thalberg ordered that the script be "cleaned up."

Brown assembled an all-star cast of actors, led by veteran performer, the stone-faced New Englander, Lewis Stone, marking the first of seven films in which he would co-star with Garbo.

Born in 1879, Stone seemed the least likely (and least handsome) of Garbo's leading men. Perhaps his biggest hit in silent pictures was his leading role in *The*

Garbo had long yearned to star in the film version of Michael Arlen's novel, **The Green Hat**, but Irving Thalberg feared he'd have a problem with the censors. The original theatrical version had confronted homosexuality, suicide, abortion, adultery, and venereal disease.

As a play, it was already notorious. Its protagonist, Iris March, defined as one of the "Bright Young Things" of the Lost Generation, had already been essayed in theaters by Tallulah Bankhead and Katharine Cornell.

Thalberg bought the movie rights to *The Green Hat* for $50,000, and then ordered that the script department "clean it up."

Prisoner of Zenda (1922). As moviemaking moved into the 1930s, he found a less rugged, more "domestic" niche playing Judge Hardy, father to Mickey Rooney in the Andy Hardy series.

Thalberg ordered that all mention of venereal disease be cut from the script, and homosexuality, if depicted at all, had to be very subtle, reduced to mere furtive glances from the characters portrayed by Douglas Fairbanks, Jr., and Johnny Mack Brown.

Fairbanks, of course, was the son of that screen swashbuckler, Douglas Fairbanks, Sr., who reached the peak of his fame during his marriage to Mary Pickford, then hailed as America's Sweetheart. At the time that his young son worked with Garbo, he had become engaged to the former porn star, Joan Crawford. His stepmother, Miss Pickford, viewed her as "common."

The cast of *A Woman of Affairs* included that dashing football player turned movie star, Johnny Mack Brown before he became typecast as a cowboy hero.

On the first day of the shoot, he startled Garbo by rushing up and giving her a big kiss. He had nicknamed her "Sugah." His Alabama accent amused her, as he invited her to visit his home state with him some time. "We'll feed you possum and grits."

The plot is pure soap opera melodrama. The three main characters, depicted as playmates when they were children, were born into the English aristocracy. Garbo was cast as Diana Merrick, Gilbert as Neville, and Brown as David.

As they grow up, Diana and Neville fall in love, much to the annoyance of his father (played by Hobart Bosworth). He banishes his son to Egypt, where he establishes a business that makes him rich.

Neville returns to England after a long absence. In the meantime, Diana has married David, with the horrible after-effect that during their honeymoon, David committed suicide. As Diana says, "He died for

By the time **Garbo** and **John Gilbert** co-starred again in *A Woman of Affairs*, their love interests had moved elsewhere. He told her, "When I think of you, and I do on occasion, I have thoughts of what might have been."

"Some things in life are better left as dreams rather than realities," she cautioned him.

"Until I met **Johnny Mack Brown,** I was unfamiliar with Southern boys," **Garbo** said.

"At first, I thought I'd be repulsed by him—after all, weren't people from the South known as 'rednecks?' But I found him handsome, sexy, and full of magnolia blossoms coming from his beautiful lips."

decency." The real reason, it's revealed, after lengthy steerage from the censors, is that he was a thief pursued by the police. *[In the original Broadway & London stage versions, he died after a virulent battle with a venereal disease.]*

The film ends on a tragic note after Diana (Garbo) drives her automobile into a tree, dying instantly.

Pare Lorentz, writing in *Judge*, claimed, "For the first time, I respected the performance of Greta Garbo." *Variety* proclaimed, "*A Woman of Affairs* is the best thing Greta Garbo has ever done. John Gilbert, an idol of the Flappers, has an absolutely *blah* role. Without the eloquent acting of Garbo, the film would go to pieces."

Shot on a budget of $350,000, the picture had a box office gross of $1,370,000.

When John Gilbert was starring in *A Woman of Affairs*, he was having a fling with **Beatrice Lillie.** Ironically, she would add Greta Garbo to her list of lovers that also encompassed Tallulah Bankhead, Katharine Cornell, Judith Anderson, Buster Keaton, Eva Le Gallienne, Gertrude Lawrence, and Rudolph Valentino.

Mercedes de Acosta went to see *A Woman of Affairs* three times, longing for the day when she could meet the goddess who had starred in it. "As a screen heroine, she was always reckless, but always gallant. Gallant and dangerous were in a sense the passwords of the 1920s. One could actually do anything as long as one lived gallantly and dangerously."

During their honeymoon in Europe, Irving Thalberg and Norma Shearer discovered **Eva Von Berne** (both photos above).

Each of the Thalbergs, along with virtually everyone in MGM's production department, thought that Eva had the makings of a star. How wrong they were.

***

During the filming of *A Woman of Affairs,* both Garbo and Gilbert were conducting affairs with other men and women. He was dating the Canadian-born Beatrice (Bea) Lillie, a bisexual, and making frequent visits to a bordello in Beverly Hills. The house was unusual at the time in that it always kept on the floor at least a dozen handsome young men, who came to Hollywood to become stars but didn't make it, ending up having to prostitute themselves. The night madam later reported that Gilbert was bisexual, often selecting both a young girl and a young man as his bedmates.

In the meantime, Garbo was having a brief fling with the newly christened "Eva Von Berne," a young actress born in Sarajevo, then part of the Austro-Hungarian Empire. While on his honeymoon with Norma Shearer, Irving Thalberg had discovered Eva and brought her to Hollywood.

Smitten with her seductive powers, he planned to promote her as "The New Garbo." The original, when not demanding pay raises, was always threatening "I'm going back to Sweden."

Thalberg welcomed Eva Von Berne—who had had very little training as an actress and very little grasp of English—to Culver City, and announced that he was starting her at the top, casting her in John Gilbert's latest movie, *The Masks of the Devil* (1928).

Also in the cast was the doomed Alma Rubens, by now hopelessly addicted to heroin. The director was Garbo's Swedish compatriot, Victor Sjöström. Eager to sniff out the competition, Garbo asked Sjöström, her friend and compatriot, if she could have lunch with Eva.

The director arranged it, and Garbo, instead of being jealous of the young starlet, bonded with her, going so far as to invite her to spend the weekend with her in Palm Springs. Eva eagerly accepted. Using her inner radar, Garbo had assumed that Eva was bisexual likerself.

That weekend in the desert proved it: The two MGM actresses spent most of the time locked inside Garbo's bedroom.

The beautiful **Alma Rubens** was John Gilbert's co-star in *The Masks of the Devil* (1928).

Self-destructive, she could not handle the pressures of stardom. Eventually, she devolved into a hopeless drug addict, the effects of which led to her premature death.

The Eva Von Berne/Greta Garbo affair was about as brief as a summer breeze on a hot August day. It came and went as fast as Eva's career at MGM. After watching the final cut of *Masks of the Devil,* Thalberg concluded that Eva could not act. He gave her $300 and shipped her back to Europe.

In a response to her acting in *The Masks of the Devil,* a contemporary critic wrote that Von Berne "reminds one of those oval-faced expressionless ladies so often found in Italian primitives."

For the German-speaking market, she made four more movies before fading from the screen at the age of twenty. She wasn't heard from until 2010 when a newspaper reported her death at the age of one hundred in a small town in western Hungary.

WILD ORCHIDS (1929)
GARBO DALLIES WITH A SEXY BUT SADISTIC JAVANESE PRINCE

Made as a silent at the dawn of the talkies, *Wild Orchids* was based on *Heat,* a novel by John Colton, and directed by Sidney Franklin, a native of San Francisco. Franklin was known for adapting both literary works and Broadway stage plays into films.

Wild Orchids would be Garbo's eleventh silent movie, her second with Lewis Stone and her first with a new leading man, Nils Asther.

Like her, Asther was a good-looking Swede, celebrated for his male beauty and publicized in the American press as "The Male Version of Greta Garbo."

In 1916, director Mauritz Stiller had cast him in *The Wings,* a gay-themed silent film that led to a series of spin-off roles for Asther in Sweden, Germany, and Denmark. During the filming of *The Wings,* Stiller put Asther on the casting couch.

By 1927, Asther was working in Hollywood, where he played opposite such stars as Anita Page, Johnny Mack Brown, Dorothy Sebastian, Pola Negri, and Marion Davies. His most popular film was *Our Dancing Daughters* (1928), opposite Joan Crawford.

To conceal his homosexuality, he proposed marriage to Garbo, but she rejected him. She even protested having to execute, before cameras, various love scenes with him, telling Franklin, "I don't know where his mouth was last night."

Asther was the veteran of a string of homosexual affairs beginning with Stiller. In 1930, he entered into a lavender marriage with Vivian Duncan, one of the co-stars in *Topsy and Eva* (1927), his first American film.

During his filming of *Wild Orchids,* Asther became involved in a torrid affair with the former football star, Johnny Mack Brown, Garbo's former leading

Garbo appears in a torrid love scene with the handsome and gay (Swedish) actor, **Nils Asther.** Some critics labeled their on-camera emoting as pornographic.

man. News of Asther's homosexuality reached the ears of Louis B. Mayer, who summoned him to his office. There, he called Asther a "Swedish *fagelah*," demanding that he grow a mustache as a means of appearing more masculine.

The plot of *Wild Orchids* spun around another love triangle: Garbo was cast as Lillie, married to John Sterling (Lewis Stone), who portrayed her dull, middle-aged husband.

Sailing to Java to check out a tea plantation, they meet a young Javanese royal, Prince de Gace (Asther). Garbo first sees him when he's whipping a Chinese servant.

The prince befriends this May-to-December couple, and invites them to stay at his lavish palace. There, behind Stone's back, he pursues Lillie (i.e., Garbo) and seduces her. When her husband learns about this adulterous betrayal, he plans to sail away without his wife, but at the last minute she decides that she loves him and is waiting for him in his departing car.

In *Wild Orchids*, **Lewis Stone** starred as **Garbo's** husband.

Many viewers, however, presumed that he looked more like her father.

Many religious groups denounced the film as pornographic and objected to a twenty-three-year-old married to a man who was almost fifty.

Variety wrote, "Sex is the meat and marrow of this movie's drama. Dames will probably feel that having (Garbo's) marital fidelity tested and tempted by a natty sheik like Asther is a possible source for pleasurable tremors."

Many critics noted that whereas Stone appeared boring and sexless, the prince was handsome, dashing, even thrilling.

The New York Times reported, "Miss Garbo's acting is well-timed and, as usual, effective. It is not an easy role, but she succeeds in imparting to it no small amount of subtlety. Nils Asther is capital as the Prince, a persistent individual who appears to be sadly lacking in caution. Stone does splendidly as the somewhat short-sighted husband."

Wild Orchids was one of the highest-grossing films of the year. Thalberg was so pleased that he decided to reteam Garbo and Asther in her next picture, this one with his lover, Johnny Mack Brown.

Garbo told director Franklin, "I am determined to rescue Johnny from the arms of this Asther creature."

THE SINGLE STANDARD (1929)
A WOMAN WANTS EQUAL FREEDOMS AND SEXUAL RIGHTS

Nils Asther and Johnny Mack Brown had been successful as leading men to both Joan Crawford and Garbo. Each had recently had box office triumphs in *Our Dancing Daughters* (1928) opposite Crawford. Irving Thalberg wanted to reteam them, this time with Garbo, in *A Single Standard*.

But after the first week of shooting, Crawford for some reason dropped out of the picture. Irving Thalberg replaced her immediately with Garbo, as Asther and Brown had emoted convincingly and scored big with her in *A Woman of Affairs*.

As their director, Thalberg designated John Robertson, best known for his success at casting John Barrymore in *Dr. Jekyll and Mr. Hyde* (1920).

MGM's publicity department touted Garbo in "her first one-hundred percent American role." [She had actually portrayed an American in *Wild Orchids*, but as a European "exotic," she was less easily recognized as one.]

Thalberg had bought the rights to *The Single Standard* from Adela Rogers St. Johns, the columnist who had written the novel on which the film had been based.

Its director noted, "That Alabama ex-footballer, Johnny Mack Brown, was one hell of a man. He was not only satisfying both Garbo and Nils Asther in the libido department but had a little high school sweetheart type of wife at home."

Asther and Garbo, each an avant-garde Swedish expatriate, had always had a love-hate relationship. Robertson, their director, said, "She waxed hot and cold with him. Once in a kissing scene, he got a little rough, and she broke away and slapped his face."

"Who do you take me for?" she asked him harshly. "One of your sailors?"

At the beginning of the shoot, Garbo made it clear: She wanted the set

Nils Asther and Garbo in a love scene from *The Single Standard*. Off-screen, they chased after the same man, their co-star, Johnny Mack Brown.

Garbo 375

closed to visitors, and even demanded that the extras and technicians be screened off so that none of them could see her act.

"If I am by myself, my face will do things I cannot do with it otherwise."

MGM was the last big studio to convert to sound. As its major star, Garbo was kept in silents almost until 1930. Thalberg was still worried about her Swedish accent. With the understanding that time was running out on the era of silent films, he assigned her a dialogue coach. After *The Single Standard*, she would make only one more silent.

Garbo with **Johnny Mack Brown** in *The Single Standard*. On screen, her character finds Brown "dull," but off screen, "he heated up the sheets."

According to the plot, Garbo as Arden Stuart, a San Francisco *débutante*, believes that women should have the same standards of sexual freedom as men.

In the beginning of the film, she is seduced by her chauffeur, Anthony (Fred Solm), who, although he's an ace aviator and the son of a lord, for some reason, is working in this menial job. When their "interlude on the beach sands" late one night is exposed, he's fired, and then commits suicide, a cheap (some said "absurd") plot twist that's never explained.

Recovering from her anguish at his death, Arden visits an art gallery, where she admires a painting by Packy Cannon (Nils Asther), who, the script reveals, is a former boxer and sailor- turned-painter. He invites her to accompany him during an extended cruise aboard his yacht through the South Seas. As a liberated woman who's unafraid of the consequences, she accepts his invitation. At the end of the sea voyage, he abruptly ends the affair.

Despite his gender preference for men, Asther performed his sexual scenes with Garbo with convincing ardor.

Arden (Garbo), in time, marries Tommy Hewlett (Johnny Mack Brown), although she finds him rather boring. They produce a much beloved son.

Then, Packy decides he still loves Arden and returns to tempt her to run away with him. But because of her son, she decides to remain faithful to her husband, preferring responsible motherhood to sexual fulfillment.

Two major stars were cast into uncredited roles: Joel McCrea and Robert Montgomery, the latter Garbo's future co-star in a talking picture.

Made for a budget of $330,000, *A Single Standard* grossed more than a million dollars at the box office.

Variety claimed, "What some girls do today, and a lot more would like to, Greta Garbo does in *A Single Standard*. The actress is most unfeline in her brazen directness."

Pare Lorentz, writing in *Judge,* said, "For the first time since she hit these shores, grim Greta Garbo has done a good piece of work."

THE KISS (1929)
GARBO'S LAST SILENT FILM

Garbo ended the 1920s by starring in *The Kiss,* her last silent film. Although her voice is not part of the soundtrack, an orchestral score and some sound effects were included thanks to the then state-of-the-art technology of the Movietone system.

The Kiss was the last silent film released by MGM before it switched to all-talking pictures. Based on a short story by George M. Saville, the movie took its title from an 1896 short film that shocked 19th Century audiences by depicting a passionate kiss between a man and a woman.

Its Belgian director, Jacques Feyder, handled Garbo with great sensitivity, later pronouncing her as "exactitude incarnate."

Garbo requested her compatriot Nils Asther (he had been her co-star in *The Mysterious Lady)* once again as her leading man, but Thalberg nixed the idea, awarding the role to Conrad Nagel instead. "Conrad and I never had any sexual chemistry on the screen," Garbo protested.

Set in France, *The Kiss* is the story of two clandestine lovers, the (married) Irene Guarry (Garbo) and André Dubail (Nagel), a successful attorney. She is unhappily married to a much older Lyon-based silk merchant, Charles (Anders Randolf), who is facing bankruptcy.

Her husband's partner, Lassalle (Holmes Herbert), has a strikingly handsome 18-year-old son, Pierre (Lew Ayres). He develops a powerful crush on Irene.

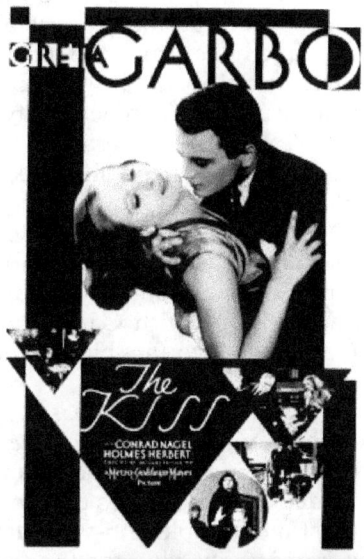

Garbo and a young **Lew Ayres** deliver *The Kiss*, as promised in the title.

In another decade, Jane Wyman would desert her husband, Ronald Reagan, for Ayres.

Although she holds him at bay, her husband suspects that she's been intimate with the ever-so-eager young man. Eventually, in a moment of ardor, the young man requests a kiss. They're interrupted by the appearance of her jealous husband. When their argument escalates uncontrollably, Irene shoots her husband with his own gun.

Brought to trial, she is defended by the lover (André) she abandoned and is acquitted of the charge. A freed woman, Irene ends the film kissing André as three old cleaning women enter, announcing, "We have come to clean the court."

During the shoot, Garbo had a brief fling with Ayres, who was three years her junior. She considered him "devastatingly beautiful," and he returned the compliment. As the director quipped, "It was a case of a female beauty meeting a male beauty."

Years later, Ayres said "I was a greenhorn of twenty, and she took me under her wing. She taught me a lot about acting." He paused. "And a lot about life. I will say no more. But I was married at the time to Lola Lane, and our union was winding down. I had no hope with Garbo, but I ended up marrying a young blonde named Ginger Rogers."

After finishing *The Kiss*, Ayres made another movie, *All Quiet on the Western Front* (1930). Gigantically popular and still included in film studies courses as one of the most memorable anti-war films ever made, it immortalized him on the screen.

Screenland wrote, "The Swedish charmer (i.e., Garbo) carries this load of a mediocre story on her splendid shoulders and so makes *The Kiss* worth seeing." The critic went on to heap even more praise on Ayres, finding him "a smouldering boy who is a real find."

Less enthusiastically, *Motion Picture* wrote, "The question of Miss Garbo's appeal is still unresolved by this picture."

The Kiss opened on November 15, 1929 in New York, just seventeen days after the stock market crash that plunged America into the Great Depression.

The film made nearly half a million dollars but caused one critic to ask, "Isn't it about time for MGM to let us hear Garbo speak?"

***

After filming *The Kiss* with Garbo, **Lew Ayres** starred in *All Quiet on the Western Front (1930)*, one of the greatest of all anti-war classics.

Lilyan Tashman in a dress that contributed to her oft-repeated designation as "Best-Dressed Woman in Hollywood."

Edmund Lowe, as he appeared with the 1935 "Signed Portraits of Famous Stars" series issued as a promotional campaign by Gallagher's cigarettes

Before the end of the 1920s, Garbo launched a clandestine affair with the once spectacularly famous actress, Lilyan Tashman (1896-1934). A tall, blonde, and slender actress "with fox-like features and a throaty voice," she had been born into a Jewish family in Brooklyn, the youngest of ten children.

Late in her teens, she became a fashion and artist's model and later, from 1916-1918, a dancer with the Ziegfeld Follies. She made her film debut in 1921 and quickly carved out a career, appearing in 66 films before her untimely death from cancer at the age of 37.

She was most often cast in supporting roles, playing a villainess or else the vindictive "other woman."

In 1925, she entered into a "lavender marriage" with actor Edmund Lowe. Born in San José, California in 1890, he, somewhat surprisingly, once thought he might want to become a Catholic priest. Instead, he evolved into an actor in Hollywood, and is best remembered for his role of Sergeant Quirt in the 1926 silent movie, *What Price Glory?* In time, he became a leading man to Mae West, Jean Harlow, and Claudette Colbert.

Their home in Beverly Hills, called "Lilowe," was the most notorious address in Hollywood, the site of weekend orgies behind locked doors. It became a secret haven for homosexuals, bisexuals, and lesbians. During the peak of its notoriety, Tashman reigned as "the best-dressed woman in the world," boasting a wardrobe that cost an astounding one million dollars.

By intent or by accident, **Lilyan Tashman** appeared in more than one girly girl-on-girl scene where satin, lingerie, and lace established a subliminally lesbian theme.

Top photo, **Tashman** with **Joan Blondell** in *Millie* (1931); lower photo: **Tashman** (right) with scantily dressed **Kay Francis** in *Girls About Town* (also 1931).

Garbo attended one of Tashman & Lowe's very permissive parties one Saturday afternoon on the arm of her leading man, Johnny Mack Brown. It was later reported that Brown and Garbo stripped down for a naked, highly visible swim in the pool. When they emerged, Tashman was waiting with a big bath towel for Garbo, and Lowe was prepped and ready to dry off Brown, whom he invited upstairs to watch what were then known as "blue movies." *[Two of them starred the actress who later evolved into Joan Crawford.]* A seduction of Brown followed. Meanwhile, Tashman "deflowered" Garbo in another part of the house.

Garbo's fling with Tashman was brief. She soon broke it off. All she said about it was, "Tashman talks too much."

ANNA CHRISTIE (1930)
GARBO—"THE VOICE THAT SHOOK THE WORLD"—TALKS!

In 1930 it seemed that half the world wanted to know if Garbo, unlike so many of her contemporaries, could master the new medium of sound. For $570,000, an astonishing amount of money back then, MGM acquired the film rights to Eugene O'Neill's *Anna Christie*. With it, Garbo would face a potentially career-wrecking instrument, the microphone, portraying an immigrant whore with a Swedish accent.

Garbo had delayed her talkie debut until the technology (specifically its audio transmission) was more sensitive and mobile.

Directed once again by Clarence Brown, Garbo, dressed in the tawdry finery of a prostitute, slouches into a riverfront bar, collapses into a chair, and says to the bartender, "*Gif me a visky, ginger ale on the side, and don't be stingy, baby.*"

The world was mesmerized by her voice. It was unlike any that movie fans had heard before. Many reviews (some of them are replicated below) focused only on her voice, almost avoiding commenting on the film itself.

The screenplay unfolds like this: A salty veteran of the sea, Chris Christofferson (George F. Marion), awaits the arrival of his grown daughter, Anna, whom he sent away, when she was five, to live with relatives in Minnesota. He is unaware that she's been making her living in nature's oldest profession, and that much of her once-joyful spirit has been extinguished. Anna needs rest and a place to stay, so Chris makes room for her aboard his barge.

Anna falls in love with a young sailor, Matt Burke (portrayed by the deeply closeted gay character actor, Charles Bickford), but dreads to reveal her background as a prostitute, Yes, there's a lot of soapy melodrama here;

GARBO TALKS, as promoted in posters, newspaper features, and on theater marquees such as this one in New York City when *Anna Christie* opened.

One critic referred to her voice as "rich, full, limpid, incredibly throaty, smoky, sonorous." Yet another defined it as "the voice that shook the world."

this is not one of Eugene O'Neill's great plays.

O'Neill told critic Richard Watts that he was not going to see the film because he heard that "Garbo was bad."

Her role, Clarence Brown's direction, and William Daniels' cinematography all earned Oscar nominations. The picture made a star of the lesbian character actress Marie Dressler in the role of a wise old wharf rat. Garbo greatly admired Dressler's acting, but spent a great deal of her off-camera time trying to fend off the amorous advances of this emotionally vulnerable old wreck whose face resembled that of a bulldog.

In reference to Garbo in the film's English-language version, critic Richard Corliss wrote: "Somehow, on the screen, picture and voice don't jell. It's not the occasional mispronunciations (on the order of '*the yudge told me to get a yob*'), it's that Garbo's acting is pitched at the wrong level. Her Anna is a travesty of despair, and the gestures of our primal ballerina are often jerkily grandiose, as if the death throes of Pavlova's dying swan have given way to *rigor mortis*." After seeing it in its completed form, she told its director, Clarence Brown: "Isn't it terrible? Who ever saw a Swedish woman act that silly?"

Before uttering her first words on a movie screen, **Garbo** told veteran actress **Marie Dressler,** "I feel just like an unborn child."

In *The New York Herald Tribune,* Richard Watts, Jr., said, "Her voice is revealed in a deep, husky, throaty contralto that possesses every bit of that fabulous poetic glamour that has made this distant Swedish lady the outstanding actress of the motion picture world."

Mordaunt Hall, writing in *The New York Times,* found Garbo "even more interesting through being heard than she was in her mute portrayals. She reveals no nervousness before the microphone, and her careful interpretation of Anna can scarcely be disputed."

John Mosher of *The New Yorker* thought it "implausible that a woman so markedly beautiful should have such an extraordinarily difficult time. She has a boy's voice, really, rather flat, rather toneless, yet growing more attractive as the picture advances. You become somewhat accustomed to it."

More than thirty years after its debut, in 1962, film historian Richard Schickel reviewed *Anna Christie,* calling it "very dull, with Marie Dressler providing the only vitality in an otherwise static and ludicrous film."

After that, a German-language version was made (Garbo was fluent in German), with Salka Viertel cast in the Marie Dressler role. Its premiere was held in Cologne. Both versions of the film were a hit at the box office, each generating $1.5 million. Garbo herself preferred her German language version, which has been judged by latter-day critics as more natural, more expressive, and more "modern" than its glossier and sometimes stilted Hollywood counterpart. Also, Garbo is obviously more at ease speaking German than English.

In an almost unheard of event for the Academy Awards, Garbo in one year received two Best Actress nominations—one for *Anna Christie*, the other for her next film, *Romance [see below]*.

The camera converted **Garbo** into a creature of elegance and beauty, even though she was big-boned, with a heavy nose and a manly stride.

Perhaps because she was competing against herself, she lost to Norma Shearer for her performance in *The Divorcée*. [The theory that an actor might lose if he or she competed against him or herself in any given year was actually disproved by Shearer. She competed against herself that year, having also been nominated for her starring role in Their Own Desire.]

Clare Booth Luce, the noted journalist, wrote: "Garbo will be forgotten as a woman in ten years, and as an actress, her memory will be dead when Helen Hayes, Lynn Fontanne, and Katharine Cornell are beginning to grow greenest. Her shadowy gigantic six-foot close-ups in the arms of a celluloid John Gilbert, Ramon Novarro, or Robert Montgomery, even Clark Gable, will be her only epitaph—fairly humorous celluloid strips of interest only to antiquarians or humorists—who may conceivably show them to their friends to provide a curious or mirthful evening."

***

Marie Dressler, a huge and much-beloved star at the time, often showed up with a young starlet, who she was putting on the casting couch with the vain promise that she might use her influence to make her a star at MGM.

Mercedes de Acosta recalled, "I knew dozens of women like Joan Crawford who advanced themselves on the casting couch. But Dressler was my first experience with a female star, who used the couch to seduce young maidens with stardust in their dreams."

In her memoirs, Mercedes later revealed that after she got involved with Garbo, she was shocked that she did not see the final cut of her films, not even some of the rushes. "She told me she never saw *Anna Christie* because she did not want to hear her own voice."

"If I see myself in film," said Garbo, "I feel it will break the dramatic quality I create within my own psyche."

According to Mercedes, "Garbo told me that it wasn't until after the war that she saw three of her films: *Anna Christie, Mata Hari,* and *Camille.*"

ROMANCE (1930)
GARBO'S "BE GAY OR DIE" INSOUCIANCE

Garbo's second talkie, *Romance,* reteamed her with director Clarence Brown and her former leading man, the stone-faced Lewis Stone. A Pre-Code drama that was to some degree overlooked after a lackluster opening, it's cited today as one of her lesser-known movies.

Romance was based on a 1913 play by Edward Sheldon. It had already been adapted into a silent film starring Doris Keane, a once-famous but forgotten actress today.

As her leading man, Garbo had been mesmerized by the looks and persona of an emerging star, Gary Cooper. But she learned through Brown that Paramount would not release him, preferring to cast him at the time in *Morocco* (1930) with Marlene Dietrich, Paramount's answer to MGM's Garbo.

Garbo rejected Irving Thalberg's pitch of Douglas Fairbanks, Jr.: "He disappointed me in our last film together. We have no magic together. Let Joan Crawford take him away."

In this her fifteenth movie, Garbo was miscast as the *prima donna* Rita Cavallini. As Richard Corliss noted in his critique: "It was a bad idea to cast her as an Italian opera singer. She does her best to get the speech patterns down right—with musical vowels, blurred consonants, and r's that roll like the Tuscan Hills. But at times, her Italian accent eludes carelessly into her natural Swedish. She smiles, frowns, winks, inhales—all mischievously—and relies heavily on extravagant hand signals, as if translating simultaneously for the deaf."

Brown opted to cast a relative unknown, Gavin Gordon, a son of Mississippi and a former railway clerk, as Tom Armstrong, the swain who falls in love with Rita. He doesn't know at the time that she's the mistress of the wealthy and ruthless Cornelius Van Tuyl (Stone).

> The press speculated about an off-screen romance between **Garbo** and her leading man, **Gavin Gordon.** "If I had the personality of a David, the gifts of Sophocles, and the appearance of Helios, I should perhaps endeavor to win Garbo's attention and favors," he famously said.
>
> Actually, he was a homosexual.

The film opens when Armstrong as a elderly bishop talking to his grandson, Harry (Elliott Nugent). Harry has fallen in love with an actress and wants to marry her, despite his parents' objections. As his grandfather, Armstrong relates the story of his long-ago unrequited love for Rita Cavallini. The film then fades into a flashback.

After a lot of melodrama, *Romance* sinks into the regret of lost love, a story familiar to thousands of people who could (and can) identify with Armstrong's plight. He and Rita come from vastly different social classes and backgrounds, and in time, their engagement proves untenable.

"On looking back to those old times," the grandfather tells his impetuous grandson, "I married someone else—your grandmother, in fact."

[At the time, the movie magazines wrongly speculated that Gordon and Garbo might be involved in an off-screen romance. Nothing could have been further from the truth. Gordon was, in fact, the lover and became the decades-long companion of Edward Everett Horton, who was fifteen years his senior. Horton became famous in the 1930s and '40s for playing prissy, nervous, and effeminate characters—i. e., veiled homosexuals.]

In *The New York Times,* Mordaunt Hall wrote: "Garbo's performance in *Romance* is as good as anything she has done on the screen."

In *Picture Play* magazine, Norbert Lusk said, "In her role as a *prima donna,* Garbo is a thing of pure beauty, an inspiring blend of intellect and emotion, a tender, poignant, and poetic portrait of a woman who thrusts love from her because she considers herself unworthy of the man who offers it."

INSPIRATION (1931)
ALTHOUGH GARBO WAS INSPIRED, THE SCRIPT WAS NOT

As one observer noted, Garbo's fans stayed with her throughout the 1930s. "They forgave her for murder, adultery, suicide, prostitution, and, until the end, bad scripts."

Such was the case with her latest talkie, *Inspiration,* in which she was directed once again by Clarence Brown. At the end of the shoot, she swore that she'd never work with him again, but didn't keep her vow.

With equal disdain, she also didn't like Robert Montgomery, her leading man. He was reasonably handsome and only a year older than her. She deeply resented his ongoing advice about how to act. At least some of his abrasiveness stemmed from when he was eighteen, when his father jumped off the Brooklyn Bridge in a suicide fall.

Author Scott Eyman later wrote that "Montgomery had an off-screen reputation as one of the chilliest, most pompous actors ever to find their way to Hollywood." He'd co-starred with Norma Shearer in *The Divorcée,* and they had had a brief fling.

After meeting Garbo on the MGM lot, Shearer told her, "Bob always looks like a naughty boy who has just swallowed a canary but isn't going to tell. Good luck working with him as your co-star. You'll need it."

During his first meeting with Garbo, Montgomery surprised her by launching into an attack on "queers and lezzies. George Cukor once made a pass at me, and I bloodied his nose."

"You will have no problem with me," Garbo answered. "The only time I'll kiss you is when the director orders it."

Lewis Stone, in addition to Montgomery, was once again her leading man, too, playing Raymond Delval, her mentor and father figure. As part of the plot, he asks her, "Are you really as heartless as you seem?"

Marjorie Rambeau, as Lulu, had the second female lead. She warns Garbo, "You will end up in the gutter."

Garbo responds, "I've known some very nice people in the gutter."

Other support was provided by the crew, none more notable than William Daniels, her top photographer. Cedric Gibbons was the art director, the most notable in the film industry at the time.

Gowns were by Adrian, who had been brought to Hollywood by Natacha Rambova, Valentino's second wife. He would design for some of the biggest stars in town, actresses who included Norma Shearer, Jeanette MacDonald, Jean Harlow, and Katharine Hepburn. He designed the clothes for Joan Crawford in twenty-eight of her films.

Inspiration was adapted from a French-

"*Inspiration* is uninspired," wrote one critic. "**Garbo's** hair is frizzled, and she wears vampiric clothing."

Another reviewer claimed, "Laurels for Garbo should be dewed with tears."

The "Eugénie Hat" that Adrian designed for Garbo in *Inspiration* became a sensation across America. Named in honor of the French Empress Eugénie de Montijo, wife of Napoléon III, who popularized it in the 1850s, it's small, and usually worn tilted forwards over the face, or angled low over one eye.

Garbo's "endorsement" of the style, as she wore it in some of her costume dramas, led to a nationwide milliner's revival that continued till the beginning of World War II.

language novel, *Sapho*, by Alphonse Daudet, published in 1884. It had previously been adapted into a silent film, *The Eternal Sappho* (1916), starring Theda Bara, the original screen vamp.

In this latest adaptation, Garbo plays Yvonne Valbret, a woman of many lovers who poses as an artists' model. She falls for André Montell, a young student of foreign diplomacy hoping for a prominent career.

They begin a love affair, but he breaks it off when he learns unflattering details about her past. Years later, he discovers her living in poverty, and he provides a cottage for her outside Paris. Their relationship at this point is platonic.

André decides to marry a woman from "the respectable class," but soon realizes that he is still in love with Yvonne. Aware that it's too late to start over again, and as he is sleeping, she leaves him a "goodbye forever" note.

Norbert Lusk, a reviewer for *Picture Play*, wrote: "Laurels for Garbo should be dewed with tears of regret. So superior indeed is Yvonne to the trite circumstances of her story that you feel that the player, aware of the disparity, is spurred to greater effort."

Variety found that "Miss Garbo has never looked or played better than in this picture." *The New York Times* claimed, "No matter what may be said of the story, Miss Garbo gives a stunning performance."

Inspiration got a lot of bad notices, the worst being from the *Hollywood Citizen News:* "Garbo has had her day. There is something about her that evokes a vitriolic past and an empty future."

Years later, Robert Montgomery was asked what it was like working with Garbo: "I never want to discuss her," he answered.

SUSAN LENOX—HER FALL AND RISE (1932)
AS A "SCREEN TEAM," GARBO & CLARK GABLE SIZZLE

In Garbo's next talkie, she co-starred with a thirty-year-old actor, a pre-mustached Clark Gable. Soon he would ascend to the throne as "King of Hollywood."

The Pre-Code plot was based on a novel by David Graham Phillips, which aroused a storm of protest because of its so-called "pornography"

The novelist had been murdered in 1911 by a crazed reader who felt that Phillips had libeled his sister in a previous novel.

As the stars from completely different worlds disliked each other intensely, Gable and Garbo saved their love-making strictly for the screen, Gable referred to her as "that stuck-up broad." She found him "crude and unmannered."

Susan Lenox was shot as Hollywood and the film industry was floundering through the final transitions from silent movies to talkies. Dozens of silent screen stars had already faded into oblivion. Gloria Swanson, as

Norma Desmond in *Sunset Blvd.*, mourned the changes, saying, "We had faces then!"

That was true back in the silent era, but no more. Since the birth of sound, actors needed faces and voices, too. And whereas Ronald Colman and John Barrymore easily made the transition to Talkies, John Gilbert, Mary Pickford, and Lillian Gish weren't faring so well. Neither was Vilma Banky. New stars were on the rise, notably James Cagney, Jean Harlow, and Gable himself.

Called "Pop," the director, Robert Z. Leonard, had once been married to the blonde, silent screen goddess, Mae Murray. This son of Chicago had been nominated as Best Director for his helming of *The Divorcée,* starring Norma Shearer.

Garbo was cast as Helga Ohlin, an illegitimate child trapped in an abusive home. Her uncle, Karl Ohlin (Jean Hersholt), wants to force her to marry a brutish lout, Jeb Mondstrum (Alan Hale, Sr.). She flees in horror and arrives during a rainstorm at the rented cabin of a mining engineer, Rodney Spencer (Gable).

He takes her in. At first, she is suspicious of him. Then he wins her heart. She falls in love. During one of his business trips, her uncle appears with her intended husband, and she's forced once again to flee.

Changing her name to Susan Lenox, she takes a train filled with circus people and becomes employed as a dancer. Of course, she has to "sing for

Two posters advertising (left) the US and (right) the German-language release of this film.

Hollywood's newest leading male sensation, rugged **Clark Gable,** privately boasted, "No matter the leading lady—Joan Crawford, Norma Shearer, Jean Harlow—The result is the same. My lovemaking has them kissing like a whore and getting wet as November in their bloomers."

He hadn't met Garbo yet. "She was as cold as Sweden in January," he said.

her supper" with the manager of the circus.

She finds the atmosphere of the circus abusive, and flees once again, this time arriving in Manhattan. Here, she becomes the mistress of Mike Kelly (Hale Hamilton), a crooked politician.

At a party at his penthouse, she has a reunion with Rodney. It doesn't go well.

A lot of melodrama follows, with arrivals and departures. The duo ends up in South America where true love finally wins out in the final reel.

The New York Times found the picture "rather disappointing, using silent film techniques, with halting and often crudely written dialogue and poorly developed episodes."

Photoplay was more positive: "If you like your romance thick, your passion strong, and Garbo hot, don't miss this. If you were mad for Garbo before, wait until you see her teamed up with this manifestation of masculine sex appeal called Clark Gable."

Privately, Gable told both Garbo and their director, Leonard, "This flicker is going to make me one hell of a box office attraction. From now on I'll no longer have to let queers like George Cukor or that so-called actor, Willian Haines, go down on me."

Two photos from *Susan Lenox*, each with a different style of male flesh (from well-groomed to scruffy) from **Clark Gable.**

After this picture, MGM's plans to forge Gable and Garbo into a romantic screen team were ditched.

In his review of *Susan Lenox*, Richard Griffith wrote: "Garbo more than betters the able performance of her rugged co-star, Clark Gable, who shines under stress but with occasional lapses into moments of amateur play-acting."

Some critics predicted that as the onscreen pairing of Garbo and Gable would become the box office dream team of the 1930s. Irving Thalberg was so pleased with their twin co-starring roles that he announced that they soon would appear in *Red Dust* (1932). That didn't happen. Jean Harlow, not Garbo, ended up in Gable's arms instead.

***

As she neared the end of filming *Susan Lenox*, Garbo met Mercedes de Acosta, who—in secret Hollywood circles—was known (in slang parlance) as a "star fucker."

Mercedes had arrived in Los Angeles in June of 1931 with ambitions of becoming a screenwriter. Along the way, she had developed a friendship with Salka Viertel, who had played the Marie Dressler role in the German-language version of *Anna Christie*.

Salka had been born in the Galicia district of Poland at the turn of the 20th Century. Her Jewish family eventually gravitated to Vienna.

Her dream was to become an actress, perhaps a writer. In Vienna, she was discovered by the legendary Max Reinhardt, and went on the stage. In 1929, with her husband Berthold Viertel, she moved to Hollywood and quickly became an important player in the expatriate colony there as a writer in the story department of MGM. She soon befriended Garbo, and, a bit later, became the acquaintance of Mercedes, too.

The Viertel home on Maybery Road in Santa Monica became a gathering place every weekend, for the European colony.

One afternoon, as Salka and Mercedes were talking, the doorbell rang. In walked Garbo, the subject of many of Mercedes' dreams, as she'd seen all of her films, some of them many times.

In her memoirs, Mercedes described Garbo's entrance: "She was remarkably beautiful—far more so than she seemed in her films. She was dressed in a white jumper and dark blue sailor pants. Her feet were bare and, like her hands, slender and sensitive. Her beautiful straight hair hung down to her shoulders, and she wore a white tennis visor pulled well down over her face in its effort to hide her extraordinary eyes, which held in them the look of eternity."

Garbo stayed to talk for nearly an hour, but Mercedes could not remember the conversation, since she was so mesmerized by the look and presence of "The Divine Garbo." After about an hour, she got up to leave, and Salka walked with her to her car. When she came back, she told Mercedes, "Garbo liked you very much."

The first time scriptwriter and actress Salka Viertel entertained **Garbo** (left) and **Mercedes de Acosta,** she told them, "What producers want in Hollywood is an original but familiar script—unusual but popular, moralistic but sexy, true but improbable, tender but violent, slick but a highbrow masterpiece. When they have that, then they can 'work on it,' making it more 'commercial' just to justify their high salaries."

Two days later, Salka called Mercedes and invited her over to have breakfast with Garbo. This time, the elusive star arrived wearing a pair of white shorts and a halter top. Mercedes later confessed that she was enchanted by her bronzed legs.

After breakfast, Salka told her guests that she and Berthold had committed themselves as hosts for a business luncheon they'd arranged in their home with a Hollywood producer. But in lieu of throwing them out, she suggested that they visit a nearby home they were "house-sitting" for an absent friend during his absence. Lovely, and with views of the Pacific, it was the property of the screenwriter, Oliver Garrett. She entrusted its door keys to Mercedes, suggesting that they spend the rest of their late morning and afternoon there, privately.

Once they were alone together inside Garrett's house, as the phonograph spun, they decided to dance. [Songs that Mercedes remembered years later from that long-ago afternoon included "Daisy, You're Driving Me Crazy," "Schöne Gigolo," and "Goodnight, Sweetheart."]

Garbo invited her to lunch, but Mercedes had other commitments, one of which was an intimate gathering at the home of Pola Negri.

Garbo scoffed at her use of the word "intimate."

"I know Pola. She'll have six-hundred guests...at least."

As it turned out, there were only one-hundred guests there for lunch that afternoon. As Mercedes was talking to Basil Rathbone and Ramon Novarro, a butler approached her, informing her that she was wanted on the phone.

It was Garbo, asking her to come over.

Mercedes said she'd drive over right away. "There are a hundred people here. No one will miss me."

As she pulled into Garbo's driveway on St. Vincent Boulevard, Garbo

Garbo (left) "California dreaming" with **Salka Viertel** (right) an *émigrée* European uncomfortably positioned in Hollywood during the peak years of the Nazi atrocities

In this scene from the silent German-made film, *Madame DuBarry* (1919), **Pola Negri,** playing the down-on-her-luck courtesan to a (disgraced) French king struggles with her captors —as directed by Ernst Lubitsch—beside a guillotine.

was waiting, clad in a man's bedroom slippers and a black Chinese dressing robe.

Sitting in the garden, in reference to the filming of *Susan Lenox*, she compared it to "my prison exile," telling Mercedes that she found Clark Gable "insufferable."

Soon, she stopped talking, suggesting that she and Mercedes sit silently in the garden, enjoying the songs of the birds and the beauty of the flowers.

As the afternoon shadows lengthened, she rose to her feet and announced that Mercedes had to go. She had to retire early for a good night's sleep before facing "Gable's bad breath tomorrow morning."

She took Mercedes delicate hand and kissed it. "Until we meet again."

And then she disappeared into the house.

***

When the final scene of *Susan Lenox* was shot, Garbo phoned Mercedes, asking her to come over to her rented home. Within minutes, Mercedes was in her car, driving to meet Garbo, who, once again, was waiting for her in the driveway.

This time, she invited Mercedes into her residence, a dark, gloomy place sparsely furnished. Mercedes looked into the living room with a fireplace, but Garbo told her, "I never use the downstairs, except for the kitchen."

She invited Mercedes upstairs into her large bedroom, which had no more furnishings than a monk's quarters. "This is where I live." Beside her bed, on a nightstand, was a children's book *Peter Rabbit*, "I read from it all the time. It is my favorite piece of literature."

Garbo told her that she'd been given six weeks off for a vacation from

Garbo's frequent appearance on the covers of film fan magazines was not lost on other members of Hollywood's European expatriate community.

A debate was raging: Was she the most beautiful woman in the world?

MGM. "I'm desperately tired, and I need to rejuvenate myself," Garbo said. "That's a new word I've learned in English. I've been given this little cabin in the Sierra Nevadas—no phone, no link to the world. I am only telling you this in case you might wonder what happened to me."

After talking with Mercedes for more than an hour, and through the open window, Mercedes heard a car pull into the driveway. She looked out to see Garbo's black Packard pulling in.

The run-down cabin at the shore of Silver Lake. That's **Garbo** stringing out laundry on the clothesline in front.

Downstairs, she met James, Garbo's African American chauffeur, who seemed to know only two words: "Yes, ma'am."

"James is my faithful servant," Garbo said. "He knows how to keep a secret. No one can pry anything about me from him,. There's a problem. When I say 'Turn right,' he turns left. Left means right. Once, I learned that, we get along just fine. I know how to direct him."

After James loaded the car, Garbo locked the house and turned to Mercedes, taking her hand and kissing her farewell. "I'm sure that the road will lead me to you again."

Holidays of long ago and far away. **Two views of Garbo** at Silver Lake, legs akimbo, topless beneath the towel, and anything but Hollywood glamourous.

Watching "the bus," as Garbo called her car, drive off into the late morning, Mercedes admitted, "I began to shed tears. I never expected to see her again. There was a finality to her departing. For all I knew, she had a lover stashed away in that isolated cabin."

Two days later, a call came in from Garbo, placed from a pay phone three-hundred miles away. "I'm so desperately lonely up here. I'm coming back with James to pick you up and take you to the cabin."

Moving nonstop except for refueling, Garbo, driven by James, arrived at the rented home Mercedes shared with her gay friend, John Colton, who had written the stage adaptation (*Rain*) of W. Somerset Maugham's novel, *Miss Thompson (aka Rain)*. When Garbo arrived, Colton invited her inside.

He had chilled some champagne and roasted a chicken for Garbo, James, and himself, serving a vegetable plate for Mercedes, since she "abhorred" meat, a result of a long-ago visit to a slaughterhouse.

When their meal was over, and as night was descending, Mercedes loaded her lone suitcase into the trunk of "the bus." With James at the wheel, they headed northwest from Los Angeles, hoping to escape the daytime heat of the Mohave Desert, which in July could register a temperature of 120° or higher.

Garbo and Mercedes, as lovers, would spend the next six weeks together in the Eastern Sierra Nevadas, at the base of Carson Mountain, about 20 miles south of South Lake Tahoe, in a cabin near the shoreline of Silver Lake. Before he headed, with the car, back to Los Angeles, James loaded their provisions into a big rowboat and Garbo with Mercedes set out together, alone across the cold waters, against a backdrop of mountains looming in the distance. Garbo told her that the cabin had been a gift from Wallace Beery, the character actor long divorced from Gloria Swanson.

James had been instructed to return in six weeks, and not to tell a soul where Garbo was, much less, reveal the identity of her companion.

Mercedes de Acosta snapped this topless photo of **Greta Garbo** during their "honeymoon" at Silver Lake. Garbo was later horrified when the private photo was leaked to the press.

Years later, her niece was not surprised that she had posed topless: "Greta is Scandinavian," was her justification.

The cabin was ramshackle and barely fit for habitation, but Garbo gravitated to its bleakness. "I didn't come here for the cabin, but for the great outdoors. Mercedes would later write that "Garbo was a creature of the wind, the storms, the rocks, the trees, and the water."

After a meager lunch, she invited Mercedes for a nude swim in the cold, clear waters that evoked Sweden for her.

That night under a full moon, Garbo roasted mountain trout on an open grill like she and her now-dead older sister, Alva, had done on a summer camping trip in her native land. Although she didn't eat meat, Mercedes or rare occasions would sample fish. Otherwise, Garbo's favorite supper was a loaf of bread, a hunk of cheese, and a glass of milk.

That night with the glow of a full moon filtering into their bedroom, Mercedes and Garbo made passionate love for the first time. As Mercedes would later tell her friend, Nazimova, "Garbo told me I satisfied her like no man ever had, especially John Gilbert." Their pattern of love making would continue without interruption for the next few weeks.

The only time they saw other people was when Garbo rowed the boat to the opposite shore of the lake where a group of burly lumberjacks were camped. From the men, they purchased fresh eggs and milk. Most of them had never seen a Garbo movie, and thought Garbo and Mercedes were simple college girls camping out.

The days passed far too quickly for Mercedes and for Garbo, too. Mercedes later wrote, "Those six weeks were like six minutes." She even got Garbo to allow herself to be photographed topless, a copy of which would later go public. Mercedes boasted privately, "I have not only seen but made love to the breasts of some of the most famous women on the planet, but none were as beautiful as those of Greta Garbo."

During the course of one hot July afternoon, Garbo for the first time in America spoke of her childhood in Stockholm, her sadness over the death of her big sister, Alva, and her desire to become an actress in Sweden and Germany.

She also revealed that her mother had caught her masturbating and told the priest on her. Later, Garbo learned that her mother, while condemning her as a "bad girl," was actually having an affair with that pastor.

After six weeks, James, the driver, reappeared at the appointed time. He was there to greet Garbo and Mercedes after they rowed from the cabin back to the point where he'd parked the bus for the next leg of their return to Los Angeles. Garbo confessed that she detested Hollywood and might return to her native Sweden. Her contract with MGM was set to expire in 1932, and she did not plan to renew it. She expressed delight that she had accumulated $1.3 million, a vast sum in a world mired at the time in a depression. "I am thinking about going back to Sweden, buying some land in Värmland, and settling down and fading into obscurity. A footnote, as you call it in English, in Hollywood history."

Mercedes urged her to reconsider. "I

This widely publicized photograph of **Mercedes** (left) and **Garbo** was snapped in 1934. A newspaper caption at the time described the sighting like this:

"An unauthorized shot of the elusive Swedish star, taken by a cameraman who waited for three hours on the running board of a car parked on Hollywood's main boulevard. He just managed to snap Garbo as she came out of her tailor's with a friend, Miss de Costa *(sic)*."

have great intuition. Your biggest pictures lie ahead of you, movies that will enchant the world. I sensed that."

As Mercedes and Garbo returned to Hollywood, MGM was immersed in pre-production for *Mata Hari,* her next picture. Her costumes would be the most provocative of her career. She'd portray Mata Hari (1876-1917), the Dutch-born exotic dancer and spy who, in France during World War I, used her seductive powers to entice members of the French military to reveal secrets which she passed on to the German command.

As a modern dancer, she was a contemporary of Isadora Duncan, Mercedes' former lover.

After only a few days back, Garbo and Mercedes learned that her three leading men in that upcoming film would be Ramon Novarro, the former lover of Valentino; Lewis Stone (again); and Lionel Barrymore.

Before shooting on *Mata Hari* began, Mercedes convinced Garbo to move out of her gloomy rented house into one on North Rockingham Road in Brentwood that was airy, filled with light, and more charming. It had a tennis court too, where the women played almost daily. "I thought I was a pretty good player," Mercedes admitted, "but Greta beat me every time."

Their days passed with horseback riding in the nearby hills, or else taking long walks into the mountains, sometimes going seven miles, with

Mercedes not only wore pants, she prosyletized them. When she "went to Pickfair dressed in a white sweater and white trousers" on her second day in Hollywood, she reports, she was pulled aside and told, "You'll get a bad reputation if you dress this way out."

According to Darwin Porter, "Mercedes was clearly cultivating a reputation, and she continued to covertly connect lesbianism to advanced ideas about clothing throughout her memoir. She claimed to have been the catalyst who persuaded both Garbo and Dietrich into pants. As she stated in her memoirs, 'When I had known Greta for a little while, I got her to exchange her sailor pants for slacks.'"

The center and right-hand illustrations are from Mercedes' diary. The pages she devoted to Garbo reveal something approaching an obsession.

the faithful James always meeting them with "the bus" at the end of their designated trail. They began to explore the "untamed" countryside of the San Fernando Valley as it existed in those days.

"We enjoyed standing on a hill in the moonlight, taking in the night air and the song of the nightingales," Mercedes said. "Sometimes, we'd remain outdoor until the first streaks of pink light brightened the sky over Southern California. Although calm and peaceful, these were the happiest moments of my often tragic life."

Mercedes, too, moved from the house she shared with John Colton. "I love him dearly, but I came to regard our house as unsafe. We used to entertain Greta there, but now I told her it was dangerous. John preferred 'rough trade,' One night, I came home and found five burly sailors sitting totally nude in the living room. As the only woman in the house, I fled upstairs and bolted my door. They next day, I moved out, having found a nice little villa next door to Greta."

Mercedes began to address Garbo's dress code. Instead of the culottes she usually wore, she got her to switch to tailored slacks, a look that was avant-garde (some said "shocking") in those days.

Once, when both of them were attired in men's clothing, they were photographed walking together along Hollywood Boulevard. That picture became notorious after its publication in *The Los Angeles Times* under a headline that read: GARBO IN PANTS.

Rumors spread quickly that Garbo and Mercedes were lesbians, although such an accusation was merely whispered about, not printed in the gossip columns.

Mercedes made Garbo more culturally aware. This devotee of music, poetry, literature, and food (vegetarian only) opened up new worlds to her. Mercedes provided her with books to wean her from *Peter Rabbit*.

In movie houses, art galleries, and in concerts, Garbo and Mercedes were spotted together as "a couple."

Garbo usually wore dark sunglasses and floppy hats to conceal her eyes. "Greta was a creature of moods," Mercedes said. "She didn't want me to live with her, but nearby. When her black mood descended, she would sit for hours staring into the darkness."

One of her most famous remarks was "I *vant* to be alone."

Mercedes soon learned about a physical characteristic that might have contributed to Garbo's retreats: She had an unusual menstrual cycle, regularly menstruating every seven or eight days. Mercedes took her to a leading gynecologist in Beverly Hills, who told her that one in a thousand women have this condition, that its reasons were unknown, and that it was not treatable.

Both pre- and post-Mercedes, Garbo was known to have had many lovers, both male and female. Before Mercedes, there had been Marlene Dietrich in Berlin. The roll call would also feature other actresses, including Fifi D'Orsay, Louise Brooks, Dolores Del Rio, Paulette Duval, Salka Viertel, novelist Carson McCullers, Beatrice Lillie, and her co-star in *A Woman of Affairs*, Dorothy Sebastian.

Her male suitors featured boxer-actor Max Bauer, photographer Cecil

Beaton (he was mostly gay), health guru Gaylord Hauser; Swedish actor Einar Hanson when he wasn't in bed servicing Maurice Stiller; conductor Leopold Stokowski; William S. Paley, head of CBS; Prince Sigurd, Duke of Upland in Sweden, and the novelist Erich Maria Remarque, who ungallantly reported that "Unlike Marlene, Garbo is lousy in bed."

MGM's publicists tried to get Garbo to be more cooperative with the press. She said, "I give everything I have on the screen. Why do I have to usurp my private life?"

Many actors remembered seeing her movies when they were in their teens. Such was the case with Marcello Mastroianni, born in 1923 and the undisputed superstar of Italian cinema. He told the press, "I thought that in most of her films like *The Painted Veil* and *Conquest,* Miss Garbo looked like the stepmother of Snow White."

On some nights Mercedes and Garbo entertained Marie Dressler, her co-star in *Anna Christie*. Overweight and quite ugly, Dressler was an amusing dinner guest. Rumors that she had a brief fling with Garbo have never been confirmed.

Born in 1868, Dressler faced a decline in her film career as a silent star, but came back big in the 1930s, winning an Oscar for *Min and Bill* (1930), co-starring with Wallace Beery. The duo also had another hit in 1933, *Tugboat Annie*. Dressler was a highlight in *Dinner at Eight* (1933), with an all-star cast. One of her scenes with Jean Harlow, walking side by side together into a very formal dining room, became one of the one hundred most iconic episodes in the history of 20th Century cinema.

HARLOW: I was reading a book the other day
DRESSLER: Reading a book?
HARLOW: Yes. It's all about civilization or something. A nutty kind of a book. Do you know that the guy said that machinery is going to take the place of every profession?
DRESSLER: Oh my dear. That's something you need never worry about.

Biographer Axel Madsen quoted Dressler as saying "When I was sad or emotionally exhausted, Greta would come to me, sensing my need for her. Standing on my doorstep, she would sing, 'Heaven Will Protect the Working Girl.' And when she was ready to leave, she would sing goodbye with the same song."

Marie Dressler, suffering from cancer, died at the age of sixty-five on July 28, 1934.

With the exception of *Anna*

Jean Harlow (left) with **Marie Dressler,** playing a *grande dame*, in *Dinner at Eight*.

In this scene, the frumpy, aging, Dressler assures the sexy platinum blonde that what she's selling will never go out of style.

Christie, Mercedes occupied a front-row seat at the filming of most of Garbo's talking films of the 1930s, concluding with her last movie, the one that was shot just as World War II had broken out in Europe and would soon engulf the United States.

MATA HARI (1931)
GARBO'S SPIN ON ONE OF HISTORY'S GREATEST VAMPS

In 1931, MGM released Garbo's 15th film, a highly fictionalized biography of the notorious Javanese-Dutch spy who worked during World War I for the German Secret Service. This wasn't one of Garbo's best films, although her headgear was the most striking she ever wore.

Directed by George Fitzmaurice, Mata Hari remains Garbo's campiest film. Adrian, the costume designer and milliner was commissioned to design the most bizarre hats of any Garbo movie: A Friar Tuck skullcap, a bishop's miter pillbox, a bonnet with spirals in the forehead, a sequined cloche inspired by a Christmas tree, and a black yarmulke destined for a courtroom episode.

It was Mercedes who suggested that Garbo wear a long black cape, with her hair straight back as she faced the firing squad.

It's true that the real Mata Hari died before a firing squad in 1917, but the rest of the events depicted in the film inspired by her life are largely apocryphal. In the movie, Garbo discovers true love in the arms of one of her victims.

The Swede was already familiar with playing the role of a beautiful spider baiting the fly. It was even suggested that she could have done the role in her sleep.

In a famous "Letter to Garbo" in the 1932 edition of *Theatre Arts Monthly,* Mary Canfield wrote: "You merely walked through it, like some superior and unperturbed mannequin."

In the press and publicity associated with its release, Garbo's power as a seductress was publicly hailed as a force more potent than that of the Virgin Mary. Although it was probably a brilliant piece of PR, it generated censor-

Left: the real **Mata Hari** in 1910; right **Garbo** portraying Mata Hari in 1931. Which of these famous women is the more exotic?

ship problems in England, thereby adding to her screen allure.

Hollywood's most notorious homosexual, Ramon Novarro, was selected as Garbo's leading man. Later, he would die violently at the hands of two brothers, both hustlers, out to rob him in his home.

Garbo's love scenes with Novarro, playing the role of a brave Russian lieutenant, were not convincing. He doesn't exactly wince by having to take a seductive woman in his arms, but it's obvious she's not a member of the gender he'd like to be romancing. One of his real life former lovers--one of whom was Rudolph Valentino--would have been more to his liking.

Except for Clark Gable, with whom Garbo appeared in *Susan Lenox: Her Fall and Rise*, many of Garbo's leading men were just too fey for her strong screen presence.

A noteworthy exception to this rule was *Mata Hari*, where Garbo is backed up by strong supporting older actors. They included Lewis Stone, cast as Andriani, who has choreographed her spy mission, and Lionel Barrymore, who plays her lover in the film. Barrymore's character, in exchange for her sexual favors (which he presumably cannot resist), betrays his country by revealing strategic military secrets that she passes on. .

During the making of *Mata Hari*, Novarro hinted to the press that he'd fallen madly in love with Garbo. Of course, that was a fabrication. At the time, Garbo was spending most nights in the arms of Mercedes de Acosta. And when she wasn't with Garbo, Mercedes was seducing Marlene Dietrich.

Perhaps the actress who was the most disappointed by the success of

Greta Garbo was never more exotic on screen than she was in her hit film, *Mata Hari*, based on the famous spy.

Author Frederick Sands wrote: "Cast for the second time as a spy, Garbo walks through *Mata Hari* like a countess slumming, curiously detached until the final unforgettable scene. Then, in black cloak, hair pulled back from her face, she appears before the soldiers who will lead her to the firing squad."

Mata Hari was Pola Negri. During the previous two years, RKO had promised that she would star in a film inspired by the life of the glamourous spy, pre-marketing her as "a woman who was unfaithful to a million men."

During the filming, Garbo kept Mercedes abreast of what was going on. She claimed that her director, George Fitzmaurice, told her that "Whereas I come across on the screen as aggressive and masculine, Novarro was coming off with passive femininity. Fitzmaurice fears the censors will demand cuts in some of my more torrid scenes."

Commercially, of the eighteen films she'd made, *Mata Hari* was Garbo's most successful, netting Metro a profit of a million dollars and becoming a sensation in both America and Europe.

The New York Times defined her performance as "flawless." *Screen Book* claimed, "Garbo has the best role of her career and sets a standard which is almost untouchable."

Variety observed that "Garbo does a polite hooch to Oriental music as a starter. In the same number, she makes a symbolic play for a large idol, with hips in motion all the while."

> When told that **Ramon Novarro** would be her leading man in *Mata Hari*, **Garbo** said, "He is a small man, and I'm a big girl. He will have to wear boots with lifts to make him taller."
>
> In one particularly suggestive scene, the viewer only saw a cigarette aglow in the darkness of the bedroom.
>
> The Hays Office demanded that the scene be cut from its 1940 reissue. That scene is now lost to history.

***

One early evening after work, during the filming of *Mata Hari*, Garbo arrived at Mercedes' new home, beaming with excitement, as if she'd scored some sort of coup. The secret she had to reveal was exciting news to Mercedes.

Late that morning, Garbo had met with Irving Thalberg, the number two man at MGM, working directly under Louis B. Mayer. She got him to agree to let Mercedes write a new screenplay for her.

A meeting between Thalberg and Mercedes had been arranged for the following afternoon.

Mercedes stayed up all night, conjuring up a possible scenario, finally inventing a character evocative of the role that Garbo had portrayed in *A Woman of Affairs*. Mercedes' script was entitled *Desperate*.

In one of its scenes, the Garbo character would make her escape while dressed as a young man. Before she reported to the studio, Mercedes ran through the plot with Garbo, who heartily approved of that scene and several others, too.

That afternoon, Mercedes was ushered into Thalberg's office. His desk was raised on a dias (platform), looking down upon three armchairs whose seats were so low they almost touched the floor. The arrangement allowed him to tower over whomever was in the office to see him.

Married to Norma Shearer, Thalberg had a boyish quality to him and was very young. He was variously called the "Boy Wonder" or "The Napoleon of Metro." Director Sidney Franklin claimed, "Thalberg was as fragile as alabaster, with an Italianate face evoking a Renaissance prince in Florence."

Irving Thalberg, left, the "Boy Wonder" of MGM in charge of production, is pictured in 1922 with his wife, **Norma Shearer**, the queen of the studio and its "super boss," **Louis B. Mayer**.

Although Thalberg hired Mercedes to write scripts for Garbo, they were never produced.

Born in Brooklyn in 1899, he eventually made it to MGM, where he rose quickly in the film world. He suffered a heart condition, a by-product of a teenaged bout with rheumatic fever. His doctor had warned him, "You will die young."

He listened to Mercedes' plot without saying anything until she got to the part where Garbo is to dress in the clothing of a young man. "Are you out of your mind?" Thalberg interrupted. Then he rose up on his platform. "At MGM, we make beautiful pictures with beautiful stars. Garbo is our prize asset. I want her beautifully gowned, not dressed as a man."

Despite his objection, he hired Mercedes to fashion a screenplay for Garbo. The next morning, Mercedes arose early and began to compose a scenario filled with action for her character, whom she'd ambiguously named "Erik."

Mercedes' script called for Garbo's character to move—fast, romantically, and recklessly—through scenes that depicted her riding with a fox hunt in Sussex; drinking beer with rough-and-tumble sailors in Marseille; hanging out with artists in seedy taverns on the Left Bank of Paris; gambling in a casino in Berlin; racing aboard a yacht off the French Riviera; and eventually and with panache, pawning her diamonds and rubies at a pawn shop on the Via Sistina in Rome.

Every evening, Mercedes would read the result of her day's work to Garbo after her return from the studio. After one of these readings, Garbo, looking disappointed, said, "So I do not get to dress as a man? Actually I want to play a man. I think I'll ask Thalberg if he'll let me play the lead in a film version of Oscar Wilde's *The Picture of Dorian Gray*."

As with thousands of other scripts and screenplays, *Desperate* would never be filmed.

***

Garbo wanted Mercedes to write a screenplay about the life of the 19th-Century French novelist, a woman who billed herself to the French as "*Geôrges Sand*." The romantic writer had been born in France in 1804 as Amantine Lucile Dupin. Amazingly, at the pinnacle of her success in the 1830s and '40s, she sold more books than Honoré de Balzac and Victor Hugo.

She became celebrated for her bohemian lifestyle and her scandalous affairs with composer Frédéric Chopin and the French Romantic poet, Alfred de Musset. She smoked cigars and dressed in mannish attire. This is why Garbo wanted to play her on the screen: "She's so unlike Camille," in her words.

In reference to his competitor, Hugo claimed that "Sand cannot determine whether she is male or female. It is not my place to decide if she is my brother or my sister."

Balzac called her "gifted with genius, one of theose exceptional women who cannot be judged by ordinary standards."

Despite her affairs with men, Alfred de Vigny referred to Sand as "Sappho, Queen of Lesbians."

"I could never quite pull off a screenplay that MGM would greenlight, in spite of repeated efforts on my part," Mercedes lamented, "but I fully understood why Greta wanted to impersonate Sand. They were so very much alike."

Although Garbo's dreams of impersonating her failed, other actresses would eventually succeed at bringing Sand to the screen. Over the course of many years, she appeared in several reincarnations: Merle Oberon portrayed her in *A Song to Remember* (1945); Patricia Morison in *Song Without End* (1960); Rosemary Harris in *Notorious Woman* (1974); Judy Davis in the British-American film, *Impromptu* (1991); and Juliette Binoche in the French film *Les Enfants du Siècle* (Children of the Century; 1999).

Biographer John Bainbridge wrote: "Like George Sand, Garbo is a child of the earth who has become one of the great ornaments of her age. She has also, like Sand, dared to live her life according to the standards of her own devising and quietly accepted the penalties imposed for failing to

Greta Garbo wanted to bring the tangled life of **Geôrges Sand**, the (female) French novelist depicted above, to the screen. Mercedes struggled in vain to create an acceptable script for MGM, but failed.

Greta and Mercedes even cast the leading men: John Barrymore as Frederick Chopin and Lew Ayres as the effete romantic poet, Alfred de Musset. Greta, of course, would have played the novelist herself.

It became another Hollywood project that never got produced.

follow the conventions of the herd. Her life has been frustrated, like Sand's and every other artist's, but here perhaps more so than most, because she is Greta Garbo, a woman who became a legend in her own time."

In 1947, an item appeared in *Variety* that Garbo would portray George Sand on the screen in a production from an independent company. George Cukor was set to direct it, with a screenplay by Salka Viertel. Laurence Oliver was assigned the role of Chopin. The movie was never made because adequate financing couldn't be arranged.

GRAND HOTEL (1932)
ROOMS FOR GARBO, THE BARRYMORES, JOAN CRAWFORD, & WALLACE BEERY

It's certainly old fashioned—after all, it was made in 1932—but Vicki Baum's bestseller was an excuse to bring together some of the great stars of the 30s, notably Garbo as Grusinskaya; John Barrymore as Baron Felix von Geigern; Joan Crawford as Flaemmchen; Wallace Beery as Preysing; and Lionel Barrymore as Otto Kringelein. Even Lewis Stone and Jean Hersholt check in, all under the direction of gay helmer Edmund Goulding. Along with Irving Thalberg, Paul Bern of the small dick and Jean Harlow-infamy produced this flick with costumes by the very gay Adrian.

Berlin's plushest hotel is the setting where "People come, and people go." There are a lot of subplots here—for example, Baron von Geigern is broke and trying to steal dancer Grusinskaya's pearls but ends up stealing her heart instead. Sure, it's pure soapy corn, but because of all these MGM legends, it's fun to watch. Regrettably, there are no scenes of Garbo and "Mommie Dearest" in the same frame. Nonetheless, Crawford was irked by Garbo's insistence on top billing and took her revenge by loudly playing Marlene Dietrich records in her dressing room.

Garbo wanted John Gilbert to play her lover but at the time, he had been designated as "box office poison." At first Garbo turned

Grand Hotel was an outstanding box office success. It was the top money-maker of the depression era of 1932, so much so that MGM became the only studio that year to report a profit.

Garbo's famous line, "I want to be alone," is ranked as No. Thirty in the American Film Institute's list of 100 best-known quotes in movies.

down the role because she believed that at 26 she was "too old" to play a prima ballerina.

But when Louis B. Mayer saw the final cut, he ordered more extra scenes shot with Garbo, fearing that Crawford (whom he never liked) would steal the picture.

The quote, "*I vant to be alone,*" spoken by Garbo in the movie, was listed at #30 in the AFI List of Top 100 Quotes from American films. *Grand Hotel* won the Best Picture Oscar, but it was not nominated for any other Academy Awards.

John Mosher in *The New Yorker* wrote, "Garbo dominates the picture, making the other players merely competent performers." Vicki Baum in *Modern Screen* wrote, "That face of wanton joy when she is happy. That face full of fear when she waits for her beloved in vain: Unforgettable! Thank you, Miss Garbo."

Sidney Carroll in *Picture Play* cast the dissenting vote: "*Grand Hotel* is worth seeing as a drum-beating exhibition for stars—each and all of them miscast."

During the filming of *Grand Hotel,* John Barrymore paid a surprise visit one night to Mercedes. They had once been friends, and he seemingly had overlooked her lesbian affair with his wife, Michael Strange.

He spent an hour talking about Garbo to Mercedes, telling her, "I am frightened to death to be working with her. She is so perfect as an artist and as a woman. And, as you know all too well, I am an imperfect man."

"But the greatest actor in the world," Mercedes assured him. "Reviewers will have a hard time determining which one of you is the more beautiful."

"Don't tell her I made this private visit with you."

"Your secrets, as always, are safe with me," Mercedes assured him.

In *Grand Hotel*, **Garbo** played a lonely Russian ballerina, **John Barrymore** a dashing baron who is, in reality, a petty jewel thief.

When Barrymore met the great diva, he said, "My wife and I think you are the loveliest person in the world."

"That shows you two have good taste," she answered.

As a blonde, **Garbo** starred in *As You Desire Me* with director/actor **Erich von Stroheim.** She was the only one in the cast who wanted him for the role, as he was "virtually hated by everyone," especially by Irving Thalberg.

Von Stroheim had undergone a serious operation and was in a weakened condition, but Garbo "mothered" him through his difficult role in which he portrayed her psychopathic captor.

As You Desire Me (1932)
Fans Want to Know: Is This Garbo's Last Film?

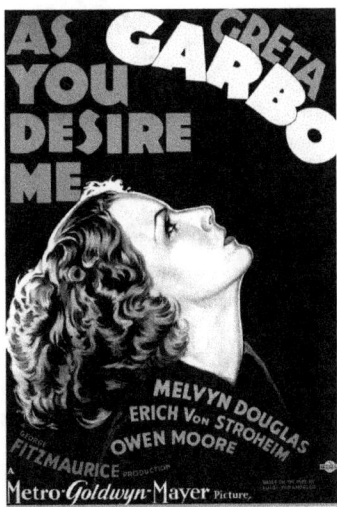

Once again, George Fitzmaurice directed Garbo (her only time as a blonde) in the Pre-Code film, *As You Desire Me*. It was based on a play by the Italian writer, Luigi Pirandello.

Her favorite photographer, William Daniels, had never made her look so beautiful, and Adrian's gowns were stunning on her well-shaped body.

Her leading man was Melvyn Douglas in the first of a trio of movies with her, including both her best and her worst. A son of Macon, Georgia, born four years before Garbo, he came into prominence in 1930s films as a suave leading man.

His father had been a Jewish emigrant from Riga, Latvia, then part of the Russian Empire. He was billed with Boris Karloff and Charles Laughton in James Whale's sardonic horror classic, *The Old Dark House* in 1932. In addition to Garbo, he also became Joan Crawford's leading man in such films as *The Shining Hour* (1938) and *They All Kissed the Bride* (1942).

Also appearing with her—as an actor, not as a director, a position he'd probably have preferred was the imperial and legendary Erich Von Stroheim. Garbo's former mentor, Mauritz Stiller, "worshipped" him, and so did Garbo, who had often been seen sitting at his feet listening to him pontificate.

According to Mercedes de Acosta, **"As You Desire Me** is the finest picture Garbo ever made. In one of its scenes, she is intoxicated. Never was a scene more superbly played. It is rare for an actress to play a drunken scene without appearing either vulgar or absurd."

"Garbo," Mercedes continued, "was neither of these. Instead, she gave a sense of being lost, like a person taking a wrong turning of a road and trying to grope her way back onto the right one."

Garbo appeared with **Melvyn Douglas,** her future leading man, in *As You Desire Me*. She was cast as Pirandello's *demi-mondaine* vamp transformed into a high-born wife.

She was more effective in scenes with Von Strohem, who played a figure inspired by Mauritz Stiller, a novelist who casts a possessive and hypnotic spell over her.

Born in Vienna in 1885, Von Stroheim was a visionary director of the silent era, helming *Greed* (1924), one of the most important movies ever made. As a director, he introduced sophisticated plots and *noirish* sexual and psychological undercurrents.

He had directed *The Merry Widow* (1925) with John Gilbert and Mae Murray, which became his biggest hit.

He'd also helmed the silent era's most disastrous film (never completed), *Queen Kelly* (1929) with Gloria Swanson. Producer Joseph P. Kennedy, faced with mounting costs, shut down the production.

Today, Von Stroheim is remembered chiefly for playing "that dumb butler role" *[his words]* in *Sunset Blvd.* (1950), starring Swanson as the demented has-been from the Silent Screen.

Cast as Zara, a *chanteuse réaliste*, Garbo plays a café entertainer in Budapest, suffering from amnesia. She is spotted by Tony Boffie (Owen Moore, Mary Pickford's former husband), who knows who she was before amnesia. He identifies her as Maria, the wife of Count Bruno Varelli (Douglas), an artist, who believes that she has been killed in a recent war between Austria and Italy.

Zara wants to flee from her "captor," Carl Slater (Von Stroheim), who seems to have her under some hypnotic spell. When she leaves him, he tries devious means to get her back. In the meantime, she has fallen in love with the count, who might (or might not, depending on a complication in the plot) be her husband.

As Garbo was shooting *As You Desire Me*, there were rumors that it might become her *adieu* to Hollywood. She was said to be returning to Sweden.

Upon its release, *The New Yorker* magazine gave the film a lackluster review, suggesting, "There is altogether too much discussion of Garbo these days."

Although admitting it was one of her lesser-known movies, Mercedes believed that in *As You Desire Me*, Garbo delivered her finest performance. Before facing the cameras the following day, Garbo spent her evenings rehearsing upcoming scenes with Mercedes.

Douglas crafted his own review of Garbo: "In the poetic intensity which she gives to banalities, she has no rival."

Richard Corliss found that Garbo as Zara was "a playful parody of Marlene Dietrich." Margorie Rosen called her performance "autoerotic intimacy, a self-caress."

***

In May of 1932, only hours before her MGM contract was to expire, Garbo announced that she was going to Sweden, and that she had booked "a one-way passage." The threat was not lost on Louis B. Mayer, who rushed to sign her to a two-picture deal, granting her $250,000 per film, an astonishing figure then, during the depths of the Depression.

Shooting on her first picture would be delayed for eight months while she was in Europe. During her time abroad, it was announced that her upcoming movie would be based on the life of Queen Christina of Sweden.

She had her choice of directors, and she selected Rouben Mamoulian, who had been born in Tblisi, Georgia, then part of the Russian Empire. His family ties were Armenian.

In time, he headed west, working in theater in both London and Broadway before moving to Hollywood. Once in Los Angeles, he helmed *Applause* (1929), one of the first talking pictures.

Upon her return to California, Garbo delayed contacting Mercedes, much to the latter's regret and disappointment. Finally, Garbo did call, inviting her on a vacation to the Grand Canyon.

On the date Garbo was set to arrive at Mercedes', she opted not to show up.

Mercedes waited and waited, but she never appeared.

Finally, Mercedes drove to Garbo's house, where she was told by her maid that she had left on a trip with Mamoulian, her upcoming director in *Queen Christina*.

Mercedes threw a temper fit, feeling betrayed. However, in less than a week, she heard from Garbo, who had returned. She had to cut short the trip because Mamoulian had given her gonorrhea, which, before the advent of penicillin, was difficult to treat. The cure for it at that time was debilitating and painful.

During Garbo's recuperation, she and Mercedes made up and spent hours discussing the character of Queen Christina. Mercedes at one time had been inspired to write its screenplay for Garbo, but the assignment had gone to Salka Viertel, another rival for Garbo's affections.

QUEEN CHRISTINA (1933)
A LESBIAN KISS, HIDDEN TRUTHS, HOMOSEXUAL TABOOS, & A BIOPIC OF A HISTORICAL FIGURE BADLY SUITED TO HER JOB

In the 1933 release of MGM's *Queen Christina*, the historical and true-to-life homely bisexual Swedish monarch was transformed into a stunning incarnation as Garbo photographed in close-up at her most beautiful.

Once again, she was teamed with her former lover, John Gilbert, after having found that she had no chemistry on screen with her first choice, another bisexual, Laurence Olivier. Nils Asther and Franchot Tone—even Clark Gable—had also been considered for the role which finally went to Gilbert. His Groucho Marx mustache did little to re-establish his career in the talkies, and this prestigious film did not halt his ignominious slide into oblivion. Within three years after the film was shot, the alcoholic Gilbert was dead.

Garbo felt some identity with the Queen who inherited the throne of Sweden in 1632 at the age of six after the death of her warrior-father, King Gustavus II Adolphus. "I looked like a boy when I was born," Garbo once said. Christina herself had been born with a body entirely covered by hair. Midwives attending the birth thought she was a boy, and as Christina matured, she developed a deep, loud voice.

Today it is believed that Christina was a pseudo-hermaphrodite—a person born with the external sex traits of one gender, but the internal reproductive organs of the other. Imitating

DIEU ET MON DROIT

A monarch (**Garbo** as Christina) erotically kisses her liege subject, portrayed by **Elizabeth Young**.

Courtier **Ian Keith** jousts for Christina's (**Garbo's**) heterosexual affections.

One of the most famous scenes in all filmdom was the closing shot of **Garbo's face** at the prow of the ship. Director Rouben Mamoulian told his star, "Think of nothing. Avoid blinking if you can, so that you're nothing but a beautiful mask. I want your face to be a blank sheet of paper. The writing will be supplied by every member of the audience."

More confusion about sexual identity: Christina, as a man, fooling **John Gilbert,** an emissary from Spain

Christina, Garbo outfitted herself as a swashbuckling cavalier to disguise her sex. Both Queen Christina and the actress who portrayed her (Garbo) were attracted to beautiful women.

MGM was subtle in dealing with the Swedish queen's lesbianism, giving her lines such "I shall die a bachelor," and "I think marriage is an altogether shocking thing. How is it possible to think of a man sleeping in the same room?"

The scene in which actress Barbara Barondess as Elsa, the sluttish servant girl, ran her hands up and down Garbo's legs ended up on the cutting-room floor. Barondess suffered great embarrassments during her filming of the scene. "I don't want to be making love to her 35 times—she's liable to like it," she told the director. In the final version, a lesbian kiss was kept in.

According to *Photoplay*, "The magnificent Garbo, enchanting as ever, is still enveloped in unfathomable mystery."

Walter Ramsey in *Modern Screen* wrote: "One of the best scenes discloses Garbo, traveling as a man, and stopping at a wayside inn, there to be placed in the same room with a nobleman from Spain (Gilbert) because all other rooms are occupied. (No reason to censor and every reason to try.)"

THE PAINTED VEIL (1934)
IN THE MIDST OF A PANDEMIC, GARBO NEVER LOOKED LOVELIER

Garbo's next picture was *The Painted Veil*, based on a 1925 novel by W. Somerset Maugham. Her faithful friend and sometimes lover, Salka Viertel, was one of the screenwriters. Once again, Garbo was united with her loyal team: Cedric Gibbons for art direction; William Daniels for cinematography; and Adrian for costumes.

For the first and only time, Garbo's leading men would include Herbert Marshall and George Brent. Supporting players were Warner Oland, Jean Hersholt, Beulah Bondi, and Cecelia Parker.

In the plot, Garbo was cast as Katrin Koerber, the daughter of an Austrian professor, who fights loneliness with daydreaming. When Dr. Walter Fane (Marshall) asks her to marry him and run away with him to China, she consents, even though she is not in love with him.

In Hong Kong, as a bored and neglected wife, she meets and falls in love with Jack Townsend (Brent), a handsome diplomat attached to the British Embassy. They begin an affair, but in time, her husband finds out. This leads to some compromises which include traveling with Dr. Fane to an inland region of China, where a cholera epidemic has broken out.

To stop the spread of the disease, he orders that a ghetto-like neighborhood be burned down. A coolie, in retaliation plunges a knife into him. Although he's badly injured, the doctor is not killed. After he recovers, Ka-

One of W. Somerset Maugham's weaker plots, *The Painted Veil*, evokes one of Garbo's earlier films, *Wild Orchids*.

It's another love triangle where an older husband migrates to the Far East with a beautiful and much younger wife. There, **Garbo** meets and falls for a handsome reprobate, George Brent.

"**George Brent** and I were savvy enough to know that *The Painted Veil* was a second-rate melodrama," **Garbo** said.

"Mercedes de Acosta warned me, it would be a failure at the box office. Brent had his own worries, telling me that with me on the screen, no one would look at him."

trin becomes resigned to a loveless, sexless marriage, and puts up a brave front.

Fifteen years older that Garbo, Marshall was born in London. During World War I, he'd lost a leg. Later, as a leading man, his slight limp was apparent.

As an actor in Hollywood in the 1930s, he appeared opposite some of its grandest female stars, not only Garbo, but Marlene Dietrich, too. His most notorious affair was with Gloria Swanson, as well as with other leading stars such as Miriam Hopkins and Kay Francis.

The Irish actor, George Brent, was only a year older than Garbo. In time, he relocated to America, first as an actor on Broadway and later as a leading man in Hollywood.

He married two famous actresses, Ruth Chatterton and Ann Sheridan. His most famous leading lady was Bette Davis, with whom he co-starred in such movies as *The Old Maid* (1939) and *Dark Victory (also 1939)*. They had a long-enduring affair.

Garbo worked smoothly with her director, Richard Boleslawski, a former Polish Lancer. In Moscow, after his military service, he opened a school devoted to Method acting. Lee Strasberg, who founded Actors Studio in New York City, was a pupil of his. Boleslawski said that "Garbo was completely thorough in her art. She is almost as marvelous as the camera itself."

The Painted Veil was a hit, grossing about $1.7 million at the box office, even though *Picture Play* reviewed it as "only tolerable."

The New York Times gave Garbo a rave. "She is the most miraculous blend of personality and sheer dramatic talent that the screen has ever known, and her presence in *The Painted Veil* makes one of the season's cinema events."

Variety, however, cast a sour note, defining it as "a bad picture—clumsy, dull, and long-winded."

***

While Garbo was occupied with filming movies, Mercedes spend nine months in 1934 working on a film script, which she entitled "the perfect vehicle for my goddess." It was a tragedy she titled *Jehanne de Arc,* a reference from medieval French for "Joan of Arc."

"I put my heart into that script," Mercedes lamented. "I worked with a passion every day, dreaming at times that when filmed, it would turn out to be Garbo's signature masterpiece."

Oddly, she never conveyed to Garbo the subject of her screen treatment, although at night, she sometimes conjured up visions of her in medieval armor. She had seen her former lover, Eva Le Gallienne, on stage performing as Joan of Arc (1412-1431) and she insisted that Garbo would be far more convincing in the role.

By August 4, 1934 she had completed her first draft, and she set up a meeting with Irving Thalberg in his office at MGM. "I have always wanted to see Garbo portraying a peasant, and not always in one of Adrian's elaborate gowns. That way, her great acting talent can emerge. Garbo is at one with nature, but in not one of her films has she ever been shown connecting with it."

She later reported that Thalberg agreed that the character of the martyred saint might be ideal for Garbo: "Definitely Oscar-worthy."

Then a surprisingly kind and generous move, Thalberg put his arm around Mercedes

Mercedes spent months of her life creating a film script in which Garbo would play Joan of Arc, only to have the Swedish actress bluntly reject it. Garbo never commented on or confronted her over any aspect of either the script or the character—a martyred medieval saint— that Mercedes had envisioned for her.

"I was flabbergasted," Mercedes dramatically asserted, "my soul destroyed. The play was my masterpiece."

and walked her to her car, something he did very rarely, if ever.

Two nights later, Thalberg phoned Mercedes shortly before midnight. "Garbo has read the script. She rejected the role, telling me she does not wish to be burned at the stake."

The rejection seemed to hit Mercedes like a fatal blow to her head.

"Perhaps you can persuade her to change her mind," he said. "Or else I can get another actress to play her, perhaps my wife, Norma Shearer. If Norma doesn't want to film it, there's always Joan Crawford."

"I thanked him and hung up," Mercedes said. "I had never talked with Garbo about the role, and I never confronted her about her rejection of my script. Even to this day, I don't know why I remained silent. In Hollywood, and elsewhere, I've had my heart broken, but this blow was devastating to me. Other actresses such as Jean Seberg or Ingrid Bergman would bring Joan of Arc to the screen, but they would never equal what Garbo could have done with the role."

Disheartened, disappointed, and rather bitter at Garbo, Mercedes decided that she could not use that as an excuse to break up with Garbo, because she was still passionate about her. "I think I could forgive her for anything."

ANNA KARENINA (1935)
TRAPPED IN A XANADU OF WHITE RUSSIAN BRIC-A-BRAC

In this 1935 release, Garbo was once again directed by Clarence Brown. He told her that in the title role, she'd be appearing opposite Fredric March, who had signed to play Vronsky in this adaptation of the Tolstoy classic.

Garbo already knew that March was notorious for attempting to seduce his leading ladies. As a counter-offensive, she wore garlic under her clothes and purposely developed bad breath as a means of staving off his advances.

In that she succeeded. Filmgoers were left pondering why her Anna would even remotely be drawn to March's stiff, colorless count. One latter-day critic noted that to his love scenes March brought the sort of sappy conviction you might expect from Merv Griffin singing "Summertime."

On the other hand, Basil Rathbone is effective as her cold, unforgiving husband, and eleven-year-old Freddie Bartholomew is quite fine as their son.

Brown lined up an impressive cast, including the very pretty Maureen O'Sullivan,

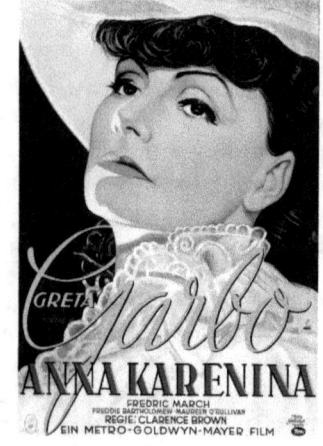

who played Kitty, and Gyles Isham, who was cast as Levin. Other players included Reginald Owen, Reginald Denny, May Robson, and Phoebe Foster. Constance Collier, "the great dyke of the Western world," was cast in the uncredited role of Countess Lidia.

Look carefully and you'll spot future movie star Dennis O'Keefe in an uncredited part as "Best Man."

Anna Karenina was Garbo's 23rd film and a remake of *Love*, in which she'd co-starred with her on-again/off-again lover John Gilbert.

Originally, producer David O. Selznick didn't want Garbo to do another period drama. Instead, he urged the screenplay for *Dark Victory*, upon her, but she turned him down. And how fortunate that was for Bette Davis that Garbo rejected what became one of Davis' most memorable performances.

After shooting *Anna Karenina*, Garbo returned to her native Sweden. "Bette Davis can have George Brent," she said. Brent had been pestering Garbo to marry him.

The New York Sun wrote, "Greta Garbo, after several years of miscasting, is back at last in her own particular province of glamour and heartbreak, of tragic lovely ladies and handsome ruthless men. Garbo's haunting beauty is what you will remember of *Anna Karenina*."

In *Anna Karenina* (1935), Garbo got a second chance to bring Tolstoy's heroine to the screen. *[Eight years before, she'd adapted the same story in the silent movie,* Love *(1927).]*

This time, eight years later, her dysfunctional family consists of **Basil Rathbone** (left), **Garbo** herself, and child actor **Freddie Bartholomew**.

In *Anna Karenina*, **Garbo** played love scenes with **Fredric March**, but stalled his sexual advances off screen. March told her, "You have the makings of another Sarah Bernhardt."

"This is a weak and dull picture, yet the persuasive genius of Garbo raises it into a class of Art," claimed *Photoplay*.

Picture Play wrote: "Garbo's greatness as supreme star of the screen is here exhibited for all who have eyes to see, ears to hear, and imagination to be stirred. And as always, the play is made to seem less important than the talent. Meticulous costumes and settings complete a marvelous reproduction of St. Petersburg society in the 1870s."

CAMILLE (1936)
THE TRANSCENDENT PASSION OF A DYING COURTESAN IN LOVE; GARBO'S FINEST ROLE

Not surprisingly, MGM teamed two of its most beautiful stars—both bisexuals—Robert Taylor and Garbo, in the 1936 version of that heart-wrencher, *Camille*. Again, not surprisingly, Garbo was cast as a courtesan. She was far more convincing as an elegant courtesan than in a hooker role.

This time, Garbo was under the skilled baton of George Cukor, the most notorious homosexual director in Hollywood.

Some reviewers impishly asked: Guess which is the pretty one? Taylor or Garbo?

Garbo was at the peak of her beauty, but so was Taylor. When not seducing Garbo on screen, he was getting regularly plowed by other beautiful men, including Errol Flynn, Tyrone Power, and Howard Hughes.

Camille originally opened at a theater in Paris on February 2, 1852, Dumas having based the character on Marguerite, a woman with whom he'd had an affair for 11 months. She died at the age of 23.

In 1936, *Camille* inspired Milton Benjamin to write a hit song called "I'll Love Like Robert Taylor, Be My Greta Garbo."

Our favorite line in the film is when Garbo asks Taylor: "You who are so young—where can you have learned all you know about women like me?"

As the courtesan Marguerite, Garbo falls deeply in love with Armand. One ad billed this film as "the gay *demi-monde* of Paris. (The *demi-monde*, in case you didn't know, and

Crowds formed at the **Capitol Theater in Manhattan** to see Greta Garbo and Robert Taylor emote in the classic *Camille*.

For their masterful performance, Garbo won her second New York Critics Best Actress Award, and in Hollywood, was nominated for an Oscar for Best Actress.

Camille also had the dubious distinction of being the favorite film of Adolf Hitler.

you probably do, translates roughly as "a jaded, decadent, stylish, and world-weary community of loose sexual morals.")

Garbo, as Marguerite Gautier, brightens her wit with champagne and seems to lead an enchanted life when Armand falls for her. Even when she descends into poverty with a terminal illness, she discovers he has not lost his love for her. It's no wonder that Giuseppe Verdi adapted the original novel by Alexandre Dumas fils, *La Dame aux camellias*, for his opera *La Traviata*. What suffering, what tragedy, what undying love...

The screenplay was mostly scripted by a woman named Zoë Akins, with help from Francis Marion and James Hilton.

One of the most eccentric figures in 1930s Hollywood, Akins was small and fat and lived with a female companion, actress Jobyna Howland. Before Howland, Akins had been in love with Ethel Barrymore, but the grand old lady of the theater wasn't in love with "the toad," as she called her.

Akins also developed a crush on Garbo, who responded by telling her that she "had to give all my love to Armand Duval," a reference to the screen role played by Taylor. And that she did, earning as a result her third Oscar nomination. The Oscar for Best Actress seemed to forever elude the luminous Swede. Lesser talent always won instead.

For our money, Garbo's death scene, where Camille collapses into a tubercular swoon, remains the finest and most touching in cinema history. One can just feel her tentative hold on life as she keeps herself alive to see her beloved once again.

With the single exception of Robert Taylor, the cast was superb. It included Laura Hope Crews. If you don't remember her name, surely you will recall her campy, sexually repressed hysteria as Aunt Pittypat (*"The Yankees are coming!"*) in *Gone With The Wind*.

Maureen O'Sullivan also appears sweet and virginal, the way Louis B. Mayer liked them before he devoured them.

Richard Corliss brilliantly summed up Taylor's role, referring to him

Repentant and in love, the courtesan (**Garbo,** as Marguerite) wears black.

She knew she was actually portraying Maire Duplessis, the real-life mistress of author Alexandre Dumas, fils, who had written the novel published in 1848 (*La Dame aux Camélias*) from which *Camille* was derived.

George Cukor claimed, "Garbo was subtle, able with a slight gesture to be enormously suggestive."

"In her erotic scenes, she never touches but kisses **Robert Taylor** all over the face. Often, she is the aggressor in lovemaking. Very original."

as "...impossibly gorgeous. Robert Taylor is usually ridiculed for playing Armand as a musical/comedy Romeo with a glistening, protruding lower lip, a crooner's smile, and a mellow, acting-school baritone. This criticism underrates the actor and overrates the role. If he sometimes suggests a choirboy lost in a bawdy house, it's because he's too intensely romantic to have a worldly sense of humor."

Years after the release of the film, in his appraisal of Taylor the actor, Cukor was rather charitable to the man Garbo herself had described as "so beautiful—and so dumb." Cukor claimed that Taylor made an "extremely good Armand," but he could have been pissed off at him. Throughout the filming, Taylor repeatedly rejected Cukor's urgent pleas to seduce him.

Other than Garbo's, the finest performance is delivered by Henry Daniell playing the Baron de Varville, Marguerite's lame-duck lover. Of the many cinematic villains of Hollywood during the 1930s, he was the most suave. We can only speculate how John Barrymore would have been in the role for which he was originally scheduled. The baron is a man "whose lips have been locked in sarcasm for so long that he cannot unpurse them even to kiss his mistress."

In *Camille*, **Garbo** (left) appears in a scene with **Laura Hope Crews,** who's cast as Marguerite Gautier's *demi-mondaine* sparring partner.

Crews would soon immortalize herself as Aunt Pittypat in *Gone With the Wind* (1939).

Lionel Barrymore overacts in one of his worst performances. Amazingly, Cukor didn't catch his onscreen blooper when he referred to Marguerite Gautier as "Margaret."

Adrian had another gay romp with Garbo's costumes, taking her from virginal white at the beginning to Grim Reaper black in her final scenes.

There was a side benefit derived from Garbo's work with Cukor. After filming was completed, Garbo asked to be taken to Katharine Hepburn's luxurious new home on Angelo Drive above Benedict Canyon in Los Angeles. Garbo was amused that Cukor had previously directed Hepburn when she was cast as a boy in Sylvia Scarlett. "I, too, want you to direct me as a boy one day," Garbo told Cukor.

"When Kate hauled Garbo upstairs to show off her new bedroom, I decided it was time for me to go," Cukor later told a group of his gay pals at a Hollywood party.

Frank S. Nugent in *The New York Times* wrote, "Greta Garbo's performance is in the finest tradition: eloquent, tragic, yet restrained. She is as incomparable in the role as legend tells us that Bernhardt was. Through the perfect artistry of her portrayal, a hackneyed theme is made new again, poignantly sad, hauntingly lovely."

Howard Barnes in the *New York Herald Tribune* gave his view: "The incomparable Greta Garbo has returned to the screen in a breathtakingly beautiful and superbly modulated portrayal of Camille. As the tragic Dumas heroine, she floods a romantic museum piece with glamour and artistry, making it a haunting and moving photoplay by the sheer magic of her acting."

CONQUEST (1937)
GARBO AS THE MISTRESS OF NAPOLÉON

Clarence Brown returned to direct Garbo in *Conquest*, based on the story of the Polish Countess Marie Walewska, the mistress of Napoléon. It was not out of love or desire, but in an attempt to get him to use his influence to help her native land free itself from oppression from Prussia and Imperial Russia.

Claude Rains was rejected for the role of Napoléan because Brown considered him too old. Charles Boyer was reluctant to play the lead. "I would have been less hesitant to play Jesus Christ. But Napoléon, My God!"

[*Boyer's statement was widely circulated in several newspapers. When he was asked to explain exactly what it meant, he told a reporter, "You figure it out." Some religious leaders objected to it, claiming, "It seemed to make Napoléon a more imposing figure than Christ himself."*]

Garbo, as Marie, was cast opposite Boyer, as Napoléon. The French actor was a well-established matinée idol, who achieved his greatest success in the 1930s in such films as *Red-Headed Woman* (1932) with Jean Harlow; with Katharine Hepburn in *Break of Hearts* (1935); and with Marlene Dietrich in *Garden of Allah* (`1936). His most famous role would come two years after working with Garbo, as Pepe Le Moko in *Algiers* (1939). [*He never said to Hedy Lamarr the most famous line attributed to him: "Come with me to the Casbah."*]

Boyer spoke to the press about working with Garbo: "She is a closely guarded mystery, enchanting but mysterious. I suspect

Conquest was the saga of Napoléon and his mistress, Marie Walewska (1786-1817).

A highly politicized Polish beauty, she was married to Count Walewska, four times her age. She first met the French dictator in 1805.

The movie flopped at the box office.

she will never unlock her heart to anyone."

Garbo and Boyer were backed up with the most talented supporting cast she'd had in any of her films—Reginald Owen, Alan Marshal, Henry Stephenson, Leif Erickson, Dame May Whitty, and the indomitable Marie Ouspenskaya as Countess Walewska.

Its worldwide gross came to $2.2 million, but its massive budget led to a loss of $1.3 million.

Gossip maven Louella Parsons claimed, "Garbo is completely overshadowed by Charles Boyer, who takes the picture, wraps it, and walks away with it."

Motion Picture Herald wrote that "*Conquest* is super colossal *magnifico*—but a dog at the box office."

The complicated relationship of Irving Thalberg and Greta Garbo came to an end on September 14, 1936. The news came over the radio and was first heard by Mercedes. He had died in Santa Monica at the age of thirty-seven.

The next day, when Mercedes reported to work at MGM, she was notified that she'd been fired.

Garbo wanted **Charles Boyer** for the role of Napoléon mainly because he was French. "As on-screen lovers, Boyer and I did not sparkle," Garbo confessed to Mercedes.

"The low point on the film came when I was summoned to Louis B. Mayer's office. The old toad made a pass at me."

Bolsheviks Abroad:
Ninotchka (1939)
At the Twilight of Her Career, Garbo Laughs

Garbo neared the end of her far-too-short career, she had one more good movie in her before oblivion. She played a hard-line Soviet Communist, Ninotchka, in this highly enjoyable comedy/romance opposite Melvyn Douglas as Leon in 1939, the year of *Gone With The Wind*. William Powell, homo-hating Robert Montgomery, and the stately queer himself, Cary Grant, were all considered as possible leading men for Garbo.

When *Ninotchka* was released, headlines across America proclaimed GARBO LAUGHS, as she'd long ago learned to talk.

She was lucky to have had the great Ernst Lubitsch, known for his light touch with comedy, as her director. But when it was time for her to actually laugh, he said that "she disliked playing the scene in front of all the extras." Rumor had it that her laugh was dubbed, but Lubitsch insisted until his death that it was not.

In spite of that laugh, Douglas later said that Garbo "didn't have an ounce of humor in her."

There's a plot here: Buljanoff (Felix Bressart), Iranoff (Sig Ruman), and Kopalski (Alexander Granach) have been sent by the communist Soviet government to Paris to sell the Imperial jewels of the recently deposed Romanoffs as a means of raising money for farm machinery. But the soft capitalist life has begun to tempt them.

Ninotchka is sent directly from the Kremlin to see what's going wrong. In Paris, she not only meets a new boyfriend, Leon (Douglas), but conflicts with the Grand Duchess Swana (Ina Claire), who owned the gems before she was forced to flee from Russia's Bolshevik Revolution. As a bit of fun casting, Bela Lugosi plays Commissar Razinin, the communist party official who sends Ninotchka to Paris.

Ina Claire and Garbo were rivals both on and off the screen. Claire was once married to Garbo's old flame, squeaky voiced John Gilbert.

Ina Claire, as the third lead, and Garbo had something in common: John Gilbert. Claire was the third of his four wives, having been married to him from 1929 to 1931. When Garbo had first heard of the union, she said, "She got John on the rebound after I had broken his heart."

Claire later claimed that during the making of their film, Garbo made a pass at her. It was not accepted. "At one point, Garbo told me she had to go to the little boy's room. Later, I used the same toilet. The seat was up. Do you think Garbo is really a man?"

Garbo confronts Comrade **Bela Lugosi,** usually the king of horror movies.

"To meet Garbo, or even to work with her, is not to know her," he said.

CAPITALISTS & COMMIES: CAN LOVE SURVIVE?

Ironies abound in the cross-cultural exchanges among **Garbo** (left), **Melvyn Douglas,** and a rich and silly socialite **(Ina Claire).**

***

"Do you want to be alone, Comrade?" one of the comic commissars asks Garbo/Ninotschka.

"No!" she replied. It's the anti-myth in monosyllable.

Mercedes de Acosta later said that "*Ninotchka* was the first gay picture Garbo had ever done." Maybe de Acosta meant something different from really, really gay.

Why, you might ask, was Lubitsch suddenly available to direct *Ninotchka*? He had recently been booted from the set of *The Women*, starring Norma Shearer and Joan Crawford, who hated each other. Lubitsch had been unexpectedly replaced with gay director George Cukor, who was known for his artistry in directing glamourous women. Ironically, Cukor himself had become available only because Clark Gable, during the simultaneous filming of *Gone With the Wind*, had refused to be directed "by a faggot" in his portrayal of Rhett Butler. Gable didn't like to be reminded of his own personal experience in Hollywood at the beginning of his career during the silent screen era, when he hustled rich men for money, usually scoring payment from them.

Ninotchka earned for Garbo her fourth and last Academy Award nomination. But on Oscar Night, Vivien Leigh snapped up the Best Actress Award for *Gone With the Wind*.

Cukor threw a party, inviting Garbo, Vivien Leigh, and her boyfriend, Laurence Olivier. Garbo and Olivier disappeared for a long time. Noting their tryst, Leigh said to the gossipy Cukor: "I hope poor Larry knows what to do. He doesn't know what to do with me, but fortunately Leslie *[Leslie Howard, who played her love interest, Ashley, in* Gone With The Wind*]* knows exactly what target to hit."

This lobby card of **Garbo** in debate with **Melvyn Douglas** was given out to theater audiences as a souvenir.

Fans of the movie went so far as to name their pets, cats in particular, after Garbo's interpretation of a humorless Stalinist in **Ninotchka**.

Comrade Ninotchka wears a hat that's much too stylish (our favorite of any in the Garbo repertoire) for acquisition by any mere *apparatchik* in the Stalinist era.

Frank Nugent in *The New York Times* filed this review: "Garbo's *Ninotchka* is one of the sprightliest comedies of the year, a gay and impertinent and malicious show which never pulls the punch lines (no matter how far below the belt they may land), and finds the screen's austere first lady of drama playing in deadpan comedy with the assurance of a Buster Keaton..... It must be monotonous, this superb rightness of Garbo's playing. We almost wish she would handle a scene badly once in a while just to provide us with an opportunity to show we are not a member of a fan club. But she remains infallible and Garbo, always exactly what the situation demands, always as fine as her script and director permit her to be."

Howard Barnes in the *New York Herald-Tribune* granted Garbo a rave: "Now that she has done it. it seems incredible that Greta Garbo never appeared in a comedy before *Ninotchka*. For in this gay burlesque of Bolsheviks abroad, the great actress reveals a command of comic inflection which fully matches the emotional depth or tragic power of her earlier triumphs. It is a joyous, subtly shaded and utterly enchanting portrayal which she creates, to illuminate a rather slight satire and make it the year's most captivating screen comedy. Ernst Lubitsch has put his famous directorial touch on the film, and it is leavened with witty lines and deft characterizations, but it is memorable as well as entertaining for having disclosed new gifts in the First Actress of our day."

To see Garbo playing a grim comrade who deviates from party doctrine on a mission to Paris, turns square briefly, and then goes overboard for romance, one would suppose that she had devoted her whole career to antic make-believe. Whether it is deadpan clowning or the difficult feat of filling a tipsy scene with laughter; whether she is trading insults with a Grand Duchess or secretly trying on one of those current hats, she is a past mistress of comedy. Meanwhile, she floods the production with her timeless and ineffable beauty, giving a rich and haunting quality to the romantic scenes and a moving intensity to the few passages of straight drama. There is an added verve and color to her personality in a role such as this which makes her even more magically lovely than in the past."

TWO-FACED WOMAN (1941)
DOOMSDAY FOR GARBO'S FABLED CAREER

Much of the success of Garbo's previous films came from her popularity with European audiences, especially French, British, and German. Now, with the world at war (the United States had not yet entered the conflict, but was on the verge), that audience had dried up.

MGM wanted a vehicle for Garbo that would appeal to American audiences. Producer Gottfried Reinhardt assigned George Cukor to direct, and once again, Salka Viertel, Garbo's close friend, was one of the writers of the script. The entire movie would emerge as an attempt to "Americanize Garbo."

The screenplay was based on a 1925 silent film, *Her Sister from Paris*, which had starred Constance Talmadge.

Because Garbo and Melvyn Douglas had gone over so big in *Ninotchka*, he once again was assigned the role of her leading man. Cukor, of course, had helmed Garbo in her finest film, *Camille*, in 1936, so MGM had high hopes.

Cast as the third lead was Constance Bennett, a major Hollywood star in the 1920s and '30s. Her career was now in decline, as reflected by her given a supporting role as "the other woman." She reminded Garbo that she had been one of the highest-paid actresses in Hollywood—"and one of the most popular."

A strong supporting cast was hired: Ruth Gordon, Roland Young, and Robert Sterling.

Garbo complained about all aspects of the film, as she was forced to take dance lessons to perform a *chica-choce*. "What in hell is that?" she asked. "Some hootch dance?"

Adrian was hired once again to design her "modern American woman" wardrobe. Garbo was not pleased. "What are you trying to do: Turn me into a Swedish Lana Turner?"

This would be the last time he would ever design her wardrobe. When leaving MGM, she told him goodbye with this: "I never liked the wardrobes you designed for me. Not in any picture we did together."

Two-Faced Woman was **Garbo's** twenty-seventh and final movie. Appearing opposite her for the third time was actor **Melvyn Douglas.**

She especially objected to a bathing suit scene she was forced to execute. The plot opens at a ski resort where Larry Blake (Douglas), a fashion magazine editor, falls in love with his ski instructor, Karin Borg (Garbo).

After a whirlwind courtship, they are married, but, as it turns out, she's an independent woman, not the dutiful wife he'd envisioned.

She remains behind as he returns to Manhattan, where he resumes his relationship with Griselda Vaughan (Bennett).

Karin arrives in Manhattan to get her husband back from the clutches of this scheming female. She adopts a ruse, claiming that she is Karin's twin sister, "a wild, amoral, modern woman."

Larry is fooled at first, but not for long. He decides to play along with her deceit.

The plot ends happily as everything works out.

When *Two-Faced Woman* was released, it was attacked by the Legion of Decency, which cited its "immoral and un-Christian attitude toward marriage and its obligations." Catholics were urged to boycott the film, and it was banned in such cities as Boston, Chicago, Milwaukee, and Omaha.

Trying for a more general release, MGM pulled it from circulation and made some vital cuts, which weakened it considerably.

The movie generated Garbo's worst reviews.

Time magazine pronounced it "an absurd vehicle for Greta Garbo. Its embarrassing effect is not unlike seeing Sarah Bernhardt swatted with a bladder. It is almost as shocking as seeing your mother drunk."

Cecilia Ager in the newspaper *PM* wrote: "The screen doesn't have an actress to compare with Garbo for loveliness, sensitivity, incandescence. She has feeling first, and she's acquired the technical proficiency and the knack of timing with which to express it. In *Two-Faced Woman* she reveals still deeper stores of humor and evanescent tenderness than ever before. Her voice has become an instrument that indicates all the emotions in their most subtle gradations. Just on the record of the sound track she's superb. And this is the woman, so unique in the movies that she's no longer a person but become now a symbol, a legend, whom *Two-Faced Woman* does everything it can to destroy. The wickedness in *Two-Faced Woman* was not in its careless disregard of what are supposed to be public morals—it had no more contempt for the conventions than a half-dozen recent movies for whose transgressions it was made an example of—its wickedness lies in its vandalism. In its story's frenzy to cover up its own emptiness, its sterility, its lack of any fine feelings, it makes Garbo a clown, a buffoon, a monkey on a stick. The fact that it's a comedy doesn't excuse its confused motivation, its repetition, its distasteful heartlessness."

In *Two-Faced Woman*, **Garbo** was called on to dance the "chica-choca" with in-house dance director **Robert Alton.**

According to Garbo, "MGM hopes that my doing this vulgar dance will attract middle-brow audiences."

Garbo found a review in *The New York Times* especially stinging: "As for Miss Garbo. this is clearly one of the less propitious assignments of her career. Though she is her cool and immaculate self in the role of the clean-limbed ski instructress, she is as *gauche* and stilted as the script when playing the lady of profane love. No doubt her obvious posturings, her appallingly unflattering clothes and make-up were intended as a satire on the vamps of history: Instead, her performance misses the satire and looks like something straight out of the movies of 1922. Mr. Douglas, who probably spends more time in pyjamas than any male lead in history, continues to look as though a brisk walk in the open air in street clothes would refresh him. Apply that rule to the whole film. Open the windows. Messrs. Cukor *et al.* This is 1942. Theda Bara's golden age is gone."

Critic Herbert Kretzner was dismissive: "Garbo, why can't she leave us alone? She has played the childish game of peek-a-boo to death. Boiled down to essentials, she is a plain mortal with large feet."

Mercedes claimed, "Although the American small town woman secretly admired Garbo, she was also baffled by her. What relation had Mrs. America to a Viking's daughter whose soul was swept by wind and snow?"

Mercedes urged Garbo not to make *Two-Faced Woman,* warning, "It is an old chestnut, having been made into a film twice before, both of them silent."

Garbo told her, "You're just jealous because you didn't write the script."

After the reviews came in, Garbo told Mercedes, "I'm sorry I did not follow your advice. The critics are trying to destroy me, or what's left of my career. Women's clubs want my film banned. Why? Because in the movie, Melvyn Douglas dates a woman he thinks is my sister. But it's not. It's really *moi.*"

George Cukor said, "*Two-Faced Woman* did not necessarily end Garbo's career. She could have gone on—and, indeed, she would be offered many comeback roles after the war. I think the truth of the matter is that she just gave up."

By mutual agreement, her contract with MGM was terminated.

In 1942, the worst year of World War II, Sir Winston Churchill, for relaxation from the tensions of a war going bad, screened Garbo movies. At Berchtesgaden, Hitler screened some of her movies, too, even though some of her films were by Jewish directors. Hitler's favorites were *Anna Christie, Mata Hari,* and *Queen Christina.*

***

The year was 1928 and Mercedes was living in Hollywood. On December 13, she was invited to a pre-Christmas party that consisted of many members of the city's gay and lesbian colony.

Cary Grant was there with his new lover, Randolph Scott, and so were a lot of lesser folk, including the director George Cukor. Mercedes met Gary Cooper and his gay lover, Anderson Lawler, a wealthy tobacco heir.

Mercedes was also introduced to Cecil Beaton, who was in Hollywood photographing the rich, the famous, and the beautiful for *Vogue* magazine and for his future anthology, *Book of Beauty.*

A rather flamboyant homosexual, Beaton was twenty-five at the time, and his photographs of English debutantes and their mothers had already made him celebrated in England. As he chatted with Mercedes, he told her. "My one goal in Hollywood is to photograph Greta Garbo. But first, I've got to meet her."

"We share the same goal," Mercedes answered.

Both Beaton and Mercedes would achieve their goal, each eventually becoming intimate with Garbo. Although jealous of him because of his eventual closeness to her, Mercedes and Beaton nonetheless became friends.

According to Beaton, "Mercedes talked jerkily in a hollow voice and was very mannish, particularly in her dress code. Her hair was short, and she wore men's clothing, always in black and white, and she looked formidable with a necktie, trousers, buckled shoes, and a cloak."

A day after meeting her, Beaton invited Mercedes to his rented apartment in Hollywood, where he showed her photographs he'd already taken of Hollywood celebrities. He also asked her to pose for him.

She was immediately impressed with his talent. Later, she wrote, "I believe in his books, paintings, and photography. I think his *oeuvre* will be considered one day as one of the most sensitive expressions of our age."

Self-portrait of **Cecil Beaton,** the noted photographer.

As early as 1923, Beaton wrote: "I adore to dance with women, and take them to theaters and private views and talk about dresses and plays...and other women. But I'm really much more fond of men. I'm really a terrible, terrible homosexualist—and try so hard not to be."

***

In years to come, details about the complicated relationship between Garbo and Beaton would fill an entire book. Indeed, one was written called *Greta & Cecil* by Diana Souhami. She viewed their relationship as a "compelling tale of a strange romance where boundaries merge between image and reality, fact and fantasy, male and female, and art and life."

The last time Mercedes heard from Cecil Beaton was when he wrote to her after Garbo had moved on to other suitors. He suffered the same fate that Mercedes did. He said, "I'm not usually critical of Garbo. But I fear she has little gratitude in her disposition—takes everything as if it's her due—and give mighty little to others. I fear she is not going to have a happy old age—but then, who is?"

"Garbo is a Virgo, which means she's high-strung, critical, intolerant, and analytical," Mercedes said. "Everything is held up to be examined through a magnifying lens."

Garbo and Mercedes would continue their friendship, on and off, for

There was an ocean of intrigue whirling through Hollywood on Oscar Night, 1939, and everyone in the industry had something to say about **Vivien** (Scarlett O'Hara) **Leigh** and her mad, passionate link to Britain's then most revered actor, (Lord) **Laurence Olivier.**

In 2011, Blood Moon published their worst nightmare, a tell-all devoted to what was REALLY happening behind the scenes with Larry Olivier and a woman we love, Vivien Leigh.

many years, with long separations. But when Mercedes published her memoirs in 1960, Garbo, enraged, never spoke to her again.

"The real tragedy of Garbo is that she is a lone wolf," Mercedes said. "No matter how much she may love a person, or try to hold onto that person's life, male or female, and be part of that life, in the end, she has to go and pursue her own lonely course."

Garbo told Beaton, "That wretched book is a horrible invasion of my privacy—and, as you know, I'm a very private person."

In a dialogue with Mercedes, Beaton said: "I hope you will not be hurt by Garbo's ruthlessness. I felt you were kind to her."

"I will not only be hurt," Mercedes answered, "but I will feel the sting of her rejection until my dying day."

On hearing of Mercedes' death, Cecil Beaton wrote in his diary: "Now, without a word from Garbo, the woman she loved more than any of the women in her life, Mercedes de Acosta, has gone to a lonely grave."

During the course of their long friendship, Garbo wrote Mercedes 181 letters, cards, and telegrams. Cecil Beaton, in his 1958 memoir, wrote, "Mercedes is Garbo's very best friend and has been for thirty years, standing by her, always willing to devote her life to her."

Desperate for money in 1959, Mercedes sold all of Garbo's letters to the Rosenbach Museum & Library in Philadelphia. "I would not have the courage to burn these letters," she told William McCarthy, curator of the museum. "I only hope the letters will be respected and protected from the eyes of vulgar people."

The museum is a repository of mainly literary memorabilia, including mementoes of Charles Dickens, James Joyce, even Chaucer.

In his diary, Beaton wrote, "Greta is at once simple, subtle, and the acme of sophistication. No one can find the truth about her."

Alice B. Toklas, the lesbian lover of Gertrude Stein, claimed, "Garbo is Mademoiselle Hamlet."

***

Garbo, an alluring *femme fatale*, would enchant future generations. As late as 2020, and perhaps for many years after that, latter-day generations might be watching her restored films. Even millions who would never see one of her movies have heard of her name.

REST IN PEACE
GRETA GUSTAFSSOHN GARBO
1905-1990

CHAPTER FIFTEEN
"The Kraut"

MARLENE DIETRICH

Cosmopolitan & Omnisexual
She Was the 20th Century's Femme Fatale

As Noël Coward phrased it, "God had a talent for creating remarkable women, and his finest creation is **Marlene Dietrich**."

No star in the history of cinema evoked erotic sophistication more than this alluring German beauty, hailed as "The Last Goddess."

Miss Dietrich, at least in the opinion of the two "love-struck" authors of this book, was the most alluring woman to inhabit the 20th Century. Certainly, she was the most glamourous in a career that spanned six turbulent decades.

A private woman of complex desires and fierce passions, she seduced some of the most famous men and women of her generation, a cast so diverse that it included John Wayne, Mercedes de Acosta, and almost everyone in between.

She never lost her ability to shock. When introduced to playwright George Bernard Shaw, she immediately knelt at his feet, unbuttoned his trousers, removed his penis, and fellated him. "I had to do that before we could talk," she said.

In the summer of 1932, Mercedes de Acosta entered that coven of men and women who enjoyed affairs with sultry Marlene Dietrich, the most celebrated *femme fatale* of the 20th Century. An *emigrée* to the U.S. from Berlin, she was one of the most glamourous women on earth, of equal appeal to both men and women.

An abbreviated list of her lovers included some of the most famous personalities at her era: Photographer Cecil Beaton, Yul Brynner, race car driver and heiress Jo Castairs, Maurice Chevalier, Colette, Edith Piaf, Brian Aherne, Ronald Colman, Gary Cooper, Lili Damita (Errol Flynn's wife), Kirk Douglas, Joseph Kennedy and his son, John Kennedy, Joe DiMaggio, John Gilbert, Howard Hughes, General George Patton, Otto Preminger, John Wayne, Edward G. Robinson, Josef von Sternberg, Orson Welles, Michael Wilding,

Cast as Lola-Lola in the German film, *The Blue Angel (Der blaue Engel)*, the relatively unknown **Marlene Dietrich** became an international sex symbol, beginning one of the most spectacular film careers of all time.

Clad in "artfully tawdry' silk stockings, suspenders, frilled knickers, and a silk hat, she was perched atop an upturned barrel as she proclaimed, "From head to toe, I'm made for love."

Marlene co-starred with handsome, dashing Gary Cooper in *Morocco* (1930), her first American film. She shocked audiences when she cross-dressed in white tie, tails, and a top hat inspired by Lola-Lola. Puffing on a cigarette, she strides through the audience, plucks a flower from a woman's hat, and then kisses her full on the lips. Then, gallantly, she tosses the flower to Cooper.

George Raft, Author William Saroyan, novelist Erich Maria Remarque, Burt Lancaster, Frank Sinatra, Claudette Colbert, Barbara Stanwyck, Mike Todd, Adlai Stevenson, Fritz Lang, Kay Francis, Tallulah Bankhead, Greta Garbo, James Stewart (who impregnated her), Eddie Fisher, and Douglas Fairbanks, Jr.

She even had a (brief) fling with Clark Gable after they'd collaborated on a radio broadcast for the Lux Radio Theatre of the Air. *[It was a staged reading of Morocco. He had played the legionnaire she followed across the desert.]*

She was born in 1901 in Shöneberg, a suburb of Berlin, the daughter of a Prussian police officer who died when she was nine. In May of 1924, she married Rudolf Sieber, an assistant director of German-language silent films. It evolved into an "open marriage" as each of them, especially Marlene, launched separate affairs. Sieber was never jealous, as he was conducting liaisons of his own. Avant-garde by anyone's standards, they discussed each other's lovers openly and without jealousy. A year after their wedding, a daughter, Maria, was born.

After years of working in German silents, mostly in secondary roles, Marlene's big break came when director Josef von Stern-

Marlene's introduction to American audiences in *Morocco* was hailed as one of the most memorable star debuts in the history of cinema. The creation of a star mystique had begun. The world was enthralled.

Later, during the bloody hostilities of World War II, Marlene had to (and did) overcompensate with proofs of her disdain for the Third Reich and her loyalty to the U.S. cause with rigorous regimes of entertaining active-duty U.S. troops "on every front of the European theater," often atop muddy makeshift stages and always at great personal danger to herself. In the process, she endeared herself to thousands of Allied soldiers, who loudly defended her and in some cases, offered to defend her with their lives.

One of **Marlene's** most ardent defenders was **Ernest Hemingway**, believed to have been the first to affectionately designate her during World War II as "The Kraut" ("The German"). In that era, in any other context, that might have been a mortal insult.

In 2017, one of his love letters—penned in August of 1952 with humor (not his usual style) and deep infatuation—reportedly sold for $30,000.

Based on deep mutual admiration, it was an affair "never consummated." Historians and fans of "La Dietrich" cite it as more or less equivalent to other deeply intimate "*amitiés-amoureuses*" that Dietrich sustained with a plethora of other famous and influential men.

berg decided that she'd be ideal as Lola, a decadent cabaret singer, in his upcoming production of *Der Blaue Engel (The Blue Angel;* 1930). *Der Blaue Engel* would make her famous in both Europe and North America, leading to a Hollywood contract.

She followed von Sternberg when he migrated to Hollywood. From there, she maneuvered her way into the arms of Gary Cooper, her co-star in the camp classic, *Morocco* (1930). In its most controversial scene, she appears enigmatically in formal menswear (top hat and tails), as part of her cabaret act. Like a cavalier and *boulevardier*, after delivering a song dripping with innuendo, she leans over the patrons assembled at a ringside table and plants a lingering kiss on the lips of a lady guest. By the standards of that era, it was spectacularly provocative and shocking. Her character later follows Cooper and the other troops into the desert, kicking off her high heels and abandoning her chic couture as the gritty winds blow her hair and makeup into primal disarray.

An early photo of her catalyst, "creator," and mentor, the ferociously autocratic **Josef von Sternberg** with an early manifestation of what the world came to know as **Marlene Dietrich.**

As critic Homer Dickens wrote, "Josef von Sternberg's Dietrich became a *femme fatale* to end all *femme fatales*. Her very presence could drive men to desperate acts, while, in most cases, she remained indifferent."

***

Mercedes began her affair with Dietrich around the time that Cecil Beaton, the noted photographer, arrived in Hollywood, Mercedes became one of the first friends he made there.

One evening, he invited her to a performance by Harold Kreutzberg, a well-known German dancer. Seated in front of them, perhaps as a gesture of German-speaking solidary among the European expatriates of Hollywood, were Josef von Sternberg and Marlene Dietrich. A few moments before it began, Dietrich turned

A BIZARRE "SOMETIMES DENIAL" OF HER EARLY GERMAN ROOTS: WAS SHE BEING COY?

Despite her bizarre insistence that she had never appeared in any films in her native Germany, here's a scene of **Marlene Dietrich** emoting with her handsome co-star, **Robert Irvine,** in *The Ship of Lost Souls (Das Schiff der verlorenen Menschen;* 1929)

around in her seat and smiled at Mercedes, giving Beaton a nod.

Mercedes was already familiar with Dietrich's allure, having seen both *The Blue Angel* and *Morocco*.

Dietrich was unlike any other screen goddess in the history of Hollywood. As described by the acerbic (sometimes lacerating) English critic Kenneth Tynan, "Dietrich exudes sex appeal, but of no particular gender. Her ways are mannish. The characters she plays love power and wear pants. She is also undomesticated. Her masculinity appeals to women, her sexuality to men."

Beaton had noticed Mercedes' sad face that night. She explained it with, "Garbo has gone to Sweden, where she'll remain for many months. Without her, Hollywood seems empty to me."

Mercedes spent the next day "slaving" over a projected film script on the life of the influential Czarist mystic, Rasputin, based on orders from Irving Thalberg at MGM.

When the doorbell rang, she thought it might be a messenger, since she had no social calls scheduled for that day. But then her maid, Anna, knocked at the door of her upstairs study, announcing, "Miss Marlene Dietrich is downstairs. If it wouldn't disturb you, she'd like to see you."

"I don't know Miss Dietrich," Mercedes said. "Perhaps she has rung the wrong doorbell."

Adventurous, distinctive, and well-mannered, but noted in some circles as a predatory lesbian with a passion for celebrities, **Mercedes de Acosta** was bowled over and enchanted by the exotic blonde sensation imported from *Mitteleuropa*.

LESBIAN CHIC

What a fine pair of rebellious and experimental and *avant-garde* iconoclasts they made: **Marlene** (left) and **Mercedes de Acosta.**

"No, she specifically asked for you by name."

"In that case, show her up here."

Withing minutes, Dietrich stood in her doorway. Dressed entirely in white, she carried a large bouquet of white roses.

"Forgive me for intruding," she said in her German-accented purr, "but I got your address from Cecil Beaton. I brought you white flowers to match your pale look. You remind me of the White Prince."

"I'm glad you're here, but it must have been difficult for you to have rung the bell of a stranger."

"It's funny, but it was not," Dietrich responded. "Somehow, I sensed that I'd be welcomed into your home. I thought I could bring some joy to you, since you looked so desolate last night. Also, you looked pale—and still do—and I thought I might cook for you. I'm good in the kitchen. I could restore some color to your face."

From there, they got to know each other, sharing stories of their respective childhoods. The only time Mercedes was startled was when Dietrich denied ever having worked in German silent pictures, insisting that *The Blue Angel* had been her first film.

[In direct contradiction to that bizarre conceit, Mercedes had recently read that before emigrating to the United States, Dietrich had starred in seventeen silent movies, including [here are their English-language names] The Ship of Lost Souls *(1929) and* Dangers of the Engagement Period, *both made the same year she'd worked on* The Blue Angel.*]*

A few hours later, at around sundown, Dietrich rose to leave, but not before Mercedes invited her to return for dinner the following night. Abandoning her writing the next day, Mercedes spent part of the day arranging a romantic, champagne-soaked dinner party, with Dietrich as the only guest. When everything was set up, she retired to her bedroom, where she dressed entirely in white.

During the course of that evening, Mercedes commented on Dietrich's natural beauty, suggesting that she should never wear rouge. "Your face has a natural moonlit glow. The rouge diminishes it."

Dietrich rose, went into the bathroom, and washed her face, never to wear rouge again.

Mercedes also suggested that Dietrich should wear slacks in her private life and promised to take her to an address in Beverly Hills the following day that could tailor-make a dozen pair for her.

Mercedes also complimented her on the two pictures she'd seen.

Dietrich brusquely dismissed the flattery. "Let's not discuss the movies. At the dance recital, when I looked at you, you seemed so lonely, even though you were with Cecil.

Martin Kosleck, one of Marlene's close friends in Hollywood, became known in World War II movies as the best actor to impersonate Josef Goebbels, the Nazi Minister of Propaganda.

Don't expect anything in the love department with that one. When I was making *Morocco*, he came onto the set and spent at least two hours locked away in Gary Cooper's dressing room."

"In America, far from Berlin, I am sad and lonely. It is not easy to adjust yourself to another country. I know, based on your own experience, that you would agree. I was drawn to you right from the beginning. Unconventional as it may seem, I came to see you because I just could not help myself."

During the peak of their passionate affair, Marlene (above) called Mercedes "The White Prince," even though that label more accurately fitted Marlene herself.

Diana McLellan, based on input from Mercedes and many other sources, wrote about their dalliance in her book, *Sappho Goes to Hollywood—The Girls:* "The first night of love between Marlene Dietrich and Mercedes de Acosta was transcendent. At last, each had found a lover whose skill, passion, sophistication, and romanticism matched her own."

McLellan went on to say: "Mercedes was Marlene's type. The tragic white face and bobbed black hair, the intensity, the tears, those slender hands, that low voice, along with chic clothes and an air of distinction—all appealed enormously to Marlene."

The morning after a night of sustained lovemaking, before returning home to check on her daughter, Dietrich told Mercedes, "I cannot sleep without the warmth of your body next to mine."

Later that same day, Dietrich sent a brief letter to Mercedes: "If you should ever cease to desire me, I will descend to my grave and cause no more trouble. When we meet again, I will kiss your hands and thank you for the happiness you have so generously given me. I want to be yours forever."

Mercedes sent a written response: "Never say 'forever.' In love, that's blasphemy. One never knows if one truly loves or whether one makes oaths one will forget. *En amour*, nothing binds you."

Later, Dietrich described her love affair with Mercedes to her husband. He was always pleased when his wife found someone to love.

Two photos of **Marlene Dietrich** snapped by Mercedes during the most infatuated peak of their affair.

"I saw Mercedes de Acosta again. Apparently, Garbo gives her a hard time, not just by playing around—which, by the way, is why she is in the hospital with gonorrhea—also she is the kind of person who counts every cube of sugar to make sure the maid isn't stealing, or eating too well. I am sorry for Mercedes. Her face was white and thin and she seemed sad and lonely—as I am— and not well. I was attracted to her and brought an armful of tuberoses to her house. I told her I would cook marvelous things for her and get her well and strong."

At the time, Dietrich had rented the beach house in Santa Monica that press baron William Randolph Hearst had built for his mistress, actress Marion Davies. Mercedes was a frequent visitor. That summer, she was introduced to Dietrich's daughter Maria. Reportedly, the girl did not like her mother's new mistress, referring to her as "the Countess Dracula."

At her rented beach house, Dietrich often entertained two German actors, a Martin Kosleck and his lover, Hans von Twardosky. According to Mercedes, "Martin was an anti-Nazi, but in the U.S. during the war he almost made a living impersonating Goebbels on the screen."

By now, Dietrich was sending her flowers at the rate of two deliveries a day. Except for the tulips, which she rejected "because of their phallic shape," Mercedes accepted them with a sense of joy. They included rare orchids shipped from San Francisco, dozens of roses, and lots of carnations. At one point, Anna ran out of vases to display them in. When Dietrich heard that, she sent Mercedes a shipment of Lalique vases. Finally, Mercedes grew tired of the excessive quantities of flowers, referring to her home as "a madhouse florist shop."

She ordered Anna to have the flowers removed and sent to patients at a nearby hospital, Cedars of Lebanon.

Switching tactics, Dietrich then began sending Mercedes gifts from Bullock's Department Store—men's pajamas, scarves, teapots, hosiery, glassware, sweaters. Mercedes kept some of them but sent others back to Bullock's for credit back into Dietrich's account.

Dietrich scribbled a note, instructing Bullock's to attach it to one of her gifts: "*Mon Amour!* Beautiful one—I adore you forever—and I kiss your hands."

Mercedes responded with a note of her own written on pink paper. She called Dietrich, "The Darling One" or else "My Goddess." She signed her name, "The White Prince." [*This letter, and others, appear in the book,* The Furious

Joan Crawford with **Douglas Fairbanks, Jr.**, in 1929 on their wedding day.

In Hollywood circles, Marlene became known for having "sex without gender preference." In time, she would seduce Crawford and have a long affair with the dashing Fairbanks, too.

Lesbian, by Robert A. Schanke.]

Mercedes, who fancied herself a poet, included some free-form verse in one of her messages to Dietrich:

> Your face is lit by
> Moonlight
> Breaking through your
> Skin
> Soft, pale, radiant.
> No suntan for you glow
> For you are the essence
> Of
> The stars and the moon
> And
> The mystery of the night.

Some of the Dietrich-Mercedes correspondence has survived. A typical one from Dietrich read:

> "Wonderful one.
> It is one week today since your beautiful naughty hand opened a white rose. Last night was even more wonderful and each time I see you it grows more wonderful and exciting. You with your exquisite white pansy face — and before you go to bed will you ring me so that I can just hear your voice?"

According to Mercedes, writing in the glow of the early days of her affair with Dietrich, "My quest for the 'eternal woman' is over."

Hollywood Rivals. No. 1 - The Dietrich - Garbo Feud
First of Six Stories Revealing Struggles Waged Behind Scenes in Moviedom.

Two Ranking Movie Stars Climb to Top of Popularity

Battle of the Divas: The competitive jockeying between **Greta Garbo** and **Marlene Dietrich** occurred within a theater that was larger and more widespread than just the pages of Mercedes de Acosta's diary.

In the 1930s, newspapers and tabloids everywhere noted them as ferocious rivals, and printed editorial pages that compared their respective popularities.

The upper photos appeared in the *Ottawa Citizen* on November 4, 1933. The lower photos appeared in the *Spokane Daily Chronicle* on December 1 of that same year.

***

During the years Dietrich became prominent in America, Hitler took over Germany. Through Goebbels, he urged Marlene to return to serve the Fatherland. She defied him, making arrangements instead to become an

American citizen.

With no intention of making Mercedes jealous, Dietrich sometimes spoke of her affairs with men. "I prefer fellatio. That way, it puts me in control. It gives me a sense of power. But most men want to put their thing in—that's all they want. I take care that no man falls in love with me unless I want him to." *[That revelation first appeared in Mart Martin's* Did She or Didn't She?*]*

Most of Dietrich's (male) lovers accepted her lesbian streak. Erich Maria Remarque, the German novelist who authored *All Quiet on the Western Front*, had affairs with both Dietrich and Garbo. *[His other lovers included Hedy Lamarr, Dolores Del Rio, Lupe Velez, Luise Rainer, and Maureen O'Sullivan (who played Jane in some of the Tarzan movies). Eventually, he married Paulette Goddard.]* Remarque found nothing shocking about Dietrich's affair with Mercedes, or with any other woman.

In contrast, Douglas Fairbanks, Jr., had a different reaction. After uncovering some of the love letters exchanged between Dietrich and Mercedes, he angrily confronted Diet-

Edith Piaf and **Marlene Dietrich:** Two impossibly famous bisexual Europeans—photographed everywhere together.

No one wore fur better than **Marlene Dietrich**...unless it was **Greta Garbo**.

On the left, above, is Dietrich as Catherine the Great of all the Russias (*The Scarlett Empress*) on the verge of storming the Winter Palace for the *coup d'etat* that will make her the most powerful woman on the planet.

On the right are two views of her rival, Garbo. Her Nordic origins seemed to adapt well—even in the heat of a California sound stage—to fur.

rich. From that point, their love affair withered and died. According to Fairbanks: "When I was married to Joan Crawford, I found out that she was a part time lesbian. I don't want to travel that road again."

During the time she was intimate with Dietrich, Mercedes bragged to her lesbian friends, "I can take any woman from any man. In fact, I have had the three most important women of the 20th Century."

That led to speculation: Members of her entourage already knew about her links to Garbo and Dietrich, but who was the third? In reference to her mysterious third famous lover, some asked "Was it Eleanor Roosevelt? Gertrude Stein? Surely not Shirley Temple? Perhaps the Duchess of Windsor?"

"Marlene was always a dear friend," Mercedes said. "Once, I was involved in a terrible car accident, and lay in pain in a hospital, recovering. Marlene was in Paris at the time, but she got through a call to me and offered to pay my hospital bill. She did everything she could to help me to recover."

From the hospital, Mercedes wrote to Dietrich:

"Golden Beautiful One. Today your letter arrived, and I was so happy to get it because it seemed to me months since I had word directly from you. I know you had a great success in Vienna and I read about you in the French papers. I also read that you are buying many feminine clothes. I hope not too feminine! And I hope that you will not give up your trousers when you return because then people can say (as they already do) that it was a publicity stunt.

Campy-vampy ladies you might have met during transit to China in its British colonial age: **Marlene Dietrich** and (in the upper-right photo) **Anna Mae Wong.** Photos are publicity stills from *Shanghai Express (1932).*

I see the 'Other Person' all the time, who is completely changed toward me—beautiful and sweet—and completely unlike last year...
I will be happy to see your beautiful little face again. Your White Prince."

The "other person" Mercedes referred to was, of course, Greta Garbo.

***

During the making of *The Scarlet Empress* (1934), Mercedes was a frequent visitor on the set. Lavishly gowned, Marlene had been cast as Catherine the Great, Empress of Russia. In one scene, she was filmed clattering up the palace steps astride a white horse.

Mercedes liked watching Dietrich perform.

Author Axel Madsen described it best: "Marlene was no less narcissistic. She knew every angle of her face, and she taught herself lighting techniques. She had herself filmed with a mirror next to the camera so she could watch her own make-believe."

The Dietrich/Mercedes affair blossomed in the spring of 1933 and continued for the remainder of that year, although Dietrich was away at times. In Hollywood, as a couple, they were seen going to the movies together, dining at Chasen's, showing up at tennis matches, and shopping. As a team, Mercedes and Dietrich often hosted swimming parties at

After the rigors of World War II and the politics she'd navigated as a loyal (but German-born) American citizen, **Marlene** returned to the screen in the French film, *Martin Roumagnac* (1946), which was unsuccessfully released two years later in the U.S. as *The Room Upstairs)*. Her co-star was her offscreen lover, **Jean Gabin**, a Free French resistance fighter and one of the greatest stars in the history of French film.

In it, Martin Roumagnac (**Gabin,** see upper photo) is besotted with love for the beautiful, charming, and sincere-hearted Blanche **(Dietrich)**, whom he murders after discovering her secret past as a high-class prostitute.

In the U.S., the Legion of Decency was outraged at the way "play for pay" was depicted and demanded massive cuts. The resulting "massacre" (it was cut from 115 minutes to 88 minutes and stripped of its pathos) pleased no one.

Dietrich's (rented) villa in Santa Monica.

They soon became part of what was called "The Sewing Circle." Charter members, by now scattered across the country, included such notables as authors Willa Cather and, Edna St. Vincent Millay; producer Cheryl Crawford, stage and screen stars Eva Le Gallienne, Nazimova, Katharine Cornell, Mary Martin, Janet Gaynor, Kay Francis, Anita Loos; and director Dorothy Arzner.

One reporter dared ask Dietrich about rumors of her lesbianism. She responded, "In Europe, it does not matter if you make love to a man or woman. We make love to anyone we find attractive. It is referred to as 'sex without gender preference.'"

It was around this time that Mercedes made Dietrich a surprising offer: In an attempt to hold onto her affection, she said, "I can bring anyone to your bed. This is not because I love you less, but because I love you more."

The last of the Dietrich movies directed by Von Sternberg was *The Devil Is a Woman* (1935), set at carnival time in Seville of the 1890s. Mercedes learned that whereas her lover's next picture, *Desire* (1936), would reunite her once again with Gary Cooper, it would be directed by someone other the Von Sternberg. With touches of grief, Mercedes concluded that Von Sternberg must have exited from (or been ejected from) Dietrich's life, and she fired off a letter of condolence.

"I am angry that anyone could hurt or wound you. I only know that I would like to keep my arms around you and to protect you from any pain. I pray that I was not the one who was the cause of this thing—that Mr. Von Sternberg did not know of me. To lose such a friend as him might harm your work. Just for loving me, you might have to pay a high price. Beautiful, thrilling firebird, do not forget your wings that belong only to you. You do not need anyone else to carry you high, up high."

***

By now, the bloom was off the rose of the Dietrich/De Acosta pairing. Dietrich told friends, "I think Mercedes is assigning herself too important a role in my life."

As was inevitable, their affair wound down, although throughout the remainder of the 30s, they would sometimes get together for a rendezvous.

After the debut of World War II, Dietrich began entertaining the American Army from makeshift stages behind the front lines of Europe. During the hostilities, Mercedes saw less and less of her, but in the late 1940s and '50s, they would, occasionally and at random intervals, remain in touch.

When Mercedes published her memoirs in 1960, Dietrich wrote to her with a very subjective "review" of its contents:

"I enjoyed your book. It evoked a time gone by, a fabulous period in my life when all of us were a lot younger and falling in and out of love with the seasons. Today, life has no longer any meaning for me. For what is life without love?"

A Writer's Notebook: Memories of Marlene

As a devoted, decades-long fan of **Marlene Dietrich**, the senior co-author of this book, **Darwin Porter** penned, in 1977, a *roman-à-cléf* based on her extraordinary life.

It was quickly designated as *Book of the Month* in the Netherlands and became "required reading" for many of the aging actresses within the orbit of Lucille Lortel, the "Queen of Off-Broadway" in whose circle Darwin at the time was regularly and frequently involved.

One member of that clique who devoured its contents, and who had it on her bedside table at the moment of her death, was ballerina Tamara Geva, the ex-wife of George Balanchine. She described its startling opening scenes (a lesbian encounter of an aging "Marlene" with a neophyte wannabe) as "a brilliant parable for the story of my life"

Arbor House, its publisher, marketed it with the following slogans: *"A fabled superstar from the glamorous era of Garbo and Dietrich,* **Marika** *was a fascinating mixture of elusive sensuality and bold innocence. Soaring from the depths of poverty to the brilliant decadence of Berlin and the sweet temptations of Hollywood, she is haunted by the looming betrayal of her own secret past."*

How did the REAL Marlene Dietrich "self-define and introduce herself" during her first encounter with Darwin at a show-biz cocktail party in Paris in the 1970s?

"Helloooooooo. My name is Marlene Dietrich, and I am a cabaret entertainer."

REST IN PEACE
MARLENE DIETRICH
(1901-1992)

CHAPTER SIXTEEN
The Confederacy's Most Famous Whorehouse Madam

ONA MUNSON

Mercedes' Torrid Affair with Belle Watling, Gone With the Wind's Kind-Hearted Hooker

---

Ona Munson, despite a body less voluptuous than that envisioned in advance by Producer David O. Selznick, was later awarded the role of Belle Watling, Hollywood's most likable madam of any movie of the Golden Age, in *Gone With the Wind* (1939), despite ferocious competition from both Mae West (left photo) and Tallulah Bankhead (right).

At the glittering Los Angeles premiere of *Gone With the Wind* (1939), it was hardly noticed that one of the stars of the film, Ona Munson, was accompanied by Mercedes de Acosta. There were too many other stars for reporters and fans to focus on that memorable night.

In *Gone With the Wind*, Munson had entered screen immortality when she was cast as Belle Watling, the owner of the local whorehouse, catering to men such as Rhett Butler, who had been on the side of the Confederacy.

David Selznick had at first wanted Tallulah Bankhead for the role—and she would have been perfect—but he was reluctant to approach her, having rejected her previously for the role of Scarlett O'Hara, selecting Vivien Leigh instead.

When Munson showed up for her wardrobe fitting and screen test for

Three views of **Ona Munson**—a woman more sensitive than Hollywood could bear.

the role of Belle Watling, she didn't look as if she'd ever set foot in Dixie—in fact, she was born in Portland, Oregon, in 1903.

She was described at the time as tall and freckle-faced, with hair cut in a sort of bob. Wardrobe and makeup went to work on her, transforming her into what one writer at the time called "a lush Rubenesque figure with creamy Ingrès skin, glossy red hair, and flashing jewels on a plunging neckline." Her voice was low, throaty, and full of sexual overtones.

After watching the screen test, Selznick said, "I've found my Belle."

In a career that spanned three decades before her tragic ending, Munson was a beauty. At times, depending on her makeup, she came close to evoking Marlene Dietrich. Over the years, she starred in twenty feature films and appeared in nine Broadway productions.

Munson in *Going Wild*. Although she was married at times, the title of the movie might have fitted her private life, which included a number of lesbian affairs, not just with Mercedes but with Marlene Dietrich, Nazimova, and the Countess Dorothy di Frasso when she wasn't in the arms of Gary Cooper.

In 1919, right after World War II, she made her Broadway debut in George White's *Scandals*. In the 1920s, she followed that with four more Broadway plays and musicals, most notably when she took over the title role of the singing and dancing ingénue, Nanette in the original production of *No, No, Nanette*.

Although mainly a lesbian, she met and married her first husband, stage actor Edward Buzzell, in the summer of 1926. The marriage was not successful. She divorced him in 1931.

She would marry once again, part of a "lavender marriage" in 1950 to Eugene Berman, a Russian-born artist and designer. Within its context, she sustained numerous affairs with lesbians, most notably with Alla Nazimova and Mercedes de Acosta.

Before Munson said farewell to Broadway, she starred in the original production of *Hold Everything!*, a musical in which she introduced the standard, "You're the Cream in My Coffee."

Moving to Los Angeles in 1930, she went to work at Warners, the studio casting her in one of its early talkies, *Going Wild*.

It was at this time that she divorced Buzzell and had an affair with director Ernst Lubitsch, prior to his marriage to Vivian Gaye.

In 1931, Munson appeared in *The Hot Heiress* with Ben Lyon, and she sang several numbers. That was followed by *Broadminded* in 1931 and *Five Star Final* that same year.

Rather disillusioned with her film roles, she returned to Broadway in *Hold Your Horses* (1933), followed by *Petticoat Fever* soon after that. Her most notable star role was in Henrik Ibsen's *Ghosts* in which she delivered a brilliant performance as Regina Engstrand. The former goddess of the silent screen, Alla Nazimova, was her director. During its rehearsal period, Munson and Nazimova had an affair, which ended amicably right before the play's Broadway opening. *[For more about Nazimova, see Chapter Six of this book.]*

Returning once more to Los Angeles, Ona found the pickings slim, but took a minor role in 1938 in *His Exciting Night*. She said, "It might be exciting for him, but not for me."

Having abandoned hopes of casting Tallulah Bankhead as Belle Watling, Selznick turned to an even more ideal choice, Mae West, whose voluptuous body fitted the description of Belle's perfectly.

West turned him down, telling Selznick, "I'm a star and have always been a star, which means I don't do cameos. But of course, let's face the truth: Had I appeared as Belle Watling, I would have doubled the gross of

Munson in *The Hot Heiress*. Originally, her role was slated for the great Broadway star Marilyn Miller, who dropped out.

Its plot swirled around an heiress who falls for a construction worker after first trying to pass him off to her swank friends as an architect. Before the end of the film, in the name of love, she agrees to live on his salary.

More press and PR photos of an actress (**Ona Munson**) desperately searching for her niche.

Gone With the Wind."

Even though her own body was less voluptuous than how the script had described that of Belle Watling, Munson auditioned for the role and won it.

***

It was a sunny afternoon in 1932 as Mercedes strolled the beach of Santa Monica with her lover, Greta Garbo. As they passed the beach-fronting homes of William Randolph Hearst and his mistress, Marion Davies, of Norma Shearer and MGM's Irving Thalberg, of Irene and David O. Selznick, Garbo decided impulsively to drop in unannounced at the home of director Ernst Lubitsch, who would, within a few years, direct her in her first (and only) comedy, *Ninotchka* (1939).

It was that afternoon that Mercedes met Ona Munson, whom she'd seen on the Broadway stage performing in Nazimova's *Ghosts* by Ibsen.

It was perfectly clear that Munson was the director's latest mistress.

As Lubitsch and Garbo talked, Munson invited Mercedes for a drink on the terrace, overlooking the pounding waves of the Pacific.

"I've been wanting to meet you for some time," Munson said. "Nazimova has told me so much about you, and she speaks of you so lovingly."

Mercedes countered by extolling how much Munson's appearance on Broadway had meant to her.

During their time together on the terrace, Mercedes had given Munson her private phone number.

"Although she was currently the mistress of a fabled director, there was a twinkle in her eye that showed a certain sexual interest," Mercedes recalled.

"Ona was small, slight, and had blonde hair. I thought she was extremely pretty, but the thing that impressed me the most were her eyes. They were very sad, and there was something about them that touched me deeply."

At sunset, Garbo was ready to leave, and she went to retrieve Mercedes. She had already announced that she was going on a six-month visit to her native Sweden.

Garbo departed early in the morning a few days later for New York, where she planned to sail to Europe. Before leaving California, she had made love to Mercedes for most of the night. "We'll meet again, dear one," Garbo had said before bidding *adieu*.

Mercedes had hoped to be invited to Stockholm with Garbo, but no such invitation was extended.

That very afternoon, the phone rang, and it was Munson. It seemed that Lubitsch, too, had departed for New York for a two-week business trip. Munson invited Mercedes to spend the time vacationing with her at the Santa Monica beach house, an invitation that Mercedes eagerly accepted.

Thus began an on-and-off affair that would stretch over a decade, with long periods of separation.

The two women turned out to be harmonious both in and out of bed, and every day, they went for long strolls along the beach. Munson claimed, "Mercedes and I shared some of the deepest spiritual moments of my life, times that far too few people ever get to share. We created an entity as sure as if it had been conceived and had borne a child."

When they were apart, as they often were, they exchanged love letters. In one, Munson wrote, "I long to hold you in my arms and pour out my love for you."

***

There was one role of a madam that Munson found so tempting, she could not turn it down. *The Shanghai Gesture* (1941) was directed by Josef von Sternberg (*The Scarlet Empress/The Blue Angel/The Devil Is a Woman*) who had launched the career of his mistress, Marlene Dietrich.

Sternberg assigned the leading roles to two emerging stars of the 1940s, Gene Tierney and Victor Mature. Walter Huston was also a co-star, with Munson cast as "Mother" Gin Sling.

Munson, in another role as a bordello's madam, a tough, ruthless, and elaborately coiffed survivor named "Gin Sling."

The film was *Shanghai Gesture* (1941).

Gigolo ("Doctor") Omar (played by Mature) bribes the local police not to jail a broke American showgirl, Dixie Pomeroy (Phyllis Brooks). He takes her to the casino operated by the Dragon Lady, Mother Gin Sling, his boss. At the casino he falls for a beautiful woman, Poppy (Tierney). Sir Guy Charteris (Huston) is a rich entrepreneur who owns a huge chunk of Shanghai, including Gin Sling's casino. The plot unfolds from there.

The movie required thirty revisions before it would pass approval from the Breen Office, the official censors of Hollywood movies of that era. Originally, the blemished noirish character of Mother Gin Sling was known as Mother Goddamn, and originally, instead of a casino, she ran a bordello.

Variety found the picture "rather dull and hazy," and wrote that "Munson could not penetrate the mask-like makeup applied for her Asian characterization."

Film critic Dennis Schwartz was more positive. "Despite the forced changes, this is still a delirious masterpiece of decadence and sexual depravity that surrounds itself with Eastern motifs that are meant to mystify rather than enlighten."

The Shanghai Gesture was the last film the great Von Sternberg ever completed. In 1950, Howard Hughes at RKO hired Von Sternberg to direct *Jet Pilot*, starring John Wayne and Janet Leigh. However, halfway through the shoot, Hughes fired Von Sternberg. The release of the film was delayed by seven years. About a year later, Hughes rehired Von Sternberg to direct *Macao* (1951), starring the busty Jane Russell and Robert Mitchum, but once again fired him halfway through the shoot.

Left photo is a piece of CBS Television press and publicity about **Ona Munson**.

The Associated Press story on the right carried the news about the actress's suicide.

After *Shanghai Gesture*, roles were few for Munson. Mercedes recalled her last weekend with the fading star when she was "morbidly depressed" and working on Poverty Row in Hollywood for Republic Pictures.

Years later, Mercedes also recalled an unhappy time in the1950s when she visited Munson in Paris. She was living with her second husband, Eugene Berman, as part of what Mercedes termed "a loveless marriage."

"She hated Paris," Mercedes said, "and longed to be back in New York. She was also in failing health, complaining of having the most horrible headaches. I tried to cheer her up, but she seemed shrouded in a veil of unhappiness. Our romantic days of the 1930s seemed far, far away. In my last visits with Ona, I left feeling depressed myself."

Munson did return to New York, but Mercedes never saw her again. She'd heard that she'd entered a hospital for some unnamed surgical procedure, perhaps a tumor. While living in an apartment in the Belnord Building on the Upper West Side of Manhattan, Munson, at the age of fifty-one, comitted suicide with an overdose of barbiturates.

Her husband, Berman, discovered her body on February 11, 1955. Next to her bed was a suicide note which read, "This is the only way I know to feel free again. Please don't follow me!"

Munson posthumously received a star on the Hollywood Walk of Fame.

BELLE BREZING
THE REAL-LIFE KIND-HEARTED HOOKER WHO INSPIRED THE CHARACTER OF BELLE WATLING IN *GONE WITH THE WIND*

The fictional Belle Watling, the owner of a bordello in *Gone With the Wind*, was based on a real life character, a woman who owned and operated an exclusive, "high-class" bordello in Lexington, Kentucky in the late 19th Century. Margaret Mitchell was inspired by her saga to create the character of Belle Watling in her best-selling saga. Ona Munson brought her character to the screen in 1939.

Now a local icon in Kentucky, she was called Belle Brezing, but that was not her real name. Born illegitimate, the future madam entered the world in 1861 as Mary Belle Cox to a poor, unmarried teenager, Sarah Ann Cox, about two months after the outbreak of the War Between the (American) States.

Sarah Ann later married George Brezing, the alcoholic, mean-spirited owner of a local saloon. Sarah's infant grew up in a household where both parents were drunk most of the time. Violent domestic disputes characterized the ill-fated marriage, which ended in 1866, a few months after the end of the Civil War.

By the time she was twelve—the age of sexual consent in Kentucky at the time—Mary Belle Cox had unofficially changed her name to "Belle Brezing."

Even at a young age, she was extremely promiscuous, finding that the men of Kentucky often preferred a twelve-year-old to a sixteen- or eighteen-year-old. Belle, who wrote poetry, some of it saucy, even penned an ode in praise of "school boys in pantalets, growing into young lads, boys who like to be kissed and to give kisses."

Belle lost her virginity to Dionesio Mucci, a local merchant who was thirty-six years old at the time. Their affair lasted two years, but she also had numerous affairs on the side, especially with two young cigar makers, James Kenney and John Andrew Cook.

Two views of Kentucky's most famous Madam, **Belle Brezing.**

Belle's life changed at the age of fifteen when she found herself pregnant but didn't know who the father was. She convinced Kenney that he was about "to become a daddy." He believed her and married her on September 14, 1875.

Shortly after her marriage, she went back to live with her mother, but then her biography grows murky. It seemed that she asked to borrow a gun from Cook, and he lent it to her without asking why she needed a lethal weapon.

Perhaps he should have, since a week later, he was found dead outside the fence in her backyard, a bullet in his skull. Mucci was said to have been the last person to see Cook alive. That very same day, Kenney fled town and disappeared for a decade.

In print, *The Lexington Daily Press* asked a provocative question: "Was it suicide or murder? If suicide, a gun would have been found next to his body. No weapon was ever discovered."

On March 14, 1876, Brezing gave birth to a daughter, Daisy Mae Kenney. Two months later, Sarah Cox died of cancer. While Belle was attending her mother's funeral, the landlord padlocked their home for failure to make payments. Returning from the ceremony, Belle and her baby found themselves homeless, with their possessions thrown out into the street. She gave her baby away to a neighbor, Elizabeth Barnett, and went to work in a house of prostitution.

As the child grew older, it became apparent that she was mentally retarded. With Belle providing support, in time, she would end up spending the rest of her life in an asylum in Detroit.

Ironically, the brothel in which Belle was employed had been the elegant former residence of First Lady Mary Todd Lincoln. Because Belle was the youngest and the most beautiful of the "working girls" upstairs, she

59 Megowan St. in Lexington, KY, Belle Brezing's third and most famous bordello, 1889-1917; **Brezing** occupied the house until her death from uterine cancer in 1940. In this blurred photo, she's visible, seated, at home, and not suffering fools lightly

A House is not neccessarily a home, and proof that Victorian clutter and "movin' on up" pretentions applied to more than just genteel parlors.

Here's a view of **one of Belle's hardworking bedrooms** in the third of her string of Kentucky brothels.

was the most requested by the local bankers and politicians, chief patrons of the brothel.

She made so much money by renting out her body that in July of 1881, she could afford to open her own "bawdy house" at 156 North Upper Street in Lexington.

She dressed in expensive gowns and attired her working girls equally well, insisting that they comport themselves elegantly and be formally dressed during their visits to the ground floor's formal parlors. On trips to New York she acquired expensive antiques, paintings, linens, and silverware. She hired two of the finest African American cooks, and served her patrons, mainly bankers, businessmen, and politicians, elegant food before they went upstairs to satisfy their libidos.

Once, she was arrested for running a brothel, but the governor of Kentucky, one of her patrons, Luke P. Blackburn, pardoned her and arranged for charges to be dropped.

With money pouring in, she purchased a mansion in Lexington at 194 North Upper Street. Her new brothel opened in July, 1882.

It was that same year that she fell in love with her bookkeeper, Billy Mabon, beginning a life-long affair.

With money acquired from industrialist William S. Singerly of Philadelphia, she purchased her finest and most elegant brothel at what is now 153 Northeastern Avenue in Lexington's red light district. It soon built a reputation as the finest in the South, drawing horse-racing fans to its premises when they came to Kentucky for the races.

Alcohol flowed freely there, but when the Temperance movement of 1915 gained strength, city ordinances were passed that forced the brothel to close, which it did in 1917, the year the U.S. entered World War I.
That was the year her lover, Mabon, died.

With money in the bank, Belle retired for life and became addicted to morphine.

Having been drug addicted for years, she was diagnosed with uterine cancer in 1938 as *Gone With the Wind* was being filmed in Hollywood. When it opened the following year, she was too ill to attend.

She learned that Ona Munson played Belle Watling, a character based on her own life.

Brezing died on April 11, 1940 as the world was once again at war. Her tombstone read—BLESSED ARE THE PURE IN HEART.

She was famous enough for *Time* magazine to run her obituary, and on its front page, *The Lexington Herald* published a eulogy.

Ironically, Margaret Mitchell's husband, John Marsh, had once lived in Lexington, working as a crime reporter for *The Lexington Herald*. He recalled how Belle Brezing used to invite members of the police and press into her elegant establishment, wining and dining them.

[Of course, if requested, she would make any of her beautiful young women upstairs available to them. It is not known how much Marsh told his wife about the establishment, but she knew enough to replicate her as a fictional character.]

Since 2009, the City of Lexington has observed "Belle's Birthday Ball" on June 16 to commemorate the former madam's birthday. She's been the subject of a documentary (*Belle Brezing and the Gilded Age of Bluegrass*) associated with the University of Kentucky, the subject of local women's studies seminars, and a figure of increasing fame within the fabric of everyday life in Lexington.

Margaret Mitchell always denied that she'd been inspired by the saga of Belle Brezing for her character of Belle Watling in *Gone With the Wind*.

But the people of Lexington know better.

Here's **Ona Munson** as Belle Watling with **Clark Gable**, cast as Rhett Butler, one of the patrons of her character's whorehouse, in *Gone With the Wind (1939)*.

WITH RESPECT AND AFFECTION,
AND WITH REGRETS FOR THE PAIN THAT DROVE HER TO SUICIDE

REST IN PEACE

ONA MUNSON
(1903-1955)

CHAPTER SEVENTEEN
MEDIA BUZZ & BOOMER/ZOOMER TIMES:
BETTER ACCESS TO A FAMILIAR FRIEND

MAGNOLIA HOUSE'S ZOOMED-IN VIEW OF
MEDIA GURU & *GRANDE DAME*

ANITA FINLEY

THE GUIDING LIGHT BEHIND ONE OF FLORIDA'S MOST
POIGNANT WELLNESS & LIFESTYLE PROGRAMS

Baby Boomers Read
Boomer Times and
They Watch
ZoomerTimes TV

"You are the salt of the earth. You have borne the pain and joy of motherhood and have earned every beautiful wrinkle and laugh line...so keep smiling and make time for your children and other children. Everyone needs a mother, but especially a grandmother, if you have reached that glorious age. Don't regret it...salivate it."
—Anita Finley

BoomerTimes
& SeniorLife Magazine

A Monthly Magazine
Serving
Active Adults in
South Florida
Since 1990

BOOMER/ZOOMERTIMES:
BETTER ACCESS TO A FAMILIAR FRIEND

WHO IS ANITA FINLEY, AND WHAT ARE PEOPLE SAYING ABOUT BOOMER/ZOOMER TIMES?

She was an early admirer of Darwin Porter. She heard about him during the publicity generated by the long-ago publication of his seminal overviews of Bogart (*The Secret Life of Humphrey Bogart*; 2003) and Katharine Hepburn (*Katharine the Great;* 2004).

She's also one of the South's leading gerontologists, a modern-day Amazon, and a Renaissance woman seemingly capable of thriving wherever she happens to land. She's a woman of influence, shaping public opinion and spreading wide her message of tolerance and love.

It's as a host on ZoomerTimes TV that Anita commands her largest audience. Darwin regularly appears on her show.

He also writes MEDIA BUZZ, an artfully gossipy monthly column crafted at Magnolia House and distributed through *Boomer Times* as a regular supplement of *The Miami Herald.* For more information about it, and the **Boomer Expo Exhibitions** she choreographs, click on *www.BoomerTimesFL.com.*

Anita Finley is one of the best educated, best informed and most charming of the many guests who have passed through my life and through Magnolia House. She's also a qualified and sought-after public speaker, promoting her personal conviction that it's never too late to learn or to try something new She also choreographs an annual symposium about wellness and health, the C.U.R.E. Symposiums. In 2020 she evolved into the creative force behind *ELearningForSeniors.com*, a website loaded with exciting stuff for Seniors and Boomers.

Blood Moon extends recognition and gratitude to Anita, a woman we love. She will always be welcome at Magnolia House.

Danforth Prince, Publisher
Blood Moon Productions, Ltd.

WHAT IS DARWIN PORTER'S MEDIA BUZZ?

It's newsy, it's gossipy, it's fun, it's produced inside Magnolia House, and it tends to generate headlines. Five reprints of *Media Buzz* appear within the pages that follow.

Headlines inspired by *Media Buzz* appeared within several major international newspapers AFTER their revelations first appeared in *Boomer Times*. Here are some pithy examples:

THE XXX-RATED LIFE OF PETER O'TOOLE
KIRK DOUGLAS, A CENTURY OF CONQUESTS
ME TOO! THE CASTING COUCH, YESTERDAY AND TODAY
JAMES DEAN: THE "OTHER" (AFTER MARILYN AND JFK) ICON OF
"THE AMERICAN CENTURY"
THEN-MARRIED VIVIEN LEIGH BEDDED GUYS—AND GALS!
PAUL NEWMAN & STEVE McQUEEN WERE LOVERS
JUNE ALLYSON SLEPT WITH TWO PRESIDENTS
HOW LIZ TAYLOR BEDDED TINSELTOWN
BILL CLINTON TRIED TO SEDUCE JACKIE KENNEDY IN A
WRESTLING MATCH IN HER NEW YORK APARTMENT
HEDY LAMARR, MOTHER OF THE CELLPHONE
JUDY & LIZA: TOO MANY DAMN RAINBOWS

How Do You Access ZoomerTimes TV?

1. Go to YouTube.com, then search for "ZoomerTimes TV," OR

2. Go to Facebook.com/Boomertimes, then search for "Zoomertimes TV," OR

3. Go to BoomerTimesFL.com

Media Buzz
By Darwin Porter
As it appeared in the June 2020 edition of *Boomer Times*

THE CENSORSHIP & BANNING OF
GONE WITH THE WIND

Censorship of films, plays, TV shows, and books, is rearing its ugly head again.

In a robust democracy, censorship is rare. As a pervasive part of a culture, it belongs more to totalitarian regimes as evidenced by what can be seen—or not—in China and Russia today. In the past, Josef Goebbels, the Nazi propaganda minister, was adept at censorship.

Since the birth of motion pictures, self-appointed American censors have aggressively tried to impose their values on their fellow citizens. In 1897, an early silent film provoked outrage by portraying a man passionately kissing his wife.

In 1907, Chicago became the first city in America to grant its chief of police the power to censor any film before it was released. That was followed with towns and cities across America appointing censorship boards *Gone*

Fearing Federal regulation, Hollywood in the 1930s imposed its own censorship board, stifling free expression until independent producers broke free in the 1960s.

Now, in 2020, new outcries of rage are being expressed as self-appointed "cultural commissars" want to decide what you can see or read.

The most notorious case calls for suppression of that enduring Amer-

Ever since its publication in 1936, **Gone With the Wind** became one of the most controversial novels ever published. Likewise, the 1939 film version raised objections from African Americans for its depiction of slavery in the antebellum South.

Yet the public devoured it. To date, it has sold more thatn 30 million copies in 27 languages. Ardent fans of the book, some of whom define themselves as "Windies," meet at periodic intervals, wearing full period costumes, to reflect on re-interpretations of (and challenges to) its content and characters. And in 1986 and 1995, the U.S. Postal Service issued stamps in honor of *Gone With the Wind* or its author as commemorations of its social impact and historical importance.

ican classic from 1939, Margaret Mitchell's film adaptation of *Gone With the Wind*.

Seen by millions upon millions, it's the highest-grossing film of all time (adjusted for inflation). Starring Vivien Leigh as Scarlett O'Hara and Clark Gable as Rhett Butler, the movie is attacked for its "romantic" depiction of the Antebellum South and its tolerance (or endorsement) of slavery.

Actually, it's not much about slavery at all. It's the saga of Scarlett, born into a bucolic life on a plantation, who is plunged into surviving a war that ravishes her land and family. Later, she charts a new life for herself as an independent woman forced into the business world during Reconstruction. It's also the story of a woman torn between two lovers.

Hattie McDaniel was the first African American woman to win an Oscar for her memorable portrayal of Mammy. Some critics single her out as the smartest woman in the movie. She even bosses Scarlett around, holding her adolescent rebelliousness in check and continually prompting her to comport herself "like a lady." During her heyday, in reference to her role, McDaniel told a reporter, "I'd rather play a maid than be a maid."

In contrast, Butterfly McQueen told me that her role as the lazy, flighty slave, Prissy, "ruined my life. I had to play Prissy in film after film after that." She immortalized herself with one of the most iconic lines ever uttered onscreen: *"Miss Scarlett, I don't know nothin' 'bout birthin' babies."*

Early in the post-Covid censorship wars, HBO stopped its streaming distribution of *Gone With the Wind*, but later enabled it for streamings with a *caveat*: Jacqueline Stewart, an African American film historian and a host of Turner Classic Movies, will narrate a brief discussion, inserted as an introduction before each screening.

Spike Lee, the best known African American director, defended *Gone With the Wind* on the TV talk show, *The View*. He also inserted a sequence from that film into his movie, *BlacKkKlansman*.

"I think people should see this movie even though it's openly racist," Lee said.

More "radical," Lee screened *The Birth of a Nation*, considered by some as D.W. Griffth's masterpiece, to students in his film studies classes at New York University. Interpreted by many as the most racist film ever made, it depicts the KKK as a heroic force for the preservation of "American values" and the White Supremacist social order.

Hattie McDaniel laces up Scarlett O'Hara (**Vivien Leigh**) and lectures her about how to behave at a pre-Civil War barbecue where she will attract the attention of eligible males.

McDaniel, later voted Best Supporting Actress of the Year, became the first African American to win an Oscar, even beating out Olivia de Havilland, who played Melanie in the same movie.

If these recent trends in American censorship prevail, virtually the entire output of films made during the first half of the 20th Century, including those with a theme of "John Wayne vs. The Indians" could be pulled from circulation.

But that won't happen without some artistic objections: Author Judith Miller wrote, "The impulse to self-censor, however powerful in such politically polarized times, is deadly to any vibrant culture. No matter how seemingly compelling its justification, it must be resisted."

Media Buzz
By Darwin Porter
As it appeared in the January 2020 edition of *Boomer Times*

THE TRAGIC, MUCH-PERSECUTED LIFE OF ALAN TURING, THE "FATHER OF COMPUTERS"

British historians estimate that the scientific breakthroughs of Alan Turing, a computer scientist (1912-1954), shortened World War II in Europe by two years and saved 14 million lives.

To its everlasting shame, Britain persecuted this progenitor of modern computing and, under Victorian laws about homosexuality, forced him to undergo chemical castration. Morbidly depressed, he committed suicide by cyanide on June 7, 1954 at the age of forty-one.

A half-eaten apple was found beside his bed. His method of dying, it has been suggested, came from his favorite fairy tale, Walt Disney's *Snow White & the Seven Dwarfs* (1937), in which the wicked queen immerses an apple in a poisonous brew.

Turing died in obscurity because his remarkable achievements were concealed at the time by the Official Secrets Code of the British government. All that has changed today—in fact, the Bank of England has announced that beginning in 2020, Turing's face will be depicted on the new £50 note.

In 2009, British Prime Minister Gordon Brown apologized "for the appalling way Turing was treated. He deserved so much better."

When President Barack Obama arrived in London, he got it right, praising this code breaker and computer visionary. He hailed Turing, placing him in "the Pantheon of innovators and discoverers from Newton to Darwin, from Einstein to Edison, from Alan Turing to Steve Jobs. Turing's goal was to embody human intelligence into an artificial form—hence, the invention of the computer."

In 2013, the Queen of England issued an official pardon.

In World War II, Turing worked with code breakers at the sprawling estate of Bletchley Park north of London. Here, he cracked the code of Nazi Germany's Enigma machine. Hitler regarded the code as unbreakable, and it remained in use throughout the entire war. That meant that the British knew in advance every major move the Nazis were going to make. Sir Winston Churchill learned that Coventry was going to be bombed but did not order the evacuation of the city, since it would have signaled the Nazis that the Enigma Code had been cracked.

Turing conceived what became known as the Universal Turing Machine, which could perform all sorts of tasks. Sir Winston told FDR of this remarkable achievement, and it was shared with American scientists working on the development of the Manhattan Project.

From that emerged atomic bombs dropped on Japan in the closing days of World War II in the Pacific. Harry S Truman learned that the Japanese planned "to fight to the last man standing" in an invasion of the home islands. He estimated that dropping those bombs, ushering in the Atomic Age, saved the lives of a million and a half American soldiers.

"Turing was a national treasure," said MP John Graham-Cunning, who worked to restore his reputation. "We hounded him to death, but his name will live forever in world history."

In June of 2019—a little late—*The New York Times* finally ran Turing's obituary. In 2014, a film about Turing's life, *The Imitation Game*, was released starring Benedict Cumberbatch.

In the post-war era, during the most intense conflicts of the Cold War, Turing was on the dawn of scientific breakthroughs that would have led to nuclear supremacy as America and Britain faced the menace of the Soviet Union. It's estimated that Turing would have advanced British technology by two decades. But while investigating a routine robbery at Turing's residence, police discovered he was having an affair with a man his own age. In March of 1952, he was convicted of "gross indecency," and, to avoid prison, he submitted to chemical castration. That meant his security clearance was lifted, and he was fired.

On the 100th anniversary of Turing's birth in 2012, posthumous tributes poured in from around the world. Today, statues honor him, wings of buildings are named after him, even bridges and roads. He is acknowledged as "the Father of Computer Science" and also as "the Godfather of All Modern Computers."

Time magazine eventually designated Turing as one of the 100 most important people of the 20th Century. "Everyone who taps at the keyboard, opens a spreadsheet or a word-processing program is working on an incarnation of a Turing machine."

In one of the most shocking and shameful acts in homophobic British history, the government forced inventor **Alan Turing** to undergo chemical castration because of his sexual orientation.

This was hardly how to treat the man who is credited for saving an estimated 14 million lives by breaking the Nazi's secret code and thereby shortening World War II.

Today, he's belatedly honored as a valiant hero, hailed by some authorities as one of the 100 most important people of the 20th Century.

Media Buzz
by Darwin Porter

As it appeared in the February 2020 edition of Boomer Times
Creative Malady

Provocative issues are being raised about the private lives of painters, actors, musicians, dancers, directors, authors and composers. Should we judge them strictly on their artistic creations, regardless of their morals?

Reputations are being destroyed by revelations about the private lives of certain artists and other creators. Morality tests are being applied to artists of yesterday who are being subjected to a 21st Century perspective of their politics and sexual improprieties.

A study of the private lives of some of the leading figures in world culture would reveal dozens of maladjusted personalities, even demented ones. Examples come to mind: Sigmund Freud, Florence Nightingale, Charles Darwin, Marcel Proust.

Should we no longer read the groundbreaking modernist novels of Cé-

CREATIVE MALADIES: i.e., eccentricities bordering on (according to their detractors) insanities. Clockwise from upper left: **Sigmund Freud, Charles Darwin** (aged 33 with his son, William); **Paul Gauguin** (self-portrait), **Tennessee Williams, Marcel Proust**, and the inspiration for modern nursing, "the Lady with the Lamp," **Florence Nightingale.**

Except for their ability to influence and improve the societies they occupied, any of them might—through uncharitable and conventional lenses—have been judged as dysfunctional, sociopathic, or insane.

line because he was an anti-Semite? Let's not look too closely into the secret beliefs, recreations, and politics of Cervantes, Richard Wagner, or even Shakespeare.

There is a condition called "Creative Malady," which suggests that great art is often produced by the psychologically damaged. It is said that mental illness, often in the form of a psychoneurosis, can sometimes lead to major success in the production of artwork.

Sir George Pickering, a brilliant septuagenarian physician and author of a book about it (*Creative Malady*, first published in 1974 and today a widely recommended academic text*)*, claimed that "great work would not have been done, or done in such splendid style, by relatively sober people leading ordinary lives."

Years ago in Key West, Tennessee Williams told me that his plays "stem from my tormented soul, my shattered dreams. I was Blanche Du Bois in *A Streetcar Named Desire* — demented, delusional, self-destructive."

In the past two years, artist Paul Gauguin (1848-1903), that self-professed "savage, exploiter, chauvinist, colonialist," has come under fire for his private life.

Moving to Tahiti in 1891, he became a notorious pedophile, fathering countless children born to girls aged twelve to thirteen. He painted them as dusky, bare-breasted, almond-eyed, mysterious, and dark-skinned beauties. He has also been criticized for promoting racial stereotypes.

Gauguin did not confine his painting to nubile Polynesian maidens. He also painted self-portraits, one of himself as Jesus Christ, another of himself as a decapitated John the Baptist, with a ruby-red glaze of blood on his neck.

Some of his sharpest critics have even demanded that museums and galleries displaying his works cease to do so. Exhibitions of his masterpieces have also been condemned. Yet reproductions of his works decorate thousands of bedrooms. His last painting, "Will You Marry?" sold for $210 million in 2014, the third-highest price ever paid for a painting.

When London's Tate Gallery presented an exhibition of Gauguin's works, many writers were highly critical of its curators for "displaying the art of a child molester." The director at the time, Vicente Todoli, said, "As a person, I might have loathed Gauguin, but as an artist, he is a genius, inspiring future painters such as Picasso and Matisse. When an artist creates something, it no longer belongs to him, but to the world."

As his legacy, Gauguin has inspired novels, operas, even movies such as *Lust for Life* (1956). It starred Kirk Douglas as Vincent Van Gogh, who cut off his ear before being incarcerated in a mental asylum. Anthony Quinn's portrayal of Van Gogh's rough-edged frenemy (Paul Gauguin) brought him an Oscar.

In 1903, the year of Gauguin's death at the age of 54, he said, "No one is good, no one is evil, everybody is both, in the same way and in different ways. It is so small a thing, the life of a man, and yet there is time to do great things."

Media Buzz
by Darwin Porter
As it appeared in the July 2019 edition of Boomer Times
Movie Stars Reveal "Their First Time"

Did you think that the life of a celebrity is easy? Think again!

Hollywood biographers face many challenges when they attempt to describe the lives of celebrities, male or female. Many readers want to know when details about how a star became acquainted with what was once politely described as "the facts of life."

In the biography I'll release in September—it's about Florida's Burt Reynolds—I was lucky to have acquired that tantalizing data when I worked for *The Miami Herald's* branch offices in Fort Lauderdale and Palm Beach.

In Palm Beach, I met this wealthy and sexually aggressive 42-year-old woman who specialized in young teenaged boys. Burt was just 14 when he began a year-long affair with her. After she sent him on his way, she took up with another 14-year-old, George Hamilton, who later evolved into the perpetually suntanned actor. George became a household word when he dated Lynda Bird Johnson, during the presidential tenure of her father, LBJ. Both Burt and George later seduced Elizabeth Taylor.

Just for fun, and because baby boomers have reached the age where we're no longer bashful about these things, here's how some other big stars were introduced to sex.

When his son turned 15, the father of Desi Arnaz took him to the best brothel in Santiago, Cuba. Milton Berle was only 12 when he lost it to a dancer in the Broadway show *Florodora*. Marlon Brando was all of 19 when a married Colombian woman, Rosa Maria Consuelo Cruz, took him into her boudoir.

During Richard Burton's first appearance on the stage, a teenaged usherette, "Lil," came into his dressing room for his introduction to sex.

In Norfolk, Nebraska, Johnny Carson tangled with "Francine, a girl of easy virtue," in the back seat of his father's 1939 green Chrysler Royal. He pronounced the experience "a disaster."

While walking down a London street, Sean Connery, 14, was picked up by a woman in her 50s who was dressed in a military uniform.

Riding a train to London, Noël Coward was seduced by actress Gertrude Lawrence, two years his senior. He was so turned off by the experience, he self-identified as gay for the rest of his life, taking up first with Prince George, the Duke of Kent.

Long before Marilyn Monroe came into his young life, Tony Curtis was eighteen and in the U.S. Navy when he visited a whorehouse in Panama City.

A teenaged James Dean surrendered it to Dr. James DeWeerd, the pastor of the Wesleyan Church in Fairmont, Indiana. Ironically, this same pastor delivered the eulogy at Dean's funeral in 1955.

Kirk Douglas, the subject of my most recent biography, *More Is Never Enough,* was seduced by his English teacher in high school, a long-term relationship that lasted on and off for years.

Singer Eddie Fisher, 14, was "assaulted" by his voracious next door neighbor, Tootsie Stern.

As a late teenager, Henry Fonda went to a whorehouse in Omaha, Nebraska. Later referring to the experience as "horrible—just a *wham-bam* that turned me off sex for years."

At age 15, Clark Gable lost his in Cadiz, Ohio, to a 58-year-old widow. The Tasmania-born swashbuckler, Errol Flynn, was only 12 when the maid entered to clean up his room and piled into his bed. That was the first of what he recalled as 14,000 seductions to come, both female and male.

Now for the women: Lucille Ball, at 14, surrendered to a local hoodlum, Johnny DeVita, 21, in the back seat of a car in Jamestown, New York. During her early years in Hollywood, she was a "gun moll."

French director Roger Vadim successfully pursued Brigitte Bardot, 15, and later married her.

Joan Blondell, the blonde bombshell of the 1930s who later married Dick Powell and Mike Todd, was 17 when an Oklahoma millionaire raped her.

Cher, 14, blamed her introduction to sex on "the boy next door, a little Italian with his brain in his crotch."

Joan Crawford, 14, was introduced to sex through a gang rape when her brother, Hal Le Sueur, brought

home three of his pals from school.

Doris Day was already married when, at age 17, she experienced "the brutality" of her first husband, musician Al Jorden.

Many actresses were raped as their introduction to sex. Hedy Lamarr, 14, was assaulted by her family's laundryman in the basement. Marilyn Monroe, 15, was attacked by a man in his forties who lived in her foster home.

Barbra Streisand was all of 18 when she surrendered to Barry Dennen, a young New York actor.

Natalie Wood was 14 when her mother ordered her fellow actor, Nick Adams, to teach her daughter "the ways of the world." Separately, each of them was later seduced by James Dean when they co-starred with him in *Rebel Without a Cause* (1955).

On a warm and long summer night beside a lake in Sweden, the future Greta Garbo was seduced by her sister, Alva.

Ava Gardner waited until her wedding night, January 10, 1942, to be seduced by Mickey Rooney. She later cracked, "Mickey lost his virginity when he was three."

Rita Hayworth, 13, "surrendered the pink" to her father, Eduardo Cansino. She survived his repeated assaults on her and went on to seduce some of the most legendary men of the 20th Century. She became so famous, her pinup image was plastered onto the *Enola Gay* the plane that carried the atomic bomb that was dropped on Hiroshima, Japan, a strike so effective (and horrible) that it led to the end of World War II a few days later.

A terrible introduction to sex was suffered by Gloria Swanson, the legendary screen vamp of the silent era. She married Wallace Beery, the ungainly, gravel-voiced, rubber-faced movie star. On her wedding night, as she confessed in her memoirs, "I was brutalized in pitch blackness by a man who whispered filth in my ear and ripped me almost in two. I spent the rest of the night huddled on the bathroom floor, swathed in towels to soak up the blood and to ease the pain."

In 2019, as a recognition of the spectacular earning power of **Burt Reynolds** as a staple in American movies of the 1980s, Blood Moon, as authored mainly by Darwin Porter, published history's first full-scale treatment of the actor's extraordinary life.

As a story with many key elements set in Florida, news of its release was broadcast throughout the Sunshine State, with special assistance from **Boomer Times** and **Anita Finley.**

Media Buzz

by Darwin Porter

As it appeared in the March 2019 edition of Boomer Times

HOLLYWOOD'S SUICIDE-SOAKED BOULEVARD OF BROKEN DREAMS, AS REMEMBERED BY
KIRK DOUGLAS

For the first time, I found inspiration in researching the life of a movie star. Kirk Douglas's amazing story is one of struggles, tragedy, and triumph. He has regained his youth, vitality, and ability to teach some primal lessons in my latest Hollywood biography, *More is Never Enough*. At the age of 102, he is the last surviving male star of Golden Age Hollywood. And unlike celebrities who died at the peak of their strength and beauty, his personal growth during his physically diminished final decades are unique in the history of show-biz.

A stroke in 1996 caused him to lose his speech, and very briefly, he contemplated shooting himself, but instead, learned to speak again with the daily help of a speech therapist.

And despite his impairments, he continued to make films, sometimes cast as a stroke victim, throughout the early years of the 21st Century. His career lasted longer than anyone else's in Hollywood. As a leading film actor, it began in 1946 opposite Barbara Stanwyck. His last screen appearance was in the poignantly titled 2009 film, *Kirk Douglas: Before I Forget*.

Kirk Douglas was the hottest actor of the 1950s and beyond. In retrospect, he was alarmed at the number of celebrity suicides, many revealing the inverse horror of the celebrity experience.

For more about Kirk's rocky road to stardom, as it specifically applied to his early days as an impoverished actor auditioning for bit parts in Broadway plays, see **Chapter Twelve** *(Katharine Cornell & Guthrie McClintic)* of this book.

Around 1910, his Yiddish-speaking parents had fled from Russia, where Jews were being killed by the Czars only to encounter anti-Semitism in the New World. But Kirk overcame it, changing his name from Issur Danielovitch to Kirk Douglas. "People thought I was Scottish."

As a star in Hollywood, he was known as a "horndog," romancing love goddesses who included Ava Gardner and Lana Turner. His second marriage to Anne Buydens clicked, and, though confined to wheelchairs, they're still wed today.

As a star, and in a strange coincidence that happened again and again, he worked with numerous directors and actors, who committed suicide when their dreams of fame and wealth and glory did not come true. Instead of reinventing themselves, they chose death instead.

As a tragic example, Kirk had a two-year affair with Irene Wrightsman, the Palm Beach socialite and daughter of Charles B. Wrightsman, the famous benefactor of New York City's Metropolitan Museum. She committed suicide. So did her younger sister, Charlene. So did their mother.

As the decades rolled on, Kirk attended endless funerals for the children of his famous colleagues. Many had killed themselves before they were 30 as part of what some insiders interpreted almost as an epidemic of Hollywood suicides.

Kirk himself had four sons, two from each of his marriages. Based on the many self-inflicted deaths he became aware of, it was painfully clear to him that being the offspring of rich and fabled stars had many pitfalls.

Kirk asked himself in some of the books he wrote, "Could the pain of all those doomed kids have been alleviated if they'd had some spiritual guidance—not just material things? Could that have enabled them to endure and conquer their suffering instead of choosing death? I could have done a lot more to help my own sons. Believe me, the list is long."

Perhaps with a sense of horror, he even compiled a list of the funerals he'd attended, with notes about the comfort he'd tried to offer to stars mourning their lost sons and daughters.

Here are some examples of suicides that influenced Kirk and for whom he grieved:

Drug overdoses killed the offspring of Mary Tyler Moore, Louis Jourdan, Carol Burnett, Ray Milland, and Paul Newman.

Kirk's friend and co-star, Carroll O'Connor (*aka* Archie Bunker), lost his son Hugh to a self-inflicted gunshot wound.

In a triple, interconnected tragedy, Charles Boyer's 21-year-old son, Michael, killed himself. Then, Boyer's wife, Pat, died shortly after that from cancer. A few days after burying them, Boyer himself committed suicide two days before his 79th birthday.

Jonathan Peck, son of Gregory Peck, shot himself, leaving no note. Bryan Englund, son of actress Cloris Leachman and producer George Englund, was found dead of an overdose in a Manhattan YMCA.

Peter, the son of Kirk's close friend and producer, Ray Stark, jumped to his death from a 14th-floor apartment in Manhattan. Jennifer Jones' daughter chose the same method, plunging from the roof of a 20th-floor hotel in Los Angeles.

Bing Crosby lost two of his seven children to suicide. His youngest son, Lindsay, shot himself when his lawyer told him that his inheritance had "evaporated." Then, his brother Dennis, deeply distraught by his own recent divorce and his alcoholism, also committed suicide.

Marlon Brando's daughter, Cheyenne, hung herself in Tahiti. Her death came four years after her half-brother, Christian, murdered her Tahitian lover, Dag Drollet.

"After all those funerals, it became my turn at bat," Kirk said. "A phone call came in from New York. A maid found my son Eric dead from an overdose. I'd sent him to 21 rehabs, but nothing worked for my boy. The world we live in makes it difficult for all children, not just the kids of stars."

"I turned to the Torah to learn how the great patriarchs raised their kids. It seems they had their problems, too. Take King David—great monarch, lousy father. Solomon was the greatest king of the Jewish people. But his son, Rehoboam, was a fool, arrogant and greedy. He told his people, 'I will flog you with scorpions.'"

In 2019, alert to the fact that no one had ever attempted a comprehensive biography of his extraordinary life and career, Blood Moon Productions, from its base at Magnolia House, produced the first grand-scale biography **(More Is Never Enough)** of the extraordinary actor known as **Kirk Douglas.**

Softcover, with about 680 pages of insights, comparisons, and commentary from dozens of Kirk's friends, frenemies, and enemies.

Kirk Douglas, More is Never Enough (ISBN 978-1-936003-61-7), from Darwin Porter and Danforth Prince.

EVERYBODY'S WATCHING ZOOMERTIMES TV, AND IF SHE WERE ALIVE, **MERCEDES DE ACOSTA** WOULD BE SCREENING IT TOO!

Boomer Times Radio
with host Anita Finley
IS NOW

zoomertimes TV
HEALTH • WEALTH • ENTERTAINMENT • LIFESTYLE

IT'S MEDIA THAT GOES
BUZZ!

AUTHORS' BIOS

DARWIN PORTER

As a precocious nine-year-old, **Darwin Porter** began meeting entertainers through his mother, Hazel, a charismatic Southern girl whose husband had died in World War II. Migrating from the Depression-ravaged valleys of western North Carolina to Miami Beach during its most ebullient heyday, Hazel became a personal assistant to the vaudeville comedienne **Sophie Tucker**, the kind-hearted "Last of the Red Hot Mamas."

Loosely supervised by his mother, Darwin was regularly dazzled by the likes of **Judy Garland, Dinah Shore, Frank Sinatra, Ronald Reagan** (at the time near the end of his Hollywood gig), and **Marilyn Monroe**. Each of them made it a point, whenever they were in Miami (either on or off the record), to visit and pay their respects to "Miss Sophie."

At the University of Miami, Darwin edited the school newspaper, raising its revenues, through advertising and public events, to unheard-of new levels. He met and interviewed **Eleanor Roosevelt** and later invited her, as part of a sponsored event he crafted, to spend a day ("Eleanor Roosevelt Day") at the university, and to his delight, she accepted. Years later, in Manhattan, during her work as a human rights activist, he escorted her, at her request, to many public functions.

After his graduation, Darwin, in a graceful transition from his work as editor of the University's newspaper and his sponsorship by **Wilson Hicks** (Photo Editor and then Executive Editor of Life magazine) became a Bureau Chief of The Miami Herald (the youngest in that publication's history) assigned to its branch in Key West. At the time the island outpost was an avant-garde literary mecca and—thanks to the Cuban missile crisis—an flash point of the Cold War.

Key West had been the site of Harry S Truman's "Winter White House" and Truman returned a few months before his death for a final visit. He invited young Darwin for "early morning walks" where he used the young emissary of The Miami Herald to "set the record straight."

Through Truman, Darwin was introduced and later joined the staff of **Senator George Smathers** of Florida. His best friend was a young senator, **John F. Kennedy.** Through "Gorgeous George," as Smathers was known in the Senate, Darwin got to meet Jack and Jacqueline in Palm Beach. He later wrote two books about them—The Kennedys, All the Gossip Unfit to Print, and one of his all-time bestsellers, Jacqueline Kennedy Onassis—A Life Beyond Her Wildest Dreams.

Buttressed by his status as The Miami Herald's Key West Bureau Chief, Darwin met, interviewed, and often befriended **Tennessee Williams. Ernest Hemingway, Tallulah Bankhead, Gore Vidal, Truman Capote, Carson McCullers,** and a gaggle of other internationally famous writers and entertainers: **Cary Grant, Rock Hudson, Marlon Brando, Montgomery Clift, Susan**

Hayward, Warren Beatty, Christopher Isherwood, Anne Bancroft, Angela Lansbury, and William Inge.

Eventually transferred to Manhattan, Darwin worked for a decade in television advertising with the producer and arts-industry socialite **Stanley Mills Haggart.** *In addition to some speculative ventures associated with Marilyn Monroe, they also jointly produced TV commercials that included testimonials from* **Joan Crawford** *(then feverishly promoting Pepsi-Cola);* **Ronald Reagan** *(General Electric); and* **Debbie Reynolds** *(Singer sewing machines). Other personalities they promoted, each delivering televised sales pitches, included* **Louis Armstrong, Lena Horne, Rosalind Russell, William Holden,** *and* **Arlene Dahl,** *each of them hawking a commercial product.*

Beginning in the early 1960s, Darwin joined forces with the then-fledgling **Arthur Frommer** *organization, playing a key role in researching and writing more than 50 titles and defining the style and values that later emerged as the world's leading travel guidebooks,* **The Frommer Guides.** *Darwin's particular journalistic expertise on Europe, New England, California, and the Caribbean eventually propelled him into authorship of (depending on the era and whatever crises were brewing at the time), between 70 and 80% of their titles. Even during the research of his travel guides, he continued to interview show-biz celebrities, discussing their triumphs, feuds, and frustrations. At this point in their lives, many were retired and reclusive. Darwin either pursued them (sometimes though local tourist offices) or encountered them randomly as part of his extensive travels.* **Ava Gardner, Lana Turner, Hedy Lamarr, Ingrid Bergman, Ethel Merman, Andy Warhol, Elizabeth Taylor, Marlene Dietrich, Bette Davis,** *Judy* **Garland,** *and* **Paul Newman** *were particularly insightful.*

Porter's biographies—at this writing, they number sixty-two— have won

Yesterday, when he was young,

Darwin Porter

A social historian feverishly fascinated by biographies and the ironies of The American Experience

thirty first prize or "runner-up to first prize" awards at literary festivals in cities or states which include New England, New York, Los Angeles, Hollywood, San Francisco, Florida, California, and Paris.

Darwin, also a magazine columnist, can be heard at regular intervals as a television commentator, reviewing the ironies of celebrities, pop culture, politics, and scandal.

A resident of New York City, where he spent years within the social orbit of the Queen of Off-Broadway (the eccentric and very temperamental philanthropist, **Lucille Lortel),** Darwin is currently at work on biographies of **Lucille Ball and Desi Arnaz** (available everywhere in the spring of 2021); and the dysfunctionally fascinating father/daughter team of **Henry Fonda** and his rebellious daughter, **Jane.**

DANFORTH PRINCE

A graduate of Hamilton College and a native of Easton and Bethlehem, Pennsylvania, he's president and founder (in 1983) of the Porter and Prince Corporation, the entity that produced the original texts and updates for dozens of key titles of **THE FROMMER GUIDES**—travel "bibles" for millions of readers during the travel industry's go-go years in the 80s, 90s, and early millennium.

He also founded, in 1996, the Georgia Literary Association, precursor to what morphed, in 2004, into **Blood Moon Productions**, the corporate force behind dozens of political and Hollywood biographies. Its vaguely apocalyptic name was inspired by one of Darwin Porter's popular early novels, **Blood Moon**, a thriller about the false gods of power, wealth, and physical beauty. In 2011, he was named "Publisher of the Year" by a consortium of literary critics and marketers spearheaded by the J.M. Northern Media Group.

Prince has electronically documented his stewardship of Blood Moon in at least 50 videotaped documentaries, book trailers, public speeches, and TV or radio interviews. Most of these are available on **YouTube.com** and **Facebook** (keyword: "Danforth Prince"); on **Twitter** (#BloodyandLunar); or by clicking on **BloodMoonProductions.com**.

Hearkening back to his days as a travel writer, Prince is also an innkeeper, maintaining and managing a historic bed & breakfast, **Magnolia House (www.MagnoliaHouseSaintGeorge.com)**. Affiliated with AirBnb, and increasingly sought out by filmmakers as an evocative locale for moviemaking, it lies in St. George, at the northern tip of Staten Island, the "sometimes forgotten"

Outer Borough of New York City. A landmarked building with a "formidable" historic and literary pedigree, it lies in a neighborhood closely linked to Henry James, Theodore Dreiser, the Vanderbilts, and key moments in America's colonial history.

Set in a terraced garden with views over New York Harbor and nearby Manhattan, it's been visited by show-biz stars who have included **Tennessee Williams, Gloria Swanson, Jolie Gabor** *(mother of Zsa Zsa, Eva, and Magda)*, soap opera queen **Ruth Warrick**, *the Viennese chanteuse* **Greta Keller**, *and many of the luminaries of Broadway. It lies within a twelve-minute walk from the ferries sailing at frequent intervals to Manhattan.*

Publicized as "a reasonably priced celebrity-centric bed & breakfast with links to the book trades," and the beneficiary of rave ("superhost") reviews (including "New York's most fascinating B&B") from hundreds of previous guests, **Magnolia House** *is loaded with furniture and memorabilia that Prince collected from around the world during his decades as a travel journalist for the Frommer Guides.* ***Since the onset of the Covid Crisis, social distancing and regular decontamination regimens have been rigorously enforced.*** *For photographs, testimonials from previous guests, and more information, click on*

www.AirBnB/H/Magnolia-House

In reference to Magnolia House, your host, handler, concierge, and problem-solver, **Danforth Prince**, says, "Come with your friends for the night and stay for breakfast. Even with social distancing, Covid cautiousness, and a lot more 'scrub-a-dub-dubbing,' it's about healing, recuperation, razzmatazz, show-biz, Classic Hollywood, sightseeing, and conversation in the greatest city in the world. Well-behaved pets (especially dogs) are welcome.

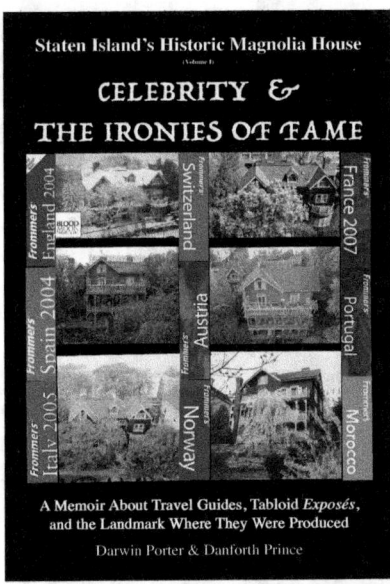 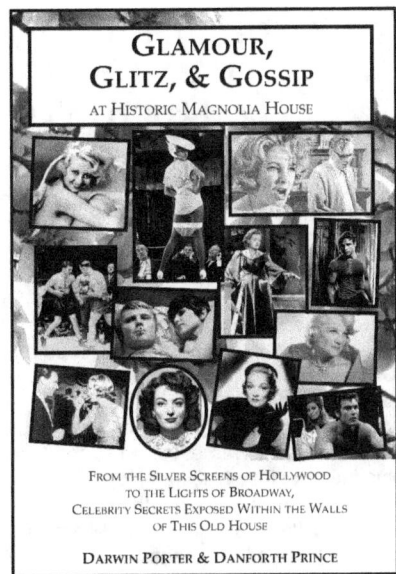

As depicted above, Volumes One and Two of Blood Moon's Magnolia House Series were conceived as affectionate testimonials to a great American monument, **MAGNOLIA HOUSE,** a nurturing and very tolerant historic home in NYC with a raft of stories to tell—some of them about how it adapted to America's radically changing tastes, times, circumstances, and values.

VOLUME ONE (ISBN 978-1-936003-65-5) focuses on its construction by a prominent lawyer during the booming (Northern) economy before the Civil War; its Gilded-Age purchase by the widow of the Surgeon General of the Confederate States of America; and later, its role as a branch office for dozens of travel titles during the heyday of THE FROMMER GUIDES, with detailed insights into the celebrity secrets their reporters (privately, until now) unveiled.

VOLUME TWO (ISBN 978-1-936003-73-0) is an *haute* celebrity romp through the half-century of Broadway, Hollywood, and publishing scandals swirling around Magnolia House's visitors and their frenemies...a "Reporters' Notebook" with everything that arts industry publicists didn't want fans and critics to know about at the time.

Each of these books is a celebration of the fast-disappearing PRE-COVID AMERICAN CENTURY.

And both are available now through internet purveyors worldwide.

BLOOD MOON PRODUCTIONS
Historically Authentic Entertainment about America's Legends, Icons, & Celebrities

LUCILLE BALL AND DESI ARNAZ BECAME THE MOST CELEBRATED DUO IN THE HISTORY OF TELEVISION

Half of America gathered every Monday night around the little black box in their living rooms to watch the antics of Lucy and Ricky Ricardo, a Cuban bandleader with his wacky, high-spirited wife.

The early struggles of Lucy and Desi were epic. As a girl, she at times was literally chained in her backyard in Jamestown, New York. As a teenager, she broke away and earned a reputation as "The Jamestown hussy," riding around with Johnny DeVita, a local hoodlum.

Born to wealth and privilege in Cuba, Desi, at the age of twelve, was escorted to the local bordello by his father to lose his virginity.

His family lost everything in the Cuban Revolution and fled to America. In Miami, Desi got a job cleaning out canary cages. He was eventually hired by bandleader Xavier Cugat because, "I beat hell out of those Afro-Cuban drums."

Meanwhile, in Manhattan, Lucy was struggling to break into show business, hustling "sugar daddies" and stage-door Johnnies who gave her money and gifts. Once, when desperate, she became a nude model. "A gal's gotta eat."

In the 1930s, she made it to Hollywood and worked making films for RKO. The executives used her as a gussied-up hooker to "entertain" out-of-town film exhibitors.

[Ultimately, she got her revenge. In one of the most ironic "fiscal revolutions" in show-biz history, she bought the studio.]

Drifting to Hollywood, Desi spotted Lucy on a sound stage "dressed like a two-dollar whore who had been badly beaten by her pimp." Their tempestuous marriage, characterized by long separations, staggered along for two decades.

By the early 1950s, the careers of both Desi and Lucy had headed south. There was a lot of resistance among TV executives who objected to his Cuban accent. But *I Love Lucy* was launched nevertheless and shot up in the ratings like a rocket, morphing into the most successful sitcom in TV history.

"With gold arriving in wheelbarrows" (Desi's words), they bought the four-block RKO Studios. Desilu Productions was launched, becoming the largest motion picture and television studio in the world.

In 1960, after their divorce, Lucy appraised her husband: "He is a Jekyll and Hyde type. He drinks, gambles, and chases the broads from thirteen to thirty, even Carrie Fisher. He's awash in broads, lots of booze, and that gay actor, Cesar Romero, is his devoted slave. Desi is destructive, but always building something. If it's big, he has to break it down."

"Love?" she asked. "I was always falling in love with the wrong man. Even Desi."

Desi, too, summed up his many years of marriage: "We were anything but Lucy and Ricky Ricardo on the tube. Those guys had nothing to do with us. Lucy and I dreamed of success, fame, and fortune. Guess what? It all led to hell."

LUCILLE BALL & DESI ARNAZ
THEY WEREN'T LUCY AND RICKY RICARDO

Darwin Porter and Danforth Prince
ISBN 978-1-936003-71-6
A pithy, photo-packed 450-page softcover, with photos,
available through Internet Purveyors (including Amazon.com),
everywhere in time for Valentine's Day

ONE OF THE 20TH CENTURY'S MOST FASCINATING WOMAN WAS SIRED BY ONE OF ITS MOST WIDELY HERALDED MOVIE STARS. AS A PRECOCIOUS BUT LOVE-STARVED CHILD RAISED AMID THE BIZARRE ABNORMALITIES OF HOLLYWOOD, JANE FONDA ADMITTED, "I SOMETIMES DID NAUGHTY THINGS TO ATTRACT MY FATHER'S ATTENTION."

In a release scheduled for the Spring of 2021, Hollywood's leading biographers turn klieg lights on two emotionally intertwined Oscar winners, the lanky and boyish American hero, Henry Fonda, and his beautiful daughter Jane, a political activist and superstar beloved by millions despite her formerly poisonous reputation as "Hanoi Jane."

This book, unlike any other previously published, reflects the private agonies of a father and daughter engulfed by the divisions of their respective generations and the ironies of The American Experience.

JANE AND HENRY FONDA
TO EACH HIS (OR HER) OWN

Available in April, 2021, through Internet purveyors,
including Amazon.com, worldwide
ISBN 978-1-936003-77-8
Softcover, 450 pages, with hundreds of photos.

DONALD TRUMP
WAS THE MAN WHO WOULD BE KING

This is the most famous book about our incendiary President you've probably never heard of. Winner of three respected literary awards, and released three months before the Presidentail elections of 2016, it's an entertainingly packaged, artfully salacious bombshell, a scathingly historic overview of America during its 2016 election cycle, a portrait unlike anything ever published on CANDIDATE DONALD and the climate in which he thrived and massacred his political rivals.

Its volcanic, much-suppressed release during the heat and venom of the Presidential campaign has already been heralded by the *Midwestern Book Review, California Book Watch, the Seattle Gay News,* the staunchly right-wing WILS-AM radio, and also by the editors at the most popular Seniors' magazine in Florida, *BOOMER TIMES,* which designated it as their September 2016 choice for BOOK OF THE MONTH.

TRUMPOCALYPSE: *"Donald Trump: The Man Who Would Be King* is recommended reading for all sides, no matter what political stance is being adopted: Republican, Democrat, or other.

"One of its driving forces is its ability to synthesize an unbelievable amount of information into a format and presentation which blends lively irony with outrageous observations, entertaining even as it presents eye-opening information in a format accessible to all.

"Politics dovetail with American obsessions and fascinations with trends, figureheads, drama, and sizzling news stories, but blend well with the observations of sociologists, psychologists, politicians, and others in a wide range of fields who lend their expertise and insights to create a much broader review of the Trump phenomena than a more casual book could provide.

"The result is a 'must read' for any American interested in issues of race, freedom, equality, and justice—and for any non-American who wonders just what is going on behind the scenes in this country's latest election debacle."

Diane Donovan, as reviewed in *California Bookwatch* and T*he Midwestern Book Review.*

DONALD TRUMP, THE MAN WHO WOULD BE KING
WINNER OF "BEST BIOGRAPHY" AWARDS FROM BOOK FESTIVALS IN NEW YORK, CALIFORNIA, AND FLORIDA
by Darwin Porter and Danforth Prince
Softcover, with 822 pages and hundreds of photos. ISBN 978-1-936003-51-8.

Available now from Amazon.com and other internet purveyors, worldwide.

www.ingramcontent.com/pod-product-compliance
Lightning Source LLC
Chambersburg PA
CBHW071949110526
44592CB00012B/1038